AF560774

SUFIS, SULTANS AND FEUDAL ORDERS

Professor Nurul Hasan Commemoration Volume

SUFIS, SULTANS AND FEUDAL ORDERS

Professor Nurul Hasan Commemoration Volume

edited by

MANSURA HAIDAR

CENTRE OF ADVANCED STUDY
Department of History
Aligarh Muslim University

MANOHAR
2004

First published 2004

ISBN 81-7304-548-8

Published by
Ajay Kumar Jain for
Manohar Publishers & Distributors
4753/23 Ansari Road, Daryaganj
New Delhi 110002

Typeset by
A J Software Publishing Co. Pvt. Ltd.
New Delhi 110005

Printed at
Lordson Publishers Pvt. Ltd.
Delhi 110007

Contents

PART 4: MISCELLANEOUS

PART 5: REMINISCENCES

Introduction

India has many reasons to be proud of one of its tallest personalities, namely, Professor Saiyid Nurul Hasan, who was not only a conscientious teacher but also known for his erudition and acumen. As an administrator, he made an exemplary contribution in whichever position he was placed. His contribution to the field of history and to the country as a whole will continue to be remembered with great admiration. This commemorative volume in honour of Professor Nurul Hasan is a humble effort on the part of the members of the Centre of Advanced Study to pay tribute to someone who has been a mentor of many talents, here and elsewhere, a patron of learning and a learned human being full of the graces of life. It was under his stewardship that the Department of History was elevated to the status of a Centre of Advanced Study and has become a leading institution in the field of history. Having started his career as a teacher, Professor Hasan had been closely attached to the teaching community notwithstanding the fact that he served the Government of India for a longer period first as an MP and then as the Union Minister of Education. He rose to be a Governor and then Ambassador, but his love for teaching and research never waned, even amidst his busy schedule as Education Minister. He not only continued to deliver lectures on medieval history particularly on his favourite subject, architecture, but he would even accompany his students to historical sites to give them an experience of varied architectural features. As Ambassador to the erstwhile Soviet Union, he often took time off to study manuscripts in the libraries of Central Asia. Many of his lectures and his thoughts on the agrarian system of medieval India have been published in the form of two books which are proof of the profundity of his thought and the depth of his scholarship. His numerous articles attest to his insightful study of medieval Indian history.

The teaching community continued to be close to his heart and even when he had left AMU, he continued to care for it. It was he who first thought of raising the salaries of the teachers to bring them at par with those of the Indian Administrative Services. It was an attempt to attract the best talent to the teaching profession and raise, in the longer run, their intellectual and academic level. For his own discipline, namely, history, he has left behind a legacy in the form of ICHR, whose conceptual framework and foundations were laid by him personally. By establishing the ICHR, he had ensured the overall development of historical studies as a variety of opportunities and financial resources began to be made available not only to scholars of repute and eminence but also to budding historians to enable them to pursue their research. As Chairman of the CSIR, his contribution to the field of science and technology was no less impressive. As an educationist, his brilliance was reflected in many branches. In fact, he himself lived like an institution—and even after his death, he has remained a legend.

A man of conviction, he not only preached the unity and solidarity of the nation and emphasized its composite culture but had also practiced the faith to the best of his capacity. He rose to the occasion whenever the nation demanded his services to strengthen its foundations.

Professor Nurul Hasan hailed from an illustrious family which had given to the nation a galaxy of eminent and competent persons. His father Mr Saiyid Abdul Hasan was the President of Courts of Ward but was deeply attracted to the cause of education. He was instrumental in the development of Shia Degree College and its affiliate institutions in Lucknow. Professor Nurul Hasan's maternal grandfather, Sir Syed Wazir Hasan was a renowned jurist and the Chief Justice in Lucknow. Each of his maternal uncles earned name and fame in their respective lives. Hasan Zaheer was a commissioner. Syed Ali Zaheer, was an intrepid freedom fighter who later became a Cabinet Minister and an elder statesman. Of his other uncles, Sayed Sajjad Zaheer, was a famous literary figure and a veteran communist leader; and Syed Husain Zaheer a renowned scientist and the first Director General of CSIR; Syed Baqar Zaheer was a member of the Railway Board.

As a student at the Allahabad University, Nurul Hasan left an indelible mark on student movements during the freedom struggle. Being a brilliant student he displayed his talents as an excellent debator, orator, organizer and an active leader. Incidentally, he was also a favourite student of my late father, Professor S.M. Zamin Ali, who happened to be a leading light of the Allahabad University at that time. He took his Ph.D. from Oxford in 1946-7. After returning from the UK he joined Lucknow University for a short while and then shifted to Aligarh to take over as Reader in the Department of History. Three years later he was appointed Professor at this Department. From 1959 onwards he served as Chairman of the Department and became the Coordinator of the Centre of Advanced Study in History, when this Centre was established through his strenuous efforts in 1968.

Be it in the field of social work or as an intellectual or an eminent historian, Professor Hasan always exhibited a scientific temper with a constantly questioning spirit and an analytical mind. Being possessed of a sensitive nature about his surroundings, he not only absorbed the most trendy currents but also accepted the challenges as and when they came his way. He held the office of Education Minister with great distinction for several years, remained member of the Rajya Sabha, served as a member of the UN delegation. He was appointed Vice-Chairman of CSIR and then later as Indian's Ambassador to the USSR. He was also appointed Governor of West Bengal, an office which he held admirably till his death in 1993. There were many academic distinctions bestowed upon him. To mention a few—he was fellow of the Academy of Sciences, USSR; Fellow of Royal Historical Society, London and Fellow of All Soul's College, Oxford. He also went to Paris as the leader of the Indian delegation to the UNESCO Silver Jubilee Celebrations.

Although Professor Hasan excelled in every sphere he was called upon to serve, his most significant contributions were as the Education Minister. Here his bold initiatives, his consummate skill in handling the most delicate problems, and his comprehensive vision found full display. As Governor, he provided a unique instance of perfectly harmonious relationship between the Head of the State and Head of the Government based on mutual understanding and accommodation.

The sphere of social welfare also benefited tremendously through the efforts of Professor Hasan and his wife. Apart from lending his personal support to welfare work, particularly to the development of the Ahmadi School for the Blind at AMU, he also established three national institutes for the disabled. Professor Hasan was married to Khursheed Laqua Begum, the eldest daughter of the then Nawab of Rampur, who herself became a historian later on. While serving as a Lecturer at Varshney Post Graduate College in Aligarh, she engaged herself in research work and secured Ph.D. degree in history from the Aligarh Muslim University. Incidentally, she developed a keen interest in social work. At the behest of the then Vice-Chancellor of AMU, Dr Zakir Husain, she took over as manager of the Ahmadi School for the Blind in 1955. Begum Sahiba was greatly instrumental in ensuring the development of this institution along modern scientific lines. Such was her deep concern for the School that even while going to Srinagar, just before her death, she took pains to take the measurements of the proposed teaching block for classrooms and bring donation from her family friends visiting the place. On 16 June 1967, the Principal of the School learnt through the then

Vice-Chancellor Nawab Ali Yavar Jung that since she had died in Srinagar, all arrangements had to be made by him for her burial. It was a heart-rending news not only for her husband but also for all our family for whom she was like a very affectionate elder, totally involved in their personal progress. Begam Sahiba had died at a young age of thirty-five. Such was our liking for her that Mr Haidar collected the money through his personal efforts and got a teaching block constructed after her name as Khursheed Laqua Building in 1968. After her, Professor Nurul Hasan himself took keen interest in the development of the school. Professor Hasan is survived by his by son Sirajul Hasan and daughter Talat Hasan. While Sirajul is an eminent physicist based in Bangalore, Talat Hasan is a renowned IT professional in California.

Professor Nurul Hasan was a legendary figure around the AMU campus, especially at the Centre of Advanced Study. A good indication of the love and respect he still generates in the hearts of his friends, colleagues and students was the deluge of articles that this editor was besieged with, once word got around that a commemorative volume was being planned and essays were being solicited.

Of the 28 essays in this volume the ones which reflect his abiding and varied interest in medieval Indian history form the bulk of the material and are placed under three categories: Sufis (a subject of great personal interest to Professor Hasan being the topic of his legendary research work in Oxford); Sultans, which deals with the administration of major ruling dynasties of medieval India; and Feudal Orders which examines the social and cultural construct of Medieval India. The fourth category has miscellaneous articles on many topics of historical importance which were dear to Professor Hasan and would be of much importance to maritime, modern and Central Asian historians. The last category has personal reminiscences of three of Professor Hasan's closest friends and relatives and they endearingly touch upon the many generous, democratic and sterling qualities of this great educator who briefly touched their lives and made it glow.

The section on Sufism starts with N.R. Farooqui's essay which traces the advent of the early Sufis along the Malabar coast in India and presents a detailed picture of Sufism at the start of Muslim rule and debunks many prevalent myths about Sufism. J.S. Grewal's pointed paper looks at the issues of gender, love and longing through the lenses of Sufi poetry as it is popular in Punjab. Muhaddith's *Zad al-Muttaqeen Wa-Saluk-i Tariq al-Yaqin*, a late sixteenth century volume on the lives of contemporary Sufi theologians, forms the backdrop of Iqtidar Hussain

Siddiqui's inquiry into the nature of Sufism in medieval India. Iqbal Sabir traces the life of Khawaja Mohammad Hashim Kishmi, an important seventeenth century Naqshbandi Sufi of Burhanpur while Maksud Ahmad Khan, in his essay, looks at the various *Khanqahs*, the Sufi centres of learning, and their impact on the cultural fabric of medieval India.

In the category broadly demarcated as 'Sultans', S. Mohd. Raza Naqvi examines Alauddin Khalji's administrative apparatus, especially his price control reforms which had a widespread impact. Ishtiyaq Ahmad Zilli and Tahmeena Javed, on the other hand, throw new light on the Saiyid Sultans of Delhi, who ruled from 1414 to 1451 and owed their rise to power to Timur. Timur is the topic of my own essay as I track his legend through the maze of myth and contemporary sources. Defence and strategic cooperation and exchange between India and Central Asia between the tenth and fourteenth centuries form the foreground of Rashmi Upadhyaya's in-depth study. Sumbul Halim Khan, in her essay on Mughal agrarian administration, looks closely at the Pargana of Udehi and the 141 villages therein. S.N. Azizuddin Hussain looks at the reign of Akbar and his complex doctrine of religious tolerance through the history of the Ibadat Khana constructed by the emperor to hold religious discussions, and also through the prism of *Mahzar* and *Sulh-i-Kul*. Mohd. Umer, in his long essay, traces the rise and fall of Imadul Mulk Ghaziuddin Khan and through it the terminal decline of the great Mughals.

The third category called 'Feudal Orders', starts with Azra Alavi examining the spontaneous uprising of 1816 against the British administration after a *chowkidari* tax was levied on the residents of Bareilly. Fatima Zehra Bilgrami in her essay reiterates the socio-economic importance of *Hidayat'ul Qawa'id*, an eighteenth century administrative manual by Hidayat'-ullah Bihari. *Tuhfah-i-Tazah*—another eighteenth century text by Maulvi Khair-al Din Allahabadi, which is an exhaustive, authentic and original source of information for reconstructing the history of Raja Dom of Banaras—forms the backdrop of Z.U. Malik's study. M.S. Ahluwalia examines feudal hierarchies in early medieval Rajasthan through a detailed analysis of four important titles, viz., *Rauta*, *Thakkura*, *Ranaka/Rana/Rai* and *Rajaputra* in the twelfth century.

The fourth category, which has essays on miscellaneous topics and eras, starts with Satish Chandra's intensive overview of India's maritime tradition through the ages. David Gilmartin, in his long essay, examines the role of irrigation in state-building along the west bank of the Indus from Darejat to Upper Sind. Surendar Gopal traces the role of Indian traders in eighteenth century Iran. Shams ud Din looks at Islamic revival in Central Asia after the dissolution of Soviet Russia in the nineties. Nirmala Joshi, on the other hand, chronicles the ups and downs of Indo-Soviet relations from Khruschev to Gorbachev and the evolution of Indian foreign policy through the cold war years. Gulfishan Khan analyses the perceptions of the West among Indian Muslims in the first half of the nineteenth century through the diary of Karim Khan Mushtaq Jhajjari, a noble who was in London during the Corn Law debates. S.M. Waseem analyses the nationalism of Sir Sayyid Ahmad Khan through his own speeches and writings.

Part five starts with the endearing tribute of S.Z. Qasim, brother-in-law of Professor Nurul Hasan and continues with his close friend former Foreign Secretary S.K. Singh's reminiscences. The section ends with Vina Mazumdar's elegiac yet lively trip down memory lane.

Professor Nurul Hasan had inspired generations of his students and colleagues and had benefited the nation immensely with his political sagacity and sage counsels. His friends found him to be imbued with the traditional Lucknowi culture, the very embodiment of courtesy and good manners, suave urbane and highly sophisticated. To him personal ties mattered a great deal which he cultivated irrespective of an individual's political ideology or religion. I certainly acknowledge my inability in doing full justice to his many-sided personality and extraordinary attainments.

In the end I express my grateful thanks to the contributors, friends, colleagues and well-wishers for their ungrudging help in this venture.

MANSURA HAIDAR

Contributors

N.R. Farooqi, Professor and Head, Department of History, Allahabad University, Allahabad.

Marc Gaborieau has retired from the Centre Nationale de la Recherche Scientifique, Paris (France).

J.S. Grewal, Honorary Director of the Institute of Punjab Studies, Chandigarh.

Iqtidar Hussain Siddiqui, Retd. Professor, Department of History, Aligarh Muslim University, Aligarh.

Iqbal Sabir, Lecturer, Centre for Advanced Study, Department of History, Aligarh Muslim University, Aligarh.

Maksud Ahmad Khan, Lecturer, Department of History, Aligarh Muslim University, Aligarh.

S. Mohd. Raza Naqvi, Retd. Professor, Department of History, Aligarh Muslim University, Aligarh.

Ishtiyaq Ahmad Zilli, Professor, Centre of Advanced Study, Department of History, Aligarh Muslim University, Aligarh.

Mansura Haidar, Professor, Coordinator and Chairperson, Centre of Advanced Study, Aligarh Muslim University, Aligarh.

Tahmeena Javed, Lecturer, Centre of Advanced Study, Department of History, Aligarh Muslim University, Aligarh.

Rashmi Upadhyaya, Lecturer, Centre of Advanced Study, Department of History, Aligarh Muslim University, Aligarh.

Sumbul Halim Khan, Reader, Centre of Advanced Study, Aligarh Muslim University, Aligarh.

S.M. Azizuddin Husain, Professor, Department of History, Jamia Millia Islamia, New Delhi.

Mohd. Umer, Retd. Professor, Centre for Advanced Study, Department of History, Aligarh Muslim University, Aligarh.

AZRA ALAVI, Reader, Centre of Advanced Study, Aligarh Muslim University, Aligarh.

FATIMA ZEHRA BILGRAMI, Reader, Centre of Advanced Study, Aligarh Muslim University, Aligarh.

Z.U. MALIK, Retd. Professor, Centre of Advanced Study, Aligarh Muslim University, Aligarh.

M.S. AHLUWALIA, Professor, H.P. University, Simla.

SATISH CHANDRA, former Chairman, UGC; Chairman, Society for Indian Ocean Studies, New Delhi.

DAVID GILMARTIN, Professor, North Carolina State University, USA.

SURENDRA GOPAL, Professor, Department of History, Patna University, Patna.

SHAMS UD DIN, Professor, School of International Studies, Jawaharlal Nehru University, New Delhi.

NIRMALA JOSHI, Professor, School of International Studies, Jawaharlal Nehru University, New Delhi.

GULFISHAN KHAN, Reader, Centre of Advanced Study, Aligarh Muslim University, Aligarh.

S.M. WASEEM, Professor, Department of Commerce, Aligarh Muslim University, Aligarh.

S.Z. QASIM, Vice-Chairman, Society for Indian Ocean Studies, New Delhi.

S.K. SINGH, former Foreign Secretary, Govt. of India.

VINA MAZUMDAR, former Director, Centre for Women's Development Studies, New Delhi.

PART 1

SUFIS

Early Sufis of India: Legend and Reality

N.R. Farooqi

Long before the birth of Islam, Arab seafarers and traders were active in Malabar. There is evidence of small Arab settlements in many coastal towns of the peninsula from the first century onwards. Flow of trade and commerce between India and the Arab world continued, with perhaps greater vigour and pace, after the advent of Islam. Arab travellers of the ninth and tenth centuries have recorded the presence of Muslims in Malabar, Gujarat, Deccan, and even in some parts of modern Uttar Pradesh. Al-Mas'udi (d. 956), who traveled in India between 915-17, has referred to a large Muslim settlement in Seymore (modern Chaul), 25 miles south of Mumbai. The ancestors of a majority of ten thousand inhabitants of these settlements, writes Al-Mas'udi, migrated from Arabia and Iraq to participate in India's lucrative spice trade, married into local families and over a period of time secured a limited degree of political autonomy from the native rulers. He has also noted the prosperity of the Muslims living in India. 'Neither in Hind nor in Sind', he asserts, 'there is a sovereign who disturbs the peace of Muslims in their own country. Islam is therefore flourishing here.'[1] Al-Mas'udi also commends the Indians for their intellectual attainments. He calls India the land of virtue and wisdom, science and philosophy. For him India was the finest example of a country that had achieved a high degree of wisdom without the aid of divine law.

Arab travellers visiting Malabar in the ninth and tenth centuries also allude to the extraordinary degree of religious freedom and political patronage enjoyed by Muslim settlers there. Ibn Battuta in the fourteenth century and then Zainuddin Ma'bari, the celebrated author of *Tuhfat al-mujuahidin* in the sixteenth century also affirm the impressions of the early Arab travellers. 'The Muslims of Malabar,' writes Zainuddin, 'lived a happy and prosperous life on account of the benevolence of the rulers, their regard to time honoured customs and their kindness.'[2] He praises the Hindu rulers of Malabar for fixing the allowance for the *qazis* (judges) and *mu'azzins* (those who call the Muslims to prayer) within their territories. Zainuddin admits that the magnanimity of the Hindu rulers towards their Muslim subjects was motivated partly by the extraordinary increase in their revenue as a result of the arrival of Muslim traders in their dominions. He censures the Muslim rulers of Gujarat and the Deccan for doing little, despite commanding large armies and wealth, to 'repel the misfortune and confusion that had befallen the Muslims' following the Portuguese penetration in Malabar. But he misses no opportunity to express his gratitude for the Samurai (Zamorin), the Hindu ruler of Calicut, for sacrificing both men and money in order to protect the life and property of the Muslims against Portuguese aggression.

Zainuddin also narrates two popular though unsubstantiated legends regarding the advent of Sufism in Malabar. According to the first, the Raja of Kodungallur (modern Cranganur), who was an ancestor of the Zamorin of Calicut, embraced Islam after witnessing Prophet Muhammad's miracle of splitting the moon. He renounced his throne, visited Arabia, had the honour of meeting the Prophet but on his way back to India died in the port city of Zofar where his grave became a popular place of pilgrimage for the devotees. Firishta, the seventeenth century author of *Tarikh-i Firishta*, claims this tradition to be closer to the truth and adds that after the king's death, his Arab friends led by the renowned Sufi Malik bin Dinar and his nephew Malik bin Habib journeyed, armed with a letter from the late king, to Malabar. They were welcomed by the local authorities and were allowed to settle in Cranganur. Freedom of worship was granted to them and their request to build a mosque in the city was allowed. Subsequently these Muslims visited Quilon, Mount Delly, Barkur, Kasargod, Mangalore, Darmadam, Pantalayini, and Chaliyam and built a mosque in each of these towns. The Muslim population of Malabar grew and over a period of time many Hindu dignitaries joined their fold.[3]

According to the second tradition, early in the ninth century a group of Sufis led by Malik bin Dinar landed, by error, at the port of Cranganur. They had an audience with the king, discussed with him the fundamentals of their religion, and convinced him of the truth of the Prophet's mission. The Raja secretly converted to Islam and decided to visit Arabia. He partitioned the empire among his relatives, ostensibly for carrying out a long cherished desire of worshipping God in a lonely and undisclosed site, and in the darkness of a night set sail for Arabia. On his return journey the Raja fell ill and died in the port city of Shihir. Before his demise, the king persuaded his Arab companions, Malik bin Dinar, his nephew Malik bin Habib and others, to go to Malabar for the propagation of Islam. Accordingly, Malik bin Dinar, his family, and dependents reached Malabar and presented a letter of the deceased king to the ruler of Cranganur. The monarch gave them shelter, land grants, and freedom of worship. Malik bin Dinar subsequently returned to his native land and left his nephew and his family in Cranganur where they lived out their lives in peace.[4]

A somewhat similar tradition is recorded in a Malyalam chronicle *Keralopatti*. According to this tradition, the king who converted to Islam and later met the Prophet was Ceraman Perumal of the Kulasekhara dynasty. Although many modern historians of Kerala question the authenticity of this tradition, M.G.S. Narayanan suggests that the last Ceraman Perumal ruled till 1122, the year of his sudden disappearance. Narayanan also states that the mosque at Hayli-Haravi (Mount Delly), reportedly built by Malik bin Habib, was completed in 1124. The erection of the mosque two years after the disappearance of the last Ceraman Perumal, according to him, lends some credence to this tradition.[5]

The exact date of the conversion of the king, however, remains uncertain. If he ruled till 1122, the question of his visiting Arabia during the lifetime of the Prophet Muhammad (570-632) does not arise. The identity of Malik bin Dinar also remains shrouded in mystery. The famous Sufi Malik bin Dinar, a leading disciple of Hasan of Basra, died in 744. Thus his visit to India either in the twelfth century or even the seventh century is beyond the realm of possibility. Arab travelers visiting Malabar between the eighth and the fourteenth centuries do not mention these traditions at all. It would therefore be not too far-fetched to suggest that the traditions in question grew after the fourteenth century only.

The Kasargod mosque inscription, discovered and deciphered in 1998 by G.S. Khawaja of the Archaeological Survey of India, refers to the construction of mosques by Muslim missionaries from Arabia in many cities of coastal Malabar. The epigraph also mentions special laws instituted by the state to take care of the legal disputes involving the Arab settlers in Malabar.[6] The inscription is undated, and thus the mystery regarding the exact date of the advent of Islam in Malabar remains unresolved. Khawaja's contention that the Basran Sufi Malik bin Dinar, whom he calls a contemporary of the Prophet Muhammad, led the Arab missionaries is also far from truth. Malik was not a contemporary of the Prophet and is not known to have visited India at all.

There is nevertheless no dearth of literary and epigraphic evidence supporting a very early presence of Muslims in Malabar. The concessions given to their Muslim subjects by the Zamorins of Calicut are also fairly well documented. A *farman* (royal edict) of the Ottoman Sultan Murad III (r. 1574-95), issued in 1576 and addressed to the Governor-General of Egypt, also alludes to an annual grant of one hundred gold coins, paid from the revenues of the port of Jidda, for the preachers of twenty-seven mosques of the port ciy of Calicut. In this *farman* the Sultan commands the addressee to pay his utmost attention to this matter and ensure the supply of one hundred gold coins annually, in accordance with the established practice, to the aforementioned preachers.[7] The allusion to 'established practice' in the *farman* suggests that the grant dated back to many decades, if not centuries.

The data regarding the activities of the Sufis on the western coast of India is unfortunately rather scarce. Ibn Battuta does mention the *khanqah* of Shaikh Shahabuddin Gazaruni in Calicut but gives no further information about the saint and his disciples. Ibn Battuta also refers to a Gazaruni *khanqah* in Quilon, managed by the saint's son Fakhruddin, where the traveller himself stayed for some time.[8] A contemporary of Shahabuddin was Pir Ma'bari Khandayat. A native of Ma'bar (modern Madurai), he is reported to have joined the army of Malik Kafur during his campaign against Ma'bar (1311). He subsequently moved to Bijapur, where he was killed in a skirmish with the local populace.[9]

Sind was another part of the subcontinent where Islam made an early appearance. Muhammad bin Qasim's conquest of Sind and Multan (712) is well known. But the Arab rule in Sind was not destined to last long. Indifference of the home government coupled with its own inner inconsistencies led to the break up of the Ummayad hegemony in Sind and two independent Muslim states in Multan and Mansura came into existence. In the early tenth century when Al-Mas'udi visited Sind, he found Multan and Mansura to be flourishing and prosperous. He describes Multan as one of the biggest frontier towns of Islam with about one hundred thousand villages subservient to it. Al-Mas'udi also refers to the celebrated sun temple of Multan where people flocked in thousands from different parts of the country to perform pilgrimage. The greater part of the income of the king of Multan, writes Mas'udi, comes from the presents offered by the pilgrims at the temple. The temple also protected Multan from the invasion of its Hindu neighbours. 'When the unbelievers march against Multan,' observes Mas'udi, 'and the Muslims do not find themselves strong enough to oppose them, they threaten to break this idol and their enemies then immediately withdraw their armies.'[10]

Shortly after Mas'udi's 'visit, it seems, the Qaramita Ismailis 'seized Multan and Mansura. Another Arab traveller Bishari Muqaddisi, who traveled in Sind around 986, found Multan under their control. The Qaramita strong man Jalam bin Shaiban is also alleged to have destroyed the Multan temple. Between 1005 and 1011, Sultan Mahmud of Ghazni (r. 999-1030) invaded Multan twice to root out the Qaramita influence from this region. In 1011 the Qaramita ruler Abul Fath Daud bin Nasr was defeated and Multan was annexed to the Ghaznavid Empire. Fourteen years later, Mahmud, while returning from the Somnath campaign, passed through Mansura whose Qaramita overlord Khafif fled the capital. He was chased and defeated. After Mahmud's death the Qaramita power in Sind seems to have revived. In 1175 Sultan Muhammad Ghauri (r. 1173-1206) finally wrested Multan from them bringing to an end the Qaramita power in Sind.

The conquest of Sind acquainted the Muslims with the intellectual attainments of the Indians and opened the way for exchange of ideas and men of letters between India and the Arab world. Indian scholars and physicians visited Baghdad, the seat of the Abbasid Caliphate, and several major Sanskrit works on astronomy, mathematics, and medicine were translated into Arabic. Sindi Muslims also contributed substantially to the progress of knowledge among the Islamic land and people. The family of Imam Abu Hanifa, the founder of the Hanafi school of jurisprudence, belonged to a Jat clan of Sind.[11] Abu Mash'ar Najih Sindi (d. 787) and Rija Ali Sindi (d. 836) were leading scholars of Hadis of their time. No less a person than the Caliph Harun al-Rashid (r. 786-809) led the funeral prayer of the former Abu Ata Sindi (d. 774) was perhaps the greatest Arabic poet of his time.

The first to spread the message of Sufism in Sind was Shaikh Abu Turab (d.788). A *tabi '-i tabi 'i* (one who personally knew a person who personally knew one of the Prophet's companions), he is reported to have settled in Bhakkar after the Arab conquest of Sind. According to the author of an eighteenth century history of Sind called *Tuhfat al-kiram*, Shaikh Abu Turab also served as the governor of the fort of Bhakkar. Not much is known about the life and activities of the Shaikh. Legends about his triumph over a local Hindu ruler Tharna, whom the Shaikh is claimed to have miraculously turned into a hillock along with his army, are still current in Sind.[12] His tomb in the village Guju, 10 miles from modern Thatta, continues to attract innumerable devotees from far and wide.

Shaikh Saifuddin Gazaruni (d. 1007) was an outstanding personality among the early Sufis of Sind. A native of Gazarun in Iran, Saifuddin arrived in Sind in the last quarter of the tenth century and founded the city of Uchch. Saifuddin's uncle and spiritual preceptor Shaikh Abu Ishaq Gazaruni (d. 1035) was a Sufi of extraordinary eminence and commanded a sizable following; Shaikh Nizamuddin regarded him as a perfect Sufi endowed with every spiritual quality. Even after the passage of three centuries, Ibn Battuta found a network of hospices on the western coast of Indian manned by Sufis of the Gazaruni order. He was amazed to find that the dead Shaikh's reputation continued to wield immense influence over the seafarers and the traders living on the Indian and Chinese coasts.[13]

There is no record of Saifuddin's activities in Uchch. His spiritual prowess however appears to have been no less than his uncle's. Shaikh Nizamuddin related the following anecdote regarding Saifuddin's triumph over a *yogi*:

> There was once a Yogi who came to Uchch. Attempting to convert Shaikh Saifuddin Gazaruni, he engaged him in a heated debate. 'Come', he said to the Shaikh, 'show me your superiority.' 'You show me your superiority' retorted the Shaikh; 'Since it is you who are trying to convert, it is up to you to demonstrate your superiority.' The Yogi soared from the ground into the air, till his head touched the ceiling. Then he came straight back to the ground. Turning to the Shaikh, he crowed, 'Now you show me your superiority.' Shaikh Saifuddin Gazaruni turned his face towards the heavens imploring 'O God, you have given this superiority to a stranger. Please grant me some miracle of like quality.' After that the Shaikh soared from his place. He flew towards the *qibla*, that is, in the direction of Mecca. Then he headed north. Reversing himself, he flew south, finally landing on his original place. Then he sat down. The Yogi was awestruck. Placing his head at the feet of the Shaikh, he said: 'I cannot display such power. I can merely go straight up from the ground and come back down. I can't turn in mid-air and fly to the right or the left, while you can turn in whatever direction you wish. This is God's work. It is divinely inspired. What I do is both false and futile.'[14]

Nearly three hundred years after the conquest of Sind, the Turks overran the neighbouring province of Punjab. The invasion was triggered by the unprovoked advance on the frontiers of Ghazni by Raja Jaipal, the Hindu-Shahiya ruler of Kabul and Punjab. Amir Subuktigin (r. 977-97), the king of Ghazni, retaliated quickly. Jaipal was defeated and Peshawar and Lamghan fell into the hands of the victor. This border skirmish blossomed into a full-fledged hostility during the reign of Subuktigin's son and successor Mahmud. The Sultan repeatedly defeated Jaipal and his successor Anandpal and Trilochanpal in several encounters. In 1010-11 Mahmud conquered and annexed Multan together with its dependencies. Moving beyond Punjab, he successfully conducted lightning campaigns against Mathura, Kannauj, Gwalior and Gujarat. He plundered the wealth and temples of the vanquished Rajas at will and thus became instrumental in generating in India, in the words of Al-Biruni, 'the most inveterate hatred of all Muslims'.[15] India had however no place in Mahmud's political ambitions. He remained content with the annexation of Punjab, leaving the rest of the conquered territories untouched.

The establishment of Muslim rule in Punjab stimulated the migration of Sufis from Iran, Iraq, Afghanistan and Central Asia to this part of the subcontinent. Lahore, which later became the administrative headquarters of the Ghaznavid Punjab, soon emerged as a popular dwelling place for Sufi immigrants. The first Sufi known to have settled in Lahore was Shaikh Ismail Lahori (d. 1057). A native of Bukhara and a scholar noted for his expertise in Koranic exegesis, hadith (prophetic traditions) and jurisprudence, he arrived in Lahore in 1005. Sufi hagiographers assert that Shaikh Ismail was not only the first Sufi of Lahore but also the town's first public preacher and instructor of the Koran. Nineteenth century Sufi authorities speak of the proselytizing zeal of the Shaikh but in the absence of contemporary evidence such assertions must be treated as doubtful.

A contemporary of Shaikh Ismail was Sayyid Husain Zanjani. An Irani by birth and a disciple of Abul Fazl Muhammad Khattali, the famous Sufi of the school of Junaid, Husian Zanjani seems to have reached Lahore shortly after its annexation to the Ghaznavid kingdom. The sixteenth century Sufi hagiographer Jamali Kanboh (d. 1537), and following him, Abul Fazl and then a host of nineteenth century Sufi writers inform us that the Sayyid lived in Lahore in the twelfth century. But in view of Shaikh Nizamuddin's testimony to the effect that his co-disciples Shaikh Ali Hujwiri (d. 1072) reached Lahore the day Husain died leaves no doubt about the fact that the former had settled in Punjab in the early eleventh century. His brother Sayyid Yaqub Sadr Diwan Zanjani is also reported to have accompanied him to Lahore. All Sufi authors speak of Sayyid Husain's extraordinary learning but none provides any information regarding his avocation in Lahore.

Sayyid Husain's junior contemporary and co-disciple Abul Hasan Ali bin Usman Ghaznavi Jallabi Hujwiri better known as 'Data Ganj Bakhsh'

(Bestower of Treasures) was by all accounts the greatest among the early Sufis of Punjab. Hujwiri's life and career are mostly hidden in mists of the past. From stray references in his book *Kashf al-mahjub*, however, we can piece together a brief sketch of his life. Born in early eleventh century in Ghazna (Afghanistan), Hujwiri passed his childhood in the city's suburbs, Jallab and Hujwir. He studied with several leading scholars of his time but had special affection and reverence for Abul Qasim Gurgani, Abul Abbas Ashqani and Khwaja Muzaffar. Abul Fazl Khattali initiated him into Sufism. After extensive travels and sojourns in Iraq, Iran, Syria and Central Asia, he settled in Lahore. The exact date of Hujwiri's arrival in Lahore is not known. But since his Shaikh (spiritual preceptor) is reported to have died in 1061 and he went to Lahore at his preceptor's instructions, it can be inferred that Hujwiri must have reached Lahore before 1061. His stay in Lahore seems to have been far from happy. He found intellectual discussion with fellow Sufis and scholars in Lahore unsatisfying and considered himself 'a captive among uncongenial folks in the district of Lahawur'.[16] He longed for the books he had left in Ghazna and took time off to visit his Shaikh there. We find Hujwiri by his side when the Shaikh breathed his last. Hujwiri eventually returned to Lahore and lived there till his death in 1072.

Kashf al-mahjub is the most outstanding of Hujwiri's ten works. The book was written partly in response to queries from a fellow townsman, Abu Sa'id Hujwiri, regarding the true meaning of Sufism and the nature of its stations and schools. An equally important objective of the author seems to have been to provide an authoritative account of Sufism. He believed that an authentic treatise on Sufism was the need of the hour, given the state of Sufism in Punjab in his days. His disenchantment with the Sufis of Lahore is clearly discernible from the following remarks: 'Know that in this our time the science of Sufism is obsolete, especially in this country. The whole people is occupied with following the lusts and has turned its back on the path of quietism (*rida*), while the ulama and those who pretend to learning have formed a conception of Sufism which is quite contrary to its fundamental principles.'[17] In twenty-five chapters of *Kashf al-mahjub*, Hujwiri furnishes a masterful narrative of the fundamental doctrines and practices of Sufism together with brief though penetrative biographies of major Sufis of the past and present. He frequently relates anecdotes from their lives, highlighting their mystical accomplishment, and quotes their saying at the end of each chapter, explaining their positions on the core aspects of Sufism. The fourteenth chapter, described by R.A. Nicholson as the most remarkable in the whole book, describes twelve schools of Sufism and their doctrines. The last eleven chapters recount various stages, the author calls them 'veils', of the Sufi path along with the 'portals of the practice and theory of the Sufis'. In each chapter Hujwiri examines the strengths and weakness of current views on Sufi concepts. He states his own opinions on these issues and constantly reminds the reader that mere observation of rituals without renouncing 'all lusts and pleasures' is meaningless.

Kashf al-mahjub demonstrates Hujwiri's mastery over Islamic religious sciences and Sufi theory. The story of the trials and tribulations he had to endure while traversing the path of knowledge was however not without its moments of passion and pain.

> 'Once I found myself', writes Hujwiri, 'in a difficulty.' After many devotional exercises undertaken in the hope of clearing it away, I repaired as I had done with success on a former occasion, to the tomb of Abu Yazid and stayed beside it for a space of three months, performing every day three ablutions and thirty purifications in the hope that my difficulty might be removed. It was not, however; so I departed and journeyed towards Khurasan. One night I arrived at a village in that country where there was a khanqah inhabited by a number of aspirants to Sufism. I was wearing a dark blue frock, such as is prescribed by the Sunna; but I had nothing of the Sufis' regular equipment except a staff and a leathern water bottle. I appeared very contemptible in the eyes of these Sufis, who did not know me. They regarded only my habit and said to one another, 'This fellow is not one of us.' And so in truth it was: I was not one of them, but I had to pass the night in that place. They lodged me on a roof, while they themselves went up to a roof above mine, and set before me dry bread which had turned green [with mildew], while I was drawing into my nostrils the savour of the viands with which they regaled themselves. All the time they were addressing derisive remarks to me from the roof. When they finished the food, they began to pelt me with skins of the melons, which they had eaten, by way of showing how pleased they were with themselves and how lightly they thought of me. I said in my heart: ' Lord God, were it not that they are wearing the dress of Thy friends, I would not have borne this from them.' And the more they scoffed at me the more glad became my heart, so that the endurance of his burden was the means of delivering me from the difficulty which I have mentioned.[18]

Hujwiri was aware of the debate between the protagonists of *sahw* (sobriety) and *sukr* (intoxication). He firmly believed that sobriety was preferable to intoxication and had nothing but contempt for the antinomian tendencies of the adherents of *sukr*. Like all great Sufis he campaigned for the supremacy of *sharia* (Religious law) over *tariqa* (Sufism). He censured the Hululis, Farisis, and the Qaramitas for their disregard of the *sharia*. His observation that 'if religion, which is the root, is not firmly based, Sufism, which is the branch and offspring of religion, must with more reason be unsound',[19] makes his position on this issue crystal clear. Hujwiri believed that *sharia* and *tariqa* compliment each other, they are like body and soul. A body without a soul is lifeless; in the same manner Sufism without *sharia* is worthless—a mere hypocrisy.

Hujwiri was not the first Sufi who sought to reconcile Sufism with *sharia*. The process had begun much before. But *Kashf al-mahjud* was certainly the first major written text of this endeavour and inspired successive generations of Sufis. The book itself is enough to ensure for Hujwiri a place along with great Sufi masters and thinkers like Abu Hamid Ghazzali and Abdul Qadir Jilani. Shaikh Nizamuddin's view that one who is not able to find a righteous guide to tread the right path, should seek guidance from *Kashf al-mahjud* sums up the value and power of that text as a Sufi document.

Another prominent Sufi of Punjab was Sayyid Ahmad. His father Sayyid Zainul Abidin came from Arabia in early twelfth century and settled in village Kursi Kot, a suburb of Multan. He married the daughter of a local landlord and Sayyid Ahmad was the offspring from this marriage. He went to Baghdad for higher studies where he is reported to have met with Abdul Qadir Jilani and Shahabuddin Suhrawardi. On his way back to India, he met Khawaja Maudud Chishti (d. 1181-2) in Chisht (Afghanistan) and received *khilafat* (certificate of authority) from him. By the time he returned to Kursi Kot, his fame had spread far and wide. Seekers of both kinds—spiritual and mundane—flocked to his residence. The Sayyid's generosity earned him the title 'Sultan Sakhi Sarwar' (Lord and Master of the Generous) and 'Lakh Data' (Giver of Lakhs). The Sayyid's growing popularity incited the jealousy of his own kinsmen and when the Governor of Multan married his daughter to him, the jealousy turned into open hostility. Shortly after this marriage, his cousins got together and assassinated him (1181). His tomb in Kursi Kot has since then been a centre of pilgrimage for his admirers. Numerous Hindu devotees, known as Sultani, attest to his popularity extending beyond the boundaries of caste or religion. As late as the nineteenth century most non-Sikh Hindus of the Jullundur division in Punjab were Sultani.[20]

A contemporary of Sayyid Ahmad was Azizudin Lahori. A Sufi of the school of Junaid and a native of Baghdad, Azizuddin reached Lahore in 1179. Two years after his arrival in Lahore, Sultan Muhammad Ghori

(r. 1175-1206) laid siege to the city. When the king of Lahore sought Azizuddin's help against the invader, he assured the king of his safety for the time being but predicted that the city would fall into the hands of the Ghorids after six years. The prediction proved to be perfectly true; Muhammad Ghori conquered Lahore in 1186 putting an end to more than 150 years of Ghaznavid rule in Punjab. Azizuddin died in 1216 and was buried in Lahore.[21]

A Punjabi Sufi whose life and career have been the subject of innumerable legends was Shaikh Abul Raza Ratan Al-Hindi or Baba Ratan Al-Hindi. Reported to have been born in Bhatinda in the sixth century, he is reputed to have visited Arabia and embraced Islam at the hands of Prophet Muhammad. Legends give him the extraordinarily long age of seven hundred years, due to the blessings of the Prophet. He is claimed to have returned to Bhatinda before his death in 1300. He is also said to have related several prophetic traditions. A treatise entitled *Risala-i Rataiya*, incorporating these traditions, was also reported to have been compiled by his followers. These stories must be treated as legend, not history. Even in the medieval period, as Abul Fazl observers, there were people who 'rejected them as the garrulity of senile age'.[22] Although the Irani Sufi Allaudaulah Simnani (d. 1336) and the Egyptian scholar Ibn Hajr Asqalani (d. 1449) were among the admirers of Baba Ratan, the renowned Indian traditionist, Raziuddin Hasan Saghani (d. 1252), rejected the traditions narrated by Baba Ratan as apocryphal. In yogic traditions Baba Ratan is identified with Gorakhnath, the chief preceptor of the Siddha cult of the *yogis*. These traditions claim that Prophet Muhammad had learnt *yoga* through Baba Ratan.[23]

Another legendary figure in the narratives of Indian Sufism is Sipahsalar Mas'ud Ghazi, better known as Ghazi Miyan and Bale Miyan. No contemporary record of his life and activities exists. The first detailed account of his career and exploits in India, *Mir'at-i Mas'udi* was written in the seventeenth century, more than six hundred years after his death. Its author Abdur Rahman Chishti (d. 1655), a well-known Sufi of the Chishti order, claims to have collected information for his book from an eleventh century work *Tarikh-i Mulla Muhammad Ghaznavi*, whose author reportedly served both Salar Mas'ud and his uncle Sultan Mahmud of Ghazna. This text is no longer extant. Abdur Rahman claims to have written the book with the assistance of the deceased Sayyid Salar Mas'ud himself, whose spirit appeared to him in a vision, commended his efforts, and vouched for the authenticity of the events narrated in the book.

Mir'at-i Mas'udi however is not a serious historical work. It is an agglomeration of facts and fiction in which the 'the great actions and exploits of other men are appropriated, without scruple, to the hero of the tale'.[24] It can at best be placed in the category of historical romance or religious martyrology.

The *Mir'at* begins with an account of the invasion of Ajmer by Salar Sahu, brother-in-law of Sultan Mahmud of Ghazni, whom the Sultan had dispatched to Ajmer in response to the entreaties of its Muslim ruler Muzaffar Khan for succour against the local Hindu *zamindars*. Sahu defeated the Hindu chieftains and was rewarded with the government of Ajmer. His wife, the Sultan's sister, also joined him and it was in Ajmer that Mas'ud was born on 14 February 1015. Two years later Sahu and his troops assisted the Sultan in his Kannauj campaign, and was confirmed in the government of Ajmer. During the next ten years Sahu undertook military expeditions from Ajmer, humbled many Indian chieftains and collected enormous revenues. When an Indian army besieged Kabuliz, in the vicinity of Kashmir, the Sultan asked Sahu to help the besieged. Sahu defeated the Indian army and was appointed the Governor of Kabuliz. He summoned Mas'ud to Kabuliz who in the meanwhile had grown into an accomplished soldier. On his way to Kabuliz, Mas'ud defeated Rai Satugan, ruler of Rawal, achieving thereby his maiden victory at the young age of twelve. During Mahmud's Somnath campaign (1027), Mas'ud fought with great distinction and subsequently travelled to Ghazni where he persuaded the Sultan to reject the pleas of a delegation of Hindus from Somnath who offered twice the weight of Somnath idol in gold in exchange for the idol of Somanth which Mahmud had plundered. Mas'ud's influence with the Sultan made the Wazir Khwaja Hasan Maimandi jealous of him who hatched a conspiracy against Mas'ud. In order to keep Mas'ud out of harm's way, the Sultan advised him to return to his parents in Kabuliz.

Returning to India, Mas'ud, now known as Sipahsalar Mas'ud, waged relentless campaigns against Multan, Ajodhan, Delhi, and Meerut, defeated the rulers of those towns, and finally camped at Satrikh (in modern Barabanki district), where he set up his headquarters. Shortly afterwards, his father joined him at Satrikh. From Satrikh, Salar Mas'ud sent armies in diverse directions to conquer the surrounding territories. Salar Sahu advanced against Kara-Manikpur while Mas'ud's two chief lieutenants Salar Saifuddin and Miyan Rajab were dispatched against Bahraich. Raja Sohil Deo of Bahraich collected a large army and prepared to give battle. The two generals therefore asked for reinforcements from Salar Mas'ud, who, against the wishes of his father, marched there in person. He reached Bahraich on 29 July 1032 and camped underneath a *mahua* tree near the sun temple situated on the bank of a tank called Surajkund. A month later Salar Mas'ud received the news of the death of his father, which however failed to dampen his resolve to root out idolatry from Bahraich. The battle for the mastery of Bahraich was fought for three days on the banks of Kosala river, and was throughout most hotly contested. On 14 Rajab 424 (15 June 1033) Salar Mas'ud was killed along with most of his followers and was later buried under his favourite *mahua* tree. The prince of martyrs, as the Salar came to be known after his death, was only nineteen and unmarried when he was slain.[25]

Needless to say, most of the aforementioned events are legend, not history. Ghaznavid histories furnish details of Mahmud's exploits in India. His campaigns against Kannauj and Somnath, among the few authentic events mentioned in *Mir'at-i Mas'udi*, are also fairly well documented. But none of these histories refer to either Sahu and Mas'ud or to their Indian campaigns undertaken ostensibly with Mahmud's blessings. There is no evidence of Muslim presence in Ajmer prior to Muhammad Ghori's campaign against Prithvi Raj Chauhan in the last decade of the twelfth century. Even the identity of Salar Mas'ud is obscure and one cannot say with a degree of confidence that a person of this name did actually exist. Sultan Mahmud of Ghazni had no nephew named Mas'ud. His son and successor was Sultan Mas'ud, and this seems to have inspired the narrators of the legend to designate their hero with this name. The evidence at our disposal also suggests that the Turks conquered the territories of Awadh and Bahraich only during the reign of Sultan Shamsuddin Iltutmish (r. 1210-36). Prince Nasiruddin Mahmud, grandson of Iltutmish, who later became the Sultan of Delhi (r. 1246-66), was Governor of Bahraich during the early thirteenth century. The *Tabaqat-i Nasiri*, the first major history of the Sultanate period and dedicated to Nasiruddin Mahmud, does not refer to Salar Mas'ud at all.

In the absence of any concrete historical evidence, a question mark must always hang against the identity of Salar Mas'ud as well as the authenticity of the events associated with him. There is evidence that even in the sixteenth century Muslim intellectuals and Sufis had reservations about the existence of Salar Mas'ud. Abdul Qadir Badauni, the author of *Muntakhab-ut tawarikh* writes that Shaikhul Hidaya, a prominent Sufi of Khairabad (modern Sitapur district) once told the chronicler's patron that Salar Mas'ud 'was an Afghan who met his death by martyrdom'.[26]

Richard Eaton in his book *Sufis of Bijapur* (1978) has suggested that the Turkish penetration in the Deccan in its initial phase (1296-1347) was abetted and supported by the Sufis, most of whom served as ordinary soldiers in the armies of the Delhi Sultans. He calls them warrior Sufis. This theory suggesting the transformation of Sufis into warriors has since been questioned because 'the principal bearers of Sufi tradition in India were in general full time religious leaders and did not themselves take part in military activities, though some of their followers did'.[27] However, in the case of Salar Mas'ud the converse process of a warrior assuming the status of a Sufi following his death seems to have taken place, at least in the pre-modern Indian imagination.

Many such legends were current in India in the medieval period. The legend of Shah Dola Abdur Rahman, for example, became popular in Maharashtra in the fourteenth century. The tales associated with the life and activities of Shah Dola bear striking resemblance to those of Salar Mas'ud. Shah Dola also is alleged to have been a nephew of Sultan Mahmud of Ghazni and was reportedly martyred in 988 while fighting a Hindu army near Achlapur in modern Maharashtra. He was also unmarried when he died. He appeared to the Bahmani Sultan Alauddin (d. 1379) in a dream in 1368 and ordered him to build his mausoleum on the site of his burial. The veneration of Shah Dola in Maharashtra as a saint probably dates back to this event. By a strange coincidence the earliest reference to Salar Mas'ud and his tomb in Bahraich also occurs in the fourteenth century work of Amir Khusrau, *I'jaz-i Khusrawi*.

Salar Mas'ud's tomb still exists in Bahraich and is one of the most popular centres of pilgrimage in northern India. The exact date of Salar Mas'ud's transformation from a warrior to a saint remains unknown. The servitor of Salar Mas'ud's tomb as well as his modern Urdu biographers would have us believe that initially Salar's grave was guarded by his family servants. Gradually the residents of the area started visiting the grave to pay their respects. But the grave became an object of popular veneration when a milkman Jasu Ahir's barren wife gave birth to a son after praying there. In 1062-3 Zohra Bibi, the blind daughter of one Sayyid Jamaluddin, came from Rudauli (in modern Barabanki district) and prayed at Mas'ud's tomb. Salar Mas'ud is said to have responded to her entreaties and her eyesight was restored. As a token of gratitude, she built a magnificent tomb over the grave of the Salar and spent the rest of her life as a servitor of the tomb. She remained unmarried and was buried near the mausoleum after her death. The fame of Salar Mas'ud as a Sufi saint can be said to date back to this episode.[28]

During his sojourn in Bahraich, more than two hundred years after Mas'ud's death, Prince Nasiruddin Mahmud is reported to have built a mausoleum on Mas'ud's grave but there is no contemporary evidence to support this. Amir Khusrau mentions Salar Mas'ud as follows: 'In the town of Bahraich, the fragrant tomb of Sipahsalar Shahid (the martyred commander of the armies), scents the entire Hindustan with the perfumes of odorous wood.'[29] This indicates that Salar Mas'ud was probably martyred in the thirteenth century in the wake of the Turkish invasion of Bahraich. This would also explain the absence of any reference to him in the pre-fourteenth century chronicles.

By the middle of the fourteenth century the legend of Salar Mas'ud had been greatly expanded prompting the first royal visit to the tomb. In 1340-1 Sultan Muhammad Tughluq (r. 1325-51) made a pilgrimage to Bahraich and donated a large sum of money to the servitors of the dargah.[30] Thirty-four years later, his successor Firuz Tughluq (r. 1351-88) visited Bahraich, shortly after the death of his favourite son Prince Fath Khan, and stayed there for some time. Shams Siraj Afif, the author of *Tarikh-i Firuz Shahi*, writes that one night the Salar appeared to the Sultan in a dream, advised him to be steadfast in the observance of the rituals, and get ready for his final journey. The next morning, Firuz had his head shaved in the Sufi fashion and began, as the chronicler puts it, his journey on the path of orthodoxy.[31] The anonymous author of *Sirat-i Firuz Shahi* informs us that by the third quarter of fourteenth century the tomb of Salar Mas'ud had earned countrywide fame as a place for providing cure to leprosy patients. The chronicler writes that Haji Ilyas, the Sultan of Bengal, who was suffering from leprosy, came to Bahraich seeking the Salar's blessing. But since he had entered the territories of Firuz Tughluq without the latter's prior permission, the Sultan retaliated by invading Bengal.[32]

By the turn of the sixteenth century, the legend of Salar Mas'ud had assumed the form of a cult in the far-flung areas of northern and eastern India. Numerous fairs and festivals commemorating the putative principal events of his life were held in modern Uttar Pradesh, Bihar, and Bengal. Replicas of the Salar's tomb sprung up in practically every town and village of these provinces. The practice of carrying green and red banners fastened on a spear, symbolizing the banners of Salar Mas'ud's army, from far-off places to Bahraich, annually on the eve of the festival held to celebrate Mas'ud's marriage to Zohra Bibi became the vogue in all these places. Although Sultan Sikandar Lodi (r. 1489-1517) banned this festival throughout his dominions, allegedly because of certain immoral practices which had come to be associated with the fair,[33] the festivities seem to have been revived subsequently. Writing about the events of June 1561, Abul Fazl, the author of *Akbar Nama*, refers to the festival of Salar Mas'ud in Agra. 'In the town of Bahraich', writes Abul Fazl, 'is the grave of Salar Mas'ud Ghazi. It is custom in India for people to make flags of various colours and convey them along with numerous presents to that place. Accordingly a large contingent starts from Agra for this rendezvous and keeps awake for several nights in the neighbourhood of the city. There is a great concourse and both the good and the bad assemble there.'[34] Abul Fazl also describes Akbar's visit to the site of the festival on the bank of the Jamuna incognito where he had to take recourse to a trick in order to keep his identity a secret when someone in the crowd recognized him.[35] The nineteenth century descendent of the emperor and his namesake Akbar II (r. 1806-37) was also an ardent devotee of the Salar. He granted the *zamindari* of the village Singha Parasi in Bahraich for the upkeep of the *dargah*.[36]

Even today the *Urs* festival (death anniversary) of the Salar is held on 12, 13 and 14 of the Islamic month of Rajab with great fanfare. Yet another festival held on the first Sunday of the Hindu month of *Jaishth* (May-June), which continues for 12 days, draws a larger crowd to Bahraich. The day is perhaps symbolic of *Jaishth* 1033 when Salar Mas'ud started his offensive against Raja Sohil Deo. The principal event of this festival is the wedding of Salar Mas'ud with Zohra Bibi. After Zohra's death her parents started the practice, which continues even in the present, of bringing a *barat* (marriage party) every year from Radauli to Bahraich and formally giving her in marriage to Ghazi Miyan. Similar processions originate from other towns of Uttar Pradesh and converge on Bahraich on the appointed day. The pilgrim parties are still called *maidni* or *barat*. The *baratis* bring wedding gifts (*jahiz*) and formally offer them at the tomb of the bridegroom Salar Mas'ud. This festival too is held on the first Sunday of the month of *Jaishth*, in numerous towns and villages of Uttar Pradesh. Drawn by the supposed healing prowess of the Salar, a large number of people afflicted with diseases, especially leprosy, participate in the festivals looking for relief and faith cure.

The unusually large number of Hindu devotees of Ghazi Miyan intrigued European observers of the nineteenth and twentieth centuries. In 1913, N.L. Rockey found to his surprise that almost 50 per cent of the pilgrims attending the festival in Bahraich were Hindus.[37] In 1849 Colonel W.H. Sleeman was struck by what was for him the extraordinary sight of Hindus and Muslims making offerings at the shrine of Salar Mas'ud, 'whose only recorded merit consists of having destroyed a great many Hindoos in a wanton and unprovoked invasion of their territory'.[38] He postulated that the Hindus 'worship any sign of manifested might or power', and explained the devotion of the Hindu masses to Ghazi Miyan in terms of his supposed influence in heaven, 'which he may be induced to exercise in their favour, by suitable offering and personal application to the shrine'.[39] The educated among the Hindus believed, suggests Sleeman, that God had used Salar as an instrument of vengeance for their wrongdoing.[40]

Abdur Rahman Chishti concludes his account of Salar Mas'ud by observing that after Mas'ud's martyrdom Ajmer once again passed into spiritual wilderness and idolatry re-established itself in the region in full force. It was only in the thirteenth century, he suggests, that the heyday of spiritualism returned to Ajmer when Khwaja Muinuddin Chishti arrived in Ajmer and led a spiritual campaign for the region's Islamization. Muinuddin Chishti is however not known for his proselytizing or crusading activities in India. In fact active proselytizing has never been a Sufi practice. Abdur Rahman's attempt to establish a link between Salar Mas'ud Ghazi and Muinuddin Chishti should therefore be seen as a means to legitimize Salar's alleged military-Islamic exploits in India. It is also plausible that Abdur Rahman Chishti deliberately chose to name Ajmer as the birthplace as well as the centre of the Salar's early activities because of the subsequent association of Muinuddin with the city.

The problem of Salar Mas'ud's real identity remains unresolved. It is almost certain that he was not the nephew of Sultan Mahmud of Ghazni. His military exploits in various parts of northern and western India narrated in *Mir'at-i Mas'udi* and other folklore are also fictitious. He was most probably a military adventurer who lost his life fighting along with the Turkish armies in the region of Bahraich in the thirteenth century. His martyr status coupled with his supposed healing prowess and the gradual process of superstition taking root among neo-Muslims which led to orthodox Islam's integration into existing popular religious structure seem to have contributed to his popularity and augmented the number of his devotees.

NOTES

1. Abdul Hasan Ali bin Al-Husain Al-Mas'udi, *Muruj al-zahab*, Eng. trans., A. Sprenger, London, 1841, p. 389.
2. Zainuddin Ma'bari, *Tuhfat al-mujahidin*, Eng. trans. S.M.H. Nainar, Madras, 1942, p. 60.
3. Muhammad Qasim Hindu Shah Firishta, *Tarikh-i-Firishta*, Lucknow, 1864, Vol. II, pp. 370-1
4. *Tuhfat al-mujahidin*, op. cit., pp. 35-9.
5. M.G.S. Narayanan, 'Political and Social Conditions of Kerala Under the Kulasekhara Empire', Ph.D. thesis, University of Kerala, 1972, pp. 185-90, 547-9, quoted by V. Kunhali, *Advent of Islam in Kerala: Special Features*, Proceedings of Indian History Congress, 1975, pp. 326-9
6. Reported in *The Times of India*, 25 June 1998.
7. *Bashvekalet Arshivi*, Istanbul, Muhimme Defterleri, Vol. 28, f. 139, *farman* no. 331, November 1576.
8. S.A.A. Rizvi, *A History of Sufism in India*, New Delhi, 1978, Vol. I, pp. 409-10.
9. R.M. Eaton, *Sufis of Bijapur 1300-1700: Social Role of Sufis in Medieval India*, Princeton University Press, 1978, pp. 28-30.
10. Al-Mas'udi, *Muruj al-zahab*, op. cit., p. 385.
11. Sayyid Sulaiman Nadvi, *Maqalat*, Azamgarh, 1966, Vol. I, p. 216.
12. S.M. Ikram, *Aab-i kausar*, Delhi, 1991 (rpt), pp. 39-40.
13. S.A.A. Rizvi, *A History of Sufism in India*, Vol. I, op. cit., p. 410.
14. Amir Hasn Sijzi, *Fawa'id al-fu'ad*, Eng. trans. Bruce B. Lawrence, Populist Press, New York, 1992, p. 138.
15. Quoted by Muhammad Habib, *Sultan Mahmud of Ghaznin*, Delhi, 1951 (rpt.), p. 86.
16. Abul Hasan Ali bin Usman Hujwiri, *Kashf al-mahjub*, Eng. trans. R.A. Nicholson, Lahore, 1982, p. 91.
17. Ibid., p. 7.
18. Ibid., pp. 68-69.
19. Ibid., p. 261.
20. Ghulam Sarwar, *Khazinat al-asfiya*, Kanpur, 1914, Vol. II, pp. 245-8.
21. Ibid., pp. 255-6.
22. Abul Fazl, *Ain-i-Akbari*, Eng. trans. H.S. Jarret, 1977 (rpt.), Vol. II, p. 401.
23. S.A.A. Rizvi, *A History of Sufism in India*, Vol. I, op. cit., pp. 320, 354
24. Elliot and Dowson, *The History of India As Told By Its Own Historians*, Allahabad, 1962, Vol. II, p. 514.
25. Abdur Rahman Chishti, *Mirat-i Mas'udi*, Eng. trans. Elliot and Dowson, op. cit., pp. 513-49.
26. Abdur Qadir Badauni, *Muntakhab-ut Tawarikh*, Eng. trans. Wolsely Haig, 1973 (rpt.), Vol. III, pp. 46-7

27. Carl Ernst, *Eternal Garden: Mysticism, History, and Politics at a South Asian Sufi Center*, op. cit., p. 101.
28. Tahir Mahmud, 'The Dargah of Sayyid Salar Mas'ud Ghazi in Bahraich: Legend, Tradition, and Reality', in *Muslim Shrines in India*, ed. Christian W. Troll, Delhi, 1989, p. 29
29. Amir Khusrau, *I'jaz-i Khusravi,* Lucknow, 1867, Vol. I, p. 155, quoted by I.H. Siddiqui, 'A Note on the Dargah of Salar Mas'ud Ghazi in the Light of Standard Historical Sources', in *Muslim Shrines in India*, op. cit., p. 45.
30. Ziauddin Barani, *Tarikh-i Firuz Shahi*, ed. Sayyid Ahmad Khan, Calcutta, 1862, p. 491; *Tarikh-i Firishta*, op. cit., p. 139
31. Shams Siraj Affif, *Tarikh-i Firuz Shahi*, Calcutta, 1891, pp. 372-3
32. Anonymous, *Sirat-i Firuz Shahi* (Khuda Bakhsh Manuscript), Khuda Bakhsh Oriental Public Library, Patna, 1999, pp. 27-41.
33. Abdullah, *Tarikh-i-Daudi*, ed. S. Abdur Rashid, Aligarh, 1954, p. 38; *Tarikh-i-Firishta*, op. cit., pp. 186-7.
34. Abul Fazl, *Akbar Nama*, Eng. trans. H. Beveridge, Delhi, 1989 (rpt.), Vol. II, p. 257.
35. Ibid., p. 225.
36. Tahir Mahmud, op. cit., p. 38.
37. Kerrin Grafin v. Schwerin, 'Saint Worship in Indian Islam: The Legend of the Martyr Salar Mas'ud Ghazi', in *Rituals and Religion among Muslims of the Subcontinent*, ed. Imtiaz Ahmad, Lahore, 1985, p. 153.
38. W.H. Sleeman, *Journey Through the Kingdom of Oudh in 1849-1850*, London, 1858, Vol. I, p. 48.
39. Ibid., p. 49.
40. Ibid., p. 49.

The *Jihad* of Sayyid Ahmad Barelwi on the North West Frontier: The Last Echo of the Middle Ages? Or a Prefiguration of Modern South Asia?

Marc Gaborieau

My interest in Sayyid Ahmad Barelwi (1786-1831) was first aroused by a series of lectures of Charles J. Adams, then Director of the Institute of Islamic Studies in McGill, on revivalism in South Asian Islam from Shah Nabiullah to Maududi: he stressed the importance, but also the enigmatic character, of this great figure of the early nineteenth century who is too often interpreted anachronistically in the light of more recent events or of later figures like Maududi.[1] I have since that time worked and published (Gaborieau 1994 to 2001a and under preparation) about Sayyid Ahmad who appears as a key figure in the modern history of South Asia: the theological landscape (Metcalf 1982) is marked by the cleavage between on the one side the Barelwis who refused his reforms and, on the other side, the schools which in one way or the other accepted his inheritance, that is to say, the Deobandis and the Ahl-i-hadith, as well as the modernists who followed Sayyid Ahmad Khan (Troll 1982: 28-57).

Sayyid Ahmad started his public career of a reformer, preacher and *jihad* fighter in 1818. This was the year which–with the fall of the Marathas and the demilitarization of India–inaugurated a period of transition which lasted up to the early 1870s from when we can date the real beginning of Modern India. In many ways Sayyid Ahmad would then seem to be entirely on the side of the modern world. Although he criticized *bid^ca* in the religious field, he did not disdain the technical innovations introduced by the Westerners. Before he started on his pilgrimage to Mecca in 1822, he had his first printing press established in Calcutta, and had the first edition of the Koran in India[2] published in 1829 (Gaborieau 1994 and 2001a); he was thus equipped to compete with the Christian missionaries with their own weapons (Powell 1993). On his return from the pilgrimage in 1824 he used a steamboat and, at his stop in Bombay, he bought firearms in view of his *jihad* which he had then announced, and which he was to start in 1826. He thus appeared, in the beginning of this period of transition, as a precursor; that is why some contemporary historians portrayed him as a harbinger of the contemporary nation-states of South Asia or in Pakistan, even as the forerunner of the Islamic state.

If these interpretations are based on patent facts, are they not in a way one-sided? Do they lay the emphasis on the right side? If we consider the whole of Sayyid Ahmad's life, we may doubt that these modern aspects outweigh the traditional ones. He was after all a very conventional Sufi *Pir* (Gaborieau 1999b), criticizing only a limited number of abuses of his predecessors like the tomb cults and the visualization of the image of one's own *murshid* (Gaborieau 1997a and 1999a).

A case in point to decide this question is the last part of life of Sayyid Ahmad with his *jihad* and his posthumous career as a *mahdi*. Was his theory of *jihad* different from the classical one? Did it anticipate the apologetic theories which flourished later in the nineteenth and twentieth centuries? Was his setting up of a theocratic State in the North West a prefiguration of modern nation-states or of contemporary Islamic states? Or was it more prosaically the last medieval utopia? I will here develop a reinterpretation which I sketched in a previous paper (Gaborieau 1999c). And I will add new arguments drawn from a previous reexamination of the posthumous career of Sayyid Ahmad as a *mahdi* (Gaborieau 2000).

Historical and Intellectual Context

Two concepts were very important in the modern history of South Asian Muslims: *daʿwa* (usually spelt *daʿwat* in Persian and Urdu) or *tabligh*, 'invitation to Islam', which has come nowadays to mean peaceful proselytization (Troll 1994; Gaborieau 1997); and *jihad*, 'war in the way of God', 'holy war', literally an 'effort' to extend the kingdom of God. The two concepts are linked: traditionally, as we shall see presently: in Sunni Islam *daʿwa* is a part of *jihad* (Morabia 1993; Troll 1994: 115-16); conversely nowadays peaceful proselytization keeps some of the spirit of *jihad* (Gaborieau 1996b; 1997: 221-2; and 2001b).

This paper revolves around the concept of *jihad*, and on its various uses and interpretations all along the nineteenth and twentieth centuries.

In order to disentangle the various usages of this concepts, it is focused on a unique episode, the *jihad* conducted from 1826 to 1831, on the North West Frontier, of what is now Pakistan, by Sayyid Ahmad Barelwi (1786-1831). We will first review the diverging interpretations of his movement which have been propounded; we will then try to ascertain what *jihad* could mean to Sayyid Ahmad and his followers in the context of the 1820s and early 1830s and even later for those who expected his reappearance as a *mahdi* and kept alive the spirit of *jihad* on the North West Frontier.

Our discussion must take into account the controversies raised in India about *jihad* during the nineteenth and twentieth centuries. They developed in three phases. Prior to the Mutiny of 1857 the medieval sunni theory held true. According to it, the Koranic verses which commanded peaceful propagation of Islam, or enjoined fighting only to repel aggression, were considered as abrogated; the only verses which remained valid were those 'enjoining an all out and un-limited war against the infidels' (Macdonald 1961; Tyan 1965; Morabia, 1993: 119-262; Friedmann 1989: 166-86). The second phase, from 1857 to around 1910, saw bold reinterpretations of the classical doctrine. At that time, in India and Afghanistan, the last indomitable Muslims kept fighting *jihad* against the British (Bosworth 1980; Friedmann 1989: 171-2) while some British administrators, like William Hunter, Christian missionaries and Hindu polemicists caricatured Muslims as spreading Islam with the sword (Friedmann 1989: 169). On the other hand Indian Muslim apologists, who had come to terms with the British domination, endeavoured to defend their community from the accusation of spreading Islam through the use of force; they developed a new interpretation according to which *jihad* was only a defensive war (Peters 1981), as did for instance, modernists like Sayyid Ahmad Khan and Chiragh 'Ali, as well as *ʿulama* belonging to various schools, the most outstanding of them being Shibli Numaʿni (1857-1914) (Peters 1981; Friedmann 1989: 169-71). Some reformers, like the Ahmadis, even declared *jihad* altogether abolished (Friedmann 1989: 172-80). The third phase, in the beginning of the twentieth century, witnessed a reaffirmation of military *jihad*, in the context of the national struggle against the British. The main artisan of rehabilitation was Abul Kalam Azad (1888-1958): in his magazine *Al-Hilal*, published from 1912 to 1914, he reaffirmed that it was an essential duty of Islam (see Douglas 1988: 140 and 171). Mahmudu'l-Hasan (1851-1920), the principal of the Deoband seminary, and an important leader of the national movement, was to write later:

'We had forgotten the lesson of *jihad*, Abul Kalam reminded us' (Douglas 1988: 100; Gaborieau 1996b). About fifteen years later Maududi (1903-79) founded his career on the reaffirmation of *jihad* (Nasr 1996: 22-3 and 74); and from him the idea passed on to the Egyptian islamists (Carre 1984: 135-42).

Sayyid Ahmad Barelwi belonged to the first of the three phases outlined above. He had the triple career of a mystical guide, a soldier and a religious reformer ((Ahmad, Qeyamuddin 1966; Ahmad, Mohiuddin 1975; Rizvi 1982: 474-97). Born in Rae Bareilly in 1786 in a family of Naqshbandi Sufis, he was trained both as a soldier and as a Sufi. He was first, and remained to the end of his life, a Sufi guide (see Gaborieau 1999b) in the line of Shah Waliullah (1703-62) and his son Shah ᶜAbdu'l-ᶜAziz (1746-1824). From 1812 to 1817 he worked as a soldier in the army of Amir Khan, the Nawab of Tonk in Rajasthan. After the defeat of the Marathas in 1818 and the establishment of the *Pax Britannica* over North India (expect for Sind and the Sikh kingdom of Punjab, i.e. roughly the present Pakistan), Sayyid Ahmad had to leave the disbanded army of Amir Khan: he started his third career of a religious reformer. He preached a purification of the religious practices of Indian Muslims, and the integral application of shariᶜa, the God given Law (Ismaᶜil Shahid, n.d. (*Siratu'l-mustaqim*): Chap. 2; Gaborieau 1999a). He particularly insisted on reviving two forgotten obligations: *hajj*, the pilgrimage to Mecca; and *jihad* or holy war. In both cases he preached by setting himself up as an example. He went on a pilgrimage to Mecca in 1822-4 with 752 disciples. And then in 1826, with thousands of followers, had a *hijra*, an 'exodus', from British controlled Ganges valley to the North-West Frontier, behind the Sikh territory, near Peshawar, in an area controlled by the Afghan kings or by unruly Muslim Pathan tribes; from there he waged *jihad* against the Sikhs, with the intention of confronting later the British. In 1831, having got into troubles with the local Pathan tribes, he left the Peshawar area to go and establish a new base in Kashmir; but he was defeated and killed on his way by Sikh army in Balakot (Shahjahanpuri 1971).

To interpret this *jihad* it is necessary to have in mind the geo-political situation of the area where it took place (Gaborieau 1996a: 268-70). It was not yet directly involved in the 'big game' of the two competing British and Russian empires. On the Indian side, the British were still far away in the East in the Ganges basin: the Indus basin (roughly what is now Pakistan) was under independent states, mainly Sind and the Sikh kingdom. On the Afghan and Central Asian side, the Russian empire was still far away: the areas now covered by Afghanistan and Uzbekistan were divided between independent Muslim principalities. On both sides traditional life continued; there was nothing of a border: merchants, scholars and pilgrims continued to move freely from Delhi to Bukhara (Gommans 1995). For Sayyid Ahmad and his *mujahidin* (i.e. *jihad* fighters) this situation could be construed as a mere continuation of the medieval world when Central Asia and Afghanistan were integral part of the land controlled by the Muslims, the *daru*'l-*islam* (Abel 1965) and when India marked a fluctuating frontier between *daru'l-islam* and *daru'l-harb*, the territory controlled by non-Muslims.

Controversies have been raging since the 1830s about the interpretation of Sayyid Ahmad's *jihad*. Chronologically it belongs to the first phase defined above when the medieval interpretation prevailed. It was seen as such by the British before 1857: they did not take seriously this holy war which they treated contemptuously as a medieval utopia (see J.R.C.1832). But after 1857 another type of militant interpretation developed: starting as a colonial caricature (Hunter 1971) it evolved into the third phase outlined above. Since the last mentioned militant interpretation is still dominant, we will first analyse it in order to understand what *jihad* could mean in Sayyid Ahmad's time, i.e. in the first phase.

Post-1857 Interpretations

There is a paradox about Sayyid Ahmad's *jihad*: the current and dominant interpretations, which belong conceptually to the third phase, were foreshadowed at the chronological time of the second phase by colonial authors, in particular William Hunter whom we examine first.

William Hunter

After 1857 there was a widely spread belief among British administrators that the Mutiny was mainly the result of a Muslim conspiracy against British rule. The suspicion increased when after 1863 it was found that disciples of Sayyid Ahmad, then called 'Wahabi', still fought on the North-West Frontier; they confronted the British directly after the collapse of the Sikh kingdom; they continued to receive money and recruits from areas as far as Bihar and Bengal. There followed, between 1863 and 1872, a series of battles and of trials which were known as the

'Wahabi trials' (Hardy 1972: 80-5) It was in the context of this witch-hunt that Hunter hurriedly wrote (Mohar Ali 1980) his book entitled *Our Indian Musalmans: Are they bound in Conscience to Rebel against the Queen*? It was published from London in 1871. Sayyid Ahmad's *jihad* is still mainly seen in India as well as in the West through this book.

Hunter's interpretation rested on two assumptions. First, an historical one: he posited that, in the matter of *jihad*, there was a continuity of inspiration from ShahWaliullah (1703-62) and his son Shah ᶜAbdu'l-ᶜAziz (1746-1824) to Sayyid Ahmad. The latter was only an obedient disciple: he carried out a mission orchestrated by Shah ᶜAbdu'l-ᶜAziz who conspired in British occupied Delhi. The second assumption is that *jihad* was not only a military fight against the foreigners, but also a social revolution of the peasantry against the rich landlords: here Hunter conflated the frontier skirmishes with the *Fara'izi* revolt in Eastern Bengal (Khan 1961 and 1965).

Nationalist Muslims

The nationalist interpretations developed in the twentieth century in the wake of Azad's reaffirmation of *jihad*. Although he himself quoted the example of Sayyid Ahmad, Azad left it to some of his associates to frame these interpretations. First ᶜUbaidullah Sindhi (d. 1944), in a book published at the end of his life (Sindhi 1941), reaffirmed the principle posited by Hunter of a continuity of inspiration from Shah Waliullah to Sayyid Ahmad through Shah ᶜAbdu'l-ᶜAziz (Rizvi 1982: 523-5; Adams 1990: 222). But it was left to a later writer, Ghulam Rasul Mehr—who was the secretary of Azad—to develop fully this interpretation in the monumental Urdu biography of Sayyid Ahmad he published in Pakistan after the partition (Mehr 1952): he repeated the first principle of a continuity of inspiration; he insisted on the second assumption of an equalitarian dimension of Sayyid Ahmad's movement. These interpretations were made known to a larger audience by the English book of Hafeez Malik (Malik 1963) and general histories of South Asian Islam (e.g.Qureshi 1962: 193-211). Harlan Pearson in his unpublished thesis (Pearson 1979) followed Mehr's lead in his emphasis on the so-called equalitarian dimension of Sayyid Ahmad's movement which he opposed to the hierarchical worldview of Shah Waliullah.

In conclusion Mehr adopted, albeit unwittingly, the colonial interpretation. For him Sayyid Ahmad's *jihad* was the culmination of the movement started in the eighteenth century by Shah Waliullah; it aimed at ousting the British and establishing a more equalitarian society. The book of Qeyamuddin Ahmad (1966) follows Mehr's lead: Sayyid Ahmad's *jihad* is seen as a nationalist struggle against the British. The same interpretation can also be found in more recent works (see e.g. Maiello 1996).

Returning to Early Nineteenth Century

Does the evidence of early nineteenth century warrant this nationalist interpretation?

The main documents are three theoretical texts in Persian: the second chapter of *Siratu'l-mustaqim* (Isma[c]il Shahid n.d.)—the first manifesto of the movement—which contains a long development on *jihad* and on political theory (see Rizvi 1982: 504-7); Sayyid Ahmad's correspondence (Ahmad Shahid Barelwi 1975); and a political treatise called *Mansab-i-imamat* (Isma[c]il Shahid 1306/1888-9 and n.d.). There were also a few popular texts in Urdu, written by disciples of Sayyid Ahmad; the most often quoted one is *Targhibu'l-jihad*, 'Incitation to Holy War' (J.R.C. 1832: 482).

Unoriginal Theory of Jihad

The doctrine contained in these sources (Pearson 1979: 93-106) can be summed up in the following way. Jihad is a war for the extension or the defence of the *daru'l-islam*, the territory controlled by Muslim rulers. This is obligatory for the Muslim community. It must be waged under the direction of an *imam*; and rules are set for the way the *jihad* must be declared (see below). There is nothing apologetic in this doctrine, in contrast to the theories presenting *jihad* as only a defensive war which were found in the second phase: these texts do not even warrant the soft interpretation later framed by the famous modernist Sir Sayyid Ahmad Khan which presented Ahmad Barelwi's *jihad* as a purely defensive war against the Sikhs (Ahmad Khan 1872). On the contrary Sayyid Ahmad Barelwi was perceived by his contemporaries, Muslim as well as Christians, as a militant figure set on fighting not only the Sikhs but also the British (Pearson 1979: 192-3; Rizvi 1982: 485; Powell 1993: 115).

We are first struck by the fact that, far from being specifically adapted to the political context of early nineteenth century, these sources are just a rewording of the medieval tradition. The classical doctrine (Macdonald 1961; Abel 1965; Tyan 1965; Morabia 1993) is summed in the same terms as in texts which were widely circulated in India at that time, be they compendia of Hanafi law written outside India (Hughes 1885: art 'jihad', 243-8), or more recent, but not more original, texts written in India as those of Shah Waliullah (Baljon 1986: 185-6). Sayyid Ahmad's theory of *jihad* is thus wholly unoriginal. We are clearly in the first of the phases described above, not only chronologically, but also conceptually.

From Shah ᶜAbdu'l-ᶜAziz to Sayyid Ahmad: Continuity or Discontinuity?

What then is specific of Sayyid Ahmad if it is not his doctrine? Here is the place to question the first assumption common to Hunter and the nationalist historians which we mentioned above: they believe that there is a continuity of inspiration from Shah Waliullah to Sayyid Ahmad through Shah ᶜAbdu'l-ᶜAziz. As stressed by Adams (1990), recent research by Indian scholars like Mushiru'l-Haq (Haq 1984), or Pakistani scholars like Shahjahanpuri (Shahjahapuri 1971) and Khalid Masud (Masud 2000), have shown that Shah ᶜAbdu'l-ᶜAziz was not hostile to the British, and was not in favour of *jihad*. A thorough analysis of his *fatawa*, show that, contrary to the belief of nationalist historians, he was not intending to fight the British when, after the conquest of Delhi in 1803, he declared India *daru'l-harb*, i.e. territory controlled by non-Muslims, as opposed to the *daru'l-Islam* which is controlled by Muslim rulers. He wanted only to determine what the legal consequences of the British take-over were, as far as Muslims were concerned, for land ownership (which was confirmed), commerce of slaves (which remained allowed) and lending and borrowing money on interest (which was licit). The twin concepts of *hijra* (exodus from a land controlled by non-Muslims to a land controlled by Muslims) and *jihad* (a holy war waged against non-Muslims to extend and defend *daru'l-Islam*)— which were later revived by Sayyid Ahmad—do not occur in his *fatawa*. In practice in North India in the early nineteenth century the obligation to wage *jihad* had lapsed.

It is precisely on these points that Sayyid Ahmad discontinued Shah ᶜAbdu'l-ᶜAziz's attitude. As we have seen above, from the beginning of his career as a reformer in 1818, he reaffirmed the obligatory character of the two forgotten obligations of *hajj*, pilgrimage to Mecca, and *jihad*. He systematically used together the twin concepts of *hijra* and *jihad*: he described his travel to the North West Frontier as an *hijra* from *daru'l-*

harb to *daru'l-Islam* in order to wage *jihad* first against the Sikhs, and ultimately against the British. He for instance developed these themes in a sermon he delivered to fighting Pathans on the Frontier (Mehr 1952;, vol.1, 277); he insisted on the same points in a letter written around 1828 to the Amir of Bukhara in Central Asia where he said:

> This humble man (Sayyid Ahmad) decided an exodus (*hijra*) from Hindustan, and resolved to wage *jihad*. He first performed the pilgrimage to Mecca. And there he got from God innumerable and incomparable favours. The most important of them was the inspiration (*ilham*) to start *jihad* and to suppress infidelity and corruption.

He adds that *jihad* is an obligation for the Muslim community and is particularly incumbent on Muslim heads of states; therefore the Amir of Bukhara must support the *jihad* of Sayyid Ahmad (see the text of the letter in Ahmad Shahid Barelwi, 1975, folios 24a-29a; comments and partial translations of the letter in Rizvi 1982: 419-22 and Gaborieau 1996a: 272-6).

In comparison with Shah ᶜAbdu'l-ᶜAziz, the originality of Sayyid Ahmad lies in the reaffirmation of a lapsed (or, one could say with contemporary islamists, 'forgotten'), obligation, *jihad*. He reduplicated for *jihad* what he had already done for *hajj*. Contrary to the second assumption of the nationalist interpretation, there was a discontinuity between Shah ᶜAbdu'l-ᶜAziz and Sayyid Ahmad.

Medieval Utopia or Nationalist Struggle?

Is then the nationalist interpretation tenable? Will it not be necessary to devise a new interpretation? To answer these questions we will now examine the main aspects of Sayyid Ahmad's *jihad* one by one.

Jihad *against Whom?*

We now come the core of the problem. Most of the commentators have reasoned in the following way: when Sayyid Ahmad reaffirmed the obligatory character of *jihad*, did he mean a war against the British? If he did, the nationalist theory would be valid. For instance, since Sir Sayyid Ahmad Khan published in 1872 his famous review of Hunter's book, commentators have focused on this question of against whom the *jihad* was directed: only the Sikhs, or also the British? The answer was: if it was only a war against the Sikhs, as Sir Sayyid first affirmed, then it was not a nationalist struggle. But if it was also against the British, then it was a nationalist struggle as Ghulam Rasul Mehr (1952) and Qeyamuddin Ahmad (1966) stated.

The evidence of the correspondence (Gaborieau 1996a: 274-80) is that the holy war was eventually to include the British. But now, to interpret it, one must realize that the real issue was not who was the adversary, but the way in which it was conducted. To clarify this question we must analyse three points: the strategy of the *jihad*, the procedures for declaring this holy war, and the status of Sayyid Ahmad as the *imam* of this war.

Strategy: Relying on Daru'l-Islam

The Strategy of Sayyid Ahmad, as explained in several of his declarations and in his correspondence, is grounded on the medieval conception of a continuous *daru'l-Islam* which must be defended and extended. He first stressed the fact that *jihad* must be waged from *daru'l-Islam*. That is why he traveled with his *mujahidin* all the way through Rajasthan, Sind and Afghanistan to the Pathan controlled territories near Peshawar, which were technically *daru'l-Islam* (Mehr 1952: vol. 1, 277). The horizon of this war is not therefore a realistic appraisal of early nineteenth century geo-politics and of the rise of colonial powers. Sayyid Ahmad acted with the medieval view in mind: the frontier between *daru'l-Islam* and *daru'l-harb* is a moving one: with the Sikhs and the British it had receded; it had therefore to be defended and progression had to be resumed to reconquer the lost territories. This point is most clearly expressed in Sayyid Ahmad's correspondence, as for instance in the already mentioned letter to the Amir of Bukhara (Gaborieau 1996a: 277-80).

The Procedures

Sayyid Ahmad had not only a medieval strategy; he also kept scrupulously to the medieval procedures as codified in law books: '*jihad*', he said, must be waged in conformity with the tradition (*sunna*) of the holy Prophet' (Mehr 1952: vol. 1, 277). He therefore insisted, as we have noted above, on starting the fight from *daru'l-Islam*. Then the law books insisted that, before attacking the infidels, the Muslims must offer them an invitation, *da^cwa*, to submit to Islam (by conversion or mere political submission) or fight to death; this is the sense in which, as indicated in the beginning of this paper, *da^cwa* is a part of *jihad* (Morabia 1993: 225). So did Sayyid Ahmad before his first battle: he addressed the Sikh general asking him either to embrace Islam, or to submit and become a protected subject (*dhimmi*) by paying the discriminatory capitation (*jizya*), or else to fight to death (Rizvi 1982: 487). After winning the battle, he insisted on enforcing the rules prescribed by the law for sharing the booty.

Sayyid Ahmad as a Caliph

But now in which capacity did he enforce these procedures? We come now to the heart of the problem. It is usually said that Sayyid Ahmad did create a theocratic state in the North West Frontier. This is an erroneous statement: his position was not that of a head of state, but something else which we must now define.

Here we come back to the theme of *jihad*: we have seen in the preceding paragraph that Sayyid Ahmad insisted that the holy war should be conducted in conformity with the *sunna*; one of the requirements of the *sunna* is that there should be an *imam*, or religious leader, to deliver the invitation (*da^cwat*) to submit to Islam. Such a leader, in the *Mansab-i-imamat* (Isma^cil Shahid 1306/1888-9 and n.d.), is called *sahib-i- da^cwat*. Sayyid Ahmad was evidently this *sahib-i da^cwat*, the religious leader who made *jihad* lawful. In his letter to the Amır of Bukhara he wrote:

> Since, from the point of view of the Law (*shari^ca*), *jihad* cannot be waged without an *imam*, for this reason all the Sayyids, *^culama*, judges (*qazi*) of lofty rank, all respected Khans and all the Muslims of the elite and of the common people, all offered allegiance (*bai^cat*) to me as an *imam*. In this way, thanks to Allah, the extermination of the Infidels, as well as the Friday prayer and the prayers of the two festivals (*^cid*) have been made lawful in conformity with the Law. (see Gaborieau 1996a, 275)

Is this office of an *imam* equivalent to that of a head of state, of a *sultan* in the medieval terminology? In other terms was Sayyid Ahmad trying to carve out one more Muslim state comparable to those of the Afghanistan of his time which was divided into several principalities, or to those of the Central Asia of his time which comprised several emirates at that of Bukhara? In a long series of texts, particularly in his correspondence, he made it abundantly and consistently clear that he was not looking for mundane power; that he was not trying to substitute his rule to the rule of the various Sultans in power in the area. For instance in a letter to the Sultan of Herat (in present Afghanistan), he said: 'There is a great difference between imamate and sultanate. The *imam* is appointed to lead *jihad* and root out rebellion. His real aim is not to govern the countries, towns and districts. His real aim is to transfer sultanate to the person to whom it really belongs' (Ahmad Shahid Barelwi, 1975: 17b; see Gaborieau 1996a: 278, and Rizvi 1982: 491).

If Sayyid Ahmad was not a sultan, what was he then? If we examine his hagiography, we soon realize that he appropriated all the symbols and roles of the classical caliph: he was called and called himself in his correspondence *amiru'l-mu'minin*, i.e. Commander of the faithful, as the Abbasid caliphs were called; his name had to be mentioned in the sermon (*khutba*) of the Friday prayer; coins were struck in his name. So he did not have ambition to become one more sultan in an area already very fragmented politically; he did not even try to unify the various emirates of the region from which he was waging his *jihad*. His ambition was to stay above all these sultans as a supreme authority which made their rule legitimate and made *jihad* against the infidels lawful. He wanted to be like the Abbasid caliph in Baghdad after the tenth century, who stood above the various Persian and Turkish sultans and gave them legitimacy. The truth is that Sayyid Ahmad in fact proclaimed himself, not a simple sultan, but a caliph.

The Millenarian Dimension of Sayyid Ahmad's Movement

To back his pretensions Sayyid Ahmad had not only the authority of the Holy Law. As I have stressed before (Gaborieau 1999b), he had also the charisma of a Sufi guide which he used to gather disciples and enrol them in his holy war. He himself emphasized up to the end of his career this mystical dimension of his life when he wrote to Muslim rulers for support in his *jihad*. For instance in his letter (Ahmad Shahid Barelwi 1975: 24a-29a) to the Emir of Bukhara, in whose town lies the tomb of Baha'ud-Din Naqshband, he stressed that he was the descendant of Shaikh ᶜAlamu'llah (1624-44), a *khalifa* of the famous Naqshbandi Shaikh Adam Banuri (m.1643), himself a disciple of Shaikh Ahmad Sirhindi; and that he himself initiated innumerable disciples who thereafter adopted a purified version of Islam and followed him (see Gaborieau 1996a: 274). But at the time of his *jihad* on the North-Western Frontier another new ground of legitimation emerged. He posed as the *mahdi*. I have studied elsewhere in detail this millenarian dimension of Sayyid Ahmad's career (Gaborieau 2000); I will here sum up the main findings which are pertinent to this paper.

It is well known that after the battle of Balakot, his disciples refused to believe he was dead; they proclaimed that he was only in concealment and would return as the *mahdi* who, in the Muslim eschatology, is expected to come at the end of history to reestablish order and justice on earth before the end of the world. A pamphlet was published by Wilayat ᶜAli of Patna to back this belief with Traditions of the Prophet. It was widely believed that Sayyid Ahmad, who was born in 1201/1786, that is to say in the first year of the thirteenth century of the Islamic era, was to be at least a *mujaddid* (Maiello 1996: 255), or better a *mahdi*. Hunter in his famous book echoed this belief by quoting a Persian poem which had been modified to suit Sayyid Ahmad's case (Hunter 1871: 55):

> I see that after 1200 years have passed, wonderful events will occur;
>
> ....
>
> Then the Imam will appear and rule over the earth;
> I see and read A.H.M.D as the letters showing forth the name of his ruler.

This millenarian posthumous career of Sayyid Ahmad was carefully studied by a British magistrate, James O'Kineally (1837-1903): he was a much better scholar than Hunter, and knew the question first hand for he sat as a prosecutor in Wahabi trials in the district of Maldah in Bengal.

His work as a magistrate, the records of which were only recently published (Khan 1961), shows the popular perceptions of the myth of Sayyid's Ahmad as *mahdi*. The Bengal peasants who had been recruited to fight on the Frontier believed that he would reappear there as the Imam Mahdi; he would chase the British from India, abolish taxes, give a *jagir* to everybody; all Muslim would get land and become rich; the Muslim religion would be exalted (Khan 1961: 283-288). These conceptions may seem naive; they in fact sum up the classical ideas about the *mahdi* who is expected to gain a victory over the infidels and bring happiness and prosperity in the world (Friedmann 1989: 167).

But O'Kineally did not rest content with this popular discourse. He also scrutinized the learned conceptions then current among Sayyid Ahmad disciples (O'Kineally 1870: particularly pp. 96-8). He was the first and, to my knowledge, the only one to reveal that their idea of the *mahdi* differed from the classical one. According to them, the Imam who will come at the end of the world will not be the real *mahdi*, but only a caliph. The real *mahdi* will appear half way between the death of the

Prophet and the end of the world according to a Tradition which says: 'This religion will not be destroyed of which I am the beginning; the Mahdi, the middle; and Christ the end', This *mahdi* is supposed to come from Khorasan (roughly speaking modern Afghanistan) where Sayyid Ahmad started his *jihad*. A Tradition thus says: 'When you will see black flags coming from Khorasan, follow them, for with them is a caliph, the Mahdi of God'.

This conception of the *mahdi* to appear in the middle of the time is not yet very clear to me; it may be connected with the Indian *Mahdawiya* of Sayyid Muhammad Jaunpuri, as O'Kineally suggests (O'Kineally 1970: 102-3); it is also analogous to the concept of the *mujaddid* of the second millennium of Shaikh Ahmad Sirhindi (Gaborieau 2000: 271). The question of the origins of this conception has still to be solved.

But we can answer the most important question for our purpose. Were these millenarian ideas really entertained by Sayyid Ahmad and his followers? They are often dismissed as fables propagated by dishonest followers after the death of Sayyid Ahmad to attract credulous peasants to fight on the frontier; or even as pure fabrications of colonial writers like Hunter (Ahmad Khan 1972: 8; Pearson 1979; 64). Now O'Kineally maintained that Sayyid Ahmad had been proclaimed *mahdi* as soon as he started his *jihad* at the end of 1826 but he did not quote any source. Can his affirmation be substantiated?

Among the doctrinal texts produced by Isma^cil Shahid only one was written at the time of the *jihad*. This is the unfinished *Mansab-i-imamat* which is not exactly dated, but is believed to have been written around 1827. This book has as yet attracted little attention; the only scholar to give a detailed summary of it was Saiyid Athar Abbas Rizvi who however did not mention the passages concerning the *mahdi* (Rizvi 1982: 514-517). This short treatise first contains an unoriginal first part on the functions of the Imam according to classical theology; and , in the conclusion, it stresses in particular his role as the *sahib-i da^cwat*, the one who calls the faithful to the holy war, an evident allusion to Sayyid Ahmad (Isma^cil Shahid 1306/1888-9: 126-42; Rizvi 1982: 515-17). The real originally of this book is to give an esoterical depth to the imamate. In the first subdivision of the second part ((Isma^cil Shahid 1306/1888-9: 59-87), the author treats of the spiritual reality of the imamate which is of three kinds: 'hidden' in the case of the saints, 'esoterical' as that of the Prophet Ibrahim who was not a ruler, and finally perfect (*tamma*) as that of the first four caliphs. But, he continues, these four caliphs were not the only perfect Imams, the *mahdi* of the end of the times will also be a perfect Imam. Then comes the decisive passage four of our demonstration ((Isma'il Shahid 1306/1888-9: 79-81): between the first caliphs and the end of the world, the time is not empty; there is place for a *mahdi* of the middle, who will come from Khorasan. Then, the author concludes, a *mahdi* can appear now among us; one has to open one's eyes to see him. This is evidently an allusion to Sayyid Ahmad.

If my interpretation is right, then this passage of the treatise, which has been up to now neglected by the commentators, proves that Sayyid Ahmad had been declared a *mahdi* in his lifetime as O'Kineally maintained. This millenarian dimension of Sayyid Ahmad's movement is not a late invention of dishonest followers, or of colonial writers. The people of his inner circle believed as himself did that he was invested with a heavenly mission to restore the rule and the glory of Islam in India. This was the most solid argument to legitimate his movement which was thus grounded on eschatological beliefs.

Conclusion

Sayyid Ahmad, as his correspondence made it clear, ultimately intended to confront the British in India. But this does not mean, contrary to the colonial and nationalist interpretations, that his *jihad* was a prefiguration of the nationalist struggle. He was not set to be a sultan, to build a state for himself; far less was he contemplating to build a nation-state in India.

The horizon of his political and strategical thought was that of the medieval *daru'l-Islam*, the fluctuating frontiers of which had to be extended or defended if the need be. He lived in a time when there was not yet a frontier between India on the one hand, and Afghanistan and Central Asia on the other hand, and in his correspondence he appealed both to Indian rulers and Afghan and Central Asian rulers; in his mind India ought to remain part of *daru'l-Islam*, as it had been during the Delhi Sultanate and the Mughal empire (for Sayyid Ahmad's geopolitical view, see Gaborieau 1996a, 278-80).

In this context, the role of Sayyid Ahmad was not that of a head of state, but of a religious leader above the various heads of state: in brief he saw himself as a caliph in the medieval sense of the term. This attitude is to be clearly distinguished from two more modern ones. Sayyid Ahmad cannot be equated with Azad and the nationalist *'ulama* like Madani who use the slogan of *jihad* to legitimate a nationalist struggle. He cannot exactly be equated either to the fundamentalists like Maududi or the contemporary Near-Eastern Islamists: the former lived resolutely in the modern context and used the concept of *jihad* to build a political, and finally not so aggressive, ideology (Nasr 1996: 74); the latter used it to form a utopian revolutionary ideology to subvert the Muslim elites who are in power in the Middle East (Carre 1984).

To return to Sayyid Ahmad's conception of restoration of the *daru'l-Islam*, its medieval outlook makes it anachronistic even in the context of the early nineteenth century. While Shah [c]Abdul-[c]Aziz tried to find realistic legal solutions to come to terms with the British presence, Sayyid Ahmad took refuge in a literal interpretation of the medieval legal texts which can be called ultra-fundamentalist. Trying to revive them in the modern context of the British presence was unrealistic; it was an utopia which took at the end a millenarian turn when after the battle of Balakot, his disciples refused to believe he was dead and waited for his reappearance as a *mahdi*. This millenarian outlook of Sayyid Ahmad's movement, like its Sufis dimension, has been neglected in the modern nationalist interpretations.

If some comparison is to be done with a contemporary movement, it would be tempting at first thought to make a parallel with Maududi and Middle Eastern Islamists who like Sayyid Ahmad—as we have already stressed—revived the 'forgotten obligation' of *jihad*. It is true that Maududi became famous in 1927 by his book *Al-jihad fi'l-Islam* which reaffirmed the obligatory character of holy war (Nasr 1986: 22-3 and 74). In the early 1940s he chose Sayyid Ahmad as one of his models and posed as a kind of *mujaddid* or *mahdi*—in the same way as the young Azad had done before (Maududi 1964: 100-15 and 139-48). But eventually, as Azad before, Maududi came to more realistic views, and took to a more moderate action in the framework of the modern nation-state of Pakistan which he tried to turn into an Islamic State. Similarly the scope of the Middle Eastern Islamists remained limited to the seizure of power in nation-states. If a parallel is to found, it would rather be in the recent events in Afghanistan and the North-West Frontier—which were also the theatre of Sayyid Ahmad's *jihad*. With the Taliban and Mullah Omar we find the same preoccupation to enforce literally the Holy Law against tribal customs, the same affirmation of the supremacy of religious men over political authorities, the same disdain of internal and international political realities, and finally the same millenarian tendencies for Mullah Omar posed as a kind of *mahdi* (Gaborieau 2002). I do not know whether the Taliban drew themselves the parallel between Mullah Omar and Sayyed Ahmad; but I am sure that there are objective grounds for such a comparison.

A last remark. It is striking that the colonial and the nationalist interpretations are based on the same assumptions. To come to a meaningful historical interpretation, two precautionary measures are to be taken. First, the events have to be replaced in their proper context of early nineteenth century when imperial frontiers had not yet been fixed between British India and Central Asia not yet threatened by Russian imperialism. Second, one has to go back to the texts produced by the movement and to reinterpret them in the light of the medieval juridical and theological thought as has been done for other figures (for instance Friedmann 1989). If these two precautions are taken, Sayyid Ahmad, far from being a realistic freedom fighter, appears as a millenarian charismatic figure.

NOTES

1. The lecture were delivered in Paris at the EHESS in April-May 1885. On the interpretaion of the figure of Sayyid Ahmed, see also Adams 1990.
2. This was not the first printed edition of the Koran to appear in the Islamic world as Garnic de Tassy believed but the second one: the first one appeared in Saint Petersburg in 1787 (see Gaborieau 2001a, pp. 102-3).

REFERENCES

Abel, A., 1965, Articles 'dar al-harb' and 'dar al-Islam', *Encyclopedia of Islam, Leiden*, E.J. Brill, 2nd edn., Vol. II, pp. 126-8.

Adams, Charles J., 'The Naqshbandis of India and the Pakistan Movement', in Marc Gaborieau, Alexandre Popovic and Thierry Zarcone, eds, *Naqshbandis, Historical Developments and Present Situation of a Muslim Mystical Order*, Istambul edn., ISIS, 1990, pp. 221-9.

Ahmad, Muhiuddin, 1975, *Saiyid Ahmad Shahid: his Life and Mission*, Lucknow, Academy of Islamic Research and Publications.

Ahmad, Qeyamuddin, 1966, *The Wahabi Movement in India*, Calcutta, Mukhopadhyay, 1966 (2nd rev. edn., Delhi, Manohar, 1994).

Ahmad Khan, Sir Sayyid, 1872, *Review on Dr Hunter's Indian Islam*, London, Henry S. King and Co., Benares (rpt. Lahore, Premier Book House, n.d.).

Ahmad Shahid Barelwi, Sayyid, 1975, *Makatib*, Lahore, Maktaba Rashidiyya, (Persian correspondence; photostat print of the Lahore manuscript).

Baljon, J.M.S., 1986, *Religion and Thought of Shah Wali Allah Dihlawi, 1703-1762*, Leiden, E.J. Brill.

Bayly, Christopher A., 1988, *Indian Society and the Making of the British Empire*, Cambridge, Cambridge University Press (The New Cambridge History of India, Vol. II/1).

Bosworth, C.E., 1980, *Jihad in Afghanistan and Muslim India*, Israel Oriental Series, vol. 10, pp. 185ff.

Carre, Olivier, 1984, *Mystique et politique. Lecture revolutionnaire du Coran par Sayyid Qutb. Frere musulman radical*, Pairs, Editions du Cerf.

Douglas, Ian Henderson, 1988, *Abul Kalam Azad. An Intellectual and Religious Biography*, edited by Gail Minault and Christian W. Troll, Delhi, Oxford University Press.

Friedmann, Yohanan, 1989, *Prophecy Continuous Aspects of Ahmadi Religious Thought and its Medieval Background*, Berkeley, University of California Press.

Gaborieau, Marc, 1994, 'Late Persian, Early Urdu: The Case of "Wahhabi" Literature', in Francoise 'Nalini' Delvoye (ed.), *Confluence of Cultures; French Contributions to Indo-Persian Studies*, Delhi, Manohar, pp. 170-96.

———, 1996a, 'L'Asie centrale dans l'horizon de l'Inde au debut du XIXe siecle: a propos d'une lettre de Sayyid Ahmad Barelwi a l'emir de Boukhara', *Inde-Asie centrale*, Tashkent–Aix-en-Provence, Edisud, nos. 1-2, pp. 265-82.

———, 1996b, 'A peaceful *jihad*? Proselytism as seen by Ahmadiyya, Tablighi Jama^c^at and Jama^c^at Islami, Workship on *Transformations of South Asian Islamic Community in the 19th and 20th centuries*, Chapel Hill, Triangle South Asia Consortium, 23-26 May 1996 (unpublished).

———, 1997a, 'Les debats sur l'acculturation chez les musulmans indiens au debut du XIXe siecle', in J. Assayag and G. Tarabout (eds.), *Alterite et identite. Islam et christianisme en Inde*, Paris, EHESS, pp. 221-37 (Collection *Purushartha*, no. 19).

———, 1997b, 'Renouveau de l'islam ou strategie politique occulte? La Tablighi Jama^c^at dans le sous-continent indien et dans le monde', in Catherine Clementin-Ojha, ed., *Renouveaux religieux en Asie*, Paris, Ecole Francaise d'Extreme Orient, 1997, pp. 211-29.

———, 1999a, 'Criticizing the Sufis: the Debate in Early Nineteenth Century India', in Frederick De Jong and Bernd Radtke, eds, *Islamic Mysticism Contested: Thirteen Centuries of Controversies and Polemics*, Leiden, E.J. Brill, pp. 452-67.

———, 1999b, 'Sufism in the first Indian Wahhabi Manifesto: *Siratu'l-mustaqim* by Isma^c^il Shahid and ^c^Abdu'l-Hayy' , in Francoise 'Nalini' Delvoye, Muzaffar Alam and Marc Gaborieau (eds), *The Making of Indo-Persian*

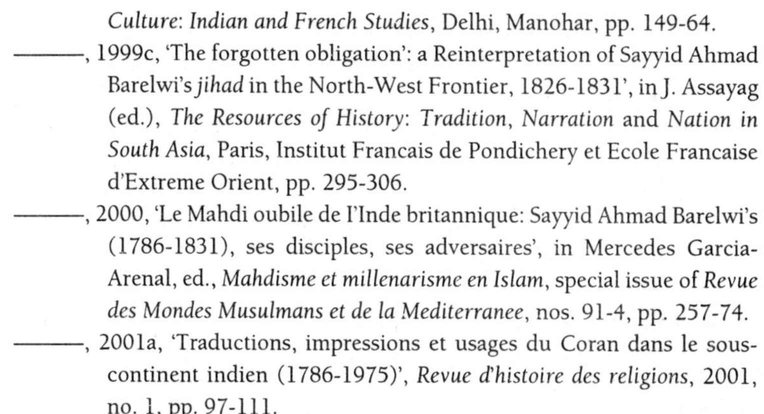

Culture: Indian and French Studies, Delhi, Manohar, pp. 149-64.

———, 1999c, 'The forgotten obligation': a Reinterpretation of Sayyid Ahmad Barelwi's *jihad* in the North-West Frontier, 1826-1831', in J. Assayag (ed.), *The Resources of History: Tradition, Narration* and *Nation in South Asia*, Paris, Institut Francais de Pondichery et Ecole Francaise d'Extreme Orient, pp. 295-306.

———, 2000, 'Le Mahdi oubile de l'Inde britannique: Sayyid Ahmad Barelwi's (1786-1831), ses disciples, ses adversaires', in Mercedes Garcia-Arenal, ed., *Mahdisme et millenarisme en Islam*, special issue of *Revue des Mondes Musulmans et de la Mediterranee*, nos. 91-4, pp. 257-74.

———, 2001a, 'Traductions, impressions et usages du Coran dans le sous-continent indien (1786-1975)', *Revue d'histoire des religions*, 2001, no. 1, pp. 97-111.

———, 2001b, 'De la guerre sainte (*jihad*) au proselytisme (*da^{c}wa*) ? Les organizations musulmanes transnationales d'origine indienne', in Jean-Pierre Bastian, Francoise Champion & Kathy Rousselet, *La globalization du religieux*, Paris, L'Harmattan, pp. 35-48.

———, 2002, 'Inaccessible Afghanistan', *Le Debat*, Paris, Gallimard (forthcoming).

——— (under preparation), *Le Mahdi incompris. L'islam indien et le millenarisme au debut du XIXe siecle.*

Gommans, Jos J.L., 1995, *The Rise of the Indo-Afghan Empire, c. 1710-1780*, Leiden, E.J. Brill.

Haq, Mushirul, 1984, 'Shah ^{c}Abdul-^{c}Aziz al-Dihlawi and his Times', *Hamdard Islamicus*, Vol. 7, no. 1, pp. 51-96, no. 2, pp. 77-103.

Hardy, Peter, 1972, *The Muslims of British India*, Cambridge, Cambridge University Press.

Hedayatullah, Muhammad, 1970, *Sayyid Ahmad: A Study of the Religious Reform Movement of Sayyid Ahmad of Rae Bareli*, Lahore, M. Ashraf.

Hughes, Thomas Patrick, 1885, *A Dictionary of Islam*, London (quoted from the reprint Lahore, Islamic Publications Limited, 1964).

Hunter, William W., 1871, *Our Indian Musalmans; Are they Bound in Conscience to Rebel Against the Queen*? London, Trubner & Co. (quoted from the reprint: Benares, Indological Book House, 1969).

Isma^{c}il Shahid, Shah, n.d., *Siratu'l-mustaqim*, Lucknow lithograph, n.d.

———, 1306/1888-9, *Mansab-i-imamat*, *Matba^{c}-i Faruqi*, Persian text with an Urdu translation entitled *Darjat-i imamat.*

———, n.d., *Mansab-i-imamat*, *Matba^{c}-i Faruqi*, Persian text only.

J.R.C. (James Russell Colvin), 1832, 'Notice on the Peculiar Tenets held by the Followers of Syed Ahmed, taken chiefly from the "Sirat-ul-mustaqim", a Principal Treatise of that sect, written by Moulavi Mahommed Ismail', *Journal of the Royal Asiatic Society of Bengal*, Vol. 1/11, 1832, pp. 479-98.

Khan, Muin-ud-Din Ahmad, 1961, *Selections from the Government Records on Wahhabi Trials (1863-1870)*, Dacca, Asiatic Society of Pakistan (Monograph no. 8),

———, 1965, *History of the Fara'idi Movement in Bengal, 1818-1906*, Karachi, Pakistan Historical Association (2nd edn., Dhaka, Islamic Foundation Bangladesh, 1984).

Macdonald, D.B., 1961, Articles 'dar al-harb', 'dar al-Islam' and 'djhad', *Shorter Encyclopedia of Islam*, Laiden, E.J. Brill/London, Luzac and Co., pp. 68-9, 89.

Maiello, Amedeo, 1996, 'Sayyid Ahmad's Imamate According to Shah Isma[c]il Shahid', in Daniela Bredi and Gianroberto Scarcia, eds, *Ex libris Franco Coslovi (Eurasiatica*, no. 40), University of Venice, pp. 251-64.

Malik, Hafeez, 1963, *Moslem Nationalism in India and Pakistan*, Washington, D.C., Public Affairs Press.

Masud, M. Khalid, 2000, 'The world of Shah [c]Abdu'l-[c]Aziz (1746-1824)', in Jamal Malik, ed., *Perspective of Mutual Encounters in South Asian History, 1760-1860*, Leiden, E.J. Brill, pp. 268-314.

Maududi, Sayyid Abul A'la, 1963, *A Short History of the Revivalist Movement in Islam*, translated by Al-Ash'ari, Lahore, Islamic Publications Limited (1st published in Urdu in 1940).

Mehr, Ghulam Rasul, 1952, *Sayyid Ahmad Shahid*, Lahore, Kitab Manzil, 2 tomes bound in one volume.

Metcalf, Barbara D., *Islamic Revival in British India: Deoband, 1860-1900*, Princeton, Princeton University Press.

Mohar Ali, 1980, 'Hunter's Indian Musalmans: a re-examination of its background', Journal of *the Royal Asiatic Society of Great Britain and Ireland*, 1980/1, pp. 30-51.

Morabia, Alfred, 1993, *Le gihad dans l'islam medieval, Le combat scare des origines au XIle siecle*, Paris, Albin Michel.

Mujeeb, Muhammad, 1967, *The Indian Muslims*, London, George Allen and Unwin.

Nadwi, Abul-Hasan [c]Ali, 1939-41, *Sirat-i Sayyid Ahmad Shahid*, Lucknow, Nadwatu'l-[c]ulama, 2 vols.

Nasr, Sayyid Vali Reza, 1996, *Maulana Mawdudi and the Making of Islamic Revivalism*, New York, Oxford University Press.

O'Kineally, 1870, 'A Sketch of the Wahabis in India down to the death of Sayyid Ahmad in 1831', *Calcutta Review*, Vol. 50, 1870, pp. 73-104.

Pearson, Harlan O., 1979, 'Islamic Reform and Revivalism in Nineteenth Century India: The "Tariqa-i Muhammadiyyah", Ph.D., Durham, Duke University (unpublished).

Peters, Rudolph, 1981, *Islam and Colonialism: The Doctrine of Jihad in Modern History*, Paris, Mouton.

Powell, Avril Ann, 1993, *Muslims and Missionaries in Pre-Mutiny India*, London, Curzon Press.

Qureshi, Ishtiaq Husain, 1962, *The Muslim Community of the Indo-Pakistan Subcontinent (610-1947)*, Paris-La Haye, Mouton.

Rizvi, Sayid Athar Abbas, 1982, *Shah ᶜAbd al-ᶜAziz and his Time: Puritanism, Sectarianism, Polemics and Jihad, Canberra*, Maᶜrifat Publishing House.

Saeedullah, 1973, *The Life and Work of Muhammad Siddiq Hasan Khan, 1832-1890*, Lahore, Sh. Muhammad Ashraf.

Shahjahanpuri, Payam, 1971, *Shahadat-gah Balakot*, Lahore, Idara Ta'rikh o Tahqiq.

Sindhi, ᶜUbaidullah, 1941, *Shah Waliullah aur unki siyasi tahrik*, Delhi, The author (rpt., Lahore, Sind Sagar Academy, 1965).

Troll, Christian W., 1978, *Sayyid Ahmad Khan: A Reinterpretation of Muslim Theology*, Delhi, Vikas.

———, 1994, 'Two Conceptions of *daᶜwa* in India: Jamaᶜat-i-Islami and Tablighi Jamaᶜat', *Archives de Sciences des religions*, no. 87, 1994, pp. 115-33.

Tyan, E., 1965, Article '*djihad*', *Encyclopedia of Islam*, Leiden, E.J. Brill, 2nd edn., Vol. 2, pp. 538-40.

Female Voice in Punjabi Sufi Poetry

J.S. Grewal

Shaikh Farid (1175-1265) was the first Sufi poet to write in Punjabi. His most authentic compositions are included in the Sikh scripture known as the *Adi Granth* or *Guru Granth Sahib*. This poetry has been published separately too by a number of scholars. The second Punjabi Sufi poet, Shah Husain, wrote in the sixteenth century as a contemporary of the Mughal emperor Akbar and the successors of Guru Nanak. His compositions also have been published by a number of scholars. Over the centuries, millions of people have heard the voice of these poets.

I

About a score of Shaikh Farid's *shloks* have a bearing on gender relations.[1] In the true Indian tradition, he uses the female voice in his verses, besides using metaphors from the life of women. Before turning to these verses we may note that Shaikh Farid talks of love as the most significant relationship between human beings and God. Two of his well known *shloks* can be rendered into English as follows:

> The lane is muddy O Farid, the home is far away, and I cherish love for the Beloved. If I move out, my shawl get drenched; if I stay in, I betray my love. Let the shawl be drenched, let the rain come in torrents. I will go and meet the friend so that my love is not betrayed.[2]

In love, the feeling of separation is painful but it is also a sure sign of the longing to meet the friend.

> All complain of the pangs of separation,but I bow to it as the King. O Farid, the body which does not know the pangs of separation is a corpse.[3]

The unfortunate person who remains alien to God is *dohagan*.[4] The gender is feminine but God's *dohagan* is not necessarily a woman.

Using the female voice, Shaikh Farid says:

I did not sleep with my husband for a night and mu limbs wither in pain. Go and ask the *dohagans* how do they spend their nights?[5]

Farid speaks as a bride in a couple of his *shloks*. Before the bride leaves her natal home her scarf is tied to that of the bridegroom. The knot symbolizes their permanent union. Farid wants to tie this knot tightly because in the whole world there is no one so important as (the husband-lord).[6] At the bridegroom's place, a ceremony is performed in which the bride takes a handful of sesame (*til*) and transfers it to the bridegroom's hand. Farid wants to be careful about the quantity to be taken out for transfer. 'Had I known that my spouse was too young, I would not have shown pride'.[7]

Shaikh Farid can use the metaphor of the bride in his own voice as well. When a young girl is engaged to be married, the exact time of wedding is fixed. In the same way, the day of death is fixed the moment one is born. Human life here is the bride (*dhan*, *vahuti*) and death, or the angel of death, is the bridegroom (*var*).[8] Much more often, however, Farid takes his metaphors from conjugal life, the relationship between the wife and the husband. The woman who washes and adorns herself to receive her husband but goes to sleep before his arrival loses all her fragrance and emits bad odour.[9] She who does not enjoy her husband in youth cannot do so in old age. She who enjoys her master acquires a new complexion.[10] She who did not enjoy the husband in youth and could not do so in old age now cries aloud in the grave that she has no hope of meeting him.[11]

The ideal woman for Shaikh Farid is the *sohagan* who enjoys her husband and has the bliss of union with him. What kind of a married woman (*sohagan*) is she for whom the spouse does not care? She has no support in her marital home and no place in her natal home.[12] The real *sohagan* does not look for anyone. She who is still searching for a husband (*sohag*) has some flaw in herself.[13] The wife must give preference to love (*preet*) over her youth, for many a youth has withered and dried without love.[14] What is that word, that quality, that *mantra*, and that manner which enable the wife to gain the husband's attention and love?[15] That word is humility, that quality is patience, that *mantra* is sweet talk—these three constitute the manner that gives power over the husband.[16]

Physical beauty is short-lived. I have seen those eyes O Farid which fascinated the world: once they could not bear a line of kohl and now a bird is hatching eggs in them.[17] When a young maid, she was keen to be wedded; when married, she faced many problems; now her regret is that she cannot regain her maidenhood.[18] Farid tells the young woman to tear off her silken scarf and to wear rough woollen shawl: the most appropriate garb is the one that leads to the husband.[19]

Only a few *shabads* of Shaikh Farid are available but even in these he does not forget women. She who does not care for the master in youth has nothing but regret when she grows old. She may yearn for the spouse but she cannot blame him; the fault lies with her. Without the beloved spouse there is no comfort. In separation from him one turns dark like the nightingale. One may meet the master only when he is kind.[20] The woman who is proud and clever hears rude words from her husband; she never unites with him. no milk oozes from her breasts.[21] To become a mother is necessary, and fortunate is the mother who gives birth to a *darvesh*.[22] The young woman feels encouraged to see that young men have crossed the river. Beside the deep well a woman stands alone without a companion, without a friend; the master shows mercy to her and ensures her association with the pious (*sadh-sang*).[23]

In the world of Farid, women are much less visible than men. The relationship of love between human beings and God does not bring in women as a matter of course. Men are explicitly asked to follow the path of love. The word *shauh* and *pir* are used for God by his male devotees too. However, the term *kant*, as well as these two terms, can be used in a neutral manner, neither specifically by male nor by female devotees of God, as in the two *shloks* on *birha*. The phrase God's *dohagan* (*dohagan rabb di*) is superbly neutral. However, when Farid addresses his companions as *sahelio*, it does not mean that he is addressing a female audience. The *dohagan* is defined as the woman who washes and adorns herself but only to slumber and not to be enjoyed by her spouse. Negatively, a woman is not a real *sohagan* if her spouse does not care for her. The real *sohangan* is devoted to her lord alone.

The domestic situation involving the relationship between husband and wife is all the time tilted against the woman. The maiden is keen to be wedded because there is no other option; marriage brings its own problems but her misfortune is that she cannot become a virgin again. The woman deserves the harsh words used by the spouse; she can only wait to be called in. The bride whose spouse is too young (to enjoy her) cannot think of offending him. The woman's love is one-sided. She who could not enjoy her spouse when she was young, dies un-enjoyed when she is old; she wails in the grave that she has failed to meet the spouse. The woman goes crazy because of her longing for the spouse and the pain of separation. But this is due to her demerit; there can be nothing wrong with the spouse.

A few verses in the female voice do carry the implication that God is accessible to women. God is all important to them but the images evoked make them subordinate to the husband. If love is meant to give parity to women, the metaphor of conjugality pulls them back into subordination in the home. However, there are other images of women in the compositions of Farid: the woman who had the world at her feet because of the beauty of her eyes, the mother who has given birth to the man of God, and the lonely woman at the well in a wilderness. The beauty of a woman is of no avail. But the woman who gives birth to men of God has to be praised. The image of the lonely woman at the well who is given the boon of *sadh-sang* by God through his grace is rather significant. She is taken clearly outside the domestic walls: she is neither a wife, nor a mother, nor a daughter; she exists in her own right as a woman, as a person.

II

The volume of Shah Husain's poetry is much larger than that of the poetry of Shaikh Farid. More than half of his verses are either in female voice or have bearing on gender relations. It is interesting to note that nearly all the ideas and attitudes expressed in the male voice are expressed in the female voice too: unity of God, his omnipotence, his omnipresence, his everlasting existence, the transitory character of human life and achievement, the futility of earthly pursuits and sensual pleasures, the importance of human life as the only opportunity in the face of inevitable death, accountability for one's deeds, remembrance of God, acceptance of his will, adoration of God, devotion to him, love for him, unification with him, longing for union with him and pangs of separation from him.

The depiction of woman in Shah Husains verses is mostly contextual, relating largely to woman as the daughter and the wife. The young girl plays with her companions; she sings and dances; she enjoys the swing in the month of *Sawan*; she keeps the hearth and the home clean; she fetches water from the well; and she spins, weaves and embroiders. To remain unwed is a misfortune. Her marriage is the responsibility of her father. She does not hope to meet the friends of girlhood after her marriage. In the home of her father and at her in-laws, she is expected to follow social conventions and the traditions of the family. She has to hear taunts if she goes to her in-laws without adequate dowry. She has to remain in veil and under some other constraints. She must not incur the displeasure of her husband. She should adorn herself to please him. She should wait for him at night. It is for the husband to decide whether or not to have union with her. The metaphors of Shah Husain, thus, evoke a patriarchal atmosphere.

Like Shaikh Farid, Shah Husain talks of the lord-husband (*shauh*). The lonely woman suffers the pangs of separation because she has not learnt how to enjoy the husband; she can become a *sohagan* only if the husband recognizes her.[24] The woman who has no merit and no beauty trembles on meeting the husband who is handsome and possesses many qualitieis: she does not know whether or not he would embrace her.[25] Shah Husain talks of the woman who has not been enjoyed by her husband for a long time in her life; she praises the *sohagans* who have their arms around their husbands. The one who keeps awake is the fortunate one; unfortunate is she who sleeps.[26] The young girl was keen to be wedded to an unknown man but does not know how he would treat her: it is a gamble.[27] The woman who has not enjoyed the husband is envious of those who have.[28] The chance to enjoy the husband should not be missed.[29] If the woman is not liked by her husband, her colourful robes lose their luster.[30] The one who remains unwedded is full of regret.[31] Every young girl has to get married and to take dowry with her.[32] After a few days in the natal home, she has inevitably to go to her in-laws.[33]

The husband (*shauh*) stands equated sometimes with the friend (*yar*). The face of the beloved friend (*yar piara*) remains imprinted on the heart of the woman who loves him; his is the whole garden and she is its nightingale. She would please him without much ceremonial by becoming the dust at his door.[34] The pangs of separation have become the lot of a woman; she addresses the *murshid*; she searches for *Lal*; and she would enjoy bliss if she meets the husband.[35] In this verse, the *murshid*, God, and the husband stand bracketed. In another verse, *shauh* is equated with God (*sahib*). Shah Husain appears to give much less importance to the metaphors of conjugality than what we find in Shaikh Farid. In fact, he can talk of a situation in which neither the natal home nor the marital home provides the context. The ways of love are strange: the Beloved does what he pleases. Sorrow and suffering gather together and there is no marital or natal home: only you are my refuge now; take hold of this innocent young girl'.[37]

Shah Husain's women address the Master (*sahib*, *sain*) and the True One (*sachcha*) directly. One woman says that she is devoted to the Master unto death; she has detached herself from everything; may the

Master not forget her.[38] Another woman carries the basket of love over her head and calls aloud at every door for a customer.[39] Only those nights are credited to the woman's account which have been spent with the Master.[40] A woman invokes the Master's grace (*fazl*) while underlining her meritlessness: He alone bestows riches or imposes poverty; He alone enables one to embrace the Beloved and keeps another a way from him.[41] In another verse, only one word, the helpless one (*vichari*), is gendered; it expresses supplication in terms which could be used by any male.[42] In yet another verse in the female voice, no epithet is used for the entity who is being addressed: *kadi tan asadada thiyo*.[43]

In some of Shah Husain's verses *sain* is equated with *sajan*, *sajan* with *sahib* or *rabb* with *piara*. Asking for grace and not justice, the woman underlines her meritlessness and prays to *rabb* that he may ignore her demerit; lying at his door, she asks the Beloved (*piara*) to keep her as he wishes.[44] 'Whether good or bad, I am your slave O Master (*sahib*). I am dyed in your colour. My firend (*sajan*) fills my eyes and I walk in the lanes without care'.[45] The friend (*sajan*) belongs to her and she belongs to him; but he is annoyed and she is suffering in his absence; she is prepared to become the slave of the one who may bring the friend back to meet her; if she meets the Master (*sain*), she would feel overjoyed.[46]

There is a smooth transition from the husband to the master, from the master to the master-friend, and from the master-friend to the beloved friend (*mahi*, *sajan*, *mittar*, *piara*) in the verses of Shah Husain. There is a message to the beloved friend (*mittar piara*) that his *jogan* would die for him and get fresh life by meeting him. With her hair let loose, she has become a *bairagan*, searching for him silently in the wilderness and in thickets on the river bank; she cannot cry aloud because of the mores of honour, but she keeps vigils day and night.[47] I am the slave girl of that friend (*sajan*) with whose name you taunt me: I am a sacrifice to him. She is the dust of his feet and she knows no other.[48] Significantly, the woman admits that she is attracted by sensual pleasures—the hens within and the peacocks outside.[49] This admission equates her with men. When the friend (*sajan*) is annoyed with her, even her friends do not care for her: she walks on to see him.[50] The beautiful friend (*sohna sajan*) has come home, and she can be congratulated. She has found the friend she was searching for. Her courtyard has become resplendent and her forehead bright.[51] Discarding social conventions and the family norms, a woman is heading towards her friend (*sajan*).[52] Like Shaikh Farid, Shah Husain speaks of dark nights and the muddy lanes; but, unlike Shaikh Farid, the woman in Shah Husain's verse meets the friend there and then as her protector and guide (*yar-sipahi*).[53]

In a dozen of verses, Shah Husain uses the symbolism of Hir and Ranjha-the popular lovers of Punjabi folklore. In some of these verses, Ranjha is equated with *shauh* or *var* (both meaning husband), or with *shauh* and *var* or with *mahi*, Ranjha and *Rabb*, or with *Rabb*, but in several other verses Hir and Ranjha stand as lovers. If Ranjha is God, Hir has a direct link with him as the symbol for human beings, booth men and women. In Punjabi literature, this symbolism appears for the first time in the poetry of Shah Husain, and it is highly significant.

'Do not talk to me of the Khedas, O mother', says Hir, 'Ranjha belongs to me and I belong to Ranjha. The Khedas have only false hopes. People think that Hir has gone crazy but the *chak* (Ranjha) is my spouse. This is known to God'.[54] 'I have found the spouse I was searching for. Crying *mahi*, *mahi!* I have myself become Ranjhan. Call me Ranjhan, Ranjhan; none should call me Hir.'[55] Ranjha is on the other side (of the river); Hir wants to cross over to meet the friend (*sajan*). She would become a *jogan* for the sake of the master and do all she can. She would distribute sweets worth lacs if she weds the beloved friend. She is grateful for the light she sees on meeting the beloved friend.[56] Hir asks her friends to bring her *mahi* to her: she is impatient to meet him. She does not want any dowry from her father; she does not want any goods from her mother. She asks for Ranjha alone every moment. But the Khedas have forcibly taken her away. She prays to God that he may enable the separated ones to meet.[57] In another verse, Hir prays that she may have sight of the Master. Her master is Sawal; she is his slave girl. People have heard that Hir has become a *bairagan*. Let them hear in lacs: what can anyone do? She would become a slave of *sadhs* and perform menial services for them (to meet Ranjha).[58] Hir wants to go to Ranjha's abode. She implores others to accompany her but she has to go alone. There are difficulties and dangers in her way. She would give the rings on her fingers to anyone who brings the news of the friend (*mittar*). Ranjha is known to be a great healer and she has crazy pains in her body. May the master (*sain*) send his message.[59]

Hir prefers Ranjha, her own choice, over the Khedas chosen by her parents. She challenges her mother to change the divine writ. She places trust in God (*qadir*), knowing that the claims of the Khedas are false.[60] Ranjha is *jogi* and *Hir* is *jogan*; she is crazy for him.[61] Hir continues to love Ranjha in spite of her parents' wishes and advice to the contrary. Her love goes back to her childhood. Nothing can erase this love. She would find peace only when she sees Ranjha. [62] She is prepared to suffer all kinds of pain in her crazy search for Ranjha everywhere. She wants to meet him at all cost.[63] Hir is not alone. All the girls of the Sials are in search of the master (*sain*). They who do not remember the master, regret in the end. We have dedicated ourselves to the master (*sahib*)'. He is also the master of Takht Hazara.[64]

In the context of what we have said so far, some of the verses of Shah Husain become significant. The symbol of the spinning wheel (*charkha*) is used to express some of his general ideas.[65] The bride is asked to wear the *salu* of *sahaj*. The ideas expressed in this composition are also of general import.[66] Shah Husain can ask the woman to wake up early and remember Ram and meditate on him.[67] He can tell the young girl that her youth is short-lived and ask her to tread the right path.[68] He can tell the innocent girl that her time is passing. Life on this earth is only for a few days. Nothing and no one can go with her. What remains for ever is the name of the Lord.[69] Shah Husain can pray for the woman that she may never forget God (*Rabb*); she may forget anything or anyone but not God; He is never to be forgotten.[70] Shaikh Farid's woman prefers love over youth; Shah Husain's woman prefers grace over youth.[71] The woman can declare that she cannot think of anything besides her friend (*sajan*).[72] Shah Husain tells the new-comer not to raise her voice in contention; she has failed to save her yarn and now she is blaming the weaver.[73] She who is in love cannot spin; why should she?[74] The sweeper woman of Shah Husain can claim to have served the master in the hope of seeing his face.[75]

III

In retrospect we may observe that Shaikh Farid adopted the female voice not as an innovation but in consonance with an old Indian tradition. Its use was appropriate for expressing the idea of loving devotion through the ideal wife sumbolized as the *sohagan*. This ideal compromises the equality embodied in the idea of mutual love. The conception of God-Husband as having all power, authority, and initiative creates the scope for union but only through the master's grace. Paradoxically, Farid creates space for women by reinforcing patriarchy. The woman has access to spirituality but essentially within the domestic walls.

Shah Husain too takes the patriarchal framework for granted. However, the metaphors of conjugal love are not dominant in his poetry. More often, the woman addresses God directly. Indeed, God tends to become more of a beloved friend than a lord-husband. The symbolism of Hir and Ranjha acquires crucial significance in this context. What is celebrated is the basic relationship of love between God and human beings. The woman is at par with man in relation to God. The patriarchal structure is marginalized. The woman as a person has direct access to God.

NOTES

1. The question of gender relations in the poetry of Shaikh Farid has been taken up by Parmjit Singh Sidhu in 'Farid da Kant' : Ratan Singh Jaggi (ed.) *Khoj Patrika: Sufi Kaav Ank*, Patiala: Punjabi University, 1989, pp. 147-53.
2. Sahib Singh (ed.) *Shalok Te Shabad Farid Ji Steek*. Amritsar: Singh Brothers, 1995 (15th edn.), p. 55.
3. Ibid., p. 60.
4. Ibid., p. 72.
5. Ibid., p. 57
6. Ibid., p. 46.
7. Ibid., p. 45
8. Ibid., p. 43.
9. Ibid., p. 59.
10. Ibid., p. 49.
11. Ibid., p. 69.
12. Ibid., p. 58.
13. Ibid., p. 99.
14. Ibid., p. 59.
15. Ibid., p. 105.
16. Ibid., p. 106.
17. Ibid., p. 50.
18. Ibid., p. 73.
19. Ibid., p. 92.
20. Ibid., p. 112.
21. Ibid., p. 114.
22. Ibid., p. 108.
23. Ibid., p. 112.
24. Jeet Singh Sital (ed)., *Shah Husain: Jivan Te Rachna*. Patiala: Punjabi University, 1995, p. 52.
25. Ibid., p. 60.
26. Ibid., p. 73.
27. Ibid., p. 75.
28. Ibid., p. 85.
29. Ibid., p. 99.
30. Loc. cit.
31. Ibid., p. 101.
32. Ibid., pp. 104 &105.
33. Ibid., p. 106

34. Ibid., p. 81
35. Ibid., pp. 87-8.
36. Ibid., p. 67.
37. Ibid., p. 109.
38. Ibid., p. 50.
39. Ibid., p. 51.
40. Ibid., p. 54.
41. Ibid., p. 55.
42. Ibid., p. 65.
43. Ibid., p. 57.
44. Ibid., p. 62.
45. Ibid., p. 72.
46. Ibid., p. 80.
47. Ibid., p. 51.
48. Ibid., p. 60.
49. Ibid.
50. Ibid., p. 88.
51. Ibid., p. 94.
52. Ibid., p. 100.
53. Ibid., p. 107.
54. Ibid., p. 76.
55. Ibid., p. 98.
56. Ibid., p. 84.
57. Ibid., p. 100.
58. Ibid., pp. 72-3.
59. Ibid., pp. 75-6.
60. Ibid., p. 77.
61. Ibid., pp. 83 & 110.
62. Ibid., pp. 84-5.
63. Ibid., p. 95.
64. Ibid., p. 89.
65. Ibid., p. 49.
66. Ibid., pp. 58-9.
67. Ibid., p. 53.
68. Ibid., p. 58.
69. Ibid., pp. 61-2.
70. Ibid., p. 66.
71. Ibid., p. 67.
72. Ibid., p. 69.
73. Ibid., p. 70.
74. Ibid., p. 84.
75. Ibid., p. 82.

Zad al-Muttaqeen wa-Saluk-i Tariq al-Yaqin: A Contemporary Work on the Lives of the Sixteenth Century Sufi Theologians

Iqtidar Hussain Siddiqui

The *Zad al-Muttaqeen wa-Saluk-i Tariq al-Yaqin* compiled in AD 1594, by Shaikh Abdul Haque Muhaddith of Delhi (d. 19 June 1642) is an important source of information about the lives and missionary work of Shaikh Ali Muttaqi (d. 1567) and his disciple, Shaikh Abdul Wahab Muttaqi. Both of them happened to be great missionaries through whom the Islamic responses in many respects, in *fiqh* (jurisprudence), in *tasawwuf* (sufism), in ethics, in *tafsir* (exegesis of Quran) and *hadith* (traditions of the Prophet of Islam) bounced back from India to the classical lands of Islam, Hejaz, Yemen, Syria, and Egypt, etc. Only two manuscripts of the valuable work are known so far. One of the them is preserved in the Raza Library, Rampur (U.P., India) while the other (and certainly of the seventeenth century) is in my personal collection. The latter is of demi size with seventeen lines on every folio, the folios being 152 in number. It is written in beautiful *nastaliq* script and its style is free from all literary embellishments.

The work under study is divided, besides a detailed preface, in three parts: the first and second, consisting of five *babs* (chapters) each, are related to the lives and works of Shaikh Ali Muttaqi and Shaikh Abdul Wahab Muttaqi in India and Hejaz, while the third part contains notices of Indian dervishes (saints) and scholars who had settled down in Mecca and Medina. Shaikh Abdul Haque Muhaddith visited many of them during his two years stay in Hejaz. Let us now briefly analyse the nature of evidence contained in the work.

The preface, comprising more than four folios, contains brief details about the compiler. Having felt in himself a compelling urge to improve his understanding of *hadith*, and benefit from the company of holy people in Mecca and Medina, he left for Hejaz (AD 1588). In Mecca, he joined the circle of the disciples of Shaikh Abdul Wahab Muttaqi, who initiated the disciples in the Qadiriyya, Shazliyya and the Madaniyya *silsilahs* (sufi orders) in the tradition of his *pir* (preceptor). Shaikh Ali Muttaqi and Shaikh Abdul Wahab Muttaqi helped Shaikh Abdul Haque in acquiring proficiency in the standard *hadith* collections, such as *Sahih-i Bukhari* and *Sahih-i Muslim*. Moreover, they guided him in performing spiritual exercises and, after two years, persuaded him to return to India (AD 1490). During his two years stay in Hejaz, Shaikh Abdul Haque availed himself of the opportunity to get in touch with a number of Sufis and scholars in Mecca and Medina.[1]

As regards the five chapters, in the first part, relating to Shaikh Ali Muttaqi, they contain authentic information that the compiler seems to have collected from the Shaikh's disciples. These chapters not only help us reconstruct the portrait of Shaikh Ali Muttaqi but also supplement the information available in other sources about other scholars and *sufis* who also played an important social role in India during the fifteenth and sixteenth centuries. Of the *ulama/sufi*, we should make mention here of Shaikh Hussamuddin Muttaqi of Tulanba, the teacher and religious guide of Shaikh Ali Muttaqi. He belonged to Tulanba but ran a seminary in Multan. Mulla Abdul Qadir Badauni and other sixteenth century writers pay compliments to him for his piety and spiritual excellence[2] but in *Zad al-Muttaqeen*, we are provided with interesting hints about the methods the great master employed to impart knowledge to his students and arouse cosmic consciousness in case they were found seriously interested in spiritual values. In fact, his sincerity and devotion to religion and learning meant a large number of people and his students who not only cherished his memory but also tried to emulate him in austerity, piety and rendering selfless service to the mankind. Shaikh Ali Muttaqi was deeply influenced by his personality.[3]

Besides, we also come across the names of certain other *ulema* who disseminated the knowledge of Islamic *fiqh* and *hadith* in different regions of India during the first half of the sixteenth century. Mention may be made of Qazi Abdullah Sindhi and his son Shaikh Hamid Muhadith. The former was a friend of Shaikh Ali Muttaqi and went to Hejaz along with the latter. Shaikh Abdullah is said to have wielded great influence on the Muslims in Sindh while his son was taught *hadith* by Shaikh Ali Muttaqi and went to Hejaz along with the latter. Shaikh Abdullah is said to have wielded great influence on the Muslims in Sindh while his son was taught *hadith* by Shaikh Ali Muttaqi. On his return from Hejaz, Shaikh Muhammad Muhaddith settled down in Gujarat and devoted his time to teaching *hadith* and other religious sciences. He also supplied information to Shaikh Abdul Haque about the life and work of his teacher in Gujarat and Hejaz.[4]

The two years spent by Shaikh Ali Muttaqi in the company of Shaikh Husamuddin Muttaqi in Multan were valuable in many respects. The great master not only supervised his study of religious works including *Tafsir-i Baizavi* and *Kitab ainal Ilm*, but also guided him in performing spiritual exercise, leading to the purification of his inner self.[5] On his departure from Multan, he settled down in Ahmedabad during the reign of Sultan Bahadur Shah (1526-37). His piety and learning attracted a large number of people of his *khanqah* but Shaikh Ali Muttaqi remained unaffected by all this. He spent most of his time in offering prayer or sitting in meditation. His admirers had a house and mosque constructed for him in Ahmedabad, outside the Shahpur gate.[6] In the tradition of Shaikh Husamuddin Muttaqi, Shaikh Ali Muttaqi also inspired his disciples through his own example. He aroused in them divine love as well as a spirit for good works. He stayed in Gujarat till the reign of Sultan Mahmud Shah (1537-54) and worked with zeal for the reform of society. He and his disciples worked for the diffusion of knowledge of *hadith* and *fiqh* in Gujarat. Having entrusted the work of reform and revival of Islamic orthodox learning to his disciples, he finally left for Hejaz. On his departure, the traditions of extreme austerity and piety set by him continued to inspire the Muslims in Gujarat for generations. The relevant evidence contained in the *Malfuzat* of Shaikh Wajihuddin Gujarati tends to suggest that the traditions set by him in Gujarat inspired the Muslims in the subsequent period as well. One day, Shaikh Wajihuddin told his disciples: 'Shaikh Ali Muttaqi was an angel in the form of man. No body would ever be able to equal him in piety'. On another occasion, Shaikh Wajihuddin paid compliments to Shaikh Ali Muttaqi in these words: 'It is beyond my capacity to attain to the level of Shaikh Ali's piety'.[7]

In Mecca, Shaikh Ali Muttaqi joined the circle of the students of Shaikh Ali Bakri of Diyar Bakr, a leading scholar of Islamic Sciences. He also visited other scholars in Mecca and benefited from his association with every one of them. Shaikh Muhammad bin Muhammad al-Sakhavi initiated Shaikh Ali Muttaqi in the Qadiriya, Shazliyya and the Madaniyya *silsilahs* (sufi orders) and also granted him *Khilafat* (permission) to enroll *murids* (disciples) in all the aforesaid *silsilahs*. Shaikh Ali achieved perfection in the understanding of *hadith* and *tasawwuf* within a short time under the guidance of his teachers and friends.[8] As a result, he gained reputation for his piety and erudition in Hejaz. People who came to Hejaz from different countries for *haj* (pilgrimage) paid a visit to him and also became his *murids*. The wealthy among the visitors, such as merchants and officers, belonging to India, Central Asia, and the Ottoman Empire offered *futuh* which was distributed among the poor and destitute people. The rich men also fixed stipends to the widows on the Shaikh's recommendation. But the Shaikh met his own expenses with the meagre income from the sale of books transcribed by himself. In an attempt to set an example of austerity and piety, the Shaikh lived in extreme poverty. He also controlled his desire for food. He took very little food and mixed water with it if he found it tasty.[10] Amongst his *murids* were included the scholars from Syria, Yemen, Hejaz, Egypt and Turkey.[11]

The biographer of the Shaikh has also incorporated certain anecdotes that cast light on the element of humour and liberalism in the Shaikh's personality. Free from religious fanaticism, the Shaikh could make concession to the Indian environment, in case it was not at variance with the Koran teaching. He would avoid opposition to certain customs the eradication of which was desirable but not easy. He also possessed a strong sense of humour. Illustrating his point, Shaikh Abdul Haque Muhaddith quotes his discussion with one of the ministers in Gujarat over the issue of remarriage of Muslim widows. Influenced by the local culture, the Muslim elite had become averse to the remarriage of the widows. It was considered unbecoming of a respectable family. Shaikh Abdul Haque writes that one day one of the ministers of Gujarat visited him and complained about the prevalence of the non-Islamic customs among the Muslims. He said that the worst of them was to keep the widowed sisters and daughters in the house and consider their remarriage as something undesirable or humiliating. Further, he said that if an effort was made by the Shaikh, this evil would be eradicated from the Muslim society. The Shaikh replied, 'By the grace of God, you are not only an influential man but also have got an estate. This evil can be eradicated with your help'. The *wazir* assured him of his whole hearted cooperation. Then the Shaikh said, 'I have heard that your mother is a widow, if you allow her to marry me, other people will be impressed and do the same'. The *wazir* got annoyed and left the Shaikh in disgust.[12]

The Shaikh is reported to have written one hundred books on *fiqh*, *ilm al-kalam* (scholasticism), *hadith* and *tasawwuf*. The first book was the *Risala-i Tabin-al-Turaq*, a treatise in Arabic on *tasawwuf*. The other important work is said to have been the *Majmu'a-i Hukm-i Kabir* in which 'the Shaikh has explained subtle points relating to Islamic mysticism. The most important contribution made by him was the re-arrangement in alphabetical order of the collection of *hadith*, *Khaz al-Ummah* compiled by Shaikh Jalal Uddin al-Suyuti (d. 1505). It was done for the convenience of the students of Islamic *fiqh*.[13]

It is also worth nothing that Shaikh Ali Muttaqi continued to take interest in the diffusion of learning in India through books and disciples. If he got hold of a standard work on any aspect of Islam, he had several copies of it made and sent one to India. Once he went out of his way to buy the book *Muwahib-ul-Dunya* (a standard work on the life of the Prophet) and sent its copy to India. Soon it gained popularity and could be found in every city.[14] He died in Mecca in 1567. On his death, his nephew Shaikh Ahmad, got his library while his mantle of spiritual succession fell on the shoulders of his disciple, Shaikh Abdul Wahab Mutaqqi.[15]

Like his Shaikh (preceptor), Shaikh Abdul Wahab also came of an aristocratic family of north India and decided to become a *sufi* at the age of twenty years. His *pir* took keen interest in his education and training. For his piety and devotion to religion, people believed that he was a special recipient of strict orthodoxy and attracted *murids* and students from Arab countries as well as India and Central Asia. The *sufis* and scholars of Mecca, Medina, Yemen, Egypt and Syria had faith in him and praised him for his spiritual attainments.[16]

Besides, we are also informed that Shaikh Abdul Wahab Mutaqqi emulated his *pir* in showing respect to the teachings and philosophical works of Shaikh Ibn al-Arabi. Shaikh Ali Muttaqi is also reported to have generally avoided any discussion of Shaikh Ibn al-Arabi's doctrine of *Wahdat-al Wujud* (unity in essence of the Creator and creation) before his students. Shaikh Abdul Wahab also remained well guarded in his criticism of the followers of Shaikh Ibn al-Arabi. Once he was constrained to tell his disciple, Shaikh Abudul Haque Muhaddith, that the works of Shaikh Ibn-Al-Arabi should be studied seriously. As for the work of Shaikh Abdul Karim Jilli, it was forbidden and called sugar mixed with poison.[17]

We are also provided interesting information about Shaikh Abdul Wahab Mutaqqi's concern for the religious reform of the Muslims in India. After Shaikh Ali Muttaqi's death, he visited Gujarat and opposed the Mahdavi propaganda there. Soon he returned to Mecca because he did not want to miss the *haj* that year.[18] Thereafter, he seems to have maintained his contact with India through his followers. Amongst his *murids* and followers were scholars and merchants of Gujarat, Deccan and the Mughal Empire. They visited him in large numbers with *futuh* (gift presented both in cash and kind).[19]

Shaikh Abdul Wahab is said to have celebrated the *urs* (death anniversary) of *sufis* and the birth anniversary of the Prophet of Islam three or four times every year. He fed a large number of people on these occasions. The death anniversary of the Prophet of Islam and the *urs* of Ghausul-Saqlain Shaikh Abdul Qadir Jilani were celebrated on a grand scale. Contrary to the tradition in India, he celebrated the *urs* of Shaikh Abdul Qadir Jilani on 9 *Rabi al-Awwal* instead of on 11 *Rabi al-Awwal* for he considered the former date as correct. Shaikh Abdul Haque Muhaddith supports his *pir* and teacher in his regard.[20] In short, like his *pir* Shaikh Abdul Wahab represented simultaneously the traditions of the sufi of *khanqah* and the orthodox *alim* teacher of a *madrasa* (college).

The last part is also important as it provides us valuable information about the emigrant saints and scholars whom the compiler met in Mecca and Medina. Some of them migrated from India. They came from families belonging to different strata of the Indian Muslim society. In their account, we find references to certain facts of sociological importance that have not been mentioned by the medieval historians of Gujarat. For instance, the Muslims in Gujarat and other provinces were divided into *biradris* (racial or ethnic groups). According to Shaikh Abdul Haque, the members of the *Naina biṛadri* (brotherhood) lived in the territorial unit of Surat. They belonged to the Saifi'i school of thought. Faqih Muhammad Naina who had settled down along with his family members in Hejaz was a scholarly man.[21] He became a devout sufi under the influence of Shaikh Ali Muttaqi. Likewise the account of Mian Khuda Baksh Daccani indicates that even the Indians of ordinary means could manage to travel to Arabia, owing to their religious commitment. In Hejaz, Mian Khuda Baksh voluntarily took up the responsibility to keep the tomb of the Prophet clean and got pleasure in serving there as a dustman. He lived in Medina along with his family members.[22] The references to the Indian *qawwals* (singers) in Mecca and Medina suggest that the community of the Indian Muslims in the holy places of Islam was quite sizeable.[23]

In the final analysis, it may be stated that the work *Zad al-Muttaqeen* is free from hagiographical embroidery. It provides us with vital insights into the social role performed, and influenced wielded by the sixteenth century sufi/*ulema* both in India and the Arab lands. But for this work we would not have got any information about the significant contribution made by the Indian celebrities to the spiritual and intellectual heritage of the Islamic world in the sixteenth century.

NOTES

1. Shaikh Abdul Haque Muhaddith Dehlavi, *Zad al-Muttaqeen wa-Saluk-i Tariq al-Yaqin*, Ms. in the personal collection of the writer, ff. 2b-4b; hereafter cited as *Zad al-Muttaqeen*.
2. Mulla Abdul Qadir Badaoni supplies in the *Najat-al Rashid*, interesting information about Shaikh Husamuddin Muttaqi's piety and religiosity. Describing his strict adherence to the Islamic *sharia*, he states that whenever he went towards the tomb of Shaikh Bahauddin Zakariya of Multan, he would not enter the tomb but stand outside, away even from its shade to offer prayer. The reason was that it was constructed with the money donated by the nobles whose means of income were hardly in conformity with the law of *sharia*. Moreover, the labourers employed in its construction were not paid wages according to the religious law. He further adds that Shaikh Husamuddin owned cultivated land in his hometown, Tulanba and paid *ushr* (one tenth of the produce) to the state in time before the officials came to collect it. He met his personal expenses with its produce. Sultan Sikandar Lodi, being fond of the company of the learned men, invited him to his court and also offered a big land grant but he refused to leave Multan. On the fall of the Langah dynasty, the conditions deteriorated and he had to abandon his land because he was required to pay taxes not permitted by the *sharia*. Thus left without any other source of income, he had to face starvation (cf. *Najat ul-Rashid*, ed. Syed Moinul Haque, Lahore, 1972, pp. 423-4). There is also little relevant evidence contained in the *Malfuzat* (collection of table talks) of Shaikh Wajihuddin Gujarati (d. AD 1588) that shows how careful Shaikh Husamuddin was in matter of his diet. He would eat only fish after he had abandoned cultivation because it was caught by fishermen in the river and its use did not go against the *sharia*, cf. Shaikh Muhammad, *Malfuzat-i Shaikh Wajihuddin Gujarati*, Ms. Habib Ganj Collection, Maulana Azad Library, Aligarh, no. 21/221, Farsi, f. 4b.
3. *Zad al-Muttaqeen*, ff. 5a-b.
4. Ibid., ff. 7b-8a, 8b-9a.
5. Ibid., ff. 5a-5b.
6. Ibid., f. 7b.
7. Shaikh Muhammad, *Malfuzat-i Shaikh Wajihuddin Gujarati*, op. cit., f. 9b.
8. Ibid.
9. Ibid.
10. *Zad al-Muttaqeen*, ff. 13b, 14a, 16a.
11. Ibid., ff. 10a-b, 27a, etc.
12. *Zad al-Muttaqeen*, f. 21b.
13. Ibid, f. 9b.
14. Ibid, f. 19a-b.
15. Ibid, f. 16a.

16. *Zad al-Muttaqeen.*
17. Ibid., f. 45a.
18. Ibid., ff. 40a-b.
19. Ibid., f. 41b.
20. Loc. cit.
21. Ibid., ff. 149b, 150a.
22. Ibid., f. 151b.
23. Ibid., f. 152b.

Khwaja Mohammad Hashim Kishmi: A Famous Seventeenth Century Naqshbandi Sufi of Burhanpur

Iqbal Sabir

The Naqshbandi silsilah[1] has played a significant role in the socio-political development of the Indian subcontinent during the medieval period. Introduced in India at the end of the sixteenth century AD,[2] its saints settled down in different cities and towns of the Mughal Empire[3] and exerted deep influence on the contemporary society.[4] Sources say they attracted a large multitude to their mystic fold. If, on one hand, they fulfilled the spiritual expectations and religious urges of the masses, on the other, they also came to wield a considerable and sobering impact on the ruling elite.[5] They enjoyed respect and reverence from all sections of the Muslim society. Among such Naqshbandi sufis, Khwaja Mohammad Hashim Kishmi of Burhanpur occupies an important place. A *Khalifa* of the renowned Naqshbandi saint of the early seventeenth century, Shaikh Ahmad Sirhindi, commonly called Mujaddid Alf Thani,[6] Khwaja Hashim made determined and strenuous efforts to develop and popularize the Naqshbandi silsilah and its teachings in Burhanpur and surrounding areas till the last moment of his life. The present paper sheds light on his biographical details and discusses, in brief, his mystical performance and literary achievements.

We don't find Hashim's date of birth mentioned anywhere in our sources. However, it appears from the contemporary and latter works that he belonged to a scholarly mystic family of the famous town Kishm in Badakhshan in Afghanistan.[7] His father Mohammad Qasim Nabghani Badakhshani had been a teacher of Mirza Shah Rukh, the ruler of Badakhshan.[8] His ancestors owed spiritual allegiance to the Kubrawi silsilah. In his youth he too had come into contact with Kubrawi saints. But later he felt attracted towards and decided to join the Naqshbandi silsilah.[9]

It was in his youth that Hashim Kishmi left Badakhshan for India. For about a year, he journeyed and wandered through various places in Afghanistan, Punjab and other places of north and central India. Finally, he reached Burhanpur in 1029 AH/AD 1619 where he came into contact with Mir Mohammad Nu'man, the famous *Khalifa* of Shaikh Ahmad Sirhindi.[10] The Mir who had been deputed by his mentor to Burhanpur for preaching and popularizing the ideas and practices of the Naqshbandi silsilah, also originally belonged to Kishm. He, therefore, accorded a warm welcome to Mohammad Hashim.[11]

His affection and hospitality left so deep an impact upon Khwaja Hashim Kishmi that he decided to permanently stay at Burhanpur. The Mir's guidance developed in him more and more interest in the Naqshbandi silsilah. Keeping the company of Mohammad Nu'man, Khwaja Hashim obtained formal spiritual training under him. Afterwards he got married to the daughter of the Mir.[12]

As Mir Mohammad Nu'man maintained correspondence with his *pir*, Shaikh Ahmad Sirhindi, in a punctual manner, he wrote to him about Hashim and succeeded in drawing his attention to and interest in Mohammad Hashim Kishmi. Shaikh Ahmad, therefore, invited him to visit Sirhindi.[13] It was in 1031 AH/AD 1621 that Hashim Kishmi reached Sirhind and stayed there for about two years in the Shaikh's company.[14] The latter initiated him into his spiritual discipline and trained him very strictly and attentively on the Naqshbandi mystic path.[15] Hashim Kashmi also looked after Ahmad Sirhindi's personal work of writing letters, etc. He sincerely served the Shaikh and frequently benefited from his spiritual assemblies. He is also reported to have accompanied the Shaikh to different places.[16] When Sirhindi was in Ajmer, Hashim was also there with him.[17]

Being satisfied with his mystical performance, Shaikh Ahmad Sirhindi conferred his *Khilafat* upon Hashim[18] and subsequently asked him, perhaps in the month of Rajab, 1033 AH/AD 1623 to return to Burhanpur and popularize the Naqshbandi silsilah there.[19] Hashim also maintained correspondence with Shaikh Ahmad and received instructions from him for his missionary activities.[20] He visited Sirhind a second time on receiving the news of his mentor's demise in 1034 AH/AD 1629 and remained there for several months keeping the company of Shaikh Ahmad's sons and other *Khalifas*.[21] Later he returned to Burhanpur where he lived the rest of his life.

As a Naqshbandi sufi, Khwaja Mohammad Hashim Kishmi remained, throughout his life, devoted to his master's spiritual mission. The popularity of the Naqshbandi-Mujaddidi silsilah in Burhanpur and the surrounding areas was the main object of his spiritual life. His achievements earned him great respect and admiration. People joined him in large numbers. According to *Hazarat al-Quda* nobles and officials also attended his spiritual assemblies and sermons.[22]

Khwaja Hashim's most important contribution to the development of the Naqshbandi silsilah lies in his producing the monumental works, the *Zubdat al-Maqamat*[23] and the *Nasmat al-Quds*[24] which are held as the most authentic sources of the history of the Naqshbandi saints of India and Central Asia. The former occupies a significant place in the sufi literature produced in medieval India. It is considered a *magnum opus* of the Naqshbandi-Mujaddidi saints. These works reflect Hashim Kishmi's scholarship and his knowledge of the religious literature of Islam. Another honour which Hashim Kishmi holds in the history of the Naqshbandis of India is that he compiled the third volume of the collections of his mentor's epistles, *Maktubat-i Imam-i Rabbani*.[25]

Hashim Kishmi was a poet as well. Almost all the contemporary and later Naqshbandi sources refer to his poetic compositions.[26] He himself has given two of his poems at the end of the *Zaubdat al-Maqamat*.[27] The collection of his verses known as *Diwan-i-Hashim* seems to have been completed in his lifetime.[28] It is a complete lyrical work of Hashim Kishmi and contains, on one hand, *Hamd* (praises of God), *Munajat* (inward conversation with God), and *qasidas* in praise of the Prophet of Islam and on the other, *ghazals* and quatrains (*rubais*) in honour and respect of Shaikh Ahmad Sirhindi. Besides, the *Diwan* also supplies a series of chronogramic verses which reveal the dates of the death of Maulana Khwaja Amkangi,[29] Khwaja Baqi Billah,[30] Shaikh Ahmad Sirhindi, etc. The author has dedicated a special elegy to his mentor's eldest son Khwaja Mohammad Sadiq[31] who died in 1025 AH/AD 1616, at the age of twenty-five. The *Diwan* also contains a number of chronogramic quatrains and poems composed on the demise of Shaikh Mohammad Fazlullah[32] (d. 1029 AH/AD1619-20) Mohammad Isa[33] (d. 1037AH/AD 1627-8), Syed Mirak Shah[34] (d. 1032 AH/AD 1622-3), Shah Ahmad Muhaddith[35] (d. 1038 AH-AD 1628-9), Shaikh Tahir[36] (d. 1040 AH/AD 1630-1), Abdur Rahim Khan-i-Khanan[37] and Mir Mohammad Nu'man (d. 1025 AH/AD 1616).[38] Some additional chronograms composed on the accession of Emperor Shahjahan, 1038 AH/AD 1628, and on the completion of the construction work of various buildings and mosques are also available in the *Diwan-i-Hashim*. Moreover, it also contains the poems entitled *Saqi Nama* and *Khargah-i-Laila*.[39]

Four or five manuscripts of the *Diwan-i-Hashim* are mentioned in the printed catalogues of different libraries of the world. One manuscript belongs to the India Office Library which is written into *nastaliq* script. It is worm-eaten and consists of 286 folios. The date of its transcription is not mentioned.[40] The other manuscript of the *Diwan-i-Hashim* is preserved in the library of the Asiatic Society of Bengal. It contains 183 folios, all in good condition. It is also in *nastaliq* script and does not give the date of its transcription.[41] The third manuscript of this *Diwan* is preserved in the Government Oriental Manuscript Library, Madras. It is also in good condition and comprises 193 leaves.[42] The Kutub Khana-i-Asafiyah also owns a manuscript of the *Diwan-i-Hashim*.[43] Moreover, it is learnt that the Maulana Azad Library of the Aligarh Muslim University also possesses a manuscript of the Khwaja Hashim's *Diwan*.[44]

Nothing is exact about Hashim Kashmi's death, for, all the contemporary and later sources are silent and supply no information in this connection. According to Sprenger, he was alive in 1056 AH/AD 1646[45] But Shah Zawwar Husain is of the view that Khwaja Hashim Kishmi died in 1054 AH/AD 1644.[46] He is sure he passed away in Burahanpur.[47] His tomb is still located there.[48]

NOTES

1. The Naqshbandi silsilah is an offshoot of Silsilah-i-Khwajgan which was organized in Turkistan by Khwaja Ahmad Ata Yaswi (d. AD 1166), whom the Turks respectfully refer to as Hazrat-i-Turkistan.

   It was in fourteenth century AD that a spiritual descendant of Khwaja Ata, Khwaja Bahauddin Mohammad Naqshbandi (d. AD 1389), revitalized the silsilah and popularized it among the Turks and Mongols of Central Asia and Transoxiana. His impact on the Silsilah-i-Khwajgan was so great that it came to be known after him as the Naqshbandi silsilah.
2. Though some Naqshbandi sufis are reported in some sources to have come to India and associated themselves with the royal courts of Babur, Humayun and Akbar, yet the real founder of this mystical order in the subcontinent was Khwaja Mohammad Baqi Billah (d. 1013 AH/AD 1603), who in fact introduced, preached and popularized the Naqshbandi silsilah in India. For his details, see Hashim Kishmi, *Zubdat al-Maqamat*; Badruddin Sirhindi, *Hazar al-Quds*, Vol. I; and the present writer's, article in *Islamic Heritage in India*, Vol. II (ed. Nazir Ahmad and I.H. Siddiqui), Jaipur, 2000, pp. 137-56.
3. Even Emperor Jahangir, who was a critic of the views and activities of the great Naqshbandi saint of his time, Shaikh Ahmad Sirhindi, in the beginning, acknowledges that his disciples and *Khalifas* (in other words the Naqshbandi

sufis) are found in every city of the Mughal Empire. See *Tuzuk-i Jahangiri*, Aligarh, 1864, p. 272

4. My revered teacher (late) Prof. K.A. Nizami is of the view that for nearly two centuries, the Naqshbandi silsilah was the principal spiritual order in India and its influence permeated far and deep into Indo-Muslim life. For details, see K.A. Nizami, *State and Culture in Medieval India*, Delhi, 1985, p. 160. According to another scholar of Sufism, 'For a time, it seemed as if the Naqshbandi Order would supercede the rest of the orders in India.' See John A. Subhan, *Sufism, its Saints and Shrines,* Lucknow, 1938, p. 275.
5. In case of their relations with the Mughal rulers, it may be mentioned here that they, ever since the time of Amir Timur, had been very much devoted to the Naqshbandi silsilah and its saints. He treated Khwaja Bahauddin Naqshband with profound respect. Timur's descendants used to receive Khwaja Obaidullah Ahrar 'standing at a distance with their eyes fixed on the ground'. Babur also inherited from his father Omar Shaikh Mirza who was a disciple of Khwaja Ahrar, a deep regard for the Naqshbandi saints and a feeling of close spiritual affinity with them, (see, Nizami, op. cit., p. 161). This tradition prevailed from generation to generation in the Mughal rulers of India as well. As mentioned earlier, some of the Naqshbandi saints of Central Asia and Afghanistan came to India and associated themselves with courts of Babur, Humayun and Akbar. For details, see *Babur Nama*, Bombay, 1308 AH, p. 229; Badayuni, *Muntakhab ut Tawarikh,* Vol. III, Calcutta, 1869, p. 40; Dara Shikoh, *Safinat al-Auliya*, Kanpur, 1884; K.A. Nizami, *State and Culture in Medieval India,* p. 162.

   Moreover, the influence of the Naqshbandi saints on these rulers may also be judged from a letter of a distinguished Chishti saint of the seventeenth century Shah Kalimullah of Delhi. Referring to the Naqshbandi influence upon Emperor Aurangzeb, Shah Kalimullah writes to one of his *Khalifas* in the Deccan who was trying in vain to influence his (Aurangzeb's) religious outlook, 'The Emperor of Hindustan is a descendant of Amir Timur and Amir Timur was spiritually attached to Shah-i Naqshband. These Turanis, all and every one of them, are connected with the Naqshbandi order and they do not attach any value to any other silsilah.' See, *Maktubat-i Kalimi*, Delhi, 1301 AH, p. 75.
6. Born in 971 AH/AD 1563-4 in Sirhind in Punjab, he holds a very special and significant position among the Muslim divines of medieval India. He played the most important role in disseminating the ideology and practices of the Naqshbandi silsilah in India. For centuries, he has been considered one of the most outstanding sufi teachers and thinkers of the subcontinent.

   Grown up to manhood during the reign of Akbar, Shaikh Ahmad Sirhindi was deeply perturbed at his religious experiments and, therefore, left no stone unturned in challenging the situation created by political interference in religious life. He established close contacts with eminent Mughal nobles through correspondence and made them realize the nature of heretical developments at the royal court.

He deputed his disciples and *Khalifas* to spread his spiritual mission in every city and town of the Mughal Empire. Apart from a large number of *ulama*, sufi, scholars and officials, many leading nobles of the Mughal court became his devotees. Emperor Jahangir consequently summoned him in 1029 AH/AD 1619 to his royal court and ordered his imprisonment in the fort of Gwalior. The Shaikh remained there for about a year.

Sirhindi's chief contribution to the development of sufi thought in Islam was his enunciation of the concept of *Wahdat al-Shuhud*, the Unity of Appearance. All his mystical ideas and practices are closely concerned with the central traditions of Islam. For this reason his contemporary *ulama* and sufis addressed him with the title of 'Mujaddid Alf Thani', the renewer of the second millennium of Islam. The Shaikh passed away in 1034 AH/AD 1624. The collection of his letters, known as *Maktubat-i-Rabbani*, holds significant position in the Muslim mystical literature throughout the Islamic world.

For his details, see Hashim Kishmi, *Zubdat al-Maqamat;* Badruddin Sirhindi, *Hazrat al-Quds*, Vol. II, and many modern works in English and Urdu.

7. Kamaluddin Mohammad Ihsan, *Rauzat al-Qaiyyumia* (Urdu trans.), Lahore, 1335 AH, p. 2.
8. Badruddin Sirhindi, *Hazrat al-Quds*, Vol. II, Lahore, 1971, p. 368.
9. Mohammad Hashim Kishmi, *Zubdat al-Maqamat*, Kanpur: Newal Kishore, 1890, p. 1.
10. *Zubdat al-Maqamat*, p. 1.
11. Ibid., p. 326.
12. Zawwar Hussain, *Hazrat Mujaddid Alf Thani*, Karachi, 1975, p. 789.
13. See *Maktubat-i-Imam-i Rabbani*, Vol. II (Turkish edition), Istambul, 1977, Letter No. 1.
14. *Hazrat al-Quds*, Vol. II, p. 370.
15. Ibid, pp. 369-70. Also, *Zubdat al-Maqamat*, p. 3.
16. *Zubdat al-Maqamat*, p. 3.
17. *Maktubat-i Imam-i Rabbani*, Vol. III, Letter No. 82. Also, *Zubdat al-Maqamat*, p. 282.
18. *Maktubat-i Imam-i Rabbani*, Vol. III, Letter Nø. 106.
19. *Hazrat al-Quds*, Vol. II, p. 370.
20. See *Maktubat-i Imam-i Rabbani*, Vol. III, Letter No. 42.

    It may be mentioned here that the *Maktubat-i Imam-i Rabbani*, contained thirteen epistles addressed to Khwaja Hashim Kishmi. See, Vol. I, Letter Nos. 310, 313; Vol. II, Letter Nos. 65, 74, 93, 97; Vol. III, Letter Nos. 42, 53, 69, 75, 90, 92, 96.

    The nature of relationship between Hashim Kishmi and Shaikh Ahmad Sirhindi may be judged from the contents of these letters. According to modern scholar of Indo-Islamic history, Yohanna Friedmann, 'This is the largest number sent to any single correspondent with the exception of Sirhindi's sons Mohammad Sa'id and Mohammad Ma'sum.' See, *Shaikh Ahmad Sirhindi*, Montreal and London, 1971, p. 21.

21. *Hazrat al-Quds*, Vol. II, p. 285.
22. Ibid., Vol. II, p. 370.
23. Hashim Kishmi started the compilation of this work just after his *pir's* demise in 1034 AH/AD 1624 on the instructions of Khwaja Mohammad Ma'sum (see pp. 4-5). It was completed in 1037 AH/AD 1627. It supplies detailed information about the lives and spiritual attainments of Khwaja Baqi Billah, Shaikh Ahmad Sirhindi and their sons and *Khalifas*. Two manuscripts of this work are listed in the printed catalogues. One belongs to the Bankipur (Khuda Baksh) Library as transcribed in the eighteenth century whereas the other, which belongs to the India Office Library, was transcribed in 1150 AH/AD 1737-8; (see C.A. Storey, *Persian Literature*, London, 1972, p. 989). Two editions of the *Zubdat al-Maqamat* have also appeared so far. One from the *Matba'-i Mahmud* of Lucknow in 1302 AH/AD 1885 at the intiative of Pandit Ajodhiya Nath, *Vakil*, High Court, Allahabad, and the other from the Newal Kishore Press of Kanpur, 1307 AH/AD 1890. An Urdu translation of this work was published from Lahore in AD 1909 (see *Persian Literature*, p. 989).
24. It is a continuation of the *Rashahat-i Ain al-Hayat* of Kashifi and contains biographies of the Naqshbandi saints from the beginning of the tenth century AH (sixteenth century AD), to the first quarter of the eleventh century AH (seventeenth century AD). The details of transcription, etc., are not available. See *Persian Literature*, p. 990 and *Zubdat al-Maqamat*, p. 285.
25. See *Hazrat al-Quds*, Vol. II, p. 370; and the preface of the 3rd vol. of the *Maktubat*.
26. *Hazrat al-Quds*, Vol. II, p. 377. Also, Abdul Haiy Hasani, *Nuzhat al-Khawatir*, Vol. 5, Hyderabad, 1976, p. 406. Thomas William Beal, *An Oriental Biographical Dictionary*, Delhi, 1971, p. 158.
27. *Zubdat al-Maqamat*, p. 399.
28. See Beal, op. cit. Storey, *Persian Literature*, p. 988. *Nuzhat al-Khawatir*, Vol. 5, p. 406.
29. He was a famous Naqshbandi saint of Central Asia and resided at the town known as Amkana near Bukhara. He was the spiritual mentor of Khwaja Baqi Billah. For his details, see *Hazrat al-Quds*, Vol. I (Urdu trans.), pp. 210-13.
30. As mentioned earlier (n. 2), he was the founder of the Naqshbandi silsilah in India and also the *pir* of Shaikh Ahmad Sirhindi. He passed away in 1012 AH/AD 1603 in Delhi. See *Zubdat al-Maqamat and Hazrat al-Quds*, Vol. I, *Islamic Heritage in India*, pp. 137-56.
31. Born in 1000 AH/AD 1591, he was the eldest son of Shaikh Ahmad Sirhindi and is reported to have acquired great spiritual power even his boyhood. See *Zubdat al-Maqamat* and *Hazrat al-Quds*, Vol. II.

32. A famous sufi saint of Burhanpur.
33. Also a sufi of Burhanpur.
34. He was a renowned mystic and exponent of the philosophy of *Wahdat al-Wajud.*
35. A famous scholar of the sciences of *Hadiths.*
36. He was a *Khalifa* of Shaikh Ahmad Sirhindi.
37. One of the renowned nobles of Akbar and Jahangir's Court.
38. See Eathe, *Catalogue of Persian Manuscripts in India Office Library*, p. 1570, No. 2698. Also, W. Ivanov, *Concise Descriptive Catalogue of the Persian Manuscripts in the Collection of the Asiatic Society of Bengal*, Calcutta, 1924, p. 338, No. 747.
39. Eathe, op. cit. Ivanov, op. cit.
40. See Eathe, op. cit.
41. Ivanov, op. cit.
42. See *Catalogue of the Arabic and Persian Manuscripts in Government Oriental Library Madras*, Madras, 1961, pp. 30-1, S. No. 221, Book No. D-64.
43. See *List of the Arabic, Persian and Urdu Books, Kutub Khana-i Asafiya*, Vol. I, p. 736, Book No. 437.
44. Mohammad Aslam, *Tarikh-i Maqalat*, Delhi, 1970, p. 168.
45. See *Catalogue of the Royal Asiatic Society*, p. 420.
46. *Hazrat Mujaddid Alf Thani*, p. 793.
47. See *Hazarat al-Quds*, Vol. I (Urdu trans.), p. 383. *Nuzhat al-Khawatir*, Vol. 5, p. 406. Zawwar Husain, op. cit., p. 793.
48. Mohammad Aslam, op. cit., p. 163.

    It may be mentioned here that Shah Waliullah's father, Shah Abdur Rahim, at the age of nine or ten had met Khwaja Hashim during his (the latter's) stay in his locality in Delhi. See Shah Waliullah, *Anfas-al-Arifin* (Urdu trans.), Deoband, n.d., p. 37.

    Shah Abdur Rahim was born in 1054 AH/AD 1644. It might have been, therefore, the year AD 1653 or 1654 (1063 or 1064 AH) when he had met Hashim Kishmi at Delhi. Hence, this information also is not sufficient to establish the correct year of his (Hashim's) demise.

Khanqahs: Centres of Learning

Maksud Ahmad Khan

Initially, the word *khanqah* denoted a hospice, where Sufis devote their time and energy in meditation and spiritual training of their disciples. But with the passage of time it acquired a much larger role. Besides being a centre of spirituality, it also served as a mosque;[1] *maktab*, asylum for the needy, the poor, wayfarers, travelers; *lungarkhana* (free kitchen). In fact this multifaceted and multipurpose institution provided spiritual solace to visitors and also acted as a centre of higher learning[2] and character building. It produced a number of eminent scholars whose contributions in the fields of *Tafsir*, *Hadith*, *Fiqh*, mystic literature and evolution of local dialects like Urdu and Hindi is beyond doubt.

It was also the *khanqah* where Sufis coming from different background got an opportunity to live together, perform prayers in congregation, eat together, talk and converse with each other. This naturally gave great impetus to the emergence of a healthy atmosphere of brotherhood and fostered the spirit of sharing each other's problems which ultimately resulted in inculcating a sense of concern for human beings at large. It thus acted as a powerful incentive for the service to humanity

Thus, the *khanqah* played the role of not only a religious seminary and educational academy but also served as the centre that gave impetus to the growth of religious harmony and vernacular languages.

KNOWLEDGE: ESSENTIAL QUALIFICATION FOR THE SUFI

Knowledge (*Ilm*) was considered to be the basic qualification for a Sufi. Most of the prominent Sufis required their disciples to first acquire knowledge before joining discipleship under a Shaikh.

According to Shaikh Sharafuddin Yahya al Maneri,[3] 'The ascetic of the past used to busy themselves in the pursuit of knowledge more than any other work, because the task of worship depends upon it. If a man of God worships Him with the devotion of the angels of the seven heavens and of the earth, but lacks knowledge, he will gain absolutely nothing.'[4] It was because of this that the Sufis came to believe that 'No illiterate man can be a Sufi.'[5]

When Shaikh Fariduddin Ganj-i Shakkar (d. AD 1267) desired to abandon his studies in order to join Khwaja Qutbuddin Bakhtiyar Kaki (d. AD 1235), the Khwaja advised the Shaikh to complete his education. According to the Khwaja, 'An illiterate mystic falls a prey in the hands of devil.'[6]

Scholarship and knowledge of great Shaikhs cannot be doubted. For instance, Shaikh Badruddin Ishaq (d. AH 670/AD 1271)[7] during the course of his studies came across some difficulties which, in spite of his best efforts, he could not solve and even the scholars of Delhi failed to satisfy him in this matter. He, therefore, decided to share his problems with the scholars of Bukhara. On his way to Bukhara he met Shaikh Fariduddin Ganj-i Shakkar at Ajodhan. The Shaikh, who was very famous for scholarship and learning, had solved almost all his problems and difficulties on the path of knowledge. He immediately joined the Shaikh and became his disciple.[8]

This was not only the case of just one prominent Sufi but generally they were always keen to see that the person their *khalifa* appointed must fulfil the basic requirement of qualifications. For instance, Shaikh Nizamuddin Auliya while offering *khilafatnama* to Shaikh Sirajuddin Usman,[9] observed, 'Education is the first stage in this work (Sufism), he (Shaikh Akhi Siraj) has not received any education.'[10] Therefore, Shaikh Akhi studied under Maulana Fakhruddin Zarraid and completed the basic required knowledge like *Kafiya, Mufassal, Quduri, Majma al Bahrain.*[11]

That is why most of Shaikh Nizamuddin Auliya's disciple connected with *jamat-khana* were erudite scholars who had specialized and established their academic reputation in one or the other branch of Islamic learning: Maulana Shamsuddin Yahya[12] was known for his knowledge of *usul* (juristic principles), *fiqh* (law) and syntax. Maulana Wajihuddin Paili[13] was an expert in *fiqh*.[14] Maulana Husamuddin Multani had memorized by heart large parts of *Hidayah*. Besides, he was well-versed in *Qut u'l Qulub* and *Ihya u'l Ulum*. Jamal Qiwamuddin says that in his erudition he had no peer in Delhi;[15] Shaikh Nasir got instruction from him in external science.[16]

Shaikh Sharafuddin Yahya al Maneri received his rudimentary education under the guidance of his father at Maner. He memorized several textbooks including chapters from *Miftah ul Lughat* (a key to words). But it was under the supervision of Maulana Sharafuddin Abu

Tamana[17] at Sonargaon[18] that he completed his higher education.[19]

Shaikh Badiuddin Madar[20] completed his education under the supervision of Hazifa Shami. He memorized the *Taurah* and the Bible. Besides that he learnt *Simiya, Kimiya, Himiya, Rimiya* (chemistry, natural magic, etc.). Saiyid Ashraf Jahangir Simnani (d. AD 1406)[21] also admitted that during his time, except for Shah Madar, no other saint had achieved superiority in *Simiya* and *Rimiya.*

In this connection we may cite the example of Shaikh Sharafuddin Yahya al Maneri who laid much emphasis on acquiring knowledge and advocated in his letter to his disciple Qazi Shamsuddin of Chausa that, 'You should display great zeal, both night and day, in acquiring knowledge. You should set to one side all tranquility, resting, sleeping, and eating, for knowledge is to activity—that is to say, struggle with self and austerities—as purification is to prayer.'[22]

PRIMARY EDUCATION OF A CHILD IN THE *KHANQAH*

Although no formal education was imparted by the Sufis in their *khanqahs* most often the ceremony of *Tasmiya Khwani* or *Bismillah* was conducted here at the request of disciples or followers of the Shaikh. When a child completed the age of four years, four months and four days he was usually brought to *khanqah* to perform the ceremony of *Tasmiya Khwani*.

An incident has been recorded in *Fawa'id u'l Fu'ad* dated 11th Muharram, AH 716/AD 1316. Amir Hasan Sijzi took a little boy to the *khanqah* of Shaikh Nizamuddin Auliya and sought his blessings before sending him to begin the study of Koran. The Shaikh wrote down *Bismillah hir Rahman nir Rahim* and then characters like A, B, C, D of the Arabic alphabet.[23]

Madin u'o Ma'ani gives the picture of a ceremony in the initial stages of medieval Islamic education as a basic religious feature. Qazi Ashrafuddin brought his sister's son and requested the great saint to instruct him to learn and in his own blessed hands commence writing something on the writing board (*Takhtah-i-Talimat*). The saint wrote the first four letters of the alphabet and gave instructions to the boy. Then he made the boy pronounce *Bismillah* which the latter did, and afterwards he was asked to repeat the four letters which the saint's uttered. Then the saint gave him his blessings. Thereupon the saint himself fed the boy with a bit of cake (*kak*) and sweetmeats while the rest of the same was distributed among others. *Ta'lim-i Koran* was the next stage. As regards the subjects taught at the earliest or the elementary stage, the saint said that he could recall faintly the contents of some of the books he had been made to learn in his youth, e.g. works on *Masadir* (sources or grammar) and *Miftah u'l Lughat* (key to vocabulary or a lexicon) of which the entire first volume he had to memorize and every now and then he was made to repeat what he had committed to memory.[24]

Ganj-i-Rashidi also mentions that the *Maktab* ceremony commenced in the *khanqah* of Rashidiya in Jaunpur with *Bismillah* (in the name of God) which was written and had to be repeated. It was followed by some of the letters of the Arabic alphabets written by the teacher, and these had to be recited by the child, usually 5 or 6 years of age. Sweets were distributed and prayers were offered for the well-being of the novice. Even when Diwan Rashid was lying bedridden and was on the verge of death, when he was told that one Rashid Khan had brought his daughter for the initiatory instruction in *Bismillah* and *Harf-i-Tahajji* (alphabet), he did not put forward any legitimate excuse. The letters of the alphabets were written on a piece of paper or on a wooden tablet called *Takhti*. Arshad himself initiated the *Maktab* of his son and successor, Ghulam Rashid, the compiler of *Ganj-i Rashidi*, and then entrusted him to Muhammad Anwar Bengali and others to help him in the recital and *Takrar* (repetition) of different pieces of the Koran.[25]

VISITORS TO *KHANQAH*

Khanqah became a centre of cultural amalgamation when the personality of the Shaikh attracted people belonging to different groups, faiths, religions, caste, creed, social and economic status without any discrimination. These visitors were not only from different parts of India but also from abroad. Here they all got a golden opportunity to discuss their private as well as religious and educational problems with the Shaikh. Thus, the *khanqah* played a role similar to modern cultural exchange programmes.

Shaikh Abdur Rashid rightly observes that

> We find from other sources that the Shaikh's (Nizamuddin Auliya), *jamaat khana* was constantly full of visitors who were taken to his room on the roof singly or in groups. The visiting hours were from sunrise to midday and again in the afternoon and evening. The Shaikh's conversations as recorded in the *Fawa'id u'l Fu'ad* range over all kinds of topics. But it was not considered proper to refer to the ruling king in the *khanqah* of a Chishti mystic, and the *Fawa'id*

u'l Fu'ad consequently makes no reference to the Emperor Alauddin Khilji and his officers. The duty of a Shaikh was to guide, to explain mystic principles, to lay down postulates for life. Shaikh Nizamuddin Auliya slept little at night, and his eyes were often red from sleeplessness. But 'he was an inspiring conversationalist and he had to discover the unspoken thoughts of men.[26]

Similarly, the *khanqah* of Shaikh Sharafuddin Yahya al Maneri was visited by people from India and abroad.[27] Shamuddin came from Khwarizm, who is reported to have stayed in the *khanqah* for sometime and started learning *Adab u'l Muridin* under the supervision of Shaikh Sharafuddin Yahya al Maneri;[28] Khwaja Mammun[29] and Hafiz Jalaluddin from Multan,[30] a dervish from Afghanistan, who attended the assembly of the Shaikh and put questions on mystic ideology like Sufi property and blood;[31] a traveller from Bukhara was impressed with the personality of the Shaikh to such an extent that he became a disciple of the Shaikh and received a cap.[32]

BOOKS TAUGHT AND PRESCRIBED IN THE *KHANQAH*

Above all it was a religious seminary and educational academy where religious sciences were studied, taught and discussed. Thus, it played a vital role in the diffusion of knowledge of the Holy Koran, its commentary, *Hadith*, books on Sufism, etc. Here an attempt has been made to evaluate the kind and standard of books generally prescribed and taught in the *khanqahs*. I have carefully analysed three popular and significant *Malfuzat* of prominent Sufis like *Surur us Sudur wa Nur al Budur*[33] of Shaikh Hamiduddin Sufi Sawali Nagauri (d. AH 673/AD 1274), better known as Sultan ut Tarikin, which was compiled by one of his descendants; *Fawa'id ul Fu'ad*[34] of Shaikh Nizamuddin Auliya and *Madin ul Ma' ani*[35] of Shaikh Sharafuddin Yahya al Maneri.

The *khanqah* at Nagaur appears to have become an important centre of learning on account of Shaikh Hamiduddin Sufi Sawali Nagauri's emphasis on acquiring proper knowledge. The books consulted in the *khanqah* were always of a high standard and written by very learned scholars. Some of the books consulted in the *khanqah* recorded in *Surur us Sudur* are as follows: *Tafsir-i-Madarik; Tafsir-i-Haqaiq; Tafsir-i-Maqatil; Tafsir-i-Zahidi; Tafsir-i-Imam Nasiri; Nahj-u'l-Balaghah; Kitab-i-Fa'iq; Maqamat-i-Shaikh Abu Sa'id Abul Khair; Kimiya-i-Sa'adat; Misbah ul Duja; Mashariq ul Anwar; Tafsir-i-Kashshaf; Qut u'l Qulub; Fusus ul Hikam; Quduri; Sair ul Mulik; Kitab Akhbar ul Samar; Ta'aruf Azhab-i-Ahl-i-Tasawwuf*

The books taught and consulted in the *jamaat-khana* of Shaikh Nizamuddin Auliya were as follows: *Ihya ul Ulum and Kimiya-i-Sa'adat* of Imam Ghazzali; *Eijaz ul Bayan; Qut ul Qulub; Kashf u'l Mahjub* of Shaikh Ali Hujweri; *Lawaih* and *Lawamah* of Qazi Hamiduddin Nagauri; *Mashariq u'l Anwar; Maktubat-i-Ain ul Quzat Hamadani; Bazdawi; Majma ul Bahrain; Ruh ul Arwah; Tafsir-i-Imam Nasir; Umda; Awarif ul Ma'arif; Hidayah*, etc.

Shaikh Nizamuddin Auliya's most favourite books were *Kashshaf* and *Tafsir-i-Imam Nasiri*. He had memorized the Holy Koran; *Mashariq ul Anwar* and *Maqamat-i-Hariri*

The books consulted in the *khanqah* of Shaikh Sharafuddin Yahya al-Maneri were also of a high standard. The following is the list of some books: *Adab ul Muridin* of Shaikh Najibuddin Abul Qahir Suhrawardi; *Awarif ul Maarif* of Shaikh Shihabuddin Suhrawardi; *Aqa'id-i-Nasafi; Qut u'l Qulub; Hidayah; Kashshaf; Bazdawi; Quduri; Tafsir-i-Imam Zahidi; Burhan; Tahmidad; Maktubat-i-Ain u'l Quzat; Zubdah of Ain u'l Quyzat; Mashariq u'l Anwar* of Saghani; *Tamhidat-i-Abu Shah us Salumi; Rauzat u'l Ulama; Sharah-i-Ta'arruf of Kalabazi; Siraj u'l Arifin; Targhin u's Salwat*

Kimiya-i-Sa'adat of Imam Ghazzali was popularized by Shaikh Hamiduddin Sufi Nagauri. In his *Malfuzat* the Shaikh used to advise his disciples: 'Baba! always keep this book before you.' Every day passages from this book were read in the *khanqah* of Nagaur.[36]

Awarif ul Ma'arif of Shaikh Shihabuddin Suhrawardi became a guide book for all those who founded or organized any *silsilah*. Shaikh Abdur Rashid says that the *Awarif ul Ma'arif* of Shaikh Shihabuddin Suhrawardi became the acknowledged textbook of all India mystics during he Sultanate period. Shaikh Fariduddin Ganj-i Shakkar of Ajodhan used to teach it to his disciples[37] and the *Siyar ul Auliya* gives the text of the certificate Shaikh Nizamuddin obtained from him. This certificate (among other things) authorizes Shaikh Nizamuddin Auliya to teach those fact of the *Awarif* which he had studied with his master. Generally speaking, medieval Muslim thought in India repeats and confirms the principles of *Awarif*.[38]

Shaikh Sharafuddin Yahya al Maneri used to teach his disciples *Awarif ul Ma'rif*. For instance, Shaikh Husain Muiz Balkhi (d. AH 844/AD 1440),[39] popularly known as Naush Tauhid Balkhi started learning *Awarif ul Ma'rif* under the supervision of Shaikh Sharafuddin Maneri. But after the death of the Shaikh he completed the book under the guidance of Shah Madar at Jaunpur.[40]

SUFIS ADOPTED PROFESSION OF TEACHINGS

From the above mentioned discussions, it seems that the Sufis and their disciples in the *khanqah* never limited and confined themselves to the study of mere Sufi literature. Their enthusiasm and love for acquiring more knowledge made them liberal and broad-minded to study *Tafsir* (Exegesis of Koran), *Hadith* (Traditions of the Prophet), *Sarf* (Arabic Declension and Conjugation), *Nahw* (Grammar and Syntax), *Fiqh* (Jurisprudence), *Usul-i-Fiqh* (Principles of Jurisprudence), *Kalam* (Dialect), *Mantiq* (Logic). Besides, the Sufis and their disciples promoted regional language by using local dialects in their day to day conversation.

After acquiring *Ilm-i-Zahir* most of Sufis voluntarily preferred the profession of teaching, rendered free education without hankering after any lucrative post, status and remuneration from State and thus they made their *khanqah* a centre of learning.

Most of the learned disciples of Shaikh Nizamuddin Auliya used to deliver lectures. For instance, Maulana Shamsuddin Yahya on *Kashshaf*;[41] Maulana Fakhruddin Zarradi on *Hidaya*;[42] Maulana Alauddin Nili was also a powerful speaker on *Kashshaf*.[43] Ibn Battuta saw a man so overpowered by emotions in his lecture that the latter died.[44] Maulana Fasihuddin[45] used to teach sons of Malik Baikaras Barbak of Sultan Ghayasuddin.[46]

Maulana Jalaluddin Manikpuri, *khalifa* of Shaikh Nizamuddin Auliya and disciple of Shaikh Muhammad, after *Chasht* (noon prayer) used to teach the students different topics of Theology[47] Shaikh Khizr Para doz, a contemporary of Shaikh Nizamuddin Auliya, established a *khanqah* in Bihar and devoted his times in imparting knowledge to the sons and the slaves of Khwaja Khizr.[48] Shaikh Jalaluddin Bukhari went to Multan for acquiring knowledge in the *khanqah* of Shaikh Ruknuddin Abul Fath.[49] Shaikh Najamuddin took lessons from Saiyid Jalaluddin Makhdum-i-Jahaniyan.[50] Shaikh Alauddin Husain Jeweri, *khalifa* of Saiyid Qiwamuddin Muhammad Hasan Ghaznawi al-Husaini (d. AH 710/AD 1310) was the first Junaidiya saint to come to Delhi. He later migrated to Daulatabad in AH 729/AD 1329 and died in AH 734/AD 1333. During this short span of time he delivered lectures on *Hidaya*, *Bazdawi*, *Miftah* and *Kashshaf* and gained much name and fame in the Deccan.[51]

Shaikh Munawwar, son of Abdul Majid and grandson of Abdur Shakur spent 44 years in the profession of teaching.[52]

Shaikh Jalal Muhammad Qadiri (d. AH 928/AD 1521), disciple of Shaikh Bahauddin Ansari of Mandu, settled in Burhanpur where he constructed a *khanqah* and devoted his time and energy in imparting teachings to people.[53]

According to Mulla Abdul Qadir Badauni, 'When, I, in the year 960/ 1553, being then in my twelfth year, arrived in company with my father at Sambhal, and there entered the service of Miyàn Hatim[54], I learnt by heart, in his hospice (*khanqah*), the *Qasida-i Burda*.' This shows that Badauni remained for sometime in the *khanqah* of Miyan Hatim to learn *Qasida-i Burda* and *Kanz-i-Fiqh-i-Hanafi*.

Shaikh Danishmund,[55] disciple of Shah Fakhruddin son of Shaikh Hamid Chishti, was a native of Lucknow but had settled at Mandu. For about 50 years he devoted his time and energy in imparting all kinds of knowledge to his students.

Shaikh Wajihuddin Ahmad Alawi, son of Shaikh Nasrullah Alawi and disciple of Shaikh Muhammad Ghaus Gwaliori devoted his time and energy in imparting knowledge for 60 years in Ahmadabad.[56]

Qazi Abdul Muqtadir (d. AH 791/AD 1388), one of the *khalifas* of Shaikh Nasiruddin Mahmud Chiragh-i-Delhi, spent his most precious time in offering lessons to his students.[57]

Qazi Mahmud Morpi (a village in Gujarat), disciple of Shaikh Lashakr Muhammad Arif, was a learned scholar under whom Hakim Usman Bobkani and Maulana Musa Bobkani, teachers of Adilpur (Burhanpur), had completed their study in Arabic and *Nahw*.[58]

Shaikh Hasan Muhammad[59] (d. AH 982/AD 1574), disciple of Shaikh Jamal Chishti whose daily routine was to devote his time after dawn (*Fair*) prayer to mid-day (*Zuhr*) in delivering lectures to students in his *khanqah*.

Shaikh Muhammad bin Tahir of Pattan (Gujarat) (d. AH 986/ AD 1578), a Bohra Sufi and *Mohaddis* wrote a number of books and taught *Hadith*.[60]

Saiyid Raji Muhammad Aini (d. AH 982/AD 1574)[61], disciple of Shaikh Muhammad Mutani, settled at Ujjain and constructed a *khanqah* and devoted 50 years to teaching and delivering lectures to his students.[62]

Shaikh Nizamuddin of Amethi, disciple of Shaikh Ma'aruf, instructed his disciples to read *Ihya u'l Ulum of Imam Ghazzali; Adab u'l Muridin* of Shaikh Abu Najib Qahir Suhrawardi; *Awarif ul ma'arif* of Shaikh Shihabuddin Suhrawardi and *Risala-i-Makkiya* of Imam Qutbuddin.[63]

Shaikh Hamza (d. AH 957/AD 1550),[64] settled down in Dharsau (a town in Haryana) and employed two teachers, one to teach Arabic and the other Persian to the children of noble origin whose parents were too poor to afford expenses in educating their children.

Shaikh Cha'in Laddha,[65] *khalifa* of Shaikh Abdul Aziz lectured on *Fusus u'l Hikam* and its commentary to students and Sufis.[66]

Qazi Ibrahim, son and disciple of Qazi Muhammad, settled in a *qasba* Panwari, *sarkar* Kalpi (UP) and remained busy in teaching for years and benefitted a number of people.[67]

KHANQAH AS A CENTRE OF 'DISTANCE EDUCATION'

The methods of education adopted by the Sufis in their *khanqahs* indirectly paved the way for the concept of 'distance education' which became a source of modern open university.

Regarding Shaikh Sharafuddin Yahya al Maneri, Dr. Ata Karim Burke says, 'he (Shaikh Sharafud Maneri) has devised a plan to educate and train his disciples. And with this end in view, he adopted for himself two systems at the *khanqah*. The first system was of prime importance as it involved a direct method of teaching wholly based on his *Malfuzat*. The second system involved a correspondence course mainly based on his *Maktubat* with the set purpose of teaching.[68]

Shaikh Abdur Rashid writes, the *Maktubat* is a popular work prepared for the mystic intelligentsia. It is in the form of letter addressed to persons, whose names are given but who are otherwise of no moment. Every letter is devoted to a particular topic, such as belief in Divine unity, repentance, prayer, fasting, etc. The language is simple and the author makes himself as clear as the subject matter permits. Manuscripts of the *Maktubat* (of Shaikh Sharafuddin Yahya al Maneri) are easy to find in India, but they differ in the number of letters they contain. Apparently from motives of economy, people who got the book copied selected the letters on their favourite topics and ignored the others.[69]

The beginning of letter writing among the Sufis started with the Chishti saints. Abdur Rashid in this connection comments that, 'In any case, Shaikh Hamiduddin Sawali, a disciple of Shaikh Muinuddin Chishti Ajmeri wrote a series of letter[70] to Shaikh Bahauddin Zakariyya, the founder of the Suhrawardi *silsilah* in India. He objected to Shaikh Zakariyya's way of life and in particular to his amassing of wealth. Copies of all these letters probably compiled into a book were in the hands of Amir Khurd, the author of *Siyar ul Auliya*. But only the paragraphs quoted by him are requoted by Shaikh Abdul Haq in his *Akhbar ul Akhyar*.'[71]

For instance, *Maktubat-i-Sadi* (collection of one hundred letters) of Shaikh Sharafuddin Yahya al Maneri was the result of the request made by a disciple, Qazi Shamsuddin of Chausa (Bihar) and collected by Zain Badr Arabi.[72] *Maktubat-i-do Sadi* is a collection of 153 letters of Shaikh Sharafuddin Yahya al Maneri by Zain Badr Arabi.[73]

Maktubai-i-Bist-o-Hasht, a collection of 28 letters of Shaikh Sharafuddin Yahya al Maneri is addressed to Maulana Muzaffar Shams Balkhi.[74]

Maktubat-i-Muzaffar-i-Shams Balkhi is a collection of 181 letters of Maulana Muzaffar Shams Balkhi, collected by his nephew and successor Shaikh Husain Muiz Balkhi.[75]

Maktubat-i-Sharafuddin Bu Ali Qalandar.[76]

Maktubat-i Shaikh Husain is a collection of 154 letters of Shaikh Husain Muiz Balkhi addressed to various disciples and is compiled by his son, Shaikh Hasan Daim Jashan Balkhi.[77]

Maktubat-i Saiyid Ashraf Jahangir Simnani of Kachchaucha is a collection of letters of Saiyid Ashraf Jahangir Simnani, recorded by Haji Abdul Razzaq Simani Jilani.[78]

Maktubat-i-Nur ul Haqq (Saiyid Nur Qutb-i Alam Pandwi) is more popularly known as *Ain u'l Ashiqin*.[79]

All the letters addressed to his sons and *khalifas* were collected by his disciple Shaikh Shihabuddin Manikpuri and put together as *Maktubat Maulana Husamuddin Manikpuri*.[80]

Maktubat-i-Shah Madar banam Qazi Shihabuddin DaulatabadiI.[81] *Maktubat-i-Shah Pir Muhammad Chishti Saloni* was compiled by Abu Muhamma.[82] *Maktubat-i-Kalim* is a collection of 132 letters of Shah Kalim u'l lah Jahanabadi.[83]

Maktubat-i-Khwaja Baqi Billah was recently published with one collection containing 8 letters and the other 44; some of the letters are to be found in *Zubdat u'l Maqamat*.[84]

Maktubat-i-Imam Rabbani Hazrat Mujaddid Alf-i-Sani is in three volumes: the first volume is a collection of 313 letters and was compiled by Maulana Yar Muhammad Jadid al Badakhshi Taliqani; the second volume contains 99 letters compiled by Shaikh Abdul Hai, written in AH 1028/AD 1618; and the third volume contains a collection of 124 letters compiled by Khwaja Muhammad Hashim Kishmi written in AH 1031/AD 1621-2.[85]

Maktubat of Shaikh Abdul Haqq Muthaddis Dehlawi entitled *Kitab at Makatib Wa'r Rasail* is a collection of 68 letters written to Mughal nobles.[86] It is interesting to note that only 18 letters from *Marktubat Shah Muhibullah* are available.[87]

According to Shaikh Abdur Rashid, while the *Maktubat* of the Shaikh of Munir (Shaikh Sharafuddin Yahya at Maneri) is concerned with academic matters, the letters of *Mujaddid Alf Sani* cover a vast field ranging from technology and metaphysics to politics and missionary activities. These letters are a mirror of the intellectual and spiritual ferment which swept over the spiritually saturated Indian Muslim society when it would either turn into the path of orthodoxy or be swallowed up in the religious revivalist movement known as the Bhakti movement which was the answer of the Hindu society to the silent spread of Islam in India.[88]

CONTRIBUTION OF SUFIS ON PRODUCING LITERATURES

The Sufis being aware of the significance of education devoted their precious time and energy, besides teaching and instructions, in producing voluminous works on various fields of learning.

TAFSIR (COMMENTARY) ON HOLY KORAN

Bahr-i-Mawwaj written by Qazi Shihabuddin Daultabadi (d. AH 849/ AD 1445).[89]

Tafsir-i-Nur un Nabi (*Nur-i-Ilahi, AA, 182*) by Shaikh Husain Nagauri[90] in 30 volumes; he also wrote a commentary on the third part of the *Miftah*.[91]

Tafsir-i-Rahman by Shaikh Ali Purwa.[92]

Tafsir-i-Muhammad by Shaikh Hasan Muhammad Chishti (d. AH 982/ AD 1575) a saint of Gujarat who also wrote notes on the Koranic commentary *Tafsir-i-*Bazadwi.[93]

Tafsir by Shaikh Haji Abdul Wahhab Bukhari (d. AH 933/AD 1526).[94]

Madarik: Maulana Ilahdad of Jaunpur wrote marginal notes on *Tafsir of* Madarik.[95]

Mir Saiyid Abdul Awwal[96] (d. AH 908/AD 1560) wrote lengthy marginal notes on the famous work *Mutawwal Ma'ani* of Taftazani.[97]

Saiyid Yusuf (d. AH 990/AD 1582) wrote commentary on *Manar* under the title *Taujiya-i-Afkar*.[98]

COMMENTARIES ON *HADITH*

Faiz ul Bari an exhaustive commentary on Bukhari written by Mir Saiyid Abdul Awwal.[99]

Majma' Bihar of Anwar fi ghara'ib al tanzil wa Lata'if al Akhbar, copious dictionary of the Koran and the traditions, written by Shaikh Muhammad Tahir bin Ali of Patan (Gujarat).[100]

Shaikh Ali Muttaqi (d. AH 975/AD 1568),[101] a prolific writer throughout his lifetime, is reported to have produced more than 100 books, a large number of them being short treatises. His magnum opus is *Encyclopaedia of Hadis* the *Kanz al Ummal fi Sunam al aqwal wa'l-af'al*; it was an attempt to rearrange in alphabetical order the *ahadis* compiled by Jalaluddin Abul Fazl Abdur Rahman b. Abu Bakr b. Muhammad as Suyuti's *Jami al Masanid* or *Jami* al *Kabir* or *Jama al Jawami.*[102] *Mashariq ul Anwar* the Commentary by Shaikh Shamsuddin Yahya, disciple of Shaikh Nizamuddin Auliya.[103]

BUZDAWI: JURISPRUDENCE

Qazi Shihabuddin Daulatabadi wrote notes on *Usul-i-Buzdawi*;[104] he also wrote a treatise on jurisprudence entitled *Risala-i-Ibrahim Shahi* and dedicated it to Sultan Ibrahim Shah Sharaqi;[105] Abu Bakr Qaraishi of Delhi wrote a commentary on *Wasya-i-Imam Muhammad* and *Usul-i Buzdawi.*[106] Maulana Ilahdad of Jaunpur,[107] Shaikh Saduddin Khairabadi (d. AH 882/AD 1584) wrote a commentary on it.[108]

HIDAYA[109]

Qazi Shihabuddin Daultabadi wrote marginal notes on *Hidaya.*[110] Maulana Abdullah alias Maulana Ilahad disciple of Raji Hamid Shah Manikpuri wrote marginal notes on *Hidaya* (Jurisprudence).[111]

TEXTBOOKS

Textbooks on *Sarf Usmani* written by Maulana Fakhruddin Zarradi.[112] Shaikh Abdul Quddus Gangohi composed *Bahr ul Ashar on Sarf* in the form of questions and answers which was appreciated by the teachers from Delhi.[113]

Saiyid Yusuf wrote commentary on *Lub ul Lubab fi IIm al Arab*, a famous book of Qazi Nasiruddin Baizawi. This book became famous as *Yusufi*. According to Shaikh Abdul Haq Muhaddis Dehlawi, *Lub ul Lubab* was a brief and very useful book in Delhi.[114]

Kafiyah[115] in commentary (*Sharah*) by Shaikh Saduddin Khairabadi.[116] *Hawashi* (Notes) is by Qazi Shiahabuddin Daulatabadi.[117] According to Ghulam Sarwar, 'this book is unique in its style and became famous in his lifetime'.[118]

Shaikh Wajihuddin Ahmadabadi also wrote notes on it.[119]

Nahw (Grammar, Syntax): Qazi Shihabuddin Daulatabadi wrote books on *Nahw* known as *Kitab-i* Irshad.[120] Shaikh Wajihuddin Alawi of Gujarat (d. AH 998/AD 1589) wrote commentaries or notes on almost all the textbooks including the courses at that time.[121] Saiyid Abdul Awwal had written many textbooks.[122]

WORKS ON SUFISM

The Indian Sufis not only prescribed and utilized some of the important early Sufi literature produced outside India but also to added them appropriate commentaries and marginal notes so that it could be easily understood and digested by the masses. Some of the works are:

Adab ul Muridin[123]

Sharah (commentary) was written by Shaikh Sharafuddin Yahya al Maneri under the title of *Sharah Adab u'l* Muridin;[124] another commentary on it was written by Saiyid Muhammad Gesu Daraz.[125]

Awarif ul Maarif[126]

Sharah Umda by Shaikh Abdul Quddus Ganegohi (d. AH 970/AD 1562).[127]

Notes and commentary were by Shaikh Ali Piru.[128]

Fusus ul Hikam by Imam Ghazzali

Hawashi (notes) by Maulana Lari (d. AH 937/AD 1530),[129] *Sharah* (commentary) by Shaikh Abdul Quddus Gangohi (d. AH 950/AD 1543);[130] and *Sharah o Hashiya* commentary and notes by Shaikh Ali Piru.[131]

Futuhat-i Makkiya

Notes and commentary by Shaikh Ali Piru.[132] Saiyid Abdul Awwal Daulatabadi could solve any problem from the beginning to the end of the book, added *Hashiya and Ta'aliqat* in it so that anyone could understand it easily.[133]

Hazrat Khams,[134] commentary by Shaikh Hasan Daim Jashan Balkhi (d. AD 1451)

Hishami, commentary (*Sharah*) by Shaikh Saduddin Khairabadi.[135]

Ihya ul Ulum of Imam Ghazzali, commentary by Shaikh Sadullah.[136]

Lamat,[137] marginal notes *Hawashi* by Maulana Samauddin Kamboh (d. AH 907/AD 1501).[138]

Lawa'ih of Maulana Abdur Rahman Jami, lengthy commentary (*tafsili Sharah*) under the title *Asbat u'l Ahadiya* written by Shaikh Amanullah Panipati (d. AH 957/AD 1550).[139]

Maktubat-i-Shaikh Abdul Qadir Jilani, commentary and notes written by Shah Abdur Razzaq of Jhunjhunu (Rajasthan) (d. AH 940/AD 1542), disciple of Shah Muhammad Hasan Qadiri.[140]

Minhaj ul Abidin (a work on Sufism) of Imam Ghazzali, translated into Persian by Shaikh Yusuf Buddha Iraji (d. AH 834/AD 1430) disciple of Khwaja Ikhtiyaruddin Umar.[141]

Mulahmat by Shaikh Jamaluddin Ahmad Hansawi (d. AH 700/AD 1300), *khalifa* of Shaikh Fariduddin Ganj-i Shakkar, a great scholar and author of several brochures. One of the brochures is in Arabic entitled *Mulahmat* which contains discussions on moral and religious teachings.[142]

Nuzhat ul Arwah commentary by Shaikh Ali Sher Bengali (d. AH 970/AD 1562).[143] *Risala Makkiyah* Shaikh Saduddin Khairabadi wrote notes on it;[144] *Risal Miftah ul Faiz* was written by Shaikh Hasan Tahir Chishti.[145]

Besides a number work on Sufi ideology, principle and thought were produced by them. *Kashf ul Mahjub* by Shaikh Ali Hujweri, one of the oldest systematical works on the doctrines of Sufis (in Persian) deals with valuable biographical notices of early Sufis.[146]

Silk ul Suluk by Shaikh Ziyauddin Nakhshabi;[147] *Anwar ul Uyun* by Shaikh Abdul Quddus Gangohi (d. AH 945/AD 1537);[148] *Risala-i-Shattaria* by Shaikh Bahauddin Shattari, explains the principles of the Shattari order.[149]

MALFUZ LITERAUTRE

According to Riazul Islam, 'The *malfuzat* or the table-talks were, so to say, an informal system of education among the mystic orders. The Shaikh would sit surrounded by the disciples. Any subject would crop up and the Shaikh would give a discourse on it; some of the keener and more enthusiastic disciple would take down portions of the discourse. Sometimes whole passages were taken down verbatim. Some of the disciples took care to show the notes to the Shaikh himself for approval. Some of the collections of *Malfuzat*, i.e. *Khair a'l Majalis* (of Shaikh Nasiruddin Chiragh-i Delhi) are arranged chronologically, while others, e.g. *Ma'din al Ma'ani* (of Shaikh Sharafuddin Yahya al Maneri) are arranged topic-wise.'[150]

According to K.A. Nizami, 'The *Malfuz* literature of medieval India which contains a record of the utterances of the Sufi saints is a mine of information for contemporary history—life and problems of the common man, the religious thought at higher and lower levels etc.'[151]

It was through the *Malfuz* literature that the Sufis used to express their ideologies, teach their disciples as well as common people. The passages from the compilers of *Malfuzat* given below clearly show the authenticity and significance of the Sufi literature produced during the medieval period.

Zain Badr Arabi, the compiler of *Malfuzat* of Shaikh Sharafuddin Yahya al Maneri, has given the technique of compilation in the following words:

> This humble person Zain Badr Arabi had the good fortune of attending the blessed sittings (*majalis*). At every sitting seekers (after knowledge) and disciples were present and they would, each of them according to his own state and work, submit queries on *Tariqat* or *Sharia*. The Shaikh would enlighten the questioners by a complete reply couched in charming language and adorned with fine suggestions. I collected these (talks) as far as I could recollect them. I have not left out a single word; but in case I forgot the exact words and remembered only the sense I put it into appropriate words. But I have not made the slightest change in the sense (of the *Shaikh's* talk), so much so that if I forgot the purport of some talk, I left a page blank (for it) and later submitted the question to the *Shaikh* and incorporated (his reply) in the book. I presented this collection to the *Shaikh* (for correction). He read it word by word and corrected a few mistakes of writing. . . . I have named this collection *Ma'adin u'l Ma'ani* (mines of meaning) and divided it into 63 chapters.[152]

The compiler of *Jami ul Ulum, Malfuzat* of Saiyid Jalaluddin Makhdum-i Jahaniyan Jahangast writes that he was intending to visit the saint *Makhdum-i-Jahaniyan*) at Uchch, but the latter himself came to Delhi.

> Beginning from the 8th *Robiu'l Akhir* up to the (17th *Muharram*), AH 782/AD 1380, I was in the blessed company of my precepter, I had observed that some disciples compiled the talks of their preceptors.... I was always waiting for the words to fall from the blessed lips to record them.... I have given dates and time ... e.g., *Tahajjud* (midnight) *ba'd Isharq* (morning) *ba'd chasht* (forenoon), *ba'd zuhur* (afternoon). I spared no pains. I deprived myself of the joys of food and drink. I undertook great trouble in compiling the work. The *Makhdum* came to know that I was recording his talks. Whenever ... (he was discussing) a difficult problem, he would turn to me and say 'My son, write down', Quite frequently

I took down (the talks) in the presence of the *Makhdum*, or I would come back to my room and write it out there.... If anybody finds any difficulty in comprehending anything in these talks (*Malfuz*), he may come to my house near the Mosque of old Delhi. Any one who wants a copy of this work (from somebody who happens to possess a copy) should not be refused one.

The last two sentences bring out the educational value of the system of compiling the *Malfuzat*. The compiler studied a number of books under *Makhdum-i-Jahanian* and this gave him further opportunity of recording his observations and remarks. The compiler gives a list of 150 branches of knowledge which have been touched upon in the compilation.[153]

The following is the brief list of some popular *Malfuzat* literatures available with different libraries in India:

Surur us Sudur, discourses of Shaikh Hamiduddin Sufi Nagauri, compiled by Shaikh Farid.[154]

Afzal ul Fawaid, discourses of Shaikh Nizamuddin Auliya, compiled by Amir Khusru.[155]

Ahsan ul Aqwal, discourses of Shaikh Burhanuddin Gharib, compiled by Hammad b. Imad Kashani.[156]

Ma'din ul Ma'ani, discourses of Shaikh Sharafuddin Yahya al Maneri, compiled by Zain Badr Arabi.[157]

Bahr ul Ma'ani or *Fawaid ul Ghaib*, discourses of Shaikh Sharafuddin Yahya al Maneri, compiled by Zain Badr Arabi.[158]

Fawaid ul Muridin, discourses of Shaikh Sharafuddin Yahya al Maneri, compiled by Muhammad Atiq u'llah.[159]

Fawa'id ul Fu'ad, discourses of Shaikh Nizamuddin Auliya, compiled by Amir Hasan Sijzi.[160]

Fawaid Rukni, discourses of Shaikh Sharafuddin Yahya al Maneri, addressed to Haji Rukhuddin.[161]

Khwan-i-Pur Nimat, discourses of Shaikh Sharafuddin Yahya al Maneri, compiled by Zain Badr Arabi.[162]

Rahat ul Qulub, discourses of Shaikh Sharafuddin Yahya al Maneri, compiled by Zain Badr Arabi.[163]

Maghz ul Maani, discourses of Shaikh Sharafuddin Yahya al Maneri, compiled by Shaikh Shihabuddin Ahmad Siddiqui.[164]

Malfuz us Safar, discourses of Shaikh Sharafuddin Yahya al Maneri, compiled by Zain Badr Arabi.[165]

Monis ul Muridin, discourses of Shaikh Sharafuddin Yahya al Maneri, compiled by Salah Mukhils Daud Khani.[166]

Mukh ul Maani, discourses of Shaikh Sharafuddin Yahya al Maneri, compiled by Saiyid Shihabuddin Imad Hatif.[167]

Jami ul Ulum, discourses of Saiyid Jalaluddin Bukhari Makhdum-i-Jahaniyan.[168] *Tahqiqat ul Maani* or *Malfuz Mubarak*, discourses of Maulana Shah Amun, compiled by Shaikh Arzani.[169]

Khair ul Majalis, discourses of Shaikh Nasiruddin Chiragh-i-Delhi, compiled by Hamid Qalandar.[170]

Jawami ul Kalim, discourses of Saiyid Muhammad Gesu Daraz, compiled by Saiyid Muhammad Akbar Husaini.[171]

Lataif-i-Ashraf, discourses of Saiyid Ashraf Jahangir Simmani, compiled by Haji Gharib Yamani.[172]

Rafiq ul Arfin, discourses of Shaikh Husamuddin Manikpuri (d. AD 1452), compiled by Pir Imamuddin,[173]

Lata'if-i-Quddusi, discourses of Shaikh Abdul Quddus Gangohi, compiled by his son Shaikh Ruknuddin.[174]

Tuhfat ul Majalis, discourses of Shaikh Ahmad Maghribi, compiled by Mahmud b. Sa'd Iriji.[175]

Ganj-i-La-Yakhfa, discourses of Shaikh Husain Muiz Naush Tauhid Balkhi, compiled by Maulana Niamatullah.[176]

Fawaid-i-Rukniya, discourses of Shaikh Ruknuddin Jandahi, compiled by Imamuddin Shattari.[177]

Malfuzat Akhi Jamshed Rajgiri, discourses of Shaikh Akhi Jamshed Rajgiri.[178]

Malfuzat-i-Shah Mina, compiled by Shaikh Saduddin Khairabadi.[179]

Malfuzat Qazi Abdul Muqtadir (d. AH 791/AD 1388), compiled by his grandson and disciple Shaikh Abul Fath Jaunpuri.[180]

Monis ul Qulub, discourses of Shaikh Ahmad Langar Darya Balkhi, compiled by Qazi Khan b. Khatib Bihari.[181]

Ganj-i-Arshadi, discourses of Badr ul Haqq Muhammad Arshad b. Muhammad Rashid Usmani Jaunpuri, compiled by Ghulam Arshad Jaunpuri, completed in AD 1721-2.[182]

TAZKIRAH

Siyar ul Auliya by Saiyid Muhammad bin Mubarak Alawi Kirmani popularly known as Amir Khurd. Biographical accounts of Chishti saints[183] *Siyar ul Arfin* by Hamid b. Fazl u'llah, better known as Darwesh Jamali. A biographical account of Chishti and Suharawardi saints[184] *Akhbar ul Akhyar* by Shaikh Abdul Haqq Muhaddis Dehlawi (d. AD 1642).[185] *Gulzar-i-Abrar* by Muhammad Ghausi Shattari, a biographical dictionary of about 600 Sufis who flourished in Gujarat and the Deccan.[186] *Akhbar ul Asfiya* by Shaikh Abdus Samad b. Afzal

Muhammad.[187] *Kalimat us Sadiquin* by Muhammad Sadiq Kashmiri Hamadani. Biographical accounts of 125 Sufis buried in Delhi,[188] *Manqib ul Asfiya* by Shaikh Shoaib, a biographical account of Firdausi Sufis, flourished in Bihar.[189] *Mirat ul Asrar* by Abdur Rahman Chishti.[190]

IMPACT OF PERSIAN LITERATURE

Most of the Persian Sufi poets and scholars influenced Indian Sufis, who used frequently the *diwan*, *masnawi* in their *khanqahs* and popularized them among the masses. Some of the Sufis produced the same style of *diwan* and *masnawi* on the Indian soil too. K.A. Nizami has rightly observed: 'we may turn to individual poets and writers of Iran who made an impact on Indian mystic thought. In fact it was the Persian poet who made the most abiding impact on the Sufi mind in India. Where logic or argument was ineffective, a single verse was enough to clinch the issue and satisfy the most inquisitive mind.' The poetical works of Shaikh Abu Sa'id Abul Khair (d. AH 440/AD 1049); Khwaja Abdullah Ansari (d. AH 481/AD 1088); Sana'i (d. AH 525/AD 1131); Ahmad Jam (d. AH 537/AD 1142); Nizami Ganjavi (d. AH 605/AD 1209); Fariuddin Attar (d. AD 1229); Iraqi (d. AH 688/AD 1289); Sadi (d. AH 691/AD 1292); Shaikh Auhaddin Kirmani (d. AH 697/AD 1298) Hafiz (AH 792/AD 1398) and Jami (AH 898/AD 1492) supplied a warm fund of emotions to Indian Sufis, and provided those moral and ethical ideas which became the *elan* of the mystic movement in India.[191]

For instance, Shaikh Ahmad Jam's verses were very popular among the early Chishti saints. It is reported that Khwaja Qutbuddin Bakhtiyar Kaki while listening to Sama' heard the verse recited by the *Qawwal:*

Kushtagane khanjar 'I' asleem ra
har zaman az ghaib jane digar ast.

To the victims of the dagger of submission,
There comes a new life at every moment from unseen source.

For four days and night, the Khwaja is reported to have repeated the verse and on fifth day he died.[192]

According to K.A. Nizami, 'The four most outstanding mystic poets whose influence on the Indian mind was the deepest were Sanai, Attar, Sa'di and Rumi. Under their influence mystic ideas got such currency that every mystic centre, *khanqah*, *jamat-khana*, *zawiya*, *ribat* and *daera* in India reverberated with Sufi songs.'[193] Moreover, he adds, 'In India his (Khwaja Sana'i) *diwan* was not merely read at the courts of the princes, it was a popular study in the *khanqahs* of Delhi, Gulbarga, Multan, Panduah and Maner.'[194]

Fakhruddin Iraqi's verses have for centuries been recited in Indian *khanqahs*. His *Lama'at* captured the imagination of intellectuals, his *diwan* fascinated the mystics.[195] Masud Bak[196] wrote *Tamhidat* like *Tamhidat* of Shaikh Hamadani which contains *Qasidah*, and *Ghazals*. Jamali (d. AH 942/AD 1535), a famous poet, wrote *Masnawi*, *Qasidah* and *Ghazals* but it is his *Qasidahs* which were more popular.[197] Abdul Hai, son of Shaikh Jamali, was a poet during the reign of Islam Shah Sur.[198] Shaikh Muhammad al-Husaini migrated from Gilan and settled at Uchch wrote *Qasida* under the penname of Qadiri mostly in praise of Shaikh Abdul Qadir Giliani and left a *Diwan* in Persian.[199] Saiyid Abu Said, son of Saiyid Raju (d. AH 966/AD 1558), who during the invasion of Rana Sanga on Chanderi left Chanderi and settled at Kalpi, is reported to have left a *Diwan*.[200] Saiyid Alauddin, a poet, wrote *Ghazals* and was also an accomplished musician.[201] Qazi Abdul Muqtadir wrote *Qasida* and *Ghazals* in Arabic. He is reported to have produced a reply to the famous *Qasida Lamiya* entitled *Qasida-i-Lamiya al Ajma*.[202] Shaikh Abul Fath Jaunpuri (d. AH 886/AD 1481), grandson and disciple of Qazi Abdul Muqtadir, completed his verses both in Persian and Arabic.[203] Shaikh Abu Said, son of Shaikh Jagan Khandauti, was reckoned amongst the famous poets of India.[204] Miran Bhik Shah Bahlul Barki Chishti Sabiri (d. AH 1170/AD 1756-7), disciple of Shah Bulaq Qadiri, settled in Jalandhar, wrote commentary on *Diwan* of Hafiz.[205] Saiyid Alimullah, son of Saiyid Atiqullah Chishti of Jalandhar, wrote commentaries on *Bustan-i-Sadi* and *Akhlaq-i-Nasiri* and was a famous poet of Jalandhar.[206]

KHANQAH AS CENTRES OF PROMOTION OF LOCAL DIALECTS

Khanqahs became a centre of cultural amalgamation when the personality of a particular Shaikh attracted people belonging to different groups, faiths, religions without discriminations of caste and creed, rich and the poor. Here they all got golden opportunities to discuss their private as well as religious and educational problems with the Shaikh. The Shaikh used to satisfy them according to their queries and needs.

Thus, to fill the gap of communication and to study and understand the problems of the masses, the Sufis carefully and minutely observed the utility of vernacular languages and local dialects. Therefore, wherever they settled, the first task before them was to learn the local dialects and use them in their day to day conversation. As Abdul Haqq has rightly observed,

> Both in north and south India and Gujarat, the Muslim saints and mystic took the lead in the study of the regional languages and dialects giving them a decided Muslim bias. If the soldiers were responsible for giving it a form as a spoken language, it was the mystic and holy men who helped in giving the new style of expression a literary garb. Some of these holy men and mystics settled and exerted their influence in tracts of north and south India long before the coming of the Muslim armies. They propagated their cult and imparted their instructions most often in Hindi and other zonal dialects, introducing Arabic and Persian words and technical terms of Sufism in the local languages and writing their memoirs in Hindi using Perso-Arabic scripts.[207]

Shaikh Hamiduddin Sufi Sawali Nagauri very often used Hindi words and *doha* in his *Malfuzat*.[208] Similarly, Shaikh Sharafuddin Yaḥya al Maneri in reply to Hafiz Jalaluddin Multani's Hindi proverb '*Bat Bhali par sankari*' (The path is good, but it is narrow) quickly said, '*Des bhala par door*' (The country or destination is good but it is far off).[209] Sometimes they composed Hindi *dohas* to popularize their ideologies and teachings. Shaikh Rizqullah Mushataqi (d. AH 989/AD 1581), whose pseudonym in Persian was Mushtaqi and in Hindi Rajan, is known for his famous Hindi verses *Paiman* and *Jot Niranjan*.[210] Shaikh Abdul Quddus Gangohi composed Hindi *dohra* which is reproduced at the end of *Lataif-i-Quddusi*.[211] It is called *Rushd Nama*,[212] and its Hindi translation is entitled *Alakhbani*.[213] Shaikh Nur Qutab Alam (d. AH 818/AD 1415) of Bengal wrote Hindi *dohrasi* which are found in his letters.[214] Shaikh Akhi Jamshed Rajgiri (d. AH 840/AD 1389) has frequently used Hindi *dohras* in his *Malfuzat*.[215] Shaikh Abdullah Abdal Dehlawi, whose Hindi *dohras* were very popular in Gujarat.[216] Shaikh Burhan of Kalpi (d. AH 970/AD 1562) composed Hindi *dohras* which became popular among the masses.[217] Shaikh Shah Ali Ahmadabadi (Gujarat) (d. AH 970/AD 1562) left *Diwan* in Hindi.[218] Malik Muhammad Jaisi (d. AH 900/AD 1493) is famous for *Padmavat*.[219] Qazi Mahmud was son of Shaikh Chialda and disciple of Shah Alam Bukhari. His original name was Shaikh Hamid, born in Ahmadabad but in AH 920/AD 1514, he migrated to Birpur and settled there. He was extremely fond of Hindi *dohra*. He also trained a group of *Qawwal* in *kamanchi* and they became famous for his Hindi *kamancha*.[220]

BENGALI LITERATURE

The Chishti saints established close contacts with the people through the open kitchen and extensive tours. Being themselves Bengalis they talked and preached in Bengali, the language of the people, and this naturally gave stimulus to the growth of the Bengali literature.[221]

DAKHANI URDU

They (Sufis) wrote in Dakhani Urdu besides the Persian language, simply because their aim was to foster the spirit of Islam among the people. It is surprising that some of the titles of their books are a happy combination of Dakhani Urdu and Persian. In an age in which the language and its grammar was important and was noted with great care, these titles must have hurt the orthodox *Ulama*, but the Sufis were not bothered about them. Their aim was to make the people understand their preachings. Therefore, they wrote books in the language of the people with titles which they could understand.[222]

KHANQAH AS A LIBRARY

According to Dharma Bhanu (Bharat), 'The Sultans of Dihli had no separate buildings for their libraries. The *maktabs* attached to the mosques the *khanqahs* and the *madrasas* were the place where books were stocked and preserved.... The only libraries of which we read during the Sultanate period are those of Shaikh Nizamuddin Auliya at Dihli and that of Ghazi Khan at Milwat, as also those of some rulers and provincial Sultans.'[223]

Shaikh Akhi Siraj established a *khanqah* at Panduah (West Bengal) that became the centre of widespread religious, cultural, humanitarian activities. Here flocked persons devoted to religion and knowledge. The few books of the library of Shaikh Nizamuddin Auliya which Shaikh Akhi Siraj carried with him to Lakhanuti[224] constituted the first library of Islamic mysticism in Bengal.[225]

Shaikh Ahmad Khattu (d. AH 849/AD 1445) of Sarkhez had a personal library in his *khanqah*. The incident recorded in his *malfuzat* says that on a certain occasion he took out *Masabih*, a work on *Hadith*, from his library and read before the audience a *Hadith*, relating to *Qasida* written in honour of the Prophet.[226]

According to N.N. Law, 'When Jahangir went to Gujarat, he took a library with him, which shows that love of books of which was so marked a trait in his father's character was inherited by him.'[227]

Emperor Jahangir in his memoirs writes that 'On, Tuesday, the 16th I again presented the Shaikhs of Gujarat, who were in attendance, with robes of honour and maintenance lands. To each of them I gave a book from my special library such as the *Tafsir-i-Husaini*, the *Tafsir-i-Kashshaf* and the *Rauzat u'l Ahbab*. I wrote on the back of books the day of my arrival in Gujarat and the date of presentation of the books.'[228]

Saiyid Muhammad Shah Alam (d. AH 880/AD 1475), a famous Sufi and scholar was very found of reading books. He had a big library in which besides ordinary books there were rare books also. When Sadr Jahan went to see him, the Shaikh showed one such rare copy of Imam Razi, of which the Maulana had no knowledge. The Shaikh was fond of reading books. Both his hands had marks which were caused by leaning during deep excessive study.[229] According to Shaikh Abdul Haqq Muhaddis Dehlawi, Mir Saiyid Abdul Awwal (d. AH 968/AD 1560) had a library which was rich with all kinds of books.[230]

KHANQAH AS CENTRE FOR SPIRITUAL TRAINING AND CHARACTER BUILDING

The *khanqah* was basically a centre where spiritual knowledge was imparted and disciples were trained in religious discipline. Thus, those disciples who had the urge could live in the *khanqah* for a specific period and practice austerities, self-mortifications and devotions prescribed by the Shaikh. According to Shaikh Langer Dariya, during the lifetime of his father Shaikh Hasan Daim Balkhi Bihari, nearly 30 to 40 Sufis used to remain busy constantly in spiritual exercise and self-mortification in the *khanqah*.[231]

Ziauddin Barani informs us about the *khanqah* of Shaikh Nizamuddin Auliya.

> [He] had opened wide the doors of his discipleship...admitted (all sorts of people into his discipline) nobles and plebians, rich and poor, learned and illiterate, citizens and villagers, soldiers and warriors, free-men and slaves and these people refrained from many improper things, because they considered themselves disciples of the Shaikh: if any of the disciples committed a sin, he confessed it (before the Shaikh) and vowed allegiance anew. The general public showed an inclination to religion and prayer, men and women, young and old, shop-keepers and servants, children and slaves, all came to say their prayers. Most of them who visited the Shaikh frequently, offered their *Chasht* and *Ishraq* prayers regularly. Many platforms, with thatched roofs over them, were constructed on the way from the city to Ghiyaspur. Wells were dug, water-vessels were kept, carpets were spread, and a servant and a *hafiz* was stationed at every platform so that the people going to the Shaikh may have no difficulty

in saying their supererogatory prayers. Due to regard for the Shaikh's discipleship all talk of sinful acts had disappeared from the people. There were no topics of conversation among most people except inquiries about the prayers of *Chasht, Awwabin* and *Tahajjud.* How many genuflections (*rak'ats*) they contained: what *Sura* of the Koran to recite in each *rak'at.* What invocations (*du'a*) are to follow each prayer? How many *rak'ats* does the Shaikh say every night and what part of the Koran in every *rak'at* and what *daruds* (blessings on the Prophet)? What was the custom of Shaikh Farid and Shaikh Bakhtiyar? Such were the questions which the new disciples asked from the old. They inquired about fasting and prayer and about reducing their diet. Many persons took to committing the Koran to memory. The new disciples of the Shaikh were entrusted to the old. And the older disciples had no other occupation but prayer and worship, aloofness from the world, the study of books on devotion and the lives of saints. And God forbid that they should ever talk or hear about the worldly affairs or turn towards . . . worldly men, for such thing they considered to be entirely sinful and wrong. Interest in supererogatory prayers alone had developed to such an extent that at the Sultan's court many nobles, clerks, guards, and royal slaves had become the Shaikh's disciples. They said their *Chasht* and *Ishraq* prayers and fasted on the 13th, 14th and 15th of every lunar month (*Ayyam-i-Biz*) as well as during the first ten days of *Zil Hijjah.* There was no quarter of the city in which a gathering of the pious was not held every month or after every twenty days with mystic songs that moved them to tears. Many disciples of the Shaikh finished the *tarawih* prayers in their houses or in the mosques. Those with greater perseverance passed the whole night standing in their prayers throughout the month of *Ramazan*, on Fridays and during the days of the *Hajj.* The higher disciples stood in prayers for a third or three-fourths of the night throughout the years, while others said their morning prayers with the ablution of their *'Isha* prayer. Some of the disciples had, by now, reached to eminence in spiritual power through this education.... Owing to the influence of the Shaikh, most of the Mussalmans of this country developed interest in mysticism, prayers and aloofness from the world, and came to have a faith in the Shaikh. The hearts of men having become virtuous by good deeds, the very name of wine, gambling and other forbidden things never came to any one's lips. Sins and abominable vices appeared to people as bad as infidelity. Out of regard for one another the Mussalmans refrained from open usury and regrating (*intikar*), while the shop-keepers, from fear, gave up speaking lies, using false weights and deceiving the ignorant. Most of the scholars and learned men, who frequented the Shaikh's company, applied themselves to books on devotion and mysticism. The books *Qut u'l Qulub, Ihya ul Ulum* and its translation, *Awarif u'l Marif, Kashf ul Mahjub; Sharh-i-Ta'arruf, Risala-i-Qushairi, Mirshad ul Ibad, Maktubai-Ain-i-Quzzat* and the *Lawaih* and *Lawama* of Qazi Hamiduddin Nagauri found many purchasers, as also did the *Fawa'id u'l Fu'ad* of Amir Hasan owing to the sayings of the Shaikh which it contains. People asked the book-sellers about books of devotion. No handkerchief was seen without a tooth brush (*miswak*) or a comb tied to it. Owing to the great number of purchasers, the price of water and leather vessels became high. In short, God had created the Shaikh as a peer of Shaikh Junaid and Shaikh Bayazid in these later days and man of wisdom. The virtues of a Shaikh—and the art of leading men (in the mystic path)—found their fulfilment and their final consummation in him.[232]

CONCLUSION

With this brief survey and critical analysis we may safely conclude that the nature and character of the functions performed by medieval *khanqahs* were not confined to academic pursuits like *Maktab* and *Madrasa*. The *khanqahs*, on the other hand, acted as centres for character building, and they trained the novices in adapting to new localities and regions, so that Sufis with vast knowledge, spiritual accomplishment and liberal policy could propagate and popularize the teachings of Islam and humanism among the masses.

NOTES

1. When Shaikh Nizamuddin Auliya settled at Ghayaspur in Delhi, he used to offer prayers in congregations along with his followers in his *jam'at khana*, except for the Friday prayers. Saiyid Muhammad b. Mubarak Alawi Kirmani (better known as Amir Khurd), *Siyar u'l Auliya* (hence *SA*), Delhi, 1885, p. 264.
2. '*Khanqah* or the shrine of Muslim saints also acted as a centre of dispensing knowledge.' Syed Ameer Ali, *The Spirit of Islam*, Delhi, 1978, pp. 471-2.
3. Disciple of Shaikh Najibuddin Firdausi and an eminent saint of the Firdausiya order. It was under his guidance and supervision that his order flourished and was popularized in India. Shaikh Shah Shoib, *Manaqib u'l Asfiya* (*MAs*), Khuda Bakhsh Oriental Public Library (KBOPL), Patna, f. 84b; Hamid b. Fazl u'llah known as Darwesh Jamali, *Siyar u'l Arifin* (*SAr*), Rotograph, Dept. of History, AMU, f. 101; Shaikh Abdul Haqq Muhaddis Dehlawi, *Akhbar u'l Akhyar* (*AA*), Delhi, 1914, pp. 117-22; Abu u's Samad b. Afzal Muhammad, *Akhbar u'l Asfiya* (*AAs*), MS. Maulana Azad Library (MAL) AMU, ff. 45b-46a.
4. *Maktubat-i-Sadi* (*MSadi*), a collection of one hundred letters of Shaikh Sharafuddin Yahya al Maneri, addressed to one of his disciples Qazi Shamsuddin of Chausa (Bihar), compiled by Zain Badr Arabi, Lucknow, 1870, Letter No. 37, p. 144.
5. *Hadis* quoted by Qazi Nur u'llah Shushtari, *Majalis u'l Mominin*, Tehran (Iran), 1881-2, *Majlis*, 6, p. 256.

6. Muhammad Qasim Farishta, *Tarikh-i-Farishta*, Lucknow, 1323 AH, Vol. 2, p. 384.
7. *Khalifa* and son-in-law of Shaikh Fariduddin Ganj-i Shakkar. He is reported to have compiled the sayings of Shaikh under the title of *Asrar u'l Auliya*. For details see. *SA*, pp. 138-9; Amir Hasan Ala Sijzi, *Fawa'id u'l Fu'ad* (*FF*), ed. and Urdu tr. Khwaja Hasan Sani Nizami Dehlawi, Urdu Academy. Delhi, 1990, pp. 42-3; *AA*, p. 67; *AAs* MS. f. 41b; Muhammad Ghausi Shattari, *Gulzar-i-Abrar* (*GA*), ed. Muhammad Zaki, KBOPL, Patna, 1994, p. 42; Mufti Muhammad Ghulam Sarwar Lahori, *Khazinat ul Asfiya* (*Kha As*), Lucknow, 1873, Vol. I, p. 319.
8. *SA*, pp. 268-71.
9. Popularly known as Akhi Siraj, he was a native of Bengal. Shaikh Nizamuddin Auliya used to call him Aina-i-Hindustan (Mirror of India). After Shaikh Nizamuddin Auliya's death he returned to his native place and made his centre of activities at Panduah (Bengal). *SA*, pp. 282-8; *AA*, pp. 86-7.
10. *SA*, p. 288, also *SA*, p. 90.
11. *SA*, p. 90; *AA*, 86.
12. One of the famous scholars of Delhi, who first tested Shaikh Nizamuddin Auliya's scholarship and then joined the circle of the Shaikh. See *SA*, pp. 223-6; *AA*, pp. 97-8; *GA*, p. 97.
13. An experienced teacher and a man of wisdom, renowned for his piety, he joined the discipleship under Shaikh Nizamuddin Auliya towards the end of his life. *SA*, pp. 296-7; *AA*, pp. 99; *GA*, p. 75.
14. *GA*, p. 75.
15. K.A. Nizami, *The Life and Times of Nizam uddin Auliya*, Delhi, 1991 p. 161.
16. *SA*, 279.
17. An erudite scholar and renowned teacher, he migrated from Bukhara towards India during the reign of Sultan Ghiyasuddin Balban (AD 1228-81). He lived for sometime in Delhi, his fame as a teacher, growing influence and popularity among the masses within a short span of time, compelled the Sultan to order him to leave Delhi and to settle at Sonargaon. Shaikh Sharafuddin Yahya al Maneri, *Khwan-i-Pur Nimat*, MS, *Majlis*, 5, f. 15; *MAs*, ff. 82b, 83a.
18. A town near *Dhaka* (Bangladesh), it was capital of the independent Muslim rulers of eastern India, during the time of the Pathan Sultanate of Delhi. See J. Wise, 'Notes on the Sonargaon', *Journal of Asiatic Society of Bengal* (*JASB*), 1874, Vol. XLII, Pt. I, p. 134.
19. *MA*, MS, 83b; See also Ata Karim Burke, 'Makhdum Shaikh Sharafuddin's Maktubat-i-Sadi' A Correspondence Course of Spiritualism, *Indo-Iranica*, 1981, Vol. 34, Nos. 1-4, p. 124.
20. Popularly known as Shah Madar, he was the founder and pioneer saint of the Madariyya order in India. Originally a Jew from Syria, after completing education in various fields he visited Makka and Madina, embraced Islam

and is said to have studied *Hadiths* there. He is reported to have travelled in the company of Saiyid Ashraf Jahangir Simnani during his journey to Makka. He ultimately migrated to India and settled at Makampur. Shaikh Abdur Rahman Rudaulawi Chishti, *Mirat-i-Madari* (*MiM*), the transcript of the MSS available in MAL (a) Habib Ganj Collection, Call No. 32/129/1-2, ff. 21, copied by Muhammad Murad in AH 1121/AD 1709-10, (b) Subhanullah Collection, Call No. 297/7/46; *AA*, p. 164; *Ain-i-Akbari*, Eng. tr. Colonel H.S. Jarreti, Delhi, 1978, Vol. 3, p. 412; Dara Shikoh, *Safinat ul Auliya*, pp. 187-8; *Kha As*, 2, pp. 310-12.

21. Born in AH 688/AD 1285, in the royal family of Simnan (Khurasan), he abdicated the throne in favour of his brother, went to Panduah (Bengal) and became a disciple of Shaikh Ala ul Haq, received *khirqah* and *khilafat* and finally settled at Kichaucha where his tomb is located. *AA*, pp 166-7; *GA*, p. 131; Ṣhaikh Abdur Rahman Rudauawi Chishti, *Mirat ul Asrar*; (*MAs*), MS, MAL, AMU, Abdus Salam, Call. No. 934/29(F) *Tasawwuf*, ff., 302a-307a; *Kha As*, Vol. 1, pp 371-7.
22. *M. Sadi*, Letter No. 55, p. 222.
23. *FF*, 24th *Majalis*, p. 257.
24. Bruce Lawrence, *The Malfuzat of Some Sufi Saints of Bihar*, pp. 612-13.
25. *Ganj-i-Arshadi*, Collected Works of Saiyid Hasan Askari, KBOPL, Patna, Vol. 1, 1985, p. 15.
26. Abdur Rashid, 'The Treatment of History by Muslim Historians in Sufi Writings', in C.H. Philips, ed., *Historians of India, Pakistan and Ceylon*, London, 1961, p. 13.
27. Ata Karim Burke has rightly observed that, 'As soon as the *khanqah* was erected at Bihar Sharif, the *Makhdum-i-Jahan's* disciples and devotees, as it has been stated, rushed to him to get religious-cum-spiritual lessons.' *Indo-Iranica*, 1981, Vol. 34, p. 126.
28. *Madin ul Ma'ani*, discourses of Shaikh Sharafuddin Yahya al Maneri, compiled by Zain Badr Arabi, MS, MAL, AMU, Call No. Habib Ganj Collection, 21/34 *Farsiya Tasawwuf*, Chap. 35, f. 155a.
29. *Khwan-i Pur Nimat*, MS, Maj. 16, f. 49a.
30. *Madin ul Ma'ani*, MS, Ch. 23, f. 108b.
31. *Madin ul Ma'ani*, MS, Ch. 30, f. 135a.
32. *Rahat ul Qulub*, MS, Maj. 2, p. 5.
33. *Surur us Sudur*, MS, MAL, Call No. 21'168.
34. *Fuwa'id ul Fu'ad*, Delhi, 1990.
35. *Madin ul Ma'ani*,
36. *Surur us Sudur*, MS, f. 25
37. Once Shaikh Farid uddin Ganj-i Shakkar was teaching *Awarif ul Ma'arif*, but at one place he found it difficult to read it because of its bad script. Shaikh Nizamuddin suggested to his master that Shaikh Najib uddin had a better manuscript. *FF*, Maj. 25th, pp 43-4.
38. Shaikh Abdur Rashid, op. cit., p. 130.

39. He was the son of Shaikh Muiz Balkhi and nephew of Shaikh Muzaffar Shams Balkhi. But he was brought up and trained in the *khanqah* under the supervision of Shaikh Sharaf uddin Yahya al Maneri. Besides acquiring mystic knowledge he had studied different branches of theology including *Sahih Bukhari* and *Sahih Muslim* and several books on jurisprudence under the guidance of renowned scholars, during his four years stay at Makka. See *Monis ul Qulub*, discourses of Shaikh Ahmad Langer Darya Balkhi, compiled by Qazi Saiyid b. Khitab Bihari, MS, Balkhi Library of Fatuha, Patna; MS, f. 357a;
40. *MM*, MS, MAL, *Farsiya* 32/129-1-2; f.26a.
41. *SA*, p. 318.
42. *SA*, p. 268.
43. *AA*, p. 93.
44. Ibn Battuta, *The Rehla*, Eng. translation and commentary by Mahdi Husain, Oriental Institute, Baroda, 1976, pp. 30-1.
45. *GA*, p. 77.
46. *SA*, p. 299.
47. *AA*, p. 178.
48. *SA*, p. 112.
49. *Jami ul Ulum* (*Ja Ul*), discourses of Saiyid Jalaluddin Bukhari, ed. Qazi Sajjad Husain, Delhi, 1987, p. 444.
50. *Ja Ul*, p. 453.
51. Muhammad Sulaiman Siddiqui, 'Shaikh Muhammad Ruknuddin: His Role in Medieval Deccan', *Islamic Culture*, Jan. 1981, Vol. 55, No, 1, pp. 52-3.
52. Son of Haji Sulaiman, s/o Israeil. *GA*, p. 432.
53. He was born in Delhi but went to Gujarat for higher education and later migrated to Burhanpur, Deccan. *GA*, p. 205.
54. Disciple of Shaikh Azizullah of Talamba (Sarai Sidhu Tahsil, Multan). *Muntakhab ut Tawarikh* (*MT*), Eng. tr. T.W. Haig, Delhi, Vol. 3, p. 4.
55. His real name was Piyara, son of Kabir. *GA*, p. 248.
56. *GA*, p. 373.
57. *AA*, pp. 150-1.
58. *GA*, p. 337.
59. His real name was Shaikh Muhammad but was popularly known as Shaikh Hasan Muhammad, son of Shaikh Ahmad (famous as Shaikh Miyanjee), son of Shaikh Nasiruddin. Ali Muhammad Khan Bahadur, *Mirat-i-Ahmadi*, Supplement, ed. Saiyid Nawab Ali, Calcutta, 1930, pp. 75-6; *GA*, p. 294; *Kha As*, 1, 436.
60. *GA*, pp. 295-6.
61. Son of Shaikh Khan by fourteenth stage his line of descendant goes to Shaikh Muhammad Hamadani. He left his home at the age of eleven and after passing his time as a wanderer he reached Bidar (Deccan) and became a disciple of Shaikh Muhammad Multani. In AH 930/AD 1523 his *pir* offered *khirqah* and instructed him to settle at Ujjain. There he married the

daughter of Saiyid Safi (Shafi Khan). *GA*, pp. 291-2.

62. *GA*, p. 292.
63. *MT*, Eng. tr, Vol. 3, p. 29.
64. Although descendant of Shaikh Bahauddin Zakariyya, he joined the Jahriya order. *AA*, pp. 186-7.
65. A native of a village Sohna, 25 miles from Delhi, now a town in the Tahsil and District of Gurgaon, Haryana. *Imperial Gazetteer of India*, New Series, Delhi, Vol. 13, p. 72.
66. *Mt*, 3, Eng. tr, p. 163.
67. GA, p. 396.
68. *Indo-Iranica*, 1981, Vol. 34, Nos. 1-4, p. 126.
69. Shaikh Abdur Rashid, op. cit., p. 132.
70. *AA*, pp. 30-1.
71. Shaikh Abdur Rashid, op. cit., p. 130.
72. Lucknow, 1870, and Kanpur, 1911. Eng. tr. Father Paul Jackson, S.J., Bombay, 1985.
73. Lahore, 1904, Urdu tr. of 101 letters by Abu Saleh Muhammad Yunus under the title of *Sabil ul Rashad* in two volumes, Bihar Sharif, AH 1386/AD 1966.
74. Newal Kishore, Lucknow.
75. MS, KBOPL, Patna.
76. *AA*, pp. 129-31; *MS Maktubat-i Sharafuddin* by Ali Qalandar Panipati is available in 131 folios, MAL, Call No. Habib Ganj Collection *21/111 Farsiya Tasawwuf* also Abdus Salam No. 918/13 (f) *Tasawwuf*.
77. MS. Patna University Library, Bankipur, Patna.
78. MS. MAL, Subhan ullah Collection, Call No. 297/71/17 *Malfuzat wa Maktubat;* Lucknow, 1309AH/
79. MS. MAL, Zamimah Subhan ullah Collection, Call No. 297/71/18, *Malfuzat wa Maktubat Farsi.*
80. *GA*, p. 94.
81. MS, MAL, Abdus Salam Collection, Call No. 915/10 (Alif) (f) *Tasawwuf*
82. MS, MAL, University Collection No. 68/8/F
83. Mujtaba Press, 1897, Urdu tr. of 91 letters by Khaliq Anjum.
84. Kanpur, 1890; Urdu tr. under the title *Kitab-i-Zubdat ul Maqamat*, Lahore, 1909.
85. Newal Kishore, Kanpur, 1891.
86. MS, MAL, University Call. No. 24, *Farsiya Mazhab wa tasawwuf wa Ikhlaq.*
87. MS, MAL, Subhanullah Collection, Call No. 297/71/13 *Malfuzat wa Maktubat.*
88. Shaikh Abdur Rashid, op. cit., p. 132.
89. His ancestors hailed from Ghazni, but he was born and brought up in Daulatabad (Deccan), completed his education under Shaikh Abdul Muqtadir at Delhi but joined the discipleship of Maulana Muhammad Khwajagi and later settled at Jaunpur. *AA*, pp. 180-1.

90. Muhammad Ghausi writes his name a Shaikh Kamaluddin Husain (GA, p. 175), a descendant of Shaikh Hamiduddin Sufi Nagauri, lived in Gujarat, after sometime went to Ajmer. When the city was attacked by the Rajput chief, Rana Sanga, the Shaikh left for Nagaur and devoted his time to teaching. He is reported to have visited the court of Sultan Ghiyasuddin, the Khalji ruler of Mandu. See *AA*, pp. 182-3, Shaikh Rizqullah Mushtaqúi, *Waqi'at-i-Mushtaqui,* Eng. tr. and ed. I.H. Siddiqui, Delhi, 1993, pp. 218-20.
91. Written by Sirajuddin Abu Yaqub Yusuf b. Abi Muhammad b. Ali as Sikkaki, d. AH 626/AD 1228. A. Halim, *Journal of Pakistan Historical Society (JPHS),* Vol. No. p. 26; see also *AA*, pp. 182-3.
92. A great scholar as well as competent authority on the works of Shaikh ibn Arabi. *AA*, p. 179; *GA*, p. 127.
93. *Mirat-i-Ahmadi*, Supp. p. 76.
94. A disciple of Shaikh Abdullah Shah Quraishi and among the descendants of Saiyid Jalaluddin Surkh Bukhari of Uchch, he strictly adhered to *Shara* and did not hesitate to even criticize Sultan Sikandar Lodi for not sporting a beard. *Waqiat-i-Mushtaqui*, Eng. tr., p. 69; Abdullah, *Tarikh-i-Daudi*, ed. Shaikh Abdur Rashid, Aligarh, 1954, p. 798; Ahmad Yadgar, *Tarikh-i-Shahi*, ed. M. Hidayat Husain, pp. 62-3; *AA*, pp. 215-19.
95. *AA*, p. 197.
96. A disciple of some of the descendants of Saiyid Muhammad Gesu Daraz. He left his native place Daulatabad, lived for sometimes in Jaunpur then in Gujarat and finally settled in Delhi where he died in 968/1560. *AA*, 253; *GA*, pp. 155-6. *Zikr-i-Jami-i-Auliya-i-Delhi*, Tonk, p. 72; Muhammad Sadiq Hamdani, *Tabqat-i-Shah Jahanii*, MS. MAL, AMU, Call No. 22/46/1, f. 191b; *Kha As*, 1, pp. 427-8.
97. *Mutawwal* is a highly esteemed work in Arabic on rhetorics written by Sadr uddin b. Masud b. Umari Taftazani. It is in the nature of an explanatory commentary on the *Takhlis ul Miftah* of Muhammad b. Abdul Rahman Khatibi Damishqi Qazwini which is itself a commentary on Sikkaki's *Miftah*. A. Halim, 'History of Persian Literature during the Saiyid-Lodi period, 1414-1526', *JPHS*, 1955, p. 26.
98. Son of Saiyid Jamal at Husaini, a saint of Delhi. His ancestors are reported to have migrated from Mashhad to Multan and during the reign of Sultan Firoz Shah Tughluq settled in Delhi. *AA*, 150.
99. *GA*, p. 253; *AA*, pp. 253-7.
100. A famous traditionalist who proceeded to Makka where he studied traditions with eminent scholars like Ibn Hajar al Haytami al Makki and became a disciple of Shaikh Ali Muttaqi in the Qadiri and Shazili order. He was assassinated near Ujjain by some followers of the pretended Mahdi in AH 986/AD 1577. *Encyclopaedia of Islam,* new edition, Vol. 7, p. 458.
101. Alauddin Ali b. Husamuddin Abdul Malik b. Qazi Khan al Shazili al

Qadiri was born in Burhanpur. He became a disciple of Shaikh Abdul Karim b. Shaikh Bajan of Burhanpur, and afterwards went to Multan where he studied with Husamuddin Muttaqi, after whom he was named Muttaqi. He also lived for a long period at Ahmadabad but left India for Makka and finally settled there after Humayun defeated Bahadur Shah (the ruler of Gujarat) in AH 941/AD 1534. *AA*, pp. 257-65; *GA*, p. 370.

102. *Encyclopaedia of Islam*, new edition, Vol. 7.
103. *Jawamil Kalim*, 30; *AA*, pp. 97-8,
104. *AA*, pp. 180-1;
105. A. Halim, *JPHS*, 1956, Vol. 8, p. 13.
106. *GA*, p. 204.
107. *AA*, p. 197.
108. Shaikh Mina (d. AH 874/AD 1469) wrote commentary on *Bazdawi, Misbah, Hisami, Kafiya and Risala Makkiya. AA*, p. 193.
109. A famous book on Muslim jurisprudence written by Burhan uddin Abul Hasan b. Ali al Marghinani (d. AH 593/AD 1196). *Encyclopaedia of Islam*, Vol. 3, pp. 279-80.
110. *AA*, pp. 180-1.
111. He received 1000 *tankas* from Sultan Husain Shah Sharqi as reward for his work which was in several volumes. He spent the entire amount on his students. *AA*, p. 197.
112. *SA*, p. 289.
113. *Lataif-i-Quddusi* about the life and condition of Shaikh Abdul Quddus Gangohi, comp. Shaikh Ruknuddin, ed. Hafiz Muhammad Usman, AH 1311/AD 1893, Delhi, p. 6.
114. *AA*. 150.
115. A well known Arabic grammar produced by Jalaluddin Abu Usman b. Umar, better known as Ibn ul Hajib (d. AH 648/AD 1248).
116. *AA*, pp. 193-4.
117. *AA*, pp. 180-1.
118. *Kha As*, 1, 380.
119. *MT*, Eng. tr., 3, 43; *Mirat-i-Ahmadi*, Supplement, Cal. 1930, pp. 68-9.
120. *AA*. p. 180; *Kha As*, I, p. 390.
121. *Mirat-i-Ahmadi*, Supplement, Cal. 1930, pp. 68-9.
122. *AA*, pp 253-7.
123. Written by Shaikh Ziauddin Abu Najib Abdul Qahir Suharawardi, founder of the famous Suhrawardi order.
124. *AA*, p. 113; MS, KBOPL, Patna, Urdu tr. Saiyid Qasimuddin Ahmad.
125. MSS, Ethe, 1863.
126. Shaikh Shihab uddin Umar Suhrawardi.
127. *GA*, p. 216.
128. *GA*, p. 127.
129. *GA*, p. 211.

130. *GA*, p. 216.
131. *GA*, p. 127; *AA*, 179.
132. Ibid.
133. *GA*, pp. 253-4.
134. This book came to be known as *Kashf ul Asrar,* written in Persian. It contains discussions on topics like the reality of knowledge and mystical knowledge. *Monis ul Qulub,* MS, Maj. 50; f. 112; Maj. 69, f. 350.
135. *AA*, 193.
136. *MT*, 3, 63.
137. A well known treatise on Sufism written by Shaikh Fakhruddin Iraqi, and nephew of Shaikh Shihabuddin Suhrawardi. He came to India and lived in the *khanqah* of Shaikh Bahauddin Zakariyya in Multan.
138. *AA*, pp. 211-12.
139. *AA*, pp. 241-3.
140. *AA*, pp. 237-9; *GA*, p. 226.
141. *AA*, p. 155; *GA*, p. 127.
142. I.H. Siddiqui, *Perso-Arabic Sources of Information on the Life and Conditions in the Sultanate of Delhi*, Delhi, 1992, p. 64.
143. A disciple of Shaikh Muhammad Ghaus Gwaliori, he claimed himself to be the descendant of Nurul Huda, a famous disciple of Shaikh Jalaluddin Mujarrad of Sylhet. *GA*, pp. 282-3.
144. *AA*, 193.
145. *AA*, 190; *Kha As*, 1, p. 409.
146. Lahore, 1923; Eng. tr. R.A. Nicholson, London, 1970, and Delhi, 1982.
147. He was a disciple of Shaikh Farid who was the grandson of Sultan ut Tarikin Shaikh Hamiduddin Sufi Sawali Nagauri. *AA*, pp. 105-9.
148. *Anwar ul Uyun fi Asrar ul Maknun*, anecdotes of Shaikh Ahmad Abdul Haq Rudaulawi (d. AH 836/AD 1434), Lucknow, AH 1295/AD 1878, Urdu tr. Khalilur Rahman Chaudhuri.
149. *AA*, pp 198-200.
150. Riyazul Islam, 'A Survey in Outline of the Mystic Literature of the Sultanate Period, *JPHS*, 1955, Vol. 3, pp. 202-3.
151. K.A. Nizami, 'Mystic Ideas of Iran and their Impact on Sufi Thought and Tradition in India', *Indo-Iranica*, 1981, Vol. 34, Nos. 1-4, pp. 115-16.
152. *Maadin ul Maani*, MS, MAL, University Collection No. 20, *Farsiya Mzhab*, ff. 2b-3a.
153. Riaz ul Islam, 'Collection of the *Malfuzat* of Makhdum Jahaniyan 1307-88 of Uchch', *JPHS*, 1961, Vol. 9, pp. 212-13.
154. *Surur us Sudur,* MS, MAL, AML, Subhanullah Collection, Call No. 21/168.
155. Delhi, AH 1305/AD 1885.
156. K.A. Nizami, 'A Note on *Ahsan ul Aqwal*', *JPHS*, 1953, Vol. 3, Pt. 1, pp. 40-4.

157. MSS, KBOPL, Patna, and MAL, AML (a) University Coll. No. 20, *Farsiaya Mazhab wa Tasawwuf wa Akhlaq*, (b) Habib Ganj Collection, 21/34, *Farsiya Tasawwuf.*
158. MS, KBOPL, Patna.
159. MS, Balkhi Library, Fatuha, Patna, Bihar.
160. Urdu Academy, Delhi, 1992.
161. Hyderabad, AD 1910; Urdu tr. Saiyid Shah Muhamad Shafiq Firdausi, Bihar Sharif, 1927.
162. MS, KBOPL, Patna, Ahamdi Press, Patna, AH 1321/AD 1903; Eng. tr. Father Paul Jackson, Delhi, 1982.
163. Agra, AH 1321/AD 1903.
164. MS. KBOPL, Patna.
165. Photostat copy of the MS available in KBOPL, Patna,
166. MS, KBOPL, Patna. Urdu tr. Saiyid Shah Qasim uddin Ahmad Sharif ul Firdausi, Bihar Sharif, 1988.
167. Agra, 1904.
168. Delhi, 1987.
169. MS, KBOPL, Patna.
170. Ed. K.A. Nizami, Aligarh, 1959. Urdu tr. Maulana Ahmad Ali.
171. Urdu tr. Muninuddin Dardai, Delhi, 1990,
172. MS, MAL, AMU, University *Zamima* No. 30, *Farsiya Tasawwuf*; Nursrat, Delhi, AH 1295/AH 1878.
173. MS. *Mujibia Khanqah*, Phulwari Sharif, Patna.
174. Mujtabai Press, Delhi, AH 1311/AD 1894.
175. Urdu tr. Saiyd Abu Zafar Nadawi, Azamgarh, 1939;
176. MS, KBOPL, Patna.
177. MS, KBOPL, Patna.
178. MS, MAL, AMU, *University Farsi Nasr* (3) 66/4.
179. *AA*, p. 193; but it is also available under the title of *Manaqib i Shah Mina or Tuhfa-us Sadiya*, comp. Muhiuddin Rizwi Husini, ed. Hardoi, 1900. MS. available in MAL, Habib Ganj Collection, Call. No. 21/244, *Farsiya Tasawwuf.*
180. *AA*, 175; *Mirat ul Asrar,* MS. f. 288a.
181. MS. Balkhi Library, Fatuha, Bihar.
182. MS, MAL, Subhanullah Collection, Call No. 297/71/14 *Malfuzaf wa Maktuabt.*
183. Delhi, 1885.
184. Delhi, 1893, Urdu tr. Ghulam Ahmad Muradabadi, AH 1319.
185. Delhi, 1914, Urdu tr. Maulana Dubhan Mahmud and Maulana Muhammad Fazil, Deoband. U.P.
186. Patna, 1994.
187. MS, MAL, Firangi Mahal, Call No. 85/3, copied in AH 1249/AD 1836, copied by Shaikh Husain Ali.
188. MS, Research Library, Dept. of History, AMU, Aligarh, Call No. 99.

189. MS, KBOPL, Patna, Calcutta, 1895.
190. MSS, MAL, AMU, Abdus Salam Collection, Call No. 934/29(f) *Tasawwuf*.
191. K.A. Nizami, *Indo-Iranica*, Vol. 34, 1981, p. 98.
192. *AA*, p. 25.
193. K.A. Nizami, *Indo-Iranica*, Vol. 34, 1981, p. 103.
194. Ibid., p. 103.
195. Ibid., p. 106.
196. His real name was Sher Khan, a relative of Sultan Firoz Shah Tughluq, was inclined towards Sufism, joined discipleship of Shaikh Ruknuddin Imam. *AA*, pp. 168-73.
197. *AA*, p. 227.
198. *AA*, p. 228; Khwaja Nimatullah, *Tarikh-i-Khan, Jahani wa Makhzan-i-Afghani*, ed. S.M. Imamuddin, Dhaka, 1960, Vol. 1, p. 377.
199. *AA*, p. 202.
200. *GA*, p. 250.
201. *AA*, p. 232.
202. *AA*, pp. 150-1.
203. *AA*, p. 175.
204. *GA*, p. 426.
205. *Kha As*, 2, p. 498.
206. *Kha As*, 2, pp. 450-1.
207. As A. Halim has quoted Maulavi Abdul Haqq (Baba-i-Urdu), '*Urdu ki ibtidai nashaw wa numa men sufian-i-Kiram ka kam*', p. 90, *JASP*, 1958, Vol. III, p. 48.
208. *Surur us Sudur*, MS, ff.
209. *Madin ul Ma'ani*, MS, *Majlis*, 23, f 103a.
210. *AA*, pp. 174-5.
211. *Lataif Quddusi*, Delhi, 1894.
212. '*Rushd Nama* is written in mixed prose and poetry; its style is similar to that of the *Lamat* of Shaikh Fakhruddin Iraqi (d. AD 1289) and of the *Lawaih* of Abdur Rahman Jami (d. AD 1492). It draws upon those verses of the Koran and traditions of the Prophet Muhammad which provide the base for Sufi beliefs and practices. It quotes Persian verses from Sufi poets such as Attar (d. 1230), Rumi (d. 1273), Sadi (d. 1292), Nakhshabi (d. 1350), Masud Bak (d. 1397-8), Abu Ali Qalandar (d. 1324) and Muhammad Qalandar. What endows the *Rushd Nama* with a distinctive character is the profuse use of Hindi verses composed by Shaikh Abdul Quddus himself and his teachers.' Saiyid Athar Abbas Rizvi and Shailesh Zaidi, *Alakhbani*, Hindi introduction, translation and annotation, Aligarh, 1971, Introduction, pp. VIII-IX.
213. *Rushd Nama*, MS, MAL, AMU, Aligarh, Subhanullah Collection,
214. *Maktubat Saiyid Nur Qutb-i-Alam Pandwi*, under title '*Ain ul'Ashquin*, MAL, AMU, Call No. Zamimah Subhanullah Number, 297/71/18 *Malfuzat wa Maktubat Farsi*.

215. *Malfuzat Shaikh Akhi Jamshed Rajgiri*, MS, MAL, Call No. *University Farsi Nasr* (3), 66/4.
216. He was a famous *majzub*, used to move in the streets of market dancing and singing Hindi *dohas*. He was a nephew (sister's son) of grandfather of Shaikh Abdul Haq Muhaddis Dehlawi. *AA*, pp. 290-1.
217. *AA*, p. 270; Mulla Abdul Qadir Badauni says, 'In AH 967/AD 1559 when I was returning from Chunar during the rule of Abdullah Khan the Uzbek, I spent a night in attendance on the Shaikh (Shaikh Burhan), whose conversation was sublime. He recited, appropriate to the occasion, some of his own Hindi poetry of which the subjects were exhortation, admonition, mysticism, the unity of God, and withdrawal from the world.' *MT*, Eng. tr., Vol. 3, p.11.
218. He was a descendant of Saiyid Ahmad Kabir Rafai' (d. AH 588/AD 1192) of Yemen. *GA*, p. 280.
219. *Encyclopaedia of Islam*, 1991, Vol. 6, p. 272.
220. *GA*, p. 214; *AA*, pp. 162-3.
221. A. Rahim, 'Shaikh Akhi Siraj al Din Usman, A Bengali Saint' *JPHS*, 1961, Vol. 9, p. 24.
222. Sadiq Naqvi, *Muslim Religious Institutions and Their Role under the Qutb Shah*. Hyderabad, 1993, pp. 148-9.
223. *JPHS*, ed. S. Moin ul Haq, Jan. 1954, Vol. 2, Pt. 1, p. 287.
224. *AA*, 86; N.N. Law has quoted *Khurshid Jahan Numahi by* Ilahi Bakhsh al Husaini, MS, Asiatic Society of Bengal, Calcutta, p. 214, in *Promotion of Learning in India (During Muhammadan rule by Muhammadans)*, Delhi, 1973, p. 37.
225. A Rahim, 'Shaikh Akhi Siraj al Din Usman, A Bengali Saint', *JPHS*, 1961, Vol. 9, p. 26.
226. *Tohfat ul Majalis*, MS, Section 38.
227. N.N. Law, op. cit., pp. 175-6.
228. *Tuzuk-i Jahangiri*, Eng. tr. Alexander Rogers and ed. H. Beveridge, Delhi, 1978, pp. 439-40.
229. *Mirai-i-Ahmadi, Supplement,* Bombay, p. 3; for details see S.A. Zafar Nadvi, 'Libraries during the Muslim Rule in India', *Islamic Culture*, Oct. 1945, pp. 329-47.
230. *AA*, p. 253.
231. *Monis ul Qulub*, Majlis, 14, f. 11.
232. Ziauddin Barani, *Tarikh-i-Firoz Shahi*, ed. Shaikh Abdur Rashid, Aligarh, Vol. 2, pp. 343-7.

PART 2
SULTANS

Sidelight on Alauddin Khalji's Price Control Measure

S. Mohd. Raza Naqvi

The reign of Sultan Alauddin Khalji (1296-1316), though brief, was marked by some very important political, social and economic developments. It witnessed the unprecedented expansion of the Delhi Sultanate, successful repulsion of repeated Mongol invasions, significant changes in the composition and role of the ruling class, emergence of a new tax structure, introduction of novel military reforms and the minimum interference of the shariat and its exponents in the affairs of the state. But the economic regulations of Alauddin Khalji have been described as the 'greatest administrative achievement of the Delhi Sultanate'.[1]

Ziauddin Barani (1285-1357), the contemporary historian, has discussed these regulations in his *Tarikh-i-Firoz Shahi* in great detail. Other historians of the period have also recorded them with some difference and the treatment of the subject.[2] However, the price control measure of the Sultan has become a matter of controversy among the modern scholars with regard to the motive of the Sultan in introducing the measure and the area of its operation.[3] But if the events that preceded the enforcement of price control regulations, recorded by Barani and other authorities, had been kept in view, perhaps, the above controversy would not have arisen. It is, indeed, surprising that the factors that forced the Sultan to take steps for the control of the prices escaped the attention of scholars. An attempt has been made in the present paper to piece together these developments.

Among the contemporary sources, Barani has linked the price control measure of Alauddin Khalji with the desire of the Sultan 'to maintain a large and well-equipped army on a low salary, as the higher pay to a vast force would exhaust his huge treasurers within five or six years'.[4] This statement of Barani has created a controversy among modern scholars: (i) whether the Sultan regulated the prices just for the military considerations, or his objective was the benefit of common people, and (ii) whether the regulations were enforced only at Delhi or at other places also because (a) as the measure was intended for the benefit of soldiers, they and their families were stationed at other places also, and (b) it would not have been profitable for the traders to import commodities at higher prices from outside and sell it at lower rates at Delhi.[5] The fact appears to be that the statement of Barani about the motive of the Sultan in enforcing the price control measure is the reasoning of a political thinker who was explaining the historical facts according to his own thinking, after a lapse of about fifty years, ignoring or forgetting the important political and economic developments which led the Sultan to initiate the step for meeting an extraordinary situation. Barani himself has recorded these developments with admirable detail and is corroborated by his contemporary friends and historians.[6] A study of these developments suggests that the price control regulations of Alauddin Khalji were meant for the imperial capital of Delhi as its population was passing through extreme hardships at that particular juncture. After the examination of these facts, the controversy appears unwarranted.

The way Sultan Jalaluddin Khalji (1290-6) captured the throne of Delhi dealt a serious blow to the developing concept of a priviledged ruling dynasty and hereditary succession. He occupied the throne by force, without any hereditary or legitimate claims.[7] The precedent established by him was soon followed by other adventures, though unsuccessfully. Alauddin Khalji, the nephew and son-in-law of Jalaluddin Khalji was, however, a different man. Illiterate though he was, he was a man of uncommon commonsense and a great schemer, as subsequent events proved, who did not just dream to occupy the throne of Delhi, but also nursed the ambition to become a Prophet and second Alexander the Great.[8] He made elaborate preparations before making any bid for the throne of Delhi. He needed a large force as well as public support to usurp the throne and legitimize his bloody coup. It required a huge amount of money. While at Kara as its Governor, he led expeditions to Bhilsa and Deogir with and without the permission of the Sultan and brought unlimited wealth in the form of horses, elephants, jewellery and cash.[9]

After treacherously eliminating the loving and unsuspecting Sultan at Kara, Alauddin started for the capture of the throne of Delhi, lavishly distributing on way the money he had brought from the south, to enlist soldiers and win over the public to his side.[10] Barani writes: 'He

(Alauddin) gave lakhs (of *tankas*) to his Khans, Muluk and Umara to recruit fresh cavalrymen ... on every stage about five *man*,[11] money was showered on public by small *minijaniqs* that had been moulded for the purpose.'[12] By the time he reached Baran (modern Buland Shahr), about 40 miles east of Delhi, he had gathered an army of fifty-six thousand *swars* and sixty thousand infantry.[13]

He ultimately entered into Delhi with a vast force. Jalaluddin's son, Qadr Khan, whom the dowager Queen had raised on the throne of Delhi, could not withstand such a large army and fled to Multan, then under his elder brother Arkali Khan, leaving the throne vacant for his brother-in-law.[14] After his enthronement, Alauddin again distributed the salary of a year or a half as *inam* among his old and new soldiers.[15] The result was, in the words of Barani: 'As unlimited wealth had been accumulated in the treasury of the Sultan, and the money had also been distributed among the masses in different ways and they have got bagsful of *tankas* and *jitals*, they were enjoying a pleasant and luxurious life.'[16] It needs no emphasis that the above developments would have caused (a) considerable inflation in Delhi, and (b) enormous increase in its population with the arrival of the large force of Alauddin (over one lakh) and their families. The two things together would have resulted in the rise of prices, if not shortage, of supplies. Further, once the new Sultan was firmly seated on the throne, he embarked upon on a campaign of conquests. Ranthambhore, Gujarat and Sehwan were captured and fresh wealth poured into Delhi in the form of booty.[17] It may be pointed out here that Alauddin had not yet changed the shariat's rule of 4/5 of the *ghanimah* (war booty) going to the soldiers and only 1/5 of its to the state.

However, before the Sultan could realize the financial repercussions of these developments, and initiate any step of check the inflationary trends at Delhi, he had to face successive Mongol raids. While the attack of Saldi and Turghy was repulsed at Jaran Maran (or Jalandhar),[18] the invasion of Qutlugh Khwaja (1299) was very serious. His target was Delhi, and he was marching fast towards it with a force of two lakhs, avoiding skirmishes on way.[19] Before he reached Delhi and besieged it, there was great panic in and around the capital. Vast population of the neighbourhood came inside the city for shelter and safety. The effects of this invasion on Delhi have been described by Ziauddin Barani in these words: 'So many people of the adjoining areas had poured into Delhi that they could not be accommodated in the streets, bazars and mosques. Because of the influx of large numbers of people (in Delhi), the provisions (*asbab*) became costlier in the city. The roads for the *caravanian* (grain merchants) and *saudagran* (traders) were blocked (due to Mongol siege of Delhi) and the people faced great hardships.' Needless to say, because of the impending attack of Qutlugh Khwaja, 'The Sultan had already summoned his generals and their armies from all directions.'[20] This observation of Barani is of great significance for the proper understanding of the price situation at Delhi and for Sultan's price control measures.

Luckily, however, the Mongols were thoroughly defeated with heavy losses to them, and the Sultan and his nobles celebrated this great victory by holding feasts and drinking parties,[21] unconcerned about the hardships which the population of Delhi, especially the poors had been passing through. It had become difficult for them to get their daily necessities of life. The crisis reached such an extent that there was heavy rush on shops, stampede and death of some people. The tragic incidents could not have gone unreported. When the Sultan was informed about them, he was holding a music and drinking party. He was shocked at the news, went into a pensive and contemplative mood and summoned his advisors to find out ways and means to bring relief to the people. Isami has described the entire episode and Sultan's response in these words:

> At that moment (when the Sultan was enjoying the music and drink) one of the royal favourites arrived. After invoking blessings on the emperor and performing the prostration ceremony, he entreated thus: 'Your Majesty! May you enjoy long life and property! Instead of indulging in the deserts, pray rescue the oppressed in your dominion lest weak should perish under your regime. Pressed by scarcity, people have thronged in quest of grain today and some of the poor have been trodden down.' On hearing this, the Emperor became depressed and desisted from drink....' Then he sent for men of experience and probity, and told them that since the people were on verge of death on account of famine and poverty, the barns should be thrown open from sunrise to sunset and grain should be sold at 'old prices', which must remain uniform and permanent. Thus it was intended that the people should be relieved of famine and the aggrieved be solaced and profiteers be sent to gallows unless they repented and desisted from hoarding so that prosperity be promoted and troubles be removed and necessaries of life provided to all.[22]

A statement in *Khair-al-Majalis*, though a bit different, in essence corroborates the account of Isami. Qazi Hamiduddin, a great businessman of his time, had access to the court of Alauddin. Once he had a long conservation with the Sultan, which he subsequently narrated to Shaikh Nasiruddin Chiragh, the senior successor of Shaikh Nizamuddin Auliya.

Hamid Qalandar, the author of *Khair-al-Majalis* has given a summary of this conversation. We quote its operative part as it throws light on both Alauddin's motives in introducing the price regulations as also the place where they were enforced.

'I then came near the Sultan and said, 'King of the Musalmans, I have a request'. 'Speak out', he replied. 'I came into the Chamber and found the Sultan thinking about'. 'Hear me', the Sultan replied. 'For sometime the idea has been coming to my mind. God Almighty has so many creatures, but he has placed me at their head. Now I, too, should do something the benefit of which may accrue to all people. I said to myself what can I do? If I give away all treasures I possess and a hundred such treasurers more—they all will not reach all the people. If I give away all my villages and my territories, they too will not suffice. So I was thinking over the problem—what should I do so that my work may benefit all the people? Just now an idea has came to me and I explain it to you. I said to myself that it I reduce the prices of grain, the benefit of it will accrue to all the people. But how is the price of grain to be reduced? I will order all the (Hindu) *Nayaks* of the empire, who bring grain 'to Delhi', to be summoned. Some of them have ten thousand transport animals while others have twenty thousand. I will summon them, give them robes and money from the treasury (for their business) and for the expenses of their families, so that they may bring grain and sell it at the rate I fix'. So the Sultan ordered and the grain began to come from all sides. In a few days its prices fell to seven *jitals* a *man*. Butter (*roghan*, *ghi*), sugar and other commodities also became cheap and 'all people' began to benefit from Sultan's work[23]

There is no mention in this conversation as to why the Sultan was so much worried and wanted to bring down the prices. Obviously it was due to the circumstances described by Barani and Isami, particularly the latter. As life had become extremely difficult for the people of Delhi, the Sultan had to take immediate steps to bring relief to the people of the city. The Sultan, with the help of his advisers, promptly promulgated price control regulations.

Barani has given a detail account of these regualtions.[24] If we carefully examine them, we will find that they were based on some sound economic principles. This partly explains the stability of prices during his reign and the success of the measure. These principle were: (i) fixation of prices of various items according to 'the cost of their production', (ii) ensuring the uninterrupted supply of all items of necessity and controlling their demand; (iii) establishing only one concentrated and wholesome market for similar items and (iv) creating an infra-structure to enforce the relevant rules and regulations. All regulations described by Barani as *zabitas*, (plural *zawabit*) separately for each of the four markets, come under the above four heads.

As regard the first step, the fixation of the prices of commodities, the Sultan made great efforts for ascertaining the prices of different items (from other places or from the place of their production) before their official prices (*nirkha-i-Sultani*) were fixed. Barani says that the prices were fixed according to *bar-awurdi*[25]. This is a Persian term still in use in Arabic and Persian institutions of north India for the bills of salary and other expenditure. It literally means, 'bringing out', and has been rightly interpreted as the 'cost of production'.[26] Fixing the prices on the basis of *bar-awurd* indicates the practical wisdom of an illiterate and autocrate medieval ruler who did not resort to arbitrary fixation of prices as they would not have worked.

However, even the fixation of prices according to the cost of production and in spite of harshness of the Sultan and strict vigilance of his officials, the officially fixed prices could not have been maintained unless the supply of all items was ensured and their demand was fully controlled. This important aspect was not ignored. The collection of land revenue largely in kind, establishment of state granaries, enrollment of *caravanian* in the register of *mandi* officials and settling them down with their families on the bank of Jamuna in Delhi, advancing the loan of a huge amount of 20 lack *tankas* to the Multani merchants, all were meant to ensure the regular and uninterrupted inflow of all necessities into the city. Similarly, the order for the collection of almost the entire surplus produce from the peasant by the revenue officials and grain merchants, ban on hoarding, permit system for fine and rare quality of cloth and the elimination of or restriction on middlemen (*dala* or brokers) from the slave and cattle markets were intended to prevent hoarding, speculation and rise in prices.

Yet another step with the same objective was the establishment of three concentrated market of *mandi*, *sarai-adl* and slave, horses and cattle market by clubbing the items of a similar nature. The general market or *bazaar-i-amma* of Barani was apparently scattered throughout the city. *Mandi* was the market for all types of grain; *sarai-adl* for salt, sugar, edible and lamp oil, fruits and cloths. Merchants of these items could unload and sell their merchandises nowhere else. This restriction would have ensured abundant availability of these important items, and would have prevented the creation of their artificial scarcity, speculation and rise of prices.[27]

Finally, the Sultan created an elaborate and effective administrative machinery for the implementation and enforcement of relevant rules and regulations. Alauddin was a fine judge of men and was lucky to have a bunch of loyal and highly capable adviser and officials. From amongst them he appointed a superintendent (*shahna* and/or *rais*) for each market, whose duty it was to vigorously enforce the *zawabit* (rules) of their respective markets and keep the Sultan informed about their functioning. They performed their duties efficiently and honestly.[28] No doubt, it was partly due to the harshness of the Sultan and his all prevailing three-tier spy system. There were the *barids*, formal intelligence officials; the *munhiyan* or the spies. Then there were the small boys whom the Sultan used to send to the markets to know whether the reports of the two state agencies were correct.[29] However, it would be unfair to the Sultan if we accept Barani's accusation of the Sultan in toto about his cruelty to his officials. Both Isami and the compiler of *Khair-ul Majalis* write that the Sultan was very considerate towards the officials and the traders. To the merchants he extended protection and huge amount of loans and to the officials he gave liberal and large *iqtas* with strong contingents of *swars* and *piadas* to enhance their status and prestige in the eyes of people. Barani himself mentions this fact.[30]

After the above discussion based on facts and statements of contemporary sources, we can conclude that the price control measure of Alauddin was meant for and enforced in the imperial capital of Delhi to bring relief to its vast population which had suffered because of inflation, manifold increase in its population, Mongol invasions, disruption of supplies and the consequent scarcity and exorbitant rise in prices. The circumstances described by Isami and *Khair-ul-Majalis* which led the Sultan to introduce price regulations do not support Barani's statement that the measure was taken by the Sultan because of military considerations. As such the controversy about the motive of the Sultan and the area of operation of the measure also appears unnecessary. The arguments that the regulations might have been enforced at places besides Delhi because (i) army and their families were living at many places, and (ii) it would not have been profitable for traders to import commodities at higher prices and sell them in Delhi at lower process do not appear tenable. These arguments presuppose that prices had risen everywhere for which there was neither any reason nor any evidence. Moreover, the significant observation of Barani that the prices were fixed (at Delhi) on the basis of *bar-awurd* (cost of production) negates this presumption. Ferishta, of course, writes that 'The prices of Delhi have been noted to give an idea of the prices of other territories.'[32] But his observation does not necessarily mean that the prices had risen at other places and that the regulations were enforced there too. It may very well mean that the prices at other places were similar (or even lower in the context of *bar-awurd*).

However, it is not the contention to totally deny the relevance between the keeping of a large army, fixation of a low salary for soldiers and the control of prices of Alauddin, irrespective of the reasoning of Barani on the matter. It appears that the economic measures of Alauddin (the market regulations, agrarian measures, the new tax structure) and the fixation of the salary of soldiers was a package deal, like the *Karori* experiment of Akbar. As mentioned earlier, before and soon after his enthronement, Alauddin gave ad hoc pay to old and new recruits under the compulsion of his circumstances. After his accession, he sent expeditions to Multan, Gujarat, Sehwan and Ranthambhore, etc. While he was still engaged in these military operations, he had to face successive Mongol attacks with grave political and economic consequences. Once the earlier raid were repulsed, the Sultan initiated steps to undo its effects, and along with other measures he also turned his attention to the reorganization of his army.

We know that no serious attempt was made by the predecessors of Alauddin Khalji to check the decay that had set in the Sultanate army under the successors of Iltutmish due to the soldiery and associated *iqtas* becoming hereditary. With the passage of time it adversely affected the strength, efficiency and fighting capacity of the army. Sultan Ghiyasuddin Balban (1266-86) who had to face internal and external threats, did attempt to resume the *iqtas* of incapable soldiers, but was prevailed upon by his old loyal and confident Fakhruddin Kotwal to abandon the move as it would cause hardship and starvation to a large number of old and aged people who had rendered valuable services to the state in the past.[32] Kaiqubad (1286-90) and Jalaluddin Khalji did not have the capacity and intention to undertake such a project.

Alauddin was a very ambitious ruler. He wanted to make extensive conquests and become the second Alexander the Great. Then the Mongol menace forced him to maintain a large and efficient army. He was realistic enough to understand that such a vast and mobile force could not be based on and tied down with cumbersome *iqta* system. Even otherwise, he was going to resume *milk, inam* and *waqf* grants to bring the heart of the empire, the Doab region, under his direct control, turning it into *khalisa*, for political and administrative considerations.[33] He, therefore, decided to pay the soldiers in cash, but on small salaries (*mawajib-i-andak*).[34] Barani writes that as prices had already been brought down by market regulations, the Sultan was able to fix low (*andak*) salary for the armymen.[35]

He fixed the pay of a regular (*murattab*) *swar* (cavalryman) at the rate of 234 *tankas* per annum. Further, the *swar* would be given 78 *tankas more if he maintained an extra horse*, becoming a *du-aspa swar*. It would, then, mean that out of 234 *tankas* that the regular *swar*, or *yak aspa* would receive, 78 *tankas* was the allowance for the upkeep of his horse, and the rest (156 *tankas*) per annum would be the salary that the foot soldier (*piadah*) would get. Barani stresses the point that the Sultan was very strict in demanding one and two horses from his *yak-aspa* and *du-aspa* soldiers respectively, and to ensure that he introduced the *dagh* system. Thus, incidentally, the credit for introducing the two important features of the army organization of the Delhi Sultanate and of the Mughal periods, namely the *du-aspa* and *dagh* system also goes to Alauddin Khalji, who is generally remembered only for his economic measures.[36]

The personal allowance of a soldier at the rate of 156 *tankas* per annum or 13 *tankas* per month, does appear to be a meagre amount. Barani himself describe it as 'a small pay'. But as we do not know as to what exactly a soldier was paid before Alauddin, or whether he was paid in cash at all, it would not be correct to say that Alauddin 'reduced' the salary of soldiers. None of our sources, not even Barani, says that the 'salaries of the soldiers were curtailed'.[37] Of course, it is yet to be examined if the above allowance was sufficient enough for a modest living of a army man with prices that were prevailing after Sultan's price control measure. However, even with this apparently small pay, Alauddin Khalji's army performed wonders. It kept the recalcitrant feudatory chiefs of the empire in check and submissive, brought almost the entire north India under his sway and forced the ruler of extreme south to accept the suzeranity of the Sultan. Above all, it repeatedly routed the Mongol hordes and saved the country, its people and civilization from their ravages and devastations.

NOTES

1. Muhammad Habib and K.A. Nizami, *A Comprehensive History of India*, Vol. V (Delhi Sultanate), p. 390.
2. Ziauddin Barani, *Tarikh-i-Firoz Shahi*, ed. Saiyed Ahmad Khan, Calcutta, 1860, pp. 302-24; Amir Khusro: *Khazain-al-Futuh*, Eng. tr by M. Habib, Madras, 1931, pp. 8-14; Isami, *Futuh-al-Salatin*, and A.S. Usha, Madras,

1948, pp. 313-15; Hamid Qalander, *Khair-al-Majalis*, ed. K.A. Nizami, Aligarh, 1959, p. 420.

3. Habib and Nizami, pp. 388-90; K.S. Lal, *History of the Khaljis*, New Delhi 1980, pp. 217-23; Irfan Habib, The Price Regulations of Alauddin Khalji, *IESHR*, 21, 4 (1984).
4. Barani, p. 303.
5. Habib and Nizami, ibid; K.S. Lal, ibid; Irfan Habib, ibid.
6. Khazain, p. 814; Isami, pp. 313-15.
7. Barani, pp. 170-5.
8. Ibid., pp. 262-3.
9. Ibid., pp. 220-4; Isami, pp. 228-36.
10. Barani, pp. 239-40; Isami, p. 239.
11. The *man* of those days consisted of 4 *sers*, and 1 *ser* was 24 *tolas* in weight. Habib and Nizami, p. 379.
12. Barani, pp. 239-40; Isami, p. 245.
13. Ibid., pp. 242-4.
14. Ibid., p. 246.
15. Ibid., p. 248.
16. Ibid., p. 247.
17. Ibid., p. 250-4.
18. Ibid., p. 250.
19. Ibid., p. 259.
20. Ibid., pp. 254-5; Khazain, pp. 120-4.
21. Ibid., p. 261.
22. Isami, pp. 315-16.
23. *Khair-al-Majalis*, pp. 240-1; Habib and Nizami, pp. 374-5.
24. Barani, pp. 304-19.
25. Ibid., p. 316.
26. Habib and Nizami, p. 377.
27. Barani, pp. 304-18.
28. Ibid., p. 312.
29. Ibid., pp. 308-18.
30. Isami, pp. 315-16, *Khair-al-Majalis*, p. 241; Barani, p. 305; Khazain, p. 9.
31. Habib and Nizami, p. 388.
32. Barani, pp. 64-5; Habib and Nizami, p. 289.
33. Barani, pp. 284-5.
34. Ibid., p. 303.
35. Ibid., p. 319.
36. Ibid., pp. 303-4, 319.
37. K.S. Lal, p. 220.

New Light on Timurid Relations with the Saiyid Sultans of Delhi

Ishtiyaq Ahmad Zilli

Saiyid Sultans of Delhi, who ruled from 1414 to 1451,[1] owed their rise to power to Timur. Khizr Khan, founder of the dynasty, had joined the entourage of Timur while the latter was marching to Delhi and before his departure from India he assigned the territories of Multan, Depalpur and Delhi to him.[2] But it was only after a protracted struggle extending over a period of fifteen years that Khizr Khan could succeed in taking possession of Delhi. It is generally acknowledged that Khizr Khan continued to recognize Timur and his successor, Shah Rukh, as his overlords, possibly nominal.[3] During his entire tenure of seven years he did not assume titles of royalty and continued to style his court as *Rayat-i A'la* (Sublime Standard).[4] But it is not very clear whether he accepted any other obligations relating to *khutba* and *sikka* as well. Similarly, the nature of the relationship of the successors of Khizr Khan and the Timurids is not clear. It is believed that the 'fiction' of allegiance of the Saiyid rulers to the Timurids was brought to an end by Mubarak Shah, the son and successor of Khizr Khan.[5] It is obvious that the problem has not been properly investigated and the evidence available on the subject in the contemporary and near contemporary sources such as *Tarikh-i Muhammadi* of Bihamad Khani, *Matla' S'adain* of Abdur Razzaq Samarqandi and *Ahsanut Tawarikh* of Hasan Rumlu, etc., has not been fully utilized.

It would appear from the evidence gleaned from these sources that, contrary to the contention of the modern historians, whatever reservations some of the Saiyid Sultans might have entertained regarding the nature of this relationship, they continued to fulfil the obligations towards the Timurids which were accepted by Khizr Khan at the time of the assignment of these territories to him. These obligations included not only allegiance to the Timurids but also entailed payment of annual tribute as well as recitation of *khutba* and coining of money in their name.[6] Contemporary history, *Tarikh-i Muhammadi*, which was compiled by Bihamad Khani in 1438 at Kalpi,[7] contains evidence that conclusively proves it. It records:

> In Delhi which is the dome of Islam (*qubbatul Islam*) and the centre of the government of Hindustan, the orders of that exalted Badshah (Shah Rukh) have been in force for the last forty years. The amount of tribute that has been customary from the time of Amir Timur has been reaching the imperial court of Amir Shah Rukh without any delay and the kings and sultans of Delhi have been graced with the robes of honour from that Monarch. Several times robes of honour and standard was brought from Heriv (Heart) to Delhi for Khizr Khan bin Sulaiman. After the death of Khizr Khan, emissaries brought throne and *chatr* for his son Mubarak Khan bin Khirz Khan from Heriv to Delhi in 827/4123. After the death of Mubarak Khan, Malik Budh, a grandson of Khizr Khan, became the ruler of Delhi and assumed the title of Sultan Muhammad. He also has been loyal to him till this date 839(1435).[8]

At another place the same author adds albeit in a rather general vein: 'In all the countries of Arab and Ajam and the territories of Hind and Sind *sikka* and *khutba* was adorned by the name of Timur and his sons.'[9]

In the light of this rather definite evidence, the nature of the relationship that existed between the Timurids and the Saiyid Sultans becomes quite clear. It shows that at least till the time of the compilation of *Tarikh-i Muhammadi* in 1438, *khutba* was recited in the name of Shah Rukh at Delhi; coins were struck in his name and regular tribute was sent to his court. Moreover, the Saiyid rulers received from the Timurids almost all those favours and insignia, which are vouchsafed by sovereigns to their subordinates such as robes of honour, throne and *chatr*. It is corroborated by some other contemporary and near contemporary sources as well.[10]

Apart from the information contained in these sources which goes to prove this position beyond any reasonable doubt, some new and definitive evidence has come to light on the subject in the form of a *farman* issued by Ulugh Beg (1447-9) and addressed to the last Saiyid Sultan, Alauddin Alam Shah (1445-51), assigning to him the government of Delhi and its dependencies.[11] This document is contained in Abul Qasim Namakin's *Munshaat-i Namakin*, an important *insha* collection coming down from the reign of Akbar.[12] Saiyid Abul Qasim Namakin, a noble of some consequence under Akbar and Jahangir, hailed from a distinguished family of Khurasan.[13] His father, Mulla Mir, is said to have been a trustee of the shrine of Imam Ali Riza at Mashhad.[14] This family background may partly explain strong presence of documents relating to Khurasan and Central Asia included in the *Munshaat-i Namakin*. The documents relating to Central Asia included in the *Munshaat* have a very wide range. These include appointment orders, *fathnamas* and a large number of letters of different categories.

This *farman* adds a new dimension to India's relations with the Timurids during the first half of the fifteenth century. It goes even beyond other contemporary and near contemporary sources in reaffirming the subordinate position of the Saiyid Sultans of Delhi vis-a-vis the Timurids. It shows that not only Khizr Khan, the founder of the Saiyid dynasty, owed his rise to power to Timur but his successors were also confirmed in their position by the contemporary Timurid rulers till the very end. In spite of the fact that some of these rulers did not apparently relish this unequal relationship and seem to have strong reservations about it, they were nevertheless obliged to live with it as their attempts to shake it off did not succeed.[15] Therefore the contents of the *farman* more than prove the contention of the author of *Tarikh-i Muhammadi* and other sources. English translation of the *farman* and a brief analysis are being presented here for the consideration of the scholars.

The text included in the *Munshaat* does not contain the name of the issuing authority as also that of the person to whom it is addressed and who is being thereby assigned the government of Delhi and its dependencies. This is clearly due to the deliberated decision of the compiler to omit names and dates of most of the documents he has included in his collection. The obvious reason for this shortcoming is that he visualized his compilation not as a collection of the documents of historical significance but simply as a volume containing illustrations of different kinds of *insha* writings for those interested in learning this art. The main criteria before the compiler, therefore, would be to make available to the readers excellent specimens of every possible kind of documents to be used as a model.[16]

However, since the *farman* contains obvious references to Timur and Shah Rukh as the predecessors of the ruler issuing the *farman* and mentions the names of Khizr Khan, Mubarak Khan and Muhammad Khan as the forerunners of the recipient, it would not perhaps be far-fetched to assume that this is a formal *farman* granted by Ulugh Beg to the last Saiyid ruler, Alauddin Alam Shah, after the latter's accession in 1445. The internal evidence, the setting of the *farman* and the language and the terms used clearly indicate that it is a copy of a genuine and authentic document. Moreover, as noticed earlier, its contents are fully corroborated by contemporary and near contemporary sources.

A closer scrutiny of the *farman* brings out some very interesting points. First, it is noteworthy that the *farman* describes the confirmation of Alauddin Alam Shah on the throne of Delhi as the conferment of a *suyurghal* consisting of Delhi and its dependencies, which could imply that Timurids considered Hindustan as a part of their dominions and regarded the Saiyid rulers of Delhi as their subordinates. As noticed earlier, the Timurids sought to reinforce this position by constantly sending robes of honour, throne and *chatr* and ensuring that the obligations accepted by the Saiyids were scrupulously discharged. In case of any default, prompt action was taken to force them to adhere to these obligations. Second, it suggests that not only Khizr Khan owed his rise to kingship to the Timurids but his successors Mubarak Khan and Muhammad Khan were also confirmed in their succession by Shah Rukh. It may be noted that the *farman* does not use any title for Khizr Khan and his successors higher than *malik*, *malik zada* and *khan*. This is clearly meant to remind them of their obligations towards the Timurids. It need not be emphasized that the words used in a formal *farman* are very carefully chosen. Lastly, confirming Alauddin Alam Shah in the government of Delhi and its dependencies, the nobles and officials are directed to consider those territories as an the *suyurghal* of the above-mentioned great Malik and to consider him as independent ruler and rightful *wali* and *badshah*. They are further directed to remit *ma-iwajib* and *huquq-i diwani* to him, season after season, and year after year. If the words like *wali* and *badshah* are not taken very seriously, and the contents of this *farman* are compared with the Mughal *farmans* of land grants, not much difference will be noticed. This does not leave much scope for speculation about the nature of relationship that existed between the Saiyid Sultans of Delhi and the Timurids.[17]

Text of Ulugh Beg's Farman *to Alauddin Alam Shah*

The roots of the royal plant, the branches of the great imperial tree, the great nobles, the powerful *wazirs*, the pillars of the mighty kingdom, the grandees of the resplendent presence, the inhabitants of the threshold of the court, the keepers of the vestibule which is the asylum of the world, the people of ranks and distinctions, the commanders of *tomans* and *hazarjat*, along with the notables of the routes and the grandees of the provinces like the eminent *naqibs*, the *imams* of the age, the officials of the territories, the protectors of the people, the *ri'aya* at large and the entire populace of such and such country may know that whereas with the assistance of the divine armies of the victory and success and the means of infinite fortune and felicity, the kingdom of Khurasan, which from ages and generations had been our inherited seat of the throne of the *khilafat* and the *qiblah* of the fortunes of the great reigning kings, came under our possession in the best way and under the influence of the most illustrious fortune, and the writer (*munshi*) of the *diwan* of 'verily we made you rulers of earth'[18] adorned and decorated the dignified *manshur* of *khilafat* in our august name with the pen of authority and permanence in accordance with 'do good (to others) as Allah has done good to you,'[19] our full determination, which is capable of achieving great things, is directed, viewing (the situation) with the eye of wisdom and the pupil of circumspection, to assign the control of the events and affairs of every country and every region to one of the discerning officials, so that, reflecting the radiance of understanding in the realm of competence and traversing the stages of the dispensation of justice and rendering assistance to the subjects with caution and vigilant steps, he might join the needs and requirements of the needy and the indigent with fulfillment and success and thereby strengthen the foundations of the requisites of peace and order and the regulations that might ensure justice and equity among the various categories of the *Ummah*, who are the best trusts of the Creator, rendering thereby the gardens of goodness afresh, bounties of the blessing unlimited, general populace happy and entire territories prosperous specially so the country of Hindustan, which is distinguished for its towns and cities throughout the world with addition of renown and esteem.

When the Wielder of the supreme authority of 'He it is who makes you travel by land and sea'[20] conferred on the victorious, triumphant conqueror of the countries, the exalted majesty of Sahib-i Qiran (Timur), the divine grace and he led his armies to the farthest regions of Hind with a view to revive the good deed of *jihad*. Wherever he reached the divine forces of victory hastened for the reception of his august person in a way account of which is boldly written on the pages of time with full detail. Many a towns and forts did he conquer and the signs of vice and infidelity did he erase from all coasts and the rest of the places of those regions. Afterwards, the great malik, the perfection of the state and the religion Khizr Khan, who before this, by the guidance of good fortune, had turned the face of sincerity towards the exalted threshold and had been graced with honour of kissing the ground, and had accompanied the imperial retinue like the good fortune, was exalted and distinguished among the equals and compeers and, being singled out for the imperial favours and considerations, the august mandate of the government of Delhi and the dependencies thereof was issued in his name out of ever-increasing favours. After his death, his sons of praiseworthy qualities, Malik Mubarak Khan, Malik Muhammad Khan and Malik Darya Khan,[21] who ere the fruits of the tree of *Siyadat* and the pupil of the eye of majesty and dominion, attained the good fortune of ruling an governing that territory during the reign of Khaqan-i-Said (Shah Rukh).

Now the worthy descendant of the Khan of the blessed family of sovereignty, the prince (*malik zada*), the most noble, the one of excellent origin, the ruler of the territories of Hind by the right of inheritance and deserts, the chosen one of the age, world-adorning chief, the successor of the kings, the binder of the enemies, the resolver of difficulties, the object of divine favours, the supporter of the state and religion . . . who is well-known for the excess of courage and firmness and possessed of extreme intelligence and discernment, the signs of whose descent for leadership and the lights of whose nobleness and ability to rule are evident from the forehead of his affairs aspirations in accordance with the dictum 'noble son follows his illustrious forefathers', getting himself enrolled in the cadre of the victorious court wishes to revive the traditions of his late father, and therefore in accordance with 'we found our fathers on a course, and surely we are guided by their footsteps,'[22] we have assigned the government (*ayalat wa sultanat*) of the kingdom of Delhi and the dependencies thereof on permanent basis (*ala sabil il istiqlal*) to him and gave the reins of administration of all affairs, administrative and fiscal (*mulki wa mali*), in his power and authority. It is the duty of the nobles, grandees and the (other) groups of the inhabitants, the commonality throughout all the cities, towns and districts, the dwellers of the deserts, throughout land and sea, that considering those territories as *suyurghal* of the above-mentioned great Malik, should recognize him as independent ruler (*hakim wa farmanrawa alal itlaq*) and rightful governor (*wali*) of those regions and remit *mal-i wajibi* and *huquq-i diwani* to him season after season and year after year in full without any deficiency, should not go against his advice and should take every care in this regard.

NOTES

1. Saiyid dynasty was established with Khizr Khan's capture of Delhi in 1414 and came to an end with the abdication of Alauddin Alam Shah in favour of Bahlul Lodi in 1451. Cf. Yahya Sirhindi, Tarikh-i *Mubarak Shahi*, ed. M. Hidayat Hossain, Asiatic Society of Bengal, Calcutta, 1931, pp. 18, 181; Muhammad Qasim Hindu Shah, *Tarikh-i Frishta*, Newal Kishore edn., Vol. I, p. 159.
2. There is much difference of opinion among the chroniclers regarding the actual territories assigned to Khirz Khan by Timur. According to Sharfuddin Ali Yazdi (*Zafar Nama*, *Bib. Indica*, Vol. II, p. 75) only Multan was conferred upon him. Bihamad Khani (*Tarikh-i Muhammadi*, British Museum Manuscript, OR 137, f. 306b) states that office of the *Shihna* and government of Delhi was given to him. Shahabuddin Ahmad (*Ajaib ul Maqdur fi Akhbar-i Timur*, Matba Usmani, Misr, 1350, p. 71) would seem to suggest

that Timur appointed him as his deputy over all his possessions in India. *Tarikh-i Mubarak Shahi* contains two different versions: according to one Delhi was bestowed upon him (p. 166) while the other describes the assignment of Multan and Depalpur (p. 167). Babur (*Babur Nama,* trans. A.S. Beveridge, Delhi, 1979, p. 481) would appear to suggest that Delhi was given to him. A *farman* of Ulugh Beg reproduced by Abul Qasim Namakin (*Munshaat-i Namakin*, India Office Ms. No 2064, ff. 28a-29a) shows that Delhi and its dependencies were assigned to him. Peter Jackson (*The Delhi Sultanate: A Political and Military History*, Cambridge University Press, Cambridge, 1999, pp. 318-19) considers Sirhindi's claim regarding the assignment of Delhi as 'apocryphal' and thinks it was an attempt to bolster the legitimacy of Sayyid dynasty.

3. For example, see R.P. Tripathi, *Some Aspect of Muslim Administration*, Allahabad, 1974, pp. 78-80; K.S. Lal, *Twilight of the Sultanate*, New Delhi, 1963, pp. 71-2; Aziz Ahmad, *Studies in the Islamic Culture in the Indian Environment*, Oxford, 1964, pp. 10, 19. Peter Jackson (pp. 318-19, 322), however, basing himself on the evidence of Bihamad Khani, says that Khizr Khan acknowledged the overlordship of Timur and paid tribute to Shah Rukh and the family continued to received orders from the Timurids for forty years
4. Abul Fazl writes that 'Khizr Khan in gratitude (to Timur) did not assume the regal title but styled his court 'The Sublime Standards'. See Abul Fazl, *Ain-i Akbari*, English translation by H.S. Jarret, Orient Book Reprint Centre, New Delhi, 1978, Vol. II, p. 312. *Tarikh-i Mubarak Shahi* (181) also refers to Khizr Khan as *Rayat-i A'la* though it uses the title of Shah for Sultan Mubarak and Sultan Muhammad.
5. Tripathi, p. 7; Aziz Ahmad, p. 10.
6. Ivaglu has in fact preserved a letter of Shah Rukh Mirza, which was written in response to an earlier letter of Khizr Khan where he had sought the permission of the Timurid Ruler to include his name in the *khutba* and *sikka*. Shah Rukh not only gave the permission but also supplied the text of the *khutba* that was to be read in the mosques. See Haider Ali Evoglu, *Majma ul Insha*, British Museum Ms., OR 3482, ff, 38b-39a cited by Aziz Ahmad, p. 19 and n. 5. For a copy of the letter of Shah Rukh containing at the end the text of the *khutba*, see Abdul Husian Nawai, *Asnad wa Mukatabat-i Tarikhi-i Iran*, Bungah-i Tarjumah wa Nashr-i Kitab, Tehran, 1241, pp. 143-5. For English version of the text of the *khutba*, see T.W. Arnold, *The Caliphate*, London, 1965, pp. 113-14.
7. For information about the book, see *Tarikh-i Muhammadi*, English translation by Muhammad Zaki, Department of History, Aligarh Muslim University, Aligarh, Asia Publishing House, Bombay, 1972, Preface.
8. *Tarikh-i Muhammadi*, ff.311b-312a.
9. Ibid., f. 304b.

10. *Ain-i Akbari*, Vol. II, 312; Nizamuddin Ahmad, *Tabaqat-i Akbari*, Newal Kishore, edn., pp. 133-4; *Firishta*, Vol. I, p. 162; T.W. Arnold, *The Caliphate*, London, 1965, pp. 113-14.
11. *Munshaat-i Namakin*, India Office MS, ff. 28a-29a.
12. So far only three MSS of the book have been noticed. These are available in India Office Library (*Catalogue India Office Library*, pp. 1141-2, No. 2064), Maulana Azad Library, Aligarh Muslim University, Aligarh (University Coll. No. 26, 27, *Farsiya Nasr*) and Salar Jung Museum, Hyderabad (*Catalogue of Persian Manuscripts*, Salar Jung Museum Library, Vol. III, pp. 78-9, No. 790).
13. For information about Abul Qasim Namakin, see Farid Bhakkari, *Zakhirat-ul Khawanin*, ed. Saiyid Moinul Haq, Pakistan Historical Society, Karachi, 1961, Vol. I, pp. 198-200; Shah Nawaz Khan, *Maasir-ul Umara*, *Bib. Indica*, Vol. III, pp, 74-6; Ali Sher Qani Thattavi, *Tuhfat-ul Kiram*, Matba Nasiri, Delhi, 1304 H., Vol. II, p. 127.
14. Ali Sher Qani, Thattavi, *Tuhfat-ul Kiram*, Vol. II, p. 127.
15. *Tarikh-i Mubarak Shahi*, p. 218; *Tarikh-i Firishta*, Vol. I, p. 167. Firishta clearly suggests that the real cause behind Shaikh Ali's expedition was Mubrak's departure from the conciliatory policy of his father.
16. For a detailed discussion on the subject, see I.A. Zilli, Department of Insha literature till the end of Akbar's Reign, in Muzaffar Alam, Francoise 'Nalini' Delvoye and Gaborieau (eds.), *The Making of Indo-Persian Culture*, Centre de Sciences Humaines, Manohar, Delhi, 2000, pp. 309-49.
17. For a detailed discussion on the relations of Saiyid Sultans with the Timurids, see I.A. Zilli, 'Relations of Saiyid Sultans of Delhi with the Timurids—A Reappraisal', in Nazir Ahmad and Asloob Ahmad Ansari (eds.), *Fakhruddin Memorial Volume*, Ghalib Institute, New Delhi, 1994, pp. 221-8.
18. Koran, 10/14.
19. Koran, 27/77.
20. Koran, 10/22.
21. Inclusion of Darya Khans name seems to be transcriber's mistake, as he did not belong to the Saiyid ruling family.
22. Koran, 43/22.

Timur's Image in the Contemporary Sources

Mansura Haidar

A close study of the sources indicates that Timur belonged to that category of unfortunate historical personalities who have been largely misunderstood and were, therefore, depicted in contemporary and later sources rather inadequately. While court historians have often been suspected of producing intentional records, the prejudiced comments of hostile historians of the consquered regions who had exaggerated the devastations allegedly perpetrated by Timur in Eastern world gained currency quite conveniently. The Indo-Persian sources were no exception in this respect. Even the authenticity of Timur's autobiography the *Tuzukat-i-Timuri* which is an account of his statesmanship and high administrative talents has been challenged. An attempt is, therefore, being made in this paper to enrich the already existing data on Timur's life and his cultural achievements and to present an objective analysis of a hitherto unknown and rare evidence contained in contemporary and later historical sources.

Timur had been denounced by certain medieval and modern historians as a 'terror', or 'viper', though he has been placed by others in the category of world's great conquerors like Chingiz, Alexander, Attila and Napoleon and his 'bigness' is said to be 'unquestionable'.[1]

The scenes on his birth are said to carry ominous forebodings[2] by some chroniclers while the presence of the power of Mars in his horoscope had been highlighted by others.[3]

While evaluating a controversial figure like Timur, that the constraints of his situation had circumstantial determinents ought not to be ignored. On the one hand, Timur 'represents the culmination of an old tradition', and on the other (and perhaps more strongly), he emerges as an epitome of Turco-Mongol and Perso-Islamic aspirations and an embodiment of their combined traditions from which he drew his sustenance alternately and almost equally. The crisis of identification created by contradictory forces which were then at work, compelled

Timur to adopt a flexible attitude in the beginning though gradually he managed to increase his sphere of influence making it more broad-based and supported by diverse elements.

On the eve of Timur's birth, Central Asia was passing through a phase of 'universal confusion'. Timur certainly deserves credit not only for carving out an empire for himself but also for providing stability to a vast region. Indeed, Timur had largely affected (if not totally transformed) the course of historical developments in and around Transoxiana during his regime. The conqueror not only deposed and appointed kings in the neighbouring regions (of Dashti Qipchaq, India) but was willingly drawn into the Eurasian politics also. His campaigns, however destructive and 'lacking in geographical coherence', were certainly beneficial for his own empire as they were productive and money generating.

It was merely through his 'courage and capacious intellect' that Timur brought under his control and into his permanent possession, the countries of Transoxiana, Khwarazm, Turkestan, Khurasan, the two Iraqs, Azerbaijan, Persia, Mazindaran, Kirman, Diyar-i Bakr, Khuzistan, Egypt, Syria, Asia Minor and other places. Like Chingiz, Timur also claimed to have waged war for higher objectives. Al Hasan the Arab says that Timur frequently boasted that 'he was born to this end, and that he must take in these exercises his principal delights: for every other thing wherein he did exercise himself was but borrowed, being appointed and called of God to punish the pride of Tyrants'.[4]

Timur's claims to such timely succour which he offered to the subjects of the conquered states are confirmed by the available sources. *Alnujumuz zahira* refers to the anarchy prevailing on the eve of Timur's invasions but even Abul Fazal also confirms that since 'all the systematic administration and knowledge of affairs ceased to exist and the government fell into discredit' 'the sublime standards approached. Notwithstanding the conquest of so populous kingdoms, the booty obtained was not important, and the invaders impelled by love of their native land, retired from the country'.

Yazdi appreciated Timur's expansionist activities in high sounding words. But Timur seemed to be wise enough not to extend his domain beyond a particular extent as he knew that the occupation and defence of these places would be difficult. In India, Turkey and other places, therefore, he contented himself with the demands of allegiance and tribute. His diplomatic skill is discernible from his letters sent to various contemporary Eastern and Western diplomatic potentates. Equally impressive was his performance in dealing with internal elements like Mongols and Sarbadars.[5]

The so-called 'treacherous attitude' of Timur towards Qara Tatars, Jalairs or Sarbadars should be viewed in true perspective. The Tatars were numerous, war-like, active and well equipped with arms. Any tribal resurgence could be a threat to peace and prosperity of the land. Fearing the belligerant spirit of such tribes, Timur 'scattered their society, emptied home, their assemblage and dispersed them in deserts and marshy valley. One such group was banished to Kashghar, another to the frontier post between the limits of Khatas and Indians and still another to Duwira near Issikkul. It could certainly be argued that this stern and harsh administration was perhaps the need of the hour. Timur suppressed all those who presented a stumbling block to the stability of the country. Thus, the other 'crowd of rogues of different sorts'—among them wrestlers, swordsmen, boxers and mounte banks with all their 'obstinacy and hostilities' were a source of anarchy and trouble for Timur in Samarqand. They too were removed through strategem.

Timur clearly perceived the blessings of enlightened despotism and evils inherent in a tribal structure and in the existence of insurgents. He crystallized them in the speech he delivered to the Tatars:

> If you are equal among yourselves, without a leader, they will plunge in their blood at their pleasure; there is no prosperity for men, who are equal among themselves, except through princes; and not even through princes, if the foolish among them rule.
>
> But I am not always with you nor have I two right hands to defend you, therefore, to strengthen your condition there is need of order and to guide your assembly laws and statues are needed, house keeping would yield the best result and safety; and the first law should be: to set up an Imam, who would bring leaders and people to imitate his actions; then to arrange the whole society in suitable order and assign to each his place of obedience, and next to administer justice, hand the reins of office and administration to those who are fit for them, advance every worthyman to that of which he is worthy and when your counsels agree and your aims are united, then your sons will be powerful and your enemies will be overthrown, and with one hand resisting, your foes, you will rise superior to your enemies and opponents.

Obviously Timur's successful political activities aroused antagonism and invited wrath and unfavourable comments from the chroniclers, some of whom say that he was 'lacking either reason or religions', that he 'acted the part of a fox'—'the advancing—climbed gradually, lame though he was, to his desired eminence', having 'no course but sedition, rebellion, ferocity and outrage until he achieved his destiny'.[6]

At least in this context Al Hasan also supports Ibni Arab by saying that Timur had once told him on the eve of a battle that 'I should not so much trust unto the lion's skin, wherein I wrap my arme, that I should not serve myself with the Foxes, to wrap therewith my head'.

It cannot be denied that Timur often resorted to unfair means though, more often than not, these were justified by the ends. Any vindication for the (mis)deeds of a medieval monarch is neither possible nor feasible. Nevertheless the greatness of such a ruler may be judged not by the preconceived notions of distorted facts presented by subjective accounts of medieval chroniclers but—retrospectively in the true perspective—to be more concrete in the light of his contribution to the world civilization, to the betterment of people in general and to the welfare and prosperity of his compatriots in particular.

Undoubtedly, Timur was somewhat different from other Easten conquerors like Chingiz and Mahmud Ghznavi, both in psyche and an attitude towards international relations and, above all, in the sphere of contribution to human civilization. Examined in the perspective of his age, with all the relative concomittants of the medieval times, Timur stands out as a conscientious and a living symbol of aspirations of his countrymen. In a world ravaged by the anti-social elements in the wake of Mongol invasion, he could bring stability, security and prosperity. The chroniclers are at times justified in praising Timur for his multifarious achievements. A review of sources, therefore, seems essential for a monarch of medieval times.

Yazdi portrays him as 'Perfectman' (*Kamil al zat*),[7] divinely inspired, divinely guided and an interpreter of unknown secrets. Abul Fazl describes Timur as *Salisul-qutbin*[8] either in the sense of 'a pole supplemental to the two poles' or that he was an embodiment of three kinds of poles, namely, *qutbul millat* (pole of religious community), *qutbud-din* (pole of faith), and *qutbud-duniya* (pole of the world or realm). It is also probable that the three circles set to shape a triangle on the special armoxial bearing to signify that 'Timur is lord of three quarters of the world'.[9] Al Hasan the Arab asserts that 'this prince was induced with such knowledge, as made him admired of the people where he commanded, who are for the most part great wonderers, in so much as this caused him to be accounted a prince accompanied with the Divine Vertue, considering the justice he used in all his actions'. The same traveller further comments upon his personal magnetism (the

'Divine beauty' of his 'majestic eyes and hair)', 'modesty', 'comeliness', 'carrying away the prizes therein whether it were in shooting with his bow, or changing horses in the middle of the courses or in breaking an iron in running at the Quitaine; he made everyone wonder at his dexterite'.

Abni Arab Shah, a contemporary chronicler who had seen Timur personally, portrays him as of 'a tall and of lofty stature though he belonged to the remnants of the Almalekites, big in brow and head, mighty in strength and courage, wonderful in nature, white in colour, mixed with red, but not dark, stout of limb, with broad shoulders, thick fingers, long legs, perfect build, long beard, dry hands, lame on the right side, with eyes like candles, without brilliance, powerful in voice; he did not fear death'.[10] Another Arab chronicler (who is said to be closely connected with Timur), however, depicted him as a man whose 'stature was of the middle sort, somewhat narrow in his shoulders, he had a fair leg and strong, the strength of his body was such as nobody surpassed, his visage was courteous and well proportioned; he had but little hair on his chin, he did wear his hair long and curled'.[11]

Timur is said to be 'firm in mind, strong and robust in body, brave and fearless, like a hard rock. He did not love jest and falsehood, wit and sport pleased him not; truth though troublesome to him pleased him; he was not sad in adversity or joyful in prosperity. . . . He did not allow in his company obscene talk or talk of bloodshed or captivity, rapine, plunder and violation of the norm. He was spirited and brave and inspired awe and obedience. . . . He excelled in plans that struck the mark and in the wonders of physiogromy; was excellent in fortune, of apt diligence firm of purpose and truthful in business. A debater, who by one look and glance comprehended the matter aright, trained, watchful for the slightest sign; he was not deceived by intricate fallacy nor did hidden flattery pass him; he discerned keenly between truth and fiction and caught the sincere counsellor and the pretended by the skill of his cunning, like a hawk trained for the chase so that for his thoughts he was judged a shining star and the arrow of every star, making straight for the mark, imitated the sagacity of his judgement.

Al Hasan adds that one could not perceive any alteration in the prince's countenance, adversity and judgement. He saw openly the vicissitudes of things, 'as one sees with keen eye a thing perceived by the senses'. In 'cunning and craft, Timur excelled Sasan (the ancestor of Sassanid Emperor of Persia) and Abu Zaid and by his wisdom and arguments surpassed Ibni Sina (Avicenna) and by his logic reduced the

Greeks to silence, when he overturned propositions against them and conciliated deadly foes and made the bitterest enemies into friends'.

Timur drank no wine. By nature, Timur spurned actors and poets though to his inner circle he admitted soothsayers and physicians and was attracted by their talk and gave ear to discourse. Since Amir Safiuddin was well versed in *qawaidi nujumi wa ahkami raml* (rules of astronomy and regulations of geomancy) his advices regarding the propriety of timings were often heeded.[12]

While Ahmad Ibni Arab says that 'Timur was an "*ummi*" (uneducated) reading writing and understanding nothing in the Arabic tongue, but of Persian Turkish and the Mughal language he understood enough but no more', another Arab Al Hasan (who was a close 'companion' of Timur), however, records that 'Timur was well instructed in the Arabian learning and exercised himself much therein'. The chroniclers, however, unanimously confirm that 'Timur was constant in reading annals and histories of the prophets of blessed memory and the exploits of kings and accounts of those things which had formerly happened to men abroad and at home and all this in the Persian tongue'.[13]

Timur himself once asserted that 'I am intimate with learned men, to whom I am greatly devoted and in whose company I delight and I have the ancient zeal for learning.' Timur was 'greatly given to reading and learning stories' with a memory so sharp that when 'readings were repeated before him and those accounts filled his ears, he seized hold of that matter and so possessed it that it turned to habit, so that if the reader slipped, he would correct his error'.

Timur had a great liking for scholars and theologians, loved learned men and admitted to his inner reception nobles of the family of Mohammad; 'he gave the highest honour to the learned and doctors and preferred them to all others and received each of them according to his rank and granted them honour and respect'. A bitter critic of Timur like Ibni Arab Shah, however, describes how after the conquest of Halab, Timur had summoned the learned men of the conquered region conveying them through Maulavi Abdul Jabbar, of the famous ecclesiastical family of Samarqand, that the former wished to put such questions to them as remained unanswered even by the *ulama* of Samarqand, Bukhara, Herat, and all the cities with a definite warning that 'do not be like them and let none reply to me except your most learned and most eminent man, who rightly what he says that these *ulama* (including Ibni Arab Shah)' had already learnt about Timur that 'he troubled learned men by putting a certain question, which he used as a reason to put them to death or torture'. Ibni Arab Shah's appeal for mercy that 'Give thanks for this fortune (of numerous conquests) by sparing these Imams and slay none' met with the explanation offered by Timur followed by assurances that 'I slay no one of set purpose but you bring death on yourselves; but I, by Allah! Will slay none of you and you will be secure concerning your lives and goods.' The event quoted by Ibni Arab finds a parallel in the accounts of Indian sources.

Timur's love for discourse had even created confusion regarding his personal faith. Ibni Khaldun depicted Timur in the following words:

> Some attribute to him (Timur) knowledge, others attribute to him heresy because they note his preference for the 'members of the house of Ali (*ahlibait*) still others attribute to him employment of magic and sorcery, but in all these there is nothing; it is simply that he is highly intelligent and very perspicacious, addicted to debate and argumentation about what he knows and about what he does not know.

The believers in the proverb '*Qui ubique est musquam est*' (he who is of all religions is of none) may criticize Timur for his Mongolian legacy of eclectic and pantheistic approach as Timur 'held all religions in reverence'. Like Chingiz he had faith both in monotheism and monism as he

> worshipped only one God creator of all things. [He] often said that the greatness of Divinitie consisted in the Sundry kinds of people which are under the cope of Heaven who served the same diversely, nourishing itself with diversitie as the nature was diverse where it had printed his image, God remaining, notwithstanding, one in Essence, not receiving therein any diversitie. This was the reason that moved him to permit and grant the use of all religions within the countrys for his obedience always provided that they worshipped only one God.[14]

Shami, Yazdi and Hafiz Abru had depicted Timur as a *dindar* (constant in religion) who removed the rust of *bidat* (heresy), respected *sharia* and religion, held the *ahlibait* dear, and did everything for propagation of Islam; remained devoted to *sadat*, *ulama*, pious and righteous men, *mufti*, recluses and saints. Intead of wasting his time in the pursuit of wordly pleasure, he dedicated himself to prayers, reading of Holy Book and to acts of human welfare. Nevertheless, Timur was not an orthodox Muslim. Ibni Arab says that there were several kinds of people and nations as he had brought with him, giving liberty unto them all to fame and build their houses, causing money to be distributed to do the same and giving all kinds of privileges and freedoms unto the prisoners for to give them a grater desire to build and settle themselves there; and having caused the streets and places to be plotted, and having appointed a place for everyone to build upon'.

Even in his army there were 'men of intellect and learning and ability, poets and those excellent doctors, and among them defenders of the truth and students of the sciences and subtle explorers thereof and men who in every sort of science and its full investigation combined the double path of enquiry, logic and perception, approving the principle of the Sufis the revival of sciences'.[15]

Shaikh Shamsuddin Kulal who is said to have greatly honoured and respected Amir Targhi (the father of Timur) due to his 'spiritual and temporal eminence', had by his 'spiritual insight' prophesied about the advent of the star of Timur. The early supporters of Timur included Shamsuddin Fakhuri who being 'of greatest authority in those parts, was consulted by all in affairs of state and religion'. Having made a pilgrimage to the tomb of Khwaja Ahamd Yarawi in 1397, Timur ordered for the construction of a mosque which in Babur's time says that the tomb was 'still dominating the town', and was a 'pilgrims's land mark'.[16] During his visit to Andikhud, Timur, 'out of good intentions and sincerity met Baba Sanku' who happened to be one of the renowned saint of his times.

Timur had asserted that 'I have not won success except by the aid of Saiyid Baraka who 'supported with his prayers what Timur did with his sword'. Such was the deep regard entertained by Timur for this revered saint that the latter's body was 'exhumed from Andikhud for reburial in Samarqand by Timur's wish and there laid in such a position that Timur's body was at its feet.

Timur believed that 'if a prince would be strong and secure, he must attach to him the religious'.[17] Nevertheless in his attitude towards the learned men and theologians, he used 'familiarity and an abatement of his majority; in his arguments with them he mingled moderation with splendour, clemency with rigour and covered his severity with kindness'.[18] The claim of certain modern writers that Timur listened to the dictates of *mullas* is not supported by the sources. It was only once that Timur had invited religious groups to assist him in his efforts to exterminate financial bungling in the revenue administration—a rare honour accorded to much neglected class of esslesiastics which was harped upon by Shami and Yazdi to vouchsafe for the piety and religious fervour of Timur. However, Timur had his own moments of uneasy relationship with the *mullas*. Shaikh Zayn u Din Abu Bakri Tayabadi (d. 791) a saint (*sahibi kamal*) Timur's contemporary did not care to pay respects to former after the conquest of Herat in AH 782 . Even Timur's messenger met with a rebuff from the saint that 'what have I to do with Timur', the world conqueror. Unlike Muhammad bin Tughlaq of India (who forcibly summoned to his court even a dying *mulla*), Timur personally visited the saint and 'upbraided' him for not advising Timur's tyrannical predecessor. The Shaikh's cool reply that 'I have indeed done so, but he would not listen, and God has now appointed you over him. However, I now advise you too to be just, and if you likewise do not listen, God will appoint another over you' struck Timur hard a second time. Timur is said to have commented later on that 'he had seen many dervishes; every one of them had said nothing with reference to himself'.[19] There were occasions when Timur out of expediency or necessity obliged the *mullas* as in the case of the Turcomans or the Indian captives who were released at the recommendation of Shaikh Ahmad Kathu.[20] Yet Timur's verdict in the context of his attitude is too unambiguous. Although he admits that a 'prince should make his laws according to the religion of his country' and that 'the teachers of the divine law should be appointed', he reaffirms that only 'the prince is the judge of ecclesiastic matters'.[21]

After his victory in Delhi, Timur ordered all the inhabitants to be made prisoners (since some of Timur's soldiers were killed by the people of the city) and took them all off towards Transoxiana. Eventually Shaikh Ahamd Kathu the famous saint of his times went along with the army and had an interview with the Great Timur and made apparent to him his condition as a dervish, and his surpassing knowledge. Moreover the Shaikh argued with the learned doctors who were with the Transoxianian forces and begged for the prisoners' lives. The Great Timur took such a strong liking for him that he acceded to his request and liberated all the prisoners. This signal service of the Shaikh remained forever as a debt upon the people of Hindustan.

In modern times to some of us the exploits of Timur seem to be obnoxious and his expansionist wars expose him to the allegations of nurturing imperialist ambitions, encroaching upon another country's freedom and violating human rights. Examined in the context of medieval scenario, Timur appears to be a paragon of humane approach and liberal values; one who managed to put down the anarchy prevalent in his country as well as in the neighbouring regions, enforce law and order and introduce justice and a benevolent government. It is generally believed that Timur's rule was that 'of an individual'. It was a 'government of overlapping structures and undefined institutions' which was 'a sign of primitivism' and which signifiy, 'the apparent failures of Timur and other normal sovereigns'.[22] In this context two things may be pointed out: the sources confirm the existence of a highly urbanized culture in Central Asia where a very well developed and nicely organized administrative system also existed ever since the days of Abbasids if not earlier. Ibni Khaldun pointed out that this region 'never ceased to have an abundant and continuous civilization and the tradition of scientific instruction has always persisted in them', and further inform us that their 'sedentary culture' was 'firmly established'. The same author has elsewhere argued that nomadism is necessitated by geographical drawbacks of a particular region and should not be necessarily a sure sign of a country's backwardness as diversity in unity is not an unusual feature in a country's cultural milieu. In this context the views expressed by Al Hasan Arab a contemporary of Timur are more explicit and relevant:

> Some of our Historigoraphers branded him (Timur) as the 'sonne of a shephered', but this have they said not knowing at all the customs of their countrey, where the principall revenue of the kings and Nobles consisteth in cattell, despising Gold and Silver but making great reckoning of such riches, wherein they abound in all sorts; this is the occasion wherefore call them shepherds and say also that this prince descended from them.[23]

The medieval chroniclers have also echoed that sedentary and pastoral (nomadic) culture coexisted in Central Asia where development of science and technology was at par (if not more) with other contemporary civilizations. Having inherited a well thought out and already practiced administrative structure, Timur need not evolve it from a scratch though certainly in the 'leisure of his declining years' and with a retrospective eye over the scenes of a long and arduous life, he is said to have compiled 'for the perpetual instruction of his imperial descendants, these rules of government and those measures of policy which himself had invariably followed; and from his history he collected several plans he had formed'.[24]

Ibni Arab Shah categorically mentions that 'after he (Timur) had settled the countries' he 'made laws for the kingdoms of Turkestan' a fact confirmed by following comments of Al Hasan that: 'The recreation he (Timur) did take were help for to ease him in the pains of his public affairs where unto God had called him. Having upon his return called together all the people he published his laws which were all reverenced of this people, as though they had proceeded from the Divinitie, so much admiration had everyone of the greatness of this prince'.[25]

Presumably these laws refer to the *Tuzukat-i Timuri* only as no other codified law is extant.

According to the prescribed norms of Timur 'a prince must be just and good as well as valiant'. Timur's stress on *Rasti Rusti* (truth is safety) shows how particular he was about imparting justice to his subjects for which he sat in *diwan khana* clad in a red robe and under him courts ceased to be venal.

Timur had introduced a very elaborate arrangement of justice. Al Hasan records that 'thṛee times in the week at Samarqand, Timur ministered open justice unto the meanest, in his imperial majesty—a thing which made him beloved of the people over whom he commanded'.[26]

There were three departments dealing simultaneously with cases of litigation and imparting justice, each in its own separate tent where the litigants and criminals were brought for hearing in civil, criminal and financial cases. While certain judges dealt with financial frauds and bungling in the government departments and revenue administration, another category of judges were in charge of the affairs of government 'Proctors' who resided in the outlying districts and cities and came all the way to present their complaints before Timur. The punishment for the crime was finally decided in the last court of application by Timur to whom all the matters were reported. Thereafter six by six and four by four the judgements were delivered. When any decree had to be put down in writing the judges ordered their 'scribes to attend and engrave it but writing is short and soon finished. No sooner it is engraved than it is copied into a register book which the scribes keep. It is charged to carry it into effect and he taking a silver seal engraved with its proper device inks this over and stamps it on the decree at its foot. Then another officer will take it and register it in his book. It is then brought back to the judge who finally affixes his own seal with ink.' When three or four of these decrees have been sealed and thus dispatched they take them and seal them with Timur's own official seal which is inscribed with the legend that proclaims 'This is the truth' or *Rasti Rusti*.

Timur ensured safety of travellers and traders by taking special measures of appointing guards at every step.[27] For him deliberation, counsel, vigilance and circumspection were 'the four assistants'.[28] Al Hasan describes that Timur dedicated four days of a week to give 'secret audience for the affairs of his state and took advice for matters of importance which were decided daily in his presence. . . .[29]

Although Persian sources stress that every class of population was well attended to and well-provided for. Clavijo describes that the condition of peasants was not very good and they were afraid of 'messengers', i.e. the revenue collectors of Timur. Similarly the artisans and the handicraftsmen were forced to sell all their goods at the rates prescribed by Timur in pursuance of the tax *tarh* which made them think that they were being 'robbed' by Timur. Contradiction is noticed in the account of Ibni Arab and Al Hasan regarding the plight of soldiers of Timur. The former highlights their miserable condition while Al Hasan says 'neither had he any other care than preserving the goodwill of his most famous soldiers'. A general picture given by the travellers and chroniclers, however, goes in favour of Timur. Clavijo who travelled throughout Central Asia in 1402 gives a very impressive depiction, his state:

> Samarqand was fertile in producing wheat in aboundance. Fruit trees with rich vineyards; livestock famous for having fat tails that weigh each some 20 lb. These flocks of sheep are so abundant that even when Timur is in camps and scarcely a couple of sheep can be had in market for the price of a *ducat*. Prices indeed are so low that for a Meri which is a coin worth 3 pence or half a *real*, you may have a bushel and a half of barley. Baked bread was plentiful, rice can be had cheap in any quantity. Richess and abundance of this great capital and its district is such as is a wonder to behold and it is for this reason that its name is rich town Simiz Kent (Lit. *Simiz* = rich, fat; *Kent* = town, i.e. rich town).

Hafiz Abru describes the major agrarian reforms undertaken by Timur.[30] Al Hasan also says that when a Chinese emperor came to see Timur, he was astonished to behold so many soldiers and the country so well replequished with people[31] and adds that the very fact of Timur using 'so little curiositie of riches in their apparel and garments, wondering that the Emperor was appareled in meane cloth of one colour, without any other fashion though to countervaile that he had about him men who seemed to be kings'. It is interesting to note that Hafiz Abru also stresses that in the *toi* where ten thousand people had assembled, none was dressed in cotton and all were richly clad.[32]

The author of *Khulasatul Akhbar* even goes to the extent of saying that at the time of Timur's death, the region of Samarqand distinguished itself as an excellent and prosperous place which was full of gold, silver, precious stones, grains, rarities, arms and encampments and regal fineries and surpassed the entire world in its wealth of learned men, scholars, artisans, competent artist, engineers, etc.[33] Apart from the immense booty[34] the revenue from customs imposed on all merchants who came form India and went to Samarqand and regions beyond was considerable to the state, since Timur was the 'sole master of the iron gate'.[35] Similarly Samarqand is 'accompanied with a fair river which causeth great traffique and makes it richer than any city within that country'.

Under Timur Samarqand was not only rich in food stuffs but also in manufacturing—such as factories of silk—both the kinds called *zaitumi* and *kimkhwab*, crapes, taffetas and stuffs which are called *tarcenals* in Spain which are all produced in great number.[36]

Clavijo found that the market of Samarqand 'amply stored with merchandise imported from distant and foreign countries'. He says that 'every year to Samarqand much merchandise of all kinds came from Cathay, India, Tartary and from many other quarters. In the countries round Samarqand and territories, commerce is very flourishing but there was as yet no place within the city where this merchandise might suitably be stored, displayed and offered for sale. Timur, therefore, gave orders that a street should be built to pass right through Samarqand which should have shops on both the sides.' During the construction of this market all the houses along the road were demolished and property holders had to quit as 'the builders erected shops each having two chambers front and back and streetway arched over with a domed roof with windows and water fountains. The cost of all this work was charged to the town council and workmen did not lack as were wanted by the overseer. In the course of 20 days whole new street was carried though.'[37]

Clavijo says that 'so great was the population now of all nationalities gathered together in Samarqand that of men with their families, the number they said must amount to 150,000 souls. Of the nations brought here together sects with Christians who were Greeks and Armenians, Catholics, Jacobites and Nestorians beside Indians.'[38]

The same traveller records that none was to be given passage from the province of Samarqand to go into the lands to the south of the river unless he was granted a 'permit' and a 'warrant' declaring 'whence he has come and whither he is about to go'. Such permits were demanded even from the free born natives of Samarqand. On the contrary any person coming into Samarqand 'may do so unhindered' and 'none need show any warrant for the passage where ferry boats have guards stationed in them, set there by the order of Timur to oversee and control the passage'. The reason being 'the immense captive brought by Timur from conquered places to collect orphans etc. forcibly to increase the population' which had 'by this fashion increased lately by him so as to number 100,000 souls or perhaps more'.[39]

Timur had taken special care to make his capital Samarqand populous and prosperous. Due to the constant efforts of this conqueror, Samarqand became a cosmpolitan city. It is in this context that the assertions of Al Hasan that Timur's conquests had brought glory to his empire seem to be convincing, Babur refers to the fact that the 'population without the city is more numerous than within the town' as beyond suburbs of Samarqand stretched great plains where there are many hamlets—all well populated for here the 'immigrant folks' are settled whom Timur has caused to be brought from the conquered lands.

Timur is said to be 'devoted to artists and craftsmen and to works of every sort if they had dignity and nobility'.[40] Timur had brought from Damascus learned men and craftsmen and 'all who excelled in any art, e.g. the most skilled weavers, tailors, gem cutters, carpenters, makers of head covering, furriers, painters, bow makers, feltcovers, in short craftsmen of every kind'. Likewise all his *amirs* and lords took multitude of lawyers, theologians, of men who knew the Koran from memory and learned men, craftsmen, workmen, slaves, women, boys and girls. All the skilled and expert professionals and handicraftsmen from Fars and Iraq were also dispatched to Samarqand.[41]

Ibni Arab also supports the view that 'In short Timur gathered from all sides and collected at Samarqand the fruits of everything; and that place accordingly had in every wonderful craft and rare art someone who excelled in wonderful skill and was famous beyond his rivals in his craft.' According to the details given by him, the list of the Musicians included: Abdul Qadir Maraghi, his son Safiuddin, and his son-in-law Nashrin, and Qutb of Mosul and Ardshir Janki and others.

Clavijo also supplements the above information. Due to its significance the entire passage is being reproduced here:

> Trade has always been fostered by Timur with the view of making his capital noblest of cities and during all his conquests wherever he came he carried off the best men of population to people of Samarqand bringing thither the mastercraftsmen of all nations. Thus from Damascus he carried away with him all weavers of that city, those who worked at the silk looms, the bow makers who produced crossbows which are so famous; likewise armourers, also craftsmen in glass and porcelain who are known to be the best in all the world. From Turkey he had brought the gunsmiths who make arquebus and all men of other crafts wheresoever he found them such as silversmiths and masons. These all were in very great numbers indeed so many had been brought together of all sorts and that of every denomination and kind you might find master workmen established in the capital. Again he had gathered to settle here in Samarqand

artillerymen both engineers and bombardiers in the capital besides those who make the rope by which these engines work.

The craftsmanship of the artisans was reflected through the account of various ceremonies. During state functions, *qurultais*, celebrations of royal weddings, these artisans were allowed to participate 'arrange a gala show—for each craft exhibition for spectators' and were 'under obligation to sell their goods and not, to return home unless permitted'. The celebration of Ulugh Beg's marriage at Kanigul in 840, for example, has been preceded by a general proclamation throughout the city inviting 'trading folks of the town' who sold stuff jewels with merchants for sale of goods of all sorts and artisans were to encamp at the Meadow with Horde, Shami, Yazdi, Clavijo, Ibni Arab Shah describe the beautiful

tents of different sort of which one had the upper and lower border interwoven with gold and were adorned within and without the finest raw silk; another was all woven of silk and decorated with various figures and flowers of diverse lines interwoven; a third was girt on every side, as by a crown, by great pearls, whose price is known to the knower of secrets alone; and another was decked with gems of various sort which set in broad curtains embroidered with gold dazzled the eye. In the midst also they set roofs of silver and stairs to ascend and doors for their houses and couches, on which they might recline; also painted leaves and tent curtains broadened with gold and marvellous tents and buildings, and in them fans of cloth of fine texture for coolness and other contrivances and cushions and keys and bolts. They also showed rare treasurers and hung there curtains of marvellous beauty and among them a curtain of cloth taken from the treasury of Sultan Aba Yazid, of which each part was about ten cubits of the new measure in breadth, decorated with various pictures of herbs, building and leaves, also of reptiles, and with figures of birds, wild beasts and forms of oldmen, youngmen, women and children and painted inscriptions and rarities of distant countries and joyous instruments of music and rare animals exactly portrayed with different hues, of perfect beauty with limbs firmly jointed; with their mobile faces they seemed to hold secret coverage with you and the fruits seem to approach as though pending to be plucked; and the curtain was one of the wonders of the world, yet its fame is naught to the sight of it.[42]

The people of Samarqand also brought forth what they had gathered of their furniture and ornament and put it opposite those tents so far as the eye could see; and each of the citizens gave his mind to what he could make; and each of the craftsmen laboured with might and main to show a sample of his art and the workmen in what concerned their work, so that a weaver of linen cloth displayed a horseman fitted with all his equipment and perfectly formed even to the nails and eyelids and showed fully even the niceties of his whole armour, as the bow, the sword and the rest of his equipment and that all out of cloth of fine linen and brought it out from the place without trouble. The cotton weavers made of cotton a tower built high, constructed in a way, raised like a mountain, stable and beautiful in appearance with a whiteness of body excelling the hours of Paradise and perfect height overtopping forts; and when they had set it up by its beauty it held the beholders and by its height, visible far and wide in that plain, men crossing were guided, so that it became a raised landmark for travellers and served as a tower over the courts of those buildings.

'Likewise did the goldsmith, ironworkers, makers of greaves and bows and other craftsmen and those who excel in every art. Then very company placed what it had made, each thing separately in its place before the tents of Timur and the tent of his court, behind which they set all the market places.'

A galaxy of talented men adorned the court of Timur Ibni Arab gives a long description certifying that Timur's judge at Samarqand were, namely: Maulana Abdul Malik (son of the author of *The Hidaya*) could simultaneously train the studious, follow a game of chess and dice and compose a poem. The theologians who were expert in jurisprudence included Maulana Saduddin Taftazani (d. 791), Shaikh Samsuddin Muhammad (whom Timur had brought from Rum), Khwaja Muhammad Zahid of Bukhara, 'the great interpreter' who 'retained the tradition in memory' and 'expounded the Sacred Koran in hundred volumes'. Apart form these two readers (and also Maulana Fakhruddin) there were those 'who knew the Koran by heart and read and recited with knowledge like Abdul Latif Damghani, Maulana Asad Sharif Hafiz Husseini, Muhammad Muhriq Jamaluddin Ahmad (both from Khwarazm) and Abdul Qadir Maraghi.

From amongst the renowned orators and public speaker were: Maulana Ahmad, who was called 'the king of elequence in Arabic, Persian and Turkish and was the wonder of the age'; Maulana Ahmad Tirmizi and Maulana Mansur Qazani were the other two who excelled in the art. Maulana Ahmad Talib Alnahas Mustakhij was one of the most famous astronomers of this period who is said 'to have drawn up astronomical tables up to 200 years as early as 808/1406'. From among the painters Abdul Hai of Baghdad was considered to be the best.

Khwaja Ismatullah Bukhari excelled in poetry—each of his word was said to be a 'treasure of secret realities and divine knowledge (*bar lafz i oo ganji maarif o haqaiq i pinhan*)' and was said to be '*Lassan ul ghaib*'.

Abdul Mulk Samarqandi was the '*malikul ulama*' of the realm of Timur. Mirza Muhammad Abdul Qadir, Mirza Mohammad Aghajan[43] were other renowned scholars.

Calligraphy was another art which flourished in Central Asia particularly during the age of Timur and his successors. Some of the well-known calligraphers were: Said Khattat, Abdul Qadir, Tajuddin Salmani.

Timur was 'constant in the game of chess, that with it he might sharpen his intellect; but his mind was too lofty to play at the lesser game of chess, and therefore, he played only the greater game, in which the chess board is of ten squares by eleven, that is increased two camels, two giraffes, two sentinels, two mantelets, a vazir and other pieces.[44] Aladuddin of Tabriz, a lawyer learned in the tradition of the Shafaite sect happened to be the most skilled in the game of chess 'who could give a pawn' to the second best player Zainal Yazdi and still beat him and could give a knight to Ibni Aqil the third best player. A commentary on *Chess and the Theory of Play* was also completed by him.

Hunting was more of a political and military necessity than a pastime. Wrestling, however, was another game by which Timur was entertained.

Since Kesh was Timur's birth place, he had tried hard to make it a green town (*Shahri Sabz*). Babur says that Timur 'erected noble building in it. To seat his own court he built a great arched hall and in this seated his commander, *Begs* and his *Diwan Begs*, on his right and on his left. For those attending the court, he built two smaller halls, and to seat petitioners to his court, built quite small recesses on the four sides of the court house. Few arches so fine can be shown in the world.' It is said to be higher than the Kisri Arch. Timur built in Kesh a college and a mausoleum in which are the tombs of Jahangir Mirza and others of his descendants.

Both Ghyasuddin Ali and Babur refer to the fact that in the Walled City of Samarqand, near the iron gate, Timur had constructed a Friday Mosque of stone. Having seen a mosque in India which was 'pleasant to the sight and sweet to the eye; with a beautifully built vault adorned with marble and the pavement likewise', Timur had immediately expressed his desire that one like it should be built for him at Samarqand.[45] Not only the Indian craftsmen, 'in order that there should be no deficiency', materials were also included among the spoils which included the consignment of stone. Many stonecutters were brought from India who showed their fine skill in its decoration. Babur says that 'round its frontal arch is inscribed in letters large enough to be read two miles away, the

Koranic verse '*waaz yerfer, Ibrahim al Qawaid ali akhara*'. Timur's-Diwan i Aala Khwaja Ghyasuddin Salar Simnani, who come to Yazd for collection of texes, constructed a luxury market (*tim*) in the middle of the market place of the town and named it as *Darul Fath*, Yazdi asserts that the cloth market (*bazaz khana*) was of such height and unique quality that in the entire world there is no other example.[46] Several canals were dug out.

When Timur found that the subjects were tired of the plundering raids of Aughanians and Zakzunis in the *wilayat* of Iriyab, which was laid waste earlier, and since the welfare and betterment of the Muslims, it was the strengthening of religion that had all along been the main objective of Timur. He had therefore, ordered that peace and security be restored to the region for the welfare of the poor and the down trodden and the safety for travellers be ensured. A group of builders, servants, artisans were therefore called for corvee (*hashr*) and within a fortnight such a large fort with all its houses, mosques and Jami Mosque was quickly renovated[47] in AH 772; Timur survived even to this day. The renovation of Qarshi was also planned by him.[48]

Timur founded towns in his realm and around Samarqand, to which he gave the names of great cities and capitals, such as Misr, Damishq, Baghdad, Sultan and Shiraz 'which are the prides of countries'. Another city was built on the near bank of the Jaxartes and where a bridge over the river with anchors and skiffs was joined to it. The city was named Shahrukhia and it was placed in open country. A number of forts were also built after leveling of valleys and low lying places and in a city called Ashbara an impregnable citadel was constructed.

Towards the end of 793 in Musik an army was sent to Khwarazm for the renovation and reconstruction of the place which was laid waste earlier. It was fortified and made populous and prosperous. In 794 Shahrukhia (which remained in a dilapidated state ever since the invasion of Chingiz Khan) was renovated.[49]

There were innumerable sculpters of glass, bronze and other material, each of whom was the most skilful one of his age and the equal of all in his craft and a marvel of his times.[50]

Although the shawl industry in Kashmir is said to have been established by Turkestani weavers invited by Sultan Zainul Abedin, another supposed founder of the shawl industry was said to be Saiyid Ali Hamadani.

Alhaj Ali Alhaj, Muhammad Hafiz both hailing from Shiraz were the famous goldsmiths. Although there were many polishers of gem but Altun excelled in this art and marvelously 'adorned gems with various figures and carved jasper and onyx with the letters of Yazd more beautifull than Yaqut'.

Timur laid out several gardens in and around Samarqand with 'beautiful, splended palaces which were all firmly constructed in a new style with marvellous beauty'. In some of these palaces there were frescoes on the walls depicting live assemblies, representations of Timur's battles, sieges and his conversation with kings, *amirs*, wise-men and magnates, hunting scenes, etc. Among the planters of trees Shahbuddin Zurdakasln surpassed others.[51] From the Mulkusha to the Turquoise Gate, an avenue of white poplar was planted. In the garden itself there was a kiosk painted inside with pictures. Another garden was Naqshi Jahan on the banks of river Kuhik above the Qarasu even though the same was in ruins when Babur saw it. The Bagh-i Chinar was laid out by Timur near the walls, shortly before Clavijo saw it and described it as Bayginear.[52]

Ibni Arab mentions a few of them namely: 'Aram', Bagh-i Shamsi, Bagh-i Bihisht 'The glory of the world', another 'The Garden of the North', and 'The sublime garden'. In the environs of Kash he built a large garden palace called Takht-i Qaracha where one of his builders lost his horse, which grazed for six months in that garden until it was found.

These gardens were open to the public particularly when Timur was away from Samarqand, the rich and poor citizens went for an excursion or a walk therein and 'found no retreat more wonderful or beautiful than those and no resting place more agreeable and secure. . . .' Strangely enough, 'its sweetest fruits were common to all, so that even a hundred pounds weight thereof would not sell for a grain of mustard'.

Timur was a lover of fine arts and a patron of handicraftsmen, innovators engaged in scientific and technological developments, and men of excellence in general. Timur's contributions to the development of painting, architecture, sculpture, wood carving, etc., have been as highly appreciated as his attempts of creating possibilities of exchange of ideas and talents. The credit for developing industries like shawl, carpet, paper and several others goes to Timur. He gave a sound administration to Central Asian lands, cultivated both natural resources and human talents and yet, ironically enough, he failed to be acknowledged as the saviour of his people.

NOTES

1. Timur is usually branded as 'a scourge of humanity' whose goodness if any were surpassed by his evils and that 'benefits which he conferred on his subjects or their posterity were not equal to the evils which he inflicted' and that 'Tamurlane had no greatness except his military geninus and that is one of the lowest kinds of greatness (J.H. Sanders, *Tamerlane or Timur the Great Amir*, Eng tr. of Ibni Arab's *Ajaibut Mqdur finawadir in Timur*, London, 1936, Introduction, p.l. He has been called by Marlowe as 'The scourge of God and terror of the world' with whom 'all Asia is in arms'. The destructions wrought by him during his external campaigns have been exaggerated. While discussing the 'bitter whirlwind of rapine and pillage', in India. Badauni describes that Timur put to the sword about fifty thousands prisoners who had fallen into the hands of his soldiery before reaching the river Ganges; and some of the ecclesiastical dignitaries of his army also who had not the slightest acquaintance with the sword' (A. Badauni, *Muntakhab ut Tawarikh*, vol. 2, Delhi, 1973, p. 356; Ibni Arab, op. cit., p. 130. Cities were badly ravaged in the conquered places 'as it were with an earthquake' (ibid., p. 358).
2. Ibni Arab Shah says, 'The night on which he was born something like a helmet appeared, which seemed to flutter in the air, then fell into the middle of the plain and finally was scattered over the ground; thence also live coals flew about like glowing ashes and collected so that filled the plain and the city; they also say that when the evil man saw light his palms were full of freshly shed blood.' When they consulted the augurs and diviners about these portents, some replied that 'he would be a guardsman, others said that he would grow up a brigand, while others said a blood thirsty butcher, finally some said that he would be an executioner' (Ibni Arab Shah, op. cit., p. 1).
3. In his *Akbarnama*, Abul Fazl asserts that 'It is a beautiful coincidence that in the horoscope of the Lord of Conjunction (Timur) Mars is in the Fifth House. Experienced philosophers have laid stress on the power of Mars in the horosphers have laid stress on the power of Mars in the horoscope of princes' (*Akbarnama*, Eng. tr., vol. I, Delhi, 1972, pp. 78-9). Like Augustus, Timur too is said to have been born under Capricorn while the Fifth House in his horoscope happened to be Taurus with the Jupiter and Mars therein and Venus was in the Third House. Timur's cusp born sun sign was Aries-Taurus as he was born on the night of Tuesday 9 April 1336 in the year of Mouse (First of the Turkish Cycle).
4. Al Hasan the Arab, *Purchas and his Pilgrims*.
5. Ibni Arab, pp. 18-19; also see Hilda Hookham, *Tamburlaine the Conqueror*, London, 1962.
6. Ibni Arab, pp. 1-3.
7. Sharafuddin Yazdi, *Zafarnama*, Tehran edn., pp. 5-10.
8. Abul Fazl, *Akbarnama*, text, p. 77, tr. p. 204.

9. Clavijo, *Embassy to Tamerlane,* ed. Denison Ross and Eiteen Power, tr. from Spanish by G. Le Strange, London, 1928, p. 208.
10. Ibni Arab, op. cit., p. 295.
11. Al Hasan the Arab, *Purchas and his Pilgrims*, vol. XI, Glasgow, MCMVI, p. 403.
12. *ZN*, I, pp.100-1; Al Hasan, p. 435.
13. Ibni Arab, p. 299; Al Hasan, pp. 401-3.
14. Yazdi, p. 205.
15. Abul Fazl, p. 203.
16. Babur, *Baburnama,* p. 356.
17. *ZN*, I, pp. 117-19, Calcutta edn.; *HS*, III, p. 82; *Tuzukat*, pp. 193, 195, 197.
18. Ibni Arab, p. 298. For details cf. Mansura Haidar, 'Timur's religious policy', *Proceedings of Indian History Congress*, 1973 session.
19. Abul Fazl, *Ain-i Akbari*, Eng. tr. Blochman, vol. I, New Delhi, p. 395.
20. Badauni, *Muntakhab-ut Tawarikh*, vol. 2, pp. 357-8.
21. *Tuzukat-i Timuri*, op. cit., pp. 177, 179, 181, also p. xxxiii.
22. Beatrice Forbes Manz, *The Rise and Rule of Tamerlane*, Cambridge, 1989, p. 19.
23. *Purchas,* op. cit., p. 403.
24. J. White, Preface to the *Tuzukat-i Timuri*, Eng. tr. by Davy, Oxford, p. viii.
25. Ibni Arab, p. 48.
26. Al Hasan the Arab, p. 467.
27. *Tarikh-i Shahrukh*, p. 16.
28. *Tuzukat,* p. 5.
29. Al Hasan, p. 468.
30. *Tarikh-i Shahrukh*, pp. 130-1.
31. Al Hasan, p. 463.
32. *Tarikh-i Shahrukh*, pp. 13-14.
33. *Khulasatut tawarikh,* f. 402.
34. Ibni Arab, Pers., p. 136; Hasan, p. 467.
35. Clavijo, pp. 204-5.
36. Ibid., p. 289.
37. Ibid., pp. 278-9.
38. Ibid., pp. 287-9.
39. Ibid, pp. 201-2.
40. Ibni Arab, p. 298.
41. Ibni Arab, pp. 162-3; *ZN* I, p. 442; Al Hasan, p. 441.
42. Clavijo, pp. 248, 233-4; Ibni Arab, pp. 216-17.
43. *Awimaqi Mughul*, Amritsar edn., pp. 317-21.
44. Ibni Arab, pp. 296-9.
45. *Baburnama*, p. 77.
46. Ibni Arab, pp. 222-4; *ZN* II, p. 386.
47. Ghayasuddin Ali, *Ruznamah-i Ghazavat-i Hindustan*, p. 25; *ZN* II; p. 324.

48. Mirza Rumu, *Timurnama*, IOST, MS No. 1526, ff. 186-90.
49. Ghayasuddin Ali, *Ruznamah-i Ghazavat-i Hindustan*, p. 29.
50. Mirza Rumu, *Timurnama*, IOST, MS No. 1526, ff. 186-90.
51. Ibid., p. 314.
52. *Baburnama*, pp. 77-8.

Some Aspects of the Administrative Setup Under the Sayyids (1414-1451)

Tahmeena Javed

The political scenario of the Delhi sultanate is marked by the uncertainties and the swift changes of the latter half of the fourteenth century itself; and the coming of the fifteenth century added even more chaos and confusion. The establishment of the Sayyid dynasty[1] ensured the survival of the Delhi Sultanate, but no more than that. The empire at that time was reduced to its narrowest boundaries and its disintegration led to the gain for the provincial kingdom to the extent that the Sultanate was reduced to the position of a regional kingdom. Sayyid rulers had to struggle very hard to maintain royal authority and collect the annual revenue even in that shrunk area.[2]

In these circumstances it seems obvious that no conscious attempt was made to transform the administration in order to make it more efficient and responsive to the needs of the time, as this kind of restructuring requires vision and dynamism from the ruler, not the unfocused outlook and vacillating tendencies which were so characteristic of the rulers of this dynasty. This personal weakness on the part of the ruler was compounded by the lack of available resources and inertia to change the existing structure. This inertia can best be explained with the help of the numismatic evidence of the period of Khizr Khan.[3] Although no conscious attempt was made to restructure the administration, there was a tendency for the simplification of the administrative setup under the Sayyids. Further, the scarcity of resources prevented the rulers from maintaining double staff like the two *shahnas* for elephants (one for the right and other for the left flank), the two chief *jandars*, the two chief *silahdars*, etc.[4]

The first ruler of the dynasty Khizr Khan ruled as the representative of Amir Timur[5] and, to make his position quite obvious (probably to avert any kind of confusion), he refrained from assuming any royal title.[6] His name was not included in the *khutba*[7] and the numismatic evidence proves beyond doubt that no coins were struck in the name of Khizr Khan for the whole seven years of his reign.[8] This attitude of Khizr Khan seems incomprehensible especially when one considers that although he was nominated by Timur,[9] he received no help from Timur to substantiate his claim, and he could establish his hold over the territory of Delhi only after more than fifteen years of Timur's departure; but a careful analysis of the situation makes sense of Khizr Khan's attitude. Although he established his hold over the Delhi sultanate, his position was quite precarious, and, to stabilize his position, he decided to declare himself as Timur's representative because it created a fear psychosis as people had not yet forgotten the magnitude of destruction that Timur's invasion had inflicted upon them. So Khizr Khan secured his actual authority over Delhi by sacrificing outward claims of sovereignty. The other possibility, of Khizr Khan's himself being in awe of Timurid rulers, could not be totally ruled out as any action can have more than one cause, but of course one cause has to be dominant. However, being a representative of Timur, he ignited sentiments of strong dislike among the masses. So to pacify the inhabitants of Delhi he had to spend a huge amount from the scarce resources.[10] Yahya, the only contemporary chronicler of the Sayyids is absolutely silent about the relationship between Delhi and Samarqand. His attitude could best be explained as an attempt to present the Sayyid rulers as more independent and in a better light (as Yahya was aiming for the royal patronage). Another contemporary chronicler, Bihamad Khani,[11] who was not writing under any such pressure, gives a brief but very significant account of the relations between Delhi under the Sayyids and Samarqand.[12] In Bihamad Khani there is reference to the annual tribute being sent to Samarqand till 1434.[13]

During seven years of Khizr Khan's reign the position of the Sayyid rulers was stabilized, and Mubarak Shah, who succeeded him, took the royal title of 'Sultan-i-Azam',[14] and later he also inscribed his name on the coins.[15] This can be seen as the attempt to assert the sovereign rights of the Sayyid rulers. Mubarak Shah's successors, Mohammad Shah and Alam Shah, were men of even lesser abilities, and although they took the royal title and inscribed their own coins, but during their reign the real power was in the hand of their powerful nobles. Alauddin Alam Shah, the last ruler of the line abandoned Delhi, as he was not able to bear the political pressure and preferred the tranquility of Badaon[16] to the uncertainties of Delhi.[17]

As the head of the armed forces, the first three rulers–the third one to a limited extent–carried out wide military expeditions. As the Sayyid rulers were quite frequently out of their capital, usually on military expeditions, they appointed a 'Naib-i-Ghaibat', or deputy in absentia, who worked as regent in the absence of the sultan from the capital. The appointment of the vazir as the 'Naib-i-Ghaibat' was not customary (as the vazir under the Sayyids was basically a military leader). Under Khizr Khan, Malik Sarup,[18] who was the 'Shahna' (governor of the city), was also the vice-regent.[19] Later, under Alam Shah, Husam Khan worked as regent when the former went for a campaign to Samana, and later when he permanently shifted to Badaon.[20]

The nobility under Sayyids comprised nobles from different nationalities and religions. To illustrate, Sayyid Salim and Sayyid Khan were Arabs, Allahabad Kaka Lodi and Malik Sultan Shah Lodi were Afghans, Malik Karamchand and Malik Bira were Hindus. There were some Indian born Muslims like Rajab Nadira, and some nobles from the provincial dynasties like Amir Ali Gujrati. But there was no predominance of any particular group. During the Sayyid period, some of the nobles who were given important assignments, *shiqq* and *iqta,* were Malik Tuhfa and his son Sikandar Tuhfa, Mahmud Hasan, Malik Sarup, Malik Sadhu Nadira, Malik Khairuddin, Zirak Khan, Sarwar-ul-Mulk, Kamal-ul-Mulk, Hamid Khan, and Husam Khan. All of these nobles were army officers and their primary duty was to maintain the armed contingent and lead the military expeditions.

The nobles were generally given the title of 'Malik' but some higher nobles were given additional titles like 'Malik-ul-Shark', 'Majlis-i-Ala', 'Khan-i-Azam, 'Ala-ul-Mulk', 'Imad-ul-Mulk' and 'Taj-ul-Mulk'.[21] Some of the nobles were given more than one title in recognition of their services: Malik-ul-Sharq Sikandar Tuhfa was given the additional title of 'Shams-ul-Mulk'[22] and Malik-ul-Sharq Mahmud Hasan was later given the title of 'Imad-ul-Mulk.'[23] Some of the higher nobles were given the right to play the military band '*maratib*' at specified times. Malik Ala-ul-Mulk and Malik Ruknuddin were the holders of honoured rank of '*maratib*' with drums (*damamas*), and others had '*maratib*' with kettle drum (*naqqara*) and fish ensigns. There is no information about the grading system of the nobles but the highest category was undoubtedly of those who were given the right to play the '*maratib*'.

The tradition of the Delhi sultanate of including the slaves of the Sultan in the nobility and assigning them high positions continued under the Sayyids. Khizr Khan right after the establishment of his government in Delhi confirmed all the slaves of Sultan Mahmud in the assignments which they were holding.[24] During Mubarak Khan's reign, the fief of Biyanah was given to Muqbil Khan, Sultan Mubarak's slave. Muqbil Khan was also given the privilege to control his territory through a regent, Malik Khairuddin.[25] The only other reference of this kind of privilege is in the case of the royal prince Mubarak Shah. Then, another slave of the lieutenant of Malik Sikandar Tuhfa was given the title of Malik.[26]

With different dynasties and with different rulers the position of vazir always remained higher than the other officials but the prestige of the vizarate vexed and waned with different dynasties. The Tughlaq period saw the heyday of vizarate in medieval India. As the later Tughlaq's were weak, the power of the vazir began to grow, and he became the head of the civil and military affairs with the king a mere puppet in his hands. During the reign of Mubarak Shah there was an attempt to reduce the king to the position of a dummy but it did not succeed.

Khizr Khan employed his vazir Taj-ul-Mulk[27] largely on military duties so much so that right after the assumption of his duty the vazir was deputed to deal with the rebels of Katehar and Badaon.[28] As Khizr Khan did not emphasize royal paraphernalia for himself the vizarate also was shorn of its glamour. After the death of Taj-ul-Mulk, the office of vazir was conferred on his eldest son Sikandar.[29] However, his appointment does not indicate that the vizarate was hereditary, because later appointments of vazir did not confirm hereditary succession. Malik Sikandar's appointment to the post of vazir appears to be a tribute to his father's services to the sultanate, as we do not get any reference of his having had any important assignments before this. Malik Sikandar was given the title of Malik-ul-Shark and was also employed largely on military duties. However, after two years, during Mubarak Shah's reign, he was deposed from the post of vazir and was posted as the governor of Lahore.[30] The next vazir to take up the duties was Malik-ul-Shak Sarwar-ul-Mulk, and immediately after his appointment he was despatched to fight the recalcitrant zamindars of Etawah and Katehar.

The civilian duties of the vazir were entirely delegated to the background under the Sayyids, as he was primarily a military leader and was given the most challenging assignments. But at the same time, he was in charge of the finance department also. As the vazir of the Sayyids was constantly engaged in the military expedition, partly for his effective administration and partly to reward Kamal-ul-Mulk for his brilliant services, Mubarak Shah bifurcated the vizarate, and the office of 'Kar-i-Ashraf' (auditor general) was given to Kamal-ul-Mulk.[31] This truncation of power rankled in the heart of Sarwar-ul-Mulk and he hatched a conspiracy and killed Mubarak Shah.[32]

After this, Sarwar-ul-Mulk put Mubarak Shah's son Muhammad Shah[33] on the throne but he did not intend to delegate any powers to him, usurped all the authority to himself,[34] and gave important assignments to his supporters.[35] A government constituted in this manner can only survive if the person who has the real authority behind the figurine king is a man of some standing and has the support of a major section of the nobility, if not of all the nobles. Although Sarwar-ul-Mulk had hatched a conspiracy and had killed the sultan, he lacked these essentials and as a natural consequence he had to face a counter revolt by the nobles loyal to Mubarak Shah and had to stand a siege within the wall of Siri.[36] Sarwar-ul-Mulk had tried to kill Muhammad Shah in order to get rid of him but again 'there were plots and counter plots and the vazir assassin band was met by a stronger party of loyal adherents, by whom they were cut to pieces' and Sarwar-ul-Mulk was killed by Kamal-ul-Mulk,[37] who became the next vazir.

After the appropriation of the vazarate by Kamal-ul-Mulk, we have no references from which to infer the power equation between the king and the vazir. Later Muhammad Shah replaced him with Hamid Khan, in order to please Bahlol Lodi, who was the governor of Sirhind at that time.[38] Though this act was not befitting the dignity of the king of the Delhi sultanate, it brings to light that the attempt to create a marionette sultan ended with the defeat of Sarwar-ul-Mulk. There is no denying the existence of court politics and the rivalry of the different factions of the nobility which continued unabated, but at the same time the Sayyid rulers remained independent of adherence to any one faction, and relenting to the pressure of Bahlol Lodi was the political expediency of the time. Under Alam Shah, Hamid Khan continued to be vazir until he gave some suggestions to the Sultan which were not appreciated and earned the sultan's displeasure,[39] and later at the instigation of the senior nobles, Hamid Khan was dismissed and imprisoned.[40] However, he escaped and invited Bahlol Lodi to attack Delhi.

For the Sayyid period, we come across such terms as *shiqq*, *khitta*, *iqta* and *parganah*.[41] Though the references to 'parganah' are not numerous, it testifies to its existence at that time. The term '*iqta*' occurs very frequently, and interpreted along with the text cannot stand for an administrative unit alone, but a unit of fiscal administration as well. Although '*khitta*' seems to be identical with '*iqta*', it is used very rarely. It is quite significant to note that within the reduced boundaries of the then Delhi sultanate, threatened by the usurping chiefs and powerful neighbouring states, the units of local administration remained more or less the same as under the earlier dynasties.

Kol, Sambhal, Doab, Multan, Dipalpur, Mahoba, Kalpi, Dhar, Samana, and Lahore are mentioned as '*shiqq*' by Yahaya. All the *shiqqs* were not uniform in size and they were slightly smaller in the Ganges *doab* than elsewhere. The *shiqdars* were designated as 'Amir' and always maintained an armed contingent. Thus, under Khizr Khan and Mubarak Shah, Malik Sultan Shah Lodi was styled as the Amir of Sirhind,[42] Mahabat Khan as the Amir of Badaon,[43] Auhad Khanor Shams Khan as Amir of Bayanath, Hasan Khan of Rapri, Ala-ul-Mulk of Multanand Malik and Sikandar Tuhfa as the Amir of Lahore. Under the Sayyids the royal princes and other important nobles were sometimes made governors of more than one *shiqq* at the same time. There are two incidents which indicate this: one when Prince Mubarak was given the *shiqq* of Firozpur and Sirhind at the same time,[44] and another when Malik Mahmud Hasan was given the *shiqq* of Multan and Siwistan.[45]

In the changed territorial setup there was no need for the big administrative units to be looked after by one single governor but for the creation of smaller units so that the maximum number of nobles could be satisfied.[46] A *shiqq* appears to have been an aggregate of two or more *parganah*, as there was variation in the size of the *parganah* also. The structural division of *shiqq* into *parganah* started at that time, and Yahya's reference to Sayyid Salim possessing many *iqtas* and *parganahs* in Tabarhinda and Doab makes it clear that *iqta* and *parganah* were separate units. During Sayyid period we also get references which show that a noble was granted fief, *iqta*, *parganah*, and fort, all at the same time, and in different regions.[47] The most plausible explanation for this seems that the rulers of this dynasty (as they were quite insecure about their territorial extent) wanted to prevent the accumulation of power by their nobles but at the same time they had to satisfy the senior ones. To handle the situation, they gave these nobles their due share but in different regions. The nobles were also transferred quite frequently from one place to another to check the consolidation of power.

The main duty of the governor or *shiqdar* was to serve as the king's deputy and act as the chief executive officer for the maintenance of law and order, the suppression of internal disturbances of local chiefs, and to extend their help to the state in case of external aggression. They were also expected to help in the task of revenue collection, and as royal authority weakened at that time, this aspect of their duty was to be taken more seriously. He was the head of the armed retinue under his jurisdiction. There is no clue to establish what the basis was for determining the number of troopers under these *shiqdars* but it seems reasonable that according to the territorial extent under their jurisdiction, they were expected to maintain the retinue. There is only one reference indicating the exact number of troopers under a *shiqdar*, when Malik-ul-Sharq Mahmud Hasan was given a contingent of 2,000 horsemen under him, at the conferment of the fief of Lahore (after the reconstruction of the fort of Lahore) during Mubarak Shah's reign.[48] *Shiqdar's* duty also included the safeguarding of the highways and providing protection to the inhabitants under his jurisdiction from the undue exaction of the local revenue officials.

As the representative of the king, these governors had to carry out his *farmans* and supervise the administration of justice in their territory. It seems that it was necessary for a governor to reside in the region which was assigned to him, for when Prince Malik Mubarak was appointed governor of the *shiqq* of Firozpur and Sirhind, he himself stayed back in the capital and instead Malik Sadhu Nadira served as his 'naib' or deputy governor.[49] Similarly, Malik Khairuddin Tuhfa served as deputy governor of Bayanah and Sikri on behalf of Malik Muqbil Khan, Mubarak Shah's slave.[50]

For this period, there is no evidence of the existence of regular prison for the detention of offenders after the verdict of the law court. Sometimes, the governors and other senior nobles were given the custody of political prisoners. During the reign of Alam Shah, the custody of the deposed vazir Hamid Khan was given to Malik Muhammad Jamal. When Hamid Khan escaped, he chased him and ultimately was killed in the encounter.[51]

At the time of the establishment of the Sayyid dynasty, the situation appeared to be quite confusing, but once the imperial authority was established in and around Delhi, the confusion gave way to stability and security for the people of Delhi, at least for the time being. Delhi sultanate survived the chaos which started from the latter half of the fourteenth century, and in ensuring its survival and continuity, the Sayyids had their share. Although reduced in area, influence and prestige, the basic structure of the sultanate was preserved under the Sayyids and was bequeathed to the succeeding Lodi dynasty.

NOTES

1. Yahya bin Ahmad bin Abdullah Sirhindi, *Tarikh-i-Mubarakshahi*, Eng. trs. H. Beveridge, Delhi, 1986, p. 189, gives the date 15 Rabiul-awwal AH 817 (Monday 4 June AD 1414); Khwajah Nizamuddin Ahmad, *Tabaqat-i-Akbari*, Eng. trs. Brajendra Nath De, Delhi, 1992, vol. I, pp. 292-3; and Muhammad Qasim Ferishta, *Tarikh-i-Ferishta*, Eng. trs. John Briggs, Calcutta, 1966, vol. I, p. 294, has same dates; Elliot and Dowson, *History of India as told by its own Historians*, Delhi, 1964, vol. IV, trs. of *Tarikh-i-Mubarakshahi*, p. 46 has 15 Rabiul-awwal AH 817 (30 May AD 1414) Al Badaoni, *Muntakhab-ut Tawarikh,* Eng, trs. George S.A. Ranking, Delhi, 1973, vol. I, p. 375 has 17 Rabiul-awwal AH 816.
2. Yahya, op. cit. His account of Sayyids is full of the details of these annual expeditions, see pp. 190, 191, 192, 193, etc.
3. 'The specimens of the Delhi mintage in more or less sustained order bear the names of Firoz Shah and other duly installed monarchs of his house dated in full figures and embracing several of the absolutely identical seven years during which Khizr Khan was ruling over Delhi', Edward Thomas, *The Chronicles of the Pathan Kings of Delhi*, London, 1871, p. 329; H. Nelson Wright, *Coinage and Metrology of the Sultans of Delhi*, Delhi, 1936, p. 239.
4. Yahya, p. 189; Nizamuddin, p. 293.
5. Ferishta, p. 295, Bihamad Khani, *Tarikh-i-Muhammadi*, Eng. trs. Muhammad Zaki, Aligarh, 1972, p. 95 (Appendix II); Nizamuddin, p. 293. Yahya is silent about the issue and so is Badaoni.
6. Ferishta, p. 295; Nizamuddin, p. 293; Yahya, p. 189. He uses the title 'Raiyat-i-Ala' for Khizr Khan (not explicitly saying that he took no royal title) whereas, he uses the title of 'Sultan-i-Azam' for Mubarak Shah and 'Sultan-i-Ahad-ul-Zaman' for Muhammad Shah, p. 199 and p. 243 respectively.
7. Yahya and Badaoni do not mention the *khutba*. Ferishta, p. 295, mentions that the *khutba* was read in Timur's name and later in Shah Rukh's name. Nizamuddin, p. 293 also suggests the same but adds that later the *khutba* was also read in Khizr Khan's name.
8. Thomas, op. cit.; N. Wright, op. cit.
9. Yahya, p. 173. 'Having conquered Delhi, I bestow it upon you', 'the victor bestowed upon Khizr Khan the Fief of Multan and Dipalpur'. Badaoni, pp. 358-9, corroborates what Yahya says. Bihamad Khani, p. 93 (Appendix), also confirms the same.
10. Yahya, p. 189, 'the inhabitants of the city, who during the course of late events had become ruined and indigent were rewarded with gifts, pensions and proper allowances'.
11. He was a contemporary of Yahya but they were not aware of each other. Bihamad Khani's work *Tarikh-i-Muhammadi* is the only source about the kingdom of Kalpi, which was established in AD 1390.

12. The Maliks and Sultans of Delhi received robes of honour and flag from Hirat for Khizr Khan. After Khizr Khan's death, one of the leading nobles brought the throne and chart for Mubarak Shah in the year AH 827 (AD 1424)', Bihamad Khani, p. 95 (Appendix II).
13. Bihamad Khani, p. 95 (Appendix II); Ferishta, p. 295, mentions the occasional sending of tributes to Samarqand.
14. Yahya, p. 199.
15. Thomas, op. cit., in the 12 R.Y., p. 329; N. Wright, op. cit., in the 8 R.Y., p. 239
16. South-western division of the Bareilly division, United Provinces.
17. Nizamuddin, p. 331. Alauddin wrote to Bahlol Lodi, 'I am contended with the one Parganah of Badaon and I am giving up the empire to you.'
18. Different MS of *Tarikh-i-Mubarakshahi* has 'Sarub' and 'Sarup'; Yahya, p. 189 has Sarup; Elliot and Dowson, vol. IV, p. 47, has Malik Sarwar; Nizamuddin, p. 293 has Malik Sarwar.
19. Yahya, p. 189.
20. Ferishta, p. 315; Nizamuddin, p. 330, refers to Husam Khan as the vazir and regent during Alam Shah's reign but it was Hamid Khan who was vazir of Alam Shan and Nizamuddin also mentions the same in further references,. Badaoni, p. 401, refers to Hamid Khan as vazir and Husam Khan as 'Umdat-ul-Mulk' (privy councellor) but not as regent.
21. There is only one reference to this title, when it was given to the vazir Malik Tuhfa at the time of the establishment of the Sayyid dynasty. Yahya, p. 189.
22. Yahya, p. 237.
23. Ibid., p. 221
24. Ibid., p. 190, 'the slaves of the ci-devant Sultan were confirmed in the pergannahs, villages and fiefs which they enjoyed in the late reign (Sultan Mahmud)'.
25. Ibid., p. 213.
26. Ibid., p. 232.
27. Yahya, p. 189; Nizamuddin, vol. I, p. 293; Ferishta, vol. I, p. 294; Badaoni, p. 377.
28. Yahya, p. 190; Nizamuddin, vol. I, p. 293; Ferishta, vol. I, p. 295; Badaoni, p. 377.
29. Yahya, p. 198; Nizamuddin, vol. I, p. 299; Ferishta, vol. I, p. 297; Badaoni, p. 380.
30. Yahya, p. 206.
31. Yahya, p. 239; Nizamuddin, vol. I, p. 320, Ferishta, vol. I, p. 308; Badaoni, p. 393.
32. Yahya, p. 241; Nizamuddin, vol. I, p. 322; Ferishta, vol. I, p. 308; Badaoni, p. 394.
33. Yahya, p. 243; Ferishta, vol. I, p. 309; Badaoni, vol. I, p. 395; 'Muhammad Shah—whom Mubarak Shah had adopted as his own son', Nizamuddin,

p. 322, also mentions Muhammad Shah as the adopted son of Mubarak Shah.

34. Yahya, p. 244. 'He (Sarwar-ul-Mulk) took possession of cash, treasure troves, royal studs, elephant and the armoury', Nizamuddin, p. 322; Badaoni, p. 395; Ferishta, p. 309.
35. Ibid.
36. Yahya, p. 248.
37. Yahya, p. 249.
38. Ferishta, p. 312.
39. Ferishta, p. 314; Nizamuddin, p. 330, "*Hisam Khan* who was the vazir of the empire—, represented that the return of the sultan, merely on hearing a false rumour of the approach of enemy, was not befitting to the dignity of his state. Sultan Alauddin was vexed and pained at these words'; 'Nizamuddin, mentions *Hamid Khan* as the vazir of Alam Shah at other places'. Badaoni, p. 401, relates the whole incident to Hisam Khan, the privy counsellor.
40. Nizamuddin, p. 331; Badaoni, vol. I, p. 401; Ferishta, p. 314.
41. Yahya, pp. 189, 190, 191, 200, 209, 222, 223, etc.
42. Ibid., pp. 202, 206.
43. Ibid., p. 207.
44. Ibid., p. 191, 'Malik Mubarak in addition to the district of Firozpur and Sirhind'.
45. Ibid., p. 209.
46. During the period of Firoz Shah, one governor for the whole area comprising Multan to Ghaznin, one governor (Hisam-ul-Mulk) for Awadh, Sandila and Kol. Yahya, p. 140. During the Sayyid period Awadh, Sandila and Kol were made separate units for governorship. Yahya, pp. 174, 197.
47. Yahya, p. 222, 'Sayyid Salim—owing several fiefs and parganahs in the Doab, besides the fort of Tabarhinda (Sirhind). Rayat-i-Ala also bestowed upon him the *khitta* of Sarsuti and the *iqta* of Amroha'.
48. Yahya, p. 204.
49. Yahya, p. 191; Nizamuddin, p. 295; Badaoni, p. 378.
50. Yahya, p. 213; Badaoni, p. 387.
51. Nizamuddin, p. 336.

Military Exchanges between India and Central Asia (*c.* Tenth-Fourteenth Centuries)

Rashmi Upadhyaya

The land of Central Asia, which has a geopolitical significance of its own, has ever remained magnificently connected with the contemporary world. The global development of the Central Asian tribes, like Mongols and others, and their interaction with the settled neighbours to the south and west such as the Chinese and the Arabs proved favourable for them. Other regions like Bactria and East Persia, bordered on Central Asian zones, had developed intermittent mutual links, so much so that the cultural differences between them could not be marked as great. The strategy of war, passed down from generation to generation by the nomads of Central Asia was a considerable factor in their military success over their neighbours. India, a country of immense wealth could not fail to attract these nomadic people. The foreign tribes, including the Bactrian Greeks, the Sakas or the Scythians, the Kushanas and the Huns, later on followed by the Turks and finally by the Mongols and the Mughals entered India across Central Asia, by way of the Hindukush. The Sakas, Kushanas and the Huns, though they did not directly belong to Central Asia, left indispensable traces of their Central Asian background. But there is no doubt of the Central Asian origin of the Turks who arrived in India as invaders in the tenth century AD. They developed a unique power of organization, military strength, and spirit to infuse enthusiasm, which enabled them to form a military among their own people and lead them to a stage of superiority over the others. They had great skill in science and technology of the military sphere which put them ahead of their other Asian counterparts. Mongol immigration into India in the form of encroachment also occurred in the thirteenth century. The consequent effect of these military onslaughts was truly destructive for India. But the Indians learnt some distinct lessons from their experiences of war and struggle with the Turks, who by then had settled in India as Sultans. Hence, they became Indianized to an extent by incorporating commendable traits and elements of Hindu military system. The nature of the military exchange and relations between India and Central Asia could thus be regarded as reciprocal as the Hindu kings of India, during a series of wars with the Turks, had also discerned a few military concepts and technological devices. In some cases they also tried to apply them on their Turkish adversaries. The success or vulnerability of these concepts and devices requires a further scrutiny.

The reciprocities of Hindu India with Central Asia were thus mutual. The impact of Turkish military technology and strategy on the Hindu military system has been a subject of interest and attention for scholars. Some of these technological transformations and modifications, including the iron stirrup and horse shoe, were introduced by the Turks from Central Asia in India during the Ghorian and Ghaznavid conquests.[1] The application of such technological devices led to a form of mounted horse archery, which combined with the superior breeds of their horses bred in Afghanistan, Iran and Central Asia, established their supremacy in cavalry. The horse dominated all aspects of nomadic life. The superiority of their horses in their awesomeness, agility and mobility was indeed unquestionable. They could launch volleys of arrows at full gallop.[2] Central Asia with its temperate climate and high proportion of rich feather grass, was best suited for breeding of horses.[3] The upland pastures of Ghuzgan, Gharechistan, Tukharistan, Khuttal, and Chaghaniyan were famous breeding grounds, from where the horses were exported as far as China in the Mongol and Timurid period.[4] Such horses were usually referred to as small, strong, thick-necked, thick-coated, surefooted, and enduring animals.[5] In Sanskrit sources also, the Central Asian horses are noted for their wisdom, speed, brightness, power, and strength.[6]

The picture of India, on the other hand, with regard to cavalry crops had been somewhat gloomy before the coming of the Turks. Sanskrit texts written before the first century AD specify that the functions of horses were to guard elephants and chariots, and not as fighting units. The fusion of Central Asian culture by the settlements of the Scythians and the Kushanas provided a significant place to cavalry in the armies in India. The concept of horsemanship had been further revived by the Huna invaders from Central Asia during the Gupta period, as a result of which chariots gradually lost a place as a wing of the army in northern India by the seventh century AD. However, the remarkable change in the mentality of the Hindus of India to maintain good breeds of horses had occurred by the coming of the Turks as fighting units.[7] Their cavalry was far superior to the Indian horses of that time. The Hindu rulers of India by coming into contact with Turkish armies got inspired to import Central Asian horses in large numbers. The Sanskrit sources of early medieval period include Central Asian horses as the best in the list of horses imported from other countries outside India, including Arabia and Persia, the neighbouring lands of Central Asia.[8] The composition of various political treatises in Sanskrit containing references to horses during early medieval period also attest to their consciousness for maintaining a good quota of cavalry. The role of cavalry in the armies is also highlighted to a great extent in these sources. Thus *Nitivakyamrita* (*c*. eleventh century) refers to cavalry as 'the moving protection line, the rampart of the army' and advises that 'the task of making advance, retreat, attack, penetration and destroying the enemy's rank could only be accomplished by cavalry'.[9] *Manasollasa* (*c*. twelfth century), an encyclopedic work of western Chalukya King Somesvara III states, 'The cavalry is the key to fame; a king in possession of a strong cavalry need entertain no apprehension regarding his territory'.[10] The epigraphic records and foreign accounts provide striking references to the position of cavalry maintained by the Rajput rulers of northern India. Much attention is provided in these compositions for the training of good horses for war. But, in spite of the maintenance of cavalry and the realization of its utility, it could not acquire a high standard of performance in Indian armies like that of the Turkish adversaries, partly owing to the absence of cross-breeding and mounted archery, due to the lack of technological devices like iron stirrups.[11]

The use of war-machines variously termed as *catapults*, *arraads*, *munjaniqs* and *maghribis*, used for throwing missiles and stones in siege warfare, owing to their far range of discharging heavy weights with great strength, was certainly introduced by the Turks on a large scale in India.[12] The Hindus had mostly used these machines from the top of their fortifications.[13] Though the Hindu kings of India came to acquire firsthand knowledge of these machines during the eighth century AD, while fighting with the Arab invaders in Sindh,[14] the use of which they had probably learnt from the Romans, but the practice of their use could not be widespread till the arrival and settlement of the Central Asian Turks in India, as the Arab invasion of Sind was short-lived and did not leave a permanent impact like the Turks, who stayed in India for a long time. Their intermingling with the Hindu Kings of India was of course much closer, than the former, resulting through a series of wars leading to the final conquest. The most authentic treatise on war, *Adab ul Harb wa Shujjat*, signifies the use of numerous types of *munjaniqs* (stone throwing machines in Persian), such as *mujnaniq i dev* (a heavy *munjaniq*), *munjaniq i ghuriwar* (a particular type, not specified), and *manjaniq i khan* (a *munjaniq* on wheels).[15] The same work also refers to *arradas* (probably the *ballistas* of Greece) of numerous types, as *arrada i ekrui*, *arrad i garda*, *arrada i kuftay*, and *arrada i khan* without specifying them.[16] In the sources of the contemporary period, there are frequent references to the use of such machines by the Rajput or the Hindu kings of India. Kalhana reports that in the siege of Bansala, the royal troops used them with success.[17] *Kanhadade Prabandha* reports that at the time of Alauddin's invasion, the bastion-guards of the fort of Siwana were equipped with a large number of stone throwing machines.[18] Amir Khusrau also refers to their use from both sides during the course of the conquest of Telang.[19] Similar references are found of the conquest of Ranthambhor.[20] Barani refers to the death of Nusrat Khan during the siege of Ranthambhor by a stone discharged from a *maghribi* from the fort.[21] Afif, too, reports that during the siege of Nagarkot, both sides were in possession of *munjaniqs* and *arradas*.[22] It is said that by the end of the twelfth century, the device had been practiced by the Hindus on such an extensive scale that the fort of every *rai* was plentifully supplied with such machines.[23]

The invaders from Central Asia, including the Ghaznavids and Timur, on the other hand, could not remain uninfluenced by the armies of their Hindu counterparts during the course of wars. The use of elephant in the Ghaznavid, Turkish, and Timurid armies is largely owed to the Hindus, whose militias were outfitted with a large number of huge and mighty elephants. By realizing their utility, they adopted elephants as an important wing of the army. They started to acquire them as tribute from the Hindu princes[24] and as war plunder. The craze for the collection of such beasts had increased even to such an extent that the Thanesar expedition of AD 1014-15 was provoked by Mahmud's desire to get some of the special breed of elephants, excellent in war. By the acquisition of elephants in such a large number, there formed a *pil-khana* to accommodate 1000 elephants at Ghazna, and, to tend them, a staff of Hindus was appointed under a *muqaddam i pilbana*.[25] The Ghaznavids had restricted the use of these elephants to royalty and an unpermitted use of elephant by a private individual was tantamount to rebellion. Utbi calls elephants as *hass-as-Sultan* and, according to him, 'when the plunder from India was being divided out, they automatically fell within the Sultan's [domain]'.[26] Owing to the great value and regal status, the elephants became an article to gift by the Ghaznavids to other rulers.[27]

The use of elephants by the Ghaznavids could really prove fruitful to them against their neighbours. The elephants then played a significant role in Ghaznavid military organization. According to Gardizi, the use of elephants by Mahmud on 4 January AD 1008 (Sunday, 22 Rabi II 338) proved miraculous in a battle against Karakhanids as the latter's army could not understand how to fight these animals and thus the result of the battle was determined.[28] The proclivity of elephants could also be assessed by them in AD 1116-17 during the battle outside Ghazna between Sanjar and Arsalanshah and Masud III, when the horses of the Seljuks were initially panicked by the elephants of the Ghaznavids. Subuktagin is also said to have used 200 Indian elephants against Fa'iq and Abu Ali Simjuri. Similarly, Mahmud is referred to as possessing a force of 400 elephants while going to battle with Altigin.[29]

The Ghorian troops also realized that their armies were weaker before the mighty elephants of Hindustan. It was on account of the realization of such a weakness that Muhammad bin Sam said to Qutbuddin Aibak:

> the horses of our army have never seen the features of elephants. Our cavalrymen suffer defeat because our horses fight shy of the elephants. You should order that some elephants of mud and wood—mountain like and steady—be made and installed in the midst of the field—all wearing arms and clad in armour. Then all our troops should mount the horses, wearing war arms and arrive in the field galloping their distance-travelling horses. When our horses become accustomed to the sight of the elephants, our cavalrymen will not be defeated.[30]

Zafar-nama also notes that the soldiers of Timur's army had never encountered elephants before invading India.[31] A similar account regarding the unawareness of elephants is also found in *Malfuzat i Timuri*.[32] The existence of the words for elephant (Mgl. *Ja'an Tkish Yaghan*) and their frequent use in Onomastic (The *yaghantigin* 'elephant-price', found amongst the Qarakhanids) indicates that the Turks and the Mongols of Central Asia were not unfamiliar with elephants. But their use in battle against horses in war before the Ghaznavids is not known from our sources.[33] Ghaznavids were the first to use elephants for battle in a large number, which they learnt from India.[34] Timur, the great Turkish invader to India, had become so impressed by the performance and qualities of Indian elephants that he ordered a number of them to be sent to Turan and Iran, and to Fars, Azur, Rum, Samarkand, Tabrir, Shiraz, Hirat, Sharwan, and Azurbaijan, so that the princes and nobles throughout his dominion might see their excellence.[35] The early Turkish rulers could also visualize the utility of elephants. They used them in the battlefield in a respectful manner. Even the great Turkish Sultan Balban considered one elephant equal to five hundred war horses.[36]

The Hindus also excelled in weapons of close combat. Their most proficient weapon was the sword. The sword has acquired the first place in the list of the thirty-six weapons of war referred to in Sanskrit and Prakrit sources related to polity and warfare.[37] The sculptural evidence from contemporary architectural remains also attests to the prominent use of this weapon.[38] The fighting scenes of warriors at Khajuraho are living proofs of the popularity of the weapon,[39] and that the sword accompanied by the shield was the most popular weapon of the Chandella foot soldier is proved by the frescoes of the Lakshman temple.[40] The sculptures of Nilakanthesvara temple (Kekind in Rajasthan) and Harsanath temple (Sikar in Rajasthan) also reveal the representation of swords in the hands of Rajput warriors.[41] Besides the procession of warriors depicted on the Dilwara temple (twelfth century AD) at Mount Abu, a figure of a warrior recovered from Bhilsa, and a relief sculpture at Chittor depicting war scenes clearly show the representation of swords and lances.[42]

India, already acquiring an unparalleled excellence in the field of iron technology,[43] had several sword manufacturing centres. Bhoja, the great Paramara ruler himself refers to Varanasi, Magadh, Ceylon, Nepal, Anga, Saurashtra, and Kalinga as the centres of sword manufacturing.[44] Further, *Agni Purana* mentions the swords, manufactured at Khat, Suparaka, Bang (Bengal), and Anga as celebrated respectively for their elegant appearance, strength, endurance, power of standing blows, and keenness.[45] Debal had also become famous as a centre of sword manufacturing.[46] Bhoja, referring to the relative value of swords produced in different countries, states that those manufactured at Benaras and Saurashtra were the best while those at Magadha, Anga and Kalinga were the worst.[47]

The key to the excellence of the Hindu sword was the quality of Indian steel. The Hindus were highly expert in the methods of welding iron. Alberuni has quoted the case of a smith, who was making a sword, applying the technique in which the cast iron was mixed with wrought iron by forging to elongate and hammering.[48] Indian sword blade had always been a subject of praise owing to its quality. Mallal, an early Arab poet describes the flight of Hemyarites as chased by a hailstorm of arrows, 'whilst hard Indian swords were penetrating them'.[49] Fakhr-i Mudabbir, who gives a long list of famous swords such as *Chini, Firangi, Yamini, Bilamni* (*sayalamani*?), *Shahi, Alai, Hindi* and *Khurasani*, mentions the *Hindi* sword as the best and most lustrous (*gawahardartar*). To a special variety of *Hindi* sword, *mawz-i darya* (waves of the sea—probably on account of the watering on the blade), he states as 'the most costly sword of all'. Further, he continues to state, that 'in the army, treasury or armory of a king there was not likely to be more than one of them'.[50] While comparing the Hindi sword with those of Khurasan and Iraq, he says, 'They (Indians) have the hardest blades of all the swords ... the swords known as *Bakhari*(?), used in Khurasan and Iraq are soft and not of well tempered steel: but in inflicting wounds they break less (than the Indian swords).'[51] It is true that the swords made of soft steel could not break easily but those made of hard steel were very effective. The same author further describing a special variety of swords 'made of soft iron to which silver and copper was added and thus more pliable on account of the silver', most possibly referred to a blade prepared by welded method in India. He also says that if a person is wounded with such a sword, it does not heal easily.[52]

The Arab traveller, Idrisi brings equal praise to both the Indian steel and the sword blades produced by it by stating: 'the Hindus excel in the manufacture of irons and in the preparation of those ingredients with which it is fused to obtain that kind of soft iron, which is usually styled Indian steel. They also have workshops wherein are forged the most famous swords in the world.'[53] The result of such a variety of sword making was that the Turkish invaders developed a great fascination for it. The fame of the Indian sword has risen to such an extant in Central Asia that Mahmud considered it worthy to include in the list of precious articles to be given to Qadir Khan, who was called by Gardizi 'the chief of all Turkistan', during the course of a friendly meeting with him, the political aim of which was to join forces in order to put an end to Ali-tagin's rule in Transoxiana and to give it to Yaghan-tagin, the second son of Qadir Khan, who was to be married to Mahmud's daughter.[54] The latter in return sent to Mahmud the products of Turkistan, which mainly included fine horses with gold trappings and Turkish slaves.[55] Timur, in AD 1399 also carried with him all the skilled expertmen and appointed them to work in the factories established at Ispahar, Khurasan, and Samarkand.[56] Thus Persia became the great supplier of swords. The steel ingots for these factories were prepared in India at several centres in Hyderabad, and at Kona Samudram and Dundurthy in the south.[57] The prepared iron blades or swords in these Persian towns were exported to other Muslim countries.[58] If the Persian literature of the eleventh and twelfth centuries can be believed 'a well equipped warrior of this period had to provide himself with an Indian sword, a Tartar lance, an Afghani horse and Persian bow'.[59] Indian sword blades, finished or half finished, and steel continued to be imported into Persia till the sixteenth century AD and also afterwards.[60]

Besides this, an exchange of Indian and Central Asian military may also be examined in the corporations of soldiers in the armies. Evidence is not lacking regarding the recruitment of Hindu troops and expertmen in the armies of Central Asian Turks. The Hindu soldiers under the command of *sipah silar i hinduyan* had their own quarter in Ghazna.[61] They were a counterweight to the Turks and seem to have been considered in many ways more reliable than them.[62] Their fidelity was tested well in AD 1030, when a defection was created within Turkish troops and it was the Indians under their commander, Suvendhray, who alone remained loyal. It is also known that a stipulate quota of 500 Indian cavalry and infantry was appointed by Mahmud to accompany him for overthrowing the Turkish troops.[63] In the same manner 500 cavalrymen were sent away to a fortress with a guard of three *muqaddams* together with a body of infantry.[64] The appointment of the Indian troops was just to avoid the sympathies of Turkish troops with fallen generals and their fellow countrymen. The Ghaznavids always praised the Indian troops for their good quality. They always found the Rajput princes tenacious opponents. In whole of Ghazna there are only some rare occurrences of the poor show of these troops. In the employment of these soldiers by the Ghaznavids religion was no bar. They took extensive part in the slaughter and violence done to the Muslims and the Christians.[65] Besides the soldiers, some of the Indian troops were also appointed as palace guards.[66]

The chief source for the supply of these soldiers was the Indian campaigns, which yielded a large number of slaves and an influx of cheap slave labour into Ghazna. It was from the Kanauj expedition of AD 1018 that a vast stream of perhaps several hundred thousand slaves reached Ghazna and were traded to other parts of the Islamic world.[67] Similarly, Timur's capture of Delhi in AD 1398-9 provided a lot of slaves to him resulting in the diminished number of slaves in India after the fourteenth century.[68] This export of slaves continued even under the Mughals.

Thus, the above evidence of mutual exchanges between India and Central Asia undoubtedly suggests an effusion of the spirit of militarism and the ingredients related to warfare from both sides, which certainly resulted through the combat of their armies on the battlefield.

NOTES

1. See Irfan Habib, 'Changes in Technology in Medieval India', *PIHC*, 1979; 'Technological Changes and Society during 13th and 14th Centuries', *PIHC*, 1969.
2. R.C. Smail, *Crusading Warfare*, Cambridge, 1956, p. 169; Robert Elgood (ed.), *Islamic Arms* and *Armor*, London, 1979, p. 81.
3. Andre Wink, *Al-Hind: The Making of the Indo-Islamic World*, Vol. II, Oxford, 1999, p. 84.
4. C.E. Bosworth, *The Ghazanavids, Their Empire in Afghanistan and Eastern Iran (AD 944-1040)*, Edinburgh, 1963, p. 113.
5. *Ancient Art of Warfare from Rames to Vauban*, Vol. I, (1310 BC/AD 1650), London, 1966, pp. 288-9.
6. *Ashvashastra* of Nakula, Tanjore Saraswati Mahal Series, No. 26, 1952, p. 75.
7. See *Ramayana, Mahabharata, Arthashastra*, etc.
8. *Manasollasa* of Somesvara, G.O.S., Vol. II, pp. 211, vv. 69-74; *Yuktilkalpataru* of Bhoja, ed. Isvara Chandra Shastri, Calcutta, 1917, p. 182, vv. 26-27; also see *Ashvashastra*, op. cit., p. 75.
9. "सरराम् अपसरणम् अवस्कन्द परानीक-भेदनम् चेत्येतत् तुरंगमैकसाध्यम्।" (*Nitivakyamrita* of Somadva Suri, tr. Sudhir Kumar Gupta, Jaipur, pp. 182, v. 7, 183, v. 9).
10. *Manasollasa*, G.O.S., Vol. I, No. 28, p. 81, v. 574. *Agni Purana* also makes a similar statement that 'horses should be purchased and collected for the purpose of virtue, enjoyment and furtherance of earthly possessions' (*Agni Purana*, tr. M.N. Datt Shastri, Varanasi, 1967, Ch.CCLXXXVIII, p. 1060).
11. See Irfan Habib, op. cit.
12. See Mohd. Habib's Introduction to Elliot and Dowson, *The History of India as told by its own Historians*, Vol. II, Aligarh, 1952, p. 47.
13. See *Rajtarangini*, ed. M.A. Stein, Bombay, 1892, VIII, 1677-9, 1685-6; B.N.S. Yadav, *Society and Culture in Early Medieval Northern India in the Twelfth Century*, Allahabad, 1973, p. 213; *Kanhadade Prabandh*, tr. V.S. Bhatanagar, New Delhi, 1991, pp. 39-40, 74; *Khazainul Futuh*, tr Mohd. Habib, Madras, 1931, p. 40; Elliot and Dowson, Vol. III, p. 308.
14. See *Chachnamah*, tr. Mirza Kalichbeg Fredunbeg, Vol. I, Delhi, 1979, pp. 81, 83, 189.
15. *Adabul Harb Wa Shujjat*, Hindi tr. A.A. Rizvi, *Adi Turk Kalin Bharat*, Aligarh, 1956, p. 271.

16. Ibid.
17. *Rajtarngini*, VIII, 1677-9, 1685-6; B.N.S. Yadav, op. cit., p. 213.
18. *Kanhadade Prabandh*, pp. 39-40.
19. *Khazainul Futuh* in Elliot and Dowson, op. cit., Vol. III, p. 81.
20. Barani, in Elliot and Dowson, Vol. III, p. 146, *Khazainul Futuh*, tr. Mohd. Habib, p. 40.
21. Barani, op. cit., p. 172.
22. Ibid., p. 308.
23. Mohd. Habib's Introduction to Elliot and Dowson, op. cit., Vol. II, pp. 47-8.
24. After AD 1009 the raja of Narayanpura made peace with Mahmud on the condition that an annual tribute including fifty elephants be paid. Similarly, the Chandella King Ganda, after the campaigns of AD 1022-3, relieved himself by promising a payment of 300 elephants. (C.E. Bosworth, op. cit., pp. 75-6). Ferishta also informs that Subuktagin accepted the proposals of peace from Jaipal on the condition of the payment of elephants and an annual tribute (*Tarikh-i-Firishta* of Muhammad Qasim Hindu Shah Ferishta, tr. John Briggs in *History of the Rise of the Mohmedan Power*, Vol. I, Calcutta, 1966, p. 10).
25. C.E. Bosworth, op. cit., p. 117.
26. Ibid.
27. Ibid.
28. V.V. Barthold, *Turkistan down to the Mongol Invasion*, Philadelphia, 1977, p. 273.
29. C.E. Bosworth, op. cit., p. 116.
30. *Futuh us Salatin*, tr. A. Mahdi Husain, Vol. I, Bombay, 1967, p. 148; Vol. III, Bombay, 1977, p. 841; also see *Chachnamah*, Vol. I, tr. Mirza Kalichbeg Fredunbeg for the absence of elephants in Arab armies.
31. Elliot and Dowson, op. cit., Vol. III, pp. 498-9.
32. Ibid., pp. 437-8
33. C.E. Bosworth, op. cit., p. 115.
34. Ibid., p. 115f.
35. The elephants in *Malfuzat-i-Timuri* are not directly referred to as Indian but those possessed by the Sultan Mahmud of Delhi and abandoned by him, when he fled and later which were captured by Timur (Elliot and Dowson, Vol. III, pp. 443-4). But these in all probability were Indian in origin because the chief source for supplying of elephants to the Turkish Sultans of Delhi had been the Indian forest. Also see *Zafarnama*, Elliot and Dowson, op. cit., Vol. III, p. 503.
36. *Tarikh i Firuzshahi* in Elliot and Dowson, Vol. III, p. 103.
37. *Yuktikalpataru*, p. 139, vv. 28-9; also see *Manasollasa*, Vol. II, p. 160, vv. 64, 70-2.
38. B.N.S. Yadav, on the basis of literary and archaeological evidences, which

show the predominant use of sword instead of bow and arrow, sees the decline of archery during early medieval period. Proving his point, he states that the bow and arrow, which was the chief weapon during the previous ages, had given its place to the sword from tenth century AD onwards. In his opinion, the sword in the twelfth century AD, as described in the *Rukminiharana* and *Kiratarjuniya,* came to be closely associated with ideal chivalry (B.N.S. Yadav, op. cit., pp. 216-17).

39. G.N. Pant, *Indian Arms and Armor*, Vol. II, New Delhi, 1980, pp. 24-5.
40. Ibid., p. 25.
41. Ibid.
42. Ibid.
43. Indians were familiar with the smelting of iron as early as BC 1100. The art was learnt by them perhaps through some skilled iron-smiths of Asia minor, where it was known from the third millennium BC. The 100 talents of Indian steel presented to Alexander in BC 326 by the tribes of Malli and Oxydrakae in order to please him, which he had carried to Greece, must had been in all possibility of excelled value, for a mere piece of iron considered worthy of presentation to the conqueror of the world itself, undoubtedly, appears a clear proof of the excellence (*Indian Arms and Armor,* II, p. 89).

    Due to its fineness, Indian steel and iron remained an important article of trade, imported by Romans from India. In the field of technology, the famous iron pillar at Mehrauli near Qutub Minar, New Delhi, the largest and heaviest single piece of iron, weighing about 8 tons and the huge iron beams (one of them over 25 feet large, 11 inches broad and weighing 48 tons) used in the Sun temple at Konark remind us of the expert workmanship of the highly skilled iron-smiths (ibid., p. 89).
44. *Yuktikalpataru*, p. 141, vv. 47-54.
45. *Agni Purana*, II, Ch. CCXLV, p. 886.
46. *Ibn Haukal*, Elliot and Dowson, op. cit., Vol. I, London, 1967, p. 37.
47. *Yuktikalpataru*, pp. 141, vv. 47-54, 170, vv. 25-28.
48. Ahmad. Y. Al Hasan, and Donald, R. Hill, *Islamic Technology*, Cambridge, 1986. p. 258.
49. G.N. Pant, *Indian Arms and Armor*, Vol. II, p. 11.
50. Simon Digby, *War-Horses and Elephants in Delhi Sultanate*, Oxford, 1971, p. 81.
51. Ibid.
52. Ibid., p. 18; also see *Encyclopedia Britannica*, 1960.
53. W. Egertan, *A Description of Indian and Oriental Armor*, London, 1986, p. 56.
54. V.V. Barthold, op. cit., p. 284.
55. Ibid.
56. G.N. Pant, *Indian Arms and Armor*, Vol. II, pp. 90, 1; also see *Studies in*

Indian Weapons and Warfare, New Delhi, 1970, p. 128.

57. *Indian Arms and Armor,* Vol. II, pp. 90-2. *Studies in Indian Weapons and Warfare*, p. 28.
58. Robert Elgood (ed.), *Islamic Arms and Armor,* London, 1979, pp. 207-8.
59. G.N. Pant, *Indian Arms and Armor,* Delhi, 1978. Vol. I, p. 69.
60. Ibid., Vol. II, pp. 90-3, 208, *Islamic Arms and Armor,* p. 208.
61. C.E. Bosworth, op. cit., p. 110.
62. Ibid.
63. Ibid.
64. Ibid.
65. Ibid., p. 110.
66. Ibid., p. 108.
67. Ibid., p. 102; Andre Wink, op. cit., Vol. I, Delhi, 1990, p. 62.
68. Ibid., also see *Cambridge Economic History of India*, Vol. I, Cambridge, 1982, pp. 84, 89-92.

Agrarian Landscape of a Mughal *Pargana*: Studying Udehi from *Taqsims*

Sumbul Halim Khan

Scholarly concern of agrarian-based issues, related in particular to agricultural production, extent of cultivation, and agrarian trade, has set aside the data on the 'uncultivable waste'. An effort to undo this segregation is increasingly being felt.[1] We need to understand the complete landscape of an area, and the use to which the land was being put. This will facilitate better comprehension of agrarian-environmental relation of a particular area.[2]

With this end in view, *pargana* Udehi is sampled. The explanation of this selection lies in the fact that Udehi was a *pargana* in *sarkar* and *suba* Akbarabad, and therefore in the core of the Mughal empire. The data is found in continuous series. It also seems that the profusion of documentary evidence[3] needs to be utilized to improve the existing knowledge of the physical geography of the area.

Morphology

Pargana Udehi is comprised of *qasba* Udehi and 141 villages. The settlements vary considerably. On the basis of an examination of total *raqba*, one can classify the villages into four types–large, medium, small and very small. The percentage distribution of the types of villages is 4.1 per cent as large villages, 70.2 per cent as medium, 11.2 per cent as small villages, and 14.5 per cent as very small villages.

Table Showing Classification of Villages

A. Large Villages

No. of villages	Name of the villages	Area in *bighas*
9	Bamanwas	33840
1	Udehi Khurd	18144

2	Qasba Udehi	17560
	Sahro	14241
2	Vardalo	12696
	Vaghor	10211

B. Medium Villages

S. No.	Name of the villages	Area in *bighas*
1.	Aluda	2904
2.	Umargarh	3750
3.	Islampur	4884
4.	Akbarpur Kohla	1775
5.	Hirnia	2352.5
6.	Owari Buzurg	2900
7.	Owari Khurd	2900
8.	Ahmadpur Imajpur	3962
9.	Astoli	1350
10.	Akodi	1314.11
11.	Ibrahimabad	4063.1
12.	Vadhlai	6504
13.	Vandhavali	1963
14.	Vabhori	2720
15.	Vadarkha	4406.14
16.	Varodgujar	3505
17.	Varodajat	3781
18.	Varodia Buzurg	2496.19
19.	Varodia Khurd	1879.15
20.	Varho etc.	2904
21.	Veenagaon	1176
22.	Vonipur	1000
23.	Varila	4774.5
24.	Bhanapur	4213.1
25.	Bhorpur	4181.15
26.	Piplai	4341.13
27.	Toksi	6648
28.	Todila	2204
29.	Thakriya	1536
30.	Tajpur	2499
31.	Jehran	3542
32.	Jivali	4181

33.	Jaribo	3700
34.	Jahangirpur	1300
35.	Jajpur	3322.17
36.	Jafarpur	1750
37.	Chandpur	2633.1
38.	Chhago	4027
39.	Chhain	1794
40.	Dharoli	4504
41.	Habibpur Gujar	3154.15
42.	Habibpur Mina	1192.17
43.	Janpur	1320
44.	Jidarpur	2904
45.	Daher Haja	2450
46.	Dupsija	3965
47.	Dobha	4408
48.	Dargahpur	1200
49.	Datasuti	3060
50.	Daulatpur	1000
51.	Dilippur	1750
52.	Rampur Thali	1654
53.	Rahsi wa Perozpur	5133
54.	Ranila wa Hinarpur	5016
55.	Ralawato	4374
56.	Ramiro	5906
57.	Rajapur	2827.15
58.	Sadapur	2300
59.	Safpur	1000
60.	Salupur	1250
61.	Sarapur Dahana	1142
62.	Salana	2904
63.	Sikandarpur	2904
64.	Sahajpur	1976
65.	Satrasalpur	6638
66.	Saldo	1006
67.	Sarai Itwarwadi	3285.12
68.	Sithora	3398.13
69.	Sumel Buzurg wa Khurd	2448.6
70.	Gaspur	5681
71.	Faraspur	1077.7
72.	Kevlaghat	6156

73.	Kevri Buzurg	4056
74.	Kevri Khurd	1837
75.	Kesavpur	1000
76.	Khotala	2827.15
77.	Khudsia	1142.13
78.	Kodi	1093.1
79.	Kacharharo	2061
80.	Gaonri Buzurg	1359
81.	Gaonri Khurd	1218
82.	Gehnorli	2157
83.	Guthli	2982.11
84.	Khorli Gunj	2904
85.	Khorli Mina	4374
86.	Kiratpur	1000
87.	Lalpur	1500
88.	Mau	2214
89.	Mirzapur	2650
90.	Mahanadpur	1844.5
91.	Modipur	1403
92.	Manpur	5400
93.	Morachi	1536
94.	Islampur 2	1260
95.	Madhogarh	4221.5
96.	Manderu	2035
97.	Navagaon	3840
98.	Nadoti Aspur Vanipur	8214
99.	Hingoipur	2825.07

C. Small Villages

S. No.	Name of the villages	Area in *bighas*	Remark
1.	Virpur	3500	0 Population attached to Bamanwas
2.	Dalapur	1750	
3.	Sarangpur	1500	
4.	Jafarpur	1750	0 Population
5.	Jahangirpur	1300	0 Population
6.	Saeedpur	2300	
7.	Jaintipur	1400	0 Population
8.	Shafipur	1000	

9.	Sarinagri	700	0 Population
10.	Dargapur	1200	0 Population, attached to Vardalo
11.	Rahro	11094	3 *bighas* attached to Vardalo
12.	Kashipur	Attached villages called *Dakhili*	Attached to Udehi
13.	Asifpur	Attached villages called *Dakhili*	Attached to *qasba* Udehi
14.	Itwarpur	Attached villages called *Dakhili*	
15.	Kamalpur	2000	Attached to *qasba* Udehi
16.	Raisingpur	2000	0 Population

D. Very Small villages

S. No.	Name of the villages	Area in *bighas*
1.	Kishanpur	952
2.	Kadipur	871.4
3.	Pirkharhari	864
4.	Jaswantpur Khurd	805
5.	Jaswantpur Buzurg	761.17
6.	Ibrahimpura	750
7.	Ratupura	674.2
8.	Golaguwari	655
9.	Silorapura	653.2
10.	Hasanpur	547.4
11.	Nohri	530
12.	Kalyanpur	500
13.	Akbarpur	219.12
14.	Wajidpur	420
15.	Sultanpur	518.14
16.	Ramsinghpur	0
17.	Raipur	0
18.	Rampur	0
19.	Mohsampur	0
20.	Madhwapura	0
21.	Harnathpuri	0

Generally speaking, large villages are a result of the extent of good cultivated land in river beds, assured water supply, and communication, location in a strategic position, with ruins of old walls of forts.[4] Seen from this perspective, one finds good water supply in at least Udehi Khurd where out of a total *raqba* of 18144 *bigha* the *talab* area was 18 per cent and *nala* area was 1.3 per cent, *kua* area .02 per cent.[5] Similarly in Bamanwas, out of 33840 *bighas* 2.9 per cent was *talab* area. Likewise, Sahro was also rich in water resources with 2 per cent in *talab* area and .4 per cent in *nadi* area. Vardalo also had .8 per cent in *talab* area.[6] The cultivable area of these villages was as follows:

Table Indicating Cultivable Area of Large Villages

S. No.	Name of the villages	Cultivable Area (per cent)
1.	Qasba Udehi	69.82
2.	Udehi Khurd	17.66
3.	Bamanwas	94.59
4.	Sahro	93.60
5.	Vardalo	96.89
6.	Vaghor	96.08

Medium villages were in a greater majority due to more favourable conditions than large villages.

Small villages so called here are basically *dakhili* villages, attached either to large or medium villages. These villages were desolate, newly founded, or not self-sufficient. The important element in this type was the absence of populated area. Mostly these villages had only cultivable area. Only in one village, namely Rahro, populated area is found, which is only three *bighas*.

Very small villages are treated separately due to their smaller *raqba* in comparison to small villages, and also because here both cultivable as well as uncultivable area is present.

Interestingly enough, the villages of *pargana* Udehi (including Udehi Khurd and *qasba* Udehi replaced by modern Udehi Kalan) are presently contained in tehsil Gangapur and tehsil Bamanwas covering an area of 248.4 sq. miles (643.4 sq. km) and 285 sq. miles (739.4 sq. km) respectively in Sawai Madhopur district.

The evolution of the village Bamanwas in sixteenth century, with small villages attached to it, becoming the biggest village of *pargana* Udehi and presently a separate tehsil with 1425 villages, is an interesting development. The tehsil population is still reported to be predominantly rural.[7]

Among other factors, the presence of the river Morel in the south of Bamanwas cannot be ignored.[8] Udehi Khurd also had 3277 *bighas* in tank yet it did not develop, so water resource cannot be the sole criterion for such a development.

Sawai Madhopur district at present comprises eleven tehsils, viz., Mahwa, Todabhim Karauli, Sapotra, Malarna chor, Sawai Madhopur, Hindaun, Nadauti, Bamanwas, Gangapur, and Khandar. The villages of medieval *pargana* Udehi are now spread in the tehsils of Gangapur, and Bamanwas of district Sawai Madhopur.

River System and Water Resources

The behavior of the water is not merely a function of rainfall–its intensity, character, seasonal distribution, etc., and topography, but is vitally affected by the nature of the land surface. Rainfall soaks into forest soil and into fields well covered with vegetation but it runs off freely from barren rock and naked hard-baked fields especially in channels prepared for it between rows of tobacco and cotton plants. The control of water does not stop at the riverbank; it takes in the entire landscape and every activity that depends on and in turn affects that landscape-agriculture, forestry, grazing, etc. Thus, water became a strategic key to full-fledged all out river valley watershed planning, i.e. planning for proper control of the water and all the other basic assets which affect its behaviour.[9]

Water is especially important in an arid region like Rajasthan. It is the primary need for any agro-economic growth. Besides rainfall, this need was fulfilled by river *(nadi), talab, nala, kua, and howd.*

The river systems that benefited *pargana* Udehi were Morel, Dhund and Khari. The Morel river is a tributary of Banas. It is joined by river Dhund and later by Khari. The Khari river rises in Todabhim and Lalsot ranges of hills about fifteen km north of Bamanwas and, after flowing south, joins the Morel.[10]

Among the streams of significance is Kareli. It loses its identity in Morel. This stream is in close proximity to Bamanwas.

Our documentary evidence alludes to villages Umargarh, Hirnia, Vadarkha, Rampur Thali, Khudsia, and Navagaon being on the bank of rivers.

Table Indicating Villages on Riverside and the Area Covered by them

S. No.	Name of the villages	Area in *bighas*	per cent to total *raqba* of the village
1.	Umargarh	500	13.33
2.	Hirnia	200	8.50
3.	Vardarkha	50	1.13
4.	Rampur Thali	100	6.05
5.	Khudsia	50	4.38
6.	Navagaon	700	18.23

We are informed by the district gazetteer that there are no natural lakes in our sample area. However, tanks were constructed by the erstwhile Raja. Ninety such small irrigational tanks are reported.[11] Our internal evidence sketches a more graphic description when it records the area covered by tanks in the villages of Udehi.[12]

Table Showing Tank Area in The Villages of *Pargana* Udehi

S. No.	Name of the villages	Tank Area in *bighas*
1.	Udehi Khurd	3277
2.	Akbarpur Kohla	40
3.	Vardalo	150
4.	Vaghor	250
5.	Vadhlai	135
6.	Vandhawali	150
7.	Vabhori	110
8.	Vardarkha	60
9.	Varod Gujar	150
10.	Varodiya Buzurg	40
11.	Vinagaon	145.5
12.	Varila	360
13.	Bhanapur	100
14.	Bamanwas	1000
15.	Pirkharhari	5
16.	Toksi	50
17.	Tudila	135

18.	Thakriya	15
19.	Jihran	80
20.	Jaribo	150
21.	Japur	50
22.	Jasvantpur Khurd	50
23.	Chonpur	75
24.	Dharoli	150
25.	Jidarpur	100
26.	Dabsija	
27.	Dobha	50
28.	Rampur Thali	30
29.	Rahsi wa Firozpur	150
30.	Ranila wa Hanapur	200
31.	Ralawato	50
32.	Rajapur	50
33.	Sahro	250
34.	Safpur	20
35.	Sarapur	100
36.	Sikandarpur	50
37	Sahajpur	150
38.	Satrsalpur	90
39.	Sarai Itwarwadi	86
40.	Sithora	125
41.	Sumel Buzurg	8
42.	Kadipur	26
43.	Kevri Buzurg	100
44.	Khoutala	50
45.	Kodli	5
46.	Gaonri Buzurg	100
47.	Gaonri Khurd	40
48.	Golagwari	20
49.	Gehnauli	190
50.	Khorli Gujar	98
51.	Khorli Mina	30
52.	Khempur	20
53.	Mau	43
54.	Modipur	4
55.	Manpur	65
56.	Manderu	200
57.	Nadoti	400

Thus, one can discern that out of a total of one hundred and forty-one villages fifty-seven had tank facility. Interestingly enough, though modern maps show proximity to Morel in Bamanwas, our evidence indicates no river area in the village. However, as we can see from the above table, tank (*talab*) area in Bamanwas is substantial. Whether this tank area was natural or artificial is not discernable from our records. In the modern context, it is reported that there are no natural lakes in the area.[13]

Surprisingly only seven villages of the *pargana* have wells and the area covered is also very small. The information contained in *taqsim*[14] is set out in the following table

Table Presenting Area Covered by Wells (*Kua*)

S. No.	Name of the villages	Area of the wells in *bighas*	Per cent to total area
1.	Udehi Khurd	4	.02
2.	Islampur	4	.08
3.	Vardalo	2	.015
4.	Tudela	9	.4
5.	Rahsi wa Firozpur	4	.07
6.	Saldo	3	.3
7.	Mau	3	.13

In three villages we come across the *chah* area being mentioned separately. The reason for specifying *kua* area and *chah* area is not clear because both the terms connote a well.[15]

Table Indicating *Chah* Area

S. No.	Name of the villages	Area of *chah* in *bighas*	Per cent to total area
1.	Hirnia	10	.4
2.	Owari Buzurg	5	.2
3.	Chhain	15	.8

The sparse nature of distribution of wells either styled as *kua* or *chah* in *pargana* Udehi indicates some correspondence to a deeper water table in the region. The villages where wells are mentioned were comparatively higher in the water table because other water resources are also seen.

The difference in the separate usage of *kua* and *chah* area is perhaps that the former is a deep well since it is found only in villages where there are tanks (*talab*) and water channels (*nala*). *Chah* on the other hand is found in villages with river *nadi* (see the table set out below)

Table Showing *Kua* in Villages with *Talab*

S. No.	Name of the villages	*Talab* area in *bighas*	*Nala* area in *bighas*	*Kua* area in *bighas*
1.	Udehi Khurd	3277	245	4
2.	Islampur	-	127	4
3.	Vardalo	150	-	2
4.	Tudela	135	30	9
5.	Rahsi	150	60	4
6.	Saldo	-	-	3
7.	Mau	45	-	3

It can also be gleaned from the above table that the area covered by *chah* was much larger as compared to *kua* area, so *chah* must be a shallow well due to which more *chahs* were dug in the mentioned villages.

So far as hillocks are concerned, only eleven villages had them. The total area covered by such hillocks mentioned in *taqsim* of VS 1713 to 1722/AD 1656 to 1665 was 2240 *bighas*.

Flora

Trees were present in most of the villages of *pargana* Udehi though the area covered varied from 1 *bigha* to 15 *bighas*. The total tree-covered area in AD 1656 to 1665 in *pargana* Udehi was 1351 *bighas*. The type of trees that grew in the area is not borne out by our documentary evidence.

Since this tree belt is categorized as tropical, dry, deciduous in the National Atlas of India,[16] and so are the forests of Alwar, we can form a fair idea about the trees that are grown from Gazetteers of the region. These forests are classified as the subsidiary edaphic type of dry tropical forests.[17]

A deciduous tree or bush is one that loses its leaves in the autumn every year.[18] It is noted that from a usage point of view, forests of this type are valuable for protection of soil and production of grass, fuel, charcoal, *katha* etc. Some of the shrubs are utilized for basket-making. Some commonly known trees and shrubs of this variety are as follows

Table Showing Trees Etc in Dry Deciduous Variety

S. No.	Botanical name	Type of tree	Hindi Name
1.	Acacia Arabica	Tree	Babul
2.	Acacia Catechu	Small tree	Khair
3.	Aegle Marmelos	Tree	Bel
4.	Anogeissus Pendula	Tree	Dhok
5.	Azanrachta Indica	Big tree	Neem
6.	Cassia Fistuala	Tree	Amaltas
7.	Cuscuta Reflexa	Leafless parasite	Amarbel
8.	Carissa Carandas	Small Bushy shrub	Keronda
9.	Capparis Decidua	Scrubby bush	Ker
10.	Dalbergia Sisoo	Tree	Shisham
11.	Danprocalanus Strictus	Bamboo	Bans
12.	Emblica Officanalis	Tree	Aambla
13.	Ficus Religiosa	Tree	Pipal
14.	Ficus Lacor	Tree	Pakar
15.	Ficus Glomerata	Tree	Gular
16.	Opuntia Dillenti	Shrub	Nagphali
17.	Pandanus Tectorius	Shrub	Kewda

18.	Phoenix Sylvestris	Palm tree	Khajur
19.	Saccharum Spontaneum	Grass	Kans
20.	Sachharum Munja	Grass	Munj
21.	Szygium Cumin	Tree	Jamun
22.	Tamarindus Indica	Large	Imli tree
23.	Vettiveria zizaniodes	Grass	Khas
24.	Zizyphus Mauritiana	Tree	Ber

Apart from providing fruits etc., forest products provided fuel; sale of trees for fuel was common. These were also taxed under *siwai jamabandi*. In some areas, like Phagi, the state share on such sale amounted to 50 per cent of the produce.[19]

Other Features

Few villages had area classed as sand dunes (*thale ret*). This area was of significant size in the villages of Imajpura, Varho, and Vadarkha in *pargana* Udehi. Total sand dune area in *pargana* Udehi was 2247 *bighas* in our period.

There was some area allocated for passage or *rah*, but what seems surprising is that every village did not have passage area, not even *qasba* Udehi. Should this passage or *rah* area be treated as Mughal route, as we find the latter crossing the *pargana*?[20]

A very common feature of the village landscape of *pargana* Udehi as seen from the *taqsim* is the land classed as *kallar*.[21] The dictionary meaning of *kallar* is barren, sterile, brackish, saline land or soil.[22] This land produces salt, gypsum and saltpeter.[23]

In the hilly and sandstone tracts, there are enclosed basins, and in these, local runoff collects. During summer months these get dry. They consist of clayey soils with deposits like sodium chloride gypsum, gypsite, nitrate and other salts.[24]

Salinity in the soil is achieved by the type of water, which was distinctly classed in the *taqsim* records of Udehi as *khalwa nadi*,[25] measuring 500 *bighas* in village Umargarh and *nala khal* of 127 *bighas* in village Islampur and 100 *bighas* in village Akodi.[26]

In modern times too, the salt manufacturing continued, as can be inferred from the agreement of 1882 concluded with the Karauli ruler by the British for the suppression of manufacture of salt in the state.[27] The national scale of the small scale industry also shows common salt manufacturing in modern rural Sawai Madhopur.[28]

A comparison of the *taqsim* documents of two different sets of years i.e. AD 1651-65 to that of AD 1712-40 poses a problem. In the first set of figures, one finds *kallar* in almost all villages of *pargana* Udehi. In the latter statistics, however, one finds the same area classed as *sor khar*. Why the two terms are used interchangeably is not clear.

The term *sorkhar* is a derivative of *Shora* and *khar*. *Shora* can be identified as potassium nitrate, chile salt petre or nitre.[29] *Khar* means alkaline earth, saline or brackish soil.[30] It appears that *kallar* indicates saltpans from which salt (sodium chloride) was extracted. However the extraction of saltpeter involved an advanced process,[31] as observed in *The Travels of John Albert de Mandelso from Persia into the East Indies*.

> They get it out of land that hath lain fallow. The blackest and the fattest ground yields most of it. . . . . they make certain trenches which they fill with their saltpetrous earth, and let into them small rivulets as much as will serve for its soaking which may be effectively done, they make use of their feet, treading it till it becomes brooth (broth). When the water has drawn out all the saltpeter which was in the earth they take the clearest part of it and dispose it into another trench where it grows thick and then they boil it continually scumming it and then put it in earthen pots where the remainder of the dregs goes to the bottom and where water thickens they take it out of the pots to set it adrying in the sun where it grows hard, and is reduced into that form wherein it is brought into Europe.

Surprisingly, one finds levy by the name of *agarkhari* on the manufacture of salt in the *arhsattas*.[32] Earlier in AD 1643 the Emperor issued a *farman* regarding the prohibition of manufacturing of salt in *pargana* Mauzabad as it incurred a loss to the state.[33] One does not come across any specific tax on manufacture of saltpeter. Should this be taken as an indication that the manufacturing took place elsewhere?

Statistics contained in the *dastur ul amal* suggest variation in the rates of state charge on carriages carrying common salt and those carrying *loon*, which is defined as nitre. The former is taxed more.[34]

Agriculture

Agriculture was carried out in almost all the villages of *pargana* Udehi. Comparatively speaking, the agricultural fields constituted the largest chunk of the total areas in the village.[35] The crops sown in Udehi were food crops like *sarso, jowar, bajra, moth, urd, barley, gram, ghan, til, baijrhi, kodo, chola, barli*; the cash crops were cotton (*van*), sugarcane (*varh*), tobacco (*tamakhu*) and jute (*sunn*). Besides, there were vegetables like opium (*post*), *ajwain, kusum*, garlic (*lehsun*), brinjal (*baigan*), cucumber (*kakrhi*), spinach (*sag lahra*), and *kaada*.[36]

These were harvested from *rabi* and *kharif* as follows:

Kharif

Bajra, jowar, moth, urd were important *jinsi* crops, while *chola*, sugarcane, cotton occupied larger areas or accounted for larger shares in revenue. Other significant crops were *til*, vegetables, *barli, tobacco*.

Rabi

Barley, wheat, and gram were principal *rabi* crops. Mixed crops such as *baijhri, gojai, gochani* were also of some significance. Another *jinsi* crop was *sarso*. Mention may also be made of vegetables, tobacco, and *ajwain*.[37]

Though the agricultural field area would not have been as saline as the area separated as *kallar*, nevertheless, the soil may still contain salinity. These days the excess soluble salts can be readily leached out of the soils. How does one then explain this phenomenon of extensive agricultural production in medieval times in such an area? The problem has to be treated on different levels. First, the observation is that if the total area of the Mughal empire is taken as a whole and it is assumed that agricultural practice has not changed, the average acre sown in Mughal times was more productive than now.[38] This view seems plausible in the light of studies on soil science and environmental chemistry that point at a multiplying number of pollutants.[390]

Secondly, in the absence of railways every region would have carried on its agriculture to cater to its local demand sometimes despite such constraints as salinity of soils.

Finally, studies on salt stress in soil indicate that salt harm varies from plant to plant. Some are salt sensitive like beans, pea and celery while others are salt tolerant e.g. crops like barley, cotton; crops like paddy, wheat etc., are considered medium tolerant.[40] Generally speaking, it is observed that saline soil decreases permeability of roots to water and disrupts functions like photosynthesis, respiration, proteins and hormones. This damage manifests in poor germination of seeds, reduced crop growth, and yield.[41]

Thus, one finds that agricultural production was a necessity as well as that it was carried out with a certain degree of care and knowledge, of which possibly the Mughal peasant was not ignorant.

People

People who lived in these spaces normally remain invisible in studies focusing on the environment. In the landscape of Udehi, our records indicate the area covered by habitation. Unfortunately, the size of the population and the number of houses in a village are omitted in the otherwise rich statistical data, though one constantly does come across *chappar* or *chapparbandi* in *taqsim* but here only area in *bighas* is provided.[42] Except for the newly founded villages where area under habitation is zero, in other villages the area under habitation is moderate. The range over all villages varies from 2 *bighas* to 200 *bighas*.[43]

Since agricultural use of land was predominant, people in *pargana* Udehi appear where differential land revenue demand is mentioned under *batai jinsi* (crop sharing) on village revenue payers. The *dastur ul amal pargana* Udehi VS 1772/AD 1715 shows that generally the land revenue demand was fixed at half of the produce in respect of all crops except wheat and *bajra*, where it was three fifths. A close scrutiny reveals that for favoured revenue payers such as *Brahmans*, *Qanungo*, *Mahajans*, *Patels*, *Bhats*, *Kamins* and *Bhomias* the land revenue ranged from one fourth to two fifth.[44]

If the data on district Sawai Madhopur and Gangapur available in the Census of 1961 is taken into consideration, it appears that broadly speaking, there were as many as twenty-seven, castes, tribes or races inhabiting Udehi. Among these *Mina*, *Gujar*, *Chamar*, *Brahman* predominated.[45]

Table Presenting the Percentage of Caste, Tribes, and Races (Based on Census 1961)

S. No.	Caste	per cent in Gangapur
1.	Mina	24.4
2.	Gujar	13.5
3.	Chamar	13.3
4.	Brahman	9.0
5.	Mali	6.0
6.	Mahajan	5.0

7.	Pathan	4.5
8.	Koli	4.0
9.	Sheikh	2.9
10.	Rajput Hindu	2.8
11.	Kumhar	1.7
12.	Jogi	1.7
13.	Khati	1.5
14.	Raigar	1.4
15.	Nai	1.1
16.	Bhangi	1.0
17.	Jat	0.9
18.	Khatik	0.6
19.	Sadhu	0.6
20.	Fakir	0.5
21.	Sunhar	0.4
22.	Teli	0.3
23.	Ealai	0.3
24.	Luhar	0.2
25.	Dhakar	0.2
26.	Daroga	0.2
27.	Bhat	0.1
28.	Lodha	0.0
29.	Naik	0
30.	Ahir	0
31.	Rebair	0
32.	Kaimkhani	0
33.	Gadaria	0
34.	Patel	0
35.	Kumbi	0
36.	Meo	0
37.	Kachhi	0
38.	Charan	0
39.	Bambhi	0
40.	Bhil	0
41.	Dhed	0
42.	Bishnoi	0
43.	Dangi	0
44.	Grasia	0
45.	Merat	0
46.	Purohit	0
45.	Rawat	0
48.	Sargara	0
49.	Sirvi	0
50.	Sondhia	0

A recent study also indicates that the caste of zamindars of Udehi in Akbars' time, as provided in *Ain,* were Shaikhzadas, while in Aurangzeb's reign, they were Panchanots.[46] The *pargana* was also a locale of zamindar uprisings between the years AD 1675 and 1718.[47]

One can conclude that the area so far treated as uncultivable waste, namely wells, water channels, salt pans, trees, and hillocks contribute in some way to the productivity of the cultivable fields; hence the latter should not be treated in isolation from the other features of the environment. A landscape vision is desirable for a complete justice to a given region.

NOTES

1. *Studies in History*, Vol. 14, No. 2, new series, New Delhi, 1998.
2. The term environment etymologically means surroundings. It is considered to be a composite term for the conditions in which organisms live and thus consists of air, water, food and sunlight which are the basic needs of all living beings and plant life to carry on their life function. B.K. Sharma, *Industrial Chemistry*, Meerut, 1995, sec. iii, pp. 1-2
3. *Taqsim* documents offer us detailed survey account of both *pargana* as well as village level. Akbar initiated the preparation of these revenue containing cultivable and uncultivable statistics for fixation of realistic *jama.* The extant *taqsim* documents in the Rajasthan state archives are *Taqsim dahsala pargana* Udehi vs 1708-1720; vs 1713-1722; vs 1789-1798; vs 1791-1800; vs 1815-1824. Also see Satya Prakash Gupta and Sumbul Halim Khan: Mughal documents: *Taqsim* (c 1649-c 1800), Jaipur, 1996.
4. R.C. Sharma, *Settlement Geography of the Indian Desert*, New Delhi, 1972, pp. 89-91.
5. *Taqsim*, op.cit.
6. Ibid.
7. C.S. Gupta, *Census of India*, 1961, Vol. XIV, Rajasthan, pt IX, A, Census Atlas, 1967.
8. *Rajasthan District Gazetteer, Sawai Madhopur*, Jaipur, 1981, p. 6.
9. Erich W. Zimmermann, *World Resources and Industries, a functional appraisal of the availability of agricultural and industrial material*, New York, 1950, pp. 572-3.
10. *District Gazetteer, Sawai Madhopur*, p. 6.
11. Office of Executive Engineer, cf ibid.
12. *Taqsim*, op. cit.
13. *District Gazetteer*, p. 7.
14. *Taqsim*, AD 1656-1665.

15. Maulvi Syed Ahmad Dehlvi, *Farhang-i Asfia*, Delhi, 1974, Vol. 3.
16. *National Atlas of India*, Calcutta, 1980, plate 103.
17. *Rajasthan District Gazetteer, Alwar*, by Mayaram, Jaipur, 1968, p. 14.
18. Ibid.
19. *Dastur ul amal* and *amal dastur, pargana* Phagui AD 1691; *dastur ul amal, pargana* Amarsar cf. S.P. Gupta, 'New evidence on agrarian and rural taxation in Eastern Rajasthan (17th & 18th c), P.I.H.C, Aligarh, 1975.
20. See Irfan Habib, *An Atlas of the Mughal Empire*, political and economic maps with detailed notes, map 6b.
21. *Taqsim*, AD 1651-1665.
22. Salt accumulation has been a perpetual problem of civilizations in arid and semi-arid regions. All natural water systems contain dissolved mineral substances commonly referred to as soluble salts. Some rainwaters, far from coastal salt sprays may be very low in salt content. As water flows over and through the soils it picks salt loads. If water rapidly evaporates as it flows on the surface, it results in increasing the concentration of salt. The predominant ions contributing to salinity of soil are sodium and chloride although ions such as calcium, magnesium, potassium, and sulphate, borate and bicarbonate are significantly high in certain regions. It is estimated that more than 20 million hectares of cultivable land is saline in India. See *Industrial Chemistry*, op. cit., pp. 176-8. In arid regions of Rajasthan and Gujarat there is a high evaporation rate which tends to further concentrate salts in soil. Restricted drainage is also a factor that contributes to salinization of soil, Ibid, pp. 170.
23. J.T. Platts, *A Dictionary of Urdu, Classical Hindi and English*, pp. 842.
24. Raj Kumar Gupta and Ishwar Prakash, *Environmental Analysis of Thar Desert*, Dehra Dun, 1975, pp. 14-15.
25. Alkanization of soil refers to the accumulation of exchangeable sodium ions in soils. Soil particles absorb and retain ions on their surface due to electrical changes in soil solutions. When enough soluble salts accumulate in these soils, sodium frequently becomes the dominant ion in the soil solution. Due to evaporation or water absorption by plants, solubility limits of calcium sulphate and magnesium carbonate often get exceeded. These salts precipitated with a corresponding increase in the sodium make all the soil alkaline which is unsuitable for plant growth. See *Industrial Chemistry*, pp. 170.
26. *Taqsim*, op. cit.
27. *Rajasthan District Gazetteer*.
28. Ibid.
29. George Watt, *A Dictionary of Economic Products of India*, Vol. VI, Pt. 2, Calcutta, 1893.
30. Platts, *A Dictionary*, op. cit, p. 867.
31. *The Travels of John Albert de Mandelso from Persia into the East Indies*, London, 1669, pp. 66-7.

32. *Arhsattas* of different *pargans*, Rajasthan State Archives, Bikaner; also see Agrarian system of Eastern Rajasthan c 1650-c 1750, Delhi, 1986.
33. *Farman* of Shahjahan addressed to Jai Singh, s.no. 51/old no. 68 dtd shawaal 1053/7 Dec 1643, R.S.A, Bikaner.
34. *Amal dastur hasil rahdari*, VS 1773/AD 1715; also *Amal dastur kotwali chabutra qasba* Phagui, VS 1770/AD 1713.
35. *Taqsim*.
36. *Dastur ul amal, pargana* Udehi, VS 1772/AD 1715. C.F. Gupta, *Agrarian System of Eastern Rajasthan*, Appendix A5, pp. 280-3.
37. Ibid.
38. Irfan Habib, *Agrarian System of Mughal India*, p. 23; also Tapan Raychaudhuri and Irfan Habib, eds., *Cambridge Economic History of India*, Vol. I, p. 220.
39. Sharma, *Industrial Chemistry*, Section III, *Pollution and its Control*, chapter I, *Environmental Chemistry*, p. 178.
40. Ibid., p. 178.
41. Ibid., p. 178.
42. *Taqsim*.
43. Ibid.
44. *Dastur ul amal, pargana* Udehi VS 1772/AD 1715. C.F. Gupta, *Agrarian System of Eastern Rajasthan*, pp. 123-5.
45. *Census of India*, 1961, Rajasthan.
46. R.P. Rana, 'A dominant class upheaval: the zamindars of a North Indian region in the late seventeenth and early eighteenth centuries', *I.E.S.H.R.*, Vol. XXIV, no. 4, 1987, pp. 402-3.
47. R.P. Rana, 'Agrarian revolts in North India during late 17th & early 18th centuries', *I.E.S.H.R.*, Vol. XVIII, nos. 3 & 4, 1987, pp. 323-4.

Ibadat Khana, *Mahzar* and *Sulh-i-kul*: An Examination

S.M. Azizuddin Husain

The gates of India were opened in 1555 for Iranian *Ulema* and *Umara*, a significant development in the history of India. This decision of Humayun (1530-40/1555-6) provided a new dimension to Indian polity, society and culture. Iranian scholars, Hakim Abul Fath Gilani, Fathullah Shirazi, Mir Murtaz Shirazi, Saiyid Nurullah Shushtari and others came and settled down at Agra.[1] Akbar gave them full patronage and support. These *ulema* were experts on *Uloom-i-Din* (religious subjects) and *Uloom-i-Maqulat* (scientific subjects). Under the imperial patronage, they laid the foundation of a new education policy and revised the syllabus of *madrasas*.[2] But in the early part of his reign Akbar was under the influence of some bigoted Sunni *Ulema*, like Makhdum-ul Mulk Abdullah Sultanpuri and Shaikh Abdun Nabi who did not follow *sharia* in their personal life. With the arrival of the Iranian *Ulema*, those *Ulema* got alarmed, seeing the presence of the Iranians at the Mughal court as a threat to their position. In 1566-7 Mir Murtaza Shirazi's dead body was exhumed from the vicinity of Amir Khusrau's grave because he was a Shia.[3] In 1569-70 Akbar had Mirza Muqeem of Esfahan[4] put to death on the charge of being a Shia.[5] Around 1569-70, Mir Turbati was also executed.[6]

In March 1575 Akbar worked out a plan and commissioned an edifice in Fathpur, named *Ibadat Khana*, for holding religious discussions.[7] According to Badauni, the site selected for the new building of *Ibadat Khana*, was the deserted *Khanqah* (hermitage) of Mian Abdullah Niazi Sirhindi. Mulla Sheri wrote in derision: 'In these days I have seen places of worship for Pharaohs and *Shaddads* being built on the property of a Farooqi.'[8]

At the beginning only Sunni *Ulema* were invited for discussions at the *Ibadat Khana*. Every Friday night discourses were held with the *Ulema* and *Mashaikh*. Akbar wanted to have discourses with ascetics and the disciples of Shaikh Moinuddin Chishti, and this was one of the reasons for the construction of *Ibadat Khana*. Akbar discussed Sufism, science, and philosophy.[9]

The Emperor sat in the centre of the hall while his four ministers Abdur Rahim, Birbal, Abul Fazl and Faizi each sat in the four corners of the hall.[10] A contemporary painting of the *Ibadat Khana* shows that it was located near the eastern gate of the Jama Masjid of Fathpur. *Ibadat Khana* had three platforms. The painting shows Akbar sitting on the top platform. The middle platform is shared by Abul Fazl, Faizi, Father Rudolf Acquaviva from Italy and Father Monserrate from Spain. The lowermost platform is occupied by *Ulema* and priests of other religions holding books.[11] Akbar asked the *Umara* to sit on the east, the Saiyids on the west, the *Ulema* to the south and *Mashaikh* to the north. The emperor made it a point to go to each side for discussion. [12] Abul Fazl gives the list of the following participants of *Ibadat Khana*, 'Sufis, Philosophers, Orators, Jurists, Sunnis, Shias, Brahmins, Jatis, Suras, Carbaks, Nararene, Jews, Sabis (Sabians), Zorastrians and others enjoyed exquisite pleasure by beholding the calmness of the assembly, the world-lord sitting in the lofty pulpit.'[13]

Akbar had brought a very good collection of manuscripts, particularly on religion, from Gujarat. These books were distributed by him to *Ulema* participating in the discussions at the *Ibadat Khana*. Badauni got *Mishkatul Anwar*, a book on the traditions of Prophet Muhammed.[14]

According to the author of *Dabistan-i-Mazahib* the following points were discussed in the *Ibadat Khana*.

1. The tradition of the camel straying out.
2. Ascent upon the caravan of the *Quresh* at the beginning of the *Hijri* era.
3. Demanding the nine wives.
4. Separation of women from their husbands.
5. The companions giving up their earthly bodies.
6. The selection of the first three Caliphs.
7. The affairs of the *Fadak*.
8. War of Siffin, etc.[15]

A serious allegation relating to Makhdumul Mulk's evasion of *zakat* was also discussed. These debates undermined the influence of Makhdumul Mulk Abdullah Sultanpuri and Shaikh Abadun Nabi.[16]

Badauni records that Shaikh Badruddin Chishti, son of Shaikh Salim Chishti, was called to the *Ibadat Khana*. Badauni believed that Badruddin was so disgusted with the atmosphere at Akbar's court that he first went to Ajmer, then to Gujarat and from there to Mecca where he fasted till he obtained spiritual union with God.[17]

Akbar tried to maintain decorum in the discussions in the *Ibadat Khana*. He entrusted Badauni with the duty of reporting to him any *alim* who did not behave properly, who spoke irrelevantly or did not maintain the decorum of the *Ibadat Khana*. One night, in the course of a discussion, tempers rose high and confusion ensued. Asaf Khan was sitting next to Badauni and he told him that if he followed the instructions of the Emperor *in toto*, there would soon be no one left in the *Ibadat Khana*. When Akbar heard this witty remark of Badauni he was amused.[18]

After this experience Akbar opened the gates of *Ibadat Khana* around 1576, to Shia Muslims also to participate in these discussions. This was the first time in India that Shia *Ulema* got such an opportunity. In the same year Mulla Muhammed Yazdi also arrived at Fathpur. Akbar invited him to take part in the debate going on at the *Ibadat Khana*. Another reason for the gradual change in the attitude of the Emperor, according to Badauni, was the induction of new entrants to the Mughal court such as the three brothers, Hakim Abul Fath Gilani, Hakim Humam and Hakim Nooruddin. These Gilani brothers attracted the attention of the Emperor by their profound theological learning and their excellent qualities as individuals. Soon Hakim Abul Fath Gilani became an intimate friend of the Emperor. Historical books were read out, especially about the first three Caliphs and it was stated that the quarrel over *Fadak* ensued because Fatima claimed it as her own, but Abu Bakr would not let her have it. They discussed the so-called war of Siffin, fought between Ali and Muawiyah.[19] Heated discussions had taken place on different issues between the Sunnis and the Shias at the *Ibadat Khana*. Faizi who was one of the active participants of these debates made a beautiful comment on the heated discussions going on in the *Ibadat Khana*: 'Always I see you busy in discussions and debate. But there has been no result of these heated discussions except perspiration.' In such arguments Badauni says that "the Shias, of course, gained the day and the Sunnis were defeated; the good were in fear, and the wicked were secure".[20] As a result of all this, Badauni elaborates, those who had earlier been in favour with the Emperor and close to him fell out, and those who were out of favour became close to the Emperor, thus his earlier companions and friends were alienated and strangers and aliens became close to him.[21] But Akbar became so perturbed by these debates that he left Fathpur in 1576 and only returned in 1578.

In 1578 Akbar also invited Hindus, Parsis and Christians to take part in the discussion at the *Ibadat Khana*. By inviting non-Muslims, he widened the scope of discussions. At the same time he also made an attempt to create understanding about Indic religions by getting translated the *Ramayana* and *Mahabharata* into Persian. A Hindu was executed on Shaikh Abdun Nabi's *fatwa*. On this execution a debate was organized by Akbar at Anup Talao where a number of scholars participated. Earlier their *fatwas* were never questioned and were considered as revealed ones. *Ulema* opposed this decision of Shaikh Abdun Nabi in the light of Islamic jurisprudence. Akbar observed to Badauni, 'Have you heard that if there are ninety-nine traditions inflicting the punishment of death for a certain offence, and one tradition allowing the accused to be set at liberty, *Muftis* should prefer that one tradition?' Badauni endorsed Akbar's statement but defended Abdun Nabi on the ground of political expediency. Akbar lost his temper for he believed that he alone should be the sole judge of political expediency.[22] Badauni became so hostile to Akbar that he even made clear his preference for the time of Bairam Khan.[23]

During the year 1579-80, Akbar spent a great deal of time in the *Ibadat Khana* and often throughout the night he was absorbed in discussing questions pertaining to religion.[24] The learned men continued to contradict and oppose one another and the antagonism of the sects reached such a pitch that they would call each other fools and heretics. The controversies gradually passed beyond the difference between Shia and Sunni, of Hanafi and Shafai. This constant fighting and the unbecoming behavior of the *Ulema* and *Mashaikh* annoyed Akbar. Actually these *Ulema* had no idea of debating any issue. They considered whatever they said to be infallible. Badauni recounts a story which reflected the true feelings and the attitude of *Ulema* like Abdullah Sultanpuri. 'One day I (Badauni), Shaikh Abul Fazl and Haji Sultan went to meet Makhdumul Mulk. We saw that he had before him the third volume of *Rauzatul Ahbad* written by a Sunni *alim* Jamaluddin Ataullah bin Fazlullah al-Husaini (d. 1520). He said to us, "See what mischief this Iranian has wrought on the faith" and thus saying he showed us that couplet which occurs as encomium to Imam Ali: 'This alone is sufficient to prove his resemblance to God, That it has been doubted that he himself was God.'

Makhdumul Mulk said,

He has passed beyond *rifz* here. I am firmly resolved to burn this book in the presence of a Shia. I (Badauni) who had never met Makhdumul Mulk before, made bold to say, This couplet is a translation of those verses which are attributed to *Imam* Shafai (d. AD 1819). He (Makhdum-ul-Mulk) looked towards me sharply and asked, 'From where are you quoting?' I said, 'From the commentary of *Imam's Diwan*. He said, 'The commentator, Qazi Mir *Husain-i-Maybuzi* (d. 1485) has also been accused of *rifz*.' I said, 'you are missing the point.' Shaikh Abul Fazl and Haji Sultan, with their fingers on their lips, were making signs to me to be silent. Again I said, 'I have heard from some trust worthy men that the third volume is not the work of Mir Jamaluddin, but is the work of his son Saiyid Mirak Shah, or some other person, and that it is for this reason that its style differs from that of the first two volumes, being poetical, and not the style peculiar to traditionalists. He answered saying, 'My child! In the second volume also I have found passages which clearly prove the *bidat* (sinful innovation) and mischief of the author's belief, and I have written notes on them. When the meeting ended and we left, Abul Fazl and Haji Sultan congratulated me for overcoming a great crisis. They added that had the Mulla decided to persecute you (Badauni) none could have saved you.[25]

Such a dictatorial attitude was followed by a section of the *ulema*. There was no space for difference of opinion. If they did not have an argument they could go to the extent of burning that book. Badauni was of the opinion that this attitude of the *Ulema* weakened the Emperor's faith in Islam. One such person was sufi, Shaikh Tajuddin, called Tajul Arifin. He called Akbar *Insan-i-Kamil*.[26] Discussions at the *Ibadat Khana* proved to be a catalyst in Akbar's fast-changing religious outlook. During this period learned monks arrived from Europe. Akbar began to take an interest in Christianity. He provided them full security because when these bigoted *Ulema* could not tolerate the followers of Islam belonging to non-Sunni sects how could they tolerate Christians, particularly those from Europe? Akbar had to convert his *Khushbu Khana* at Fathpur into a Church for Father Rudolf Acquaviva from Italy and Father Monserrate from Spain.[27] Abul Fazl; was asked to translate the Bible into Persian.[28]

During the year 1579-80 Akbar called renowned *Ulema* and *Mashaikh* from all over the country, had private interviews with each of them, and investigated several matters. Badauni felt these *Ulema* and *Mashaikh* were bribed by land grants, which was why according to him they agreed with the Emperor's interpretation of many religious problems.[29]

One major hurdle faced by Sunni *Ulema* was the *insdad-i-bad-i-ijtihad* (The Gates of *Ijtihad* were closed after the completion of four fights), as a result of which they could not go beyond it. Though this was contrary to the attitude of the founders of the four schools of jurisprudence, none of them (Imam Abu Hanifa, Imam Malik, Imam Shafai and Imam Hanbal) ever claimed the finality which later generations assigned to them. There were, however, Sunni scholars like Juwaini (d. 1085), Ibn Taimiya (d. 1328), Suyuti (d. 1505), Shah Waliullah and others who did not agree with the finality claimed by the majority of Sunni *Ulema* and insisted upon *Ijtihad*.

Badauni states that in 1579, Akbar was anxious to unite in his person, the spiritual as well as the political leadership of the state.[30] The stalemate was broken by Shaikh Mubarak through a document called *Mahzar* dated *Rajab*/August 1579, signed and sealed by Makhdum-ul-Mulk Abdullah Sultanpuri, Shaikh Abdun Nabi, Shaikh Mubarak, Qazi Jalaluddin, Sultan Khwaja and Ghazi Khan.[31]

Eminent *Ulema*, after discussing the issue in the light of *Ayat* of the Koran- 'Obey God and obey the Prophet and those in authority among you', and the *hadis* that 'it is the duty of the people to obey *Imam-i-Adil* and for this they will be rewarded and those who do not obey will be considered wrong doers'.[32] It is resolved that the status of *Sultan-i-Adil* is higher than the position of *Mujtahid*[33] and that *Hazrat Sultanul Islam Kahaful Anam Amirul Mauminin Zillillah Alaal Alameen Abul Fath* Jalauddin Muhammed Akbar *Padshah Ghazi Khuld Allah Mulkao*, is a judge, an intellectual and a scholar. Keeping in mind all these qualities of the Emperor, if there arose any difference of opinion among the *Mujtahidin*, to end that stalemate, he can on the basis of his wisdom give a final opinion which will be acceptable to all and will be binding on all to follow that.[34] If one the basis of his right thinking some *ahkam* are made which had no contradiction with Koranic injunctions and will be a cause of convenience for the *Ulema* and other persons following it will be compulsory for every individual and disobedience will be a reason for divine displeasure. To promote the rights of Islam, *Ulema-i-Din* and *Fuqha-i-Muhtadin* drafted this *Mahzar* and signed it. The *Mahzar* was signed by Shaikh Mubarak Makhdumul Mulk Abdullah Sultanpuri, Shaikh Abdun Nabi, Ghazi Khan, Qazi Jalaluddin and Sultan Khwaja. Akbar read the following *Khutba* from the *Mimbar* of the Jama Masjid at Fathpur:

> The Lord has given me the Empire,
> And a wise heart, and a strong arm.
> He has guided me in righteousness and Justice,
> And has removed from thoughts everything but Justice.
> His praise surpasses man's understanding,
> Great is his power, Allah-o-Akbar.

Badauni observes that all at once he (Akbar stammered and trembled, and though assisted by others, he could scarcely read three verses which were composed by Faizi.[35] These are very powerful verses and it would have become difficult for Akbar to control himself.

Abul Fazl comments on the *Mahzar*, '(They said) assuredly if the rank of *Ijtihad* is lower than the dignity of a *Nafs-i-Qudsi* (pure soul) be a dispeller of the darkness, a wise sovereign shall through select institutions become the pacifier of a disturbed hearts-The medicine suitable for the age, is to address the king in the style of *ijtihad* and then to represent to him the confusion of religions and creeds to beg him to untie the knot.'[36] It is quite surprising that though Badauni had given the full text of the *Mahzar* he recorded that, 'This document gave absolute authority to Akbar as *Imam-i-Adil* over the *Mujtahids*.'[37] In the preamble of the text of the *Mahzar*, the *Ulema* had quoted one *Ayat* of the Koran and one saying of Prophet in that the term of *Imam-i-Adil* is used. The *Ulema* recognized Akbar as *Sultan-i-Adil*.

The *Mahzar* was later on examined by several historians—V.A. Smith[38] followed by F.W. Buckler,[39] M.L. Roy Chaudhry,[40] S.R. Sharma,[41] R.P. Tripath,[42] S. Nurul Hasan,[43] I.A. Khan,[44] Muhammed Aslam,[45] Athar Ali,[46] K.A. Nizami,[47] S.A.A. Rizvi[48] and others. But there is a need to examine the views of these historians in the light of the text of the *Mahzar* and the accounts of contemporary historians.

It is surprising that after the fall of Mughal empire in 1857, no attempt was made by Muslim scholars to write a history of the Delhi Sultanat and Mughal empire. V.A. Smith was the first historian who examined the text of the *Mahzar* of Akbar's reign. Smith writes: 'six years later the time was considered ripe for extending the autocracy of Akbar from the temporal to the spiritual side by making him Pope as well as king.' Secondly, he interpreted the *Mahzar* as a decree of infallibility. Both these statements show that Smith failed to understand the spirit of *Mahzar*.

F.W. Buckler holds the opinion that the *Mahzar* was intended to fix the position of Akbar in the Muslim world by eliminating the religious or political control of Persia but without committing him to the allegiance of the Ottoman *Khalifa*.[49] Akbar was following the Turko-Mongol theory of kingship in which there was no place for the recognition of any Muslim ruler of Persia or the Ottomans. Secondly, the *Ulema* had only given the status of *Sultan-i-Adil* to Akbar, and that was restricted to the Mughal empire only. This status had nothing to do with Persia or the Ottomans. Buckler further elaborates his point of view by saying, 'the Mughal *Ulema* simply placed Akbar above the *Mujtahidin*—the Shia *Ulema* of Persia—and therefore, beyond Persian religious jurisdiction'.[50] These European scholars have an inadequate understanding of Islam. The concept of *Ijtihad* is basically an Islamic one. Both Sunnis and Shias recognize the institution of *Ijtihad*. Ghazali has defined *Ijtihad* and its categories at length. Shah Waliullah also believed in the institution of *Ijtihad*. Shia *Mujtahidin* of Persia had nothing to do with Akbar or the Mughal empire nor did Akbar's position as *Sultan-i-Adil* have any role in Persia. No objection came from Persia to Akbar holding the position of *Sultan-i-Adil*. But the Shah of Persia objected to Shahabuddin, the Mughal Emperor, when he adopted the title of *Shah-i-Jahan* (AD 1627-58).

Roy Chaudhry is of the opinion that, 'He (Akbar) intended to devise some means of freeing himself from the politico-religious pretentions of Iran and the religious hegemony of Rum. Thus very slyly the *Imam-i-Adil* of Hindustan was placed above the *Mujtahids* of Persia.'[51] Firstly, Akbar was the follower of Hanafi *Fiqh*. Persian rulers were following Jafari *Fiqh*. Both India and Persia had different religious jurisdictions. None of them could encroach on any body else's area. Secondly, the religious hegemony of Rum does not come into the picture because Akbar followed the Turko-Mongol theory of kinghsip. Thirdly, the position of *Imam-i-Adil* was not given by *Ulema* to Akbar. He was given the position of *Sultan-i-Adil*. The jurisdiction of *Sultan-i-Adil* was restricted to his empire. Akbar's authority had nothing to do with Central Asia or Iran at all and in that there was no place for the so-called Caliph. Mughal emperors of India did not recognize them. Further, he writes that 'The *Mahzar* made the orders of the Sultan binding on the whole nation, thus bringing the Shias under his authority.' He concludes his argument by saying that 'the *Mahzar* began by giving the Emperor Akbar the dignity of *Imam-i-Adil*, a title which no one, be it a Shia or a Sunni, could object to.[52] This title was not given by the *Ulema* to Akbar. People living in the Mughal empire whether they were Sunnis, Shias, Hindus or Christians had to follow Akbar. The Sunni *Ulema* signed the *Mahzar* and accepted Akbar as *Sultan-i-Adil*. A Shia *Alim* Qazi Saiyid Nurullah Shushtari also accepted Akbar as *Sultan-i-Adil* in his work *Risalat Luma Fi Salat Al-Juma*[53] and made it compulsory for all Shias to perform the Friday prayers in the presence of Akbar, the *Sultan-i-Adil*. Three possible reasons can be given for such interpretations by these historians. Firstly, they had no knowledge of the original language. Secondly, they relied on contemporary chronicles and did not consult the works of other *Ulema* of Akbar's period. Thirdly, they present such analysis intentionally to promote dissension between Sunnis and Shias.

R.P. Tripathi writes that, 'The *Mahzar*[54] was a challenge to the pretentious of the Sultan of Rum.' Did the Sultan of Rum exercise any religious or political control over the Mughal emperors of India? Even during the Sultanate of Delhi, some Sultans had regard for the so-called Caliph-Sultan Iltutmishand Firoz Shah Tughluq, for example. But there were other Sultans such as Alauddin Khalji or Ghiyasuddin Tughluq who did not pay any regard towards the so-called Caliph. So there was no question of considering the *Mahzar* of Akbar's reign as challenge to the pretentions of the Sultan of Rum.

S. Nurul Hasan examined the *Mahzar* of Akbar's reign and questioned the theses of earlier historians. Examining Roy Chaudhrys statement, Hasan writes that 'The statement of Mr. Roy Chaudhry that *Imam-i-Adil* of Hindustan was placed above the *Mujtahids* of Persia[55] and that 'Shias could not object to Akbar being given the title of *Imam-i-Adil* is based on some misconceptions.'[56] The term of *Imam-i-Adil* was not used in *Mahzar*, which makes the whole debate redundant.

Hasan raised some points which highlight the significance of *Mahzar*.

1. Abdullah Khan Uzbek had banned all schools of law except the Hanafi school.
2. The Shahs of Iran were ardent upholders of Shiaism (Jafari Schools) and recognized no other branch of law.
3. The Ottomans were no less bigoted in their outlook.
4. The *Mullahs* had formed a class of their own and had become very powerful.[57] The history of their securing power goes back to the days of Umaiyads.

No doubt Akbar wanted to create a congenial atmosphere in his empire and wanted to accommodate people of diverse religious groups. That could not be done without making the *Ulema* powerless. Secondly, as Badauni observed, there was so much difference of opinion that it was impossible to find one's way. Akbar, therefore, decided to accept the final authority of the *Ulema*.

I.A. Khan had also examined the issue of *Mahzar*. Khan writes, 'In the *Mahzar* the king's title as head of the orthodox Muslims (*Amirul Mauminin* and *Badshah-i-Islam*) rested on the sanction given by the leading *Ulema* of the realm.'[58] The title of *Badshah-i-Islam* is not given in the text of the *Mahzar*, the *Ulema* had given Akbar the title of *Sultan-i-Islam*. There is marked difference between *Badshah* and 'Sultan'. Khan writes, 'This phase of Akbar's policy ended some time around 1580. Apparently, the attempt to project Akbar's image as *Badshah-i-Islam* proved abortive. The revolt of 1580-1 showed that it failed to create the desired impression upon the Turani and Persian nobles, a new mode of revenue collection, and such other administrative reforms as affected their income and power. The dismissal of Shaikh Abdun Nabi and Makhdum-ul-Mulk (December 1579), and the abolition of *jizya* for the second time, in the tense political atmosphere indicate a sudden collapse of the policy pursued so vigorously during the preceding thirteen years.'[59]

Akbar's image was projected by the *Ulema* as *Sultan-i-Adil* and not as *Badshah-i-Islam*. This observation of Khan suggests that he did not read and examine the text of the *Mahzar*. It is not indicated where Khan had found this title. So his thesis that the *Mahzar* proved to be an abortive attempt falls to the ground because Akbar abolished *jizya* in 1564. In the same year an attempt was made on his life near the *Madrasa* of *Khairul Manazil* in Delhi. But Akbar had to re-impose *jizya* in 1575 under forced circumstances because the *Ulema* were very powerful. After getting empowered with the authority of *Sultan-i-Adil*, Akbar finally abolished the *jizya* in 1580, because the *Ulema* could not check or challenge Akbar's decisions. *Dagh* or the new mode of revenue-collection had nothing to do with Islam. No doubt some Turanis and Iranis joind the revolt against Akbar, but the majority of the Iranian and Turani *Ulema* and *Umara* also supported Akbar. That is why Akbar became successful in crushing this revolt.

Again, Khan writes, 'The turning point might well have come immediately after the *Mahzar*. This document not only failed to strengthen Akbar's hands but was responsible for reopening a very sensitive issue by seeking to provide a theological justification of his sovereignty. It is noteworthy that a *fatwa* of *Kufr* against Akbar appeared only after signing of the *Mahzar*. It is understandable that Akbar soon realized his mistake in issuing the *Mahzar* and took a decision to put it into cold storage.'[61]

It is not possible to agree with Khan that the *Mahzar* failed to strengthen Akbar's hands. In 1578 Akbar brought the issue of the execution of a Brahmin for discussion in the *Ibadat Khana* when the *Ulema* decided that the decision of Shaikh Abdun Nabi was not according to Islamic law. Akbar observed to Badauni, 'Have you heard that if there are ninety nine traditions inflicting the punishment of death for a certain offence, and one tradition allowing the accused to be set at liberty, the *Muftis* should prefer that tradition?' In Islam polity and religion is one and this *Mahzar* made Akbar the sole judge of political and religious authority. Badauni endorsed Akbar's statement but defended Shaikh Abdun Nabi on the ground of political expediency. Akbar lost his temper for he believed that he himself was the sole judge of political expediency.'[62] The *Mahzar* gave Akbar the power of the sole judge by declaring him as *Sultan-i-Adil* whose status was higher than *Mujtahidin*. The *fatwa* of *Kufr* against Akbar challenged the decision of those *Ulema* who recognized him as *Sultan-i-Adil* because once Akbar was declared a *kafir*, the *Mahzar* would automatically become redundant. But there were *Ulema* like Shaikh Abdul Haq Muhaddis Dehlavi, who declared Akbar as *Khalifa-i-Ahd* and *Sultan-i-Zaman* and a Shia *Alim* Qazi Saiyid Nurullah Shushtari who accepted Akbar as *Sultan-i-Adil*. There was a large number of eminent *Ulema* who were staunch supporters of Akbar. The action of few *ulema* should not be given so much weightage. So the *Mahzar* never proved to be abortive, and basically strengthened the hands of Akbar. As Badauni observed, Akbar must have realized that it was essential that a decree be promulgated to give him supreme powers in religious matters also and it was keeping this in mind that the *Mahzar* was promulgated.[63]

Khan further elaborates his point by saying, 'the policy behind the *Mahzar* ended in a debacle, this very failure liberated Akbar from the fetters of a pro-Islamic policy. Subsequently, there was, more or less, a smooth unfolding of Akbar's enlightened religious policy based on his philosophy of *Sulh-i-kul*.'[64]

The *Mahzar* was not a debacle. Khan contradicts himself by saying, 'It liberated Akbar from the fetters of a pro-Islamic policy'[65] and 'Akbar's enlightened religious policy was based on his philosophy of *Sulh-i-kul*.'[66] Akbar never followed an anti-Islamic policy. We do not find any difference in his religious policy before or after 1580. Akbar only liberated himself from the clutches of the bigoted *Ulema* or in the words of Abul Fazl, 'little minds.' Akbar's policy of *Sulh-i-kul* was based on Maulana Rum, Hafiz Shirazi and Shaikh Saadi's concept of *Sulh-i-kul*, which were within the spirit of Islam. So we cannot accept the view of Khan that Akbar liberated himself from the fetters of a pro-Islamic policy, Akbar gives his own observation about his position in one of his verse: 'My place is neither among pagans nor Muslims' Unfit as I am both for hell and for heaven, what should I do?'[67]

Badauni's observation also goes against Khan's thesis when he records, 'As a result of all this, those who (*Ulema*) had earlier been in favour with the Emperor and close to him fell out, and those (*ulema*) were out of favour became close to the Emperor, thus his earlier companions and friends were alienated, and strangers and aliens became kin to him.'[68]

Athar Ali in his article on the religious ideas of Akbar writes, 'There is no doubt that Safavid Iran exercised considerable influence on the minds and manners of Akbar's court. The Safavid Shah was also a religious figure, a representative of the *Imam*, and thus superior to all religious divines of the country.'[69] This is factually incorrect because among Shias the *Naib Imam* of Imam Mehdi will always be the superior religious authority. Every Shia whether he is a ruler or a subject will be under the *Taqlid* of *Naib Imam*. Secondly, the Safavid Shah was not the representative of Imam Mehdi but the representative of the *Naib Imam* of Imam Mehdi. There is a marked difference between Sunni and Shia belief, relating to the concept of *Imam*.

Athar Ali makes two comments

(1) 'But we can see how that the *Mahzar* did not ultimately meet Akbar's ambitions: and (2) Abul Fazl in his *Akbar Nama* passes it by very casually.'[70] It is not clear as to what type of ambitions of Akbar, Athar Ali, had in mind. The *Ulema* recognized Akbar as *Sultan-i-Adil*, whose status was higher than that of the *Mujtahidin*; he became the highest authority both in religious and political affairs. For example after getting empowered by this authority he finally abolished *jizya* in 1579. In the Koran there is an *Ayat*, 'Obey God and obey the Prophet and those in authority among you'. The *Ulema* recognized Akbar as *Olil Amr* (authority).

Secondly, Abul Fazl makes a significant comment on *Mahzar*, but he does not believe in repetition. 'Assuredly if the rank of *ijtihad* which is lower than the dignity of *Nafs-i-Qudsi* (Pure Soul) be a dispeller of the darkness, a wise sovereign shall by choice of institutions become the pacifier of disturbed hearts-The medicine suitable for the age is to address the king by the style of *Ijtihad* and then to represent to him the confusion of religions and creeds to beg him to untie the knot.'[71] Abul Fazl makes an apt comment because he was a scholar of repute. He does not copy the words and the titles used by *Ulema* in the text of the *Mahzar*. In the text of the *Mahzar*, the title of *Sultan-i-Adil* is used. He uses the title of *Nafs-i-Qudsi*. The text states that the status of *Sultan-i-Adil* is higher than that of a *Mujtahid*. Abul Fazl writes that the rank of *Ijtihad* is lower than the dignity of *Nafs-i-Qudsi*. In Abul Fazl's words this

Mahzar will remove the confusion of religions and creeds to beg him to untie the knot.'[72] This comment of Abul Fazl is sufficient to negate Athar Ali's statement.

Again, Athar Ali writes, 'Akbar had already begun looking towards other religions, first out of animosity, and after the *Mahzar*, out of increasing desire to put his own position beyond the narrow framework of traditional Islam.'[73] There is nothing like 'The narrow framework of traditional Islam.' Basically Akbar escaped from the clutches of some short-sighted and bigoted Sunni *Ulema*.

Athar Ali states that, 'There is need, first of all, to establish accurately what views Akbar held or developed after the failure of his appeasement of Muslim orthodoxy that had culminated in the *Mahzar* of 1579, i.e. during the period 1581-1605'?[74] The idea, of *Mahzar* had been mooted by Shaikh Mubarak who was also an *Alim* and not party to Sunni orthodoxy. Bigoted Sunni *Ulema* like Makhdum-ul-Mulk Abdullah Sultanpuri and Shaikh Abdun Nabi were forced to sign the *Mahzar*. The *Mahzar* snatched power from Sunni orthodoxy, so there was no question of 'appeasement'. We do not find any significant change in the policies of Akbar after 1581, and historians who write 'Muslim orthodoxy' should correctly call it 'Sunni orthodoxy'. Sunni orthodoxy was in power, and other sects of Muslims had nothing to do with it.

Athar Ali writes, 'It is significant that throughout the *Akbar Nama* and *Ain-i-Akbari*, a very neutral terminology is adopted in reference to Islam. Islam is not stepped as such at all. It is usually called '*Ahmedi Kesh*', i.e., the Muhammadan doctrine, as one may say in English. *Ahmedi Kaish*[75] is clearly a term coined by Akbar or by Abul Fazl with his approval. No other work in Persian ever uses such a designation for Islam. Was it that the word Islam, implying peace as the characteristic element of the faith, was thought by Akbar to be too value-loaded, to be used for it?[76] But the term *Ahmedi Kaish* and *Din-i-Muhammadi* is used by many Muslim scholars and Persian poets for Islam, and it is difficult to believe that these terms were coined by Akbar or Abul Fazl, as is suggested by Athar Ali. Secondly, Islam does not mean 'peace', its meaning is 'obedience'.

Athar Ali comments, 'The implicit but repeated suggestions by Athar Abbas Rizvi in his recent work that Akbar was hostile to Sunni orthodoxy, has little basis. Shia theologians were by no means more liberal than the Sunnis in their attitude to non-Muslims'.[77] This explains why Athar Ali writes 'Muslim orthodoxy' rather than 'Sunni orthodoxy' Makhdumul Mulk was the first Indian Sunni *Alim* who wrote a book-

Minhajud Din wa Mairajul Muslimin, to prove that Shia faith is *batil* (false). Badauni writes, 'He (Makhdum-ul-Mulk) always strenuously, exerted himself to enforce the holy (Sunni) law, and was a bigoted Sunni. Owing to his exertions many *Malahida* (heretics) and *Rawafiz* (Shias) went to the place (hell) prepared for them.[78] Shaikh Hamid, a famous Sunni *Alim*, asked Humayun whether his entire army consisted of *Rafizis* (Shias). Humayun requested the Shaikh to spell out the reasons for such an opinion. He said, 'Everywhere the names of your soldiers are of this kind: Yar Ali, Kashf Ali, Hyder Ali. I have not found a single man bearing the name of any other companion. Humayun calmly explained to the Shaikh the purity of his Sunni faith.'[79] On the other hand Abul Fazl comments on the personality of Mir Abdul Latif, 'From his lack of bigotry and his broadmindedness he was called in India a Shia. In fact he was journeying towards the serene city of universal tolerance.' Abul Fazl expresses his opinion about Shah Fathullah, a Shia scholar, 'The company of that spiritually great man had wrought a revolution in his own ideas.'[81] Badauni calls him, 'That wonder of the age Shah Fathullah.'[82] Up to the end of the sixteenth century no Shia Alim wrote any book against the faith of Sunnis and Hindus. While Mir Murtaza Shirazi's dead body was shifted from the vicinity of Amir Khusrau's upon the *fatwa* of Sunni *Ulema*, Ahmed Thattaiv was killed by a Sunni because he was a Shia. In the Mughal empire Shias were not implicated for similar actions as Akbar was hostile towards the bigoted Sunni *Ulema* because since the days of *Umaiyads* they had dominated Muslim rulers and politics. Shias never shared power ever since the foundation of Sultanat in India upto the first half of Akbar's reign.

Athar Ali writes, 'Certainly there was no exaltation anywhere of the person or status of Ali in any of the happy sayings of Akbar or in Abul Fazl's works.'[83] 'Exaltation of the person and status of Ali' is found in the writings of a large number of Sunni *Ulema, sufia* and poets of Akbar's reign. Their writings are proof of this. Athar Ali quotes the letter of Mirza Aziz Koka written in 1594 from Mecca. Aziz Koka warned Akbar that there were insincere nobles, who 'prefer the infidels to the Muslims.'[84] This letter itself strengthens the argument that Sunni orthodoxy was very powerful and trying to influence Akbar. The text of this letter shows that a section of Sunni orthodoxy was against Akbar's policy of *Sulh-i-kul*.

The determining force was not religion but interests in land. Akbar modified rules for *Madad-i-Maash* grants.

These new rules were made to check fraud by the holders of *Madad-i-Maash*[85] grants.

(i) All land grants of above 500 *bigahs* were held forfeit unless approved afresh by the Emperor.

(ii) In grants of above 100 *bigahs*, three-fifths of the area was to be resumed, except in the case of grants held by Irani and Turani women.

(iii) All lands held in grant were transferred to specified villages.

(iv) If anyone asked for a transfer of land for convenience, he had to lose a fourth part of it.

(v) Upon the death of a grantee holding a land grant exceeding 15 *bigahs* of land, the land was to be resumed until the heirs proved their descent before the Emperor.

(vi) Even less than 100 *bigahs* were to be rechecked by the *Sadr* and Abul Fazl would himself verify that these were not obtained by undeserving *Ulema.*[86] Higher grants would be given by the Emperor on the basis of merit and scholarship, not on the basis of hereditary right of succession. So it was a loss to the sons of those *Ulema* who were not scholars, who wanted to hold these grants after the death of their father. Secondly, women got a concession while male *Ulema* were deprived of this concession. Male *Ulema* considered themselves superior to women, and wanted all privileges to be enjoyed by them. So the *Ulema* also felt hurt by this attitude of the Emperor. Even grants of less than 100 *bigahs* were to be checked by the *Sadr* and Abul Fazl, so that they should not be held by undeserving scholars. As Abul Fazl writes, 'those turban-wearers of evil heart and long-Sleaved ones of little minds.'[87] The effect of these regulations relating to grantees of *Madad-i-Maash* grants can be imagined. Through these positive measures Akbar had reduced the insolent *Ulema* to order and had restrained them within bounds as closely as a nut is enclosed in its shell, and to such a degree that stricter discipline could not be imagined. Badauni believed that things reached such a pass that very often Abul Fazl held religious arguments with old men like the *Sadr*, the Qazi, Hakim Ainul Mulk and Makhdum-ul-Mulk and did not hesitate to humiliate them.[88] It also reflects the depth of their scholarship. There are instances when they came across any book which went against their belief they used to burn it.[89] As a result of all these reformist steps of Akbar, the majority of ignorant *Ulema* adopted a hostile attitude towards him. I agree with Athar Ali's view, 'Critics of *Sulh-i-kul* were naturally prone to denounce it with much exaggeration.'[90] A section of Sunni *Ulema* believed in creating divisions, and doing all sorts of injustices against those who did not agree with them. So since the concept of *Sulh-i-kul* was against the fundamentals of their ideology, Akbar was declared a *kafir*.

Prof. Athar Abbas Rizvi writes, 'Shaikh Mubarak through a document called *Mahzar* dated *Rajab*, 987/September 1579 had the powers of the *Imam-i-Adil* (the first ruler) reaffirmed by *Ulema* within the framework of Sunni law.' Rizvi is not correct when he says that Akbar was given the authority of *Imam-i-Adil*. Secondly, he is not right in saying 'the powers of the *Imam-i-Adil* were reaffirmed by the *Ulema* within the framework of Sunni Law.' Concept of *Imam-i-Adil* is part of the *hadis* of Prophet Muhammed and comes within the framework of Islam. It cannot be restricted to Sunnis only. Shias are also bound to follow the *hadis* of Prophet Muhammed. In the *Mahzar* the *Ulema* had empowered Akbar with the authority of *Sultan-i-Adil* and that had been accepted by a Shia *Alim*, Qazi Saiyid Nurullah Shushtari.

Abul Kalam Azad holds the opinion that Akbar could no longer be called as *Imam-i-Adil* because it could be impinged from the Shia belief that their twelfth *Imam* alone is *Imam-i-Adil*. Maulana Azad was also faced with the same problem that when the title of *Imam-i-Adil* was not given to Akbar then there is no question of discussion on that.

During the Sultanat Shias could not get positions in the administration because *Ulema* like Ziauddin Barani were of the view that no non-Sunni Mulsim should be accommodated in the administration of the Sultanat. Several books were written against the Shia faith. Ibn Taimiya (d. 1328) wrote *Minhaj al-Sunnat al-Nabawiya fi Naqd Kalam al-Shia al-qadriya* around AD 1320, Ibn Hajar al-Haysani (1504-67) wrote *Sawaiq al-Muhriqa Fi Radd ala aklil rafz wal zandaqa* in 1544. Mirza Makhdum Sharifi wrote *Nawaqiz Fil Radd ala al-Rawafiz* in 1579-80 in Baghdad and dedicated it to the Ottoman Sultan Murad III (1574-95) The first book on Shia-Sunni polemics was written in India, by Makhdumul Mulk Abdullah Sultanpuri-*Minhajud Din wa Mairajul Muslimin*. Akbar must have read these books because all of them were available in India.

With the establishment of the Mughal empire, there was total domination by Chaghtais and Turani nobles. Humayun was defeated by Sher Shah and had to take refuge under the patronage of the Shah of Persia. With the help of the Shah, Humayun became successful in re-conquering his lost empire. Humayun was convinced of the inability of the Turanis to collaborate with Iranis. He, therefore, made three divisions in his army. The biggest under his own command comprised

202 officers. Of these not more than 15 were Iranis. The second division consisting of 56 officers was placed under Akbar. Of these only half a dozen were Iranis. The third contingent was placed under Bairam Khan. It consisted of 54 officers who were, with the exception of about six, all Iranis. It shows that there were tensions in the Mughal nobility between Turanis and the Iranis from the very beginning.[92]

After Humayun's death, Bairam Khan appointed Mir Abdul Latif as Akbar's tutor. Abul Fazl who was deeply impressed with the intellectual attainments of Mir Abdul Latif says, 'From his lack of bigotry and his broadmindedness he was called in India a Shia and in Persia a Sunni. In fact he was journeying on towards the serene city of universal tolerance and so the zealots of each sect used to censure him'.[93] It seems that Mir Abdul Latif left a deep impression on Akbar's mind.

After becoming familiar, with the role of Makhdum-ul-Mulk and Shaikh Abdun Nabi, reading the books on the polemical debates between the Shias and Sunnis outside India, and listening to discussions in the *Ibadat Khana*, Akbar concluded that he would follow the policy of *Sulh-i-kul* (Peace with all). This policy was a threat for the bigoted *Ulema*. Since the days of the *Umaiyads* they had enjoyed power and had indulged in discriminations of the basis of being Arab/non-Arab/*Ajami*/*Mawali* (new Muslims) and belonging to any other sect. The polity developed by the *Umaiyads* was based on all sorts of discriminations, and they had given full power to the *Ulema* to practice it freely and fearlessly. The Abbasids came to power to raise a hue and cry against these discriminations but they also followed policies based on discrimination. The Sultans of Delhi also followed the *Umaiyads* and Abbasids. During the early years of Akbar's reign Badauni writes, 'He (Makhdum-ul-Mulk) always strenuously exerted himself to enforce the holy (Sunni) law, and was a bigoted Sunni. Owing to these exertions many *Malahida* (heretics) and *Rafzis* (Shias) went to the place prepared for them.'[94]

Akbar made religious tolerance an essential element of his policy of *Sulh-i-kul* which he declared in 1580. As a result of this policy, a healthy atmosphere was created. Akbar had given full financial support to meritorious *Ulema* irrespective of their sectarian affiliations. He did not restrict his policy of *Sulh-i-kul* to political affairs only. He linked it with culture. In the second half of the sixteenth century Akbar changed the old concept of state, as defined by Barani in *Fatawa-i-Jahandari*. He tried to create unity in Indian society and culture. Jahangir explains Akbar's policy of *Sulh-i-kul*, in these words, 'As in the wide expanse of the divine compassion there is room for all classes and the followers of all creeds, so on the principle that the shadow must have the same properties as the Light, in his dominions, which on all sides were limited only by the salt sea, there was room for the professions of all opposite religions, and for beliefs good and bad, and the road to altercation was closed. Sunnis and Shias met in one mosque, and Franks and Jews in one Church, and observed their own forms of worship.'[95] Faizi's poetry buttressed Akbar's ambitions to allow all religious communities to promote their spiritual aspirations in an atmosphere of peace and amity. Things reached such an extent that Badauni observes, 'Fathullah Shirazi used to perform Shia prayers with great composure in the *Diwan Khana-i-Khas*.'[96]. Badauni believed that if the bounty of all the former rulers of Hindustan were thrown into one scale, and the liberality of Akbar's age was thrown into the other, still Akbar's age would be far heavier than the past and present combined.[97]

NOTES

1. Agra is an old town situated on the bank of river Yamuna. It is around 180 kms. from Delhi. Sikander Lodi had shifted the capital from Delhi to Agra. Mughals also made Agra the capital of their empire. During the reign of Akbar large number of Iranian *Ulema* came from Iran and settled down in Agra. As a result of the settlement of large number of *Ulema* in Agra during the second half of sixteenth century, Agra emerged as a centre of learning. Several *Madarsas* were established by eminent scholars in Agra. Mughal emperors, princes, princesses, *Umara, Ulema* and others had taken interest in building monuments of various categories in Agra. Qazi Saiyid Nurullah Shushtari's tomb is also situated in Dayal Bagh, Agra. Shah Jahan shifted the capital back from Agra to Delhi.
2. *Madrasa* is a centre of learning. These centres were founded to impart education. With the establishment of Turkish rule in India several *Madrasas* were established. The famous *Madrasa* of Delhi Sultanat was that of Firoz Shah Tughluq which he established at Hauz-i-Khas.
3. Mir Murtaza Shirazi was an Iranian scholar and a Shia. He died in Delhi and was buried near the tomb of Amir Khusrau in the campus of the *dargah* of Nizamuddin Aulia. Some Sunni *Ulema* objected to his burial. Abdul Qadir Badauni, *Muntakhab-ut Tawarikh*, Vol. II, p. 203.
4. Esfahan is a town in Iran. It has beautiful monuments. Esfahan is called as '*Nisf-i-Jahan*' (Half of the World).
5. Badauni, op, cit., Vol. II, p. 124.
6. Ibid., Vol. II, p. 255.
7. In history books and also the Archaeological Survey of India, records

pointed to another building as *Ibadat Khana* which it is not. Recently Mr. Muhammed K.K., Superintending Archaeologist, ASI, Agra Circle, with the help of a contemporary painting of *Ibadat Khana*, and its description given by Badauni, established its real location and has also excavated the structure of *Ibadat Khana* in front of the eastern gate of Jama Masjid at Fathpur.

8. Badauni, op. cit., Vol. II, p. 201.
9. Ibid., Vol. II, p. 25.
10. Ibid., Vol. II, p. 299.
11. Please see the painting of *Ibadat Khana*. Recently Mr. Muhammed K.K., Superintending Archaeological Survey of India, Agra Circle, has excavated and developed the platform of *Ibadat Khana*.
12. Badauni, op. cit., Vol. II, p. 299.
13. Abul Fazl, *Akbar Nama*, Vol. III, p. 365.
14. Badauni, Vol. II, p. 202.
15. *Dabistan-i-Mazahib*, Vol. I, pp. 99, 100.
16. Badauni, Vol. II, pp. 207, 208.
17. Ibid., Vol. II, p. 212.
18. Ibid., Vol. II, p. 201.
19. Ibid., Vol. II, pp. 211, 308.
20. Ibid., Vol. II, p. 308.
21. Ibid., Vol. II, p. 308.
22. Ibid., Vol. III, pp. 79-83.
23. Ibid., Vol. III, p. 33.
24. Ibid., p. 33.
25. Ibid., Vol. III, pp. 113-16.
26. Ibid.
27. Abul Fazl, Vol. III, p. 365.
28. Ibid., Vol. II, pp. 255-60.
29. Badauni, Vol. II, p. 285.
30. Ibid., Vol. III, p. 83.
31. Ibid.
32. Please see the text of *Mahzar*.
33. Ibid.
34. Ibid.
35. Badauni, Vol. II, p. 268.
36. Abul Fazl, op. cit., Vol. III, p. 397.
37. Badauni, Vol. II, p. 270.
38. V.A. Smith, *Akbar, the Great Mughal.*
39. F.W. Buckler, *JRAS*, 1924.
40. M.L. Roy Chaudhry, *Din-i-Ilahi*, Calcutta.
41. S.R. Sharma, *The Religious Policy of the Mughal Emperors*, Bombay, 1962.
42. R.P. Tripathi, *Some Aspects of Muslim Administration.*

43. S. Nurul Hasan, *The Mahzar of Akbar's Reign.*
44. I.A. Khan, *The Nobility under Akbar and the Development of his Religious Policy 1560-80*, *JRAS*, 1963, No. 1.
45. Muhammed Aslam, *Din-i-Ilahi Aur Uska Pas Manzar.*
46. Athar Ali, *Sulh-i-kul and the Religious Ideas of Akbar.*
47. K.A. Nizami, *Akbar and Religion.*
48. S.A.A. Rizvi, *Religious and Intellectual History of the Muslims in Akbar's Reign.*
49. Buckler, op. cit., p. 591.
50. Ibid., p. 591.
51. Roy, op. cit., p. 119.
52. Ibid., p. 119.
53. Qazi Saiyid Nurullah Shushtari, *Risalat Luma Fi Salat Al-Juma.*
54. Tripathi, op. cit., p. 143.
55. Hasan, op. cit., p. 11.
56. Ibid., p. 11.
57. Ibid., pp. 17, 18.
58. Khan, op. cit., p. 34.
59. Ibid., p. 35.
60. Badauni, op. cit., Vol. II. p. 60, Abul Fazl; op. cit., Vol. II. p. 313.
61. Khan, op. cit., p. 35.
62. Badauni, op. cit., Vol. III, pp. 79-83.
63. Ibid., Vol. III. p. 83.
64. Khan, op. cit., p. 35.
65. Ibid., p. 35.
66. Ibid., p. 35.
67. Verses of Akbar quoted by Prof. Hadi Hasan.
68. Badauni, op. cit., Vol. II, p. 308.
69. Ali, op. cit., p. 28.
70. Ibid., p. 29.
71. Abul Fazl, Vol. III, p. 393.
72. Ibid., Vol. III, p. 393.
73. Ali, op. cit., p. 29.
74. Ibid., p. 29.
75. Ibid., p. 29. Spelling of 'Kesh' is wrongly written by Prof. Athar Ali. Correct spelling is 'Kaish'.
76. Ali, op. cit., p. 32.
77. Ibid., p. 35.
78. Badauni, op. cit., Vol. III, p. 70.
79. Ibid., Vol. I, pp. 468, 469.
80. Abul Fazl, op. cit., Vol. II, p. 35.
81. Ibid., Vol. III, pp. 848, 849.
82. Badauni, op. cit., Vol. II, pp. 379-82.

85. Abul Fazl, *Ain*, Vol. I, p. 198.
86. Ibid., Vol. I, p. 198.
87. Ibid., Vol. I, p. 198.
88. Ibid., Vol. II, p. 263.
89. Badauni, op. cit., Vol. III, p. 70.
90. Ali, op. cit., p. 39.
91. Rizvi, op. cit., p. 217.
92. Bayazid Bayat, *Tazkira-i-Humayun Wa Akbar*, pp. 176-87.
93. Badauni, op. cit., Vol. II, p. 70.
94. Ibid., Vol. II, p. 70.
95. Jahangir, *Tuzuk-i-Jahangiri*, Vol. I, London, 1909, pp. 37, 38.
96. Badauni, op. cit., Vol. II, p. 315.
97. Ibid., Vol. II, p. 71.

Imadul Mulk Ghaziuddin Khan: His Rise and Fall

Mohd. Umer

Imadul Mulk was the son of Ghaziuddin Khan Firoz Jang,[1] the eldest son of Nizamul Mulk Asaf Jah.[2] As an extremely reserved and godly man, Firoz Jang spent his days in the company of theologians and his nights in vigils; the life of his household was strictly puritan. These qualities he had inherited from his mother, who was the daughter of a pious *shaikh* of Gulbarga. He himself was married to Zeb-un Nisa, the daughter of the *wazir*, Itmad-ud Daula Qamaruddin Khan.[3]

As far as the early life and bringing up of Imadul Mulk is concerned, there are two versions. One, Saiyid Ghulam Ali Khan informs us that when Ghaziuddin Khan was about to depart for the Deccan after the death of his father Nizamul Mulk Asaf Jah in 1748, he wanted to hand over his son, Mir Shihabuddin, who was also called Mir or Khwaja Habshi, as well as Khwaja Narwari,[4] because he was born there on 1 February 1736, to the eunuch Jawid Khan, but his high sense of self-respect did not permit him to do so. Hence holding his hand, Ghaziuddin Khan entrusted his young son, Mir Shihabuddin in the care of Safdar Jang, and thereafter he left for the Deccan. Till the age of 16 or less, Mir Shihabuddin used to come to Safdar Jang, and he treated him as his father. Mir Shihabuddin was brought up by his pious father with utmost strictness. He spent his days with tutors and theologians. He was never allowed to mix with the boys of his own age, or with the eunuchs, nor to attend any performance by dancing girls though this was the universal amusement of all classes in that age and almost a matter of course at every social gathering. Saiyid Ghulam Ali Khan comments that the wise men never allowed their sons to get accustomed to such things. If Firoz Jang had not imposed such restrictions on him, it would not have been possible that his son in infancy had learnt seven styles of calligraphy. He mastered several languages, including Turkish. As a scholar, he was versed in several branches of knowledge and composed poetry of some note, both in Persian and *rekhta* (Urdu) under his penname 'Nizam'.[5] He had a deep knowledge of the secrets of men. None of the sons of the noble men of the age had acquired such a training and culture at this young age, still under teens, and he was even envied by the sons of the learned men and the *ulama*. Afterwards he rose to political power and gained the titles of Imadul Mulk, Ghaziuddin Khan Bahadur Firoz Jang, *Mir Bakhshi*, *Aminul Umara*, Nizamul Mulk Asaf Jah.[6]

When the news of the death of Ghaziuddin Khan Firoz Jang at Aurangabad on 29 October 1752, reached Delhi, Intizam-ud Daula Khan-i Khanan, the uterine brother of Shihabuddin's mother, instigated the emperor that he (Shihabuddin) should be imprisoned and his house be demolished and the wealth Firoz Jang had hoarded in his Delhi mansion be seized. Half of it should be confiscated to the imperial exchequer and the other half be left for his family. In the meantime, Aqibat Mahmud Khan Kashmiri, a man of great wisdom and ability was the tutor of Shihabuddin. As coached by his tutor, Shihabuddin at once went to the *wazir*, Safdar Jang's house, spent there the whole night and next day in weeping. Taking pity on the orphan, Safdar Jang embraced him. Consoling him he said, 'My son, you sit contended in your home and I regard you more than Shuja-ud Daula (his own son). You are my one eye and the other your brother Shuja-ud Daula.' Thereafter, Safdar Jang went to the emperor and reminded him that during the reign of the emperor Muhammad Shah, Nizamul Mulk Asaf Jah had rendered meritorious services and Firoz Jang likewise had served him loyally. Now his son, Mir Shihabuddin, hoped that under the shadow of your Majesty, should serve the state like his grandfather and father. He should now be bestowed the *khilat* of the *Mir Bakhshi* and the title of *Amirul Umara*. The emperor Ahmad Shah retorted by saying that, 'Do you not know the condition of these Turanis? They were the main cause for the ruin of the empire and disgrace of my illustrious family, and they are, too, a thorn in your path. You should keep silent in this matter. I want to confer the *khilat* of *Mir Bakhshi* or Shuja-ud Daula. Being a well-wisher of the court, what is the need that you should say something against my wishes?' In short, Safdar Jang prevented Firoz Jang's property being confiscated under the law of escheat by the king and persuaded the reluctant emperor to appoint Shihabuddin as *Mir Bakhshi*, with the title of Ghaziuddin Khan Bahadur Firoz Jang, *Amirul Umara* and Imadul Mulk, on 12 December 1753. Later on Nizamul Mulk Asaf Jah was added to his former titles. Till then, he outwardly professed to be the *wazir's* partisan.[7]

The second version about Shihabuddin's early life has been given by the emperor Ahmad Shah himself, who had to suffer much humiliations and intimidation at the hands of his nobles particularly from Safdar Jang, Intizam-ud Daula and Imadul Mulk. During the civil war between the emperor and his *wazir*, Safdar Jang, the former had expressed his bitter views about the disloyalty and betrayal of the above mentioned three nobles of his court before the Raja Madho Singh, whom he had summoned for his assistance. Contrary to the statement of Ghulam Ali Khan, that Shihabuddin Khan was brought up by Safdar Jang, the emperor said that,

> It is well known to the gentry and commonalty alike that I took up these as infants from the care of Hazrat Firdaus Aramgah (emperor Muhammad Shah) and brought them up as my own sons. The first was Imadul Mulk, s/o Nizamul Mulk Fath Jang (Ghaziuddin Khan Firoz Jang), the second was the *khan-i khanan* (Intizam-ud Daula), s/o Asaf-ud Daula Qamaruddin Khan Chin Bahadur and the third was Abul Mansur Khan Safdar Jang, the son-in-law of Burhanul Mulk Saadat Khan. Firdaus Aramgah, who was an unparalleled physiognomist, later on told me that these three infants were unworthy and their disloyalty radiates from their foreheads. A time came when it appeared as if their ruin had become imminent, but I saved them. Firdaus Aramgah told me that in no case should they be given any office of power. Qamaruddin Khan, too, did not like them to be raised to prominence. I, however, ignoring their advices, kept them with me day and night as my own sons. First of all, I made Abul Mansur Khan as my *wazir*. Since the foreboding of my father were based on truth, disloyalty came out from his deeds. Hence, I dismissed him and appointed Intizam-ud Daula *khan-i khanan* as my *wazir*. I appointed Imadul Mulk on the post of *Mir Bakhshi*. All their activities were against my wishes'.[8]

By saying that the above-mentioned three infants had been brought up by him, Ahmad Shah actually meant that at first they had enjoyed favour and patronage from the emperor Muhammad Shah and thereafter from him. In fact they were brought up in their respective families and with the passage of time when they grew up, they were raised to high positions of power, but despite these favours, they proved to be disloyal and caused much humiliation to Ahmad Shah and acted against the interest of their master and the state.

To understand properly the party politics at the court of Ahmad Shah and his ultimate downfall, we should briefly study the prevailing conditions in the court during the *wizarat* of Safdar Jang.

REIGN OF AHMAD SHAH: NEW OFFICIAL APPOINTMENTS

Mirza Muhammad Muqim (later on Abul Mansur Khan Safdar Jang), was the son-in-law of Saadat Khan Burhanul Mulk, whom in 1723 he had appointed his deputy in Awadh and obtained for him the title of Abul Mansur Khan from the emperor Muhammad Shah.[9] After the death of Saadat Khan (1739) Muhammad Shah conferred on Abul Mansur Khan, the title of Safdar Jang and confirmed him in Awadh with all its *sarkars*, granting him the *jagirs* held by his uncle.[10] In 1744, Muhammad Shah appointed him as *Mir-i Atish* on the recommendation of Umdatul Mulk Amir Khan *Anjam*, who headed the Irani party at the court.[11] In short, holding the post of *Mir-i Atish*, Safdar Jang must have seen that the Turani party was very powerful during the reign of Muhammad Shah and there existed great rivalry and hostility between these two parties to gain and retain the political power at the court. It was due to this background that when Safdar Jang was appointed as *wazir*, in place of the former *wazir*, Qamaruddin Khan, who was killed in the battlefield with Ahmad Shah Abdali in 1747, he was so much afraid of Nizamul Mulk Asaf Jah, who headed the Turani party that his appointment was kept in top secrecy. It was when the news of Nizam's death reached the court in 1748, that he formally began to attend the office of the *wazir*.[12]

Notwithstanding the fact that the atmosphere at the court was surcharged with intense rivalries between these two parties, Safdar Jang committed a great blunder from the very beginning of his *wizarat* in the distribution of the offices in the Central government. For instance, in addition to the governorship of Awadh, which he held since the death of Saadat Khan (1739), he secured the governorship of Agra and Ajmer for himself. Later on he secured the governorship of Allahabad in place of Ajmer, because this *subah* was adjunct to Awadh. Thus in addition to the post of the *wazir*, he became the governor of three most important and prosperous provinces of northern India.[13]

The other important office of *Mir Bakhshi* was held by Nizamul Mulk Asaf Jah and after his departure to the Deccan, his son Ghaziuddin Khan Firoz Jang held this post at the court as his deputy. After his death in 1748, instead of confirming Ghaziuddin Khan in that post, it was given to Sadat (Salabat) Khan Bahadur Zulfiqar Jang (a friend of Safdar Jang and a Shia) with the rank of 8000/8000.[14] Safdar Jang's son replaced his father as the *Mir-i Atish* with the title of Jalaluddin Haidar Khan Shuja-ud Daula Bahadur Jang.[15] Ahmad Ali Khan, an adopted son of one of the sisters of Safdar Jang, was appointed as the *Bakhshi-i Ahdiyan*.[16] Abdullah Khan and Saduddin Khan were retained to the posts of *sadr* and *khan-*

i saman respectively.[17] Najm-ud Daula Muhammad Ishaq Khan held the post of *divan-i khalisa*, after the death of his father, Mutamad-ud Daula Muhammad Ishaq Khan, during the reign of the emperor Muhammad Shah. He was now confirmed on the same post because he was the brother-in-law of Shuja-ud Daula.[18] Among the Turani nobles, Intizam-ud Daula *khan-i khanan*, son of Qamaruddin Khan, the late *wazir*, was appointed as the *Bakhshi II*, in succession to his father. He was also given the governorship of Moradabad with the same title held by his father, Itmad-ud Daula. Muinul Mulk Muinuddin Khan Bahadur was confirmed as the governor of Multan and Lahore.[19] Ghaziuddin Khan Firoz Jang, son of Nizamul Mulk Asaf Jah, was appointed governor of the Deccan in place of his brother, Ahmad Khan Nasir Jang.[20] In short, by ignoring the Turani nobles, who had not been given important posts at the centre, Safdar Jang had sowed the seeds for sharp conflicts and rivalries at the court as will be seen.

Besides the above appointments, a new unprecedented element was introduced in the peerage. For instance, Jawid Khan,[21] a eunuch,[22] who enjoyed the patronage of the Queen-Mother, Udham Bai,[23] as well as Safdar Jang, who had allied himself with him, was appointed *darogha-i diwan-i khas* with the rank of 6000/4000 with the title of Nawab Bahadur. He was rewarded with the highest possible insignia of honour, namely, the *mahi-o maratib*, standard, banner, kettledrums and fringed *palki*. A Delhi historian of the time reflects with sadness, 'No eunuch had ever been so exalted before, and no noble had been given the title of *nawab* (at court)'. He further observes, 'Never since Timur's time had a eunuch exercised such power in the state; hence the government became unsettled. The hereditary peers felt humiliated by having to make their petitions through a slave and to pay court to him before any affair of state could be transacted'.[24] Another eunuch Roz Afzun Khan was given the *mansab* of 6000/4000.[25]

Besides, according to old established traditions of the Mughal emperors, whenever a grandee died, his *jagirs* and moveable properties reverted to the state under the law of escheat. It was the prerogative of the emperors to redistribute it as he liked.[26] But during the reign of Ahmad Shah, there was a departure from this law. The powerful nobles at the helm of affairs divided such *jagirs* among themselves without the prior approval of the emperor. For instance, the big *mahals* of Nizamul Mulk Asaf Jah and Itmad-ud Daula Qamaruddin Khan's *jagirs* fell under the category of *pai baqi* (vacant to be reassigned) after their death. These *jagirs* were divided among the *wazir*, Safdar Jang; the *Mir Bakhshi* (Sadat

Khan) and Jawid Khan as an appendage of their other *jagirs*. The best and fertile villages were not set apart for the *khalisa* land and estates of the emperor's privy purse. The very life and sustenance of the emperor and his household depended upon this source of income. But during this reign all powerful nobles such as Safdar Jang and Jawid Khan and during the last years Imadul Mulk began to misappropriate the revenue collected from these lands, leaving only a pittance for the expenditure of the emperor. They even sent their agents to plunder the peasants and traders, so that even this last source of revenue was cut off, and the emperor, his family, his personal servants and guards were reduced to starvation. Not a single *dam* was remitted to the imperial Exchequer.[27]

Neither was any land included into the *khalisa* lands nor any maintenance allowance fixed out of it for the sons of Nizamul Mulk and Qamaruddin Khan. Roz Afzun Khan, too, was ignored, though his *mansab* was raised, but he held a very small *jagir*. The other nobles at the court also had not been given any *jagir* out of it.[28] In this way, all important posts and *jagirs* were held by three men – the *wazir*, the *Mir Bakhshi* and Jawid Khan. No one else specially the Turani nobles, the heirs of Nizamul Mulk and Qamaruddin Khan, had been given any important position or *jagir*.[29]

Besides, there were other factors which made Safdar Jang's position of unusual difficulty. He was a foreign-born adventurer whose uncle had been the first of the family to enter the imperial service of Delhi and could not establish aristocratic connections in course of one generation. The old nobility whose pedigree went back to the reign of Aurangzeb or even earlier, considered Safdar Jang as an interloper. Public offices had now come to be regarded as the inheritable property of their holder's families. The late *wazir* Qamaruddin Khan's son, Intizam-ud Daula, regarded Safdar Jang as having deprived him of his father's legacy – the *wizarat*. Intizam's sister had been married to Ghaziuddin Khan, the eldest son of Nizamul Mulk Asaf Jah. Besides this tie, the great grandfather of those two nobles had been full brothers. The Nizam's son had in addition a grievance of his own. His father had held the post of *Mir Bakhshi* (from 1739 to his death in 1748) and he looked up on it as his birthright. The appointment of an outsider Salabat Khan Bahadur Zulfiqar Jang, to that post after Nizam's death, was resented as an act of dispossession.

The clash of personal interest was aggravated by racial enmity. Nizamul Mulk, Qamaruddin Khan and Zakariya Khan (the governor of the Punjab) were all Turks from Central Asia, closely knit together by inter-marriages; while Safdar Jang was born in *wilayat* (Persia).

Religious differences further embittered the enmity between the two parties. Safdar Jang was a Shia while the Turks were all Sunnis.

The Iranians considered themselves superior over the Turks in general intelligence, generosity, style of conversation and polished manners. They scoffed at the Indian Muslims' manners as clownish and their Persian idiom as barbarous.[30]

Besides the Turks, the Afghans and the Hindustani Muslims, who lived in Shahjahanabad since its foundation had the same faith as the Turanis (Sunni).[31] They were also convinced that in case Safdar Jang got the upper hand, he would annihilate them. Hence they did not like his rise. In addition, there were some Indian Shias, who, due to difference of nationality, had turned against him and had joined the Turanis. The entire population of Shahjahanabad, not to say the whole of Hindustani Muslims became his enemy because till then the political power had been held by the house of the Turanis.[32]

Besides the tussle between the Turani and Irani nobles, there arose a struggle for the exercise of the political power between the *wazir* and Jawid Khan, because for all practical purposes, all the administrative powers passed into the eunuch's hands as the emperor sank deeper and deeper into indolence and sensual pleasures, leaving the reins of administrative affairs into the hands of Jawid Khan and his mother Udham Bai. She conducted the state business. 'Daily the high officers used to go and sit down at her porch and she used to hold discussions with them from behind the screen (through the medium of eunuch); all petitions of the realm read out to her and she passed orders on them, which were final'. The result can be inferred from the court historian's sarcastic comments. 'Oh God! that the affairs of Hindustan should be conducted by a woman so foolish as this'. About Jawid Khan, the same historian exclaims, 'Oh God! Where emperors personally had fought and *wazirs* had day and night attended to state business, this eunuch, ignorant of everything, who had never seen a battle in all his life nor even heard (its sound) in his ears, now became sole ruler'.[33]

ATTEMPT ON *WAZIR'S* LIFE (30 NOVEMBER 1748)

After the distribution of the offices and the Turani nobles being sidelined and deprived of their rightful claims,[34] Intizam-ud Daula desirous of supplanting the *wazir*, hatched a plot against his life. He concealed some light guns, muskets, rockets, swivels and other combustibles on the invisible roof of a house situated inside a covered passage, known as *chatta-i nagambodh*. Usually Safdar Jang passed through it on his way to and back from the court. On the day of Id (1748), the *wazir* after the congregational prayers with the emperor at Idgah, and after conducting the latter back into the royal fort, while returning as soon as he reached the dark covered passage, the plotter's agents set fire to the arranged artillery. There was a sudden explosion. Safdar Jang's own horse was struck by a bullet and fell down on the ground with its master, but the *wazir* escaped unhurt. It was generally believed that Intizam-ud Daula was the author of this plot. This event created a misunderstanding between the *wazir* and the emperor, as the former suspected the latter's connivance at the Turani nobles' hostility. Safdar Jang feeling a danger ahead, ceased to appear at the court.[35]

The object of the conspirators–the emperor, Jawid Khan, Intizam-ud Daula, Ghaziuddin Khan Firoz Jang and Nasir Jang et al.–was to get the dismissal of the *wazir* by military pressure and the *Mir Bakhshi*, Sadat Khan Bahadur Zulfiqar Jang and to get Intizam-ud Daula and Nasir Jang (the governor of the Deccan) appointed to their respective places as soon as the latter had arrived with his big force from the Deccan.[36]

When the hatred and hypocrisy became deep-rooted, the emperor apparently began to behave with the *wazir* with courtesy and flattery, because the posts of *darogha-i topkhana* and *ghusal khana* were held by the *wazir*. On that account, he did not want to annoy the *wazir*. But covertly he also regarded Intizam-ud Daula as his well-wisher. The emperor did not heed the complaints of the *wazir* against him.[37] Sometimes these two factions openly clashed but the situation was never allowed to take an ugly turn.[38]

On the other hand, a third group was formed comprising Jawid Khan and the Queen-mother Udham Bai, since due to his indolence and indifference to the affairs of the state and deep indulgence in sensual pleasure, the emperor handed over the reins of the administrative affairs of the state in the hands of the above mentioned duo. Consequently, there arose a power struggle between the *wazir* and Jawid Khan with the support of the Queen-mother.[39]

As there were two centres of power at the court, in this situation Safdar Jang, the *wazir*, found himself in a precarious position owing to the interference and the powers wielded by Jawid Khan into the day-to-day administrative matters. It became impossible for the *wazir* to carry on effectively the affairs of the state. His complaints against this state of affairs to the emperor fell on deaf ears. The emperor politely told the *wazir* that whatever he had to say, he should say it to the Nawab Bahadur, who would communicate it to him. This reply filled the *wazir* with disgust and frustration. He went back thinking that the emperor himself was responsible for Jawid Khan's usurpation of administrative powers.[40]

MURDER OF JAWID KHAN (27 AUGUST 1752)

The court of Ahmad Shah turned into a hotbed of intrigues and conspiracies. On the one hand, the *wazir* and on the other, the Nawab Bahadur and Turani nobles with the clandestine backing of the emperor remained all the time busy in plotting and planning to overthrow each other. Safdar Jang now realized that in practice, he was left *wazir* only in name. All the authority and prestige of his office had been usurped by Jawid Khan in alliance with the Queen-mother, transacting all important matters and was a stumbling block in his way. It was in sheer desperation to save his position from his combined opponents, that he decided to remove Jawid Khan from his way.[41] He, thus, hired the services of Suraj Mal Jat to perform this job. Jawid Khan was treacherously murdered. The killers severed his head and his trunk was thrown on the sandy bank of Jamuna.[42] All the stores and treasures of Jawid Khan within and without the fort were sealed and his various offices were at once taken charge of by Roz Afzun Khan.[43] According to Jadunath Sarkar, the murder of Jawid Khan was a political blunder committed by Safdar Jang. 'It antagonized the Emperor and his mother and all the imperial household against Safdar Jang beyond hope of reconciliation. Worst of all, it transferred the leadership of the court party and the control of the puppet emperor from the hands of a foolish and timid eunuch to those of a noble of the highest birth and the ablest, most energetic, most farsighted and most ruthlessly ambitious man in the empire'.[44]

On hearing the news of the assassination of Jawid Khan, the emperor became much perplexed, agitated and suspicious about the motives of the *wazir*, but being helpless he could not do anything.[45] After this incident, the emperor tightened his belt to oust the *wazir* and began to think of a strategy to do this work.[46] It is recorded that Udham Bai observed the rites of mourning, put on white robes and took off jewels and ornaments from her hands and neck (as if she had really became a widow only now). Following her the female servants of Jawid Khan also wore white garments.[47]

After eliminating Jawid Khan, Safdar Jang became thirsty for the blood–*khan-i khana* Intizam-ud Daula and Imadul Mulk – whom he regarded as his main rivals in future. Therefore he asked the emperor to hand them over to him. On his part, the emperor thought that it would lead to the bloodshed of the innocents and also about what reply he would give to the God in this matter on the Day of Judgement, hence he turned down the demand of the *wazir*.[48] Thereafter, Safdar Jang took measures to establish his own domination. Jawid Khan's property was escheated and his estate managers and personal servants were confined and tortured to disclose his hidden treasures.[49]

Besides, the *wazir* proceeded on to secure his hold over the imperial fort and surrounded Ahmad Shah's person with his own men such as Abu Turab Khan *qiladar* who replaced Haji Muhammad, a loyal hereditary servant of the emperor with the explicit instructions not to admit anybody armed or on horseback except his own partisans. Raja Lachchimi Narayan was posted at the gate of the *diwan-i khas* to restrict admission to the presence of the king.[50] The *wazir*'s orders were so strictly carried out that no noble or official, who was not his partisan, could have an access to the king or even came inside the fort. When those restrictions were imposed on the entry of men, except his partisans, Hakim Alvi Khan and Hakim Ali Khan, who lived day and night in the fort, went back to their houses.[51]

The king now realized that he had been reduced to a captive, confined within the four walls of the palace and cut off from the society. In short, in this situation, the king went to the house of the *wazir* and unwillingly under duress surrendered all the imperial powers to him. Thereafter all the appointments were made with the consent of the *wazir*. The *wazir* nominated several of his favourites to important posts inside the fort and outside, the old imperial servants were forced to make room for them. The emperor assigned four important posts held by Jawid Khan to Shuja-ud Daula, the *wazir*'s son, namely, *bakhshiship* of Ahadis, superintendentship of confirmation of appointments, grants; command of the mace-bearers and the charge of personal riding establishments (*jilau-i khas*). Traditionally all the above mentioned posts had always been entrusted to men of trust and confidence. Similarly, the offices like the superintendentship of drinking water for the king, betel leaves and perfumery held by Jawid Khan till his murder, were given in the charge of *wazir*'s nominees.[52]

MIR SHIHABUDDIN'S APPOINTMENT AS *MIR BAKHSHI*

About this time on the death of Ghaziuddin Khan Firoz Jang at Aurangabad on 29 October 1752, Safdar Jang got his adopted son,

Shihabuddin appointed as *Mir Bakhshi* with the titles of *Amirul Umara* Imadul Mulk Khan Bahadur on 12 December 1753, who till then outwardly professed to be *wazir*'s partisan.[53] It is for the first time that we find Shihabuddin holding an office of importance.

Despite the fact that Safdar Jang had established his complete hold inside the fort, his mind was not composed. He suspected that Udham Bai, his avowed enemy was secretly corresponding with Turani and Afghan nobles. So, besides keeping strict watch at the Queen-mother's activities, Safdar Jang sent 8 women spies to reside in the royal seraglio as domestic servants and find out the contents of all letters sent out of it. Udham Bai was highly enraged at this act and dismissed the women with rewards.[54]

Now the emperor began extending his favours to the *wazir*'s opponents and enemies and finally fell completely into the hands of Intizam-ud Daula and his companions.

CONSPIRACY AGAINST SAFDAR JANG

The popular indignation at Delhi against Safdar Jang's dictatorship had reached its climax. On that account a conspiracy was being secretly brewed to bring his downfall. Owing to his natural aversion to the business of the state as well as by *wazir*'s galling bondage, the emperor Ahmad Shah, after the murder of Jawid Khan, left all the administrative affairs into the hands of his mother Udham Bai. She now became the *de facto* head of the state, transacting all important state business, granting audience to high officials from behind the *purdah*. She used her position of supreme authority and power to form under her own leadership a coalition of disgruntled nobles against the *wazir*. *Khan-i Khanan* Intizam-ud Daula, Imadul Mulk, Hisam Khan Samsam-ud Daula, Aqibat Mahmud Khan Kashmiri and some other nobles were gradually won over, although outwardly professing to be the *wazir*'s partisans, they covertly joined the conspiracy against their benefactor. It was decided that first of all, they should liberate the emperor by depriving Safdar Jang's son and his retainer Abu Turab Khan of the offices of *mir atish*, the *qiladar* of the fort, and by ending *wazir*'s hold over the imperial citadel and thenceforth they should concentrate on measures to procure the latter's dismissal and downfall. Ahmad Shah was in secret sympathy with Intizam-ud Daula and assured him his assistance.[55]

Thus with the assistance of the emperor, Intizam-ud Daula openly declared himself against the most powerful *wazir* and his determination to fight the matter to its logical conclusion. This action of Intizam-ud Daula, in fact, strengthened the side of the imperialists.[56]

After strengthening his position with the support of the nobles of the coalition Ahmad Shah dismissed Shuja-ud Daula from the post of *mir atish* and replaced him by his loyal partisan Hisam Khan Samsam-ud Daula.[57] Shuja-ud Daula's deputy Musawi Khan and his deputy Abu Turab Khan were turned out from the fort. With him, Safdar Jang's men, who were still inside the fort were also turned out and its gates were closed at Ahmad Shah's orders. In this way, the *wazir* was deprived of the command of the fort palace. The big pieces of cannons arranged on the battlement of the fort were then loaded and turned towards Safdar Jang's house.[58]

Finding himself outmanoeuvered by his opponents and that his house was within the range of the gun fire from the fort, Safdar Jang shifted to another house he had built at some distance away. With the aim of conciliating him, the emperor presented him the turban worn by him, which Safdar Jang accepted respectfully. But he sent a petition to the emperor, requesting him to give permission to go to his provinces.[59] The emperor readily granted his request, permitting him to go to his *subahs*.[60] Now the emperor was set free, the nobles and other subjects regained access to him. Every noble and officer in Delhi flocked to him.[61]

SAFDAR JANG'S ATTEMPT AT CONCILIATION

But before departing for his *subahs*, Safdar Jang made two attempts to arrive at a conciliation and rapprochement with Intizam-ud Daula whom he regarded as his main opponent. But unfortunately on both the occasions he sent Imadul Mulk, whom he had raised to the second most important position in the empire as his emissary to Intizam's house to negotiate the terms with him. But this ungrateful youngman secretly came to an understanding with his maternal uncle (Intizam-ud Daula), and although still openly professing to be the *wazir*'s follower, he had really joined the deadliest enemy of his benefactor. Keeping in mind the treachery Safdar Jang had displayed in the case of Jawid Khan, Intizam-ud Daula refused to visit the house of the *wazir*.[62]

Realizing that the situation had gone beyond the stage of negotiation and reconciliation, Safdar Jang decided to quit Delhi. On 26 March 1753, with his family and baggage, he set out. Outside the city, he encamped at Ismail Khan's garden. When his hopes shattered that the emperor would call him back to the court, he felt compelled to prepare for the battle, following the example set by Saiyid Abdullah Khan, the *wazir* who had challenged the authority of his master, emperor Muhammad Shah after his brother Saiyid Husain Ali Khan, the *Mir Bakhshi*, had been treacherously killed by the Turani nobles. Safdar Jang now summoned Rajender Giri Gosain and Suraj Mal, the Jat leader, for his assistance, who came with 1500 Jat horsemen.[63] Most of the nobles, big and small, had thrown in their lot with the *wazir*, who personally commanded 25000 troops.

PREPARATIONS FOR A CONTEST

Desiring to avoid a contest at the last moment, the emperor made an attempt to come into terms with the *wazir*, who due to his arrogance, wealth and military strength, said in reply that he would first kill Intizam and Imad. Safdar Jang actually sent two troopers to shoot his enemies. They fired their muskets at Intizam-ud Daula and Imad, when they were on the way to the court, but they missed their target and fled. Imad now became determined to fight to the last and he said, 'Now there is an open enmity between me and the *wazir* and I must fight'.[64]

Since a civil war became inevitable, the emperor sent letters to all sides calling upon the *zamindars*, feudatory princes, Rohillas and even noted Jat, Mewati, Gujars and robber chieftains to assemble under his banner against the ex-*wazir* and the pretender to the throne. A large number of the Pathans, Saiyids of Barha, Gujars, Belochis, the leaders of mercenaries, Rajput soldiers, and other chiefs ambitious of a career of prosperity and desirous of securing grants of land, joined the emperor.[65]

Najib Khan, the Rohilla chief, arrived with 2500 cavalry and infantry. The emperor asked them to join him but Safdar Jang also tried to win them over to his side. He also sent his men to them with the message that if they would join him, he would pay them twenty lakh of rupees. In short, despite this allurement, Najib Khan joined the side of the emperor which strengthened the position of the imperialists.[66] The response of the different sections of the Mughal subjects to the call of the emperor Ahmad Shah shows that despite the fact that the Mughal royalty had lost much of its power and prestige, it still enjoyed the loyalty of its subjects whatever their motives had been.

Imadul Mulk played an active role in enlisting and collecting a great number of the soldiers. Besides the two crores of rupees which Udham Bai placed at Imad's disposal, he was also considered a wealthy man. He possessed seventy lakhs of rupees hoarded by his grandfather and father. Whosoever came to him, he gave him fifty rupees as a reward and fifty rupees in advance as one month's salary and employed him. If any great man came to him with his contingents, he took him to the emperor, got him exalted with the grant of a *khilat*, jewels, and a respectable *mansab*. In short, Imad, despite being under the age of 17 or 18 years, in collecting the soldiers displayed so much exertions that he spent all the ancestral hoarded wealth. Besides, he distributed horses from his stable and clothes from his wardrobe.[67] Imad gave religious colour to the impending civil war. He worked upon the Sunni fanaticism by making a proclamation in the city and called upon all the true Muslims, who honoured the first three Caliphs (cursed by the Shias) to join the *jihad* (holy war) against the heretic leader. The green banner of the Prophet was unfurled. Thousands assembled under the banner and raised the slogans–*chahar yar*. The public enthusiasm was raised to boiling point in favour of the war. Most of the Rohillas hated Safdar Jang for being a *Shia*, rose against him at the passionate appeal by Najib Khan.[68] They numbered forty to fifty thousand.[69]

SAFDAR JANG SETS UP A RIVAL PRINCE

Ahmad Shah dismissed Safdar Jang from the office of the *wazir* and replaced him by Intizam-ud Daula, with the title of Qamaruddin Khan Bahadur, the title held by his father and Imadul Mulk as *Mir Bakhshi* with the title of his grandfather Nizamul Mulk Asaf Jah.[70]

Thereafter on the same day following the example set by Saiyid Abdullah Khan, the former *wazir* during the civil war against the emperor Muhammad Shah, who had raised the Sultan Muhammad Ibrahim to the throne with the title of Abul Fath Zahiruddin Muhammad Ibrahim,[71] Safdar Jang placed a eunuch of handsome features, sometime before purchased by Shuja-ud Daula, on the throne, entitling him Akbar Shah declaring that he was the grandson of Kam Bakhsh, son of Aurangzeb.[72]

SURAJ MAL ATTACKS OLD AND NEW DELHI

Safdar Jang instigated his allies like Suraj Mal and Rajendra Giri Gosain to plunder Old Delhi, especially the grain markets and houses outside Lal Darwaza of Shah Jahan's New City. Here the houses of middle class and poor men were plundered and their families maltreated. All those, who could leave their houses in the Old City, flocked to within the walls of New Delhi for refuge. Thereafter the Jats spread their devastations to other suburban settlements like Saiyidwara, Bijal Masjid, Tarka Ganj and Abdullah Nagar, ruining the humble people but withdrawing where the inhabitants combined and offered resistance or where a few soldiers were present to hearten and guide them. 'The Jats thus plundered upto the gate of the city, lakhs and lakhs were looted, and houses were demolished. All the suburbs (*puras*) and Churania and Wakilpura were rendered totally lampless.'[73] These ravages were long afterwards remembered by the Delhi populace under the name of *Jat-gardi*, on a par with the raids of the Marathas and the Afghans.[74]

Every day the Jats plundered the city of Old Delhi: Only those places were saved where the imperial detachments arrived in time or which lay within the range of the imperial artillery. 'All the people of Old Delhi and other suburbs fled to the New City with whatever property they could carry off; and the inhabitants of the New City, too, in fear of plunder, carried their valuables on their persons. They roamed from house to house, lane to lane, in despair and bewilderment, like a wrecked ship tossing on the weaves; everyone was running about like a lunatic, distracted, puzzled and unable to take care of himself'. The king very considerately ordered the Sahibabad garden (in Chandni Chowk), the garden of thirty thousand, and other gardens and houses belonging to his government to be vacated and given up to the people who wished to live in them. Vast crowds of people both high and low went there. Shopkeepers and artisans set up stalls in them and engaged in their trades.[75]

The Jats had ruined Jai Singhpura and many places were set on fire.[76] All the ruined people, too, who escaped came over to the new city. A great number of the people of Shah Ganj and Abdullah Nagar, with the women came to the city. All the *havelis*, lanes and bazars of the city were so crammed with the men and women that nothing was seen but the crowd of men. The *haveli* of Harim-un Nisa Koka, *Katra* Hamid Khan, *Katra* Ali Hamid Khan, Saiyidwara, the *risala* of the Dargah of Nizamuddin Auliya, the grave of Muhammad Shah, the *mamdavi* of Shahzada, the *haveli* of Nar Singh Dass and other *mohallas* of the Old Delhi were plundered.[77]

PEACE CONCLUDED

The civil war continued for six months and both the parties were exhausted and their resources fell short. The imperial troops, the Rohillas, Balochis and Gujars were clamouring for their salaries which had not been paid for a long time. Safdar Jang himself was hard pressed due to heavy expenditure incurred and tired of the fruitless warfare in which he was the principal loser. Thus both the sides desired peace. The nobles of the court and Ahmad Shah being exhausted and powerless sent a message for peace. Towards the end of the June, 1753, Intizam-ud Daula began to negotiate with him. Notwithstanding that Imadul Mulk was not in favour of it, and wanted the war to continue, the negotiations had to be given up.[78] In the meantime, Ahmad Shah in utter helplessness had appealed to Madho Singh, the Raja of Jaipur, the greatest of his feudatories, to come and save him, because this quarrel between his *wazir* and the *Mir Bakhshi* was threatening to ruin his state. Madho Singh arrived with a big army to use his good offices to bring the war to an end. The Raja had a personal interview with the king in the private chamber where he held consultations with him. Ahmad Shah complained bitterly about Safdar Jang, Intizam-ud Daula and Imadul Mulk who had been brought up by his father as his sons and he himself did the same, but they were now working against him.[79]

Finding that the king was bent upon to conclude a peace, Imad himself opened negotiations. Intizam in order to spoil Imad's plan, sent the king to visit the garden of Khizrabad and Madho Singh should bring Suraj Mal to secure his pardon.[80] The *wazir* (Intizam) rejoiced that the peace was not concluded through Imad.[81] In the end Madho Singh's officer Fath Singh conveyed to Safdar Jang an imperial *farman*, a robe of honour, an aigrette, a jewelled crust – ornament, a pearl neclace and a horse from the emperor. Thus the war ended. Safdar Jang left for Awadh. Madho Singh's work as peace-maker was done. He was permitted to return to his state.[82]

THE SITUATION AFTER THE DEPARTURE OF SAFDAR JANG AND THE DOWNFALL OF AHMAD SHAH

After the peace was concluded and Safdar Jang departed for Awadh, Ahmad Shah became very happy and the occasion was celebrated. The new *wazir*, *khan-i khanan* and the *Mir Bakhshi* Imadul Mulk, were honoured with the *khilats* ornamented with jewels. Other nobles and military commanders were bestowed *khilats* and exalted according to their exertions. The *subahdars*, including the Rajas of the empire, were rewarded. In short, besides the distribution of the charities, one crore rupees were spent in this function from the personal treasury of the emperor.[83]

After the departure of Safdar Jang, Ahmad Shah ruled only for six months, and there prevailed increasing disorder, lawlessness in and outside the capital. It did not bring peace, prosperity and stability to the Delhi government. The war had exhausted the wealth of the emperor and dried the sources of revenue, because the refractory *zamindars* in the meantime had occupied even the *khalisa* lands, and the rest of the country was divided among themselves by the powerful nobles and seditious people. The government was overburdened with debt. To the utter bankruptcy of the state treasury[84] was added the mortal jealousy between the *wazir* Intizam-ud Daula and Imadul Mulk, the *Mir Bakhshi*, because the *wazir* had foiled the attempt of Imadul Mulk so that the peace could not concluded through him and Intizam had rejoiced in it.[85] The timid powerless emperor placed between two strong rivals, whom he regarded as two serpents,[86] tried to save himself by lying to Imad and he secretly followed Intizam's counsels.[87] Besides, the emperor could not get loans from the *sahukars* because they argued that as no tract of land was left under his effective control and even the *khalisa* lands had been occupied by the refractories, from where the revenues would be realized and their debt would be paid.[88] The court historian with great anguish remarks, 'The nobles had divided among themselves the entire conquered country and they did not remit a single *dam* into the imperial treasury. At present, the emperor was not in a position to pay even a month's salaries of the soldiers. I was always present there and was looking at the changes that had taken place. I have been shedding tears as being the old loyal servant'.[89] In short, the last six months of Ahmad Shah's reign were continually disturbed by violence, tumult and *dharnas* of the starving unpaid soldiers. The officials and menials of the palace had remained unpaid for thirty two months.[90]

The Marathas had been invited by Imadul Mulk during the war and he had sent Mahboob Ram, the *wakil* with letters to bring Malhar Rao Holkar, who was at that time near Aurangabad in the Deccan.[91] Thus the Marathas arrived in the north. Both the *wazir* and the *Mir Bakhshi* tried to win over the Marathas to their side.[92] But the Marathas sided with Imad. Subsequently along with Imad, they attacked Suraj Mal Jat.

Since Suraj Mal had allied himself with Safdar Jang in the war, notwithstanding he had caused much ruin and devastations in the Old and New Delhi[93] as recorded above, he had been pardoned by the emperor at the instance of the *wazir*, Intizam and Madho Singh.[94] Hence, Imad and his Maratha allies – Holkar and Jai Apa – all the three led an attack on him. Suraj Mal fortified himself in the fort of Kumbher and the fort was besieged. As the cannons were regarded the best weapon to capture the fort, Imad petitioned the emperor to dispatch an artillery. Intizam opposed the request of Imad and counselled the emperor against sending the artillery.[95]

About this time, Suraj Mal, who had escaped in a wretched condition from the besiegers, begged assistance from the emperor. The emperor came out from Delhi, outwardly for a hunting excursion and to make some administrative arrangements in the *Antarbed*, but in reality he intended to extend his help to Suraj Mal.[96]

THE EMPEROR ATTACKED BY HOLKAR

Since an artillery was not sent, Imad advised Holkar to attack the imperial camp. Holkar liked this idea,[97] because the emperor had come out and it was befitting that his supplies of food and fodder should be stopped and this way he might get hold of the cannons. In short, without taking Imad and Jai Appa into confidence, Holkar came near the imperial camp and in the darkness of the night discharged some matchlocks. The imperial forces thinking it was Aqibat Mahmud's mischief, did not prepare themselves for an encounter. In the morning it became certain that Holkar had come. They all lost their senses, became confounded, neither to fight or fly. The emperor, his mother, Samsam-ud Daula, the *mir atish*, the *wazir*, Intizam, leaving their women and property there, ran away to the capital with a few followers.[98] Holkar entered the encampment and plundered much of the royal property–cash and goods worth about crores of rupees.[99] Malika-i Zamani, the wife of the late emperor Muhammad Shah, Sahib-i-Mahal, Roz Afzun Khan, the *wazir*, and other ladies of the imperial female apartments and most of the army were captured by the Marathas. Many of the *raths* of the women were overtaken by the Marathas, who tore off their screens and took away the money from their carriages and ornaments from their body. Many women were outraged. Some escaped to different directions and some reached Delhi on foot. The women of the *haram*, high and low, who remained captives in the camp suffered extreme hardships.[100] In short, sitting on *raths*, whose screens were old and torn in pieces, like which they had never used as carriages in their life, they reached the Delhi fort.[101]

When Imadul Mulk came to know of this disaster of the imperial camp, the ladies being taken prisoner and maltreated, albeit all that had happened had been on his suggestion, he outwardly felt ashamed and reached the camp of Malhar Rao Holkar. Thereafter he went to the camp of Malika-i zamani, presented to her five thousand *mohars*, laid his turban on the ground before her, tearing his collar and like the heretic *kufians* in deceit, shedding crocodiles tears, crying loudly, professing shame and disgrace to himself at the hardships that had befallen on her, and pleading for excuse, he said that, 'I was helpless in this matter. The Deccanis listened to none. . . . My face has been blackened'. The ex-queen stoically laid the blame on Fate.[102]

In the meantime, owing to the disruptive activities of Imad which were against the interest of the state, a complete estrangement had taken place between the emperor and his *Mir Bakhshi* and an open conflict between the duo was precipitated which culminated in the ruin of Ahmad Shah.[103] In the months following Safdar Jang's departure, Imad's one main difficulty was lack of money. He had exhausted all his ancestral hoards and had saddled himself with debt during the six months life-and-death struggle with Safdar Jang. The public treasury was empty, and revenue had ceased to come in from the provinces. The only course open to Imad was to seize the rents of the *khalisa* lands and other nobles' *jagirs* in the districts within an easy distance of the capital.

When the civil war was broken out, it was agreed upon in the presence of the emperor and his ministers that all the wealth of the realm should be first devoted to the work of crushing the rebel and after his defeat the revenues of the Deccan should be paid by Imad into the imperial treasury. The *wazir* (Intizam) agreed to do so in respect of the revenues of his provinces of the Punjab and Kashmir; the *subahs* under Safdar Jang would be taken away from him and Awadh would be equally divided between the new *wazir* and the *Mir Bakhshi* and the *subah* of Allahabad would be left for the payment of the salaries of the *sindagh*. But this agreement did not work. Hence the trouble about money continued to grow worse. Imad gradually turned disloyal and in the pride of his power even dreamt of seizing the throne.[104] Imad terrorized the emperor with the help of the Marathas.

AHMAD SHAH DETHRONED AND ALAMGIR II ENTHRONED

In this critical situation the emperor was confounded and helpless. Aqibat Mahmud Khan came to the emperor and secured his consent to appoint Imadul Mulk as the *wazir* and Roz Afzun Khan, superintendent of the Privy Council, thus depriving Intizam of both of his high offices. In return, Aqibat Mahmud Khan swore on the Koran that Imad and

Madho Rao Holkar would never play him false nor trouble him and his kingdom in future.[105a]

It is not clear whether before or after assuming the office of the *wazir*, Imadul Mulk had made up his mind to dethrone Ahmad Shah. He had taken into confidence Aqibat Mahmud Khan in this regard, who argued that this state had suffered a fatal misfortune and the apparatus of the state had been plundered and sacked by the Marathas. At this time, it was in the best interest of the country that Ahmad Shah was to be relieved from the heavy burden of the state and another prince was to be made *khalifa* in his place. After that the law officers were collected and they were asked to justify the removal of Ahmad Shah from this high office and putting in writing his shameful activities on the basis of the evidence from the Koran and *hadis* of the Prophet. On the *fatwa*, the seals of the law officers and others who were present on that occasion were put on its margin. Muhammad Ali Khan informs us that after securing the *fatwa* of the law officers, the servants of Imad sent Ahmad Shah from the throne of delight to the prison of disappointment.[105b]

In short, on 2 June 1754 (Sunday), Imad went to the court with Tatya Gangadhar (Holkar's *diwan*), Aqibat Mahmud Khan and his brother Saifullah. Ahmad Shah first placed the Koran in the hands of Imad and called upon him to swear that he would not resort to treachery against him. Imad took the strongest oaths, and was next invested with the robe of the *wizarat*. Then he went to the office of the *wizarat* where Raja Nagar Mal, the *diwan-i khalisa-wa tan* and other clerks were in attendance. He signed a few papers, and retired to an ante-room behind it dismissing the *mir atish* (Samsam-ud Daula) and other officers present. Then he summoned Lala Thakur Dass Pundit and the *nazir* Roz Afzun Khan, whispering something in their ears; immediately after this he sent Aqibat Mahmud Khan with the *haram* superintendent's assistant with a guard of 50 Badakhshi soldiers to the gate of the princes' quarters in the palace where all the grandsons of the former emperors lived in confinement. Aqibat Mahmud Khan sent his own eunuch inside, who brought out Muhammad Azizuddin, son of Muizuddin, son of Shah Alam Bahadur Shah I, and went back to his master with him. Imad came out of the *wazir*'s office, made humble obeisance to the prince and followed him. They entered the *diwan-i am*, where this prince was seated on the throne, the royal umbrella was held over his head, and he was proclaimed *padshah* Alamgir Sani (II).[106]

The new emperor immediately ordered that his predecessor, Ahmad Shah to be brought under arrest. Saifullah with his *Badakhshi* soldiers entered the *haram*, discovered Ahmad Shah and his mother, who was regarded as the prime cause for all the confusion and calamity, hiding among the trees of the small garden in front of the *Rang Mahal*. The soldiers first seized the ex-emperor and confined him in a small room outside, and then throwing *shawl* to cover his mother's face, dragged her into the same cell. The deposed monarch cried out for water in the agony of thirst and mental anguish. Saifullah held up to his lips some water and the king of the kings of an hour ago, was glad to drink it. The court historian cried out: 'What a revolution of fortune'?[107]

In short, after a week's imprisonment, both Ahmad Shah and his mother were blinded by Aqibat Mahmud Khan. Ahmad Shah passed 10 years as a blind man in the prison and died a natural death in AD 1771.[108]

MUHAMMAD AZIZUDDIN ALAMGIR II

Alamgir II, the successor of Ahmad Shah on the throne of Delhi, was an old man of fifty-five years. Born at Multan on 6 June 1699, he lost his father at the age of fourteen, in the civil war, which gave the crown to Muhammad Farrukhsaiyar. Since then he had passed his days in poverty and neglect, imprisoned in the rooms of *deorhi-i-salatin* within the Delhi fort. He had been denied any opportunity for learning about war or administration or practical experience of the outer world, but he guarded himself from vice by devoting his time to study and meditation, taking Aurangzeb for his ideal. He hated the usual diversions of royalty, such as dance and music.[109]

On account of above mentioned reasons Alamgir II left the reins of administration of the country into the hands of his *wazir*, Imad-ul Mulk. He openly used to declare himself as a puppet in the hands of his *wazir* without any power to guide the government which was in a chaotic and unsettled condition. Intoxicated with unlimited powers as he enjoyed, Imad-ul Mulk soon became very arrogant and began to indulge in disruptive activities causing great damage to the state affairs.[110] Samsam-ud Daula continued to be the *Mir Bakhshi,* with the title of *Amirul Umara,* about whom Mir Taqi Mir remarked that he was merely illiterate and lacked common sense.[111] Shaikh Qudratullah Shauq Siddiqi informs us that Alamgir II had been reduced to a puppet by the *wazir*. The empire remained only in name. Only the city of Delhi and a few *parganas* of the adjacent regions were in his effective control. He also received a small amount by way of tribute from the Nawab of Bengal, while the rest of the country was in the control of the *wazir* and the refractory *zamindars.*[112]

THE AFFAIRS OF THE PUNJAB

Ahmad Shah Abdali had inherited four *mahals* of the Punjab-Gujarat (Aimanabad), Aurangabad, Parsurur and Sialkot – ceded by Muhammad Shah to Nadir Shah in 1739. The Abdali king led an attack on India in 1752 and after defeating Muinul Mulk, then the governor of the Punjab, he again appointed him to his previous position as governor of Lahore. After the sudden death of Muinul Mulk in 1753, the Abdali had appointed Mir Momin, two years, infant son of the deceased as the governor of Lahore. Muinul Mulk's wife Mughlani Begam took the reins of the administration of the *subah* and the real powers were exercised by the regent mother.[113]

IMAD INVADES THE PUNJAB

In 1756,. Imad undertook the ill-judged Punjab adventure which ultimately drew upon his head the wrath of the Abdali. In stead of lending support to Mughlani Begam, who was his mother's brother's wife, and also his prospective mother-in-law, as her daughter Umda Begam had been betrothed to him in their childhood,[114] to consolidate her position and establish law and order, and crush her opponent court nobles, with the intention of occupying the provinces of Lahore and Multan from the representatives of the Abdali, Imad attacked the Punjab. He overpowered the forces of Mughlani Begam and took her into custody. He then appointed Adina Beg as governor of Lahore on the payment of thirty lakhs of rupees and he returned to Delhi.[115]

ABDALI INVASION (1756)

On hearing that Imad had destabilized the administrative setup established by him there, and had misbehaved with Mughlani Begam, the Abdali immediately came to Lahore. Adina Beg fled and took shelter in thick jungles. Finding himself in a great danger, Imad put many excuses before Mughlani Begam for his early misdeeds. In Delhi, the Abdali censured the inconsiderate Imad[116] in harsh words, but on the recommendations of his *wazir*, Shah Dil Khan, Mughlani Begam and on receipt of handsome presents, he confirmed him in his post of the *wazir*.[117] Besides, the Abdali extorted crores of rupees from Imad in cash and goods.[118] Due to his enmity with Intizam-ud Daula, Imad told the Abdali about his ancestral hoarded wealth as his family had held important posts for the last forty years. So, he, too, was forced under intimidation to surrender his wealth.[119] The Abdali entitled Imad as a *farzand-i khas.*[120] Imad requested the Abdali that if he was sent with his army to *Antarbed*, he would collect huge wealth for him from that region.

IMAD'S EXPEDITION AGAINST SHUJA-UD DAULA (1757)

Imad had to settle old scores with Safdar Jang and his successors, so he sought the help of the Abdali to collect money from that region, but his real intention was to liquidate Shuja-ud Daula. He marched towards Awadh with Jan Baz Khan, including two royal princes – Hidayat Bakhsh and Mirza Babar. On hearing this, Shuja-ud Daula came out with his army and encamped on the plains of Sandi and Pali. Twice engagements took place between the two parties. In short, on the mediation of Sa'dullah Khan Rohilla, peace was concluded on the condition of a payment of five lakhs of rupees – a small portion in cash and a promise for the rest.[121]

It was during his stay in India that the Abdali led an expedition against Suraj Mal Jat and caused much plunder and atrocities. But unfortunately, there was an outbreak of cholera in his army. He quickly had to return to his country Afghanistan.[122] When he to Delhi, Alamgir II and Najib Khan came to the tank of Maqsudabad and had an interview with him.[123] The emperor made strong complaints against the misconduct of Imad. Accordingly the Abdali gave the office of *Mir Bakhshi* with the title of *Amirul Umara* to Najib and Imad continued to be the *wazir*.[124]

After the peace treaty with Shuja, while returning Imad was encamping at Farrukhabad, but due to his anxiety about Najib Khan being appointed as *Mir Bakhshi*, he hastily proceeded to Delhi. He was also accompanied by Ahmad Khan Bangash, whom he had lured to get him appointed *Mir Bakhshi*, Malhar Rao Holkar and Raghunath Rao.[125]

LADY MEMBERS OF THE ROYAL FAMILY LEFT WITH THE ABDALI

Malika-i-Zamani and Sahiba-i-Mahal, two widow wives of the emperor Muhammad Shah had suffered much humiliation and hardship at Udham Bai's hands. At the instance of Imad, when the Marathas had brought about extensive devastations in Delhi, they decided to leave

Delhi. Ahmad Shah Abdali married Hazrat Begam, the daughter of Muhammad Shah.[126] He also married his son Timur Shah with Gauhar Afroz Bano Begam, the daughter of Alamgir II.[127] The Abdali took with himself these two ladies, including Mughlani Begam and sixteen other ladies of the Mughal *haram*.[128] This was perhaps the first example in the history of the Mughal rule in India that the ladies of the royal family sought asylum and married the Afghan king owing to the hardships they had to suffer at the hands of Imad-ul Mulk.

After the departure of the Abdali, Imad hurriedly reached Delhi, with his allies as mentioned above. In conjunction with the Marathas, he besieged the city to dislodge Najib Khan, the *Mir Bakhshi*. The emperor and Najib responded by fortifying themselves. For 45 days, artillery fire went on. At last taking a heavy bribe from Najib, Holkar concluded peace with him. He brought out Najib with honour and with his baggage from the fort and lodged him near his tent. Holkar gave him Saharanpur, Buriya, Chandpur and whole of Barha townships and sent him there. The emperor allowed Najib to leave Delhi. Thereafter with the help of the Marathas, Imad again took up the reins of the administrative affairs of the state and regained his position in Delhi. After the departure of Najib, Imad got appointed Ahmad Khan Bangash to the office of *Mir Bakhshi*, *Amirul Umara* with the title of Ghalib Jang in his place.[129]

PRINCE ALI GAUHAR ESCAPES FROM DELHI (1758)

Since both the emperor and Najib had grown sick of Imad due to his high handedness and coercion by acts and deeds, they sent Ali Gauhar to his *jagirs* in Hansi, Hissar and Rewari in the Punjab with a view to establishing law and order there and raising a big army to counter the moves of Imad. After the expulsion of Najib from Delhi, Imad compelled the emperor to call back the prince to foil his strategy. Imad's selfish ambition would not allow the chance of recovering a province. On the summons of the emperor, the prince had to come back and he took up his residence in the *haveli* of Ali Mardan Khan in the city instead of in the fort. Imad, who had also turned against the prince as well, treacherously besieged the *haveli*, but luckily the prince boldly cut his way out, took shelter with the Maratha general Vithal Shivdev for sometime. Thereafter Ali Gauhar went into wilderness in utter destitution and helplessness. Staying for sometime with the Rohillas, he went to Shuja-ud Daula in 1759, thenceforth to the eastern provinces to subjugate them with his assistance.[130]

THE MARATHAS ATTACK NAJIB KHAN (1759)

At the instigation of Imad, who was bent upon liquidating Najib by any means, the Marathas under the command of Dattaji Sindhia[131] entered the Rohilla territories. Finding himself unable to enter into an open conflict with the invader, Najib took shelter in the fort of Shukartal. The siege continued for four months. In this critical condition, Najib informed Shuja-ud Daula about the ulterior motives of the Marathas—that after crushing him, they would target him in their policy of expansionism. Realizing the gravity of the situation, Shuja immediately dispatched a 10,000 strong army under the command of Umraogir and Anupgir Gosain. Rumours about the arrival shortly of the main body of the Awadh army, 30,000 under the command of Shuja himself, aggravated the terror felt by the invaders. The Maratha soldiers offered no resistance and fled pell-mell abandoning all their provisions, baggage and spoils and reached Dattaji's camp. In this situation Dattaji wrote to Imad saying, 'In what sleep of negligence are you sunk?... I am engaged here in fighting at your request, and you are planning to flee to Bharatpur'. On the receipt of this letter, Imad took leave from the emperor and went upto Muradnagar en-route to Shukartal. But on reaching there, he received the definite news of the Afghan invaders having taken possession of the entire Punjab upto Sirhind and of the Marathas having everywhere fled away before them without striking a blow.[132]

After his arrival, Shuja-ud Daula defeated the Maratha army under the command of Govind Pundit. The Marathas were so overawed and demoralized that they concluded a peace treaty with him.[133]

IMAD MURDERS ALAMGIR II AND INTIZAM-UD DAULA

As mentioned earliar, failing to crush Najib even after six months of exertions, Dattaji had summoned Imad post-haste for assistance from Delhi. Imad was dissatisfied with the activities of the emperor as well as Intizam, the ex-*wazir*.[134] He was convinced that both of them kept up a secret correspondence with the Abdali and were making devices for the victory of Najib over Dattaji and were supporting his plans for his liquidation. Having documents and letters in his possession in this regard, he became all the more suspicious about them and turned disloyal. Shakir Khan informs us that those letters were, in fact, written by Najib-ud Daula, but the *wazir* attributed that they were written by the emperor and Intizam-ud Daula.[135]

In short, before going to assist Dattaji, Imad saw the danger of leaving the emperor in Delhi, to be captured by the Abdali, who was coming again, and he would be used as his tool against the *wazir*. Therefore, Imad got the emperor murdered[136] and his powerless old rival Intizam was strangled the next day.[137]

Analysing the causes which ultimately led to the murder of Alamgir II by Imad, Jadunath Sarkar remarks, 'Imad's administrative failure and daily increasing poverty, impotence and humiliation through insolvency, drove him mad, and when he learnt that sole remaining hope, the Marathas had failed to crush Najib after five months of exertion and had also lost the Punjab, and that Abdali was coming again, he in utter desperation murdered his master Alamgir II (29 November 1759). The reign ended and with it Imad's office as *wazir*, though he desperately clung to the name for some years after'.[138]

SHAH JAHAN SANI (II)

Imadul Mulk, the regicide, crowned the prince Muhiul Millat; son of Muhiul Sunnat, son of Kam Bakhsh, the youngest son of Aurangzeb, under the title of Shah Jahan Sani.[139] After Alamgir II and Intizam-ud Daula had been removed from the scene, Imad hastened to Dattaji for his assistance. About this time, there was an uproar about the near approach of the Abdali. Raising the siege from Shukartal, Dattaji went off towards Sirhind to encounter the Abdali. Imad thereafter returned to Delhi. When he heard of the encounter between Dattaji and the Abdali skirmishers, becoming certain that the latter would be victorious, he left the new king alone in Delhi, and himself went to Suraj Mal Jat, who extended a hearty welcome to him and performed the duties of a host.[140]

After his famous victory over the Marathas at the battle of Panipat (1761), the Abdali came to Delhi. He deposed Shah Jahan Sani, the nominee of Imad and nominated Mirza Jawan Bakht as the deputy of his father, Shah Alam II. Besides, he appointed Shuja-ud Daula as an absentee *wazir* and Najib-ud Daula as *Mir Bakhshi*, with the title of *Amirul Umara*. Coins were struck and the *khutba* was read in the name of Shah Alam Sani.[141]

From this time onward, we do not hear anything about Imad, who was nobody in the politics of Delhi. He continued to stay with the Jats even after the death of Suraj Mal. When Suraj Mal's son Jawahar Singh attacked Najib-ud Daula, the dictator of Delhi, to avenge the death of his father, who had lost his life in a battle with him, Imad sent his surplus retinue and family to Farrukhabad, while he himself accompanied Jawahar Singh to fight against Najib. After sometime alongwith Malhar Rao, he, too, went to Farrukhabad to take shelter with Ahmad Khan Bangash, whom he had once got appointed as Amirul Umara during the reign of Alamgir II.[142]

LAST DAYS OF IMAD-UL MULK AND HIS DEATH

Sometime after leaving the company of Jawahar Singh in a very wretched condition, Imad went to Chittor, but the company of the Raja did not prove congenial for him. Then he went to the Rana of Gohad.[143] There, too, he did not find peace of mind. Finally he returned to Farrukhabad and completely retired from active political life. After the death of Ahmad Khan Bangash (1771), he did not think it advisable to stay there anymore.[144] Besides, about this time, the news spread that Shah Alam II (1772) was intending to return to Delhi at the invitation of the Marathas to occupy the ancestral throne. In that situation, he thought it imprudent to stay on in that region, because Shah Alam II would pass by that way in his journey to Delhi. Hence leaving there some of the members of the family and retinue, Imad with some reliable men and cash, jewellery and necessary goods left for Surat Bandar. About that time Colonel Goddard was on the way to take possession of the Deccan, therefore an encounter took place between them near Surat Bandar. Due to some reasons, Imadul Mulk did not think it advisable to stay in that region and he left for Mecca.[145]

Khairuddin Muhammad Allahabadi informs us that from Farrukhabad, Imadul Mulk went to the Deccan and sought refuge with his uncle, Nizam Ali Khan, the ruler of Hyderabad, but due to his reputation as a mischievous conspirator and as being false to the salt of his masters, the courtiers of the Nawab nursed a grudge against him. They conspired to oust him from there and got him expelled. It is said that thenceforth, he went on a pilgrimage to Mecca embarking on a ship. Without any elaboration, it is recorded that during his stay there he sought help from the rulers of that region, especially from the ruler of the Rome, but in vain. After sometimes returning via Basra, he came down to Kabul and Qandhar. There he sought the help of Timur Shah Durrani, the son and successor of Ahmad Shah Abdali, but as his courtiers nursed enmity against him, because they knew his natural villainy, they did not allow him to attend the court. However, being disappointed, he returned to Surat Bandar. From here he sought the favour of the English authorities at Calcutta through the Englishmen of that region, but as the English commanders were full of sagacity, they put forward the argument that whosoever proved disloyal to his master, he lost his own credibility and whosoever committed villainy to his master, he would do no good to anyone. Hence he was disappointed.[146]

There is another version given by Muhammad Ali Khan. The author informs us that while Imadul Mulk was still at Kabul, by chance, a royal prince Mirza Ahsan Bakht,[147] son of Shah Alam II, who after his father was blinded and atrocities were perpetrated on the king and the members of the royal family by Ghulam Qadir Rohilla, son of Zabita Khan, escaped from the Red Fort of Delhi. After roaming in the wilderness of Rajputana, Jai Nagar, Bikaner and Multan, he happened to reach the country of Shah Timur, who in honour of the fact that he was a descendent of Amir Timur, and considering he was related to Shah Alam Padshah, and that he had wandered out from his own country, he extended great honour to him and kept him as his guest. Thereafter along with his army, Timur Shah sent the prince with Imadul Mulk to Multan and promised that he himself would reach there shortly to subjugate India, but in the meantime, he died and was succeeded by his son Zaman Shah, who became busy in the suppression of the Sikhs.

When the prince reached the country of Sindh Timur Shah had died and the army of the Shah leaving the prince alone went back to Kabul. Ghaziuddin Khan Imadul Mulk went to Nasir Khan Beloch at Bhawalpur. It is said that Imad did not live for a long time in the company of the prince because their relations did not remain cordial as the companions of the prince comprised of low-born people. Thereafter, the prince came back to Multan. From Bahawalpur, Imad came down to Ali Bahadur, a Maratha chief, son of Shamshir Bahadur, a commander of an army and a great chief. He was given a small *jagir* in Kalpi, where he passed the last days of his life. He died of cholera in Kalpi in 1800. According to his will, his body was taken to Pakpatan (in the Punjab) and buried in the precinct of the tomb of Shaikh Fariduddin Ganj-i Shakar.[148]

The *tazkira* writers of the latter half of the eighteenth century have included Imad's name as a poet in Persian and *rekhta* (Urdu), under the penname Nizam. Rai Lachchmi Narayan Khattari 'Shafiq' writes that the *wazir* (Imad) was second to none in several accomplishments. He wrote eloquently and spoke Arabic, Persian, Turkish, Kashmiri, Afghani and other Indian languages. He used to enjoy the company of the *Ulama*, scholars and *mashaikh*. For sometimes, he kept Mir Shamsuddin 'Faqir', a poet, in Delhi with himself. He had left a *diwan* of his poetic compositions in Persian and *rekhta*.[149]

Mir Taqi 'Mir', the poet, lived in Delhi during that period and he had seen the rise and fall of Imad. Mir regarded him as unequalled in several excellencies despite the fact that he was not of much age. Even then he wrote five or six excellent styles of calligraphy. He composed verses in Persian and *rekhta* of high taste and standard. Imad had extended much favour to Mir and gave him financial help.[150]

It appears that Imad was much devoted to and cherished much faith in Shah Fakhruddin Delhavi, a *Chishti* saint. The credit of writing the biography of the Shah under the captions of *Manaqib-i Fakhriya* goes to him.

Paradoxically, almost all the contemporary historians and writers had denounced, cursed, censured and criticized Imad in strong words for his villainy, wickedness, vindictiveness, ruthlessness, mischievousness, ingratitude, treachery and inhumanity. He had no regard for human beings and due to his high ambitions and greed for wealth, he did not even spare his maternal uncle Intizam-ud Daula and prospective mother-in-law Mughlani Begam to achieve his selfish ends.[151]

NOTES

1. For biographical notices, see Shah Nawaz Khan, *Maasirul Umara* (1780), ed. Abdur Rahim and Ashraf Ali, Calcutta, 1888, 3 vols. (Bib. Indica), Eng. trans. H. Beveridge, revised edn., annotated and completed by Dr. Beni Prasad, Calcutta, 2 vols. Other editions by Janki Prakashan, Patna, 1979 (Reprint); (Text) I, pp. 361-2; Eng. trans. I, pp. 592-3; Ghulam Ali Azad Bilgrami, Mir, *Khizana-i Amira,* Newal Kishore, Kanpur, 1871, pp. 49-50.
2. For biographical notices, see *Maasirul Umara* (Text), III, pp. 837-48; Eng. trans, Vol. 2, part, I, pp. 409-54.
3. Jadunath Sarkar, *Fall of the Mughal Empire*, I (3rd edn., 1964), Calcutta, 1964, pp. 279-80.
4. A town in the district of Gwalior State, Central India, *Today and Tomorrow*, New Delhi (n.d.), Vol. XVIII (new edition), p. 396.
5. We find the name of Imadul Mulk under the penname 'Nizam' as a poet almost in all the *Tazkiras* of Persian and Urdu poets compiled during the latter half of the eighteenth and nineteenth centuries.
6. Ghulam Ali Khan, Saiyid, *Imadus Sa'adat,* Newal Kishore, Kanpur, 1897, pp. 60-1; Ghulam Husain Khan Tabatabai, *Siyarul Mutakhkhirin,* Nawal Kishore, Lucknow, 1886, 3 vols., Vol. III, p. 46. Anonymous, *Tarikh-i Ahmad Shahi,* Rotograph No.149, AMU, Aligarh, f. 54a.
7. *Imadus Sa'adat,* pp. 62-3; *Tarikh-i Ahmad Shahi,* ff. 42b-43a, 54a; Shakir Khan, *Tarikh-i Shakir Khani* (Rotograph, No.7, Department of History, AMU, Aligarh, ff. 62ab; *Teen Tazkire,* ed. Nisar Ahmad Faruqi, Maktaba

Burhan, Urdu Bazar, Delhi, 1968, p. 270. But during the civil war, Imad had turned away from his benefactor. *Imadus Sa'adat*, p. 63.

8. *Tarikh-i Ahmad Shahi*, ff. 79b-87a and 101b.
9. *Imadus Sa'adat*, p. 90.
10. Ibid., pp. 10 and 31.
11. Har Charan Dass, *Chahar Gulzar-i Shujai*, Rotograph No.35. Department of History, AMU, Aligarh, f. 382b.
12. *Tarikh-i Ahmad Shahi*, ff. 3a-9b, 14b and 17b; *Khizana-i Amira*, pp.78-9; *Chahar Gulzar-i Shujai*, f. 19b and *Siyarul Mutakhkhirin*, III, pp.868-9.
13. *Tarikh-i Ahmad Shahi*, ff. 14b. *Khizana-i Amira*, p.76; *Siyarul Mutakhkhirin*, III, pp. 868-9 and Mir Taqi 'Mir', *Zikr-i Mir* (1783), ed. Abdul Haqq, Aurangabad Deccan, 1928, pp.68-9.
14. *Tarikh-i Ahmad Shahi*, ff. 13b-14ab and *Tarikh-i Shakir Khani*, f. 60a.
15. *Tarikh-i Ahmad Shahi*, f.15a; *Tarikh-i Shakir Khani*, f. 60a; *Siyarul Mutakhkhirin*, III, p. 872.
16. *Tarikh-i Ahmad Shahi*, f. 15a.
17. *Fall of the Mughal Empire*, I, p. 213.
18. *Tarikh-i Ahmad Shahi*, f. 15b; *Siyarul Mutakhkhirin*, III, pp.858 and 872.
19. *Tarikh-i Ahmad Shahi*, f. 15b.
20. Ibid., ff. 24b and 29 ab.
21. Like other eunuch servants of the palace he had access to the female apartments. He was about 50 years of age but quite illiterate. For details, see *Tarikh-i Ahmad Shahi*, f. 15ab and 29a.
22. There were three kinds of eunuchs. First, the *sandali* or *atlasi*, whose penis and testicles were removed from the very root; second, *badami*, a small part of whose penis was left to enable them for cohabitation; third, *kapuri*, whose testicles were castrated in infancy. Qazi Murtaza Husain, *Hadiqatul Aqalim*, Nawal Kishore, Lucknow, 1879, pp. 651-52.
23. In her early life Udham Bai was a public dancing girl. Later on she found an access to the imperial *haram* and the emperor Muhammad Shah married her. Ahmad Shah was born from her. After her son's accession to the throne, she was successively given the titles of *Bai-Jiu Sahiba, Nawab Qudsiya, Sahib-uz Zamani, Sahib-i Jiu Sahiba, Hazrat* and *Qibla-i Alam*. A *mansab* of 50000 (a nominal rank) was also conferred on her. Her birth anniversary used to be celebrated with great pomp and show and lavishness of expenditure as compared to the emperor himself. For details about her early life and subsequent life during the reign of Ahmad Shah, see *Tarikh-i Ahmad Shahi*, f. 15ab-17a, 29a and 107b-108a.
24. Subsequently his *mansab* was raised to 7000/7000 *zat* and *sawar* and made *Naib-i Sultanat*. *Tarikh-i Ahmad Shahi*, ff. 14b, 15b, 25a; *Chahar Gulzar-i Shujai*, ff. 19b and 20 b.
25. *Tarikh-i Ahmad Shahi*, ff. 14a, 15a.
26. Bernier, Francois, *Travels in the Mogul Empire* (1556-68), translated and annotated by Archiliald Constable, S. Chand and Co., Delhi, 1968 (Reprint), pp. 211-12.

27. *Tarikh-i Ahmad Shahi*, ff. 44ab; *Fall of the Mughal Empire*, I, pp. 215-16.
28. Ibid., f. 15a.
29. Ibid., f. 21b and *Siyarul Mutakhkhirin*, III, p. 883.
30. *Imadus Sa'adat*, p. 60.
31. Ibid., p. 60.
32. Ibid., p. 60.
33. *Tarikh-i Ahmad Shahi*, ff. 17b, 25a, 28b, 29a, 45a.
34. Ibid., f. 16a.
35. Ibid., ff. 17b-18a.
36. Ibid., f. 36b.
37. Ibid., ff. 47ab.
38. Ibid., f. 18ab. Sukh Rai, *Majmaul Akhbar*, MS. No. 130. *Fahrist, Urdu Farsiya*, II, Azad Library, AMU, Aligarh.
39. Ahmad Shah passed most of his time in drunken orgies, visiting the gardens in the Red Fort and in the suburbs of the capital. His *haram*, which was more than one square mile in area, abounded in a large number of beautiful women, and he lived there for weeks and months on end, without seeing any man. *Tarikh-i Ahmad Shahi*, ff. 16a, 25b, and 108a.
40. *Tarikh-i Ahmad Shahi*, ff. 16a, and 17ab.
41. Saiyid Ghulam Ali Khan informs us, if he is to be relied upon, that the emperor felt extremely oppressed owing to an unworthy omission on the part of Jawid Khan. Hence he whispered into the ears of Safdar Jang that he should be killed, but in such a manner that it should not be known that it was done on his behest or hint. *Imadus Sa'adat*, p. 60. and cf. *Chahar Gulzar-i Shujai*, f. 119b.
42. For details, see *Tarikh-i Ahmad Shahi*, ff. 39b-40b; *Chahar Gulzar-i Shujai*, f. 118b; *Tarikh-i Shakir Khani*, f. 60b and *Fall of the Mughal Empire*, I, pp. 233-4.
43. For details, see *Tarikh-i Ahmad Shahi*, ff. 39b-41b; *Tarikh-i Shakir Khani*, ff. 60b and 66b.
44. *Fall of the Mughal Empire*, I, p. 234.
45. Tarikh-i Ahmad Shahi, ff. 40b-42b, 118a; Ghulam Ali Khan Ansari, *Tarikh-i Muzaffari*, MS. No. 364/134-365/135, 2 Vols. Abdul Salam Collection, Azad Library, AMU, Aligarh, I, f. 328b; *Chahar Gulzar-i Shujai*, ff. 118 ab.
46. Ibid., f. 41a.
47. Ibid., f. 41a.
48. Ibid., f. 45a.
49. Ibid., ff. 40b-41ab.
50. Ibid., ff. 41a-42b.
51. Ibid., ff. 13b, 41ab.
52. Ibid., f. 42b.
53. Ibid., ff. 42b-43a.
54. Ibid., ff. 41b-42b.
55. Ibid., ff. 46a, 47ab and 48ab and 53ab.
56. *Tarikh-i Ahmad Shahi*, ff. 48ab and 53ab.

57. Ibid., f. 53a.
58. Ibid., ff. 48b-49a and *Khizana-i Amira,* p.50.
59. Ibid., ff. 49ab.
60. Ibid., ff. 49ab and *Chahar Gulzar-i Shujai,* f. 118b.
61. Ibid., ff. 47b-49a; *Chahar Gulzar-i Shujai,* f. 408b and *Siyarul Mutakhkhirin,* III, p. 46.
62. Srivastava, A.L., *The First Two Nawabs of Awadh,* Agra, 1954.
63. *Tarikh-i Ahmad Shahi,* ff. 49b and 50a.
64. Ibid., ff. 52ab.
65. Ibid., f. 55a.
66. Ibid., f. 56a.
67. Ibid., ff. 55b.
68. Ibid., ff. 54a-55a, 56a; *Siyarul Mutakhkhirin,* III, p. 892. *Imadus Sa'adat,* p. 63; Saiyid Nuruddin Husain Fakhri, *Sarguzasht-i Najib-ud Daula,* Aligarh, 1924, p.2 and *Chahar Gulzar-i Shujai,* f. 121a.
69. Mirza Muhammad Bakhsh Ashob, *Tarikh-i Shahadat-i Farrukhsiyar-wa Julus-i Muhammad Shah.* Rotograph No.152, Department of History, AMU, Aligarh, II, ff. 250a and 261a and *Siyarul Mutakhkhirin,* III, p. 854.
70. *Tarikh-i Ahmad Shahi,* ff. 55ab and *Zikr-i Mir,* p.73.
71. Khafi Khan, *Muntakhab-ul Lubab,* ed. Khairuddin Ahmad and Ghulam Qadir, Calcutta, 1860, 2 vols. (Bib. Indica), II, p. 914.
72. *Tarikh-i Ahmad Shahi,* ff. 55a; *Siyarul Mutakhkhirin,* III, p. 892 and *Chahar Gulzar-i Shujai,* f. 409a.
73. *Tarikh-i Ahmad Shahi,* ff. 51b-55ab; *Tarikh-i Shakir Khani,* f. 69a; *Siyarul Mutakhkhirin,* III, p. 892 and *Imadus Sa'adat,* p. 63.
74. *Imadus Sa'adat,* p. 63.
75. *Tarikh-i Ahmad Shahi,* ff. 54a and *Chahar Gulzar-i Shujai,* ff. 122b-23a.
76. Spreading all over the city, the Jats perpetrated cruelty and oppression on the poor inhabitants and plundered their houses. *Tarikh-i Ahmad Shahi,* ff. 54b.
77. *Tarikh-i Ahmad Shahi,* ff. 54ab.
78. Ibid., f. 73b.
79. Ibid., f. 81a.
80. Ibid., f. 82b.
81. Ibid., ff. 82ab.
82. Ibid., ff. 83a-84b; *Tarikh-i Shakir Khani,* ff. 67b-70a; *Siyarul Mulakhkhirin,* III, p. 893 and *Chahar Gulzar-i Shujai,* ff. 118b-125a.
83. *Tarikh-i Ahmad Shahi,* ff. 95b-96a.
84. Ibid., f. 102a.
85. For the causes of hostility between the *wazir,* Safdar Jang and Imadul Mulk, see *Tarikh-i Ahmad Shahi,* ff. 81a-82b.
86. Ibid., ff. 114ab.
87. Ibid., ff. 81b-82b.

88. Ibid., f. 49b.
89. Ibid., f. 67b.
90. Ibid., f. 116b. For the wretched condition of the servants of the state, see ibid, ff. 19ab, 20ab, 21b and 30ab. Due to not getting their salaries, the imperial army had become a restless and powerless lot. For three consecutive years they had been passing their life on loans from the *sahukars* and selling off and mortgaging their household goods and weapons. Even for their daily expenses they had to borrow money from the *sahukars*. Consequently, the soldiers had dispersed. *Chahar Gulzar-i Shujai*, ff. 151ab. Muhammad Rafi Sauda, *Kulliyat-i Sauda*, 2 vols., ed. Abdul Bari Asi. Newal Kishore, Lucknow, 1932, pp. 363-7.
91. *Tarikh-i Ahmad Shahi*, ff. 49b-50a.
92. Ibid., f. 94a.
93. Ibid., ff. 43ab, 44ab, 50b, 51-b-55ab, and 120ab.
94. Ibid., f. 82b.
95. Ibid., ff. 108ab, 109ab, 113b, 116; *Khizana-i Amira*, p.51; *Zikr-i Mir*, pp. 73-4 and *Tarikh-i Shakir Khani*, f. 81a.
96. *Tarikh-i Ahmad Shahi*, ff. 127a-29b; *Khizana-i Amira*, p.51 and *Zikr-i Mir*, p. 130.
97. Ibid., f. 130a.
98. Ibid., ff. 128a-132; *Khizana-i Amira*, pp.51-2; *Tarikh-i Shakir Khani*, f. 71a; *Zikr-i Mir*, p. 74. When Raja Bhakht Mal and other men went to pay their respects to the king, he inquired from them why he had left his wives and other females there, why they did not bring them under their escort. The *wazir* replied that in the darkness of the night nothing could be seen and known and nobody informed him about the situation. *Tarikh-i Ahmad Shahi*, ff. 128a-130a.
99. *Tarikh-i Ahmad Shahi*, f. 129b and anonymous, *Tarikh-i Alamgir Sani*, MS. No. 2604. Khuda Bakhsh Public Library, Patna, pp. 6-7.
100. *Tarikh-i Ahmad Shahi*, ff. 126a-130a.
101. Ibid., ff. 126a-130ab and *Tarikh-i Alamgir Sani*, pp. 6-7.
102. Ibid., f. 130b. *Sara Bustan*, ff. 191a-192a.
103. Ibid., ff. 95a to 134b.
104. Ibid., ff. 95ab.

105a. Ibid., ff. 131b-134b.

105b. *Tarikh-i Muzaffari*, II, ff. 3ab.

106. *Tarikh-i Ahmad Shahi*, ff. 134b-135a; *Tarikh-i Alamgir Sani*, p. 22; *Tarikh-i Shakir Khani*, f. 71b; Ghulam Ali Khan, *Shah Alam Nama*, ed. A. Al-Mamun Shurawardy and Aqa Muhammad Kazim Shirazi, (Bib. Indica), Calcutta, 1914, p. 21; *Tarikh-i Muzaffari*, II, ff. 3ab, 20a-21ab; Mirza Ali Bakht Bahadur, Mirza Muhammad Zahiruddin Azfari, *Waqiat-i Azfari*, Urdu trans. By Abdul Sattar. Oriental Research Institute, Madras University, 1937, pp. 187 and 190.

107. *Tarikh-i Ahmad Shahi*, f. 135b; *Sara Bustan*, ff. 192ab.
108. *Chahar Gulzar-i Shujai*, f. 181b; *Tarikh-i Shakir Khani*, f. 71b; *Tarikh-i Muzaffari*, II, ff. 26b-27ab; *Waqiat-i Azfari*. The *wazir* got the king and his mother blinded and confined him in seclusion in the *mohalla-i nau*. There remained still some light in one of the eyes of the king. He was able to write (pp. 187 and 189-90).
109. *Tarikh-i Alamgir Sani*, p. 5; *Fall of the Mughal Empire* (3rd edn.), Calcutta, 1966, II, p.1.
110. Bhagwan Dass Hindi, *Safina-i Hindi*, ed. Saiyid Shah Muhammad Ataur Rahman 'Ata' Kakovi, Patna, 1958; p.2; *Tarikh-i Muzaffari*, II, ff. 3b, 24b, 30b-31a and *Sara Bustan*, ff. 192ab.
111. *Zikr-i Mir*, pp. 74-5.
112. Muhammad Qudratullah 'Shauq', Shaikh, *Jan-i Jahan Numa*, Ms. No. 1856, Raza Library, Rampur, p. 502.
113. *Tarikh-i Ahmad Shahi*, ff. 30ab-31a. 85ab, 92a, 105a, 110ab and 112b; *Khizana-i Amira*, pp. 98-9; *Tarikh-i Shakir Khani*, f. 72a and *Shah Alam Nama*, pp. 26-27.
114. *Fall of the Mughal Empire*, II, pp. 74-6.
115. *Khizana-i Amira*, p. 99; *Tarikh-i Shakir Khani*, ff. 73ab, 81b-82a; *Shah Alam Nama*, p. 27 and *Siyarul Mutakhkhirin*, III, p. 898.
116. *Shah Alam Nama*, p. 27.
117. *Khizana-i Amira*, pp. 52-3, 62-3, 90, *Tarikh-i Shakir Khani*, ff. 73ab-81a; *Tarikh-i Muzaffari*, II, f. 40b; *Siyarul Mutakhkhirin*, III, pp. 898-9 and *Chahar Gulzar-i Shujai*, f. 153b.
118. *Chahar Gulzar-i Shujai*, f. 152b.
119. Ibid., ff. 152ab.
120. Ibid., f. 152b.
121. *Khizana-i Amira*, p. 87; *Zikr-i Mir*, p. 80, *Shah Alam Nama*, pp. 31-2 and *Siyarul Mutakhkhirin*, III, pp. 899-900.
122. *Tarikh-i Alamgir Sani*, pp.107-8; *Zikr-i Mir*, p. 76; *Shah Alam Nama*, p. 28 and *Teen Tazkire*, p. 271-2.
123. *Tarikh-i Alamgir Sani*, pp. 94-5.
124. Ibid., pp. 107-8; *Shah Alam Nama*, pp. 32 and *Teen Tazkire*, p. 272.
125. *Khizana-i Amira*, p. 53; *Shah Alam Nama*, pp. 31-32; *Tarikh-i Muzaffari*, II, f. 42b-3a and *Teen Tazkire*, p. 271.
126. *Tarikh-i Alamgir Sani*, pp.108; *Shah Alam Nama*, p. 28 and *Zikr-i Mir*, p. 76.
127. *Tarikh-i Shakir Khani*, f. 81b and *Fall of the Mughal Empire*, II, pp.89-90.
128. *Khizana-i Amira*, p. 100; *Tarikh-i Shakir Khani*, ff. 81ab and *Siyarul Mutakhkhirin*, III, pp. 899-900.
129. *Khizana-i Amira*, pp. 53-4; *Tarikh-i Muzaffari*, II, ff. 44b-45a; *Tarikh-i Shakir Khani*, ff. 81b, 83b-84a; *Shah Alam Nama*, p. 33; *Siyarul Mutakhkhirin*, III, p. 904 and *Teen Tazkire*, p. 272.
130. *Khizana-i Amira*, pp. 91-2; *Tarikh-i Shakir Khani*, ff. 82ab-83ab; *Tarikh-*

i Muzaffari, II, ff. 31ab, 67b-72a; *Shah Alam Nama,* pp. 30-1, 34-9, 44-9 and *Zikir-i Mir,* p.80.

131. Janku, A Marathi chief. *Tarikh-i Shakir Khani,* ff. 83b-84b.
132. *Chahar Gulzar-i Shujai,* ff. 170ab and *Tarikh-i Shakir Khani,* ff. 83b-84a.
133. Ibid., f. 170a; *Tarikh-i Muzaffari,* II, ff. 75a-78a; *Khizana-i Amira,* pp. 87-8 and *Zikir-i Mir,* p.81.
134. For details regarding the causes of rivalry and enmity between Imadul Mulk and ex-*wazir,* see *Tarikh-i Ahmad Shahi,* ff. 74a-75a, 82b-83b.
135. *Tarikh-i Ahmad Shahi,* ff. 75b, 82b-83b; *Shah Alam Nama,* pp. 92-3 and *Tarikh-i Shakir Khani,* f. 84b.
136. Alamgir Sani was greatly devoted to the dead and living saints and holy men of repute. He used to visit the tombs of Shaikh Nizamuddin Auliya, Khwaja Qutbuddin Bakhtiyar Kaki and Shaikh Nasiruddin Chiragh Dehalvi. He attended their death and birth anniversaries and performed the rituals of circumambulation. Likewise, whenever he heard of the presence of any saint of eminence in the city of Delhi, he made it a point to go to him and pay his respects. Sometimes he did so without verifying whether the saint he had heard of was a genuine one or an imposter. Besides, he also visited the graves of the Mughal kings, princes and ladies of the royal *haram* buried near the shrine of Khwaja Qutbuddin Kaki. Among the living saints, he used to pay respects to Muhammad Darvesh and Saiyid Murtaza. In short, as said above, Imadul Mulk being dissatisfied with the activities of the king Alamgir II wanted to kill him. He deputed Mehdi Quli Khan and Balabash Khan to do that job. Since this plan of eliminating the king could not have successfully materialized within the fort, so there was a need to find a pretext to get him out of it. One day Mehdi Quli Khan went to the king and met him in the *tasbih khana.* During the conversations, he informed him that some saints of repute either from Baghdad and Balkh or Lahore had arrived and they had taken up their abode at Firoz Shah Kotla. He motivated him to go there to meet them. Without any hitch, the king readily agreed. With the convoy of the king, there were Zafarullah Khan, some eunuchs and the prince Mirza Babur. When the king reached at the Kotla, he saw that the Mughal followers of Balabash Khan, the commander of the contingent of the *wazir,* were already standing there. They directed the king that the saints were staying in that chamber. The convoy moved to that direction. When he reached the door of the chamber, he alighted from the *takht-i rawan* and went inside the chamber of the tower. The Mughal soldiers attending on him did not allow anyone else from his companions to go in except Ali Khan Mahalli. The prince Mirza Babur, who was also with the king, was detained outside. The other followers going to the other side sat down there. The prince spreading the carpet began to offer the *zuhr* prayers. In the meantime, Balabash Khan went inside the chamber and came out after

killing the king with a stroke of a dagger. He asked the prince to rise up and to accompany him. The prince inquired where he was taking him. Balabash Khan in reply said to the king. The prince said what business he had with the king. He answered that he was to be taken to the fort. Saying this he snatched the dagger from the prince's waist. Taking hold of the prince's arm, he moved on. The dead body of the king was thrown on the sand of the Jamuna river below. Thereafter they publicized that the king had gone to meet the *faqirs*. From above the rampart his legs slipped, he fell down and died. Seating the prince Mirza Babur on someone's horse, Balabash Khan brought him to the fort and entrusted him in the custody of Munawwar, the deputy *nazir* of the gate of the *deorahi* of the *salatin*. On the first day, the prince was guarded at the door by the footmen throughout the day and night and detained him there without food and water. Next day, on the instructions from Mehdi Quli Khan, he was taken to *asad burj* to join his other brothers.

Tarikh-i Alamgir Sani, pp. 26,27,37,38,39,40,51,221; *Zikr-i Mir*, pp. 81-2; *Hadiqatul Aqalim*, p. 137; *Waqi'at-i Azfari*, pp. 166-8; *Waqa'-i Alam Shahi*, 5,17; *Khizana-i Amira*, p. 90; *Siyarul Mutakhkhirin*, II, pp. 676-7; *Ibid*, III, p.908; *Chahar Gulzar-i Shujai*, ff. 169b-170a; *Tarikh-i Rahat Afza*, p. 343; *Majmaul Akhbar*, f. 464a; *Tarikh-i Muzaffari*, II, ff. 71b-76ab, *Shah Alam Nama*, pp. 93-5; *Tarikh-i Shakir Khani*, ff. 84b-85b and *Teen Tazkire*, p. 272.

137. The ex-*wazir* had been in confinement for some years in the fort. It is recorded that when he was offering his prayers in the prison, the Mughals deputed by Imadul Mulk for this task going there in the night strangled him, while his mother weeping, pleaded for his life. His dead body was thrown in the Jamuna river with heavy stones tied to his foot. For details, see *Tarikh-i Alamgir Sani*, p. 222; *Shah Alam Nama*, p. 91 and *Tarikh-i Muzaffari*, II, ff. 27b, 71b, 76ab-77a.
138. *Fall of the Mughal Empire*, II, p.10.
139. *Tarikh-i Muzaffari*, II, ff. 76b-77a.
140. *Khizana-i Amira*, pp. 53-4; *Tarikh-i Muzaffari*, II, ff. 44b-45; *Zikr-i Mir*, p. 82; *Tarikh-i Alamgir Sani*, p.222; *Teen Tazkire*, pp. 272-3; *Shah Alam Nama*, pp. 95 and *Chahar Gulzar-i Shujai*, f. 170a.
141. *Tarikh-i Shakir Khani*, f. 86; *Tarikh-i Muzaffari*, II, ff. 77a, 85b, 91a; *Khizana-i Amira*, p. 106; *Zikr-i Mir*, p. 88; *Siyarul Mutakhkhirin*, III, p. 916 and *Waqi'at-i Azfari*, pp. 167-8.
142. *Tarikh-i Muzaffari*, II, ff. 132b-33a; *Tarikh-i Shakir Khani*, ff. 86b; *Khizana-i Amira*, p. 54; *Teen Tazkire*, p. 273; *Siyarul Mulakhkhirin*, III, p. 908. Imadul Mulk, who was thinking to withdraw, coming out with his family from the fort of Bharatpur, sending the surplus men to Farrukhabad, he himself joined Jawahar Singh. *Zikr-i Mir*, pp. 88 and 112.

143. Rana of Gohad was a Jat prince independent of Bharatpur. *Fall of the Mughal Empire,* II, p. 337.
144. Har Charan Dass informs us that while Imad was staying at Farrukhabad, Ahmad Khan Bangash used to give him Rs. 12000/- per month for his personal expenses. He stayed there for a long time. *Chahar Gulzar-i Shujai,* f. 229b. Also see, *Sa'adat Jawid,* f. 182a.
145. *Tarikh-i Muzaffari,* II, ff. 324a-25b. It is said that Colonel Goddard found Imad at Surat in 1780 disguised as a pilgrim and that he was for a time put into confinement. He did go to Mecca, and returned via Basra and Qandhar. He died at Kalpi on 1 December 1800. *Maasirul Umara,* Eng. trans. H. Beveridge (Patna ed. 1979), I, p. 677, fn.3.
146. *Sara Bustam,* ff. 194ab.
147. After Shah Alam II was blinded, dethroned, and tortured, the members of the royal family were subjected to inhuman cruelties, and thereafter they suffered from financial difficulties, some of the royal princes left the fort of Delhi and dispersed to other places. Mirza Sulaiman Shukoh went to Lucknow and Mirza Ahsan Bakht to Multan. Rai Tek Chand, *Roz Namcha-i Shah Alam,* MS. Khuda Bakhsh Public Library, Patna, ff. 64b, 69a and 80a.
148. For details, see Khairuddin Muhammad Allahabadi, *Sara Bustan,* ff. 194ab. MS. No. 556/7, Abdul Salam Collection, Azad Library, AMU, Aligarh, *Tarikh-i Muzaffari,* II, ff. 324a-25b; *Hadiqat-ul Aqalim,* p.175; Harnam Singh Nami, *Tarikh-i Sa'adat Jawid,* Rotograph No. 40, Department of History, AMU, Aligarh.
149. *Teen Tazkire,* p. 273.
150. *Zikr-i Mir,* p. 113. Also see *Teen Tazkire,* pp. 270-2; Mir Hasan Delhavi, *Tazkira-i Shu'ara-i Urdu,* ed. Muhammad Habibur Rahman Khan Sherwani, *Anjuman-i Taraqqi-i Urdu* (Hind), Delhi, 1940, p. 109; Ghulam Hamadani 'Mushafi', *Iqd-i Suraiya,* ed. Maulana Abdul Haqq, Delhi, 1934 (1st edn.), p. 58; Qudratullah Qasim (Hakim), *Tazkira-i Majmua-i Naghz,* ed. Mahmud Sherani, Lahore, 1933, 2 vols., II, p. 277 and Qudratullah Shauq, *Takmilat-ush-Shu'ara* MS. Raza Library, Rampur, pp. 628-34.
151. *Tarikh-i Ahmad Shahi,* ff. 95a, 101b, 102b, 104a and *Shah Alam Nama,* pp. 23 and 32.

PART 3

FEUDAL ORDERS

Social Protest and Cultural Defence: The Bareilly Uprising of 1816

Azra Alavi

In April 1816 a *chowkidari* tax was levied on the residents of Bareilly. It was an extension of Regulation XIII of 1813, already imposed in parts of Bengal and Bihar. A resident in each quarter or ward of the city was to be made responsible for its collection. The tax revenue was intended to pay for the establishment of city watchman, to be appointed and controlled exclusively by the taxpayers. The poor were exempt from payment. The tax, up to a maximum of four rupees per annum, was to be determined on the basis of the property owned.[1]

The leading residents of Bareilly strongly opposed the measure. The efforts by the Magistrate to explain that it was indispensable in order to free the police from city duties and to ensure safety of the roads, which was essential for their trade, failed.[2] The success of earlier protest movements like the one at Benares in 1810-11 in opposition to Regulation XV of 1810 must have influenced this attitude of the people.

On 16 April 1816 when the Magistrate arrived to fix the tax on each household in Bareilly, he was surrounded by a large mob, led by the *Mufti*, Muhammad Aiwaz, protesting against the measure. The Magistrate ordered the road to be cleared for him: in the ensuring confrontation, six or seven persons were killed. In the evening Muhammad Aiwaz, Muhammad Isa and a large number of other residents of Bareilly left the town and assembled at a mosque on the outskirts where they hoisted the green flag of Islam and declared a *jihad* against the English East India Company. They sent written invitations to the people of other major towns in Rohilkhand to join the *jihad*. Large numbers of armed men from Rampur, Pilibheet and other places rallied to their call and on 21 April, 12,000 men proceeded to attack the military detachment stationed at Bareilly.[3]

The uprising was put down severely. Indiscriminate arrests were made and many people not even involved in the uprising languished in jails for years.[4] However, the whole affair brought to the fore the groundswell of discontent against British rule in all its dimensions. It also reflected the pressures, tensions and conflicts that beset the Muslim society following the decline of the old order and the establishment of British supremacy.

Two significant features of the uprising were first, that the movement (though focused in Bareilly) was sustained by sympathy and active support from different parts of north India; and, second, the *chowkidari* tax served merely as a spark that ignited and inflamed other more deeply felt social, economic and religious grievances. Major General Cunningham, on the basis of personal experience concluded that Delhi being the centre of Muslim aspirations was the place where the Bareilly insurrection was planned.[5] Some officials suspected the Nawab of Rampur and his Minister Hakim Ghulam Hussain of being responsible for sending reinforcements.[6] The Enquiry Committee which was set up to investigate the causes of the uprising, however, exonerated them of this charge.[7] Connections between the Bareilly activists and Amir Khan of Tonk were also emphasized.[8]

Prior to the uprising, officials had suspected that:

> In the actual state of the public mind in Rohiklhand . . . an attempt might be made to assist movement against the British Government by the followers of Amir Khan, a large body of whom were connected by birth with the people of Bareilly and other parts of Rohilkhand and including Rampur and who had lately shown symptoms of a common feeling. . .'[9]

It is noteworthy that during this period Amir Khan had in his service a famous disciple of Shah Abdul Aziz and the future leader of the Mujahidin movement, Sayyid Ahmad Barelwi. It is probable that some of this 'common feeling' might have been due to the activities of Sayyid Ahmad.

Muhammad Isa, an important leader of the uprising, had served under the Nawab of Tonk for some time.[10] In his meeting with Major W. Richards, Commander of the 1st Batallion, prior to the uprising, he is reported to have said that if ever Amir Khan were distressed (by the British) 'he would assuredly be joined by every Pathan in the region'. And he seems to have given the impression that 'some measures had been taken by the Mussalmans to create disturbances in Rohilkhand'. It is significant that the uprising took place soon after some three to four thousand Pathans, discharged by Amir Khan, had returned to their homes in Rampur. The Nawab is reported to have told the disbanded soldiers that he would not be able to employ them if they failed to find service with the company for the British are 'inimical to the existence of any Mussalman power in India'.[11] Links between the principality of Tonk and the Bareilly insurgents are further emphasized by the fact that, after the failure of the uprising, many Bareilly activists took refuge in Tonk.[12]

The Bareilly uprising, sparked by local, municipal factors soon came to epitomize the discontent of Muslims in other parts, who were acquainted with the Bareilly happenings. The vernacular newspapers reported soon after the disturbances that all the Pathans in Amir Khan's service had applied to him for leave to proceed to Bareilly 'for the assistance of their brothers whom they understand to be at war with the Europeans'.[13]

The Bareilly uprising was not an isolated incident. It had as its immediate precedent the Allahabad uprising which was also, it appears, an attempt to resist the tax, though it did not assume a similar magnitude.[14] Indications of resistance to the measure had been manifested in Agra, Moradabad and Bundelkhand as well.[15] During November 1814 the inhabitants of Moradabad held nightly meetings at mosques and other places to decide upon the best means of evading Regulation XIII. Hence it was widely believed that the Bareilly uprising was not merely a spontaneous reaction to the imposition of the *chowkidari* tax, rather, that Muslims had made preparations to create disturbances in Rohilkhand.[16] The Magistrate of Bareilly later confessed that he did not expect so much opposition to the new measures and blamed some 'ill-disposed' persons for having been 'long employed in poisoning the public mind and in associating the new rules for a regulated establishment of Chowkeydars [*sic*] with the idea of a House Tax and other demands of a more exceptionable nature which would be made in the event of a concession to this. . .'.[17]

Some documents testify to the preparations that proceded the operations. Before the imposition of the *chowkidari* tax a proclamation was issued stating:

> In these ill-boding days there is a general report that the English have it in contemplation in a day or two to establish a tax. Notice is hereby given that should the Hindus or Mussulmans, whether Saiyyids or Shaikhs or Moghuls or Afghans or Brahmins or Rajputs or Khatrees or Bakkauls consent to pay the tax let them regard it as dishonourable . . when this tax is demanded to rise up unanimously and refuse a compliance. . . .[18]

The organizers took great pains to emphasize the similarity of Hindu-

Muslim interests and to use apparently vague but, for nineteenth century Muslim society, extremely potent and eruptive concepts of 'honour' and 'dignity' to their advantage. Captain E. Cunningham, Commander of the 2nd Regiment, later testified to the most canny fashion in which the lower strata of the Muslim population had been mobilized by emphasizing the significance of martyrdom and the Hindus by leading them to believe that, after the overthrow of the British, their lands would be assessed at a much lower rate.[19] The massive response that these mobilizing tactics elicited is evident, in terms of material, from the 8,000 matchlocks that appeared on the day of the uprising. British officials were amazed at the sudden appearance of so many guns: earlier, Colonel Gardener, while raising men for service in the hills, could with great difficulty gather only 2,500 matchlocks.[20]

After the disturbances a Committee of Enquiry was set up under E. Colebrooke to determine the causes of the uprising. The report and proceedings of the Committee contain invaluable information both about the causes and about Muslim 'perception' of the effects of British rule on their society and culture. The account of the nature of the movement identifies the channels of mobilization in Muslim societies, and how religion served not only as a medium for the articulation of social and economic grievances but also intertwined with cultural notions and became the driving force of the movement.

The Enquiry Committee pointed out the deep resentment felt by the Muslims due to the haughty and arrogant attitude of British officialdom. It concluded

> This want of personal influence over the bulk of higher classes among the inhabitants of Bareilly is attributed to the repulsive distance at which he [the District Magistrate] has kept them and the mode of reception adopted by him, which as they consider it derogatory to the rank (a point in which the natives are particularly tenacious) preclude their availing themselves of his permission to visit him[21]

Rank, prestige and honour were immensely powerful concepts and were manifested and reinforced by the tradition of patron-client relationship, by the acquisition of religious knowledge and the social power that it entailed, and by certain privileges, i.e. in relation to payment of taxes and execution of justice. The intensity with which the higher classes felt degraded due to the imposition of the *chowkidari* tax is evident from the case of Nawab Mustajab Khan, a junior of Hafiz Rahmat Khan's family, who tried his best to seek exemption from the tax for his family from the Governor-General's Agent at Fatehgarh. The agent later testified that 'the earnestness with which he repeatedly urged his request evinced the sense of degradation which these men felt from having been promiscuously confounded with the generality'.[22]

Respectable sections of society were horrified when the *Kotwal* threatened that every person failing to pay the tax, irrespective of his rank, would be liable to imprisonment.[23] This merely reminded the upper classes of the equalizing principle of the criminal code which had created unease amongst them and created a terror due to the personal harassment that legal suits could entail. Ironically, the legal reforms were not popular even among the common people, as they had made justice 'tardy and highly taxed' as opposed to the earlier quick and gratis system.[24]

The report of the Enquiry Committee endorses the view that the establishment of the English East India Company's rule meant the gradual dismantling of the urban aristocratic culture with disastrous consequences for both the aristocratic classes around whom the culture revolved as well as the peripheral urban economy of artisans, musicians, etc. The ruin of families was such an endemic problem in the Rohilkhand region that it was considered a major factor behind the uprising. F. Hawkins, Senior Judge at Bareilly, pointed out that the opposition to the Company's rule stemmed from the fact that: 'the high orders (had been) degraded in personal consequence and deprived of those lucrative offices which under the former government they used to enjoy and which to lower classes serving under them were likewise sources of livelihood'.[25]

Another British official acknowledged:

> In Bareilly there are numerous families who from a state of affluence and consequence, have fallen into insignificance and extreme poverty and to whom no situation under government is open by means of which they might be enabled to maintain in any degree their former respectability and from their education and habit of life being of the Mahommedan tribe they are unqualified to fill any situation of business or responsibility. . . .[26]

Members of these ruined upper classes were (naturally) not favorably inclined towards the Company's rule. The descendants of Hafiz Rahmat Khan were actively involved in fomenting general discontent.[27] Muhammad Isa, one of the leaders of the uprising, came from a family which had been reduced from a state of high respectability to abject penury. Other examples such as that of Shaikh Kabir, once a rich *jagirdar* of Etawah, who was later found to be living in dire straits in Rampur, are easily found.[28] The Collector of Moradabad also endorsed the view that 'the heads of certain Pathan families were the general instigators, aiders and abettors of the late commotion. . .'. Army and district officers were all agreed that the ruin of families was the main cause of discontent.[29] Bareilly being the major urban centre of the region and the place where the chief Muslim families resided, it is no wonder that the uprising took place there.[30]

Statistics for the level of unemployment are not available. However, Company officials as well as Indians both refer to a high level of unemployment. With regard to the army, Captain Cunningham wrote:

> . . . I have daily, I may say hourly, applications for admission into my Corps from men of the above description. It I tell the applicant there is no vacancy, if he choose to wait till there is one which may occur in 3 or 4 months, he is perfectly satisfied and will patiently wait that period and longer mortgaging which will be his pay perhaps for 2 months. . . .[31]

It is no wonder that about 15,000 Pathans who had lately been disbanded from the irregular Corps joined the insurrection.

Large sections of the 'Pathan gentry' were idle and the Magistrate characterized the population of Bareilly as 'full of criminals with two or three exceptions', and hence prone to rebel against the Company's authority.[32]

The general decline and the tremendous economic pressure on the various sections of society is reflected in the petition submitted by the inhabitants of Bareilly in 1231 AH.

> The people of every description resided in perfect ease and safety under the shadow of protection from the reign of the Emperor to the government of the English Company. They never suffered any oppression from the local rulers, nor experienced grief or oppression from them. Now from a reverse of fortune, and from unpropitious fate, many persons are in want of daily bread who have no measure of subsistence are perplexed in their circumstances whilst others to keep up an appearance of respectability are obliged to be decently clad. . . .[33]

The *Mufti* in his submission before the Enquiry Committee referred to the economic burden of the *chowkidari* tax and quoted the townsmen as saying 'we poor people are in want of daily subsistence (how is it possible) to pay 1 and 2 annas a month according to the Regulation . . .'.[34]

The resumption of *madad-i-mash* lands further aggravated the situation. As early as 1816 the Senior Judge at Bareilly confirmed that rent-free lands were no longer considered secure from resumption.[35] The threat to *maafi* holdings had far-reaching implications for Muslim society and culture. The imposition of Stamp and Town duties in Bareilly did not help ameliorate this pressure. But the last straw was the enhancement of the land revenue demand. It was increased to an unprecedented level and the *zamindars* were hard hit.[36] Those *zamindars* who did not accede to the terms of the settlement were obliged to surrender their lands to the Collector who held 'them or let them as security to other persons for a certain number of years, without any provision of *malikana* percentage to the real proprietors'.[37] The land revenue was collected with great vigour and no provision was made for misfortune or calamity of season. Leases were made for short periods and hence losses could not be easily made up. The Magistrate remarked: 'Our Regulation establishing a certain *jumma* (not adjusting it to the actual produce) a proceeding to realize it by . . . duress and sale have reduced almost every large landed proprietor to beggary, to say nothing of the indignity complained of in being sent to jail.'[38]

Besides the economic consequences of the loss of land, disgrace of imprisonment and the humiliation of expulsion from paternal property was particularly galling to the Muslims.[39] The resistance of these measures was particularly marked out and forceful in this region because Rohlikhand was one of those parts of the country where Islam, from the eighteenth century onwards, had started expanding vertically and had permeated those sections of the Indian social structure where it was earlier conspicuous by its absence. This process of ruralization of Islam is particularly evident from the first half of the eighteenth century when, under Daud Khan and after him Ali Muhammad Khan, roving bands of Afghans of the Gangetic Doab had carved out Afghan power at the cost of local *zamindars*. The rural landscape thus dotted with Muslim *zamindars* is a feature quite unique in its extent. George Campbell testifies to the existence of 'Pathan villages' and the establishment of Rohillas as the dominant village *zamindars* or independent cultivators.[40] Brodkin also refers to Rohillas as net gainers of land.[41] It can thus be argued that resistance to British rule was more marked in those places where Muslim society had spread further.

The economic and social grievances had created discontent at different levels of society and for different reasons. While the grievances cut across social and religious differences, discontent was expressed within particular social groups. What was needed was an ideology to create an identity of interests or, at the least, a common hostility to the same 'enemy'. Religion provided that ideology. People in different parts of Rohilkhand acted in concert due to what officials described as 'the connecting principle of religious persuasion unassisted by any common interest in pecuniary matters'.[42] It is particularly striking how religious symbolism was used to mobilize the masses. Indeed, there is almost complete unanimity on the view that large numbers of people joined the insurrection only because the green flag of Islam had been hoisted and religion was the rallying cry.[43] The *Mufti* in the letters that he wrote to different parts called upon people 'to stand forth in the defence of their insulted religion'. Imposition of the tax, of course, did not amount to an insult to religious but the moral authority that the *Mufti* commanded annulled any possibility of awkward questioning so that, for the masses, it was a *jihad*.[44] In fact, the Commander of the 2nd Regiment testified that 'this tax was considered an infringement in religion. . .(and). . .from Rampur about 150 men out of which 40 were mullahs came out to oppose this tax immediately'.[45] In its report the Enquiry Committee dismissed speculations that the Nawab of Rampur incited his people to participate in the uprising and argued that, like others, the Rampur Pathans came out in the cause of religion. In fact, the Bilaspur contingent was headed by the *Qazi* of the town.[46] This consciousness of religious duty extended beyond Rohilkhand and the Magistrate of Bareilly noted the desire on the part of some troops of Nawab Wazir of Awadh to join the uprising.[47]

The respect that the *Mufti* commanded among the masses became a major factor. It facilitated the mobilization of the people, and the conversion of a resistance to a local, municipal arrangement into a virtual *jihad* against the East India Company. The Governor-General agreed that the serious nature of the insurrection was as much due to religion as 'defence of an individual of reputed sanctity, of great influence and held in extraordinary respect, whose personal safety was supposed to be endangered'.[48] In fact, the *Mufti* had come to symbolize religion in his person and any insult or threat to him was interpreted as the same against Islam itself. It is reported that enthusiasm due to religious zeal was so great in some instances that: 'during the interview of the Magistrate's officers with the Mooftee [*sic*], many persons are stated to have interrupted the conference declaring that they had come in the express search of martyrdom and would admit of no negotiation. . . .'[49]

It is particularly significant that the Islamic flag was resorted to by both the Hindus and Muslims. The argument that the uprising was mainly a response to the deprivation of certain classes does not hold up when one finds that even people with jobs under the Company as well as servants of individual Englishmen participated in the uprising.[50] The Judge of Bareilly, in his deposition before the Enquiry Committee observed about this uprising:

> . . .but feeling which must be called indefinable drew them into it. It is a most peculiar feature of the insurrection that men who had been protected in private services in contradiction to the general fidelity we look to and very justly too from actual and repeated experience, never perhaps disappointed till this occasion—were actually in the business and actively arranged against you in the ultimate conflict. . . .'[51]

It is this 'indefinable' feeling which gives this movement a special significance, particularly the role in it of the religious and the landed classes. The mechanics of the organization of the movement shows how the religious infrastructure could be used to mobilize people. The insurgents collected at mosques or tombs of saints and this did help in rallying people. The charisma that the *Mufti* exercised is also noteworthy. However, this response of the religious elite was not uniform and the *Qazi* infact did not join this movement. Even the *Mufti*, it can be argued, took up a stance of opposition only when, in Eric Stokes' words, the first phase of collaboration had gone sour.[52] Stating his grievances before this Enquiry Committee the *Mufti* remarked:

> But from the time of Nawab Rahmat Khan Bahadur and Nawab Wazirul Mulk to the present day every ruler has treated me with the greatest respect. Whenever I interceded on behalf of the people they consented to my request and particularly under the administration of the British Government Mr. Seton and other gentlemen. . . . always listened to me whenever I had occasion to intercede in any cause and issued such orders as were satisfactory to the people.[53]

With the gradual tightening of British control certain sections found themselves being systematically eased out of positions of authority. This was naturally aggravated with loss of employment and threat to social status. Muhammad Isa is reported to have told E. Cunninghan prior to the uprising of the widespread discontent amongst the Muslims due to these policies.[54] The imposition of the *chowkidari* tax was thus merely a pretext for an attempt to regain former power and status.[55] This is particularly true when one finds that the insurgents came from villages as far as Jahanabad, Pilibheet and Rampur where this tax would not have been extended anyway.[56] Moreover, the level of taxation was not so high as, by itself, to draw even well-off people to oppose it.[57]

The discontent and unease amongst the Muslims was transformed into active opposition due to 'apprehensions of an intention on the part of the British Government to subvert their religion'.[58] The Company's official, however, failed to detect the psychological turmoil and attributed the discontent to the 'war-like habit' of the Pathans.[59]

Only rarely did officials detect that the revenue and judicial systems were perceived to be interfering with the 'national habits and social feeling' of the Muslims.[60]

Religion articulated the widespread economic and social grievances, but its functional role was confined merely to providing an idiom for the expression of grievances. It created an awareness of deprivation amongst the Muslims. British rule and the political and administrative culture that it had had promoted served as an 'alter', in Weberian terms, for the self-perception of the Muslim society. Religion became the most tangible distinction between Muslims on the one hand and the British on the other. No doubt, Hinduism and Islam were more different than Islam and Christianity, yet in the case of the former co-existence for nearly seven centuries had created an attitude of acceptance, and the growth of Indo-Persian culture had sought at least to reduce the tensions between the two communities. In the case of the British, religion stood out as the separating, divisive distinction, and the absence of a common ethos which could blur the edges of religious differences tended to make distinctions more pronounced. It is no wonder then that Muslim looked upon the British as 'foreigners' with 'difficult language, habits and religious persuasion'.[61]

The Bareilly uprising is a particularly good example of an event which brings out clearly the British rule on the Muslims and also typifies Muslim 'oppositional' attitudes: how they were formulated, how the religious elite sustained them, and how they were expressed.

NOTES

1. *The Private Journal of the Marquess of Hastings*, ed. *The Marchioness of Bute*, 2 vols., 2nd edn. (London, 1858), I, p. 115.
2. Ibid., I, p. 116.
3. To the Court of Directors, Judicial Department, 31 May 1816, *Boards Collections*, Vol. 640, 17691; also see, *Bengal Letters Received*, Vol. 96, 1 January-28 March 1817.
4. *Bengal Despatches*, Vol. 707, Judicial Department, 13 September 1822.
5. Major General Cunningham to Ellis, 24 September 1831, *Home Miscellaneous Series*, Vol. 708.

6. *Bengal Letters Received*, Vol. 96, Political Department, 1 January-28 March 1817.
7. Ibid.
8. To Sir E. Colebrooke and J. Perry from I.O. Oldham, *Bengal Criminal and Judicial Consultations*, Range 132, Vol. 47, 11-25 October 1816.
9. Political Letter from Bengal 1 January 1817, *Boards Collections*, 17691, Vol. 640.
10. Major Richards to Com. of Bareilly, 3 July 1816, *Boards Collections, 17692*, Vol. 640.
11. To Sir E. Colebrooke et al. from Major W. Richards, Bareilly, 3 July 1816, *Bengal Criminal and Judicial Consultations*, 25 October 1816, Range 132, Vol. 48.
12. *Boards Collections*, 17691, Vol. 640.
13. Report on Bareilly Disturbances, ibid.
14. Extract Judicial Letter to Bengal, 19 August 1818, ibid.
15. Ibid.
16. *Bengal Criminal and Judicial Consultations*, 25 October 1816, Range 132, Vol. 48.
17. Magistrate of Bareilly to W.B. Bayley, Secretary to Government Judicial Department, 18 April 1816, *Bengal Criminal and Judicial Consultation,* 3 July-24 May 1816, Range 132, Vol. 41.
18. *Boards Collections*, Vol. 640, 17692.
19. Capt. E. Cunningham to Colebrooke, August 1816, *Bengal Criminal and Judicial Consultations*, Range 132, Vol. 48.
20. Ibid.
21. Report on Bareilly Disturbances, *Boards Collections*, Vol. 640, 17691.
22. Ibid, para. 24.
23. *Bengal Despatches*, Vol. 707, Draft No. 253.
24. Ibid., pp. 181-2.
25. Ibid.
26. Francis Low, Collector of Bareilly to Colebrooke, 24 August. 1816, *Bengal Criminal and Judicial Consultations*, Range 132, Vol. 47.
27. Report on Bareilly Disturbances, *Boards Collections*, Vol. 640, 17691, para 24.
28. Capt. E. Cunningham to Colebrooke, 10 August. 1816, *Bengal Criminal and Judicial Consultations*, Range 132, Vol. 48.
29. To Colebrooke from Capt. E. Cunningham, 10 August 1816, *Bengal Criminal and Judicial Consultations*, Range 132, Vol. 48.
30. *Boards Collections*, Vol. 640, 17691, p. 258.
31. To Colebrooke from Capt. E. Cunningham, 10 August 1816, *Bengal Criminal and Judicial Consultation*, Range 132, Vol. 48.
32. Also see, *Bengal Criminal and Judicial Consultations*, Range 132, Vol. 47.
33. Petition from Hindu and Mussalman inhabitants of Bareilly dated 27 Rabi al Awwal, *Bengal Criminal and Judicial Cnsultations*, Range 132, Vol. 48.

34. Letter from Mufti Muhammad Aiwaz to Sir Edward Colebrooke, *Bengal Criminal and Judicial Consultations*, Range 132, Vol. 48.
35. To Colebrooke, Commissioner of Bareilly from F. Hawkins, *Boards Collections*, Vol. 640, 17691, p. 276.
36. Ibid, pp. 275-7, also p. 256.
37. Ibid, p. 276.
38. H. Dumbleton to E. Colebrooke, 31 July 1816, *Boards Collections*, Vol. 640, 17691, p. 257.
39. Report on Bareilly Disturbances, *Boards Collections*, Vol. 640, 17691, pp. 186-87.
40. George Campbell, *Modern India: A Sketch of the System of Civil Government*, (London, 1852), p. 57.
41. See Eric Stokes, *The Peasant and the Raj* (Cambridge, 1978), p. 132.
42. *Bengal Despatches*, Judicial Separtment, 19 August 1818, para 61.
43. Francis Lau to Commissioner, 18 July 1816, *Boards Collection*, Vol. 640, 17691, p. 352.
44. Report on Bareilly Disturbances, *Boards Collections*, Vol. 640, 17691, p. 169.
45. To Colebrooke from E. Cunningham, 10 August 1816, *Bengal Criminal and Judicial Consultations*, Range 132, Vol. 48.
46. Report on Bareilly Disturbances, *Boards Collections*, Vol. 640, 17691, p. 198.
47. Magistrate of Bareilly to W.B. Bayley, 29 April 1816, *Bengal Criminal and Judicial Consultations*, Range 132, Vol. 41.
48. To E. Colebrooke, C. Elliot and T. Perry from W.B. Bayley, 25 October 1816, *Bengal Criminal and Judicial Consultations*, Range 132, Vol. 48.
49. Report on Bareilly Distubances, *Boards Collections*, Vol. 640, 17691, p. 169.
50. To members of the Commission of Enquiry from W. Leycester, 21 July 1816, *Bengal Criminal and Judicial Consultations*, Range 132, Vol. 47.
51. Ibid.
52. Ibid.
53. Address from Mufti Muhammad Aiwaz, 27 Rabi al Awwal, *Boards Collections*, Vol. 640, 17691, p. 368.
54. To Colebrooke from E. Cunningham, 10 August 1816, *Bengal Criminal and Judicial Consultations*, Range 132, Vol. 48.
55. *Bengal Criminal and Judicial Consultations*, Range 132, Vol. 47.
56. Ibid.
57. Report on Bareilly Disturbances, *Boards Collections*, Vol. 640, 17691, pp. 186-7.
58. Ibid.
59. Ibid.
60. Bengal Despatches, Judicial Department, 19 August 1818, para 61.
61. To E. Colebrooke from F. Hawkins, Senior Judge, Bareilly, 12 July 1816, *Boards Collections*, Vol. 640, 17691, pp. 275-7.

Hidayat'ul-Qawa'id: An Administrative Manual of the Early Eighteenth Century

Fatima Zehra Bilgrami

The importance of *Hidayat'ul-Qawa'id* by Hidayat'-ullah Bihari was noticed for the first time by Sir J.N. Sarkar who considered it to be a valuable source of information about the Mughal administration and 'a guide book, . . . about the duties of officers'.[1] After Sarkar, many historians, writing on various aspects of Mughal administration utilized this work. The socio-economic importance of this work was highlighted by some scholars.[2] Although only scanty information is available about the compiler of the work, internal evidence suggests that presumably he was an administrative officer, since the work is 'based on actual experience and the long observed practices of the Mughal administration' which mere theoretical treatises cannot give us.

Sarkar[3] noticed the following three manuscripts of the work:

(i) The one donated by William Irvine to the India Office Library, London. It is called *Hidayat'ul Qawa'id*.
(ii) The second is available in Abdus Salam Collection of Maulana Azad Library, Aligarh which is called *Hidayat'ul Qawanin* on the fly leaf, and
(iii) His own MS secured from an old Kayastha family of Patna.

It may be mentioned that Maulana Azad Library possesses the two manuscripts, one noticed by both Sarkar and Sri Ram Sharma.[4] This manuscript belongs to Abdus Salam collection and is listed under *Farsia* No. 379/149. The other manuscript of the Library belongs to University Collection (*Farsia Ulum* No.108) entitled *Hidayat'ul Fawa'id* and Shah Munawwar has been mentioned as its author.

Out of these available manuscripts. Aligarh manuscripts are more detailed and complete, written in clear *nastaliq*.

Hidayat'ul Qawa'id was written by Hidayat'-ullah Bihari, during the reign of Farrukh Siyar in 1126/1713 as is evident from the chronogram in the introduction. The only information which the writer provides about himself is that Makhdum Shah Munawwar, a descendant of Makhdum Shah Sharful Haq Ahmad Yahya Maneri was his spiritual preceptor (*murshid*). He was the *sajjadanashin* of the *khanqah* of Shaikh Ahmad Yahya at Maner Sharif (Patna district). Hidayat'-ullah died in 1716-17. From the contents of the work, it seems that he would have served in some administrative capacity, probably in the Revenue Ministry.

Regarding the object of compiling his work he tells us that some of his ancestors who had resources, constructed mosques, bridges, tanks, gardens and houses in order to leave a good name behind. Others who were scholars or mystics, wrote works of scholarly eminence to ensure lasting fame.

As the author had neither money to erect sacred structures, nor enough knowledge to write works of literary eminence, he contented himself to write a brief account of the duties of officers (*Ahli khidmat*) for the aspirants of jobs and named it *Hidayat'ul-Qawa'id*.

The work is divided into five chapters. The first, second and third chapters have eleven sections each. The fourth chapter has been divided into nine sections and the last chapter into eight sections.

Chapter I

1. Qualities of a perfect man
2. *Derveshes*
3. Manual of work for the rulers
4. Functions of *Wakil* and *Wazir*
5. *Khan-i Saman's manner* of Business Transaction
6. About the Duties of *Bakhshi*
7. Mode of Work by *Darogha* of *Ghusal Khana* and *Diwan Khana*
8. Manual of *Subedar*'s work
9. Account of *Faujadar*'s duties
10. Account of the duties of *Darogha of Top Khana*
11. Duties of *Munshi*

Chapter II

1. Manual of *Sadr's* duties
2. About the functions of the *Qazi*
3. Manual of Duties for *Mufti*
4. Manual of *Muhtasib*'s duties and of *Nirkh Navis*
5. Duties of *Waqai Nigar*, *Sawanih Nigar*, *Narkara* and *Darogha-i-Dak Chauki*
6. Duties of *Peshkar*

7. Distinction among the officers
8. Duties of *Amin* and *Karori*
9. Manual of *Kotwal*'s duties
10. Mode of work by *Mir Imarat*
11. Duties of *Mushrif*

Chapter III

1. Duties of *Darogha-i-Kachehri*
2. Duties of *Darogha-i-Adalat*
3. Duties of *Darogha-i-Dagh wa Tashiha*
4. Duties of *Darogha* of *Darul Zarb* (*Mint*)
5. *Darogha-i-Khazana*
6. *Darogha* of *Ajnas* and *Baitul Mal*
7. *Darogha* of Elephants, Camels and Cows
8. *Darogha* of *Tosha Khana*
9. *Darogha* of *Farrash Khana*
10. *Darogha* of *Sair*
11. Duties of *Tahvildar*

Chapter IV

1. Duties of courtiers
2. Treatment of servants by the master and vice versa
3. Treatment of disciples by religious preceptors, teachers and vice versa.
4. Treatment of children by parents and vice versa
5. About companionship
6. The middle path
7. Etiquette in the present of the rich
8. About expenses and income
9. About dress

Chapter V

1. About Travel
2. About *Jamadar*
3. About Trade
4. Duties of *Mastaufi*
5. About Clerks and Accountancy
6. Manual of *Qanungo*'s duties
7. About *Zamindars*
8. Spectators at shows and other matters[7]

DESCRIPTION OF THE VARIOUS MANUSCRIPT COPIES OF THE *HIDAYAT'UL-QAWA'ID*

1. Manuscript A: Abd'us Salam collection, *Farsia* No. 379/149, AMU Library, Aligarh. On the cover of this manuscript, the title of the work is mentioned as *Hidayat'ul-Qawanin* and the name of Diwan Basir Ali is written in black ink surrounded by a margin in black ink.

The work was copied in 1241-1826 by Karam Ali at the request of Lala Luchcha Lal Dubey, for his sons, Ram Sahai and Har Sahai. The scribe claimed to have consulted several manuscripts while preparing his copy and yet requests for indulgence from the readers for any errors (which are many) in the text.

The MS begins with the praise of God:

Hamd behad bar Khudai iz o Jal ra

Though the author in his preface mentions its name as *Hidayat'ul-Qawanin* but the subscriber named it *Hidayat'ul-Qawa'id*.

No. of Folios 86. Size of the pages 7.6" x 4.4" contains 13 lines per page. The heading of all the chapters and sections are given in red ink. The paper used is oriental. The writing is *nastaliq* and the manuscript is in a very good condition.

2. Manuscript B: Aligarh, University collection. *Farsia Ulum*, 108, No. of folios 88. The manuscript is entitled as *Hidayat-'ul-Fawa'id Dastur ul Amal-i Qadim Fawa'id*. The name of the scribe is not given. In the end the ownership of the work is declared. The work belongs to Thakur Singh, son of Himaiat Lal of Madhupur (*pargana* Mongher, province Bihar), who happens to be the elder brother of Ram Kunwar Singh who had transcribed the manuscript at Banaras. At the end of the text, there are two seals, one of Thakur Singh (changed to Thakur Chand) dated 1242 and the other is of Muhammad Abul Hasan dated 1293. Chapters and section numbers are given in red but not the headings of chapters. The manuscript is in good condition and complete in all respects. Although it contains all the sections, some details about different officers have been left out.

3. I.O. 3996 A (Referred to as C): This manuscript belongs to Irvine collection. It is a copy made for William Irvine on 8 January 1898 from a manuscript acquired from Jaunpur by his agent Abdul Aziz of Ghazipur.

It comprises 19 folios, is written in *nastaliq*, each page having sixteen lines. The headings are in red ink.

The preface is the same as in other manuscripts. The text starts without any list of contents. It seems to be a selected version of *Hidayat-'ul-Qawa'id* (though the colophon does not mention it). Neither the chapter numbers nor the section numbers are given. The fourth chapter is completely missing. While the section about *munshi* is absent from the first chapter, the sections on *Ifta*, *Mushrif* and *Mir-i Imarat* are not included in Chapter II. From Chapter V also several portions (except *jamadar*, *siyaq* and *qanungo*) are missing. Even in the available text, information is given in a more concise form though the manuscript is very fine.

4. Sarkar's Manuscript, National Library, Calcutta, No. 94 (Referred to as D), photocopy Aligarh University collection, *Farsia* No. 417: Sarkar describes it as 'wanting in two leaves at the beginning and at the end'. It is a small book with twelve or thirteen lines per page. The list of contents and the first two pages are in a different hand from the rest of the manuscript. The original starts from page 3 with certain verses, then comes the list of contents as given by the author. The last heading is about *zamindari* and it is incomplete. Section seven about spectators is completely missing. The manuscript comprises 53 pages.

Page nos. 11 and 12 have been supplied by the same person who had copied the first two pages.

Heading of the fourth section of the first chapter has been put down, but the account of *wakil* is missing, and the duties of the *wazir* start with the sentence '*dar mahelat-i-raiyati tankhuwah dehad*'.

The manuscript is written in *nastailq* but some pages are in *shikasta* script.

In most cases the section numbers are missing. The information is more concise. Some sections start abruptly. There are a number of spelling mistakes. Sometimes the section headings are different from the two Aligarh manuscripts. Chapter V is divided into seven sections instead of eight. The last section about the spectators is not mentioned at all. At the end the date of the transcription of the copy and the name of copyist are also missing.

TRANSLATION FROM *HIDAYAT'UL-QAWA'ID*
CHAPTER I, SECTION IV TO SECTION XI

Section IV: About *Wazir*'s Duties

The *wazir* should know the nature of his work and be conversent with the manner in which all the imperial business should be carried on, so as not to be dependent on anyone about the affairs concerned. He should be sweet tongued and upright in conduct with the people of high status and firm with people of low status. For high born people understand the word and remember it, while low born cannot be controlled without firmness. He should keep a written record of all the imperial business on some paper with him, such as the annual income and expenditure, a list of officials and their salaries, a summary of the expenses of *Buyutat* (state workshops and factories), annual revenue of all the *subas-parganas* and villagewise, description of the *peshkash* of *zamindars*, offering and presents of officials and the distance of each province, etc., all important places with details of rivers and hills and central places and the number of forts. So that when questioned about any matter he should not have to consult the papers.

A fourth part of the *jagir* of the *diwans*, *nazims*, etc., should be granted in the *zortalab mahals* (rebellious areas) and three-fourths in average *mahals*, half the *jagirs* of the high *mansabdars* should comprise the average *mahals* and half of *ra'ayati mahals*. A fourth part of the *jagir* of *raiza mansabdars* should be granted in the average *mahals* and three-fourths in the *raiyati mahals*. He should discriminate in the annual income and expenditure and spend according to resources; if he finds the inclination of the ruler otherwise, he should be careful. He should adopt diplomacy and keep aloof to save himself from trouble.

When the officers are despatched on their duties he should behave in the following manner. After their appointment, whenever the *nazims* of *suba* come to take leave, the *diwan* should keep in an eye to their dignity and position, should advise them to keep all the residents, great and small in his jurisdiction happy, and protect the weak from strong, hear the complaint of the innocent and avoid avarice. As his recommendations concerning *mansabdars* serving in the provinces are acceptable he should be careful so as not to make complaint out of enmity and concessions out of intrigue.

Whosoever works with sincerity should be recommended. The rebellious and recalcitrant *zamindars* should be punished so as to set an example to others. He should send reports of the provincial matters twice a month through the *dak chauki*. The rebels, robbers and highwaymen should be set at liberty after taking bribe. This would sow the seed of sedition, and other richmen, considering that freedom could be bought, would create so great a trouble that it would be very difficult to control.

He should also advise the *diwans* of the provinces when they proceed on their business that they should be pious, polite, patient, responsible, and trustworthy so as to perform their duty shrewdly and devotedly, try to rehabilitate the *rai'yat* and keep the people of gentle birth happy by their good behaviour; select and appoint honest and hard-working *amins*, and avoid appointing greedy and wicked ones. They should send the report of the *suba* with an inventory of the treasury, twice each month through the *dak chauki*. The *karori* should be a good collector so that he is able to collect the revenue from the tax-payer diplomatically and without the use of force so as to keep him happy and the revenue dues be collected in time. He should not remit the revenue without permission. He should not be a spendthrift.

While giving leave to the *waqai nigar* tell him to write the reports fully and send them weekly, avoid writing complaints of people out of enmity, and recommendations for concession. He should write reports in such a manner that if investigation is made, it should be confirmed and add to his credit.

While giving leave to *swanih nigar*, the same instructions should be given as to the *waqai nigar* except that he should send to the court eight *nalwas* in a month that is two in a week comprising the report of the province. He should tell the *harkara* to write the truth and not the rumours. For he should keep in mind that if some nobles suffer because of his report and it is not proved, the *harkara* would lose his life, so that others make not such mistakes. Through honesty he will get promotion.

Section V: *Khan Saman's Manner of Business Transaction*

The newly appointed *khan saman* should acquire the talent of discernment. After taking charge of the work he should check the cash and the available stock in the department which is mainly the *diwani* of expenditure from the inventory list bearing the seal of the former *khan saman*, *mushrif* and *tahsildar*. If it tallies, well and good, if it does not tally he should take the former *khan saman* and *mushrif* to task and get restitution from the *tahvildar*. He should know all the aspects of his job. He should keep a copy of the annual expenses, factorywise. He should know the number of robes available in the workshop concerned. In the same way he should know about the available stock in all the factories. If there is shortage, he should make a list of the requirements, present it to his employer and take from him an order addressed to the *diwan* to advance money in accordance with the need and do the requisite. It is the duty of the *khan saman* that whatever stock is required he should buy it from the state money if available, and if he has money he should stock the things needed and take the money later at the market price, so as not suffer the royal displeasure because of the lack of things. To avoid backbiting of the *mansabdars* that he takes profit for himself by setting stock to the government, the *khan saman* should inform the Sultan, in advance that sometimes the material needed for the workshops are available and sometimes not and in the preparation of things delay occurs. There is a suggestion that if money is provided by the government, everything can be bought and stored in advance. If money is not available he could even take loan from the *mahajan* (moneylender) to buy the material and provide it to the government at market rate. If the employee is good natured, he would understand that all this is being done for the benefit of the government. He should ask for quotations from nearby places and buy from the place where the price is low and hence there is saving. It is incumbent on all the servants of the state to economize. Whatever government material is used, it should be recorded. He should keep the *taliga* containing the recorded price of the material, when sold with the knowledge and seal of the *muqim*. Any stock of weapons, etc., that he finds of good design should be brought to the notice of the employer (person concerned) and whatever is appreciated should be bought and he should realize that these types of things are acceptable to the government. The robes of honour required for the occasion of ' Id ul Fitr and 'Id uz Zuha should be kept ready one or two months in advance, so that at the time they are required people are not inconvenienced. He should try to keep the artisans like goldsmiths, workers in stone, inlay workers and experts in perforated work, *chikan* workers and the like that know their professions, happy and satisfied. For it is a well-known maxim that 'a satisfied labourer works harder'. All work should be performed in a nice manner keeping an eye on savings, for by performing his duty in this manner he would become popular with the government.

Section VI: About the Duties of *Bakhshi*

The *bakhshi* should select people of high birth, of reputed families and of experience while making appointments. He should bestow special favour and concession on people of gentle breed. During enlistment, the work of the days should be performed in two months. It is the wish of most of the wealthy people that the *diwan* should in the payment of salaries perform ten days work in one month, and the *bakhshi* should take two months for a work of ten days, but the *khan saman* should expedite the work of one month in ten days. For the transaction of the work of the army, it is necessary that the list of soldiers and the salary papers should be kept by the *bakhshi* himself, so as not to offer excuses when questioned by the person concerned. He should impress on his staff that they should not delay the work of soldiers as a little carelessness hurts much. He should know the worth and unusual qualities of each soldier and bring them to the notice of the employer (i.e. ruler) in such a manner, as to benefit them. He should see that the soldiers are present to accompany (the ruler) and to do guard duty. Encourage and prompt the soldiers to bravery at the time of battle. If they do not possess that quality they will acquire it. If the duty is performed in this manner, he would endear himself to all.

Section VII: Mode of Work of *Darogha* of *Ghusal Khana* and *Diwan Khana.*

The *darogha* of *ghusal khana* should be a man of dignity, knowing the temperament and status of people. After appointment he should acquire the knowledge of the time when each noble, great or small has to pay respect at court and where he has to stand. Better still he should keep a (written) record with names and times of paying respect by each, with him, so as to guard against anyone ill-timing his presence at court. He should come to court earlier than all and stand in the *atish khana* (artillery room). When the Sultan has entered the *ghusal khana* he should pay his respect and stand at the allotted place. The *nazir* (supervisor) and *chobdars* (mace-bearer) should be apprised before hand about the nobles who regularly attend the court. If somebody new comes to the court the *nazir* should inform the *darogha* and the latter should bring it to the notice of the ruler and act according to his orders. He should inform the *nazir* that the person will pay respect from such and such a place, and tell the *mir tuzuk* that such and such a place to stand has been assigned to him and they would act accordingly.

He should impress on the said *nazir*, that petitions and presents, etc., for the nobles that are present, and goods and presents sent by the *nazims diwan* and other officers from the provinces will be presented to the court through the *darogha*. The *daroghas* at the court of nobles should also act in the like manner. If possessed of these qualities, the *darogha* would be appreciated.

Section VIII: Manual of *Subedar's* Work

When a *nazim* of a *suba* (province) is appointed, he should take into service a proficient and trustworthy *diwan* who has acquired experiences in the service of some nobles, knows thrift and is proficient in accounts. He should appoint a talented *munshi* conversant with etiquettes, a calligraphist who has served in the estate of some great noble. He should have a trusted agent to convey the reports of the province promptly to the court and get response. He should send gifts and present to expedite the response as this is the way of the world. He should consider the presents as essential for solving his problems. He should ascertain the condition of the *zortalab* (rebellious) and *raiyati zamindars* and how many soldiers would be required for revenue collection from those who reside in the *suba*. If his troops are insufficient for revenue collection, he should report the matter to the court with other important affairs, through a trusted agent. If he receives a reply in accordance with the revenue requirements, well and good; if not he should depend on his own resources.

If his wishes are granted by the officers to the courts he should take heart and go to the province. Whatever contingent he is allotted, out of it he should recruit from the people of good families and with experience in war. When he has traversed half the way to his *suba*, he should recruit further 1/4 men (*ta'binan*). These who desire service and are experienced he should carry them with him with the promise that they will be taken in service on the date he reaches the *suba*. Out of these he should keep half with himself and the other half, with half of the troops already enlisted, should be sent in advance to the *suba* with grant of favours. After reaching the *suba*, they should try to endear themselves to the intelligent persons of the place and inquire from them about the *zamindars* and native officers and find out whether they are rebellious or loyal. They should report to their court master that so and so *jamadar* gave concession in revenue to the *zamindar* and that the *zamindar* had given so much money to the former *nazim* over and above the due revenue. When a quarter of a journey to the *suba* remains to be made he should despatch sagacious riders with *parwanas* to summon the *zamindars*, to present themselves at their appointed place: when he reached the boundary of the *suba* the aspirants to service should be employed from that date. For some months special care should be taken of them as the first impression is the last impression.

The leaders of the *zortalab zamindars* should be punished to set as an example to others. When he has settled the administration, he should keep only the requisite quota of troops, the rest should be dismissed. An eye should be kept on the soldiers. If some salary is due to them, it should be paid. Instructions should be given to the *diwan*, to spend within means and be thrifty. He should appoint honest and diligent *amils* (collectors) in the *mahals* and *jagirs* and fix their salary according to their needs so that they should not take recourse to dishonesty. He should assess the villages of the *zamindars* before sowing (*ayyam-i-taraddud*) and lay emphasis on the cultivator to increase the cultivation. If the assessment is made in advance, the *zamindar* will work more deligently. Revenue should be fixed so that the cultivators will put in more effort the next year. He should not be ostentatious so as to deprive the *rai'yat* of their total income, for they are the source of material prosperity. If he finds them affluent he should tax them in some other way. The legal *zamindars* should be favoured with robes and horses. Winning the hearts of the people through kindness and concession is the way of the wise. If this method does not succeed, he should maintain troops for the purpose of keeping them loyal. He should not extend the hand of oppression in *khalisa* lands as it would lead to unpleasantness with the *diwan-i-khalisa*; complaint would be lodged, dues would be asked and he would suffer royal criticism. He should keep royal officers like *qadis* happy with favours. *Mashaikh*, great and small, should be treated with kindness. The *derveshes* (anchorites) who live at one place must be provided monetary help. The Indigent should be given charity. The weak should be protected the from strong. Innocent ones, who had been tyrannized over must receive redressal, as justice is the true mode of governance. He (*nazim*) should keep all this in mind to get good results in this and the other world for then only will he have a firm hold over his jurisdiction.

Section IX: Account of *Faujdar's* Duties

A *faujdar* should be brave and considerate towards troops. He should recruit soldiers from amongst the known families of dauntless and brave soldiers. When the reaches his jurisdiction he should enquire about the former officers of the place, *qanungos*, etc., and console and favour them to discover the nature of the soldiers as to who are in control and who are linked with rebellious *zamindars*. He should know about the revenues and seditious behaviour of the *zamindars* in the past, treat the leader of the rebellious *zamindars* with kindness. If he is won over, well and good, otherwise he should be reprimanded till be obediently pays the revenue. If he wants to control the rebels with a small force, he should win over those who are the enemy of the seditious ones with the promise of the *mahals* of the latter and with the help of their troops crush the rebels. His administration will get a good name and rebels will be afraid and pay regular revenue. He should gain favourable opinion of *wagai nigar*, *swaniah nigar* and *harkara*, as their reports would lead to his promotion. He should practice archery, spear throwing, etc., the weapons of war and hunting. Hunting will enable him to get to know all the good and bad routes and other affairs and he should therefore get habituated to this skill. He should practice riding, and carry weapons, and always administer justice to the innocent. It would do him good in both the worlds.

Section X: Account of the Duties of *Darogha* of *Top Khana*

When he is appointed, he should take an inventory of the existing stock connected with the *top khana*, bearing the seal of former *darogha*, *mushrif* and *tahvildar*. If he finds the material available and the men present according to the list, well and good; if not he should ask about the stock from the *tahvildar* and about the presence of men from their comnanders *sardars*) of thousands. He should keep in humour the cannoneers and gunpowder men (*barut sazan*) who may be commanders of thousands, by his behaviour and concessions and try to win their devotion. As the cannoneers are perverse and bold, they are inflamed by word. They should be treated in such a manner that at the time of action (battle) they should be obedient and dauntless. If the cannoneers are favoured they will not neglect their duty. Their efficiency and good name will bring credit to the *darogha*. He should keep a record of the weight of gunpowder, etc.

He should keep a written list with him of the number and weight of each cannon and of each cannon ball, of each *hathnal* (guns), *shutrnal* (a camel swivel) and *ramjungi*, so as to be prepared when questioned about the available stock. If he performs his work in this way, he would be appreciated by the commander of the forces.

Section IX: Duties of *Munshi*

The *munshi* should be sagacious, eloquent, be a good companion, liberal, generous, having full command over words and vocabulary elegant in style, and punctual in affairs. As the *munshi* shares the secret and knows all important matters he should guard his tongue. He should have a knack of writing in a concise but intelligible manner what has been detailed to him verbally. But he should not reveal the matter to anyone. He should keep a record of the status, titles of all officers and concerned persons. The difference between a *munshi* and a *diwan* is this that the former is asked to write about matters unknown to the *diwan*. The *munshi* should have a glib tongue and also be good at keeping secrets. He should select a secluded place for his work where there should be no gathering of people, so that nobody should caste an eye over what he writes. People should avoid going to him when he is at work as the secrecy would be revealed and he would be accused. When he is asked to write about some matter he should reveal its pros and cons to his employer and write after his approval is gained. He should cultivate the company of intellectuals and try to increase his wordpower. The employer should fix a high salary for the *munshi* so that he should have no monetary problem.

NOTES

1. *Mughal Administrations, Calcutta*, 1963, p. 250.
2. Qiyamuddin Ahmad 'Some Norms of Social and Economic Behaviour—A Late Seventeenth Century Indian Point of View', *Indian Historical Review*, vol. VIII, No. I, Delhi, 1982, pp. 19-34.
3. *Mughal Administration*, p. 252.
4. *A Bibliography of Mughal India*, p. 124.
5. Chronogram of his death is *Kushad bab-i-Hidayat Miyan-i-Ahle-i-ram.*
6. Qiyamuddin Ahmad has translated the *adab* portion of *Hidayat'ul Qawa'id* in his article, see *Indian Historical Review*, vol. VIII, Nos. 1-2, pp. 19-34.
7. For further details, ibid., p. 20.

Perspectives from Eighteenth Century Regional Historiographies: A Study of *Tuhfah-i-Tazah*

Z.U. Malik

INTRODUCTION

The principal feature of intellectual life in the eighteenth century was, besides a general interest in religious studies, philosophy and literature, the study of history and history-writing of widely different categories and on a larger expanded scale. Historical studies developed in this period tended to reveal the state of society as it was in previous centuries and broaden the perspectives to apprehend what realities were behind the current crisis of change in politics and economy in the colonial context. A new pattern of historiography emerged after the mid-eighteenth century that was characterized by regional specificity and gradual eclipse of miscellaneous histories of the declining empire with their common thrust on its central structure and functioning. The growing trend of portraying the regional past, though not viewed as separate entity, is amply illustrated in the two major contemporary works, *Mirat-i-Ahmadi*[1] written in Gujarat and *Siyarul-Mutakhkherin*[2] in Bihar. These are directly concerned with the political milieu in which their authors lived and experienced, and provide detailed delineation of administrative systems and socio-economic structures as operating in the two respective regions. Some underlying factors may conceivably be attributed to this steady growth of this genre of historical literature. With the collapse of Mughal imperial edifice and disintegration of its socio-cultural institutions, numerous scholars, writers and poets migrated from Delhi to the capital towns of successor-states, large and minor alike, in quest of employment and patronage. Under the stimulating influence of chieftains and nazims these men of letters devoted their literary talents to the compilation of brief historical accounts of a particular territory, focusing mainly on achievements of its rulers in diverse fields of their activities. When the power and influence of regional *satraps* and nawabs began to wane, the British administrators appeared to show keen interest, both out of intellectual curiosity and administrative needs, in the collection and classification of information pertaining to political history, geography, and social institutions of the region, district or city they now governed.

Consequently, new channels of inspiration and encouragement were opened to this class of writers, trained in the art of composition in Persian and qualified on account of service background for accessibility in the expanding colonial dispensation. The impulse given to the continuing intellectual movement induced the historians to venture upon fresh lines, evolve different methodology and assemble rich data on a variety of non-political subjects such as geography, topography, architecture, religious and racial stratification, arts and crafts and urban centres.

Yet, the other source from which impetus came was the general public of north India, distracted and distressed by the rapidly changing scenario of their environments. They were eager to understand the causes of the transitoriness of regional kingdoms and resultant deprivation of their own economic security and social position. The kind of discourse introduced by these and other related problems enhanced the popularity of regional histories, promoted their circulation and helped the diffusion of historical knowledge in all its many facets in North India. Most notably, a substantial part of material collected by the regional chroniclers proved useful for the nineteenth century ethnographers and compilers of district gazetteers. Here it will not be possible to give even a summary view of the innumerable chronicles, treatises, and administrative manuals compiled at Hyderabad, Lucknow, Banaras, Patna, and Murshidabad, the flourishing centres of cultural and literary activities in the second half of eighteenth century. Of all the regional historiographies *Tuhfah-i-Tazah*,[3] also entitled *Balwant Nama* (I.O.L.Ms. Ethe No. 483), written by Maulvi Khair-al Din Allahabadi (1751-1827) at the suggestion of Abraham Willand, District Judge of Jaunpur,[4] 1795, is the most exhaustive, authentic and original source of information for reconstructing the history of Raja Dom[5] of Banaras from its establishment in 1740 to the annexation by the Company's government, 1780, under the personal command of Warren Hastings, the Governor-General (1772-84).

Maulawi Khair-al Din writes in his introduction to the book that Abraham Willand one day expressed his desire to have detailed information about the profile of Balwant Singh and the history of Banaras. The Maulawi told him that sometime back he had started writing on the subject but could not finish it on account of his other engagements. At that time he was serving Abraham Willand as his secretary (*diwan*) and called him the wordly lord (*Khavind-i-majazi*), and it was for his sake that he laboured day and night, and composed a new history of Banaras under Raja Balwant Singh with the title, *Tuhfah-i-Tazah*,[6] or 'A Fresh Gift' and presented it to his master. He further writes that for writing it he wholly depended on his treasured memory, reminiscences, and oral evidence deduced from his conversations with a number of participants in or observers of the historical events—the English officers and descendants of Raja Balwant Singh (1740-1770), without borrowing the relevant material from any other book. His identification with the cause and interests of English patrons and normative descriptive framework based as it was on classical paradigm, circumscribed the approach to attempt a critique of colonial exploitation, inchoate colonial administrative structure and measures, illumine the scenes of impoverishment across the rural landscape, or portray the plight of the urban poor, artisans and jobless middle class. He, however, claims that he maintained impartiality in recording the events in the face of conflicting objectives of the rival parties—nawab wazir of Awadh, the rajas, and the East India Company—in their mutual feuding to impose hegemony over the region of Banaras,[7] the fertile and productive territory, unaffected by any foreign invasions (Nadir Shah, Ahmad Shah Durrani) or Maratha raids in the past.

The author has described in a succinct manner the pattern of political and diplomatic relationships the rajas maintained with the nawabs of Awadh and governors of the Company, their real sovereign masters in succession.[8] It provides an extensive account of the social formations of landholding castes and groups, the extent of their control, economic condition, alliances and counter-alliances with officers at Banaras. He has devoted much space in delineating the vigorous, persistent efforts of Raja Balwant Singh to establish his hold over powerful local chiefs, and eliminate small *zamindars*, *jagirdars*, and tax-free grantees by usurping their landholdings.[9] In between the all-embracing political and military themes the survey of local administrative institutions and socio-economic structures bearing the stamp of Mughal origin is of great significance to deepen our understanding about the modes and manners in which they were operated, and the changes wrought by the establishment of the British rule.[10] Moreover, the work contains a vivid account of communal strife that had erupted in Jaunpur in 1776 over the construction of a temple by a local *mahajan* adjacent to an old Muslim shrine.[11] The author has also mentioned the widespread repercussions of Raja Chait Singh's revolt in 1781 felt in Bihar and Bengal.[12] To add the biographical material produced in the book, even in sketchy and anecdotal way, offers insights into diverse social facets of Muslim professional middle class comprising civil officers, soldiers, servants, and increasing trends of social mobility in the lower middle strata in a region dominated by Hindu Rajas, big *zamindars* and great *mahajans*.[13]

He has arranged his laboriously collected material into five chapters:

(a) History of Raja Mansa Ram and his relations, and their decline.
(b) The Government (*hakumat*) of Raja Balwant Singh and events which occurred during his regime.
(c) The affairs of Raja Chait Singh and occurrences that took place in those days.
(d) The events pertaining to the government of Mahipat Narain.
(e) The government of Udit Narain Singh and other contemporary happenings.

Compared with other works[14] composed by Khair-al-Din, *Tuhfah-i-Tazah* seems to be at its best level partly because he has restricted the scope of his narrative to a specific territory, and partly because he has paid serious attention to the accuracy of historical data. Educated in Islamic theology, and philosophy, he started his career as a teacher in some *madrasa* of Allahabad, but later he went to Banaras where Jonathan Duncan, the British Resident, appointed him *munshi* (scribe), and in the course of interaction he motivated him to apply his talents, vast knowledge and command on Persian language, to history-writing. By the time he composed *Tuhfah-i-Tazah* he had attained maturity of thought, precision and coherence in the configuration and articulation of the data available to him. These features marked the standard of the work and gave to it a distinguished place in the regional histories of eighteenth century.

Modern historical researches on Banaras are primarily based on English records to the exclusion of Persian source-material including *Tuhfah-i-Tazah*, and centred on its history during the post-annexation period (1781-95). Both V.A. Narain[15] and K.P. Mishra[16] are concerned with the agenda of administrative reforms introduced by Jonathan

Duncan (1787-95) in the indigenous land-revenue, judicial and police systems, and state of trade, commerce and local industries. Dr. Shayesta Khan's work deals with the career, personality, and achievements of Ali Ibrahim (1740-93), the Chief Magistrate and Chief Judge of the city courts of Banaras, appointed by Warren Hastings in 1781.[17] Bernard S. Cohn has analysed the institutional changes and impact of British rule in the region of Banaras and how its lineage dominated political units in the context of Mughal political and administrative institutions. He has explained how the British policies in Banaras created new economic and social conditions in which the emergence of new urban and rural classes became possible.[18]

The present essay seeks to briefly analyse the historical information as gleaned from *Tuhfah-i-Tazah* on the following topics:

I. Career of Khair-al Din and His Encounter with Babu Durga Charan.
II. Description of His Visits to the Cities of Patna, Murshidabad and Calcutta.
III. Shaikh Abdullah, *Amil* of Ghazipur, Banaras.
IV. Hindu-Muslim Tension in Jaunpur.

I. CAREER OF KHAIR-AL DIN AND HIS ENCOUNTER WITH BABU DURGA CHARAN

Maulawi Khair-al Din was born in 1751 in Allahabad and received primary education there, but for higher studies in theology, law, medicine, rhetoric and astronomy he went to Jaunpur, the old seat of Muslim learning and culture. He returned to his hometown and began teaching in a school which he continued only for a few years, and moved to Banaras to find out avenues to raise his income and status. One morning while he was walking on the bank of Ganges he saw a crowd of people following a tall, majestic figure, and on inquiry it was reported that he was Babu Durga Charan, formerly *diwan* of a British Officer, held in high esteem at Banaras on account of his learning, religious devotion, and political clout in officials circles. He was further informed that he had no liking for Muslims and avoided even the shadow of the adherents of Islam. He decided to meet that Bengali gentleman for the sake of enjoyment as he had no serious work to attend to at that moment.[19] The author has given a graphic account of his dialogue with Babu Durga Charan and his companions which Elliot has dismissed as irrelevant and frivolous.[20] The encounter, however, reveals his deep interest in comparative religion, study of Hindu faith and philosophy and ability to expound his viewpoint on religious controversies. It also throws light on the prevalent norms of social behaviour, cultural attitudes, and religious tolerance unaffected by changing perceptions of continuing shifts of power relationship between the two communities.

Briefly put, the Maulawi went to the residence of Durga Charan and there found him surrounded by at least one hundred persons apparently engaged in some religious discussion, and, therefore, no one took notice of his coming. When he approached nearer, Durga Charan looked at him and spontaneously stood to welcome him and so did every body in the gathering. Durga Charan asked the visitor about his credentials, his education, profession, and the cause of his visit to Banaras; but the answers pertaining particularly to advanced studies having completed at the age of 17 years created doubts in their minds. To test his scholastic attainments one of the Pandits enquired about his views on the origin of mankind, and Durga Charan became so profoundly impressed by the scholarly discourse and perspicuous articulation of the Maulawi that he remarked, 'You are a Pandit of our religion and you stay with us for sometime'. Forthwith a room on the second storey of a beautiful and spacious building in the locality of silk merchants (*katra raisham*) was acquired, four months', rent at the rate of six rupees per month paid in advance, and the room was furnished with carpets and curtains. Shortly afterwards, the servants of Durga Charan presented two *shawls*, four pieces of white cloth and cash to the honourable guest in conformity with traditions of hospitality prevalent in that period.[21]

Next day Babu Durga Charan went to pay respects to Col. Jonathan Duncan, British Resident of Banaras at Chunargarh, and in the course of conversation he referred to the arrival of Maulawi Khair-al Din in the city, his interaction with him and praised his noble character and erudition. Col. Duncan was highly pleased to hear what Durga Charan told him and invited the young scholar of Islam and comparative religion by sending a *palki* to take him to his residence. Khair-al Din found Col. Duncan a person of pleasant disposition, polite and sweet-tongued. Duncan also put normal, familiar questions concerning his antecedents and purpose of coming to Banaras, and stated that presently he was engaged in the study of the celebrated *Masnavi* of Maulawna Rum and intended to translate it into English. In the perusal of the text he had discovered some couplets which even the learned scholars could not explain, and sought his help in understanding their real meaning in simple words. The text was brought and difficult couplets were read out;

Khair-al Din easily removed the complexities and made their meaning thoroughly clear and intelligible to him. Duncan felt satisfied with the interpretation and reasoning put forth by the Maulawi, and asked him to stay at Chunargarh for the days he was to teach him the *Masnavi*. Khair-al Din lived in the fort for one month during which he received five rupees per day, besides free board and lodge, as well as footmen (*harkaras*) to carry his *palki*.[22]

This was the beginning of his contact with colonial establishment in Banaras that grew closer over the years, ushering in his rise both as an important collaborator and prominent historian in the late eighteenth century. Though a scholar of theology and law, Khair-al Din was free from religious fanaticism and the conceit of the *Ulama*: open-minded, pragmatic in outlook, and capable of apprehending ground realities of the world around him. He was also a man of goodwill and sympathy for the oppressed. He played a minor social role within his limited sphere of influence by helping the inhabitants of Banaras whom the officers of government exploited in collecting fees far in excess to the sanctioned rate. This had resulted in much outcry and tumult in the city, but no individual dared approach the British Resident to seek redressal of their grievances against the highhandedness of government officers and bankers. However, a few persons met Khair-al Din in the belief that he enjoyed the confidence of Col. Duncan and requested him to draw his attention to the deteriorating situation of public peace. Khair-al Din in his next meeting with the Resident reported what was actually happening in the city and requested him to take steps to relieve the inhabitants from unlawful exactions and severe hardships in order to win their goodwill and cooperation, so essential for stability and prestige of the new regime. Duncan responded to his sincere suggestion by announcing that those who had paid extra money in the form of bribes could take it back from the treasury, and in future they would pay only one rupee per hundred title-deeds of their landed and urban properties to *qazis* and *muftis* for verification. Previously, the landholders and revenue-free assignees had to pay seven rupees per hundred documents instead of five rupees to the accountants of treasury and two rupees to the servants of judiciary as fixed by government. This measure had opened the doors to exploitation of the propertied classes which fostered commotion, vitiating the peace in the city. The name of the city *Qazi* was Rahmat Ali Khan.[23]

On the eve of his departure from Chunargarh to Patna and other cities Duncan made all necessary arrangements for his safe and comfortable onward journey, gave letters of introduction addressed to his English friends in Calcutta, and supplied five hundred rupees for expenses towards the journey through Gopal Das Sahu, the banker.[24]

II. DESCRIPTION OF HIS VISITS TO THE CITIES OF PATNA, MURSHIDABAD AND CALCUTTA

He writes that the city of Patna is prosperous and splendid, and the people are friendly and sincere. The gentry of the city came in large numbers to meet him; they even organized a few meetings to welcome him, where discussion on current religious polemics and new trends in literature and poetry took place. In Patna he went to pay respects to Raja Kalyan Singh,[25] deputy *nazim* and son of Raja Shitab Rai, along with Hadi Ali Khan and Maulawi Faiz Ali Khan. The Raja greeted him in Muslim fashion and after exchange of customary courtesies he began discourse on the concept of *Imamat* from Shia viewpoint, and showed his book entitled *Huliyat-ul Fatamin* which Khair-al Din regarded an excellent work on the doctrine of oneness of God (*tauhid*), proofs of the prophethood (*risalat*) of Prophet Muhammad (peace be upon him), *Imamat* of Hazrat ali, and matchless qualities and virtues of Fatma, the daughter of the Prophet. After going through the book Khair-al Din remarked, 'if in reality it has been written by you, God may grant grace and bless your end'. The Raja offered him costly gifts and asked him to stay at Patna, start teaching in a school, and that he would bear all the expenses and assign a *jagir* worth five thousand rupees per annum.[26]

He declined to accept any of the gifts or assignments, but stayed on for sometime more in Patna, paying visits to English officers and assisting them in their academic pursuits. He met David Anderson,[27] member of the provincial council of Bihar who was busy in translating *Hidaya* into English. Later on, Anderson was promoted to the department of *Khalisa* in the Council of Calcutta, and went there to take charge of his new assignment. In Murshidabad Khair-al Din met Nawab Saiyid-ul Mulk Asadullah Khan, a learned scholar and leading noble of the district. Both interacted on academic problems, topics of mutual interests, and developed friendly relations. Another eminent person of the city whom he mentions was Sadr-ul Haque,[28] *faujdar* of Murshidabad. He was so deeply influenced by Khair-al Din's knowledge of affairs, learning and integrity of character that he expressed a desire of employing him as his deputy (*naib faujdar*), but he did not accept the offer and set out for Calcutta in 1779. He was welcomed by Meer Saiyid Ali to whom Nawab Muzaffar Jang, deputy-governor (*naib nazim*) to Bengal, had written a letter of introduction to make necessary arrangements for his comfortable dwelling. Meer Saiyid Ali acquired a house in the locality of Chaitpur and posted his brother Maulawi Ghulam Husain Muhyi-al Din to look after him.[29] There he met David Anderson who took him to George Vansittart (Hoshyar Jang),[30] a learned young scholar of Persian and Arabic. He was courteous, goodnatured, competent and handsome, bearing marks of leadership on his forehead. In those days he was studying *Shrha-Mullah* and one Bengali Maulawi was under employment to teach the text. He asked Maulawi Khair-al Din to clarify the meanings of some ambiguous passages which he did, and later wrote for him one hundred stories in simple Arabic which he memorized in no time and translated them into English. In Calcutta he also visited Armenian market, large and flourishing, where every commodity that he or his companions wished to buy was available.[31]

It appears that Khair-al Din had set his heart from outset to serve under some English officer in preference to an Indian nobleman; and at long last his ambition was fulfilled when he joined government services as scribe first of Captain Bruce and then as secretary to James Anderson. When Captain Bruce seized Gwalior in 1780 he acted as private secretary to Anderson, the British Resident at Sindhia's court, and took part in negotiations for peace settlement with the Maratha Chief. His brother, Salah-al Din, was also present at Gwalior serving in a subordinate position under the Resident. In the last week of March 1787 Khair-al Din left the service on account of illness and came to Jaunpur and began to live there. He also served Shah Alam in Delhi, and for sometime was attached to the court of Awadh in the regime of Asaf-ud-Daulah, the Nawab Wazir (1775-97).[32]

III. SHAIKH ABDULAH, *AMIL* OF GHAZIPUR

The author has furnished considerable historical information in respect of the position, interests, and roles of Muslim landholders, civil officers, armymen and subordinate servants associated with the process of governance in Banaras during the period the work under review deals with. But eminent among them was Shaikh Abdullah whose career, relations with *subedars* of Awadh, Rajas of Banaras, and socio-cultural activities are prominently reported in the narrative. He is depicted as a brave warrior, an efficient administrator, builder of houses, founder of towns, and patron of writers and poets. He served as an *amil* of Ghazipur[33] for four years. It is on its basis that these aspects of his personality are briefly analysed in the following pages.

Majority of Muslim servants employed by Raja Balwant Singh (1740-70) and his son Raja Chait Singh (1770-81) were of Indian origin: Afghans and Shaikhs like Shaikh Abdullah and his son Fazal Ali Khan, the *amils* of Ghazipur, Nauroz Ali Khan, *amil* of Sultanpur, Haji Sarfraz, a close companion of Balwant Singh, Meer Abdullah, *wakil* of Chait Singh, Meer Ghulam Husain Khan, superintendent (*darogha*) of artillery, Lal Khan, Dalel Khan and Rasul Khan, the Afghan captains in the army, Shaikh Iezad, and Maulawi Amarullah Khan who served in the government of Balwant Singh.[34] Cohn holds that most of the Muslim officers were of Persian origin and background as they or their ancestors had migrated from Persia to India to build their fortunes. He briefly refers to the careers of Mehdi Ali, and Ali Ibrahim Khan[35] who served under Jonathan Duncan in the post-annexation period. But they all, he writes, disappeared from the scene by the close of the century, and their places were filled by Hindu or British officers, judges, *amils*, *serishtadars* and scribes. For instance, Jacob Rider, the Judge of Ghazipur appointed eight Persian writers who were all Hindus—three Kayasthas, one Bengali Brahman, two Bhumihars and two Rajputs. In the Nagri writers' office there were also eight Hindu scribes. Only the *nazir* of the criminal court was a local Muslim, Maulawi Amarullah, the Muslim Law Officer, and his counter-part, a Hindu Law officer, was a Pandit trained at the Hindu College at Banaras.[36]

Abdullah Khan was the son of Muhammad Qasim, a Shaikh Siddiqi and *zamindar* of Dharwar in *pargana* Zahurabad. He received his early education at Delhi and obtained a job in the central government in the reign of Farrukh Siyar (1712-19). By sheer dint of dedicated service and latent talents he rapidly rose to higher grades, and attracted the attention of Sarbuland Khan, governor of Bihar, to appoint him as *naib subedar* of that province in 1717. This important position of trust and power he held for more than a decade during which he displayed great abilities as benevolent administrator, and concern for the well-being of people but without losing any opportunity to carve out a vast *jagir* for himself in the province.[37] When Fakhr-ud Daulah (1727-37), a man made of sterner stuff, began to confiscate *jagir* lands unlawfully acquired by officers of government, powerful *zamindars* and big nobles, a clash between the governor and these chief components of the existing land revenue structure arose. He also took all such lands back which Shaikh Abdullah had appropriated without royal sanction (*sanad*) and threatened to imprison him in case of defiance to his authority.[38]

In order to avoid confrontation with the mighty governor, Shaikh

Abdullah escaped into Ghazipur, a permanent centre of refuge for nearly all rebel *zamindars* from north Bihar, but shortly afterwards proceeded on the invitation of Saadat Khan Burhan-ul-Mulk, governor of Awadh (1721-39) to Faizabda. He was appointed a captain (*risaladar*) in the army and later entrusted with the administration of Gorakhpur, Bahraich and Khairabad districts. In the year 1737-8 he accompanied Saadat Khan to Delhi who having been deeply impressed by his loyalty and selfless service recommended to his deputy and nephew Safdar Jang to place the management of Ghazipur into the hands of Shaikh Abdullah. After the death of Saadat Khan in Delhi, 1739, he returned from Delhi to Ghazipur and took charge of its administration in 1740. He regularly deposited the stipulated amount of three lakhs of rupees into the Awadh treasury. He imported silk from Bengal and sold it in Banaras and out of the profits earned from this brisk trade considerable amount of money was spent on the construction of several buildings under the supervision of his deputy Shaikh Shamsul Haq. He built forts at Jalalabad, in *parganas* of Shadiabad, and Qasimabad, a town which he founded and named after his father. He built a bridge over the highway, a mosque, and Imambara, besides several other buildings and the extensive garden called Nawab Bagh. The most costly and beautiful monument erected by him in Ghazipur was Chihal Satun or palace of forty pillars admired by all who came to see it from different places.[39]

Shaikh Abdullah died in 1745, leaving four sons, Fazal Ali Khan, Karm-ullah Khan, Saadullah Khan, and Said-ullah and all remained attached to the court of Awadh. Fazal Ali Khan, the eldest, was appointed the executive head of civil and revenue administration of Ghazipur but was removed in 1747, and again in 1754 for reasons of default in payment of dues now fixed at five lakhs of rupees, but was reinstated. It was in 1757 that Shuja-ud Daulah finally dismissed him because of non-payment of arrears, and the charge of Ghazipur and Azamgarh districts was handed over to Balwant Singh on an annual revenue of eight lakhs of rupees. In compliance with the orders of Awadh government Balwant Singh invaded Ghazipur to expel Fazal Ali Khan from it, thoroughly sacked it and destroyed its buildings. Fazal Ali fled to Patna where he died; Azam Khan, his nephew and grandson of Shaikh Abdullah was awarded a pension. According to Khair-al Din the English collector on his visit to Ghazipur expressed grief over the ruination of the city and its old monuments, and ordered for the repair and reconstruction of Chihal Satun and few other buildings. Raja Balwant Singh divided the twenty-two *parganas* of Ghazipur among his own companions, and they were: Babu Baijnath Singh, *parganas* of Kunda, Chaunsa, and Zamaniya Lala Nandkishore, Sedpur; Bhai Ram Mahajan, Mahmudabad; Nand Ram, *diwan* Lal Khan, *haveli* Ghazipur; Muzaffar Khan, Sikanderpur; and Jagar Dev Singh, Shadiabad, Zahurabad.[40]

IV. HINDU-MUSLIM TENSION IN JAUNPUR, 1776

In 1776 Sevan Mahajan, an inhabitant of Jaunpur, Mohallah Hammam, constructed a new temple near the gateway between two Muslim sacred shrines—Asar Sharif and Panja Mubarak in village Khenipur, and surrounded it with the plantation of mango trees, and Hindus began to perform regular prayers accompanied with musical instruments. The building was beautifully decorated, and on the tower of it a tirsul of iron with gold plating was erected. The attendants at the shrines protested against the innovation but their complained was not heeded. This fomented tension in the city affecting peaceful life of people not involved in the dispute in any way. One day two students, Baqar Ali Khan and Muhammad Naqi Khan, came to the place and seeing the new temple felt surprised at the innovation, and they aroused religious sentiments of their companions in a bid to start agitation against it. Shortly afterwards came the month of Muharram, but they did not go as a mark of protest to perform mourning (*matam*) in the mourning house (*Matam Khana*) at the shrine. On the fifth of Muharram crowds of devotees from the city and its suburbs thronged the shine of Panja Mubark as they had done in the past; in the meantime multitude of other Muslims also congregated at the site and great commotion ensued. In that moment of excitement one Mian Abdullah, a *chela* of Sidi, announced that 'he will attempt to target the *tirsul* with his matchlock (*bondooq*); if the shot could hit it by the will of God and His Prophet and it falls down, in that event demolition of temple may be considered proper (from his viewpoint), otherwise, he will silently return to his home'. It was by sheer dint of chance that the shot fired by him struck the *tirsul* and it fell on the ground, evoking the cry of *Ya Husain* from everyside. Then, believers in the supposedly divine omen propagated that it was the bidding of Shah Mardan (Hazrat Ali) to dismantle the temple. The Muslims in response to clarion call assembled in large numbers and subsequently destroyed the sacred building of religious worship.[41]

This hideous act sparked violent reaction among the Hindus who closed their shops, collected in thousands on streets, and incited by their leaders, Bhawani Das Dasturiya and Vishnu Prasad, they decided to bring down the structure of Panja Mubark, while Muslims formed a crowd at both Qazi Gate and Jama Masjid of Jaunpur, and thus a stand-off between the two communities seemed inevitable. Fearing that the conflict might turn into a major conflagration inviting British intervention who now exercised controlling authority over Banaras,[42] some Muslim leaders—Rahim Khan and Dhund Khan—approached Hindu prominent activists and pleaded with them to settle the dispute amicably to prevent the outbreak of communal riot. They said, 'Hindus and Muslims had always lived together, and in future, too, they will have to live together in peace and harmony'. But no settlement of the dispute could be arrived at, and anarchic conditions subsisted. A group of Hindus went to Banaras to apprise Raja Chait Singh of the perilous situation prevailing in Jaunpur and requested him to restore normalcy in the strife-torn city and ensure justice to their community outraged by the demolition of the temple. Their account of the frightful events obviously perturbed the Raja, but he acted cautiously to bring the situation under control by sending his trusted secretary Jai Kiran Jauhari with instructions to investigate into circumstances leading to the turbulence and find out the real culprits responsible for the demolition of the temple.[43]

On 15 Muharram Jai Kiran Jauhari arrived in Jaunpur and set up his office of inquiry at Jama Masjid, where he summoned Namdar Khan, the *faujdar*, Nisar Khan, the *kotwal*, and several other opulent and influential persons of both the communities. He asked every one present there, who had demolished the temple, and who had precipitated communal tension. But every one of them expressed his ignorance in the matter, and, therefore, the identity of the perpetrators of the crime could not be established in that meeting. He recorded their statements on oath in the name of God, prepared a detailed statement (*mahzar*) that was duly attested with signature and seals of the witnesses, and submitted the documents to Raja Chait Singh. However, some Hindus in an interview with the Raja disclosed the names of persons openly or clandestinely involved in the destruction of the temple. They were: *qazi*, *mufti*, Shah Ajmeri, Shaikh Nazr Muhammad, Alam Husain, chiefs of weavers, Roshan Baluch, Rustum Khan and Dhund Khan. Believing their version genuine the Raja issued written orders (*parwana*) to Nisar Ali Khan, Commandant of garrison to arrest and bring these culprits to his court. Hussain, the head of weavers, did not agree to go to Banaras; on the other hand, he collected his fellowmen and brought all of them outside Jaunpur and stayed there, saying that if the Raja wanted to punish them, they would migrate from his country. The armymen having failed to secure their voluntary surrender, the commander (*qaladar*) himself visited their camp, but realizing that use of force will only complicate the problem, rather than solve it, and that their migration had the possibility of jeopardizing economic interests of the government, he held his hand from executing the orders and accordingly reported his inability in the matter to his master, the Raja.[44]

At this juncture Raja Chait Singh and his ministers were informed that a section of Muslims had outlined the plan to build mosque in the enclosure where recently the temple stood, and as a counter-measure to this sinister design Hindu *zamindars* had mobilized their individual militia and marched in that direction. The confrontation between forces of communalism on both lines seemed imminent threatening eruption of lawlessness on a wide scale the prevention of which necessitated military action against the miscreants. The Raja lost no time in dispatching troops to be deployed at the scene of conflict with strict instructions to chastise and punish all those found guilty of rioting and impeding enforcement of law and order. The bold, determined measure taken by the Raja's government yielded positive results, for no incident of killing or arson occurred, and the turbulence that had continued for more than a month subsided, and slowly calm came to settle on the town. The local manufacturing industries, badly affected by the impact of tumult, started functioning, and social, and commercial contacts of pre-riot days between communities revived, gaining good opinion of both the people and the British Resident for the regime of the Raja.[45]

But the intrinsic interest and importance of *Tuhfah-i-Tazah* is not limited to the above topics alone, it contains materials to understand aspects of cultural ethos, Hindu-Muslim symbiosis, patterns of social behaviour, religious superstition and fiction, besides additional evidence regarding political transactions generally dealt with in a perfunctionary manner in other historical writings of the period.

For instance, the author has given a detailed account of the forcible deposition of Raja Chait Singh in 1781, foundation of British rule over the territory of Banaras, and political repercussions the change gave rise to. It focuses on the nature and form of widespread insurrection by local *zamindars* and common men in support of the Raja the British authorities had to face in parts of the extensive area stretching from Allahabad to north Bihar. His perception of colonial expansion in this region as elsewhere in India is essentially British oriented, revealing his bias for foreign domination of which he was a beneficiary. He has compared the

Raja's troops with the disciplined infantry under the command of Major Popham as between grass (*kah*) and mountain (*koh*).[46] In support of his faith in the invincibility of the British armed forces he has set forth the reasoning given by Shaikh Ali Hazen (1692-1766) to Shuja-ud-Daulah and Meer Qasim, the deposed nazim of Bengal (1760-63) when they went to pay respects to the saint (*Awliya-i-Asr*) in Banaras on their march towards Buxur, 1764. The Shaikh had advised them to make settlement with the British on terms they had offered, and predicted their utter defeat in case the two chiefs ventured to fight in the open battlefield. Khair-al Din writes:

> In reply to the question as to what the purpose of their visit to Banaras was, Nawab Shuja-ud Daulah said that they had resolved to expel the British from Bengal and other dominions of Hindustan and in that noble cause they prayed for his blessings. The Shaikh smiled and said, 'most of the Hindustani soldiers in your army have recently learnt how to draw sword and hold spear into hands, but gained no experience in a straight fight with powerful warriors in the open field of battle. The English are, on the other hand, far superior, more experienced, in the art and technique of warfare, who have surpassed all other powers in this sphere. They have invented and adopted a new musket which no other war weapon can match. Therefore, they should never intend to fight with them, but try to find out means for a settlement which the English also wanted. In case war became inevitable, they should resort to the tactics of hit-and-run, blocking supply lines, and surrounding small groups of the adversary, with the help of their strong cavalry. The Nawab of Awadh on hearing this discourse of the saint felt displeased, out of regard for him remained silent, and forthwith stood up and left the place.[47]

NOTES

1. Ali Muhammad Khan, *Mirat-i-Ahmadi*, completed in 1761, published, (Baroda, 1927-8).
2. Ghulam Husain Tabatabai, *Siyar-ul Mutakhkherin*, written in 1781, published (Lucknow, 1886).
3. Ghulam Husain Khan bin Himmat Khan also wrote a history of Banaras and gave it the title of *Tuhfah-i-Tazah*, Khuda Bakhsh Library, Patna. This author was in the service of Raja Balwant Singh, his constant companion, and enjoyed his full confidence. Yet, there is another anonymous history of the *zamindars* of Banaras from the time of Raja Mansa Ram to the deposition of Raja Chait Singh in the Khuda Bakhsh Library, Patna, Ms. No. 608.
4. *Tuhfah-i-Tazah*, p. 2.

5. In the first half of eighteenth century Banaras *sarkar* constituted a *faujdari* jurisdiction, comprising Jaunpur, Ghazipur, Chunargarh, the districts of Azamgarh, Ballia and eastern part of Mirzapur. Its *faujdar* was directly appointed by the central government. Formerly it was a part of Allahabad province, but now the governors of Awadh began to excise their superior authority over the administration of Banaras, treating it as part of their province. In 1738-9 Safdar Jang, deputy- governor of Awadh in the absence of Saadat Khan Burhan-ul Mulk, the *subedar*, dismissed the deputy *faujdar* of Banaras, Rustum Ali Khan, and divided the territory into two units. The charge of three divisions—Jaunpur, Ghazipur and Chunargarh—was given to Mansa Ram a Bumihar Brahman of Gautam sub-caste, for an annual revenue of Rs.13 lakhs per annum, while the administration of the remaining districts was placed into the hands of Shaikh Abdullah for Rs. 3 Lakhs. After the death of Mansa Ram in 1740 Safdar Jang confirmed Balwant Singh in the possession of the above-mentioned divisions. Balwant Singh sent a tribute of Rs. 31,775 to the Mughal Emperor who bestowed upon him the title of Raja and *Zamindar* of certain *parganas* in Banaras.
6. *Tuhfah-i-Tazah*, p. 2
7. Ibid., p. 272.
8. *Tuhfa-i-Tazah*, pp. 111, 112, 113-14.
9. Ibid., pp. 9-10, 20, 22, 34, 35, 114, 115.
10. Ibid., pp. 103-40.
11. Ibid., pp. 115-24.
12. Ibid., pp. 231-42; For a recent detailed study on the topic, Rajat Kanta Ray, 'Colonial Penetration and the Initial Resistance', *The Indian Historical Review*, July, 1985, January 1986, Vol. XII, nos 1-2, pp. 94, 95-8.
13. *Tuhfah-i-Tazah*, pp.142-5, 162, 165.
14. He was the author of 14 books. But only few of them are known and available in the libraries. For instance, *Ibrat Nama*, 2 vols., Aligarh Ms; *Tarikh-i Jaunpur*, Aligarh Ms.; *Gwalior Nama*, Rieu, III, Add. 1850, India Office Lib., Ethe, 3947; *Sarabastan ba. Zikr Badshahan-i Hindustan*, Aligarh Ms.
15. V.N. Narain, *Jonathan Duncan and Varanasi* (Calcutta, 1959).
16. Kanta Prasad Mishra, *Benares in Transition* (New Delhi, 1975; also, B.R. Mishra, *Land Revenue Policy in U.P.* (Benaras, 1942); P.J. Marshall, for 'Economic and Political Expansion', *Modern Asian Studies*, 9, 4 (1975), pp.6465-82; C.A. Bayly, *Rulers, Townsmen, and Bazars* (Cambridge, 1983).
17. Shayesta Khan, *A Biography of Ali Ibrahim Khan*, Khuda Baksh Oriental Public Library (Patna, 1992).
18. Bernard S. Cohn, 'Initial British Impact on India', *Journal of Asian Studies*, Vol. XIX, 1959-60, pp. 418-31.
19. *Tuhfah-i-Tazah*, pp.128-272.
20. *The History of India*, Elliot & Dowson, Vol. VIII, rpt. (Allahabad, 1964), p. 416

21. *Tuhfah-i-Tazah*, pp.130-5.
22. Ibid, pp.137-8.
23. Ibid, pp.141-2.
24. Ibid., p.142.
25. Kalyan Singh, son of Maharaja Shitab Rai, was appointed in 1773 *naib nazim* of Bihar and succeeded to the *jagir* of his father in south Bihar and *sarkar* Champaran with the title of Maharaja Bahadur. In 1778 he was honoured with the title of Intizam-ul Mulk Tahavvur Jang by Emperor Shah Alam. In 1783 arrears of revenue against him mounted to more than Rs. 6 lakhs, and his *jagirs* were attached for five years from January 1784. Kalyan Singh was the author of *Khulasat-ut Tawarikh*, a contemporary history of Bihar. For details, *Journal of the Bihar and Orissa Research Society*, Vol. V, 1919, pp.345-441; *Calendar of Persian Correspondence*, Vol. VII, p. 3; Vol.XI, p.142.
26. *Tuhfa-i-Tazah*, p.149.
27. He was sent by Warren Hastings as an embassy of the Company's government to Mahadaji Sindhia in 1782 along with his brother James Anderson to assist him. In 1785 James Anderson was appointed the Political Resident at Gwalior. *Dictionary of Indian Biography*, p.13.
28. He came from the city of Gujarat, where he was born. Accompanied by his father he went to Delhi, and upon his death he arrived at Murshidabad to improve his economic condition. Here he joined service under Mahabat Jang Aliwardi Khan who appointed him *darogha-i adalat* (superintendent of court), after Qazi Muzaffar Ali. During the Maratha invasions of Bengal (1742-51) he was sent to the Poona court (Deccan) to settle conditions of peace, and the way he conducted peace parleys (1750-1) won the admiration and gratitude of both the parties. Later, he formed a corps that gave him some status and a name. After the death of Aliwardi Khan (1756) he continued to flatter and cultivate favour of whoever came to power in Bengal. He died in 1779. For details, *Siyar-ul Mutakhkherin*, op.cit., p. 807.
29. *Tuhfah-i-Tazah*, p.134.
30. Ghulam Husain Tabatabai also met him at Deenajpur where he held the post of District Collector. About George Vansittart he writes that in reality he was a man of quick perception, farsighted, endowed with noble qualities of character, possessed a clear comprehension of intricate, complex matters of administration, liked and admired by his colleagues and members of the Council at Calcutta. *Siyar-ul Mutakhkherin*, p.783. Arthur Vansittart was the son of Henry Vansittart. *The Transition in Bengal*, pp. 157n., 201, 245n., 260.
31. *Tuhfah-i-Tazah*, p.151.
32. Ibid., pp. 152-5; for the life and career of Muzaffar Jung, Abdul Majid Khan, *The Transition in Bengal, 1756-1775, A Study of Saiyid Muhammad Raza Khan* (Cambridge, 1969).

33. *Sarkar* Ghazipur contained 19 *mahals*, with the total revenue of 13,431 *dams* and area 2,88,770 *bighas*, 7 *biswas*. The *Ain-i-Akbari*, English translation, H.S. Jarret, Vol. II (1978), p. 173. Ghazipur was administered by the collector of Banaras from 1795 to 1818 and it became a separate charge from Banaras in 1818 with the appointment Robert Barlow as its first District Collector. H.R. Nevil, *District Gazetteer of Ghazipur* (Allahabad, 1909).
34. *Tuhfah-i-Tazah*, pp.16, 25, 29, 37, 42, 55, 165.
35. He was born and brought up by his maternal uncle Zair Husain Khan at Shikhpura in the district of Monghyr (Bihar). For details of Indian origin of his family, see *A Biography of Ali Ibrahim Khan*, op.cit., pp. 31-9.
36. Bernard S.Cohn, *Journal of Asian Studies*, op.cit., pp.419, 421, 424, 425.
37. *Tuhfah-i-Tazah*, p. 142; for a biographical note on Sarbaland Khan, *Maasir-ul Umara*, text, Vol. III, pp. 801-6.
38. *Tuhfah-i-Tazah*, p.16; *Maasir-ul Umara*, III, pp. 833-5.
39. *Tuhfah-i-Tazah*, pp.26, 172.
40. Ibid., pp.25, 27-32, 58, 61, 62, 173.
41. *Tuhfah-i-Tazah*, p.15.
42. On the death of Balwant Singh in 1770 his son Chait Singh succeeded to the *zamindari* of Banaras, and both Shuja-ud Daulah, the nawab wazir of Awadh and Warren Hastings, the Governor-General, confirmed the succession. The annual revenue of its district Banaras, Jaunpur and Ghazipur, was fixed at Rs. 22,48,419 or an increase of Rs. 21-2 lakhs on the rent paid by Balwant Singh. After the death of Shuja-ud Daulah in 1775 his son and successor Asaf-ud Daulah was forced by the Governor-General to cede the territory of Banaras to the Company's government because the nawab had expressed his inability to pay the subsidy amount now raised from Rs. 2,10,000 to Rs. 2,60,000 per *mensum*. Sovereignty over Banaras was in this way transferred from the nawab of Awadh to the British government. Francis Fowke was appointed Resident of Banaras.
43. *Tuhfah-i-Tazah*, p. 115.
44. Ibid., pp. 115-16.
45. Ibid., pp. 115-24. Also 'modern studies on the disquisition of Hindu-Muslim quarrels on religious places of worship and symbols in the late eighteenth and early nineteenth centuries', Gyanendra Pandey. *The Construction of Communalism in colonial North India* (New Delhi, 1997), pp.66-108; Shashi Joshi, Bhagwan Das, *Struggle for Hegemony in India*, (New Delhi); Herjot Oberoi, *The Construction of Religious Boundaries*, (New Delhi, 1994); C.A. Bayly, 'The Pre-history of Communalism: Religious Conflict in India,' *Modern Asian Studies*, Vol. 19, Part I, Feb. 1985; Lakshmi Subramaniam, 'Capital and Crowd in a Declining: Asian Port City: The Anglo-Bania Order and the Surat Riots of 1795', *Modern Asia Studies*, Vol. 19, Part I, February 1985; Imtiaz Ahmad, *Ritual and Religion among*

Muslims of the Sub-continent (New Delhi, 1985); C.A. Bayly, *Rulers, Townsmen, and Bazars: North Indian Society in the Age of British Expansion, 1770-1870* (Cambridge, 1983).

46. *Tuhfah-i-Tazah*, pp.231-42; also Rajat Kanta Ray, 'Colonial Penetration and the Initial Resistance', *The Indian Historical Review*, July 1985, Vol. XII, nos. 1-2, pp. 94, 95-8.
47. *Tuhfah-i-Tazah*, p. 77.

...in tax — 20% of the total savings subject to a maximum of Rs. 12,000

...ge — 10% of the net tax payable. (1999)

...an annual income of Rs. 88,000 during a year (HRA not included) ... Rs. 800 per month towards Provident Fund account and ... premium of Rs. 1,000 towards Life Insurance Policy. Calculate ... tax payable in the last month if she had been paying Rs. 100 ... towards income tax for the first 11 months.

...following for calculating income tax:

...d Deduction — 1/3rd of the total income subject to a maximum of Rs. 20,000 (Rs. 25,000 if income is less than Rupees one lakh).

...income tax

Slab	Income Tax
Upto Rs. 50,000	No tax
From Rs. 50,001 to Rs. 60,000	10% of the amount exceeding Rs. 50,000
From Rs. 60,001 to Rs. 1,50,000	Rs. 1,000 + 20% of the amount exceeding Rs. 60,000

...in tax — 20% of the total savings subject to a maximum of Rs. 12,000.

...rge — 10% of the net tax payable. (1999)

...an annual income of Rs. 88,000 during a year (H.R.A not included) ... Rs. 800 per month towards provident fund account and ... premium of Rs. 1,000 towards life insurance policy. Calculate ... tax payable in the last month if she had been paying Rs. 100 ... towards income tax for the first 11 months.

...following for calculating income tax:

...d Deduction — 1/3rd of the total income subject to a maximum of Rs. 20,000 (Rs. 25,000 if income is less than Rupees one lakh).

...f income tax

Slab	Income Tax
Upto Rs. 50,000	No tax
From Rs. 50,001 to Rs. 60,000	10% of the amount exceeding Rs. 50,000
From Rs. 60,001 to Rs. 1,50,000	Rs. 1,000 + 20% of the amount exceeding Rs. 60,000

...in tax — 20% of the total savings subject to a maximum of

Archaeological Evidence of Feudal Hierarchy in Early Medieval India: Rajasthan— A Case Study

M.S. Ahluwalia

An attempt is made in the present paper to study a few important feudal titles of the twelfth century, which were used commonly in northern and western India. The study is confined only to the extent of knowing the relative position of four important titles, viz., *Rauta*, *Thakkura*, *Ranaka/Rana/Rai* and *Rajaputra*, in the feudal hierarchy of the twelfth century.

A number of ruling dynasties in Rajasthan, all of which later came to be designated with the common epithet of the 'Rajput', seem in fact to have been formed out of an assimilation of the various tribes or clans, each of whom claimed a different origin but gradually turned into a ruling group. It may be pointed out that the term 'Rajput', in the sense we use it now a days, is not found in the literary or epigraphic sources prior to the fifteenth century. Even in the late twelfth and the early thirteenth century Persian chronicles, next to the term 'Hindu', the most common term used for the various 'Rajput' clans was the *Rai*, *Thakkura* or *Rana*.[1]

By the time of the Turkish invasions at the close of the twelfth century, many of the well known 'Rajput' clans of the time, had come to be recognized as belonging to the Kshatriya caste. Some of these clans began to connect themselves with Sun, Moon, Fire and Sea etc.,[2] with a view to prove their high martial status. Very little is known about the system of the ruling order of these 'proto-Rajput' clans. What one can dimly discern is the emergence of distinct categories of autonomous or semi-autonomous feudal chiefs under the rulers designated with the titles such as *Rajaputra*, *Thakkur*, *Rauta* or *Rana*.

The most characteristic element of feudalism is the lord-vassal relationship. The germs of this *ism* are found in India as early as the Saka-Kushana period[3] but the climax is reached in early medieval period as a result of the Turkish invasions in the north-western India. The common term *Samanta* used for feudal lord is found in a number of literary as well as epigraphic sources during the period under review. However, the first reference to the term *Samanta* in Rajasthan is found in the Prakrit texts and epigraphs of the eighth century.[4]

Since its growth in the post-Gupta period, the feudal elements further developed during the eighth century due to the rise of the celebrated clans like the Gurjaras,[5] Guhilots[5a] and Chauhans[6] etc. The internal feuds between these clans and the Arab, Ghaznavid and the Ghorian invasions, contributed largely towards the intensification of the feudalistic tendencies. The climax was reached in the eleventh century with the break-up of the great Pratihara empire. Again, at the close of the twelfth century, the then ruling clans of the Chauhans,[7] Gahadvalas[8] and Chandelas[9] were involved in a 'tripartite' struggle. Their chronic warfare and external pressure put by the Turkish invasions, proved a congenial soil for the development of feudal structure and relationship.

By the close of the twelfth century, the concept of vassalage became clearer. It consisted of the conquest by some foreign invader and conversion of the existing ruling chiefs and princes into vassals, leading to an extension of the tributary system. Thus the reasons for the rapid growth of the feudal elements in the late twelfth and early thirteenth century are not too far to seek. One important reason was the Turkish invasions, which led to the dislodging of the ruling hierarchy, which being uprooted, was obliged to accept the subordinate position of vassalage.

The eleventh and twelfth centuries may be characterized as a period of continued struggle for supremacy. The chief contenders for power were the Chalukyas of Anhilwara, the Paramaras of Malwa,[10] and the Chauhans of Sakambhari. Apart from this, the Chauhans of Nadol, the Paramaras of Abu and the Guhilots of Mewar also played a subordinate but important role.[11]

Another important aspect of feudalism, which further developed the lord-vassal relationship is traceable in the practice of granting land-grants to some[12] relatives and members of the clan, military commanders and other officers. The system was fairly popular from the Gupta period onwards, particularly under the Pratiharas and the Chauhans.

Although there is too much controversy over whether there was a tribal or a feudal society during the Rajput rule in western India, yet the tribal pattern may also have given rise to feudal relationship.[13] However, land grants may not be called fiefs because a fief meant a property granted against an obligation to render some personal or military service.[14] There are several such instances of assignments of land for military services. During the rule of the Pratiharas, the Chauhans, Guhilas and the Chalukyas, we find several references to estates held by scions of ruling clans or other civil and military officers.

As against this, there are also a number of literary and epigraphic references about the land grants made by way of gifts or maintenance of certain individuals without any service conditions.[15] On the other hand, there are also many instances of grants explicitly conditioned by obligations including military service, or maintenance of law and order.[16]

Although the Chauhan records indicate permanent hereditary assignments made to the members of the royal family,[17] some literary sources like *Kathakosha* and the *Lekhapaddhati* suggest that the non-religious grants were generally forfeited after the death of the vassal or in case when he failed to render the required military service. However, in actual practice, it all depended on the strength or weakness of the overlord.[18]

The hierarchical system of vassalage during the twelfth century is analysed in the *Aprajitaprichcha*, on the basis of the number of villages held by them in the following order:

Mahamandaleshwara
Mahasamanta
Samanta
Laghusamanta

The last feudatories were petty kings and below them were the *Rajaputras*[20] who were village chiefs.

There is no denying the fact that all the above titles were those of the vassals connected with land. Some were conquered and reinstated in their territories, whereas others were granted lands for their military services, a function which both (types) had to provide to their overlords.[21] Although more than a dozen grades of vassals are found in epigraphic and literary records,[22] the most common titles are *Rajaputras*, *Rautas*, *Thakuras*, *Ranakas*, *Samantas* and *Mandalikas*, each having a different size of territory.

It will thus be seen that during the post-Harsha period, a series of states and rulers appeared on the Indian political scene. The process gradually led to feudalization in the socio-economic life of the Indian society.[23] The most important aspect of the various titles of the landed aristocracy, from being the overlord down to the local governor, exhibits the existence of a 'well-developed' feudal administration[24] at work during the twelfth century, which in turn characterizes the climax as well as the downfall of feudalism in Indian history.

In the literary source, *Lekhapaddhati*, we find some important feudal titles beginning with *Rajan*, the others being *Ranaka*, *Mahamatya* and *Rajaputra* in descending order, on the basis of the land-grant documents classified as under:

(i) The charter of a king (*Rajan*) granting a country (*desh*) to a *Ranaka*;
(ii) The charter of a *Mahamatya* (high officer) granting fief to a donee, who became entitled to receive all dues from the *Ranaka*;
(iii) The charter of a *Ranaka* granting a piece of land to a *Rajaputra* on his application and obliging him to provide 100 foot soliders and 20 horsemen to the *Ranaka*, besides collecting dues and maintaining law and order in his fief;
(iv) The grant or lease of a *Rajaputra* farming out the villages to merchants and their associates, who approached them for this purpose, against a fixed amount of the revenue.[25]

Rajaputra

The most common title signifying vassalage, prevalent in Rajasthan and elsewhere during the period under review, was the *Rajaputra*,[26] which meant the son of Raja. It was used both in the literal sense as a prince or as an honorific. In the latter case, the *Rajaputra* was a kind of a vassal, who was supposed to render a personal or military service to the state in return for land granted to him.

Writing in the middle of the eighth century, the Arab traveler Sulaiman has referred to a system of sub-infeudation, wherein the conquered prince carried on the government in the name of the conqueror. A twelfth century document of the 'Marwar Chauhans' refers to a group of twelve villages which a junior *Rajaputra* received from the reigning chief.[28] Two other records[29] mention a couple of junior *Rajaputras* as the possessors of two villages.

The Nadol plate of AD 1161[30] records the grant of twelve villages with full ownership rights to a *Rajaputra* Kirtipala by Alhanadeva and Kalhanadeva Chauhan grant of AD 1176[31] records the two sons of

Kirtipala, *Rajaputras* Lakhanpala and Abhayapala. During the reign of Samar Simha, his maternal uncle *Rajaputra* Jojala acted as *Rajyachintika*, i.e. as minister or a general administrator.[32] Reference is made to another record about an allotment to a *Rajaputra* called Ajayadeva.[33]

In some other cases, the *Rajaputras* become full-fledged *Samanta* rulers. There are also instances of hereditary officers creating chiefships obviously by self-aggrandizement, by taking advantage of the weakness of the overlord. For example, a junior *Rajaputra* Kirtipala, who had obtained only a group of twelve villages from the reigning Chauhan prince Kalhana of Nadol, became the founder of the famous Jalor dynasty of the Chauhans in the twelfth century AD.[35]

Incidentally in the twelfth century literary source the *Aparajita-parichcha*, the *Rajaputra* is listed at the bottom in the descending order, on the basis of numbers of villages held by the feudatories. The *Raja-putras* were thus petty chiefs holding a few villages only.

On the authority of Dhanpal's *Tilakmanjari* (again of the twelfth century), it may be inferred that the practice of sub-infeudation among the *Rajaputra* was fairly common. It is mentioned therein that the princes Harivahana and Samarketu became *nishchinta* (i.e. free from anxiety) by distributing the towns and villages of their own *Bhuktis* among the *Rajaputras* who served them. The distribution was made on the basis of the merit of the recipients.[37]

The *Lekhapaddhati* too has classified the *Rajaputra* at the bottom next to *Rajan*, *Mahamatya* and *Ranaka* in the feudal hierarchy. It is further established from the same source that the land grants were made over to respective recipients for performing military or administrative duties. The *Rajaputras* were obliged to provide a fixed number of contingent to the *Ranaka* besides revenue collection and maintaining law and order in their fiefs.[38]

The *Rajaputras* who thus received *Jagirs* from the *Ranaka*, were bound to help him in times of war and pay him the fee at the time of accession.[39] The *Rajaputras* were on the whole quite independent in their respective territories and cultivated land through slaves, serfs or forced labour.[40] Two things become clear from the charter contained in the *Lekhapaddhati*. One, the *Ranakas* sub-infeuded land to the *Rajaputras*; two, the *Ranakas* made over the grant to the *Rajaputras* on the condition of maintaining law and order, collection of land-revenue and furnishing of a fixed number of contingents. Furthermore, the *Rajaputras* were authorized to lease out their villages to merchants and their associates for revenue collection.[41]

Since in most of the cases the *Rajaputras* held more than one village from which they could collect taxes personally, the responsibility was entrusted to rich merchants on contract basis. The real owner was in all cases, the *Rajaputra* who could sub-infeud, or increase taxes arbitrarily.[42] Thus it can be fairly concluded that the term *Rajaputra* was not the name of the caste, as we understand it today. There are also no instances to show if the different tribes regarded each other as anything other than Kashatriyas.

Rauta

Rauta or *Rawat* was the counterpart of the *Rajaputra*. This title too indicated a class of military vassals. The term *Rauta* appears frequently in the Chandela and Gahadvala inscriptions whereas in the Chaluklya and Chauhan records, the titles mostly used is the *Rajaputra*.[44]

The title *Rauta* seems to be the early vernacular form of the Sanskrit *Rajaputra* and possibly indicated a rank.[45] It has also been suggested that the title of *Rauta* is a corrupt form of *Rajyachyuta*, i.e. one deprived of a royal authority.[46] The Chandela grants indicate the grant of land to *Rautas* for military services, which was also the major obligation of his counterpart, *Rajaputra* as corroborated by the *Lekhapaddhati*.

In some cases the title of *Rauta* was conferred on the Brahmans who rendered religious services in the state as *Purohits*.[47] Govindachandra Gahadvala, for instance, conferred the rank of *Rauta* on Brahman Jaju Sharma, the chief priest of the Gahadvala court. In AD 1133, Govindachandra conferred a village on Brahman *Rauta* Jatesha Sharma. Incidentally, this Brahman's father was a *Rauta* whereas his grandfather was a *Thakkura*. From this epigraph it may be inferred that the rank of a *Rauta* was higher that that of a *Thakkura*.[48]

In AD 1177 Jayachandra Gahadvala granted a village to a Kshatriya *Rauta* Rajyadharavarman, who was the son of *Thakkura* Shri Vidyadhara and grandson of *Thakkura* Shri Jagatdhara.[49] The number of *Rautas* was far greater under the Gahadvalas than under the Chandelas.[50] A Gahadvala pillar inscription of AD 1197 makes the position of *Rauta* and *Ranaka* clear. The epigraph records the creation of a pillar by *Rauta* Ananda in reign of *Ranaka* Vijayakarna.[51]

On the basis of the existing evidence about the two titles of *Rajaputra* and *Rauta*, we may draw the following conclusions:

(i) The title *Rajaputra* was mostly popular among the Chauhans and the Gahadvalas, whereas its counterpart *Rauta* popular with the Chandelas.

(ii) Both *Rajaputra* and *Rauta* were mostly military beneficiaries.
(iii) There are hardly any instances to show if the *Rajaputras* or *Rautas* were essentially the kinsmen of their overlord.
(iv) The rank of *Rauta* was, in all probability, higher than that of a *Thakkura*.
(v) A *Rajaputra* received land grants from a *Ranaka* on certain conditions such as providing a fixed contingent to his overlord besides collection of landrevenue and maintaining law and order in his fief.
(vi) Sometimes the title of a *Rauta* was conferred on the Brahmins in recognition of their services to the State.

The title *Rauta* was thus generally applied to a *Rajaputra* in early medieval Chandela and Gahadvala records. Although the title has been mostly applied in cases of the Chauhan and Chalukya royal families, it was also common among the Brahmin, Kshatriya and Kayasthas of Bundelkhand during the period under review.

Thakkura

Another title used synonymously was the *Thakkura*. This title is found in early medieval records from the eighth to thirteenth century. The term *Thakkurs* denoting a feudatory continued to be in use in the Persian works until the early thirteenth century,[52] which may suggest the continuation of this title at the time of the Turkish invasion of northern India.

The *Thakkura*, it appears, did not possess a princely status and was possibly identified as such when he had fallen from some royal status. Epigraphic evidence suggests that some Brahmin and Kshatriya families who were related to the royal families, but could not succeed to the throne for some reasons, were thus placed in a subordinate position and were identified as such.[53]

A number of medieval inscriptions, mostly from Central India, record the grant of villages by different kings to the *Thakkuras*.[54]. As in case of *Rauta*, the title *Thakkura* applied both to the Brahmins as well as the Kshatriyas. While the former received the land grants for performing certain religious duties, the latter were recipients of land grants for their chivalrous deeds of martial services.[55] However, whether the title *Thakkura* was used as a surname or as a designation by the Brahmins and the Kshatriyas is still uncertain.

The early medieval records mention that those Brahmans who were primarily engaged in the worship of some deity, were also conferred the title of *Thakkura*.[58] It would be equally interesting to note that there are also several epigraphs wherein it is recorded that while a Brahman bore the title of a *Rauta*, his father or grandfather were known as *Thakkuras*.

It is possible that in the early period, the ancestors of the Brahman *Rauta* once functioned as priests while the grandsons rose to the position of a fief-holder due to the property gifts to that family. It is also possible that the Brahman family was a part of the aristocracy and the grandson had simply been given the title of *Thakkura* to differentiate him from his father and grandfather. The title of *Thakkura* continued to be in use till the end of the Gahadvala dynasty.[59] In many cases, while the author of the grant was a *Thakkura*,[60] the recipient of that grant was also a *Thakkura*.

The *Thakkuras* were subordinate to the *Ranakas* who possessed the land grants on their behalf.[61] Again, the title of *Thakkura* appears to be lower than that of a *Rauta*.[62] In northern India, the term *Thakkura* became common feudal epithet and was applied indiscriminately to the officials of the different castes and categories.[63] It appears that the title of *Thakkura* which began to be used from the nineth century onwards,[64] had come to connote a chief, warrior or lord in general by the twelfth and early thirteenth centuries.[65] It was applied to the class of ruling landed aristocracy, which was divided into many grades such as the *Rais*, *Ranas* *Rautas*.[66]

It is also generally believed that the titles *Thakkura*, which was prevalent only in northern India, is of foreign origin. It is also held that the word is derived from the Tartar word *Tigara* or *Tegor*. It is also opined that *Thakkura* is a word of Yuoh-chi-Thokari language, which was brought by its speakers to India.[67] The title is also found in the twelfth century literary source the *Rajatarangini*.[68]

An inscription of AD 1130 from Rajasthan records that a *Thakkura* called Rajadeva of the Guhila family acted as a vassal of Rayapala, the Chauhan king of Nadol,[69] who is turn owed allegiance to the Gujarat king Kumarapala.[70] Jayachandra's son and successor Harishchandra is mentioned in the Machhlishahr grant[71] to have granted a village in AD 1197 to one Rahiyaka, son of *Thakkura* Madanu of Kashyap gotra. Incidentally the writer of the land grant is also a *Thakkura*.

Ranaka, Rana, Rai

The early medieval Sanskrit and Persian chroniclers have used the title *Rai*, *Ranaka* or *Rana* for a powerful Hindu chief. The *Lekhapaddhati*[71] has defined the obligations of a fief-holder in early medieval Gujarat and Marwar. According to one of its charters, the king could grant a *Ranaka*, a country (*desha*) probably meaning a *Mandala*. In the second charter, the *Ranaka* undertook to pay all the dues to the grantees. Last the *Ranaka* sub-infeuded a village to a *Rajaputra*, who was to furnish a fixed number of contingents to the *Ranaka*.[73] Thus a *Ranaka* came next to *Rajana* and *Mahamatya* in feudal hierarchy.

The title *Ranaka*, like other feudal titles, was conferred on a vassal connected with land. The *Ranakas* have been referred to as feudatory vassals of Prithviraj Chauhan.[74] There are instances when a person of lower rank like Mahttara (one associated with the local affairs) rose higher in status and acquired the rank of a *Ranaka*.[75]

Although, originally the title of *Ranaka* applied to the members of the ruling family, in course of time, it came to be extended to other categories also.[76] The Chandela grants refer to the *Ranakas* who were of considerable importance and were being served by the *Thakkuras*.[77] Under the Gahadvalas[78] the *Ranakas* who received land grants gradually set up their independent principalities by the end of the Gahadvala rule.[79] Thus the title *Ranaka* referred to one of the grades of vassals and came next to *Samanta*. He appears to have enjoyed a fair degree of autonomy in his territory and even executed religious grants without the permission of the overlord.

Conclusion

The above study of a few important feudal titles of the twelfth century which were commonly used in northern and western India, particularly in Rajasthan attempts to ascertain the relative position of *Rajaputra*, *Rauta*, *Thakkura* and *Ranaka* in the feudal hierarchy.

By the time of the Turkish invasions (at the close of the twelfth century), many of the well known Rajput clans came to be recognized as belonging to the Kshatriya caste, having connected themselves with Sun, Moon, Fire and Sea, etc., with a view to proving their hierarchical status.

Second important aspects of feudal hierarchy during the period under review shows that there was the practice of giving land grants to sons, relatives or other members of the clan, which further led to the development of the lord-vassal relationship. The system became fairly popular during the chief contenders of powers like the Chauhans of Sakambhari, Chalukyas of Anhilwara and Paramaras of Malwa as is established on the basis of contemporary archaeological and literary evidence.

To sum up, the socio-economic factors leading to hierarchy and power, with special reference to western Indian state of Rajasthan, characterizes the climax as well as the downfall of feudal hierarchy during the twelfth century.

NOTES

1. Fakhruddin Mubarak, *Tarikh-i-Fakhruddin Mubarak* or *Fakhr-i-Mudhir*, Aligarh Rotograph, p. 22; Hasan Nizami, *Tajul-Maasir* (MS. copy of late Prof. Mohammad Habib), pp. 94, 108, 184, 185 and 227; Ziauddin Barani, *Tarikh-i-Ferozshahi*, Calcutta, text, 1862, pp. 36, 52, 59, 125, 163, 213, etc.
2. For further details, see Dashratha Sharma, *Early Chauhana Dynasties*, Delhi, 1959, p. 245 who cites the examples of the Rashtrakutas who described themselves as Yadavas of lunar family, though their earlier records have nothing to say about it and the Pratiharas became Raghuvamsis describing themselves as Lakshmana's descendants. The Paramaras too adopted a myth from the *Ramayana*, *Rajasthan Bharati*, Vol. III, part ii, p. 28.
3. For a detailed study of the feudal elements prior to the twelfth century, see B.N.S. Yadava's chapter on the 'Ruling Landed Aristocracy', in *Society and Culture in Northern India*, Allahabad, 1973. The information in this paper is largely based on the above mentioned book.
4. Dashratha Sharma (ed.), *Rajasthan Through the Ages*, Bikaner, 1966, p. 341. The term used here is *avalgana* in context of the personal as well as military feudal service. The epigraphic reference of this term is found in the Dudhpani inscription of the eighth century and literary sources such as the *Bharateshwara Bahubali Rasa* of Salibhadra; the *Kanhadadeprabandha* of Padmanabha and *Virataparya* of Sali Suri. Dashratha Sharma, ibid. See also L. Gopal, 'Samanta—Its varying significance in ancient India', *Journal of Royal Asiatic Society*, parts I-II, April 1963.
5. For the rise of the Gurjaras, see K.M. Munshi, *Glory that was Gurjaradesha*, Bombay, 1955; R.C. Majumdar (ed.), *History and the Culture of Indian People*, Vols. IV and V, Bombay, 1951; B.N. Puri, *History of the Gurjara Pratiharas*, Bombay, 1957.
5. For details about the Guhilas see G.H. Ojha, *Udaipur Rajya Ka Itihas*, Hindi, Ajmer, 1932; *Rajputana Ka Itihas*, 3 vols, Ajmer, 1936.
6. For the Chauhans, see Dashratha Sharma, *Early Chauhana Dynasties*, Delhi, 1959.
7. For details, see R. Niyogi, *History of the Gahadavala Dynasty*, Calcutta, 1956; S.K. Mitra, *The Early Rulers of Khajuraho*, Calcutta, 1958.
8. For the detailed history of the Chandelas, see N.S. Bose, *History of Chandalas*, Calcutta, 1956.

9. For details, see A.K. Majumdar, *Chaulukas of Gujarat*, Bombay, 1956.
10. For Paramaras, see D.C. Ganguly, *History of the Paramara Dynasty*, Dacca, 1933.
11. Dashratha Sharma (ed.), *Rajasthan Through the Ages*, Bikaner, 1966, Vol. I, pp. 261-2.
12. R.S. Sharma, *Indian Feudalism*, Calcutta, 1965; D.C. Sircar (ed.), *Land System and Feudalism in Ancient India*, Calcutta, 1980.
13. The tribal view is held by A.C. Lyall and Daniel Thorner in *Feudalism in History*, p. 142 whereas the feudal view is held by Baden Powell, *Indian Village Community*, London, 1896; and Max Weber, *The Religion of India*, pp. 53-4) cited in B.N.S. Yadava, op. cit., p. 184.
14. Marc Bloch (tr.), *Feudal Society*, London, 1965, Vol. I, p. 167. The Kamauli Plate of AD 1134 records the grant of a tract of land to a chief by one of the ancestors, Govin Chandra Gahadvala. Vatsraja, one of the descendants of this chief, has been mentioned as a feudatory of the emperor, *Epigraphica Indica* (*E.I.*), Vol. IV, no. 12.
15. A number of land grants were made over to the Brahmana or religious institutions for spiritual welfare of their ancestors with little or no obligations on the donees. B.N.S. Yadava, op. cit., p. 147; for such land grants see also R.S. Sharma, op. cit., *passim*.
16. The principality given to a vassal in return for military service is mentioned as *Bhatabhukti*: Dashratha Sharma (ed.), op. cit., p. 340 fn. 3. The feudatories owed an obligation to join their overlord whenever the latter marched against an enemy.
17. B.N.S. Yadava, op. cit., p. 147.
18. Ibid.
19. P.A. Mankad (ed.), *Aprajitapracch*, Baroda, 1950, p. 201.
20. *Chaturamsika alparajah shestu Rajapurakah*, ibid., p. 188.
21. R.S. Sharma, op. cit., pp. 85-6.
22. See list in R.K. Chaudhary's article in *Journal of Indian History*, Vol. XXXVII, p. 389.
23. K. Antonova, et al., *A History of India*, Eng. tr. K. Judelson, Moscow, 1979, Vol. I, p. 189. The authors have described Indian feudalism during this period as a two tier process: On the one hand more and more lands were being distributed as grants; on the other hand the village officials frequently gained powers among the villagers and assuming the role of petty feudal land-owners, ibid., pp. 189-90.
24. Ibid., pp.189-96.
25. C.D. Dalal and G.K. Shrigondeker (eds.), *Lekhapaddhati*, G.O.S., no. XIX, pp. 7-9.
26. For reference to *Rajaputra* in Gupta records, see *E.I.*, XII, p. 142; *Indian Antiquery* (*I.A.*) XIV, p. 102; XVIII, p. 136.
27. Sulaiman, *Sisilat-ut-Tawarikh*, tr. Elliot and Dowson, *History of India As Told by Its Own Historians*, Allahabad, 1968, Vol. I, p. 7.

28. *E.I.*, IX, no. 9b.
29. Ibid., XI, p. 4, nos. xvi and xvii.
30. Ibid., IX, no. 9 b.
31. Ibid., XI, pp. 1-5.
32. Dashratha Sharma, op. cit., p. 202.
33. *E.I.*, XIII, no. 18 b.
34. Ibid., IX, no. 9 b.
35. H.C. Ray, *Dynastic History of Northern India*, Vol. II, p. 1183.
36. See n. 19.
37. Dashratha Sharma, op. cit., p. 340 fn. 3.
38. *Lekhapaddhati*, p. 7.
39. Buddha Prakash, *Aspects of Indian History and Civilization*, Agra, 1965, p. 224.
40. Ibid., p. 225.
41. According to the *Lakhapaddhati*, the merchant or accountant is entrusted with the work of collection on condition of paying 3,000 *drammas* as main revenue; 216 *drammas* as reward to the *Panchakula* and 40 *drammas* for sundry expenses. Furthermore, the main revenue is to be paid in three instalments. Ibid., p. 9.
42. R.S. Sharma, op. cit., p. 202.
43. For example, see *E.I.*, VI, no. 20; XX, no. 14 c; II, pp. 3-4; For reference to the *Rautas* in the Cahadvala inscriptions, see *E.I.*, III, pp. 19-21, XV, pp. 7-8; II, pp. 16-22.
44. R.S. Sharma, op. cit., p. 193.
45. Ibid.
46. D.C. Sircar, *Indian Epigraphy*, Delhi, 1965, p. 343.
47. R. Nyogi, *History of the Gahadavla Dynasty*, Calcutta, 1956, Appendix B, nos. 50, 52-6, 58.
48. R.S. Sharma, op. cit., p. 133, fn. 5.
49. *I.A.* II, pp. 27-8.
50. R.S. Sharma, op. cit., p. 175.
51. Cunningham, *Archaeological Survey of India (A.S.I.)*, *Reports*, Vol. IX, pp. 120-30; R. Niyogi, op. cit., Appendix B.
52. *Fakhri-Mudbir*, op. cit., text., p. 33.
53. V. Upadhyay, *The Socio-Religious Conditions of Northern India*, Varanasi, 1964, p. 52.
54. *E.I.*, IV, pp. 111-12; XX, pp. 133-4; *I.A.*, XV, pp. 7-13; XVIII, pp.138-9, Cunningham, op. cit., XXI, p. 49.
55. *E.I.*, XX, p. 133.
56. Ibid., Cunningham, op. cit., XX, p. 49; *I.A.*, XVIII, pp. 138-9.
57. *E.I.*, XDI, pp. 275-6; ibid., XX, pp. 232-3.
58. Ibid., IV, p. 131; VII, p. 131; VII, p. 100; XIII, p. 217; XIX, p. 292.
59. See Govindachandra's grant of AD 1197, *E.I.*, X, pp. 93-100.

60. Ibid.
61. Ibid., II, pp. 20-1.
62. See supra fn. 48.
63. R.S. Sharma, op. cit., p. 197.
64. Buddha Praksh, op. cit., p. 240; B.N.S. Yadava, p. 182.
65. Ibid., p. 137.
66. M. Habib, Int. to Elliot and Dowson, *History of India*, Vol. II (Aligarh edition), p. 38.
67. Buddha Prakash, op. cit., p. 260.
68. *Rajatarangini*, VIII, p. 554; M. Habib, op. cit., p. 44 has compared the *Thakkuras* and *Rajaputras* with the knights of medieval Europe.
69. Cunningham, *A.S.I.* (Western Circle), 1908-9, p. 45.
70. B.N.S. Yadava, op. cit., p. 151.
71. *E.I.*, Vol. X, pp. 93-130.
72. C.D. Dalal et al. (eds.), op. cit., p. 7.
73. Ibid.
74. *Khartaragachhapatavali*, tr. in *Indian Historical Quarterly*, Vol. XXVI, 1950, p. 227.
75. *E.I.*, Vol. XVIII, p. 257.
76. R.S. Sharma, op. cit., p. 163.
77. *E.I.*, Vol. II, pp. 20-1.
78. *I.A.*, Vol. XVIII, pp. 18-19; II, pp. 10-28.
79. R.S. Sharma, op. cit., p. 174, fn. 4.

PART 4

MISCELLANEOUS

India's Maritime Tradition: A Review

Satish Chandra

Many wrong myths and legends regarding India's maritime traditions have been sedulously fostered over a long time especially during the colonial period. Scholars, both Indian and foreign, examined them in the period following the end of the colonial rule, and a number of them have been cast aside or radically revised. Thus, notions such as reluctance on the part of Indian, specifically Hindu traders to travel across the salt seas on account of *dharmik* inhibitions and, in consequence, leaving overseas trade first to the Arabs, and later to the Portuguese and their European successors, or that the Indian traders were mere peddlers, have been largely discarded. However, there is a persistent belief that throughout history, Indians showed little spirit of sea venturesomeness and sea-daring. Also, that the contribution of the Indians in charting sea-lanes or undertaking long sea-voyages has been marginal. A quick review shows these notions to be largely unfounded. The spirit of sea-daring was not the preserve of any one nation, but has passed from one to the others in response to challenges and opportunities. Thus, the Phoenicians were famous for sea-daring in antiquity. They were followed by Egyptians, Greeks, Romans. Later, the Arabs, Norse-men, Venice, Genoa, Spain and Portugal came into the picture. The English forged ahead in the time of Queen Elizabeth I. English sea-daring was made famous by the 'pirate' Drake. Pirates like Drake have been called the first 'free enterprisers'!

It is now accepted that the Indian maritime tradition goes back to the third millennium BC, when people from the Harappan civilization had an active sea trade with Mesopotamia. Cuneiform achival texts, royal decrees, temple inscriptions, etc., refer to continuous arrival of ships from Dilmun, Magar and Meluhha. Meluhha has been identified as the lands constituting the Harappan civilization. The ships from Meluhha

* Based on a talk given at the Centre for Advanced Study, National Institute of Science, Bangalore, January 2003.

not only brought timber, stone, cereals, oils, etc., which were lacking in Mesopotamia, but also textiles and ivory. There are references to water-buffalo and peacock which were of Indian origin, and had perhaps been sent as gifts. On their return voyage, the ships brought not only woollens, and perishable manufactures produced by the skilful artisans of Mesopotamia, but possibly copper from the copper-rich mines of Oman from Dilmun (Bahrain). This must have supplemented the copper-mines of Rajasthan. The extent of this two-way trade is testified to by the discovery of interpreters of the Meluhhan language in Mesopotamia. From this scholars have concluded that a colony of Meluhhan traders must have been living in Mesopotamia at the time.[1]

It is clear that the Meluhha-Mesopotamian sea-trade represented almost the first extensive sea-trade in the world. As a modern historian points out 'The result of urbanization and the growth of trade was the establishment of occupational groups such as merchants, sailors, artisans and moneylenders around the market place who, in time, would forge wider land and sea contacts linking the disparate economics and cultures of the Indian Ocean'.[2] Before the beginning of urbanization, fishermen were only farming the seas and exchanging their produce with food gatherers and hunters. Urbanization, as we know, began first in Mesopotamia along the Euphrates, in Egypt along the Nile, in India along the Indus river, and in China along the Yagtezekiang river. Since China was far away and largely self-sufficient, trade, including sea-trade, began first between the first of these three, viz., India, Mesopotamia and Egypt. We have little evidence, at present, of sea-trade between the Harappans and ancient Egypt via the Red Sea. But such a possibility cannot be ruled out. Lothal in Gujarat was the main Harappan port, but there were other ports also.

Although the Harappan civilization collapsed by the middle of the second millennium BC, Indian maritime skills survived, as is evident from oral traditions preserved in later literary works. The Indus and Ganga river systems provided a nursery for the learning of boat skills.[3] References in the *Rig Veda* are also cited as evidence of a continued maritime tradition. The *Rig Veda* uses the word *sindhu* fifty times, and refers to sea going vessels with oars and sails, high sea-winds and rough seas leading to ship wrecks, etc. the sea-god, Varuna, helped these sea-farers in distress. Thus, the Aryans, were not unfamiliar with the high seas and sea-fearing.[4] The first millennium BC is considered to be a period of rapid expansion of trade between the Persian Gulf and the Mediterranean due to the rise in West Asia of the Assyrian empire, followed by the Sassaian empire. Their contribution in linking the Indian Ocean to the Mediterranean in trade has been largely forgotten. The pioneering role of these empires in building sea-trade with the Orient was followed by the Greeks and the Romans. Undue emphasis continues to be given to the Greek and Roman trade with India, largely because of the book *Periplus of the Erithrean Sea* which emphasizes Greek sea-trade. The finds of Roman gold-coins in South India has led to the wrong belief that this was the main focus of India's overseas trade in early historic times.[5]

Monsoon and Sea-voyages

Long sea-voyages seen to have begun in the first millennium BC in the Indian Ocean. This was on account of the gradual understanding and utilization of the monsoon winds.[6] The monsoon itself was not the discovery of any one individual, but the result of a slow accretion of knowledge and experience over a long period of time by sailors, sea-men, etc., living around the Indian Ocean rim. The establishing of the regularity of the wind system shortened the time of the journey to Sri Lanka, and also opened the way to trade with South-East Asia. As F.F. Armesto, observes, 'The reason for the long sea-faring, sea daring tradition of the Indian Ocean lies in the regularity of the wind system. The predictability of a home-ward wind made the Indian Ocean the most benign environment in the world for long range voyaging.' He concludes , 'When sailing conditions in the Indian Ocean are compared with those elsewhere, the extraordinary role of (this) ocean becomes intelligible. This is where long range navigation was probably born'.[7]

Apart from the long distance voyaging from Basra in the Persian Gulf and the Suez harbour in the Red Sea across the western coast of India to Sri Lanka, and along the coast to Burma. Malaysia and South-East Asia, cross ocean voyages across the Indian Ocean, both in the eastern and the western parts, began during this period. Using the 5-8 degree north equatorial counter current which goes east to west from September to February, and reverses itself in the monsoon season, the Austronasian speaking people travelled from South-East Asia to East Africa and to the Madagascar Island for trade. They also settled there, as their physical remains, musical instruments, etc., testify. However, this did not lead to the establishment of any regular sea trade between South-East Asia and Africa. What did begin, and grew was the Indian connection with Java and Sumatra using the 5-8 degree north equatorial counter current, across the Andaman Sea. This was aided by the strong Indian tradition of astronomy which enabled the charting of the seas with the aid of stars. The Andaman Islands crossing was a trecherous one, and it seems, was the spot for many wreckages. The memories of these wreckages are to be found in later literature including references from the lost *Brihat Katha-Sarit Sagara*. There is a speculation that these early voyages provided the basis of the stories of Sindbad the Sailor—his discovery of the coconut, and of cannibalism in some of the islands (Andamans, possibly Papua New Guinea) are an index of this. But this is still speculative.

India and South-East Asia and Beyond

There is a strong tradition that following Ashoka's Kalinga War in second century BC, 2000 families from Orissa (Kalinga) migrated to Bali. Their journey is commemorated by the annual Beth or Bali Yatra which commences/culminates on Kartika Purnima. These voyages used the 5-8 degree north equatorial counter-current, and also travelled from Tambralipti across the Bay of Bengal, as a modern study shows (Figure 1). Ashoka is also supposed to have sent his seminarists to Malaya and Java-Sumatra for the spread of Buddhism.

During the first millennium AD, trade and cultural contacts between India and South-East Asian countries grew rapidly. We are told that the technique of rice transplantation was brought to Java-Sumatra from India. This led to the growth of agricultural production and helped in the rise of monarchical states, as distinct from local chieftainship. These new kingdoms were strengthened by the introduction of Hindu rituals, cosmic Gods, and the preparation of genologies by brahmans. While the chiefs and their landed associates were the main beneficiaries of Hindu influence, Buddhism grew apace during the period by emphasizing social equality and individual effort. Both Hinduism and Buddhism interacted with each other, as is shown by the Buddhist temple of Borobadur in Java where there are panels containing scenes from *Ramayana*. Thus, trade and cultural interaction with India were important factors in the rise of local kingdoms in South-East Asia. The rise of these kingdoms, in turn, strengthened trade and cultural contacts between India and this region.

Movement of goods, human beings, ideas and institutions between India and the countries of South-East Asia, was a two way traffic. It was the product of remarkable sea venturesomeness and daring on the part

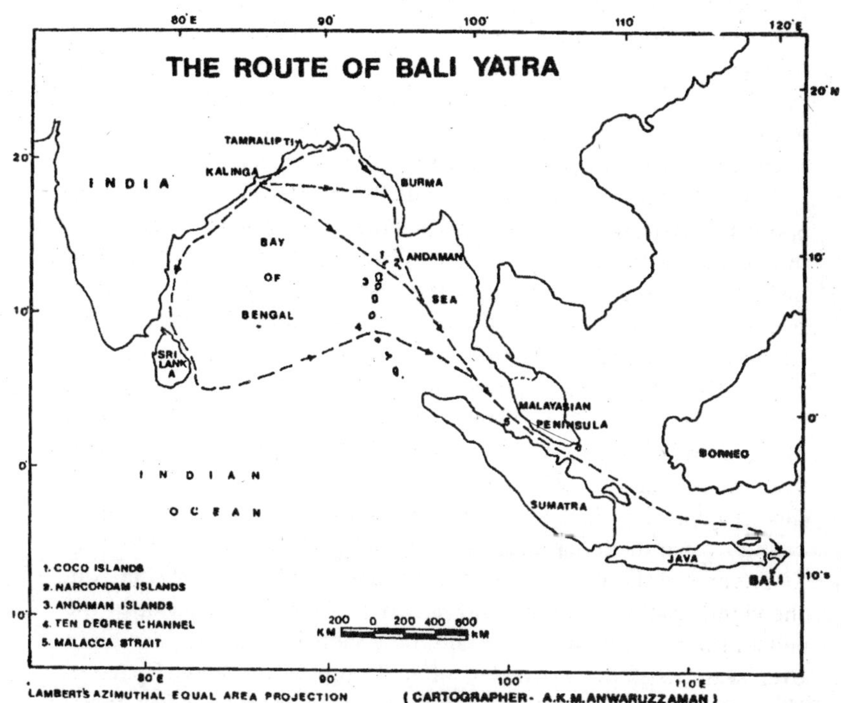

Source: *JIOS*, Vol. 1 (ii), March 1994.

Figure 1: The Route of the Bali Yatra—A Scientfic Appraisal

of the Indian and Austronasian sailors and navigators. The range, magnitude and mutually beneficial nature of this interaction is without parallel in the ancient world, and even in the pre-modern world. However, unlike the European advent into America, it did not lead to the decimation of the local peoples, or of their cultures.

While Indian's cultural contribution to the countries of South-East Asia is recognized, that it was made possible by a strong Indian maritime tradition in largely ignored. Indian trade and cultural influence extended from South-East Asia to the Asian mainland upto Annam or Cambodia, as exemplified by the Ankor Vat temples, and the Thai capital Ayuthia (Ayodhya) which was destroyed by its Burmese rivals in 1767. From South-East Asia, Indian traders and merchants extended their activities upto China, with Canton (Guangdzu) being a major centre for Indian trade. Colonies of Indian traders settled there. Here, again, the initiative seems to have been taken by the Indian traders and navigators. Later, Chinese traders sailed up to South-East Asia and Malacca. In the thirteenth century there were colonies of Chinese traders in Bengal and Malabar, though by far and large, Chinese traders did not go beyond Malacca. Indian and Arab traders carried Chinese porcelain, silks, etc., from Malacca and Malabar to the Persian Gulf and Red Sea ports. They further expanded their direct trade with China, after the fourteenth century when the Ming rulers banned foreign trade for the Chinese.[8]

The arrival of the Arabs as traders in South and South-East Asia from the eighth century onwards did not lead to the displacement of the Indian traders. Although the Arabs did establish a leading position in over seas trade, the expansion of trade provided enough space of Hindus, Jews, etc., to participate in the intra-Asian trade. In fact, intra-Asian trade reached the highest level by the fifteenth century which, precisely, was the reason why Europeans sought a direct entry into it. Till then, although there was rivalry in trade between the Europeans and Arabs, no European country had made any attempt to cut out other traders or to establish domination or control over a port, much less a part of the sea. As K.M. Panikkar, says, 'the idea of sovereignty over the sea except in narrow straits was unknown to Asian conception'. He points out that following their belief in the freedom of the seas, many Indian rulers, such as the Pallavas and the Cholas, maintained strong navies, but used them only for the protection of the coast, for putting down piracy, and for transporting troops when needed to fight on land.[9] The expeditions of Rajendra Chola I to Java, Sumatra and the Malay Peninsula during the eleventh century, and the seven grand expeditions of the Chinese Admiral, Cheng He, between 1405 and 1433, have to be seen in this context. The Chola naval expeditions did not aim at any conquest of territory, though the capital of the powerful Sri Vijay kingdom was attacked. As B. Arunachalam has shown by interpreting the place names mentioned in the inscription of Rajendra Chola, the Chola navy went through the Sunda straits between Sumatra and Java, reached the Malacca Channel, and travelled to the Malay coast (Figure 2). Malacca and Sunda were the two main choke points for trade with China. Perhaps the Chola ruler wanted to free them from the stranglehold of Sri Vijaya. That trade to China was gaining in importance at the time is shown by many studies. Close link with Malabar, and the numerous trade embassies exchanged by it with the Chinese rulers were an indication of this. Of the three Chola mission to the Chinese Emperor, the mission sent in 1077 consisted of 72 persons, most of whom were traders.[10]

The question is: Why did the Chola naval expeditions to South-East Asia cease? The answer seems to be that apart from domestic factors, there was no longer need for such expeditions because by the end of the eleventh century, the power of Sri Vijaya empire had declined, and there were no barriers to trade between India and China, and between India and the Spice Islands where spices were exchanged for Indian textiles with the help of local traders.

Again the question arises: What were the objectives of the Cheng He expeditions which, at its height consisted of 62 to 137 ships and upto 28,000 sailors, soldiers, etc.? It was not to convert the Indian Ocean into a 'Chinese Lake', as some modern Western observers have proposed. For that it would have been necessary to set up fortifications and naval bases, as the Portuguese were to do later. But no such attempt was made by Cheng He. Nor was any attempt made to control or divert trade. The expeditions were meant to, and did demonstrate the power and majesty of the Middle Kingdom. They also forced a few rulers, including the ruler of Sri Lanka, to acknowledge Chinese suzerainty. But the Chinese suzerainty sat light. In most cases, it only implied sending tribute. In Chinese tradition, any embassy implied sending of tribute, which meant accepting Chinese suzerainty. Thus, even trade goods specially high quality items such as precious or semi-precious stones, aromatics, spices, etc., were called tribute. The grand and enormously costly expeditions of Cheng He, apart from demonstrating Chinese naval superiority, were thus of little advantage. No wonder the cost conscious bureaucrats but a stop to future expeditions in Cheng He's own life time,

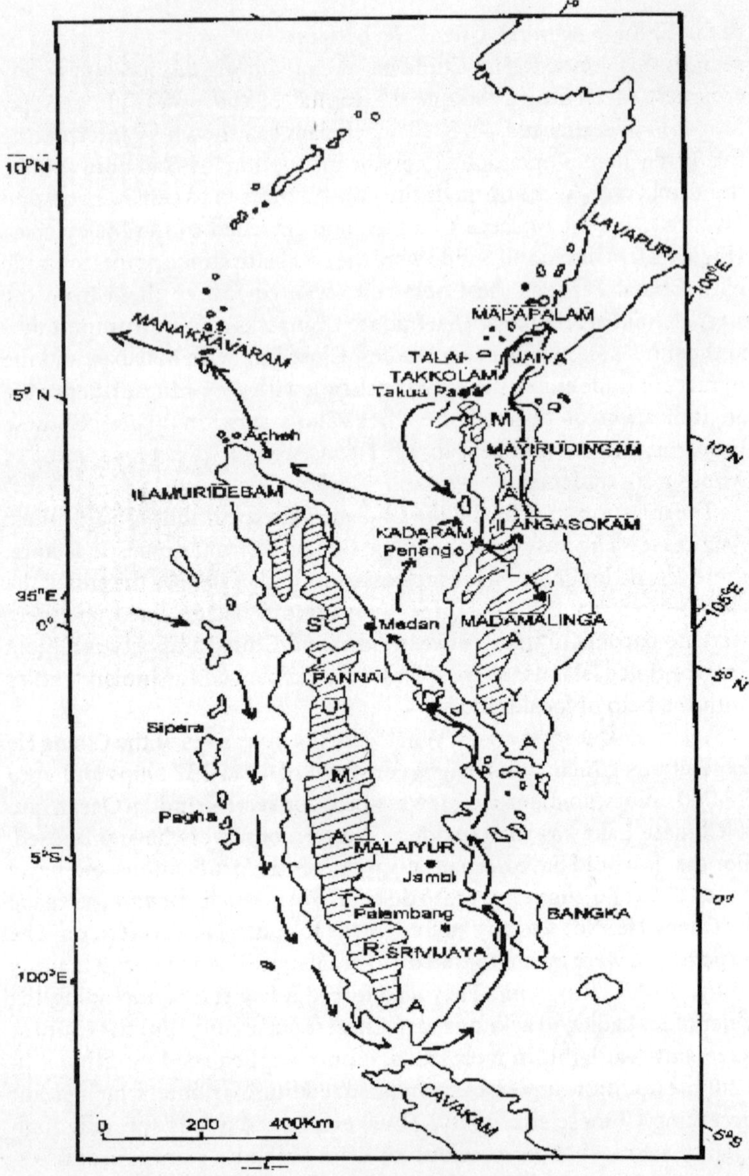

Source: *JIOS*, Vol. 10 (iii), December 2002.

Figure 2: Conquest Areas of Rajendra Ghola in South-East Asia
(Arrows indicate detection of movement)

and that Cheng He was largely forgotten. In the process, the Chinese ruler also banned Chinese foreign trade to prevent export of silver to pay for import of foreign goods. Such a ban was never imposed by any India ruler, despite their preoccupation with domestic wars and conquest.

Portuguese and Indian Maritime Tradition

Unlike Cheng He, the Portuguese were very clear about their objectives in seeking a direct sea passage to India: they wanted to exclude the Moors, i.e. the Turks from the profitable Oriental trade in spices, and to establish Portuguese domination on the lands and the seas beyond. The conversion of the heathens was also mentioned, almost as a sop to the Pope—but never seriously pursued, except in Goa. None of the major objectives of the Portuguese could be realized. Although the trade in spices was declared a royal monopoly, and enforced by brutally sinking or confiscating all those ships which defined it, the blockade was found leaking like a sieve. As in now well established by the middle of the sixteenth century, as much spices were reaching Europe over land via the Persian Gulf and the Red Sea as before.[11] The Portuguese found that the intra-Asian trade was several time more profitable than the entire Asian trade to Europe, and that Indian and Arab traders could not be displaced from it, because they knew the local markets and had local contacts. Also, the Portuguese were too few in numbers—the total population of Portugal at the time was two million! In addition, in South-East Asia, spices could only be procured in exchange for Indian textiles.

Hence, for the Portuguese the Asian trade became more important than expanding trade to Europe. In consequence, their earlier effort to exclude Indians and Arabs (Moors) from trade had to be modified by introducing a system of *cartaz* or permits. Thus, the Portuguese hardly changed the pattern of intra-Asian trade but adjusted themselves into it. What, then, was their contribution? By discovering the direct sea-route to India, the Portuguese opened the way for a structural change in Asia's trade with Europe. Om Prakash, points out 'The overcoming of the transport technology barrier to the growth of trade between the two continents (meant that) the volume of this trade was no longer subject to the capacity constraints imposed by the availability of pack-animals and river boats in the Middle East'.[12] The beneficiaries of this, however, were not the Portuguese, but the Dutch, the English and the French who during the seventeenth and eighteenth centuries expanded Asia-

European trade by introducing new items of trade to Europe—textiles, indigo, tussar, silk, tea, etc.

What about the other naval achievements of the Portuguese and of Vasco da Gama personally? There has been a lively controversy in the matter. The traditional view was that Vasco da Gama's voyage to India was made possible by 'great advances made by the Portuguese in the fifteenth century in navigation and nautical sciences—in ship-building, cartography, and the making of navigational instruments. However, modern research has refuted most of these notions. With regard to navigational instruments, it has been pointed out that of the two Gujarati pilots given to Vasco da Gama at Malindi in East Africa by the local ruler, 'the elderly one was familiar with the use of the quadrant and the kamal, and perhaps also with the astrolabe. Apparently, he was more familiar with these new fangled instruments than were Vasco and his men'.[13]

The astrolabe and the quadrant are considered to be Greek instruments which had been modified and developed further by the Arabs. The astrolabe was a highly versatile observational and computational instrument and has been called the computer of the middle ages. With it time could be determined both in the daytime and at night, both in seasonal hours and in equal hours. The height of heavenly bodies and the height of distant bodies could also be measured. These were vital aids for navigation. We are told that it was possibly al Biruni who introduced the astrolabe into India where it was enthusiastically received by Hindu and Jain astronomers.[14] Firuz Shah was so impressed with the *ustarlab* (astrolabe) that he had installed two of them next to one of his minars.[15] It was at his instance that Mahendra Suri translated a Persian work on astrolabe into Sanskrit in 1370 and called it the *yantra raj* or kind of instruments.[16] This shows its widespread use and knowledge in India much before the coming of the Portuguese.[17]

Regarding cartography, with the help of astronomical calculations use, of latitudes, and knowledge of wind and ocean currents, Indian and Chinese astronomers had charted out the sea-routes from the Indian Ocean to South China Sea much before the coming of the Portuguese. The Arab geographers had greatly added to it. The Gujarati pilot abroad Vasco's ship had a map of the west coast of India 'marked in the manner of the Moors'. Likewise, when Vasco da Gama's successors reached Malacca, there were Malay and Javanese pilots they could employ. In fact, we are told that the sailing directions compiled by Francis Roderigue in 1512 was partly based on a Javanese chart which was among the treasures of Alburque's ship which went down off the coast of Sumatra in that year. Alburque says in a letter to that it was one of the best things he had ever seen. It showed the Cape of Good Hope, Portugal, the land of Brazil, the Red Sea, the Persian Gulf, the Spice Islands, the navigation of the Chinese, 'all the names marked in Javanese script'.[18]

Likewise, we have reference to the Arab *Rahnama* going back to the twelfth century showing the sea-routes of the Indian Ocean. Ibn Majid the leading Arab geographer of the time, and himself a keen navigator, who has been wrongly identified as the pilot who guided Vasco's ships to Calicut,[19] says '. . . everyone knows his own coast best, although God is all knowing, and it is certain that the Cholas live nearer to those coasts (the Bay of Bengal) than anyone else, so we need them, and their *qiyas* (techniques of stellar measurements) as a guide'.[20]

Thus, in the field of sea-charting, the Portuguese used the knowledge acquired by the navigators and the sea-men of the region. As a navigator, Vasco da Gama's knowledge and expertise was indifferent. Thus, for two weeks he was lost in the South Atlantic equatorial sea on account of wrong charting on his part. As a modern critic, F.F. Armesto, remarks: 'Curiously, perhaps, Vasco's real importance might be thought to be outside the Indian Ocean. . . . By revealing the nature of the wind system of the South Atlantic, Vasco's voyage created the possibility of maritime link between Europe, Africa and much of South America'.[21]

The crucial question is the navigational superiority of the Portuguese ships and their cannons. In terms of sea-worthiness and carrying capacity, the ships Vasco brought to India were not superior to those operating in the Indian Ocean region. The three ships—two *naus* and a *caravelle* which Vasco brought with him to Calicut, were quite small. The tonnage of the two *naus* was 150 tons each, while the *caravelle* was smaller. The total number of sailors, gunners was 148 or 178 only. As against this, the ships operating in the Indian Ocean were upwards of 250 tons, with the Chinese junks going up to 1,000 tons. However, Vasco's ships carried 20 bronze guns between them, and the hulls of the Portuguese ships had been strengthened to cope with the shock of their discharge. Although the Chinese had used naval guns from the thirteenth century, and Cheng He's ships had carried and used guns, the Indians had never seen their use. They did not even try to copy the Chinese junks, and their superior rudder and sails. We can only ask the question: why such lack of curiosity on the part of the Indian? Perhaps, this was because Cheng He's voyages did not effect in any way the existing pattern of trade or political relations in the region. Anyhow, armed with guns, the Portuguese easily dispersed the three naval expeditions of the Zamorin of Calicut between 1490 and 1504. In 1506 the Zamorin's navy consisted of, 60 *naus* and hundreds of *paraus*. In the last engagement, he had two guns. But these guns only threw stones![22]

It is argued that apart from guns, the Portuguese ships were also more manoeuverable than the Indian ships on account of superior rigging. This has been emphasized by K.N. Chaudhury, who contrasts the quadri-lateral lateen sails of the Indian ships with the multiple square sails of the Portuguese. He says: 'As a means of propulsion, the lateen sail was capable of achieving high speeds. The main drawback of the lateen rig was the size of the sail area, and the difficulty of tacking the ship in a head-wind. Even a small ship of 250 tons or so had a mainyard nearby as large as the mast itself. The main sail attached to the yard was enormously heavy and cumbersome for the crew to handle when the wind was fresh. To move from star-board tack to the port-tack, the sailors had to release the mainsheet and the tack purchase and move the entire sail to the opposite side. It was a difficult and dangerous operation and not often undertaken'.[23]

Despite the author's careful study of ships and ship construction in the region, his argument cannot be fully accepted without a deeper study of ships operating in the Indian Ocean at that time. It may also be noted that the Portuguese ships used the lateen sails for the caravel which was a fighting ship. The lateen square-rigged sail was adopted by ships in South and South-East Asia, which had a different naval tradition than that of the Arabs. The parau of Malabar was a small cargo ship, while we have reference to the prau used in the Tamilnad and North Sri Lanka, which had square sails, warts and hull ribs.[24]

For almost half a century during the early part of the sixteenth century, the Portuguese had to meet the naval expeditions of the Ottomon Turks, assisted by the Zamorin, the ruler of Gujarat and others. By 1505, the Zamorin had been able to recruit two renegade Venetians who undertook to train local artisans in the making of naval guns. In 1509, the Turks brought with them ships of the Mediterranean types and guns aided by the Venetians. In a hard-fought battle near Gujarat wherein the Zamorin joined, the Portuguese triumphed. Portuguese historians rate it as important as the battle of Lepanto (1570), for it gave them the mastery of the Indian Ocean. In repeated naval battles with the Turks till 1556, in which both sides used the same type of ships and guns, the Portuguese won—except in 1522 when the Turks defeated them outside the Red Sea, and closed the Red Sea to them. We can conclude that the Portuguese were superior in the art of navigation and seamanship, not in the construction of their ships or guns. They lost to the Dutch and the English only when the latter brought faster ships with a lower bow-line, and iron guns which had a flatter trajectory.

The Mughals and the Question of an Indian Navy

The question is: Why, despite its skilful artisans and fabled wealth and rich navigational traditions, India did not, following the advent of the Portuguese, use their example to build new types of ships and manufacture naval guns so that a navy could be brought into being in order to challenge the European domination of the seas? No easy answer can be given to this question. Regarding ship-building, recent research shows that the Indians were fairly quick to copy the Portuguese style of ships. Portuguese or Iberian style ships began to be built in the shipyards of Cochin, Bassein, etc. According to K.N. Chaudhury[25] '. . . After 1500 a new class of ships appeared in the Indian Ocean which had many of the characteristics of the Iberian galleons. The new ships were called "baghlas". In northern Gujarat and Malabar they were called "kotias". Thus, the hull design was changed in order to withstand the vibrations of the simultaneous firing of guns.' The adoption of the frame building tradition of European ships-building also strengthened the carrying capacity of the ships, and we hear of ships of upward of 1,600 tons being used for carrying of the ships, and we hear of ships of upward of 1,600 tons being used for carrying pilgrims and goods for *haj*. Using Indian teak which was superior to the oak and pine used for ship building in Europe, Indian built ships in the seventeenth century were in no way inferior in workmanship and finish, if not superior to the European built ships. In fact, many ships for the European companies were built in India.

The question of naval guns is however more complicated. From the sixteenth century, Indian ships had started carrying cannons, largely to cope with pirates. The number of guns carried by these ships had increased from 30 to 40. By the end of the seventeenth century, they were carrying fifty guns each. But the quality and positioning of the guns, the quality of the gunners and seamanship were uncertain factors. According to a French observer, the guns were for show only, and would not be able to withstand a single European ship. However, in 1690, a French ship *Legier* of forty guns ran off Goa into two ships of the ruler of Musqat in Oman of sixty and eighty guns respectively. The action and cannonade continued till nightfall when, under cover of darkness, the French ship escaped and arrived at Goa, in a shattered condition. Similarly, the Maratha naval chief, Kanhoji Angre, had guns with a striking capacity which could engage enemy ships before their guns could strike his ships.

Thus, technologically both ships and guns appear to have kept pace with the developments in these fields in Europe. Bronze guns were replaced by iron guns, and the shape and size of the ships suitably altered. It should be remembered that till the sixteenth and seventeenth centuries, there was no separate standing navy. Ships which carried cargoes were also armed with cannons and rowers, and could be called upon and used as a navy whenever needed. The construction of Indian ocean going ships had steadily increased, so that while there were 50 ocean going ships at Surat in 1650, their number had increased to 112 by the end of the century. So also the number of guns they carried. Thus technologically it would not have been difficult for the Mughals to bring together a navy, *if they had so desired.*

It appears that the Mughal Emperor did, on several occasions, discuss the feasibility to building a navy. According to the Italian, Niccolai Manucci, 'Having arranged the affairs of the kingdom with sufficient completeness, Aurangzeb, relying on the victories he had gained on land, thought of establishing the fear of himself at sea. He, therefore, resolved to set up a fleet with a considerable numbers of ships'. An Italian, Ortensio Bronziono, built a small ship fitted with guns, and demonstrated the capacity to fire in all directions. But Aurangzeb abandoned the project. Manucci says it was because he considered that 'to sail over the fight on the ocean was not the thing for the people of Hindustan but only suited European altertness and boldness'.[26]

Perhaps, Manucci was putting forward his own ideas and prejudices, because Aurangzeb considered the matter a number of times. As his correspondence shows, he noted that the Rumi Turks (Ottomon) and the Ferangis (European) were in a state of perpetual clash and conflict on the seas, and that the ruler of Musqat, who were Kharjites but Muslims 'have a well equipped fleet for battle on the sea'. He therefore instructed the Mughal *mutasaddi* of Surat port of 'strike an alliance with the Musqatise and provide them with a few ships and "ghurab" fighters, fully equipped with arms'. The purpose of this was 'to serve as convoy and guards on the sea, (and) enjoin upon him to drive off the ships of the hat-wearers, including the English and the Dutch robbers . . .'.[27]

However, Aurangzeb resiled even from this limited option, for fear that any action which would unite all the European powers—Dutch, English and French and the Portuguese against him, would be harmful.

Aurangzeb's refusal to build a navy can, perhaps be explained best by the reply of his wazir, Jafar Khan, to such a project. The wazir said 'There is no deficiency of money or timber or other materials to form a navy but there is lack of men to direct it.'[28] What the wazir implied was that only persons from the class of nobles could be asked to command ships. But the Mughal nobles, who were used to control land through their jagirs, and to be commanders of cavalry, would consider it demeaning to be asked to serve on the sea on board a ship.

The Mughal refusal or reluctance to build a navy was not due to their Central Asian origin. The Ottoman Turks who built a strong navy in the Mediterranean had also come from Central Asia. Nor was it due to absence of a maritime traditions, or absence of technological means—ships, guns, navigational instruments, etc. The reason was essentially sociological—based on the attitude of an essentially landed elite. On land, it refused to see the significance of the infantry armed with flint lock guns which was more than a match for the cavalry. However, command of cavalryman was considered a symbol of esteem.[29] The Mughals did however, by diplomacy and judicial use of force, ensure that the Indian Ocean remained open for the Indian traders, the situation being reversed only with the establishment of colonial rule over India.

Apart from Shivaji's limited efforts, and the effort of Kanhoji Angre, the only Indian ruler who tried to build a navy was Tipu. He set up a shipyard, provided it with training manuals, and planned to build 1,000 war ships. But he was the son of a mere soldier, no a Mughal nobleman. The English were alert to the threat posed to them by Tipu more than the Marathas who largely relied on light cavalry and swords. Hence they look steps to nip in the bud the challenge that Tipu's naval ambitions could pose to them.

NOTES

1. See Shirin Ratnagar, 'Meluhha in the Third Millennium B.C'., Paper presented to the Indian History Congress, Amritsar, 2002 (mimeo).
2. K. Mc Pherson, *The Indian Ocean, A History of Peoples and the Sea*, Delhi, O.U.P., 1993, p. 21.

3. See R. Mookerjee, *Indian Shipping: A History of the Sea Borne Trade and Maritime Activity of the Indians: From the Earliest Times*, London, 1912.
4. R.N. Nandi, *Aryans Revisited*, Delhi, 2001, pp. 101-5. According to him, Dwaraka and bet-Dwaraka were two of the ports used by the Aryans, some of whom had settled in the Kathiwar region. He argues that some Aryans came to India from Iran by sea, and knew the Persian Gulf and the Arab Sea.
5. Himanshu Ray, 'An Interpretation Essay on Maritime History', *Journal of Indian Ocean Studies*, Delhi, Vol.3, No. 2, March 1996, pp. 167-74.
6. The 'discovery' of the monsoon was for long attributed to a Greek, Hippalos, in AD 45 (almost like Vasco da Gama's 'discovery' of India in AD 1498). It is evident from the account of Pliny that Hippalos was the Greek word for the monsoon. Pliny, *Natural History*, VI, 26, pp: 100-1. See also Charles Verlinden in Satish Chandra (ed), *The Indian Ocean: Explorations in History, Commerce & Politics*, Delhi, Vikas, 1987, p. 33.
7. F.F. Armesto, 'The Indian Ocean in World History', in *Vasco da Gama and the Linking of Europe and Asia*, eds. Anthony Disney and Emily Bouh, O.U.P., 2000, pp. 14, 16.
8. See H.P. Ray, *Trade and Trade Routes between Indian and China, c. 140 BC–AD 1500*, largely using Chinese sources, Calcutta, 2003, pp. 242-6.
9. K.M. Panikkar, *Asia and Western Dominance*, reprint, Delhi, 1999, p. 29.
10. K.A. Nilkantha Shastri, 'The Colas', in *The Colas, Calukyas and Rajputs AD 985-1206*, eds. R.S. Sharma, K.M, Shrimali, Comprehensive History of India, Delhi, 1993, pp. 38-39; H.P. Ray, 'Maritime Relations between Tamil Nadu and China', *JIOS*, Vol.VI, No. 1, No. 1998, pp. 59-71, Vol. VII, No. 1, Nov. 1999, pp. 48-54, idem. 'Sino-Indian Historial Relations—Quilon (Kollam) and China', *JIOS*, Vol. VIII, No. 1, Aug. 2000, pp. 116-28.
11. Om Prakash, *European Commercial Enterprise in Pre-Colonial India*, C.U.P., 1998, pp. 45-6.
12. Ibid., p. 2.
13. John Villiers, 'Ships, Sea-Faring, and the Iconography of Voyages in the Age of Vasco da Gama', in *Vasco da Gama and Linking of Europe and Asia*, loc.cit., pp. 72, 74.
14. S.R. Sarma, 'Yantraraj: The Astrolabe in Sanskrit', *Journal of Indian Sciences*, 34 (1999), pp. 145-8.
15. Afif, *Tarikk-i-Firuz Shahi*, p. 370.
16. S.R. Sarma, 'From Yavani to Samskrtam Sanskrit Writing Inspired by Persian Works', *Journal Institute of Oriental Culture*, University of Tokyo, Tokyo, 2000, pp. 80-1.
17. Between the fourteenth and eighteenth centuries, more than a dozen manuals were composed in Sanskrit on the astrolabe. Many of these were based on Arabic and Persian sources (ibid).
18. John Villiers, loc. cit., pp. 75-6.

19. For the controversy about Ibn Majid, see Sanjay Subramanyam, *The Career and Legend of Vasco da Gama*, C.U.P., 1997, pp. 121-8.
20. Ahmad Ibn Majid, *Kitab ul Fawaid fi Usul-al bahr wa'l qawaid* (1490), tr. G.T. Tibbets, as *Arab Navigation in the Indian Ocean before the Coming of the Portuguese* (London, 1971). Ibn Majid was also the first to adjust the compass needle to move freely. (See Anwar A. Aleem, 'Aarb Navigation in the Indian Ocean', Ocean Dept., University of Alexandria, Cairo, p. 262.)
21. F.F. Armesto, loc. cit.
22. See K.S. Mathew, 'Navigation in the Arabian Sea during the Sixteenth Century—A Comparative Study of Indigenous and Portuguese Navigation', in *Ship Building and Navigation in the Indian Ocean Region*, AD *1400-1800* (ed. K.S. Mathew), Delhi, 1997, pp. 26-43.
23. K.N. Chaudhary, *Trade and Civilization in the Indian Ocean*, C.U.P., 1985, p. 156.
24. See V. Vitharana, *The Oru and the Yatra, Traditional Out-Rigger Watercrafts of Sri Lanka*, Dehiwell, 1992. Also K. Mc Pherson, *Indian Ocean*, loc. cit. p. 34.
25. K.N. Chaudhary, *Trade and Civilization*, op. cit., p. 151.
26. Niccolai Manucci, *Storia do Mogor*, tr. W. Irvine, II, p. 47.
27. S. Hasan Askari, 'Mughal Weakness and Aurangzeb's attitude towards the Robbers and Pirates on the Western Coast', *Proceedings of the Indian History Congress*, 1960, reprinted in *Journal of Indian Ocean Studies* 2(3), July 1995, pp. 236-42.
28. Ibid.
29. Satish Chandra, *Parties & Politics at the Mughal Court, 1707-1740*, Introduction to 4th edn., O.U.P., 2001, p. xiv.

Irrigation and the Baloch Frontier

David Gilmartin

This paper is an examination of the role of irrigation in state-building along the west bank of the Indus. Though its major focus is on the role of irrigation in the construction and definition of British imperial power in the middle decades of the nineteenth century, it begins by examining briefly the role of irrigation in earlier efforts at state-building in the area. This paper argues that irrigation works represented a critical field through which state-building was negotiated.

The geographical focus for the paper is the middle Indus region, an area stretching 200 miles along the right bank of the Indus from the Derajat to Upper Sind. In climate, the region was an extremely arid one, with rainfall at Dera Ghazi Khan averaging only a bit more than six inches a year, and showing a very high degree of variability. Though an area of mixed population when the British arrived, the people of the region were predominantly Baloch and Pakhtun, with the Baloch predominating in the hills to the south (Upper Sind and Dera Ghazi Khan) and Pakhtuns in the north (Dera Ismail Khan). Baloch and Pakhtun tribal organization shaped political loyalties in the hills of the region, with most of the tribes practicing some combination of pastoral herding, agriculture, trade, and raiding as foundations for their livelihoods. It was in the southern half of this area that significant canal investment along the Indus first began to shape the definition of British power, first on the far side of the Sulemans in Upper Sind, and then, more significantly, along the Dera Ghazi Khan frontier of the Punjab, and it is this area which will be the focus of this paper.

Early British images of the Baloch did not often associate them with irrigation and agriculture. As Frederick Fryer wrote in the 1870s, 'the Biloches are robust and manly, but they look upon war as their trade, and despise agriculture and the arts of peace.'[1] But, as the earliest records and travelers accounts indicate, political structures among the tribes along the frontier had long been closely connected to forms of adaptation to the environment based on both pastoralism and agriculture. Pastoralism played a central role in Baloch life and shaped many of their customs and political institutions. As Pehrson notes, 'pastoralism was central to the Baloch's own sense of identity and provided the framework in which many features of Baloch culture found their clearest expression'.[2] But irrigated agriculture was also central to the dynamics of Baloch economic and political organization. Indeed, interactions between pastoralism and agriculture had long moulded both Baloch identity and Baloch roles in state-building.

Water Control and Tribal Organization

Though forms of water control and Baloch relationships to their environment had shifted over time, we can identity various methods of controlling water for irrigation that had long influenced life in this region. Before discussing the ways that irrigation shaped developments on the Indus plains, we will begin with a brief description of forms of water control in the hills, and of their relationships to tribal organization and life.

Methods of irrigation in the hills were essentially of three types.

Of first importance for Baloch tribes in the hills were irrigation waters derived from the numerous perennially flowing streams found in the mountain valleys of the Suleman range. Though the flow of most of these streams was limited (and disappeared in the heat of the lowlands before reaching the Indus), the agriculture from *kalapani* irrigation (*syap* in Balochi, that is, irrigation from 'black water': clear, perennially running streams) was critical to the structure of many tribes. The relative stability of *kalapani* irrigation encouraged the emergence of fairly elaborate, if relatively small, systems of watercourses, with distribution calculated often on the basis of water shares, based on timed water use.[3] Though irrigating relatively small aggregate areas, these systems of canal irrigation were important in providing a relatively stable, if limited, agricultural base supporting the establishment of small towns and the authority of tribal chiefs. These chiefs provided protection for traders (usually Hindus), who in turn transformed the towns into regional markets.[4] The towns thus became the centres of tribal networks, providing a focus for the circulation of pastoralists (who were sometimes periodic cultivators as well) in the surrounding districts, and, at the same time, they often became centres for the authority of the tribal chiefs. *Kalapani* irrigation thus often was a key to the definition of centers of Baloch tribal circulation, though its overall contribution to Baloch livelihoods was limited.

Kalapani irrigation was supplemented in some parts of the Baloch hill country by *karez,* which were underground watercourses carrying water through tunnels dug into the slopes of hills. *Karez* were, in the words of the author of the 1907 *Loralai Gazetteer*, 'a very ancient method of artificial irrigation' in Baluchistan and were widely used. However, they were far more common in the western parts of Baloch territories, however, which were more strongly influenced by Iran. Though they were sometimes constructed by powerful individuals, they were often developed also by communities of co-sharers, who paid to have them periodically cleaned by itinerant labourers, and their presence thus sometimes supported relatively stable agricultural communities.[5] But they played an insignificant part in shaping the productive capacities of the Baloch tribes that inhabited the middle Indus region, who are the main focus of our attention here.

More important generally to the adaptation of the tribes of the Derajat to their environment were the less fixed forms of agriculture practised in response to the uncertain patterns of rainfall in the region. These also provide us our best insight into the relationship between forms of water control and the structure of Baloch tribal organization. The construction of small *bands*–earthen embankments to trap water after periodic rains–was common throughout the hills. Cultivation was most fully developed on the hill torrents that dominated the skirts (*daman*) of the mountains all along the Derajat frontier. Though usually dry during most of the year, these torrents filled with silt-laden, fertilizing water between May and August, allowing *kharif* crops to be sown on inundated lands (called *rodkohi* cultivation). Distributaries from each torrent were filled by the construction of earthen dams at the distributary mouths, which were broken in turn to allow water to pass to distributaries further down the torrent once higher lands were thoroughly inundated. Irrigation from hill torrents thus required a relatively high degree of communal cooperation both in the construction of the earthen dams and in the building of the high earthen *bands* (also known as *laths*) around fields, which were necessary to deeply soak the plots, catching the silt and readying the fields for planting. They also required cooperation between those who controlled the various distributaries on these torrents.[6]

Such cooperation was not always easy to attain. Most torrents operated on the basis of a distinction between upper irrigators (*moond* or *saroba*) and lower irrigators (*pand* or *paina*), the upper irrigators having the right to take as much water as they required before the lower irrigators were allowed to break the upper dams to bring the water down to their own distributaries. But, since torrents were highly unpredictable, shifting their courses and sometimes bringing water down from the hills so powerfully that dams were suddenly and unexpectedly broken, stable cooperative arrangements around these torrents were rare. Conflicts were so frequent that, as one British official noted, 'every attempted dam was known as *khuni band* (bloody dam).'[7] Sometimes tribal ties provided the basis for cooperation. Many distributaries were dominated by (and named after) the tribal sections that had originally built them.[8] In some cases, Baloch *sardars*, leaders of tribal sections, or others, controlled large quantities of land on these torrents and exercised strong influence on their organization. Sometimes, however, cooperative arrangements were dictated by the needs of a mixed groups of cultivators, who, as the first regular British settlement officer of Dera Ghazi Khan put it, appointed their own local officials, called *maimars*, to oversee distribution and cooperative work on the torrents.

Nevertheless, *rodkohi* cultivation bore a critical relationship of Baloch tribal life, for it was integrated into the dynamics of Baloch tribal organization. *Rodkohi* cultivation was so variable that preparing fields for cultivation was in some ways a speculative endeavour. It could return handsome profits when successful, but it paid off, as one official estimated in the mid-nineteenth century, approximately one year in three.[9] It thus tended to be the province of a generally mobile and semi-pastoral population, as dependent on cattle as on agriculture.[10] Cultivators lived, according to Fryer, in 'scattered encampments',[11] and kept herds that could be taken to the Indus riverain to graze when *rodkohi* cultivation failed. Protection from tribal leaders, who could guarantee access to grazing land for cattle and provide support in lean years (sometimes through raiding expeditions), was thus critical to the widespread practice of *rodkohi* cultivation. For their part, tribal leaders, including not only Baloch chiefs, but also their *mukaddams* (or heads of tribal sections), benefited from the high returns from torrent cultivation, for when the water supply, with its fertilizing silt, proved adequate, the return from *rodkohi* cultivation could be excellent. When it did not, they underscored their chiefly position among their tribesmen by making grain or cash advances,[12] or by organizing tribal raiding parties.

The uncertainty associated with *rodkohi* cultivation underscored one of the critical dynamics that shaped Baloch tribal organization. Though forms of water control were central to Baloch adaptation, communities of water control on the frontier were generally not self-contained, but were often composed of semi-pastoralists and temporary cultivators, who depended on political and ecological relationships extending well beyond the structures of water control that supported most Baloch agriculture. Stability and protection in Baloch life depended on structures of political solidarity transcending attachment to the land, for few strategies of settled production offered certain returns. Baloch political organization was structured, therefore, by an ideology of segmentary descent that transcended any particular form of attachment to the environment, offering to Baloch households protection in a shifting world of both pastoralism and cultivation.

Indeed, the power of 'blood' shaped a world of reciprocal obligations stretching across the boundaries of pastoralism and settlement. Though kinship ties structured the social organization of small Baloch pastoral bands, they played a different role within the larger and more diverse world of the Baloch tribe. With few secure sources of water in the hills, (apart from limited centers of *kalapani* irrigation), Baloch tribal chiefs tended only rarely to control stable hierarchies of authority within fixed landed boundaries. To the contrary, the authority of chiefs was constrained by the influence of segmentary section chiefs, who were themselves constrained by the 'elders of the section they represent'.[13] Chiefs and followers were bound largely by an ideology of reciprocal obligation adapted to their highly uncertain environment.[14] Nothing symbolized the protective power of a Baloch chief more clearly than his generosity and hospitality to his fellow tribesmen. Lavish generosity, of course, also required wealth, which itself tended to legitimize chiefly authority, as did heroic leadership in raids, which could bring in booty. Successful management of trade relations with states could also greatly enhance a chief's reputation. But whatever the economic foundations, it was protection of Baloch livelihood that energized tribal loyalties, and gave meaning to chiefly claims to authority based on heroic genealogies. Tribal leadership thus operated in counterpoint to the uncertainty of the Balcoh environment.

Tribal configurations could thus rapidly change in such circumstances, as the history of Baloch tribes along the Dera Ghazi Khan frontier indicaters.[15] So it is not very surprising that chiefs and their followers frequently responded to shortages of water or access to grazing grounds by moving into new territories, searching for new productive environments, and new sources of water.

No account of Baloch environmental adaptations can thus remain confined to the hills. Baloch interactions with the Indus plains date at least back to the fifteenth century, and probably much earlier. Virtually from its earliest recordings, Baloch history and tribal organization was shaped by the search for irrigation water derived directly from canals on the Indus river.

The Baloch and Canals on the Indus Plains

The story of Baloch interaction with the plains begins with the stories of Baloch migration that, in many crucial respects, brought modern Baloch identity into existence. As Longworth Dames has argued, the great Baloch migration out of Mekran and into both the Suleman range and Indus plains in the fifteenth and sixteenth centuries was preserved in Baloch ballads as something of a 'national migration, a charter for Baloch ethnicity after a period of internal strife. Initially, it was probably the recruitment of Baloch chiefs into the service of Indus plains states in this era, including the Langahs in Multan, the Mughals, and a series of states in Sind, that opened the Indus plains to this migration, though the nature of these migrations changed over time.[16] Many ballads thus charted the exploits of the great tribal chiefs, such as Mir Chakar Rind, who led the Baloch into the plains. Chakar, who, according to tradition, along with his son, aided Babur and Humayun in securing the Delhi throne, in fact lived on in Baloch legends as the image of an ideal chief.[17] At the same time, however, elements in these ballads suggested also the connection between the memory of this great migration and the search for productive autonomy among Baloch tribesmen. 'The Rinds and Lasharis [Baloch tribes of the time] made a bond together, one poem of the migration declared, 'and said: "Come, let us leave this barren land; let us spy out the running streams and sweet waters, and distribute them among us; let us take no heed of tribe or chief"'.[18] As in the hills, control over water (and access to grazing grounds) remained a critical imperative for the Baloch as they moved onto the plains.

The impact of Baloch movement to the plains on Baloch tribal organization and culture, however, was mixed. Many Baloch gained powerful positions with the states of southwestern Punjab and Sind in the following centuries, and waves of Baloch migrations left Baloch settlements scattered by the nineteenth century over much of western Punjab and Sind. Chakar and his descendants received land grants from the Mughals, particularly in the Punjab.[19] In the eighteenth century, the

Kalhoras in Sind offered numerous grants to Balochis for service to the state, thus laying the groundwork for the emergence of a powerful class of Baloch military *jagirdars* in Sind, a class from which the Talpur Mirs, themselves Baloch, ultimately emerged as rulers of Sind in the late eighteenth century.[20] But it was not the increasingly powerful military aristocrats of Sind or the increasingly dispersed Baloch migrants of the Punjab who played the most important roles in the reformulation of Baloch tribal culture and organization in response the migrations of this period. Indeed, there was a tendency over the centuries for many Baloch migrants to Punjab and Sind to become increasingly assimilated into Punjabi and Sindi culture, a tendency particularly marked in the western Punjab.[21] 'Those who followed Chakur [that is, who migrated to Sind and Punjab] have become Jatts,' a Baloch proverb declared, 'while those who stayed behind have remained Baloches.'[22] The hills, in fact, remained the stronghold for the protection of Baloch identity.

Even for the tribes that occupied the hills, however, developments on the plains proved critically important. And no development was more important for the middle Indus frontier than the emergence of an important regional state on the Indus in the sixteenth century controlled by the Mirrani Baloch of Dera Ghazi Khan, for it was the Mirranis who pioneered the new forms of water control that first introduced irrigation canals on the plains into Baloch history. Ghazi Khan Mirrani, of the Dodai branch of the Baloch, had come to the plains in the fifteenth century in the train of Dodai leaders taking service with the Langahs at Multan, and had later established himself (with a state land grant?) on the Indus; he was, according to Fryer, 'a great cattle-owner', who was 'attracted by the grass',[23] But, to establish a foundation for his authority, he began to construct small inundation canals from the Indus. Water that was of course plentiful in the Indus was notoriously fickle, and the direction and nature of the floods (and of the their silt deposits) varied from year to year, rendering cultivation and fixed agricultural settlements, even with the supplemental use of wells, precarious. As the *Ain-i Akbari* observed in the sixteenth century, 'The river Sind (Indus) inclines every few years alternately to its southern and northern banks and the village cultivation follows its course.'[24] Kacha wells certainly existed; the plains were probably dotted with wells associated with temporary cultivation and with the herds brought down to the Indus riverain by pastoralists.[25] But only by building inundation canals from the Indus to water lands beyond the direct reach of the Indus floods were the Mirranis able to establish a relatively fixed agricultural base for themselves, and in the process, to transform the political foundation for their authority. Indeed, canal construction provided the foundations ultimately for a new form of Baloch state in the middle Indus basin, linked increasingly closely to the state systems of the Indus plains. According to the *Ain-i Akbari*, the Mirranis commanded, by the end of the sixteenth century, a brick fort, a large army, a substantial revenue and an important position as a tributary within the Mughal state system.[26]

Canal construction thus played a critical role in defining the position of the Mirranis as players in the larger world of Indian power relations. But, in spite of Dera Ghazi Khan's absorption into the Mughal world, the social technology that established the new canals of Dera Ghazi Khan did not come primarily from models provided by the Mughal Empire, but from the ongoing interaction between pastoralism and agriculture that had long shaped Baloch affairs. Local documents and oral traditions collected by British officials in the nineteenth century suggested that the processes of canal construction under the Mirranis—and under their eighteenth century successors—were closely related to these interactions. In seeking to secure their power on the plains, the rulers of Dera Ghazi Khan projected the routes of potential canals largely along routes defined by the presence of pre-existing wells on the plains, wells associated not generally with long-settled cultivators (for village communities were very few on the Dera Ghazi Khan plains) but rather with semi-pastoralists, both Jats and Baloch, who had regularly taken their cattle to the riverain to graze and who also practiced temporary, well-assisted cultivation. Many of these were men who probably already had considerable experience with the temporary and uncertain *kharif* cultivation practiced on hill torrents.

By defining wells as units of land ownership, however, the rulers sought, in effect, to draw the labour of the mobile population of the region into fixed canal projects, an effort that had a potentially transformative effect on the state's social base. As Fryer described the process, the rulers assembled those who laid claims to these wells and paid them a monthly cash sum or a *seer* of flour while digging the canal, usually dividing the work into sections (*dakhs*) and assembling those who had claims (based on old wells) on each section for the work. Fryer wrote,

When the canal was dug, the branch canals and cuttings were made by the people themselves, who divided the water by their own communities, and each proprietor became the owner of an estate possessing the advantage of canal irrigation, as a return either for his own labour in excavating a portion of the canal, or else as a return for the capital he had sunk in paying some one else to dig his share of the canal.[27]

By providing supervision, some capital, and political leverage (as, for example, in taking up land for canal heads), the Mirranis established an important agricultural base, while relying only partly on their own agents for the construction of new canals.

The result was the emergence both of relatively autonomous local irrigating communities and of an increasingly powerful Baloch state. These were generally communities defined, in their basic form, neither by tribal descent (though that was certainly important in some cases) nor by their relationship to the land. As later British officials observed, landed rights in Dera Ghazi Khan generally originated in access to water, and, as a result, there were no 'village communities' in the usual sense, apart from sharers in water.[28] The structure of mutual relations among sharers in water was determined largely by the inter-relationships between water rights and labour obligations that had shaped the original construction of the canal. Indeed, this relationship was continually reasserted by the need for annual silt clearance or inundation canals, which depended on the labour (or, in some cases, capital) of the water sharers, who were known in this capacity as *chhers*. The Mirranis and their successors, as rulers, played vital roles in supervising and organizing *chhers* for annual silt clearance. But in matters of canal maintenance and water distribution, the irrigators were generally supervised by a *maimar* selected on a particular branch or watercourse by the water sharers themselves. Tribal bonds played an important role in the establishment of some branch canals, but the basic structure of irrigating communities was shaped by the relationship of sharers to the source of water itself.[29] Defined by their roles in irrigation, these communities thus made possible the local administration of irrigation (though they offered otherwise no political challenge to the emerging state authority).

The construction of inundation canals thus enhanced considerably the Mirranis' power. New canals increased the revenue, and also more importantly, provided lands for settling supporters of the rulers and building tribal supports. Such lands came largely from wastes taken up along the routes of canals, on which both kinsmen of the Mirrani rulers and Baloch chiefs from the hills were given rights in return for early support for the Mirrani state. The Khosa chief, for example, married into the family of the Mirranis and was given a grant of land on the plains, through which a canal (called the *haibatwah*) was later constructed.[30] Evidence concerning the successors to the Mirranis at Dera Ghazi Khan suggests even more clearly how rulers drew their relatives and supporters into the process of canal building in order to stabilize the state's political base. Eighteenth century evidence, for example, suggests how canals were periodically expanded or resuscitated (as the river's set shifted or canal heads and channels silted), in efforts to enhance or re-establish state power. This was evident, for example, in the policies of Mahmud Khan Gujar, a former *wazir*, who, in the late eighteenth century usurped power from the Mirranis. In seeking to stabilize state authority after a long struggle for power, sometimes in alliance with both the Durranis and the Kalhoras, Mahmud Khan encouraged an extensive new program of canal building and re-excavation. He not only bought up canal lands, but also encouraged the settlement of his own supporters on newly opened canal sections, and like the Mirranis, apparently claimed the right to assume unclaimed canal sections for himself, which could be distributed to supporters, and thus secure his power.

Nor was Mahmud Gujar alone in the eighteenth century in taking advantage of changing political conditions to define new claims to state authority in the process of organizing canal constructions. In the southern portion of Dera Ghazi Khan, Makhdum Rajan Shah of Sitpur, *sajjada nishin* of a prominent sufi shrine on the Indus and governor of Sitpur, also became active in canal building after gaining control of much of the southern part of the district around 1740.[31] Shortly thereafter he excavated a large canal, known as the Dhundi, that ran a distance of almost 70 miles, and was said to have cost the Makhdum a lakh of rupees. Though the canal passed partly through already settled areas, the Makhdum underscored his own power by settling large numbers of his own supporters at the tail on a tract of wasteland that the Mukhdum claimed under the authority of a *sanad* from Nadir Shah.[32]

Canal construction also strengthened centralized power in other ways, particularly by providing a framework for drawing commercial capital into alliance with the rulers. Evidence from deeds collected by the British in the mid-nineteenth century suggested that sales of canal sections of Hindus (who in Dera Ghazi Khan were primarily traders or lenders) were important in expanding and encouraging commercial production on some canals, and in the process drawing commercial men into political alliance with the state. Among these deeds was one dating from the 1740s in the name of one of the later Mirrani rulers of Dera Ghazi Khan selling certain ownership rights on wells of the Manka canal to Hindus. The importance of channeling capital into canal projects was suggested also by the evidence of what were known as *adhlapi* tenures on canals; tenures shaped by the original claimants to canal sections agreeing to give up to outsiders half of their land (and, presumably, of their claims on canal water) in return for the provision of capital or labour to excavate the required section of the canal and to open cultivation. Deeds confirming such arrangements were found from the 1750s, for example, transferring *adhlapi* rights on the Manka canal to certain Hindus, 'in consideration of donees supplying the *dhak* or section of the excavations assigned to donors by the Nawab (Ghazee Khan)'. Such tenures were also used by Makhdum Rajan Shan on the Dhundi, and were almost certainly used extensively by Mahmud Gujar as well, thus defining a structure in which Hindu capital could move relatively easily into canal investment.[33]

Though it is likely that such tenures existed from the earliest canal constructions, these land sales to Hindus probably increased in significance in the eighteenth century when, after the establishment of Afghan power, the town of Dera Ghazi Khan increased in commercial importance due to its place in the trade to Kandahar and Kabul, and due to the increased presence of both Afghan and, particularly, Shikarpuri Hindu traders in the town. As Alexander Burnes noted in the 1830s, the town had once been known along with Shikarpur as one of the 'gates of Khorasan'. That Hindu capital found its way into agricultural production on canal lands is suggested by the importance of indigo in canal production on the better inundation canals, a commercial crop that also played an important role in the town's exports, and one in which traders usually had a high stake.[34] Relations between Baloch canal-builders and Hindu men of capital were, in fact, probably quite close. Documents collected by the British in the mid-nineteenth century for one small indigo and cotton-producing canal, for example, showed that the entire canal, along with its watercourses, was mortgaged in the early nineteenth century to one Bhae Oodo Dass Shekarporia, before being re-mortgaged, in the 1840s, to an important Baloch chief. While relatively late in date, this evidence hints at the ongoing presence of both Hindu commercial capital and Baloch interest in many canals.[35]

Although perhaps most important to the power of the Mirranis and their successors, canal construction also played a critical role also in defining the extremely dangerous relationship of the state to the hill Baloch, whose presence had a continuing, critical influence on the politics of the plains. For the rulers of Dera Ghazi Khan, the incorporation of Baloch leaders into the canal systems of the plains not only drew additional capital and labour into plains agriculture, but also proved vital to stabilizing their power. Baloch hill leaders were often given important roles in excavating branch canals on new canal projects. Both the Mazari and Drishak chiefs, for example, were given lands on the plains and they excavated canals in the southern part of the region, allowing their tribesmen to move in large numbers to the plains. The Mazaris had 'long brought their cattle down every winter to graze near the Indus', but moved in large numbers to the plains after the Mazari *tumandar* excavated a canal known as the Hamalwah, perhaps initially in the seventeenth century, on the tract of land between Rojhan and the Indus. In the case of the Drishaks, as Fryer described it, 'an ancestor of the present Dreeshuk Tomandar, excavated [the Mobarik branch of the Dhoondee, the Makhdum of Sitpur's canal] for the use of his own tribe'.[36]

Critical to the larger history of the Baloch, however, the new forms of local state power rooted in the construction of canals on the plains also influenced the political organization of the frontier Baloch themselves as they came into increasingly close relations with Indus plains states. As Dames argues, this period of agricultural expansion on the plains was also the period in which the organized *tumans*, each with its own state-recognized chief (or *tumandar*) had crystallized in the adjacent hills, a process suggesting the increasingly close interactions with plains states that characterized the period. For many of the emerging *tumandars*, an irrigated agricultural base in the plains came to be as important as a base derived from *kalapani*- or *rodkohi*-based agriculture in the hills or *daman*. The role of *tumandars* as assertive military leaders in the hills, commanding the military allegiance of tribal sections while protecting Baloch grazing grounds and dispensing largesse, in fact remained central to Baloch organization, whatever their relations with the plains. But access to production from canal lands helped to provide for many the material base to make this role effective, even as it drew them into more important roles in the plains economy.

Relations between *tumandars* and the rulers at Dera Ghazi Khan were of course not without tension. For the leaders of the *tumans*, the importance of access to irrigated land was balanced by the importance of autonomy and the need to maintain flexibility to mobilize tribesmen for raiding to protect the *tuman* and to maintain the reputation of the chief. In the time of Mahmud Gujar, for example, the Drishak *tumandar* was granted revenue rights over a portion of the villages on the Dhundi canal, but only after a bitter feud with Mahmud Khan in which, as Bruce relates it, the Drishak had raided near Dera Ghazi Khan to steal cattle, killed Mahmud Khan's brother, and defeated a force sent against them.[37] State recognition of rights in canal lands was also associated with other measures of control. Rulers sometimes gave charge over to *tumandars* of the mountain passes along the trading routes to Afghanistan, paying them for the safety of the *kafilahs* (caravans), while drawing them under state influence with the simultaneous grant of revenue rights on lands on the plains. Bruce records, for example, that during the time of Ahmad Shah Durrani, the Gurchani *tumandar* (and his leading *mukaddams*) were offered the right to collect the government's share of the produce (*masul*) in kind on several villages on the plains, and to collect a tax on camels coming into the plains in return for the safety of the Hurrund and Dajil frontier. It was because of this, as Griffin and Massy write in *Punjab Chiefs*, that the *tumandar* 'moved down into the plains, and built himself a fort at Lalgarh, where the Gurchani chiefs now live'.[38]

In this context, the structures of association that shaped most canal construction and organization in Dera Ghazi Khan were critical, for the canals brought semi-pastoral Baloch into an external framework of canal organization, which yet allowed considerable initiative and autonomy to Baloch chiefs (and others) in the processes of canal construction and organization. Evidence on the roles of Baloch *tumandars* and *mukaddams* suggests that on some canals they played important roles in silt clearance and water distribution, and perhaps also in the appointment of the *maimars* (or *mirabs*) who supervised the collection of *chhers* for canal clearances and arranged distribution.[39] At the same time, however, communities of irrigators (including Baloch tribesmen) often exercised considerable autonomy themselves, with respect to Baloch chiefs and to the state alike, and often selected their *maimars* independently. While access to canal lands often gave Baloch chiefs and their *mukaddams* political leverage, it was hardly sufficient to fully stabilize their authority. The continuing self-assertion of the chief as a protector and warrior—and negotiator with the state—remained critical to the maintenance of tribal authority.

Nothing suggested this more clearly than the conflicts that erupted in the face of a general breakdown in canal irrigation on the Dera Ghazi Khan plains in the late eighteenth and early nineteenth centuries. At the heart of this was the major shift in the course of the Indus that occurred around 1790 as the river broke through its right bank south of Kinjur and moved to a more westerly course, shifting its junction with the

Chenab from a site south of Shahr Sultan to a site near Mithankot, about 60 miles downstream.[40] The effects of this shift on the operation of nearly all the canals in the southern part of the Derajat was devastating. As Bruce notes, 'the heads of the Bisharut and other canals in the south of the district were carried completely away, while inundations which had never been known before overspread the face of the country from the north to the south', in the process disrupting cultivation completely in many of the canal villages of the region. Broken down canals had, of course, been reconstructed before. But now the disruption of irrigation on the plains was associated with a period of significant conflict among the Baloch. Not coincidentally, as Bruce observes, 'it was about the same period that the Belooches, who had gained a firm footing in the plains, commenced that series of wars and blood feuds which lasted for over forty years, and devastated the country'.[41]

It is in fact impossible to draw a direct correlation between the increase in conflict among the frontier Baloch and the shift of the Indus, for this period was also one of escalating conflict within Baluchistan after the death of Nasir Khan of Kalat, and on the plains between the Nawabs of Bahawalpur, the Talpur Mirs in Sind, the Durranis, and the Sikhs, which strongly influenced conflict along the frontier. But the conjunction of a serious environmental disruption with a time of considerable political conflict on the plains suggested the close interaction between environmental and political factors in shaping Baloch organization. With the disintegration of an effective state at Dera Ghazi Khan, it was impossible to reconstitute the social structures for resuscitating or reconstructing the canals. The results were not only increasing conflicts among the Baloch tribes over access to resources, but in many cases challenges to tribal leadership as the environmental foundations of many of the *tumans* were disrupted. Many of the conflicts of this period involved not just conflicts for resources between Baloch tribes, but conflicts over leadership within particular tumans, with states on the plains using alliances with some tribes to defeat others, and rivals within tribes using alliance with other tribes to gain state recognition as leader (*tumandar*) within their own tribes.[42]

The nature of the conflicts of this era were in part captured by the Baloch ballads of the era (later collected by Longworth Dames), many celebrating the valor of tribal chiefs and heroes who fought over territory, water, and grazing grounds in this period. Each tribe claimed its own 'lands and running water, wealth and cattle.' But it was the self-assertion of the tribes in battle that in effect validated their status and helped to legitimize their myths of common descent, even as new leaders and new tribal configurations emerged. Chiefs tried to emphasize their own steadfastness and traditions of valor as they summoned their warriors from different tribal segments, calling, as did the chief of the Tibbi Lund, 'to my whole tribe, from the hills to the rich lands of the plains' to assemble to defend their territory. In a ballad extolling the heroism of the Lunds, for example, the warriors of the tribe fought 'like mighty warriors of old' against their enemies, the language of the ballad suggesting at the same time their tribal identification with both pastoral and agricultural resources: 'Thronging forth like a herd of cattle, . . . the heroes of the Lunds and Gurchanis came together [for battle] as the water of a torrent comes against an embankment.'[43] But the stories of both warriors and chiefs, which emphasized above all bravery and success as the markers of tribal identity, suggested the fluidity of Baloch political configurations even within a context in which claims to descent (and to the heroism of one's ancestors) defined the legitimate currency of assertions of tribal unity. Not all tribal segments, of course, always united readily, particularly in the face of different patterns of relations to the productive environment and of potential alliances with states and other tribes. Indeed, the establishment of unity remained an evanescent ideal extolled in many ballads, a measure itself of the strength and virtue of a Baloch chief.

Some *tumans*, in fact, disappeared entirely under the pressures of this period, facing both concerted attacks from other tribes and the loss of their ecological base, their members dispersed and attached themselves to other groups. As Bruce notes, the Jistkanis, who held land on the Shoree Nullah, 'were not able to hold their own on their former lands,' and having lost both their *tumandar* and their environmental base, 'broke up and scattered themselves amongst all the other Beloch tribes,' partly under pressure from the Drishaks who had themselves lost much of their irrigated agricultural base on the plains. Similarly, the Hussains, who lived on the Nisao plain in the hills, were besieged by both the Drishaks and the Marris, and after the death of their *tumandar* broke into parts that joined other tribes, losing, in the process, their 'name and place amongst the Beloch tribes'.[44] An important group of Hussains attached themselves as a segment to the Khetrans, a *tuman* composed of a number of segments of differing origins, which, although without lands on the plains, emerged as an increasingly important tribe in this era as a result of their productive *kalapani* agricultural base in the Barkhan valley in the hills, and as a result of their increasingly important role in marketing raided property and directing trade between the hills and the plains.

When the British arrived on the Baloch frontier, they thus found a region in flux. As Bruce wrote: 'At annexation the whole of Dera Ghazi Khan District was marked by immense jungle tracts, which were found intersected with lines of old canals, and the remains of what had once been large flourishing villages.'[45] In fact, this situation was worse in the south of Dera Ghazi Khan than in the north, which had escaped the most serious effects of the shift in the Indus. Diwan Sawan Mal had also done much to try to improve the canals and stabilize the country north of Dera Ghazi Khan in the 1830s.[46] As elsewhere, the British probably exaggerated the disorder they encountered on their arrival on the frontier. Nevertheless, the evidence of irrigation's political importance in an earlier era of Baloch history was on the plains for the British to see.

British Irrigation and the Myth of the Baloch Frontier

Still, as the British established their control along the Indus frontier in the 1840s and 1850s, their approach to irrigation reflected a vision shaped largely by their self-image as colonial rulers and their image of the 'pastoral' Baloch. As they moved into the Indus Basin in the mid-nineteenth century, many British observers tended to view the emerging colonial frontier as a moral divider separating the advance of civilization from the turbulent world of Baloch 'marauding'. Indeed, irrigation represented for many early administrators a critical element not only in the definition of the frontier but also in the moral definition of the British colonial state itself.

The vision of a clear divide between settled, irrigated agriculture and frontier hill life first captured the British imagination as they established their authority on the upper Sind frontier, the first section of the frontier along which the British made their administrative presence felt after the annexation of Sind in 1843. The Marri and Bugti, who occupied the Suleman range facing Sind, controlled important centers of *kalapani* irrigation in the hills that were central to their tribal organization, though they did not hold significant canal lands in the plains nor control much torrent irrigation.[47] Their wealth lay overwhelmingly in their cattle, which were susceptible to raiding by other tribes. Raiding into the plains was common in the period immediately preceding the arrival of the British, and the Talpur Mirs of Sind (themselves Baloch by origin) had attempted to control the hill Baloch largely, as Lambrick put it, by hiring 'Baluchis of one tribe to guard their borders against Baluchis of another'.[48] In confronting these Baloch in the years immediately following annexation, early British administrators thus tended to draw a sharp line between the uncivilized territory of the frontier and the settled lands on the plains controlled by the British. Indeed, control of the Marri-Bugti frontier tended to revolve initially around military operations, and in the early years the British relied heavily on the establishment of frontier military posts and the use of force to punish raids from the hills and to force recognition by the frontier tribes of superior British military power.

But the transformative vision of agricultural settlement, a vision predicated on the myth of a Baloch world separated from that of the settled plains, increasingly played an important role in defining British frontier policy and in ensuring a critical role for irrigation within it. The peculiar importance of irrigation and agricultural settlement on the frontier was conceptualized most clearly by John Jacob, whose influence dominated the upper Sind frontier in the late 1840s and 1850s. For Jacob, the demarcation of a clear 'moral' frontier between civilization and the 'roving' cattle keepers of the hills was important not only to controlling the frontier, but in defining the legitimacy of British power. Jacob was strongly imbued with mid-nineteenth century ideals of political economy, and saw the progress of the British themselves as exemplifying, in the words of his biographer, Lambrick, 'the infinite capacity of man for steady self-improvement'.[49] Nothing was therefore more important for the progress of Sind than the construction of roads, bridges, and canals—all of which separated British Sind both physically and morally from the 'uncivilized' frontier. And among these, no words were more important than those for irrigation. Irrigation was, for Jacob, an instrument transforming pastoral wandering into a peaceful, industrious, settled life. The transformative power of irrigation and agricultural settlement defined for Jacob the moral identity of the British as colonial rulers, even as it separated British Sind from the Baloch frontier. It fit into a structure of thinking in which the laws of political economy, themselves natural laws, defined the meaning of human advance.[50]

These ideas were reflected in early British efforts to use resettlement onto irrigated lands as an instrument of transformation to physically control the Baloch from beyond the border. The first British attempt to force the settlement of hill Baloch in the plains as a mechanism of control came after Sir Charles Napier's 1845 military expedition into the hills shortly after annexation.[51] After defeating several small Baloch tribes in a military campaign, Naiper sought to solidify British victory by resettling kept groups of defeated Baloch on the plains. It was Jacob, however, who stressed most strongly the critical importance of irrigation in this transformative endeavour. In both a physical and a moral sense, only the complete immersion of formerly hill Baloch in irrigated agriculture could achieve, in Jacob's view, the definitive separation of these Baloch raiders from their wandering life in the hills—and thus assure their absorption into the British political order. Jacob criticized the early results of Napier's efforts, which, having failed to give proper attention to irrigation, failed also to break decisively the links of settled Baloch to the hills.[52] Taking them into hand, Jacob sought to disarm and immobilize them (allowing only the chiefs and a small body of guides in government service to leave periodically), while at the same time organizing them for the clearance of an old channel of the Begari canal, the Nurwah (a channel originally dug by the Kalhoras[53]), to bring adequate canal water to their lands. For Jacob, this was the key to the whole policy. Nothing expressed Jacob's concern more clearly, as he put it himself, than the vision of Baloch 'digging merrily at a canal'.[54] 'From the time they took to agriculture,' Jacob wrote, 'they were really conquered and commenced to be reformed.'[55]

The same policy animated much of early British relations with the Bugti tribe, in spite of the difficulties that Bugti resettlement policies encountered. After the military defeat of the Bugti *tumandar* in 1847, Jacob himself took a hand in encouraging the settlement of the Bugti *tumandar* and his followers on the plains, urging their separation (both physically and morally) from the life of the hills as critical to further control. Indeed, having moved a group of Bugtis led by the *tumandar* to a settlement on revenue-free lands near Larkana, the government began almost immediately to organize them in the opening of an old canal to bring an adequate water supply to their lands and to engage them in the discipline of irrigated farming. But, from the beginning, the history of the settlement was troubled. Within a year, the *tumandar*, Islam Khan Bugti, had fled the settlement and, in defiance of the British, returned to the hills. For some officials, this event suggested simply that the degree of physical separation from the hills at Larkana had been inadequate to facilitate the transformation. Larkana was situated too near the frontier, they argued, and they recommended moving the Bugtis yet further from the frontier, to lower Sind. But the dilemmas in the process of forced settlement were summed up more generally by Bartle Frere, the

Commissioner in Sind: the Larkana settlement, he noted, was 'far enough from the border, and sufficiently surrounded by comparatively civilized and well disposed cultivators, for the colonists to feel they were strangers and exiles, a marked and distrusted people in the midst of temptation to thieve and be idle; yet not far enough to prevent their keeping up all their old border connections and feelings'. Indeed, Frere's comments suggested the intended subversion of ethnic distinctiveness and identity which was at the heart of this British settlement policy.[56]

Experience with the Bugtis indicated the problems inherent in forced separation from the hills as an expression of the British vision of transformative irrigated settlement. Though forced separation from the hills continued to be used as an element in frontier control, it attracted increasing criticism and skepticism from administrators in the ensuing decades. But this did not mean that the vision of irrigated agriculture as a foil to the life of the hills was abandoned. To the contrary, Jacob's ideas found continuing expression in the concept of an irrigated agriculture cordon paralleling (and in essence defining) the frontier. In the eyes of Jacob in Upper Sind—and in the eyes of many later administrators in the Punjab as well—the successful establishment of an irrigated, agricultural barrier to hill 'marauding' provided the best practical means of protecting the frontier, by defining a clear line for military protection and by enlisting settled agriculturalists in the protection of their irrigated lands. Equally important, it defined a visible moral line of demarcation between the settled society of British colonial India and the less 'civilized' lands outside, creating, in effect, a membrane through which the Baloch could gradually (and voluntarily) be drawn into the colonial regime's agricultural world.

The influence of the frontier on Sind irrigation development in this era thus proved to be substantial. The first major canal project undertaken by the British in Sind was Jacob's scheme for the rehabilitation of the Begari canal, for which the Bombay government sanctioned Rs. 1,30,000 in 1852. The canal, which ran roughly along the border between the upper Sind frontier and Sukkur District, was intended, when cleared out and re-dug, to provide water for re-populating the upper Sind frontier district as a prosperous, settled bulwark against the insecurity of the hills (from which the canal was separated by an intervening desert tract). The concern for a cordon along the frontier drove yet more centrally Jacob's subsequent proposal for a new desert canal, running through the desert north of the Begari and much nearer the Baloch frontier. The foundations for the canal were begun when a small zamindari watercourse from the Indus was acquired by the government and extended into the desert in the late 1850s. For various reasons, the completion of the canal was delayed until the 1870s.[57] But Jacob's commitment to the project proved unswerving. As James Outram wrote to reassure Jacob, 'I will yet be done I trust, and the desert annihilated; tempting the hill tribes to become solely cultivators of the plain.'[58] Indeed, the moral power of irrigation to reclaim the Baloch, drawing them from the 'predatory' roving life of the hills, remained central to the official ideology of the project. 'From the time when Sind was first taken by the British Government,' a later irrigation department report declared in discussing the origins of the desert canal that 'it has always been the object of the authorities to induce the roving predatory Baluch tribes, inhabiting the Bugti hills, the desert at the foot of them, and portions of the Upper Sind Frontier District, to take to peaceful agricultural pursuits.'[59]

In fact, the importance of the frontier in shaping Jacob's thinking on irrigation generally became clear when he became the acting Commissioner in Sind in the mid-1850s. Among Jacob's most important acts as acting Commissioner was his decree in 1856 abolishing the use of 'statute labour' on all Sind canals. The long-standing role of statute labour in Indus basin canal operation was complex [and will be discussed later]. But for Jacob, the issue was straightforward. British reliance on the mobilization of forced canal labor was unacceptable because it undercut the powerful linking of irrigation development with the advance of natural laws and civilization. Not only was statute labor a 'great evil, crushing energy [and] stopping real improvement,' in Jacob's words,[60] but its use also threatened to undermine irrigation's transformative cultural meaning. For Jacob, the configuration of settled, peaceful, irrigated agriculture in opposition to the uncivilized life of the Baloch in the hills, helped to justify the legitimate political foundations and the moral purpose of the British colonial state itself.

The Expansion of Irrigation in Dera Ghazi Khan

But, however powerful and influential, these ideas jostled uneasily with the more complex reality of irrigation in the middle Indus basin. Irrigation was, in fact, not just a sign of difference between settled and tribal life, between colonial civilization and tribal marauding, but a central element itself in the complex ecological reality of Baloch tribal organization and ethnic identity. If irrigation played an important role in British thinking as a marker of the advance of civilization, it had long played an equally critical role in interaction with pastoralism, in the self-definition of Baloch identity and in structures of Baloch authority and tribal organization. Irrigation and pastoralism were *together* critical to the balance of authority and egalitarianism that shaped the descent-based ideologies of Baloch identity and tribal life. Indeed, from this perspective, irrigation provided less a structure of transformation than a critical field of political negotiation between the Baloch and the British in the early years of British rule, as the British and Baloch negotiated not only their own identities, but also the structural relationship of ethnicity (of 'blood') and colonial rule itself.

Not even Jacob, of course, had ever imagined that in practice the world of irrigation in upper Sind could be separated fully from the world of Baloch tribal life, and many others were even less willing to assert this separation so strongly. Jacob was well aware of the importance of control over irrigated lands in underscoring the power of Baloch chiefs, even as these same chiefs maintained their authority in the hills. Even on the plains, Sind police reports stressed the interaction between settled agriculture and cattle stealing as a regular feature of the upper Sind Frontier.[61] And when the desert canal was completed in the 1870s, the British distributed grants of land to many Bugtis from the hills, which were not intended so much to encourage the abandonment of pastoralism in favour of settlement, as to shore up the power of headmen within the different sections of the tribe, and thus reduce reliance on plunder. Grants to the Baloch on the desert canal in fact prompted considerable debate among Sind authorities about residence requirements, thus suggesting the continuing tension over the role of settlement as a mechanism of frontier control. But in the end many grants were made which did not require permanent residence. Islam Khan Bugti, for example, the *tumandar* at one time confined on the plains, was himself ultimately given a *jagir* on these terms, as was his grandson, Shahbaz Khan Bugti, the future head of the tribe and a man later central to British frontier policy, who came to control a separate branch canal.[62] Control over canal lands thus became an element in shoring up the authority of Baloch chiefs, whose authority continued to rest primarily in the hills.

The contradictions in frontier irrigation found fullest expression, however, in British policies along the Dera Ghazi Khan frontier further north, annexed to the British Empire with the Punjab in 1849. There, many Baloch chiefs and their tribes had long straddled the frontier. The

Baloch had long held substantial canal lands on the plains in addition to *rodkohi* and *kalapani* cultivation in the hills, grazing their flocks and controlling water on both sides of the frontier. History thus defined a somewhat different set of relations between the plains and the hills in the Derajat than in Sind.[63]

Still, just as in Sind, most Punjab officials initially saw the definition of a frontier barrier between settled society and the hills as critical to the establishment of colonial control. As the Deputy Commissioner of Dera Ghazi Khan noted in the late 1850s, the extension of cultivation was central to the establishment of such a barrier:

> It is the immense tracts of waste and jungle that render it so easy for hill marauders to leave the passes and penetrate unobserved for many miles towards the river, returning with stolen cattle to the thick jungle, and during the . . . night to the hills. Every new settlement renders this kind of theft more precarious, and reduces the labor of our police.[64]

The construction in the 1850s of major *bands* along the Indus in Dera Ghazi Khan was in fact intended not only to protect, for military reasons, the Dera Ghazi Khan cantonment and station (which were carried away by a major floods in 1856), but also to encourage the spread of agriculture, by protecting irrigation works from the effects of floods.[65] Irrigation and military security were thus strongly linked, in the 1850s, in defining a line of protection from the hills (even though direct state expenditure on irrigation in the 1850s was severely hampered by a lack of available state funds).[66]

But British policy in Dera Ghazi Khan eventually came to depend on irrigation not just to define a line separating the plains from the hills, but, far more than in Sind, as an element drawing Baloch leaders into direct investments on the plains—and thus more directly into the ambit of British authority. In fact, the potentially close interrelationship between British control over the frontier and the roles of Baloch chiefs and their tribesmen in agriculture, was recognized clearly by Major C.C. Minchin, who took control of Dera Ghazi Khan as Deputy Commissioner in 1860. Minchin's comments on early British military forays against the Bozdar, a predominately pastoral tribe occupying the north of the Dera Ghazi Khan frontier, suggested a growing British awareness of the importance of agriculture (and irrigation) in defining relations with frontier Baloch chiefs. The British initially viewed the Bozdar, at annexation a tribe confined largely to the hills, as 'inveterate plunderers and cattle thieves'[67] (in spite of their controlling several rent-free villages on the plains originally given to them by Diwan Sawan Mal). But after an expedition against them in the late 1850s revealed that they also controlled considerable *kalapani* cultivation in the hills, Minchin saw the British as possessing levers of control over them. Irrigated agriculture, in fact, drew them inevitably into the orbit of British power. 'We have the whole game in our hands now that we have visited and surveyed their country,' Minchin wrote. 'We have not only learnt the road into their country, but also the fact that it contains valuable crops, the destruction of which causes more loss than the plunder of several seasons could compensate for.' Minchin thus recommended that the Bozdar be given additional lands in the plains to strengthen further the British hand.[68] The lesson of the Bozdar was that the key to controlling the tribes lay not in separating the chiefs from the hills, but in drawing them into the framework of British administration surrounding agriculture (and irrigation) by taking advantage of the role that agriculture had long played in Baloch power and tribal life.

Minchin thus launched a policy in the early 1860's encouraging direct, voluntary canal investment on the plains by Baloch chiefs *themselves*, that was intended to build on the role that agriculture already played in Baloch society. To provide an example to others, Minchin initially turned to Mussoo Khan Nutkani, a wealthy Baloch chief from the north of Dera Ghazi Khan, who had been closely allied with the Sikhs before annexation, and who already had large agricultural investments on the plains.[69] Though Mussoo Khan's canal-building efforts were only partially successful, his example nevertheless soon attracted the attention of others. Several chiefs now promised, as Minchin put it, 'to excavate new canals or extend old ones, the cost to be defrayed by the applicants, who solicit only the rent-free lease for a term of years of the waste lands to be brought under cultivation by these canals.'[70] As Sir James Lyall later wrote, 'The leading men of the district were persuaded, in some cases not erroneously, that with his ['Minchin's] assistance they were going to make their fortunes by [canal construction and] canal extensions.'[71]

Baloch chiefs, of course, had their own reasons for investing in canal projects. Though reasons varied in most cases, the attraction of canal investment in the plains related directly to the jockeying for chiefly power that characterized most of the Baloch tribal systems. For many chiefs, or aspirants to chiefly power, control over stable agricultural income was a key element in the exercise of the largess necessary to command tribal authority (and to the maintain the access to credit necessary for such largess[72]). The dynamics of ongoing competition for leadership within the Baloch tribes provided the framework in which much of the Baloch interest in voluntary canal investment emerged, particularly after the British had made it clear that they would support such investment with favorable leases. Among the first to propose canal excavations following Massu Khan's example, were leaders in the Loond and Khosa tribes, both of whom faced critical internal challenges to their leadership in these years. Faced with the uncertainties of dependence on torrent cultivation (and its failure for several years running in the late 1850s and early 1860s), both responded to Minchin's initiatives by mobilizing their tribesmen in reopening old canal routes on the plains to secure agricultural income that could stabilize their positions in competition with rivals.[73] Though investment in canal-building by no means obviated the need for legitimizing claims to authority based on descent and on the mobilization of Baloch warriors, it provided critical political leverage in stabilizing tribal authority.

The most dramatic example of investment in canal-building in the wake of Minchin's efforts, however, and one that suggested clearly the context provided by ongoing jockeying for tribal position, was that of Jamal Khan Leghari, *tumandar* of the Legharis. During the period before the British, the Leghari tribe had emerged as one of the most powerful among the Derajat Baloch tribes, as the result of a series of alliances with states on the plains and armed conflicts with other tribes, notably the Khosas and Gurchanis.[74] At the time of annexation, the Leghari *tumandar* could command about 5,000 fighting men from five segments (four of which lived at least partly on the plains and one, the Haddianis, that lived entirely in the hills).

Equally important, Leghari chiefs claimed access to a range of diverse sources of income. With their seat established at Choti, below the hills, the Leghari chiefs had access both to hill torrents and canal lands on the plains, as well as grazing lands in the hills. They controlled, in additon, *kalapani* lands in the Barkhan valley in the hills, which had provided a retreat for the *tumandar*'s family in the early nineteenth century, when the Legharis' position on the plains had been challenged during the period of disruption and conflict preceding the extension of Sikh rule. This position had been cemented by the establishment of marriage ties with the Khetrans, who from Barkhan played an important role in the trade of the region. Further, through close relations with the Sikhs, the Legharis had gained recognition (through state payments) as protectors of the Sakhi Sarwar pass and had close connections with the shrine of Sakhi Sarwar, collecting a tax on shops and on livestock sales at the

Sakhi Sarwar fair, in return for maintaining order at the fair and acting as military guardians of the shrine.[75]

But in the years following the British annexation of the Punjab, the Leghari chiefship had come to be a subject of sharp dispute. Jamal Khan Leghari was a leader of a branch of the Aliani segment of the tribe, which had long maintained a prescriptive right to provide the tribal *tumandar*, but his position as tribal chief had been challenged in the early years of British rule by leaders of other Aliani branches. The British had initially sought to mediate conflicts over leadership within the tribe (in part by appealing to the intervention of a family of Sayyids).[76] But it was, in the end, primarily by entrepreneurial skill in canal investment on the plains that Jamal Khan was able to secure his position as *tumandar* against his internal chiefly rivals, surpassing all of them in access to wealth, and thus to the honor of largess, command of warriors, and ultimately, firm recognition from the British.

Jamal Khan's most important canal investment was a scheme for the extension of the Manka canal, launched in the early 1860s in the wake of Minchin's encouragement to Massu Khan Nutkani. The Manka canal was one of the largest and most important canals in Dera Ghazi Khan district. Probably first excavated under the Mirranis, the Manka was reexcavated under Mahmud Gujar and ran nearly eighty miles across the center of the district. By the time of British annexation, however, the southern tail portion, which ran through Leghari lands, had seriously decayed. This land, lying between Choti, the seat of the Leghari chiefs, and Dajil, was, according to Minchin, wasteland 'covered here and there with thick jangal'.

The British and the Leghari chiefs alike had a potentially strong political interest in the agricultural transformation of these lands. For Minchin, the transformation of such 'jangal' was critical to the consolidation of British power. For Jamal Khan Leghari, on the other hand (whose notion of 'jangal', which had long played a part in the semi-pastoral economy of the Leghari tribe, was probably different from Minchin's), the agricultural transformation of the area held the key to a successful strategy for the consolidation of chiefly authority in the Leghari tribe. With much of the land on the Manka tail already claimed under prescriptive rights by the Leghari chiefs, Jamal Khan proposed widening and extending the Manka to Dajil, if the government would agree to pay half the cost and to grant him, in addition, other unclaimed wastes to be watered by the extension. This the government agreed to, and paid Jamal Khan Rs. 29,000 as half the proposed cost, viewing this as an investment to leverage the other half of the cost from Jamal Khan. Whether Jamal Khan actually paid this much was unclear; later evidence suggested that he carried out the excavations by dividing the proposed extension into *dakhs*, and engaged his own tribesmen (and others) in the project, offering them, in turn, rights to cultivate lands on the newly extended canal, and sharing with them the costs of opening cultivation. Since the tract now opened to cultivation lay directly to the east of Leghari-controlled torrents, the opening of opportunities for cultivation on the Manka strengthened Jamal Khan's control generally over Leghari *mukaddams* and tribesmen, who now had access to more secure irrigated lands to supplement uncertain torrent cultivation. At the same time, Jamal Khan underscored his position as the Leghari *tumandar* by claiming superior rights, and was empowered by the British in this capacity to take collection in kind on the new canal lands.[77]

The Manka extension proved critical to the consolidation of Jamal Khan's power. But it was not the only project in which he had a hand. Indeed, Jamal Khan's interest in canal-building suggested the importance of such investment not only in consolidating his leadership of the Leghari tribe but also in gaining power and precedence among the Baloch chiefs more generally. Probably the most lucrative field for canal expansion in this period lay in the southern part of Dera Ghazi Khan, where the course of the old Dhundi, the great canal constructed by the Makhdum at Sitpur in the mid-eighteenth century, could still be traced, though its lower reaches had long since silted and fallen into disuse. The country was, according to Minchin, 'in great portion a dense jungle' that sheltered robbers from the hills. In the late 1850s, proposals for reopening had been mooted by the larger zamindars of the Rajanpur tahsil on more than one occasion, but it was only in 1861, following government approval for the Massuwah, that Minchin received a petition from Massu Khan Nutkani, Jamal Khan Leghari, and Nur Muhammad Khan Bozdar, a local zamindar and later tahsildar of Rajanpur, offering to pay half the cost of the re-excavation of the Dhundi, in return for the government's paying the other half and giving the petitioners the right to control canal clearance, and a twenty-year revenue-free lease on the waste lands to be opened at the tail. Through the Dhundi project, Massu Khan and Jamal Khan sought to use the new British canal policy to extend cash cropping and gain increasing political influence along the Dera Ghazi Khan frontier as a whole.[78]

Not all, of course, were happy with this effort. The petition of Jamal Khan's group was followed in quick order by a second group of petitioners, headed by one of the largest landowners in Rajanpur, Mir Shah Nawaz Khan Serai, seeking to block Musso Khan and Jamal Khan and requesting permission to re-excavate the canal themselves on similar terms.[79] After some negotiations, the government, seeing reclamation of 'jungle' as the main desideratum, decided to put together the two groups of petitioners, along with others with claims to lands along the route of the canal, and to form 'a sort of joint-stock company' in order to maximize the capital available for the excavation. Sharers in this endeavor put up altogether Rs. 60,000 for the project, of which Jamal Khan Leghari contributed one-third. Three other shareholders, Imam Bakhsh Mazari (the Mazari *tumandar*), Mussoo Khan Nutkani, and Mir Shah Nawaz Khan Serai, each put up Rs. 5,000, with the rest of the capital provided by over twenty different shareholders, among them the Drishak *tumandar*. British officials thus mediated the construction of a sort of Baloch-dominated entrepreneurial coalition, structured by British property law, intended to reclaim the southern Dera Ghazi Khan frontier.

In practice, of course, the sharers in the Dhundi excavation 'company' represented a wide variety of interests. For Jamal Khan and Mussoo Khan in particular, the Dhundi excavation was predominantly a form of speculation, intended to increase their wealth, their control over land, and their influence in the district—their major concern lying in the so-called 'Dhundi *pattis*,' the 'wasteland' (totaling approximately 70,000 acres) at the tail of the canal which would be opened for settlement by the re-excavation of the canal. Others were interested in resuscitating their own Rajanpur estates. For the Drishaks and Mazaris in particular, the canal also promised to open additional cultivable lands in Rajanpur for their Baloch tribesmen. The Dhundi *pattis* were in fact immediately to the east of the Drishak *tuman*. Though further from the Mazari lands, the canal also promised additional agricultural opportunities for the predominantly pastoral Mazari, many of whom also practiced precarious forms of cultivation dependent on river flooding in the Indus riverain. As Minchin noted, the riverain lands in Rajanpur were only cultivatable during the *rabi* after the Indus floods subsided, and the tenants on these lands were thus left without employment during the *kharif* season, and free 'to plot mischief'. Many Mazaris who cultivated in the riverain during the *rabi*, moved with their animals to the hills in the summer. By allowing the cultivation of commercially valuable *kharif* crops, including indigo and cotton, the opening of canal lands would thus provide critical income and employment during the hot season.[80] An important benefit in British eyes of the re-excavation of the Dhundi was thus the promise of increased power within the Mazari tribe for the Mazari chief—and thus the potential for greater British control over the Mazari tribe.

Conflicting interests, however, created serious problems for the Dhundi project, just as they did on Jamal Khan's extension of the Manka. Not only did the sharers have potentially conflicting political interests, but British canal officers faced serious technical problems in balancing the demands of those interested in newly opened 'wastelands' on the canal tails with those depending on irrigation near canal heads. As on the Manka extension, British canal officials had to significantly reorient irrigation arrangements near the head of the Dhundi in order to facilitate extension of the canal. On the Manka, Jamal Khan's extension required the British to sever several branch canals from the Manka in order to get adequate supplies to Leghari lands on the tail, and to supply these old branches from other canals or from new cuts taken from the river. This created considerable resentment against both Jamal Khan and the British among other Baloch chiefs whose own irrigation concerns were affected.[81] On the Dhundi, the role of the government in providing administrative assistance in an effort to assure the success of the 'Dhundi Company' was even more wide-ranging. Not only did the British provide oversight for the excavation, even using the government's powers to impress labor to carry out the project, but the irrigation department also moved, as on the Manka, to reorient irrigation arrangements on the upper reaches of the canal to try to assure adequate water for the Dhundi *pattis*. When the project was hampered by large inundations from the Indus, the British paid for the construction of a new *band* on the Indus, the Shah Jamal embankment, to protect the canal. When this required further reorientations of irrigation arrangement behind the *band*, the government re-negotiated with the Dhundi Company, granting it rights to take water rates from newly irrigated lands on the upper Dhundi. Indeed, Jamal Khan, acting, at least ostensibly, in the interests of the Company, continued to negotiate throughout the 1860s for increased concessions, in spite of the ongoing controversy between the Company and many of the zamindars towards the head, and in spite of the fact that problems with adequate water supply continued to hamper the expansion of cultivation in the Dhundi *pattis*.[82]

The political and economic interests of Baloch chiefs thus drew Baloch capital and labour into frontier canal investment in the early

1860s—even as the technical pressures of this process defined for the British a new role as the technical and legal arbiter of Baloch irrigation. Indeed, the tapping of Baloch energy into frontier irrigation development, as Baloch leaders themselves maneuvered for power within their own ecological and descent-based systems, opened new vistas of agricultural expansion on the colonial frontier. Whatever the difficulties, the initiatives from Baloch chiefs produced sufficient irrigation expansion that by the mid-1860s it was hailed by British officials as evidence of a spectacular colonial success. 'It is roughly estimated,' the Commissioner of the Derajat wrote in 1865, 'that the cultivated area irrigated from the [Indus] inundation canals is *three times* as large as it was at annexation.'[83] The Deputy Commissioner of the district extolled in the mid-1860s the political and social value of canals, which now ran along the whole border of the district, except for the area in the extreme south. The advantage of canal extension, he said, had been enormous, 'affording a nomad population the means of settling to fixed pursuits, reclaiming wastes; and last, but not least, making an artificial barrier against inroads from hill robbers, who are afraid to cross running water.'[84]

Perhaps equally important, canal projects had drawn several of the more important Baloch chiefs increasingly into the political and moral orbit of the colonial government. 'We have in the Baloch tribes of the Derajat a manly chivalrous race, and amongst their Chiefs some liberal-minded, public-spirited individuals, who thoroughly appreciate the efforts made to improve their position. . . .'[85] Nothing showed this 'liberalism' more clearly, in the eyes of a man like Minchin, than Baloch investment in canal irrigation within the new framework of administration developed by the British in the district. Indeed, it suggested that, in spite of the continuing role of these chiefs as tribal leaders beyond the irrigated plains, they had, by investing in irrigation, in a sense, 'crossed the frontier,' to take part in the new British empire.

Sandeman, Irrigation and the 'Forward Policy'

But the political implications of this process were nevertheless ambiguous and suggested on a broader scale the contradictions inherent in the British approach to frontier irrigation. However strong the connection between investment in settled agriculture and investment in the British regime, experience in Dera Ghazi Khan had also shown that chiefs invested in canals for reasons that had relatively little to do with 'liberalism' and with the principles that for many British officials defined and justified their rule. However 'liberal' some chiefs appeared to be in their willingness to invest in agriculture, to step up 'in the scale of civilization,' as Minchin put it,[86] the power and position of Baloch chiefs depended on the place of agriculture within a Baloch ecological system in which pastoralism, raiding, and violence also played critical roles. Indeed, the balance between control of agriculture and pastoral movement was, it can be argued, central to the dynamic of descent-based Baloch ethnic identitiy.[87] As Bruce pointed out, there was little to suggest that the Baloch were less likely to keep arms when farming than when moving with their animals; the strength of even the most 'liberal-minded' Baloch chief lay in his ability to 'turn out his clan of good guerilla warriors'.[88] All this suggested that for the Baloch, plains canal investment was linked to a larger trans-border cultural framework.

The cultural suppositions underlying British and Baloch interests in irrigation 'development' thus probably differed in critical ways. One example of this lay in perceptions of 'wasteland' and '*jangal*'. For the British, the distinction between 'waste' and productive agricultural land remained central, and strongly shaped the manner in which they viewed the increasing Baloch investment. Though well aware of the importance of long fallows in much of this arid region, and of the existence of temporary cultivation within largely pastoral tracts, they nevertheless widely used the term *jangal* to signify land that was, in effect, morally outside the sphere of agriculture, and that could be reclaimed for productive uses only if it were cleared of *jangal* (that is, uncontrolled, scrub growth) and subjected to irrigation. *Jangal* thus represented the abode of unsettled Baloch marauders, and to become cultivated it had to be morally transformed. But, for the Baloch, investment in irrigation hardly defined a moral transformation of the land from an unsettled world of 'marauding' to a world of settled agricultural production. Pastoralism and agriculture were, in fact, two interrelated elements in the ecological system in which Baloch identity and organization were rooted. *Jangal*, in the sense in which the British used it, thus encompassed for the Baloch a variety of lands, ranging from those used for pastoral grazing and periodic agriculture, to those which were used for cover during raids. Indeed, many of these lands probably went through periodic cycles as they were used alternatively in different ways depending on security, pastorage and availability of water.[89] It was thus unlikely that, for the Baloch, investment in irrigation on the plains heralded the same moral transformation of the land that it did for Minchin.

The nature of Baloch canal investment in the 1860s thus began to raise questions for some British officials about the cultural and political meaning of irrigation and settlement and about the nature of the contrasts between British rule and the realm across the frontier that had helped to shape British perception of their own colonial identity. Question were raised, for example, about the relationship of the canal department to the new patterns of irrigation development created by Baloch canal investment. As in Sind, the transfer of administrative control over canals to a specialized irrigation officer, linked to the provincial canal department, signaled a view of irrigation as a pre-eminently technical subject. The British had already appointed an officer to survey the existing canals of the Derajat frontier in the early 1850s, and in 1858 the management of these canals was brought directly under the authority of an officer of the Punjab Irrigation Department, thus incorporating it in a larger technical world. But, in this context, Minchin's reliance on the initiative of Baloch chiefs for the expansion of canal building appeared all the more problematic.

These questions came to a head most clearly with the arrival of Robert Sandeman as Deputy Commissioner of Dera Ghazi Khan in 1866. Sandemen shared many of Minchin's (and Jacob's) assumptions about the transformative nature of the British presence in the Indus basin, but he also realized that the irrigation investments of Baloch chiefs like Jamal Khan Leghari contradicted in some respects the basic logic of long-standing British thinking about the frontier and frontier policy. Jamal Khan Leghari had acquired considerable political influence as an intermediary between the British and the hill Baloch as a direct result of his increasing investment in irrigation on the plains. And yet, so long as the British conceived of the irrigated plains and the hills as separate moral and administrative worlds, his growing influence as a Baloch tribal chief served neither unequivocally to 'improve' and settle the Dera Ghazi Khan plains as a cordon against the hills, nor to provide the British an effective lever to directly control the Baloch across the frontier.[90] Military force continued to be critical to frontier protection. The ambiguities in his position thus suggested the contradictions in British frontier policy.

Sandeman, for this and other reasons, gradually developed in Dera Ghazi Khan in the late 1860s what became known as the 'forward policy', a new British approach to the frontier that ultimately had a profound impact on British policy along all the frontiers of north-western India. The key to Sandeman's policy was the notion that intermediaries like Jamal Khan could only be controlled if the British attempted to encompass fully the system of which the Baloch were a part—a system of power that spanned the frontier.[91] Sandeman thus rejected the colonial taboo against crossing the frontier, except on punitive military expeditions. He sought to cast a net around the systems of Baloch political orbit of the British administration, mediating their disputes in meetings both in the hills and on the plains, and offering their followers paid 'tribal service' as a regular form of income. The key to the new policy lay in an expansion of British knowledge about and mediation among the tribes on both sides of the border.

But Sandeman's policy depended not just on an expansion of British knowledge and presence, but critically also on a new frontier myth. Indeed, this new myth was perhaps most dramatically launched by a celebrated unarmed tour across the border undertaken by Sandeman himself in 1867. Formerly, British officers had been prohibited from venturing across the frontier, except on armed punitive expeditions. But after laying the foundations through consultations on the plains with Baloch chiefs and headmen, Sandeman embarked in 1867 on a tour of the headquarters of the leading Baloch tribes and classes in the hills, accompanied by leading *tumandars*, and traveling, in the awestruck and italicized words of his Victorian biographer, '*without military protection of any kind*'.[92]

The self-assertion embodied in this act defined symbolically, in effect, the new frontier power and policy of the British. The colonial state was not to be defined by a clearly bounded, physical frontier (as might be a nation-state) separating it from 'outsiders,' or even by the clear moral divide between settled, productive agriculture and the wandering life of the hills (however important that notion remained for many British officials). Rather, the power of the British—and their distinctive claim to authority—was defined by the British ability to encompass the Baloch tribal system within a net of British knowledge and power spread through the self-assertion of men like Sandeman—by a combination, in other words, of administrative science and the force of British moral character. The self-assertion of the British (embodied by Sandeman) was thus as important to the myth as was the power of British sciences of administration, and the British saw this as helping to draw even the Baloch themselves (for whom chiefly self-assertion was the key to legitimate leadership) into the spirit of their empire. As Dames noted in recording a Baloch poem in praise of Sandeman's 1867 expedition, the event had 'struck the Baloch imagination as deserving celebration in song as fully as a successful raid.'[93] The frontier was thus defined, in British eyes, not by the intrinsic differences of those without and within, but by the reach of Britain's power of assertion, understanding and incorporation. This was not, then, a policy of ethnic subversion of the Baloch, but one of incorporation. And the result was a policy pushing British agents ever more deeply into affairs beyond the Punjab and Sind frontiers.[94]

Critically, however, the 'forward policy' also had implications for British thinking about the place of irrigation in the society that they ruled on the Indus plains. By extending their own authority into the hills to encompass a Baloch world that spanned the frontier, the British also recognized, by implication, the legitimate intrusion of the world of the hills into the management of Baloch irrigation on the plains. Indeed, the reverse side of Sandeman's 'forward policy' of extension into the hills was the view that the management and expansion of irrigation of the plains could not be treated as a technical subject defining a realm wholly divorced from the politics of Baloch tribal identities and politics. Neither Sandeman nor most other British officials abandoned wholly, of course, the vision of irrigation and settlement as particularly associated with transformation and moral 'improvement'. But the powerful vision of irrigation as a foil to the life of the hills was compromised by the acceptance of a vision of Baloch ethnic identities that encompassed both investment in plains irrigation and raiding in the hills simultaneously. Closely bound up with Sandeman's move toward a 'forward policy' into the hills, was thus a critique of the developing British system of irrigation management on the plains of Dera Ghazi Khan.

Canal administration in Dera Ghazi Khan when Sandeman arrived was under the control of a district canal officer under the authority of the Punjab Irrigation Department, D. Kirwan. Kirwan had, in fact, worked closely with previous deputy commissioners in brokering the arrangements that had led to the great expansion of Baloch investment in canals beginning in the early 1860s. He had provided critical technical planning that had shaped Baloch canal-building in those years. Though sensitive in political issues, he had defined a system of canal administration that, at least rhetorically, put technical assessment and improvement at the heart of canal management. In Kirwan's report, the problem of managing canal heads, rationalizing the distribution of the water between canals, installing regulators, and arranging for timely silt clearance to maintain proper levels represented the official business of canal management. Among the first problems Sandeman confronted on arriving in Dera Ghazi Khan was thus the question of how to reconcile the management of canals under the authority of the canal department, with the imperatives of the 'forward policy'.

The management of silt clearance came to be an issue of considerable contention after Sandeman's arrival in the district, as he began to focus on the relationship between clearance arrangements and the structuring of Baloch power. The organization of canal clearance on virtually all inundation canals was critical to effective canal operation. The annual maintenance of canals depended on silt clearance during the cold weather. But in Dera Ghazi Khan, as in Sind, the British had directed in the 1850s that canal clearance be carried out not by *chhers*, but by wage labour, the cost of which was (in theory) split between the irrigators, who paid a special rate, and the government.[95] This rate was fixed until 1857, when the Punjab Chief Commissioner ruled that, as the rate had proved inadequate to meet half the costs of clearances, it should fluctuate to represent a true half cost. When Sandeman arrived in the district, he found that the total cost of canal clearance had risen steadily since annexation, more than tripling in the decade between 1857 and 1867, thus increasing greatly the financial burden of canal administration on both the government and the district's revenue payers. Though the increase was due in part to rising wage rates in the district (and an expansion of cash-cropping?), Sandeman blamed also the role played by prominent Baloch sardars, such as Jamal Khan Leghari, in taking up the contracts for canal clearances. The technical rhetoric of the canal department only masked, in Sandeman's view, the reality that Baloch politics already affected profoundly not only silt clearance, but almost all aspects of the operation of canal management—thus placing the canal officer in an anomalous position.

Indeed, Sandeman argued in 1868 that there was 'a regular traffic' in canal clearance contracts and estimates being carried on in the district in the interests of powerful Baloch zamindars like Jamal Khan. Though contracts for canal clearance were ostensibly auctioned in public, most were delivered (often by what Sandeman called 'private bargains') to prominent Baloch chiefs who could afford (or who could draw on credit with Hindu *banias*) to pay the required securities. These chiefs then in turn assigned them to their *mohtibars*, or resold them to *ods*, local contractors, often at rates that secured substantial profits to the chiefs. As the testimony of contractors themselves indicated, such profits were often further inflated by complicity between the surveyors and contractors in rigging the clearance estimates. Chiefs such as Jamal Khan thus profited in various ways. They profited directly from their ability to secure clearance contracts that had, as Sandeman saw it, increasingly been given out at inflated rates, allowing them to sub-contract and make handsome profits. They profited also from the leverage that control of clearance gave them on canals on which their own lands were situated. As one *lambardar* put it to Sandeman, Jamal Khan was able to get the zamindars on a canal entirely in his power by clearning out as 'little or much of the canal as suited him', thus presumably securing the maximum reliable water supply for his own lands.[96] Indeed, the extent of Jamal Khan Leghari's influence on the Dera Ghazi Khan canals was indicated by the fact that in 1867 he 'and his friends, by his own admission,' held 'the contracts of the Manka, Shoria, Dhingana, Dhoondee, and several branch canals, the amount of which came to nearly half a lakh of rupees.'[97]

What particularly disturbed Sandeman, however, were the potential political problems that this system of canal administration created for his overall system of frontier control, particularly in light of the developing 'forward policy.' And for this he blamed not only Jamal Khan but the district canal officer, Kirwan, whose position Sandeman increasingly saw as politically untenable. Not only had Kirwan allowed the costs of canal administration to escalate, but his canal clearance policies had, inadvertently or otherwise, also influenced politics beyond the frontier. In bitter correspondence with the Punjab government, Sandeman suggested that canal administration on the plains now held the capacity to wholly disrupt frontier administration, as there was 'not a single frontier chief who does not speculate extensively in the canals, and whose very position depends on the supply of water he receives'.[98] Careful manipulation of water administration on the plains was thus critical to the larger political purposes of British rule on the frontier, but by approaching such problems officially, as if they revolved only around technical improvement issues, the canal department exacerbated the problem. As Minchin himself had written in 1864, disputes about water often caused both the District Officer and the Superintendent of Canals great difficulty; though often appearing technical, these were generally 'more political than agrarian'; indeed, politics were often 'disguised', he wrote, 'under claims for canal cuttings'.[99] The very separation of 'technical' matters from those of indigenous power relations undermined British power.

A case in point was the disputes surrounding the irrigation of the Mazari tribe. Though still in the late 1860s a relatively poor and largely pastoral tribe occupying the southern part of Dera Ghazi Khan, the Mazaris and their chief, Imam Bakhsh, were increasingly prominent in Sandeman's plans for controlling the Dera Ghazi Khan frontier, particularly the frontier facing the Marri-Bugti hills. Sandeman saw Imam Bakhash Mazari as a critical intermediary in dealing with the Bugti chiefs, with whom the Mazaris had close relations. The Mazaris often grazed their cattle in the Bugti hills, while the Bugtis, in dry seasons, brought their cattle down to the river into Mazari lands. To cement his own influence with the Bugtis, Imam Bakhsh Mazari had negotiated with the British in the early 1860s, on the Bugtis' behalf, for lands on the canal projects in which the Mazaris were involved, including the Dhundi and the resuscitation of the Gamul, a branch of the Kadra canal.[100] Like attempts to settle sections of the Bugtis in Sind, however, these attempts to create Bugti settlements on the plains in Dera Ghazi Khan proved unsuccessful.[101] But the potential role of the Mazari chief as an intermediary in British relations with the Bugtis nevertheless remained vital to Sandeman's frontier strategy. He thus proposed in 1867 the reworking of the Gamul project (which had not been an initial success) to shore up the position of the Mazari chief, developing with the canal engineer a technical plan to solve long-standing water problems in the Rajanpur *tahsil* (exacerbated by on-going problems with the supply of the Dhundi canal as well). Sandeman proposed a new 'joint-stock' scheme involving not only the re-opening and extension of the Gamul, but the construction of a new head and a protective Indus *band* for the Kootub canal, which would be tailed into the Gamul to give it a secure supply. This would not only allow the increasing settlement of some Mazari tribesmen (who continued to be the most heavily dependent of the Baloch tribes on the plains on cattle and pastorage) but would also draw labour and cultivators onto irrigated lands controlled by the Mazari chief, including former tenants (presumably Jats) from Bahawalpur, thus increasing and stabilizing Imam Bakhsh's income. The result would be enhanced power within his tribe and enhanced leverage for the British in dealing with the Mazaris—and by extension, increased leverage for Sandeman in dealing with the Bugtis.[102] Technical improvements in irrigation works were thus critical to Sandeman's political vision for a system of control on the Mazari frontier.

But the political benefits of such technical improvements could in practice be undercut, in Sandeman's view, by the very reliance in these projects on the technical expertise of the district canal engineer. Neither design nor operation problems were free of broader implications relating to the tribal politics of the Baloch. In the case of the Mazaris the increasing influence of the district canal officer in Mazaris' affairs had come with a clear political cost. In early 1869, even as new canal projects in Rajanpur were underway, Sandeman discovered that the executive engineer had sold contracts for clearing existing canals in Rajanpur to a relative of Jamal Khan Leghari, in spite of the delicate problems facing Sandeman in composing relations between the Legharis and the Mazaris, who had interests in these canals. Strains had, in fact, been exacerbated by previous conflicts between Imam Bakhsh and Jamal Khan Leghari over canal investments in Rajanpur, not all of which had turned out successfully. Kirwan, of course, defended his actions as necessary to maintaining good canal operation. He declared that since no Mazaris had come forward when the contracts were auctioned, he had given the contracts to a man who could do the job. But Sandeman complained that this hardly answered the political objections, for whatever the difficulties in letting the contracts, such actions greatly complicated his political dealings with the tribes, a position with which the Punjab Lieutenant-Governor ultimately agreed.[103]

Even more serious, however, were the political conflicts over water distribution that developed as Baloch and British canal investments advanced, not only in Rajanpur but in other parts of the district as well. A representative example of this was the dispute between the Legharis and Khosas that centered on Jamal Khan's extension of the Manka canal. In reorienting the upper branches of the Manka to ensure the delivery of adequate water to Jamal Khan's extension at the tail, Kirwan had effectively severed the Dhori, which watered Khosa lands, from the Manka, installing masonry heads (*moris*) on the Manka to do this. For Kirwan, this was justified by the fact that the Dhori now was connected to the new Fazalwah, built by Fazal Khan Loond, which supplied water to the Khosas as an alternative. But in the eyes of Sandeman, this played into the bitter feuds that had long disrupted politics within the Khosa tribe, and fanned long-standing enmities between a section of the Khosas and their 'hereditary blood-enemies', the Legharis. The shift in the source of water for the Dhori led into a battle for power within the Khosa tribe between Sikander Khan Khosa, who was related by marriage to the Loond *tumandar*, and Ghulam Haider Khan Khosa, the son of the Khosa chief, who was not. To Ghulam Haider, locked in a bitter dispute with Sikander Khan for influence within the Khosa tribe, the severing of the Dhori's ties to the Manks, particularly at the behest of the chief of the Legharis, and its connection to the Fazalwah, seemed deliberately calculated to undercut his ability to control tribal access to water, and with this, his ability to claim legitimate chiefly authority in the tribe. Seeing the loss of his control over Dhori water, Ghulam Haider Khan protested strongly to the British, and failing to gain redress, carried his protest outside the tribe, 'wander(ing) about complaining of his grievances.' Ghulam Haider Khan, in fact, accused Sikander Khan, the Loond *tumandar* and Jamal Khan of all being allied in a conspiracy against him, a conspiracy which was being aided by the executive engineer. Though the Khosas were among the largest landowners in the district, and long tied to agricultural lands on the plains, the episode, in Sandeman's estimation, seriously disrupted their relations with the British government.[104]

The potential significance of such conflicts for frontier security was demonstrated to Sandeman by the emergence of a violent challenge to British authority on the frontier in the mid-1860s. Shortly after Sandeman's arrival, the frontier witnessed the rise of an 'outlaw band' in the hills led by Ghulam Husain Bugti. Ghulam Husain had challenged the authority of the Bugti chief, and gathering around him tribesmen of the Marris, Bugtis and Khetrans, numbering at times as many as 1,200 men, had launched a series of raids along the border, raiding as far as Kelat and Jacobabad in Sind. The chief problem in bringing Ghulam Husain under control lay in the fact that the chiefs of the various tribes in the hills were able to exert little control over him. Perhaps most critical to Ghulam Husain's success was the asylum and support he received in disposing, in the hills, of the property and livestock plundered in raids on the plains. Ghulam Husain was given asylum by the Haddiani Legharis and Khetrans, and much of the property he plundered was sold to the Khetrans at Barkhan, who, in the words of Sandeman, 'sent it for sale into our territory with their annual *kaflahs* (caravans)', which passed through Sakhi Sarwar with the safe conduct of Jamal Khan Leghari.[105] Sandeman was convinced that Jamal Khan knew well of Ghulam Husain's movement, but 'for purposes of his own', concealed them from the district authorities.[106] Indeed, his wealth and leverage with other chiefs in canal affairs had given him power, as Sandeman saw it, to defy the district authorities. 'Sandeman used to say,' wrote his protege, Richard Bruce, 'that when [Jamal Khan] came for interviews he used to sit with his tongue in his cheek looking superbly insolent. . . . His power on the frontier galled Sandeman. 'Pat, my boy,' Sandeman supposedly told Bruce, 'until we can smash up Jamal Khan and his little game we shall never do any good either in the district or with the Border tribes.'[107]

Asserting his 'forward policy' in the late-1860s, Sandeman thus sought, in dealing with Ghulam Husain, to build a new alliance of *tumandars* along the border. Using the Mazari *tumandar*, Imam Bakhsh, as an intermediary, he established direct relations with the Bugti chief, Ghulam Murtaza Khan, even though the Bugti *tuman* lay entirely beyond the ostensible (British-defined) Dera Ghazi Khan frontier. After a *darbar* at Jampur with all the Bugti headmen, Sandeman turned his alliance against Ghulam Husain and almost three hundred of his men at Hurrund in one of the most dramatic frontier encounters of the early British era.

The result was a sensation. This 'brilliant affair', the Punjab government subsequently wrote, ending as it did 'in the dispersion of an organized and extensive robber confederacy', and in heralding a new era in frontier policy in Dera Ghazi Khan. The Hurrund raid in fact marked a critical turning point in the history of the Dera Ghazi Khan frontier, for the door to the ascendancy of the 'forward policy' was now opened. It was shortly afterward that Sandeman sealed his reputation as the new star of British frontier policy with his celebrated unarmed stroll through the hills.[108]

But, as Sandeman wrote stormily to the government in the aftermath, one of the chief lessons of the Hurrund raid was the interconnection between frontier control and administration on the plains, and particularly the control of irrigation. Indeed, central to Sandeman's view of the proceedings was that Jamal Khan's influence on both sides of the frontier had been so strengthened in the period before the Hurrand raid by his role in the district's canal system—in which virtually all the frontier chiefs were involved—that it had undercut his role as an intermediary for the administration on the frontier and unsettled the frontier in general.

In the period following the Hurrund raid, Sandeman thus moved aggressively to try to exert more political control over canal administration in the district, even as he pushed his 'forward policy' into the hills. And he did this not just with an attack on the position of Jamal Khan Leghari, but with an assault as well on the reputation of the canal department's executive engineer. The pervasive—and inevitable—intrusion of politics into a department that operated ostensibly on the basis of technical knowledge had in practice, Sandeman now argued, produced only a system of deeply entrenched corruption, in which the engineer, Kirwan, was fully enmeshed. Indeed, by 1870, Sandeman had succeeded in putting Kirwan into the dock at the chief court of the Punjab in Lahore for accepting bribes, charging him with being in league with Jamal Khan Leghari in a massive scheme of canal corruption. According to the charges, Kirwan had from the early 1860s acted in concert with Jamal Khan and leading Hindu bankers of Dera Ghazi Khan to siphon off canal allocations and to channel canal contracts to Jamal Khan at concessional rates in return for the transfer of large sums to Kirwan's bank accounts. It was the result of this corrupt bargain that had resonated all along the frontier in the run-up to the Hurrund raid. 'I believe the largest raid that ever occurred on this border, in which 300 men were killed and wounded,' Sandeman now wrote in high outrage, 'was instigated to a great extent by those concerned in these canal fraud cases.'[109]

Among numerous charges, the major ones centered on Kirwan's handing of expenditure and contracts for the clearance and extension of the Dhundi and Manka canals. Sandeman charged that a sum of Rs. 16,000, authorized by the government for the Dhundi project, had been endorsed by Mr. Kirwan not directly to the tahsildar overseeing the work, but to a 'Dhoondee Canal Account' with Chimmun Lall & Loodu Ram, leading bankers of Dera Ghazi Khan—an account that was in fact controlled by Jamal Khan Leghari. From this account Rs. 6,000 was subsequently transferred to the tahsildar for actual Dhundi canal expenses. But the remaining Rs. 10,000 was transferred to another account of Jamal Khan's entitled 'Cotton Deposit Account.' Augmented by an additional Rs. 10,000 of Jamal Khan's own money, this account was then used by Loodu Ram to engage in cotton speculations, a venture in which Jamal Khan Leghari and Loodu Ram were sharers in profit and loss. When these speculations proved successful, Jamal Khan transferred from his profits of the following year a sum of Rs. 4,000 to the personal banker of Mr. Kirwan, who drew up *hundis* to transfer the amount to Kirwan's bank accounts in Agra and Lahore. The evidence thus suggested that Kirwan and Jamal Khan had been in complicity from the beginning.[110]

Equally disturbing were the alleged arrangements worked out between Kirwan and Jamal Khan for the disposal of the Manka silt clearance contracts. From Kirwan's arrival in the district, the prosecutors charge, he had encouraged corrupt arrangements for silt clearance contracts. Though instructed to sell the clearance of the Manka by public auction, Kirwan,

> according to an understanding between himself and two native contractors, Jamal Khan, chief of the Lugaries[*sic*], and Ahmed Khan, his agent, gave them year after year a monopoly of the contract on the most favorable terms, stipulating that he, Mr. Kirwan, should receive a share of the profits.[111]

Right up until 1869, Kirwan had continued to receive kickbacks while

Jamal Khan retained control of the clearances. Most importantly, as Sandeman saw it, Kirwan's corruption explained more clearly than any earlier evidence the dramatic escalation in the cost of canal clearances in Dera Ghazi Khan since the time of annexation. The revelations of 1870 thus only confirmed what Sandeman had long suspected. The corruption of the executive engineer had encouraged corruption, as he saw it, at all levels of the district canal administration.

Conclusion: Empire, Irrigation, and Tribal Identity

But the lessons of this scandal were far larger. Kirwan himself was acquitted of most of the charges against him at Lahore, a result, as the prosecutors saw it, of the supposed perjury of key witnesses among the Hindu bankers. Nevertheless, the charges against Kirwan and Jamal Khan resulted in critical changes in the framework for irrigation in Dera Ghazi Khan. In immediate terms, Kirwan's official career was brought to an end. The British also reprimanded Jamal Khan officially for his involvement, and stripped him of his position as an honorary magistrate. But more significant were the larger changes that came in Sandeman's wake. The scandal involving Kirwan and Jamal Khan provided the occasion for the reformulation of frontier irrigation in ways more fully reflective of the redefinitions of the frontier—and of the meaning of water control and British rule—implicit in Sandeman's 'forward policy'.

The subsequent administrative triumph of the 'forward policy' on the frontier was in fact marked by the ascendancy of Sandeman and his ideas in dealing with the Baloch from the mid-1870s into the 1880s. Sandeman moved on from Dera Ghazi Khan to become eventually the Agent to the Governor-General for Baluchistan, a position from which he directed a policy seeking to incorporate the whole Baloch political structure, including the influence of the Khan of Kelat, into a British colonial framework.[112] But the impact on irrigation on the Indus plains was equally telling. The British increasingly began to view the processes of irrigation expansion and agricultural settlement on the Baloch frontier as shaped and constrained by their interaction with the tribal systems of the Baloch themselves.

One measure of this was the almost categorical rejection by many of Sandeman's supporters of the idea of trying to separate sections of the Baloch from the hills and from their tribal cohorts in the interest of frontier control or moral transformation. 'With regard to the independent

Biluch tribes on this border,' Richard Bruce wrote, 'nothing but evil would ensue from trying to settle particular sections or individuals, or indeed, from dealing with them in any other way independently of the main body. . . .' To the contrary, the authority of Baloch settlement on their own tribal lands, 'which are finer than any we could offer them . . . .' Bruce argued, in effect, that settlement could occur (and, in fact, was occurring) within the existing frameworks of Baloch structures of tribal adaptation to their environments. The Bugtis, Marris, and Khetrans, he noted, had been steadily grazing their cattle and extending cultivation on lands that, except for short periods, had previous to British rule long been waste—a response now, he implied, to increasing frontier order.[113] Critical for the expansion of agriculture was thus the strengthening, within this context, of Baloch tribal authority and the position of the Baloch chiefs, not the breaking up of tribes. What was needed was an imperial framework within which the connection between Baloch ethnicity and settlement on the land could be maintained—not the subversion of Baloch ethnicity to effect a moral transformation.

Critically, this process also involved a new British emphasis on the importance (and legitimacy) of Baloch cultural identity within the operation of politics and irrigation on the Indus plains. In sharp contrast with the pre-existing concern to morally transform Baloch leaders by drawing them across the border, some British officials now seemed to imply that Jamal Khan Leghari's fault was not that he had brought Baloch politics into district canal administration, but that he had compromised Baloch identity as he had done so, that his dealings with Kirwan had become corrupt because he had strayed too far in his canal machinations from being truly 'Baloch'. T.H. Thornton, Sandeman's biographer and himself a high British offical, thus noted that Sandeman's reliance on Imam Bakhsh Mazari in the late 1860s as a political counter to Jamal Khan, had reflected not only that Imam Bakhsh was strategically situated on the Bugti frontier, loyal to the British and 'singularly upright', but that he was also 'a Baluch to the backbone'.[114] This was, by implication, in sharp contrast to the image of Jamal Khan embodied in the tales of complex finance emerging from the Chief Court in Lahore. Ironically, this reflected, of course, a continuing British stereotype, shared by many Baloch themselves, that pastoralism, in which the Mazaris were heavily involved, was connected to true 'Balochness'. But noteworthy also was that being 'Baluch to the backbone' was viewed now as offering no challenge to full participation in the colonial political structure and in the expansion of irrigation on the plains; to the contrary, it was seen by some as a vital element in the process of agricultural expansion.

Indeed, Jamal Khan Leghari's subsequent career itself illustrated the importance of these attitudes. In spite of being censured and denied magisterial powers after the revelations of Kirwan's trial, Jamal Khan retained an important position in British frontier policy in the 1870s, precisely because he remained one of the most important players both in Dera Ghazi Khan irrigation and in tribal affairs. It was no surprise in this context that Sandeman himself ultimately played the critical role in rehabilitating Jamal Khan by using him as an intermediary in his political dealings with the Khetrans in the early 1870s, and finally employing him in 1875-6 on his mission to Kelat, a service for which Jamal Khan was rewarded not only by the restoration of his magisterial powers, but also by the honorary title, 'Nawab', a strong signal of his continuing political importance to the British.[115]

Bythe time of his death, Jamal Khan had thus regained his reputation as one of the most heroic of the Baloch tribal chiefs. This was illustrated by an elegy in Balochi written in response to a contest sponsored by an assembly of Baloch chiefs to commemorate Jamal Khan's death at Dera Ghazi Khan in 1881.[116] Jamal Khan's position of influence with the British was now recognized as one of the foundations of this reputation. He was as splendid a presence when he 'sat with the English on a chair of state,' as 'when he drew his sword and made war on his foes,' the poet wrote. But his chiefly image was derived equally from his ability to mitigate the uncertainties of the diverse environment in which his tribesmen lived, an ability that hinged on his control over water. Water, of course, ultimately depended on the will of God. 'May Allah protector of thousands bring the pleasant rains' the poet exhorted, 'may they come in their season and rain upon Choti's mountain-skirts [near the seat of the Legharis], may the river [Indus] rise in flood and the creepers burst into flower.' But the successful appropriation of this bounty depended on the construction and management of the torrents and inundation canals necessary to take advantage of these gifts.[117] Nothing symbolized Jamal Khan's primacy in this more clearly than his ability to tap into God's bounty to secure his reputation as a master of largess for his followers and tribesmen.

> Of all chiefs of tribes the Choti Nawab is the first with sharpened knife in hand . . . to kill the fatted kine, sheep and goats, that nothing should be lacking in hospitality. . . . Hand-mills and bullock-mills perpetually grind corn, and

processions of trays with golden covers pass in; and minstrels in numbers overflowed the place, bringing deputations into the assembly-hall in Jamal Khan's dwelling. . . .

This was, in fact, the cultural currency of Baloch power. 'Many thousands of enemies and friends,' the poet wrote, 'abase themselves.' Though images of pastoralism and animal-keeping continued to be prominent, the successful collection and munificent distribution of the produce of irrigated agriculture were clearly now critical to Jamal Khan's reputation.

Jamal Khan's position made clear the degree to which, even for the British, tribal power and irrigated agriculture had now come to be intimately related. The spread of agriculture, and agricultural development, remained central to British visions of morally civilized life, and of their own transformative power in India. But the definition of imperial power, particularly in the Indus basin, was increasingly linked also to the British vision of themselves as patrons of a tribal social order. Central to the state's own self-definition was thus an ability to reconcile its identity as a force for moral transformation with its identity as a tribal patron. Indeed, irrigation had become a critical field–perhaps *the* critical field–in which the interrelationships between these visions were negotiated and played out.

The contradictions in British policy were, of course, numerous. As the history of canal-building along the frontier suggested, irrigation development involved complex relationships between a variety of actors: tribal leaders, cultivators, pastoralists, itinerant labourers, traders, men of capital, and state officials. It involved negotiations of power not only between the British and tribal leaders, but between competing tribal leaders, between such leaders and their kinsmen, between pastoral leaders and monied Hindu traders, and between competing state officials. Such negotiations had shaped pre-colonial state-building, and the British made critical use of them as well. British officials had thus used personal influence–and the structure of British law (including the facilitation of joint-stock companies)–to draw both tribal leaders and indigenous men of capital into canal investments that would strengthen British power and influence along the frontier.

But as the British defined their own authority in relation to frontier tribal structures–and mobilized tribal chiefs such as Jamal Khan as key players in irrigation development–they had sought not only to patronize the spread of agriculture, but also to define a simplified vision of tribal leadership that would effectively facilitate new forms of tribal encapsulation within their imperial structures. This was implicit in Sandeman's forward policy. Tribal leaders, as Sandeman saw them, were defined preeminently by genealogy, patronage of their kinsmen, and the upholding of tribal honor, which included a strong emphasis on the value of loyalty. This was critical to Sandeman's vision of imperial incorporation.[118] Nothing had so upset Sandeman about the canal scandals of the late 1860s as the fact that Jamal Khan had seemingly acted in ways that defied his vision of tribal honor and chiefship, striking entrepreneurial deals with Hindu traders even as he conspired behind Sandeman's back with the district canal engineer. Though such actions were entirely in keeping with long-standing Baloch strategies for securing wealth and power, they were at odds with the vision of tribal leadership that men like Sandeman now saw as central to the emerging structure of imperial power.

But reconciling Sandeman's vision of tribal organization to the effective management of water did not prove to be an easy undertaking. To avoid a repetition of the scandals of the 1860s, the government subsequently dictated administratively that the oversight of canal management could no longer be left wholly to the Irrigation Department engineers. Although 'the officers of the Canal Department' would continue to have 'primary' responsibility for the technical administration of canals, the Punjab Lieutenant Governor directed in 1874, their decisions would subsequently be subject to direct review by the Deputy Commissioner of Dera Ghazi Khan, who held primary responsibility for the political management of the district's tribes.[119]

But such administrative expedients were hardly enough to resolve the issue, for, in practical terms, effective canal administration and the maintenance of tribal leadership were not always easy to balance on the ground. To encapsulate tribal authority within the evolving structure of imperial rule involved a more sweeping definition of a structure of rights and law that was consistent *both* with the imperatives of agricultural expansion *and* with the imperatives of tribal leadership and identity. And this involved not only the definition of water rights, but also the larger question of defining rights to land, to which water rights were closely linked. Tribal chiefs such as Jamal Khan Leghari and Imam Bakhsh Mazari had, in fact, gained large landed estates during the processes of canal construction, a circumstance central to the redefinition of their authority within the framework of British imperial rule. Investment in canal-building, and the spread of agriculture, had gone hand in hand in Dera Ghazi Khan with the fixing of legal rights.[120] But although this served to stabilize Baloch chiefly authority, it hardly encapsulated fully the influence of Baloch tribal chiefs. As Sandeman and others had understood well, chiefly power often hinged on the ability to cross such fixed boundaries, to negotiate open access to land and water, and to mitigate uncertainty amidst diverse environments. While in some ways facilitated by the fixing of property boundaries, chiefly authority thus derived, in other ways, precisely from the ability to transcend them.[121] The challenge for the British was to define a legal structure within which the imperatives of tribal identity and the fixing of rights could thus be reconciled.

Subsequent British policy in Dera Ghazi Khan clearly reflected these tensions. Defining the nature of the extent and limits of the tribal authority of men such as the Leghari and Mazari *tumandars*–and of their rights in irrigation–remained an ongoing subject of discussion and debate in British correspondence. Though British officials took increasingly direct roles in the management of Baloch canals after 1870, stabilizing agriculture and fixing water rights, they attempted at the same time to maintain, by various expedients, the distinctive claims to authority of Baloch chiefs within the district's irrigation system.[122] But the tensions arising from frontier irrigation development in Dera Ghazi Khan also point us toward the larger tensions shaping British law and policy in the second half of the nineteenth century in the Indus basin as a whole. Imperial authority in the Indus basin hinged both on the spread of agriculture (and the settling of property rights) and on the patronage of a tribal social system. To understand how these concerns interacted to shape the larger structure of British law and power in the Indus basin we must move, therefore, from the Baloch frontier to the emerging heart of imperial authority and agricultural expansion on the plains of the Punjab. For it was there that the political implications of the interactions between property, water control, tribal organization, and imperial authority, can be most clearly seen.

NOTES

1. F.W.R. Fryer, *Final Report of the First Regular Settlement of the Dera Ghazi Khan District (1869 to 1874)*, Lahore: Central Jail Press, 1876, p. 66.
2. Robert N. Pehrson, *The Social Organization of the Marri Baluch*, compiled and analysed from his notes by Fredrik Barth, New York: Wennar-Gren Foundation for Anthropological Research, 1966, p. 4.
3. For a discussion of the divisions of time used for *kalapani* irrigation in the

hills (though in an area occupied predominantly by Pakhtuns and Khetrans), see *Loralai District*, Baluchistan District Gazetteer Series, Vol. II, Allahabad: Pioneer Press, 1907, pp. 187-92.

4. The subordination of Hindus was indicated by dress, but their protection was critical to Baloch honor. As one British official put it in the 1860s, 'Amongst the Baloch the good treatment of Hindoo traders and their families, through whom all monetary transactions are carried on, is a point of honour.' This was so important that when the Mazari chief visited the Bugti chief at Schaf (the Bugti seat in the hills), and heard rumors that he had violated Hindu women, he responded that the Bugti chief must have gone mad and should be sent away for treatment. NAI, Foreign Dept. Procs. (Pol A), June 1863, nos. 123-5 (Settlement of Sections of the Boogtee in the DGK Plains).
5. For a detailed discussion of the operation and construction of *karezes*, see *Gazetteer of Loralai District*, pp. 180-6.
6. For a good description of the operation of *rodkohi* irrigation, and its problems, see Henry St. George Tucker, *Settlement Report of the Dera Ismail Khan District* (1872-79), pp. 5-8, 197-203
7. The comment is from L.J.H. Grey, who worked on torrent irrigation, in Dera Ghazi Khan in the 1860s. F. and C. Grey, eds., *Tales of Our Grandfather, or India Since* 1856, London: Smith, Elder, 1912, pp. 97-8.
8. Fryer, *SR*, pp. 59, 60.
9. This was the estimate of Major C.C. Minchin in 1861. He added, however, that 'the produce of one good year will more than cover the losses of the other two years, yet during this period the zamindars must remain idle and unemployed—a fruitful source of mischief—unless they can obtain service in other parts of the country'. Punjab Board of Revenue, file 251/106 (Purchase of the Nur & Dhundi canals), p. 10.
10. M.L. Dames, DC, DGK to Comm & Super, Derajat, 17 April 1888, Punjab, Rev. and Agric., Agric., A procs., no. 1, August 1888. IOL.
11. Fryer, *SR*, p. 38.
12. As Minchin noted of the Khosa *tumandar*, when torrent cultivation failed, he assisted 'his distressed clansmen from his own granaries making small money advances in addition'. Capt. C. Minchin, *Memorandum on the Baloch Tribes in Dera Ghazi Khan District*, Selections from the Records of the Government of the Punjab, new series, no. 3, p. 12.
13. Fryer, *SR*, p. 61.
14. For a discussion of Pakhtun tribal society stressing the tension between the search for productive household autonomy and the dependence on tribal leaders, which in its central aspects seems equally applicable to the Baloch, see Asger Christensen, 'Organization, Variation and Transformation in Pukhtun Society,' *Ethnos*, Vol. 46, nos. 1-2, 1981, pp. 96-108.
15. As Pehrson notes in his discussion of the Marri Biloch, the tribes confronting the British in the nineteenth century had been shaped by a pattern of

ongoing splitting and fusing segments, and by the roles of tribal leaders in protecting and expanding grazing grounds. Yet, awareness of the differing origins of tribal segments did not prevent the maintenance by emerging Baloch tribes of a unifying political ideology of segmentary descent. Pehrson, *Social Organization of the Marri Baloch*, p. 3.

16. There may, in fact, have been two separate waves of migration into the Indus Basin, one in the thirteenth-fourteenth centuries that carried Baloch from Makran into Sind, and a second, in the fifteenth century, that took them into Punjab, Brian Spooner., 'Baluchistan: Geography, History, and Ethnography,' *Encyclopedia Iranica*, Vol. 3, 1988, p. 609.
17. Dames, *Popular Poetry of the Baloches*, Vol. I, p. xxiii.
18. M. Longworth Dames, *The Baloch Race: A Historical and Ethnographic Sketch*, Asiatic Society Monographs, no. 4, London: Royal Asiatic Society, 1904, p. 47. The importance of the search for water as a critical trope in Baloch poetry generally is also suggested by Dames. See L. Dames, *Popular Poetry of the Baloch*, Vol. I, p. xvii.
19. Inayatullah Baloch, *The Problem of 'Greater Baluchistan': A Study of Baloch Nationalism*, Stuttgart: Stenier-Verlag-Wiesbaden-GMBH, 1987, p. 97.
20. For a discussion of the emergence of Baluch as a sort of military aristocracy under the Kalhoras and the Talpurs, see Richard Burton, *Sindh and the Races that Inhabit the Valley of the Indus,* Lahore: Khan Publishers, 1976; reprint of 1851 edition, pp. 235-7. According to Burton, the advent of the Baloch into the Kalhora aristocracy came in the 1740s when the ruler of the Kalhoras, who also claimed religious authority as *pir*, indeed two of his powerful Baluch *murids* to settle in the low country.
21. In Sind, as compared with Punjab, continuing migrations strengthened tribal organization among Baluch in the eighteenth and nineteenth centuries, a fact reflected in the significant number returned as speaking Baluchi in 1901. E.H. Aitken, *Gazetteer of the Province of Sind*, Karachi: Government Printing, 1907, rpt., 1986, p.189. But even in Sind, as Sorley remarks: the Baluch tribes 'have not retained an organization, comparable among their neighbours in Baluchistan regions . . .'. H.T. Sorley, *The Gazetteer of West Pakistan . . . Sind,* Karachi: West Pakistan Government Press, 1968, p. 240.
22. M. Longworth Dames, *The Baloch Race*, p. 48.
23. Fryer, *SR*, p. 39. According to the Gazetteer of Dera Ismail Khan, Malik Sohrab Dodai entered the service of Sultan Husain Langah of Multan in the fifteenth century, and received large land grants along the Indus to help to protect the country against robbers. This attracted the Mirranis, who established Dera Ghazi Khan, while Malik Sohrab founded Dera Ismail Khan, named after his son. *Gazetteer of the Dera Ismail Khan District, 1883-84,* Lahore: Arya Press, 1884, pp. 29-31.
24. *Ain-i-Akbari*, trans. by Col. H.S. Jarrett and corrected by Jadunath Sarkar, Delhi: Low Price Publications, 1989 reprint, vol. II, p. 331.
25. See Dames, p. 34, and suggestion that use of *jhalars* on the Indus

represented a form of asserting political control of lands in early days of Mirranis.

26. *Ain-i-Akbari*, Vol. II, p. 333. I assume that the listing for Dudai in the *Ain* refers to the Mirrani of Dera Ghazi Khan, though Inayatullah describes a 'Dodai confederacy' including not only the Mirrani but also that of Dera Ismail Khan and the Kolachi of Dera Fateh Khan as well. He cites Sujan Rao Batalwi, writing in the time of Aurangzeb, as noting that the Dodai country showed 'no sign of poverty and robbery', and that they commanded an army of 80,000 soldiers and 50,000 horsemen, a figure significantly larger than that given in the *Ain-i-Akbari*. Inayatullah Baloch, *The Problem of 'Greater Baluchistan'*, pp. 99-100. See also Muzaffar Alam, *The Crisis of Empire in Mughal North India*, Delhi: Oxford University Press, 1986, pp. 143-4. None of these sources explicitly mentions the building of canals.
27. F.W.R. Fryer, Settlement Officer, DGK to Comm. & Super., Derajat, 11 February 1871. IOL. Ag. Rev & Commerce, A procs. September 1872, no. 15, Appendix. The terms in which this process is described reflect of course, the revenue preoccupations of the British in the nineteenth century, but there is no reason to doubt this account as a general outline of the process.
28. 'Private property,' as James Lyall put it, 'originated in water, the scarcer article, rather than land.' Village commons were therefore virtually unknown, as land only gained value with the sinking of a well or access to canal or torrent water. J.B. Lyall, Settlement Comm, Multan and Derajat, 13 October 1875, Fryer, *SR*, p. 10.
29. This paragraph is based generally on Fryer's report on canals. F W.R. Fryer, Settlement Officer, DGK to Comm. & Super., Derajat, 11 February 1871. IOL, Ag. Rev & Commerce, A procs, September 1872, no.15, Appendix.
30. R.B.J. Bruce. 'Notes on the Dera Ghazi Khan District and its Border Tribes'. p. 92: Major W.G. Davies. Officiating Settlement Comm., Multan and Derajat to Officiating Sec to Fin Comms, Punjab, 27 November 1874. IOL, Foreign Department. A procs., August 1875, no. 41. According to Munshi Hukum Chand, 'Haibat Khan Mirrani first had the canal dug from the river in the time of Nawab Ghazi Khan' (though it later became buried). Munshi Hukum Chand, *Tawarikh-i-Zilla Dera Ghazi Khan*, Lahore: Katoriya Press, 1876, p. 516.
31. Give political background here, demise of Nahars in south of DGK, role of other eighteenth century states, particularly Durranis.
32. Munshi Hukum Chand, *Tawarikh-i-Zilla Dera Ghazi Khan*, pp. 522-4.
33. Fryer file for Sitpur.
34. 'Report by A. Burnes on the Trade of the Upper Indus, or Derajat', Foreign Dept. Procs., 25 September 1837, no. 94. National Archives of India, Delhi. Burnes noted that the numbers of Hindus and Muslims in DGK was about equal, as there were 125 temples and 110 mosques in the city. The role of Shikarpuri merchants and indigo trade is also discussed by Mohan Lall,

who traveled through DGK to Shikarpur in 1836 and reported back to the Company. Foreign Dept. Procs., 1 August 1836, nos. 32-4.

35. This was the Gamoowala canal. Though its exact date of construction is not given in the documents, it was probably built in the late eighteenth century by a local zamindar, Gamoo Jhakkar. The first mortgage occurred about 1814. IOL, Punjab PWD, Civil Works—Irrigation, December 1868. A procs. no. 1.
36. Neither of these involved relations with the Mirranis, but reflected the general pattern. Lepel Griffin and C.F. Massy, *Chiefs and Families of Note in the Punjab*, Lahore: Civil and Military Gazette Press, 1910, Vol. II, p. 334; F.W.R. Fryer, Settlement Officer, DGK to Comm. & Super., Derajat, 11 February 1871. IOL, Ag., Rev. & Commerce. A procs, September 1872, no.15. [Check PA file on Gurchani canal under British to show how the process potentially involved not only the chiefs but the heads of tribal sections.]
37. Bruce, p. 33.
38. Bruce. *Notes on the Dera Ghazi Khan District*, p. 43; Griffin and Massy, *Punjab Chiefs*, Vol. II, p. 363.
39. Example of Jahan Khan Khosa.
40. The most likely date for the shift, according to the gazetteer, was 1787, though not all were in agreement on this. According to tradition, the shift was precipitated by the construction of a canal by the Nawab of Sitpur, into whose bed the river shifted. *Muzaffargarh District*, 1908, pp. 5-6.
41. Bruce, p. 130.
42. Give examples—Mazaris, Gurchanis, Drishaks, Legharis—these included marriage alliances.
43. The quotations are from 'The Attack on Tibbi Lund', a ballad concerning a thirteenth century (AH) conflict between the Tibbi Lund on the one side and the Gurchanis and Legharis on the other. The ballad, as Dames notes, 'is probably the composition of a Dom or professional minstrel', M. Longworth Dames, *Popular Poetry of the Baloches*, pp. 63-6.
44. Bruce, p. 32.
45. Ibid., pp. 22-3.
46. Capt. C. Minchin, *Memorandum on the Baloch Tribes in Dera Ghazi Khan District*, Selections from the Records of the Government of the Punjab, New Series, no. 3, p. 48.
47. The area below the Suleman range, which on the Sind side fell away to the west at almost right angles to the Indus, was open to large, uncontrolled river inundations that, before the construction of the Kashmore *band*, sometimes inundated the entire country as far as Shikarpur, thus rendering canal operation extremely uncertain and difficult. At the time of the British arrival, the Marri-Bugti hills were thus separated from the area of settled cultivation in upper Sind by an approximately thirty-mile strip of largely uncultivated desert.

48. H.T. Lambrick, *Johan Jacob of Jacobabad*, 2nd edn, Karachi: Oxford University Press, 1975, p. 35. Many Baloch had . . . long been settled on irrigated lands on the Sindi plains, and had served the Kalhora and Talpur states. In fact, the Kalhoras had considerably expanded irrigation in the eighteenth century, particularly in upper Sind, in part to provide canal lands for Baloch leaders whose assimilation to a military aristocracy was critical to the Kalhora state. The Baluch Talpur Mirs also encouraged canal-building and Baloch immigration settlement in Sind though probably not to the same degree as the Kalhoras. Border affairs of the Talpurs were further complicated by their relations with the Brahui Khan of Kelat, who claimed authority over the Baloch tribes settled in the plain of Kachhi, but in the 1830s and 1840s exercised relatively little of it.
49. Lambrick, *John Jacob*, p. 381.
50. Though sharing many of Jacob's ideas, not all of his contemporaries of course shared his elevation of natural laws over the imperatives of religion, nor his willingness to see transformative power in the application of laws of political economy to India. Others saw the transformative moral power of roads, bridges, and irrigation in more limited terms. As one contemporary responded to Jacob's arguments: 'a moral government requires a moral nature in the people to be governed, as well as in the governors . . .'. Even most settled *Sindhi* in this view lacked such a 'moral nature'. Still, Jacob's views reflected a powerful strand in British thinking. Lambrick, *John Jacob*, p. 381.
51. These tribes, the Jakhrains and Dombkis, two Baloch tribes from Kachhi, were settled at Janidero in upper Sind, where, in the later words of Aitken Napier 'hoped that they would reform and become peaceful husbandmen'. Aitken, *Sind Gazetteer*, p. 143.
52. Jacob found, for example, that most 'settlers' maintained control over their horses, and continued to participate in occasional raids. Though government had required them to sell their horses, most had arranged sales to nearby zamindars who, in return for a share in plunder, kept the horses for the Baluch to use on occasional raids. He also found that these 'settled' Baluch, like their hill brethren, maintained regular accounts with Sindi *banias* for the disposal of plunder, usually in return for grain. Lambrick, pp. 136-9.
53. See Chablani, *Economic History of Sind.*
54. Lambrick, pp. 138, 151, 237.
55. National Archives of India, Foreign (Pol.), 19 Janurary 1855, nos. 268-9. A subsequent grant of land near Kashmor was also made to one of the leaders of the Dombkis in 1850, who resettled many of his followers on a tract opened by Baluch labour and irrigated through the clearance of another old canal, Lambrick, p. 240.
56. Organizing the Bugti to construct irrigation works and clear canals was hardly enough in these circumstances to overcome resistance. In 1851, the British reached an agreement with the Bugti *tumandar* allowing him to

remain in the hills, and with those in Larkana to return to the hills if they so wished, contingent on certain good conduct guarantees. In the end, about three-quarters returned to the hills. NAI, Foreign (A Political E), July 1883, nos. 267-340.

57. Maksudwah extended in 1870s (see Bugti settlement file, p. 6)—relation of Maksudwah to Desert Canal not completely clear.
58. Lambrick, *John Jacob*, p. 270.
59. Maharashtra State Archives, Bombay, Public Works Dept., Irrigation, no. 50 of 1899. 'Desert Canal, Remodelling Project'.
60. Selections from the Records of the Bombay Government, no. XXXIV, New Series.
61. Selections from the Records of the Bombay Government, no. CXVI, New Series. 'Annual Police Report for 1868, Province of Sind', 1870.
62. As Bruce wrote later in explaining the political importance of Desert Canal grants, some of the Bugti headmen 'occupy positions in the tribe which they consider they are bound under their tribal notions of honor to maintain and live up to'. And yet, 'circumstances over which they have no control make it impossible for them to do this honestly or by fair means, so that wherever they find an opening for plunder, they do not allow it to escape them'. Income from agricultural lands on the plains tended to encouage them to break this cycle. Bruce, Pol. Agent, Thal-Chtiali to Agent to G-G in Baluchistan, 22 April 1883, NAI, Foreign (A Political E), July 1883, nos. 341-4.
63. This was also shaped by the fact that there was a far larger, barren tract separating the hills from cultivation on the Sind side than there was on the DGK frontier.
64. Selections from the Public Correspondence of the Punjab Government, Vol. IV, no. 4; Memorandum on the Dera Ghazi Khan District, 1860.
65. The 1856 flood was so severe that it was from this flood that, a dozen years later, the residents of DGK calculated their date. 'The Dera Ghazi Khan Cantonment and Civil Station were swept away by this flood,' Fryer wrote, 'and it reached some ten miles inland, demolishing villages and destroying the cattle and crops.' Three great *bands* were erected in this era, the Kala, Bahar Shah and Shah Jamal embankments. The largest of these, the Kala embankment was completed in time for the 1857 flood season at a cost of approximately Rs. 70,000. Fryer, *SR*, p. 5.
66. Schemes for government expenditure to improve and extend DGK inundation canal were repeatedly rejected in the mid-1850s for want of funds. See Minchin, Memo on the DGK Distt. 1860.
67. *DGK Gazetteer*, p. 28.
68. Minchin, pp. 37-8.
69. Mussoo Khan Nutkani's earlier interest in irrigation was suggested by his having gained a mortgage on a small commercially productive canal, the Gamoowala, in the 1840 (see n. 38). In 1859, he joined with Jamal Khan

Leghari in re-executing a mortgage bond on this canal, negotiating in the process leases on lands near the canal that brought them considerable profits. IOL, Punjab Public Works Procs (Civil Works-Irrigation), May 1868, no. 16; October 1868, no. 27; December 1868, no. 1; May 1870, no. 22.

70. Punjab Board of Revenue, file 251/106 (Purchase of the Nur & Dhundi canals), p. 10.
71. Nur & Dhundi file (Lyall, p. 34).
72. That the British themselves saw working through the chiefs as a way of tapping local capital for canal investment was suggested by the comments of the Punjab Financial Commissioner, who noted that, although the 'native capitalists' would not readily loan to government to build canals, 'the zamindar, or at all events, the chiefs, could secure loans [for canal investment] at the usual market rate'. Fin. Comm. Punjab to Sec. to Govt. Punjab, 5 March 1864. Punjab Archives, Revenue, 9 July 1864, nos. 28-30.
73. Both the Loond and Khosa canals appear to have made use of the route of the old Haibatwah Canal, dug originally during the Mirrani period, a canal taking off directly from the river that had long since fallen into disuse. More recently, the part of the Haibatwah running through Khosa lands had been known as the Dhori, and had been attached as a branch to the Manka. Fazal Khan Loond, the Loond *tumandar*, re-excavated part of the old Haibatwah from the river, and Sikander Khan Khosa 'reexcavated the Dhori portion, severing it now from the Manka and reattaching it to Fazal Khan's canal'. The implications of these developments for internal tribal conflicts, particularly within the Khosa tribe are discussed below. Davies (see earlier note on Haibatwah) and Nur & Dhundi file, p. 14; Fryer file, p. 17. See also Hukum Chand, p. 516.
74. In the period immediately before the British arrival, the Legharis had been closely allied with the Sikhs. Note also previous relations with Kalhoras; the Talpur Mirs were in fact themselves a branch of the Legharis.
75. Griffin and Massey, vol. II, pp. 341-5; Fryer, *SR*, p. 50; NAI, Revenue & Agric (Land Rev), February 1904, part B, no. 8 ('Allowances and Privileges of Leghari Tumandar'). Conflict with the Marris had in fact forced the Legharis to give up the cultivation of most of their *kalapani* lands in Barkhan by the time the British arrived, though they were later to try to reclaim these lands through the courts.
76. Minchin, pp. 17-18. Though long ruled by a collateral branch (Rahim Khan), in the early years of British rule, Jamal Khan Leghari and his uncle—Jalal Khan, were engaged in a struggle over the *tumandarship* of the tribe. Jalal Khan's claims rested in part on his marriage into the Rahim Khan branch.
77. The exact terms of agreement and excavation are not totally clear. For discussion, see IOL, Foreign, August 1875, no. 41.

78. See evidence on Jamal Khan's purchase also of indigo vats–Nur and Dhundi file, p. 38.
79. According to Lyall, Jamal Khan and his 'outsider confederates' probably timed the submission of their petition to try to forestall the Rajanpur zamindars, p. 34. The Serai family of Rajanpur were not Baloch, but descendants of the Kalhoras. Griffin and Massy, *Punjab Chiefs*, pp. 346-351.
80. Imam Bakhsh Mazari's concern with opening another canal near Rojhan suggested the importance to his control of the opening of new agricultural lands in Rajanpur Tahsil. Minchin noted the fear of loss of tenants to lands opened in Kashmore further south. See Nur & Dhundi file, p. 14. *Patti* was the word used for a well estate (a block of land in other words), with a well already in it.
81. The greatest problem was with the Khosas. Fryer, *SR*, p. 57 (see below).
82. Nur & Dhundi file, pp. 34-9.
83. IOL, Punjab Public Works, Irrigation, September 1865, no. 15.
84. DC, DGK to Ex Eng, Indus Canals, 17 December 1864. IOL, Punjab Public Works, Oct. 1865. Civil Works, Agric, A proc., no. 5.
85. Minchin, pp. 37-8.
86. Ibid.
87. For a statement of this basic argument, see Brian Spooner, 'Insiders and Outsiders in Baluchistan: Western and Indigenous Perspectives on Ecology and Development,' in Peter D. Little and Michael M. Horowitz with Endre Nyerges, eds., *Lands at Risk in the Third World: Local Level Perspectives,* Boulder, Westview, 1987. As Spooner notes of Makran, the interaction between pastoralism and settled agriculture is central to the Baloch's conception of 'ethnic provincial autonomy,' defining the link between the conception of the people and a territory (p. 36). One might argue also here that the Baloch had their own myth of the frontier that played an important role in shaping their identity. The life of the hills, pastoralism and raiding was viewed as the morally superior life in comparison with the settled life of the plains, even as control of settled land was critical in defining the structures of leadership that made the successful maintenance of Baloch identity and leadership possible.
88. R.B.J. Bruce, 'Notes on the Dera Ghazee Khan District', p. 120.
89. At times this was recognized by the British themselves. For a discussion of *jangal*, see also Michael R. Dove, 'The Dialectical History of "Jungle" in Pakistan: An examination of the Relationship Between Nature and Culture', *Journal of Anthropological Research*, Vol. 48, 1992, pp. 231-3.
90. Robert Isaac Bruce, *The Forward Policy,* Lahore: Longmans Green, 1990, pp. 14-15.
91. This is why the differences between Sind and Punjab frontier control policies were of such concern to Sandeman.

92. T.H. Thornton, *Colonel Sir Robert Sandeman: His Life and Work on Our Indian Frontier*, p. 36. The mythology surrounding Sandeman in British administrative lore is thick. Thornton opines that Sandeman's recent loss of his wife and children to diptheria had perhaps prepared him for his bold and reckless undertaking. See also the assessment by Ronald Wingate in his introduction to the 1979 reprint of Thornton's book: Sandeman succeeded in the late 1860s, Wingate writes, 'without military assistance, but simply by force of his personality, by an almost reckless disregard for danger, in three years bringing order to the [DGK] district' . . ., p. x.
93. A critical part of the Sandeman myth rested on British assumption about the effect that Sandeman's actions had on the Baloch. Recording a Balochi poem by a Drishak bard, Dames noted that, 'The event was a new development in Baloch history, as a successful attempt by a ruler of the plains to manage the hill-tribes by peaceful methods.' Dames, *Popular Poetry*, p. 100.
94. The long-term career of Sandeman's 'forward policy' hinged on a debate with British officers in Sind over whether the Khan of Kalat, the most powerful chief in Baluchistan was to be viewed as a centralized ruler or simply as the head of large tribal confederacy. This issue, of course, had critical implications for whether the boundaries between the British and Baluchistan were viewed as fixed or highly permeable. Though Sandeman came to be the arbiter of policy in Dera Ghazi Khan in the late 1860s, his ideas were at first rejected by the Government of India, in favour of those of the Sind administration. See the discussion of the 1871 Mithankot conference on this issue in Inayatuallah Baloch, *The Problem of 'Greater Baluchistan'*, pp. 137-8. By the mind-1870s, however, Sandeman had triumpled, and in 1877, when the Baluchistan Agency was created, Sandeman became the first Agent to the Governor-General for Baluchistan. The 'forward policy' ultimately had an important impact also on relations with Pakhtun tribes in the NWFP.
95. In this, the British followed the policy of Diwan Sawan Mal, who had decided to clear the DGK canals with paid labour, rather than *chhers*, and who had established the policy of the state paying half the cost and the irrigators the other.
96. Also profited by fact that his lands on Manka were held rent-free so that as clearance costs were apportioned according to revenue, he didn't have to pay.
97. IOL, Punjab Public Works, Civil Works, Irrigation, February 1869, proc. no. 1.
98. Sandeman to Commissioner, Derajat, 16 June 1868. Punjab Public Works, Civil Works, Irrigation, July 1869, proc. no. 1.
99. DC, DGK, 1864 (blue book, p. 59).
100. NAI, Foreign Dept. Procs. (Pol A), June 1863, nos. 123-5 (Settlement of

Sections of the Boogtee in the DGK Plains). According to Minchin, writing in 1863, the close relations of Imam Bakhsh to Ghulam Murtaza Khan Bugti had helped to guarantee the peace on that border in previous years. Imam Bakhsh and Ghulam Murtaza had periodically fallen out over various causes: attempt by the Mazaris to aid in Bugti settlement reflected Imam Bakhsh's concern not only to solidify his relations with the Bugti but also to increase his importance to the British.

101. As Bruce wrote, the Dhundi lands were divided between the headmen of the Mussoori and Shambani sections of the Bugti, but although they put some money into sinking wells and improving the canal, they never did enough to open cultivation and no hillmen ever really settled. Bruce implies that this was because profits from cattle (both their own and stolen) were potentially greater, and because these Bugtis had long obtained only a very small part of their livelihood from agriculture. 'Without skilled labor and the expenditure of money in erecting *bunds* and cutting watercourses to bring them into culturable order, [their lands] could not possibly yield any profits,' Bruce also implies that uncertainty of water supply made this investment problematic, though he did try to get Jats to put in labor and take up cultivation when it was clear and Baloch would not. J.R. Bruch, Asst Comm. Rajanpur to DC, DGK, 16 Dec. 1867. IOL, Punjab Foreign Procs, January 1874, no. 12.

102. IOL, Punjab Public Works, Civil Works, Irrigation, proc. no. 20, March 1868.

103. Kirwan defended himself by noting that one contract given to the chief of the Drishak tribe, local allies of the Mazaris, had resulted in inadequate clearance. Further, he noted, 'the man who takes the contract does not take the labor of his own tribe to clear the canal, but employs the people of the country through which the canal runs.' But this hardly answered the larger political objections. The Lieutenant-Governor ultimately urged the executive engineer in future to gain the Deputy Commissioner's concurrence before giving any clearance contract 'for a canal belonging to one tribe to an individual belonging to another'. Punjab Public Works, March 1869, Irrigation Branch, no. 3.

104. Files to check here include: blue book, p. 79.

105. NAI, Foreign Department Proceedings, Political A, June 1868, nos. 82-6. (Arrangements made with Khetran, Boogtee and Murrce since the Hurrund Raid of 1867). The Legharis and Khetrans had a variety of connections, including links of intermarriage.

106. Punjab Public Works, Civil Works-Irrigation, July 1869, no. 1, pp. 4-5.

107. Bruce, p. 16.

108. T.H. Thornton. *Colonel Sir Rebert Sandeman: His Life and Work on Our Indian Frontier*, p. 32. Most of the account of the Hurrund raid and its background is taken from Bruce, *The Forward Policy*, pp. 24-32. Despite the triumph of his policy in Dera Ghazi Khan, Sandeman's overall

'forward policy' was not, of course, accepted by the Government of India for several more years.

109. Punjab Judicial, August 1870, no. 13.

110. IOL, Punjab Judicial, February 1871, no. 15. Much of this occurred during the period of the American civil war, when cotton speculations at Bombay could be extremely profitable.

111. J.B.B. Boyle, Bars-at-law, to Govt Advocate, Punjab, 25 August 1870. IOL, Punjab Judicial, October 1870, no. 29.

112. The concern to incorporate Baloch ethnicity within a framework of British administration developed nowhere more fully than in British approaches to the law, most notably with the development of the tribal *jirga*. But the process of encapsulation of these systems within the structure of British power had many facets, which it is impossible to elaborate on here.

113. In discussing settlement of the Bugti, Munro, the Derajat Commissioner had in 1872 complained that the attempt to settle groups of Bugtis in DGK had failed not only because of inadequate water supplies on their lands, but because the Bugtis never appreciated the offer of lands for settlement, preferring plundering, and 'were not disposed to settle down to labor on the plains forsaking their former haunts and abandoning the marauding habits inherited from their ancestors.' To this Bruce replied that the problem was not indisposition to agriculture but the separation of settled sections from the Baloch as a whole. This did not mean, of course, that British officials now rejected entirely a view of the division between hills and plains as a marker of the effective boundaries of 'civilization.' This attitude was still evident, for example, in Fryer's descriptions in his first regular settlement report, pp. 72-4.

114. Thornton, p. 30.

115. *Punjab Chiefs*, p. 343.

116. 'Elegy on the Death of Nawab Jamal Khan', Dames, pp. 105-10. On Jamal Khan's death while returning from haj, 'an assembly of Chiefs', as Dames put it, 'offered a prize for the best elegy and this was won by Panju Bangulani (a member of the Lashari clan of the Gurchanis)'. All quotations in this paragraph are from this poem.

117. Interestingly, in terms of irrigation works, the poet made direct reference only to Jamal Khan's construction of a *karez* (or underground water channel), rather than to his far more significant role in constructing inundation canals. This was probably because *karez*, which were common in the interior and western parts of Baluchistan but almost unknown in Dera Ghazi Khan district, had stronger hill-Baloch cultural connotations. Jamal Khan had built one important *karez*, at Chou Bala, modeled on works in Quetta District. See *Punjab Chiefs*, p. 343.

118. The long-term direction of Sandeman's policy is suggested by the

comments of a twentieth century anthropologist. As Pehrson observed of the Marri, the effect of almost a century of British policy had been to define a form of tribal organization that had, for practical purposes, put 'the extra assistant commissioner', rather than the Marri chief, at 'the apex of Marri tribal organization'. Pehrson, *The Social Organization of the Marri Baluch*, p. 4.

119. IOL, Punjab Foreign, January 1874, no. 7.

120. The limits of the new estates of the Baloch chiefs in Dera Ghazi Khan—in many cases significantly shaped by the processes of canal-building—were demarcated at the time of the regular settlement in the 1870s. Jamal Khan Leghari's was the largest. The best figures for the Leghari chief's estate come from later files of the Court of Wards, which took over the estate of Jamal Khan's grandson, also named Jamal Khan, in the 1920s. By then, the total was approximately 114,000 acres, the great bulk located in Drea Ghazi Khan and Jampur *tahsils*. Of this land, about 96,000 acres were listed as 'uncultivated.' Approximately 12,000 acres were returned as canal-irrigated land and 2,500 acres as irrigated by *rodkohi* (though figures for this form of production were, of course, quite variable). The estate also claimed (in addition to some new lands) *ala milkiyat* rights on lands in the Barkhan Valley (which had been the subject of long-standing litigation in the British courts), and an indeterminate amount of unmeasured land in the DGK tribal areas. Attachment to A.V. Askwith, DC. DGK to Commissioner, Multan, 23 February 1928. Punjab Board of Revenue, file 601/1/29/71 ('Management of the Estate of K.B. Nawab Jamal Khan Leghari Tumandar').

121. British recognition of the imperatives of tribal authority was suggested by their treatment of *inams* awarded to tribal chiefs at the settlement in the 1870s in compensation for their former rights to collect revenue from their tribesmen on their *tumans*. The largests *inams* of Rs. 10,000 per year, went to the Leghari and Mazari *tumandars*. The British attempted to underscore the continuing tribal authority of these men by allowing them to collect these *inams* directly in kind in order to strengthen 'the patriarchal or tribal system of administration in the Baloch *tumans*,' as one official put it. 'The authority of the *tumandar*,' he continued, 'depends partly on his hospitality, and partly, like all authority, on his power to make himself unpleasant when the authority is questioned.' The direct collection of revenue in kind from Baloch villages (known as *jagir batai*) was intended to facilitate this. See 'Note on Jagir Batai System, BOR, 311\?. But the British also noted the degree to which the very fixation of revenue rights for tribal chief tended to undermine, in the long run, their chiefly authority.

122. Asserting the importance of 'a well-ordered, economical' system of 'professional management' for irrigation, the British in fact moved in the

1870s and early 1880s to bring under direct government control many of the major canals built by Baloch chiefs in the 1860s, including the Massuwah, the Fazalwah, the Dhori, the Manka tail, and the Dhundi, among others. Many of the Baloch chiefs themselves supported this, for shifts in the Indus had made the technical management of many of the canals so expensive and difficult that they saw a more regular water-supply (administered by the canal department) as outweighing any political advantages derived from direct control over canal operation. At the same time, however, they pushed for a recognition of their rights to water within the structure of government management. For some discussion of these takeovers, see IOL, Punjab Foreign, August 1875, no. 41; Punjab BOR, file 251/106 (Purchase of the Nur and Dhundi Canals); IOL, Punjab Foreign, June 1878, no. 4; and Punjab Foreign, November 1878, no. 20 (Purchase of Dhori and Fazalwah Canals).

Indians in Iran in the Second Half of the Eighteenth Century

Surendra Gopal

Indian traders had a substantial presence in Iran in the seventeenth century.[1] They were able to keep up their numbers in the first half of the eighteenth century despite adverse political situation, both in Iran and India. In Iran the Safavids passed into history after the Afghan invasion. In India after the death of Emperor Aurangzeb in 1707, the Mughal rule rapidly lost control over the country. The rule of Nadir Shah brought no cheers to Indian traders in Iran but still they did not leave the country. After the assassination of Nadir Shah in 1747, the Indians tried to regain their lost position. The present essay attempts to explore how far the Indians succeeded in their objective. It also sheds light on the business practices of the Indians.

After the assassination of Nadir Shah in 1747, Iran once again plunged into deep turmoil. The Empire created by Nadir Shah disintegrated fast.

The Afghans declared their independence under Ahmad Shah Abdali. And the Russians decided to nibble at the Caucasian frontier.

But on the whole, Iran remained free from internecine wars that had ravaged the country following Afghan occupation in the 1720s. Karim Khan ensured political stability to the country for the next three decades. Hence, the languishing trade once again revived. Several other factors also enabled Indians to intensify their commercial activities in Iran.

The Abdalis who had come to power in Afghanistan established peace within the country. Ahmad Shah Abdali founded a new city of Qandahar; he emulated Nadir Shah when he extended the Afghan empire to the vicinity of Delhi in India. Sind, Punjab and Kashmir formed part of the Afghan empire. Sindhi and Punjabi traders who formed the majority group among Indian traders in the interior of Afghanistan could now have easy access to Central and North Iranian cities. Moreover, as was the case in 1720s, the Afghan rulers, Ahmad Shah Abdali, Zaman Shah and Timur Shah depended heavily on Hindus for managing the state finances and also the finances of important members of the nobility. The Hindus occupied high positions in the Departments of Finance and Revenue. All over Afghanistan Hindu traders, moneylenders and bankers prospered and they established themselves in all the towns and big villages of Afghanistan. The strong and widely dispersed presence of the Hindus in Afghanistan enabled Indians to undertake journeys to both Iran and the trans-Oxus region of Central Asia with greater security and confidence. Their channels of communications back home remained open.

After the death of Nadir Shah, the seizure of power by Karim Khan in Iran and the establishment of the Abdali rule in Afghanistan and a spell of political stability in the region from Yamuna to the Caspian, helped the revival of commercial and allied activities of the Indians in both these countries.

Another political factor helped the process. After the 1750s, parts of the Indian subcontinent gradually came under the occupation of the English East India Company. The English rulers largely controlled and regulated India's overseas trade. But they were in no position to interfere with the activities of Indians hailing from Kashmir to Sindh as they traveled across the land frontier, not under European control. Indians continued going to Iran and Central Asia unhampered by British interference.

Beside the pull factor, a push factor also operated and forced Indians to go to Iran and Central Asia for trading purposes.

After the demise of Nadir Shah in 1747, the Afghans in Afghanistan had declared their independence; under their leader Ahmad Shah Abdali, they repeatedly entered into the Punjab and its neighbourhood and devastated the country. Between 1747 and 1764, Ahmad Shah Abdali attacked the Punjab seven times.[3] Even the Marathas and the Rohillas from Delhi made the Punjab a target of their plunder.[4] This was an additional factor which prompted Indians in Iran to turn more and more to the Caucasus region and Russia.

Political exigencies forced Indian traders in Iran and Astrakhan to continue their mutual trade with much greater intensity even in the second half of the eighteenth century. Small wonder, then that Indians remained active in Russo-Iranian trade even in the second half of the eighteenth century.

The Indians in Astrakhan continued to carry on trade with Persia. They employed or entered into a variety of arrangements with Armenians, Persians and even their compatriots to bring goods on their behalf from Persia.

A list of passengers on board the ships *Sv. Petr* and *Selafin* which arrived at Astrakhan in April 1755 shows that an Armenian Nikita Martinov, a Persian Musa Hanali Muhammad from Mashhad and Indians Chesu Dadlaev, Uvna Ramchandov, Chilram Negondaev and Dunichand Pervomaidov carried goods for resident Indians of Astrakhan such as Chuvala Nanuev, Amardas Multaniev, Bulakiev, Lachiram, Galabriev, Baliram Fatichandov, Jivan Tolochandov, Marwari, Dulachandov, Chamandini Multaniev, Chantu Nanuiev and Gulab Nanuev, etc.[5] Persian goods generally consisted of varieties of silk and cotton textiles, paper, dry fruits, copper, etc.[6]

The trade to Persia across the Caspian Sea was fraught with risks. In one instance, the ship on which an Indian trader Magandas was traveling across the Caspian with goods worth 30,000 roubles, sank. He lost his life and property.[7]

Several Indians having stayed for some time in Astrakhan would return to India via Persia. In 1765 some Indians traders put in an application for a Russia passport and sought permission from Russian authorities to leave for Persia. They had come to Astrakhan on a Persian passport.[8]

In the last quarter of the eighteenth century, Indians faced a number of difficulties in carrying on their trade operations in Astrakhan. The Russians, jealous of their prosperity, petitioned to their government to adopt measures to curb trading activities of Indians. The Indians, devoid of governmental patronage both at home and in Russia had to put up with a number of impositions levied by the Russian government.

For example, in 1777, a proposal was mooted to restrict the stay of Indian in Astrakhan up to three years only.[9] Adverse circumstances did not, however, dampen the spirit of the Indians; they stuck tenaciously and continued to trade with Persia and carried on other business activities. Dolontri Raganatov, Chekurdas Tularamev, Kishandas Gulabriev, Mengre Multaniev sent goods on various ships and galleots to Persia in 1778.[10] The goods were mostly of Russian origin, and included iron nails.[11]

Twenty years later, we find a request by an Indian trader Magudas to the Governor of Astrakhan to allow him to load his ship *St. Anna* with good for sale in Persia.[12] Obviously, he had prospered to become a ship-owner. But he was an exception and was the last of the prosperous Indian merchants in Astrakhan.

The colony of Indian merchants in Astrakhan was languishing; it no longer played any significant role in the Russo-Persian trade as it had done during the past 170 years. The Indian merchants in Iran lost a stable market in Russia with the winding up of the 170 year old Indian merchant colony in Astrakhan in the opening decade of the nineteenth century.

By the last decade of the eighteenth century the international political situation had dramatically changed. The Revolutionary and Napoleonic Wars had transformed the European perception of geo-politics. Persia in the eyes of England, France and Russia had acquired a strategic importance; it was looked upon as a launching ground for a full-fledged invasion on India. Iran had turned into a cockpit of European rivalry with England, France and Russia dispatching their missions to woo the Shah.[13] Simultaneously, the onset of the Industrial Revolution was also transforming the international economic scene. The role of Indian merchants in Russo-Persian trade was reduced to insignificance and within the next few years they faded away from the scene, except as small time retailers or as moneylenders.[14]

Though Indian participation in Russo-Persian trade had been minimized, they still remained active in almost all the cites of southern, south-eastern, central, north-eastern and north-western Iran and on the western and southern shores of the Caspian Sea.

On the shores of Persian Gulf, Bandar Abbas was abandoned in 1760: the European trading companies shifted their factories to Abu Shehr, which emerged as a new centre of sea-borne trade of Persia.[15] Basra in Iraq was another port which served as a transit point to Iranian cities. Hence, the Indians continued coming to Iran by the sea-route as in the past though it is difficult to estimate their numerical strength. Of course, Bandar Abbas ceased to be a centre of concentration of Indians.

Franklin, who boarded the ship going from Surat to Iran in 1787 found a large number of Indian passengers bound for different places in the Gulf. Franklin disembarked at Abu Shehr and then travelled to Shiraz. In Shiraz he found a special *caravanserai* for the use of Indian merchants. The Indian merchants paid rent for staying and carrying on business from this place.[16]

From other accounts, it is clear that Indians continued to be active in the major cities of Iran. One may note an important shift in the composition of the Indian trading community in Iran.

At this point of time Shikarpur in the upper Sindh was emerging as an important entrepot with strong trade links with Iran and Central Asia by overland routes. Writing about Shikarpur around 1783 Moulai Sahdai stated: 'The caravans of Central Asia and Khorasan that come in winter, used to come up to; Shikarpur, Sukhpur, Rohri, Larkana, Kandiaro, Nasarpur, Sehwan Thetta and Karachi were the centres of trade.'[17] This was facilitated by the policy of religious toleration pursued by the Afghan ruler of Qandahar, Timur Shah, who in 1785 extended his protection to the Hindus and encouraged them to settle in town promising 'that they should carry on their trade without dread of indefinite extortion'.[18] Shikarpur now rivaled Multan as a centre of Indo-Persian trade. It was definitely the financial capital of the region extending from the Caspian Sea through Iran, Central Asia and Afghanistan to Sindh.[18a]

Foster found in Herat about one hundred Hindu merchants, chiefly from Multan residing in two *caravanserais*.[19] On route to Persia, he met another Kashmiri who was going for business to Mazandran.[20] Here he found one hundred Hindus chiefly from Multan and Jaisalmer.[21] [This statement is the clearest indication that Rajasthanis from the border region of Sindh were a significant part of the Indian diaspora in Iran and Astrakhan.] He noted that 'they (Hindus) occupy a quarter in which no Mahometaum is permitted to reside, and where they conducted business without molestation or insult, and I was not a little surprised to see those of the Bramin sect, distinguished by the appellation Peerzadah, or title which Mahometans usually bestow on the descendants of their prophet'.[22]

In Baku he found a *caravanserai* of Indians where mostly merchants from Multan lived. While leaving Baku for Astrakhan, Foster was accompanied by five Hindus 'two of them were merchants of Multan, three were mendicants, a father, his son, and a Sunyassi [ascetic] (brought to Astrakhan)'.[23]

The Hindu Multani merchants, he found, had no compunction in 'drinking the cask water and preparing victuals in the ship-kitchen.'[24] When they were told by Foster that they were contravening the caste-rules, they replied that they had already become impure by crossing the forbidden river,[25] beyond which all discrimination of tribes ceased.

The Hindu mendicant was described by Foster as a 'spirited Youngman, who impelled by an equal alertness in mind and body, blended also with a strong tincture of fanaticism, was making, it may be termed, the tour of the world, for he did not seem to hold it much a matter of much concern whither his course was directed, provided he was in motion'.[26]

The young man received all his requirements from his compatriot Hindus at Baku. Those Hindus had also given him letters of introduction to their agents in Russia.[27]

The reality of the strong and longstanding presence of Indian merchants in the port as well as inland cities was realized by the English East Indian Company as well as the high authorities of the Persian government. None of them wanted their removal as the Indians were serving the interests of both the powers and contributing to the economy of both the countries. The fact was enshrined in the commercial and political treaty signed by the authorities of the English East India Company and the Prime Minister of Iran in 1800.[28] The terms of the Commercial Treaty stipulated that 'English and Indian Traders and Merchants should be permitted to settle, free from taxes, in any Persian seaport, and should be protected in the exercise of commerce in the Shah's dominions'.

The Persians respected the terms of the commercial treaty in the beginning of the nineteenth century. We have reports on the activities of the Indians in the various cities of Iran such as Isfahan, Shiraz, Tabris, Yazd, Mashhad, Kashun, etc. Fazil Khan, the author of *Tarikh-i-Manzil-i-Bukhara* and also Pottinger, Fraser, Vigne, Mohan Lal, etc.,[29] who visited Iran in the first two decades of the nineteenth century met Indians in all the important commercial centres of Iran.

A word about the caste composition of the migrant Indian (Hindu) traders to Persia. By and large the Hindu traders hailed from the trading castes of Gujarat, Rajasthan, Sindh and the Punjab.

The Punjabi Hindu traders mostly belonged to the Khatri and Arora castes. Some were members of the Vaishya caste. They were vegetarians. The traders form Rajasthan and Gujarat were Vaishyas and Jains. The latter formed a distinct religious group but they inter-married with the Vaishyas; they were strict vegetarians and refrained from meat-eating.

The Hindu traders from Sind cannot actually be said to come from a trading caste because of the peculiarity of the caste system in the province. In the nineteenth century they were known as Lohanas.[30] They were not vegetarians. They were described as 'businessmen and scribes' (*Qaumi-i-navisandah*).[31] Fryer had in 1670s found them eating both meat and fish but like other Hindus considered beef taboo. A recent writer has also said, 'they were so lax in their eating habits that they ate practically every meat, including that of dead animals excepting beef and cats'.[32]

Economically the traders did not constitute a homogeneous group.

Those who acted as agents and collaborators of the European trading companies were rich. Their range of business was vast: they combined long-distance wholesale trade with moneylending, discounting of *hundis*, issue of letters of credits, etc. They employed agents. Coming next to them were a group of affluent traders who concentrated on wholesale and retail trade and moneylending. The poorest of them managed to eke out a living: they were retailers, acted on behalf of their rich compatriots and engaged in petty moneylending.

Moneylending was an integral part of the activities of the Indian traders as was the case with the Armenian, Georgian and Jew businessmen, since Islam forbade usury to its followers.

Small moneylenders served the need of the poor citizens as described by Tavernier.[33] The rich moneylenders assisted the traders, the European companies, the local nobility and in case of need, even the royalty. One is reminded of Father Krusinski's remarks, '. . . the first Indians that dwelt in *Persia*, came from the city of Multan: this [*sic*] drive the principal trade at Isfahan and are great moneylenders.'[34]

In view of such a sharp economic differentiation within the ranks of Indian traders, one cannot describe them as belonging to the elite category. These migrant Indians were distinct from Indians who went abroad during the same period and whose activities have been described by Sanjay Subrahmanyam in 'Iranians Abroad: Intra-Asian Elite Migration and Early Modern State Formation'.[35] We do not come across instances of these Indians occupying high positions in the state administration and influencing state policies. Of course, occasionally they were consulted by the local authorities to elicit certain information and were asked to render specific services.

Among these Indians, some prospered and could move into the 'elite category'. The instance of Sutur[36] illustrates this. The process continued throughout the seventeenth and eighteenth centuries under review.

The Indian community always remained a heterogenous group in terms of religious, regional, linguistic and caste affiliation and in the scale and range of business operations. Their command over capital and their investment capabilities differed. Hence the community never developed a unified aim since the interests of the members never coalesced. They seldom developed joint-stock ventures.

The Indian did form partnerships but mostly with their own countrymen and relatives and only occasionally with others. But these ventures were mostly *ad hoc* and for specific purposes. Only family business partnerships endured for any length of time. The conclusion is inescapable. *In case of Indians the 'elite class solidarity' was missing.*

The migration basically resulted from the desire to earn a living; the quest for material gain was another motive. Of course, the exodus also satisfied the restless spirit of adventure. It was never forced or planned from above, except, say when Nadir Shah sent Indian artisans to Persia and Central Asia to construct grandiose buildings for him.

The presence of the community of the Indian traders in Iran could not be described as the result of any diaspora. The Indians had gone to earn a living and better their material prospects. They had not left the soil of India because of persecution, ethnic, religious or political. They were free to stay on or come back subject to their own perceived material interests, inclination or security considerations of the projected journeys.

Some of them (Hindu traders) who decided to integrate themselves with the host societies encountered no resistance. The Hindu traders in Astrakhan became christians.[37] Some married local Tatar women and raised families. The children born out of such marriages were known as *Agrizhanets*.[38] These Indians generally lived with their families away from the place where the Hindu Indians had their collective residence. They continued to carry on business both with and/or as agents of their compatriots.

Numerically the Indians were so small in comparison to the 'host societies' that neither their integration nor desire to retain their identity caused any ripple. The early modern state dealt with them purely in terms of protecting and promoting its economic interests and respecting and ensuring its religio-social and cultural sensibilities. For example, nothing should be done to undermine Islam, the religion of the region. In the process, one point came out, i.e. the early modern state had to accept religious pluralism and refrain from insisting on the practice of one faith and one set of rituals if their large economic interests had to be safeguarded and promoted.

The Safavids, their predecessors, and their successors in Iran in the seventeenth and the eighteenth centuries permitted Christians, Hindus/ Jains from India, Parsis (local as well as Indians) to worship publicly in buildings constructed for the purpose in accordance with their own customs. These non-Muslims could follow rituals, prescribed by their faith in social intercourse among themselves as well as with the outsiders. Religion or race was not a handicap in conducting trade and allied activities as long as the trader conformed to broad state policies. This was the message of the early modern state. It was loud and clear both in India and Iran in the seventeenth and the eighteenth centuries.

Lack of data prevents us from describing in detail the nature of the credit system run by Indians in Iran. However, something can certainly be said about the system which operated when trade was carried with Persia by Indians in Astrakhan or when Indians in Persia established trade contacts with Indians of Astrakhan. One is emboldened to speculate on this after Ruquia Hussain published her paper 'Credit Techniques in Armenian Commerce in Mughal India'.[39] It cannot be forgotten that the Armenian trading in India had close contacts with their compatriots in Persia. At the same time, the Indians in Persia and Astrakhan repeatedly entered in trade relationship with the Armenians.

Ruquia Hussain mentions *avak*, *bottomry*, *respondentia* and *commenda* deferred payment, etc., as forms of credit practised by the Armenians in India.

Commenda type of credit can be seen in the arrangement made between the Indian Bugari and Nagi Shafiev, an inhabitant of Derbant.[40] *Respondentia* type of loan was also resorted to.[41] *Bottomry* was also prevalent.[42] A case of deferred payment/*avak* was reported when Rajaram Marwari lent money to an Armenian Melkun Bagiev in Persian currency in Tabriz; the amount was to be repaid in Russian currency along with the stipulated interest in Astrakhan.[43]

We have several other examples of the business arrangements entered into by Indians in course of their ventures in the Perso-Russian trade.

In 1725 a Georgian Armenian Andrey Egorov was given a loan of 2,600 roubles by an Indian Tavar Balakiev in Astrakhan so as to purchase goods to be sold in the Persian city of Gilan. When he returned after trading, the profits would be equally shared after the capital had been returned.[44] In this case the Armenian was acting as a trader on *commenda*.

The Astrakhan Indian traders frequently hired local Tatars to carry their goods to Gilan. In 1727 two Indians, Ramchand Lyachiramov and Bansiram Basanstov engaged four Tatars to carry goods to Derbent and thereafter to Gilan. They were to be paid 20 roubles.[45]

These borrowings were sometimes of a complicated nature and would give rise to legal wranglings. This is evident from a case instituted by an Indian trader Chandyerban Kolichandov (Chanderbhan) in Astrakhan against an Armenian Astur Agasiev from the Georgian capital Tiblisi, in course of proceedings, it came out that Agasiev had borrowed in the Persian city of Tabriz from an Indian Rajaram Marwari a sum of 600 roubles in 'Persian money' and promised to repay the amount along with interest in Russian currency to him in Astrakhan.[46] Agasiev died before he could repay the loan and his family members sent from Tiflis another Armenian Asatur to repay him. Astur went to Gilan where a complaint was filed against him by Chandyerban's Indian relative Dayal and Asatur returned to Astrakhan but did not pay back the borrowed sum. During interrogation Asatur claimed that he did not have any money with him since he had paid off other claimants. However, the judge justified the claim of Chandyerban and ordered the effects of Asatur to be sold for compensating Chandyerban.[47]

A law suit instituted in 1729 by an Indian Petr Ivanov (a new convert to Christianity) reveals a new dimension of business relationship subsisting between Indians and Armenians in Iran. Vartan Grigoriev, an Armenian from Julfa (a suburb of Isfahan in Iran) during a visit to Astrakhan borrowed a sum of 300 roubles in Persian coin Abbasi from Indians Matu and Abichand and pledged goods belonging to a resident of Astrakhan, Tikhon Loshkarev. These items were kept in an Indian store-house under a seal. Vartan died without paying customs duties and his borrowings to many others. On Vartan's death, Andrel Ilyu and Peter Maksimov forcibly removed the pledged goods from the Indian store-house. The Indians Matu and Abichand went to Gilan to press their case.

The Persian magistrates ordered that the remaining goods belonging to Vartan be sold and all his creditors be paid.[48]

The question arises: Could Indian trading activities be described as western scholars from the days of Van Leur and Meilink-Roelofsz do as 'pedlar's trade'?[49] Niels Steensgaard admits, it was carried on in a very sophisticated manner. Personally I am inclined to dub it as 'trade pure and simple' with large variations in range and capital deployment depending upon the capability and capacity of the particular trader. The absence of state patronage was a crucial factor in forcing the Indian to act in his individual capacity rather than to form companies as the Europeans, the Portuguese, the Dutch, the English, the French, etc., did. Judged in his individual capacity he was a trader 'par excellence' for did he not survive the onslaught of the Europeans and revolutionary political upheavals in Iran, Afghanistan and India for more than two centuries.

Steensgaard has explained his survival in terms of his desire to remain content with smaller margins of profits between 10 and 5 per cent against the Europeans who needed at least a gain of 60-70 per cent to break even. He has alluded to the rigid structure of the companies; it denied them flexibility in their operations as against the Indian who could always improvise and who enjoyed greater mobility.[50] Of course, these reasons do explain the survival of the Indian traders in Iran. But an additional factor must also be taken note of.

The internal towns of Iran, especially those situated in east, central and north-eastern Iran and also those lying on the rim of the Caspian Sea were almost equidistant from Indian exit points of Multan and Kabul and from the Gulf ports. As we know within Iran there were no navigable rivers or wheeled carriages.[51] All the goods meant for the internal cities were transported by pack animals. Hence, the largest number of important internal cities of Iran, Yezd, Mashhad, Nishapur, Qazvin, Kum, Kashan, Teheran, Tabriz, etc., could be reached roughly at the same cost from Multan or Kabul as from the Persian Gulf ports. The economics of transporting merchandise did not militate against the overland route.

It should also be remembered that the overland route was well supported by a string of *caravanserais,* situated at convenient distances. These offered facilities for rest, food, fodder and water and conditions of security of life and property. The Persian *rahdar* or 'guard of the roads' saw to it that the travelers were not molested and their person and property remained safe. Thus there was little hesitation by Indian traders in using the routes radiating towards the Iranian cities.

Also politically till the forties of the nineteenth century, the British rulers in India were in no position to interfere with the Indian traders bound for Iran. Only when they conquered Sind in 1843 and the Punjab in 1849 could the British impose a semblance of control over these intrepid traders and influence their operations. By then the railways and steamships had appeared and were being introduced in India. The revolution in the transport system completely tilted the economics of trade against the Indians. But even in these altered situations, the Indian traders managed to survive by introducing change in their mode and scale of operations.

NOTES

1. Surendra Gopal, 'Indian Traders in Iran in the Seventeenth Century', *Journal of Historical Studies,* Patna University, Patna, No. 2, pp.18-36.
2. Idem, 'Indian Traders in Iran in the First Half of the Eighteenth Century', in Quddusi et al. (eds), *Pura-Prakasa* (Z.A. Desai Commemoration Volume) Vol. 2, pp. 434-42.
3. L. Lockhart, *Nadir Shah*, London, 1938, p.174.

4. N. Baqui, *Lahore Past and Present*, Lahore, 1984, pp. 192, 193, 197.
5. Ovchinnikov and Sidorov (compilers), *Russko-Indiiskiye Otnosheniya XVIII Vol.* (hereafter cited as *R.I.O. XVIII v.*), Moscow, 1965, Doc. No. 161, pp. 317-19.
6. Ibid., pp. 317-20
7. Ibid., Doc. No. 163, p. 320.
8. Ibid., Doc. No. 183, pp. 350-1.
9. Ibid., Doc. Nos. 192 and 193, pp. 364-9.
10. Ibid., Doc. No. 194, pp. 369-75.
11. Ibid. The consignment also included some goods of German origin. Ibid., p. 373.
12. Ibid., Doc. No. 206, p. 395. The owner of the ship Mugundas Teridasov was probably the last great Indian merchant of Astrakhan towards the end of the eighteenth and the beginning of the nineteenth century.
13. John Malcolm, *The History of Persia*, Vol. II, London, 1825, pp. 316-18.
14. *R.I.O., XVIII v.*, Doc. No. 216, dated AD 1800, p. 417.
15. Malcolm, II, pp.135, 144; Francklin noted that Indian goods were brought chiefly to Abu Shehr, William Francklin, *Observation Made on a Tour from Bengal to Persia*, Calcutta, 1788, p. 59.
16. Francklin, p. 25.
17. Iqbal Ahmad Memon, 'Shikarpur, the Eighteenth Century Commercial Emporium of Asia', in M. Yaqub Mugul (ed.), *Studies on Sindh*, University of Sind, Jamshoro, 1988, p. 99.
18. Ibid., p. 7

18a Claude Markovits, *The Global World of Indian Merchants, 1750-1947*, Cambridge, 2000, p.138. The author feels that Shikarpur was the 'financial capital of the Durrani Empire'.

19. George Foster, *A Journey from Bengal to England*, Vol. II, Patiala, 1970, p. 151.
20. Ibid., p.184.
21. Ibid., p.186.
22. Ibid.
23. Ibid., p.187.
24. Ibid., p.291.
25. Ibid., p.292.
26. Ibid.
27. Ibid.
28. Malcolm II, p.127.
29. Hafiz Muhammad Fazil Khan, *Tarikh-i-Manazil-i Bukhara*, Srinagar, 1981; Henry Pottinger, *Travels in Baloochistan and Sind*, London, 1816; James B. Fraser, *Narrative of a Journey into Khorasan in the Years 1821 and 1822*, Delhi, 1984; G.T. Vigne, *A Personal Narrative of a Visit to Ghuzni, Kabul and Afghanistan*, Delhi, 1983; Mohan Lal, *Travels in the Punjab, Afghanistan and*

Turkistan, to Bulkh, Bokhara and Herat and to Great Britain and Germany, Calcutta, 1977.

30. Humaria Dasti, 'Multan as a Centre of Trade and Commerce During the Mughal Period', *Journal of Pakistan Historical Society*, July 1990, pp. 251-2.
31. Ansar Zahid Khan, p. 246.
32. Ibid.
33. Ruquia Kazim Hussain, 'Indian Trade and the Indian Merchants in Persia in the Middle of the Seventeenth Century', *Proceedings*, Indian History Congress, 53rd Session, Warangal, pp. 284-7.
34. Father Krusinski, *The History of the Late Revolution of Persia*, Vol. II, London, 1834, p. 197.
35. Sanjay Subrahmanyam, 'Iranians Abroad: Inter-Asian Elite Migration and Early Modern State Formations', *The Journal of Asian Studies*, No. 2, May 1992, pp. 340-63.
36. Goldberg, Antonova and Lavrentsove (eds), *Russko-Indiiskiye Otnosheniya, XVII vol.* (hereafter cited as *R.I.O., XVII v.*), Moscow, 1958, Doc. No. 45. Sutur, the Indian merchant was imprisoned on the Persian soil but was released on the intervention of the Russian ambassador as he was carrying money of the Russian government for buying silk and other commodities on its behalf in Persia.
37. *R.I.O., XVIII v.*, p. 80. Marwari Barayev, the most important and the richest Indian trader in Astrakhan became a Christian and was renamed as Petr Fedorov. Ibid., p. 327. Some Indian merchants had accepted Christianity on Russian soil earlier as well.
38. Ibid., Doc. No.112, pp. 207-8. See also in ibid., pp. 64, 70, 583.
39. Ruquia Hussain, 'Credit Techniques in Armenian Commerce in Mughal India', *Proceedings*, Indian History Congress, 51st Session, Calcutta, 1990, pp. 327-31.
40. *R.I.O., XVIII v.*, Doc. No. 41, pp. 63-4. The document dated 1725 explains that Nagi Shafiev would purchase goods out of the borrowed money and sell them. After sale, he would return the principal amount and the profit would be divided into three parts. The Indians would get two parts and Shafiev would retain one part.
41. Ibid., Doc. No. 44, pp. 69-70. In 1726 Tatar Bamamet borrowed from Marwari Barayev 440 roubles. He was to go to Gilan in Persia and purchase goods there. On return he was to sell these commodities at Astrakhan as desired by Marwari Barayev. The latter retained the option to purchase the entire consignment at prevailing prices in Astrakhan.
42. Ibid., p. 71. Stepanov took from Gulyab Otomchand 34 puds of sandal wood. He was to transport this commodity overseas on the boat of his master Yakov Petrov. On return the profit was to be divided into three parts: two parts going to Otomchand and one part to Stepanov. In case the

boat sank and the goods were looted, Stepanov was not required to pay anything to Gulyab Otomchand.

43. Ibid., Doc. No. 48, p. 75.
44. Ibid., Doc. No. 42, pp. 65.
45. Ibid., Doc. No. 49, pp. 82-3.
46. Ibid., Doc. No. 48, pp. 75-7.
47. Ibid.
48. Ibid., Doc. No. 53, pp. 98-100.
49. Niels Steensgaard, *The Asian Trade Revolution in the Seventeenth Century*, Chicago, 1973, p. 406.
50. Ibid., pp. 410-11.
51. G.L. Strange (tr. and ed.), *Don Juan of Persia*, London, p. 50. 'The Persians make use of no wagons, coaches nor litters of any sort; nor indeed are there any ships or galleys, for the more special purposes of navigation, and only a kind of light boat is in common use.'

Islamic Revival in Central Asia

Shams ud Din

In the aftermath of the Soviet Union's disintegration in December 1991, it was widely believed that the five Central Asian Republics (CARs), on the basis of their common Islamic heritage, would unite or come very close to the wider Islamic *Umma*. As a result there would arise a solid Islamic fundamentalist bloc as there had been a rapid growth and revival of Islam and Islamic groups in Tajikistan, Uzbekistan, Kyrghyzstan, and to a lesser extent in Turkmenistan and Kazakhstan as well. However, such a widely held view was not based on any objective reality or on the basis of any fundamentalist traditions in Central Asia. Anti-West or anti-Russian movements and ideas in Central Asia were weak. On the contrary, the ruling elite sought to identify its interests with secular and modern Turkey, and the West. Moreover, there were many groups and influential personalities that saw the salvation of Central Asia with continued close cooperation with Russia. This is, however, not to deny the upsurge of Islam or, to be appropriately called, the restoration of Islam.

Suppression of Islam during the Soviet Period

During the Soviet period, particularly beginning from 1927, Islam was brutally suppressed. Anti-religious propaganda was a characteristic feature of Soviet Marxist propaganda, religion being the 'opium of the people'. Slavic republics of the Soviet Union, namely, Russian Federation, Belarus, and Ukraine, however, did not experience the violent anti-religious vandalism experienced by the Central Asian Republics, where the mosques were physically destroyed, Islamic seminaries and madrasas closed, Sharia courts abolished, and Islamic monuments burned. Caricatures of Islamic teachings and practices and of Prophet Mohammed were a regular feature. According to the Marxist dogma, religion was the opium of the people, an obstacle to modernization and social development. However, Marxism itself was being propagated and imposed like a fanatical belief. Usually, scholars blamed J.V. Stalin for excesses, and believed or projected V.I. Lenin as a liberal ideologue and statesman. In fact, it was Lenin who was opposed to any cultural or political autonomy to any region. But, during the initial post-Soviet period, political conditions were so unstable that even if Soviet Russia had tried to impose the doctrinaire policy, it would have further created a gulf between Moscow and the periphery. Lenin was a pragmatic politician and he understood the prevailing mood and situation, and pleaded for restraint. In those days, even Stalin sought to allay the fears of Central Asian people and promised that the Soviet power would give them equal status. But it was not to be. When a group of natives led by Mustafa Chokaev captured Kokand and demanded the right to self-determination, being propagated by the Soviet communists, Stalin wrote back to him that he was free to exercise it if he had power. Moscow was striving to re-establish its control over the far-flung regions that had been cut off due to the civil war. By the time Moscow established its control and consolidated its power in Central Asia, Lenin had died and Stalin had faithfully implemented Lenin's grand design of creating and consolidating a centralized state. Soviet anti-religious campaigns continued until the breakout of the Second World War. On the eve of the World War II, Stalin himself denounced the anti-religious campaigns and assured the masses that they were free to practice religion, and he appealed to them to pray for the success and victory of the motherland against the fascist Germany. Later on, after the end of the Second World War, anti-religious campaigns were once again revived. Reiterating Marxist dogma, Nikita Khrushchev said that communist education must liberate the peoples' mind from religious prejudices and superstitions which, he felt, still hampered some Soviet people (Central Asian Muslims) from full demonstration of their creative faculties and unflinching belief in Marxism-Leninism.

Notwithstanding the violent anti-religious and anti-Islamic campaigns and persecution of Islamic clerics—a large number of them were physically liquidated—Islam survived in the minds and hearts of the people.

Perestroika and Revival of Islam

When Mikhail Sergeyvitch Gorbachev came to power in 1985, he set out to transform the USSR through radical reforms, known as *perestroika* (restructuring of economy) and *glasnost* (openness or political liberalism). As a consequence, there was a respite from anti-religious campaigns and a gradual process of revival of Islam in Central Asia. The trend towards political liberalization resulted in qualitative changes for Islam in Central Asia: the old and dilapidated mosques were renovated and a number of new mosques were built. The ideologically motivated bureaucratic impediments in the opening and normal functioning of mosques were removed. According to some estimates, by 1992 in Uzbekistan about 3000 mosques had been reopened, in Tajikistan 130 mosques were functioning in large towns, and in Turkmenistan about 500 mosques were reopened or built in towns. The Islamic traditions and customs were now being openly observed. To begin with, the appearance of Islamic slogans and banners was seen as something new and it attracted the attention of media the world over. Some commentators saw in them the seeds of Islamic fundamentalism.

The Revival of Islam in Central Asia

With the collapse of the Soviet Union the world witnessed a resurgence of Islam in Central Asia. During the Soviet areas, as we observed above, Islam was brutally suppressed, surviving mainly in family rituals and in the form of national custom. In rural areas it had a relatively less hostile environment. With independence in 1991, the Central Asian leadership rediscovered the significance of Islam as an important aspect of national identity and national consciousness. This is not only reflected in the phenomenal increase in the number of newly built mosques and opening of religious seminaries (madrasa), but also provides legitimacy and relevance. The leaders now take the oath of office on the Holy Koran. Islam now provides a universal bond to overcome or supplant tribal, ethnic, and linguistic divisions.

Islam has, thus, acquired a new status–an essential element of national identity. Islam is the bedrock of nationalism in Central Asia. Islamic resurgence and national rebirth are two sides of the same coin. Growing Islamic consciousness is thus seen as an indicator of consolidation of nationalism as well as a unifying force among the artificially divided ethno-national republic. But the resurgence of Islam in Central Asia has also its darker side as manifested in the civil war in Tajikistan. The sudden release of Islam from the totalitarian grip threatened the stability of the region, first creating a psychosis among the Russian minority which, already suffering from the demise of the

USSR, felt threatened by the rise of Islam. The leaders of the Russian Federation also made loud outbursts in favour of the Russian diaspora in Central Asia. The ruling elite in Central Asia, which largely comprise the former nomenclature, though willing to accept Islam as a quintessential component of their history and culture, felt uneasy because of the support various Islamic groups were getting from the Afghan *mujahideen*, the Wahabbis, and the Taliban of Afghanistan. The involvement of Islamic fundamentalists in violent terrorist attacks in Tajikistan, Uzbekistan and Kyrghyzstan left no doubt in the minds of Central Asian leaders that they were faced with the grim task of navigating between the twin threat of national chauvinism from the north and Islamic fundamentalism from the south.

In Central Asia, Islam can become a political force only if the existing regimes fail in their efforts towards economic development and democratization of polity. Already seen as remnants of former communists the failure of the exerting regims to provide employment to the youth, and give opportunity for genuine political participation tended to discredit the ruling elite and push the youth in the fold of growing Islamic movements. Thus, the ruling elite finds itself in a difficult situation. They have themselves lifted the curbs on religion in order to promote nationalism and establish their Islamic credentials, but fundamentalists now challenge their secular regimes.

President Nursultan Nazabaev of Kazakhstan decided very early to distance himself from the possible spill-over effect of Islamic fundamentalism when in 1991 he established the separate *Muftiat* of Kazakhstan. During the Soviet period there was a combined *Muftiat* for whole of Central Asia with its headquarters in Tashkent. The head of Kazakhstan's *Muftiat* spoke against the formation of an Islamic party, as it would be, he felt, 'a breach of peace'.

Following the collapse of communism, ideologues and opinion makers in the West, particularly the United States of America, turned their attention towards Islam. During the Cold War period, Islam was seen both as a victim of Soviet anti-religious policy as well as an effective instrument for the rollback of communism. After the Soviet invasion of Afghanistan, they found the much-awaited opportunity to use Islam against their rival superpower. The Americans provided training, arms, and ammunition to Islamic *mujahideen* in Afghanistan to fight against the Soviets.

Subsequent to the Soviet withdrawal from Afghanistan in 1989 in accordance with the Geneva Accords, the USA washed its hands off from the Afghan conflict, leaving the field to the *mujahideen* to fight it out with the communist regime of President Najibullah. Afghanistan posed no threat to the vital interests of the western world. All attention in the Western world, particularly the United States America, was fixed towards the Islamic Republic of Iran. Iran was considered as the bastion of Islamic fundamentalism. When the Soviet Union finally collapsed two years later the Central Asian Republics became independent. While four of the five republics of Central Asia managed to preserve political stability, Tajikistan—the southernmost and non-Turkic republic—plunged into civil war in May 1992. As the Tajiks are descendants of ancient Persians, who largely inhabited the region before the arrival of Turkic people, the international media 'discovered' the hands of Islamic republic of Iran in the Tajik civil war. The Islamic Renaissance Party (IRP) did play a significant role in the Tajik conflict and initially achieved considerable success against the old communists. Using Islamic slogans, it, along with the democratic parties, mobilized public opinion in certain regions that had been neglected during the Soviet period. The Tajik conflict was basically a violent clash of interests between clans and regions rather than Islamic *jihad* against the atheist-communist regime. By December 1992, the communists with the support of Russia and Uzbekistan regained ascendancy and pushed the rebellious clans and tribes back to the south from Dushanbe. Thousands of Tajik refugees fled to neighbouring Afghanistan, swelling the number of Tajiks in Afghanistan. Historically, Afghanistan has provided refuge to fleeing Central Asians, mostly Tajiks and Uzbeks, since the October 1917 revolution in Russia. In the 1920s, hundreds of thousands of Uzbeks and Tajiks, when Soviet Russia was tightening its totalitarian grip, escaped to Afghanistan. In Central Asia, the Tajiks largely engaged in guerilla warfare in the twenties of the preceding century against the Soviet Union, popularly known as Basmachi movement. From the hideouts of the mountains of Tajikistan, the Basmachis continued their struggle against the Red Army. When crushed by the Red Army, the Tajiks and Uzbeks crossed the porous border into Afghanistan.

Indo-Soviet Relations: From Khrushchev to Gorbachev

Nirmala Joshi

In the evolution of India's foreign policy, relations with the Soviet Union and now the Russian Federation have always constituted a major component. Since the mid fifties Indo-Soviet relations began growing and for the next three and half decades went from strength to strength. This enduring relationship had acquired a multi-dimensional character by the time the Soviet Union broke up in 1991. The relationship covered an entire gamut of areas such as strategic, political, defence, economic, science and technology and culture. If the two countries were able to forge a steady and a stable relationship it was largely due to the ties being firmly anchored on the area of shared vital interests. This compatibility of interests augured well for Indo-Soviet relations. The Treaty of Peace, Friendship and Cooperation of 1971 symbolized the all-round character of the relationship. The present article attempts to understand the relationship.

Beginning of a New Era: The Khrushchev Period

India's first Prime Minister and architect of Indian foreign policy, Jawaharlal Nehru envisaged close and friendly ties with the Soviet Union. This was partly because he had carefully observed the October Revolution and the new socialist experiment unfolding in the Soviet Union. Nehru's visit to the Soviet Union along with the members of his family left a lasting impression on his mind. His book *Soviet Russia* written after his return from the Soviet Union in 1927 has lucidly recounted his impressions. The Indian National Congress adopted a socio-economic programme as one of its goals largely due to the ideas generated by the October Revolution. The Congress Socialist Party and the Communist Party were wholly inspired by the ideals of the October Revolution. Importantly as Indian independence was nearing Nehru was keen to develop a strong relationship with the Soviet Union. In a very perceptive comment made in the late thirties Nehru had said: 'Russia is our neighbour, a giant sprawling half over Asia and Europe and between such neighbours there can be either amity or enmity. Indifference is out of question.'[1] That Nehru had opted for amity was obvious from his untiring efforts to build a meaningful relationship with the Soviet Union. The geographical proximity and its potentialities to emerge as a major power were the important factors in Nehru's consideration. In line with this thinking Nehru appointed his sister Smt. Vijayalakshmi Pandit as independent India's first Ambassador to the Soviet Union. Perhaps due to a proper understanding about developments in the newly emerged colonial countries including India the Soviet Union misperceived the domestic developments. In the case of India, its decision to join the Commonwealth, or its policy of non-alignment, or the banning of Communist Party in 1948 led the Soviet Union to wrongly evaluate these developments. Consequently Indo-Soviet relations in the Stalinist period remained distant and frozen.

It was only in the mid-1950s that India and the Soviet Union began to come close to each other. It was primarily the geopolitical factors that compelled the Soviet Union to reconsider its policy towards India. An area of shared vital interests was emerging between India and the Soviet Union. This brought about a fundamental shift in Soviet foreign policy which was formalized at the Twentieth Congress of the Communist Party of the Soviet Union (CPSU) in 1956. The first such area was Pakistan. Since inception Indo-Pakistani relations were embittered due to the traumatic experience of partition, the unprecedented violence that accompanied partition, the human suffering, and the Kashmir issue. This left India's western boundary highly vulnerable. Hence, in India's strategic thinking and in its foreign policy goals Pakistan came to acquire a high priority. Nevertheless India was confident of dealing with Pakistan and ensuring its security. India's security scenario underwent a sea change when Pakistan joined the US-led military alliances, namely, the Central Treaty Organization (CENTO) and the South-East Asian Treaty Organization (SEATO). As a member of these alliances Pakistan brought into the Indian subcontinent an external player and thereby, complicated India's security scenario. No doubt India was not the target of CENTO and SEATO, but it had every reason to be worried over Pakistan's membership. Pakistan's main purpose, in Indian view, was to obtain arms from the US and use them in Kashmir with the objective of separating the territory from India. The extension of Cold War to South Asia was viewed with equal concern by the Soviet Union. The containment strategy of the West seriously undermined the security of Soviet southern periphery—the Central Asian region was vulnerable. The U-2 spy plane incident of 1960 proved that Soviet apprehensions were not baseless. India's refusal to endorse the alliance system was welcomed by the Soviet Union, at least its southern periphery was not completely encircled. In the process the Soviet Union acquired a vital stake in Indian foreign policy, especially in its non-alignment. From the Soviet perspective a non-aligned India was preferred than an aligned Pakistan. The emergence of these geopolitical factors brought India and the Soviet Union closer to each other. The result was that both the countries supported each other in areas of critical importance. One such area was Kashmir. The Soviet Union extended full support to India on this issue. In a significant speech at Srinagar in December 1955 Khrushchev said: 'that Kashmir is one of the States of the Republic of India has been decided by the people of Kashmir.' This was reiterated by Prime Minister Nikolai Bulganin in his report of the Supreme Soviet on 29 December 1955.[2] Consequently, India received valuable support for its stand on the Kashmir issue both in the United Nations and elsewhere. From India's point of view close relations with the Soviet Union were an affective means of thwarting all attempts by Pakistan to seize Kashmir with the support of the countries of the West. This was the beginning of an eventful relationship that scaled new heights with the passage of time.

The area of shared geopolitical interests widened further in the late fifties over China. Tensions between India and China had been mounting mainly over the boundary problem. Throughout the fifties India engaged China in an effort to solve the boundary problem. The Panchshila Agreement or the Five Principles of Coexistence signed in 1950 hoped to solve all existing problems in an amicable way. That such hopes were belied was obvious by the end of fifties and in 1962 the Sino-Indian conflict broke out. Nehru expressed satisfaction, however, at the stand taken by the Soviet Union. He told the Parliament on 25 September 1959 that the Soviet Union was taking a 'more or less dispassionate view of the situation'. Nehru was referring to the TASS statement of 9 September over Chinese objections to Soviet impartiality in the border incidents. The Chinese deeply resented the statement which, they were to charge later, had revealed the Sino-Soviet rift to the world.[3]

In fact Sino-Soviet differences were also simmering in the fifties. The uneasy Sino-Soviet relationship of the early fifties turned bitter with the ideological differences that surfaced at the Twentieth Congress of the CPSU in 1956. China was opposed to the fundamental changes initiated at the Congress. At the Moscow Conference of eighty-one Communist Parties in 1960 the Sino-Soviet rift came out in the open. Some analysts believe that the developing friendly relations between India and the Soviet Union was one of the factors that contributed towards this schism. Since the Sino-Soviet differences coincided with Sino-Indian hostility the symmetry between India and the Soviet Union strengthened further. Even on the question of Indian military action in Goa, Daman and Diu the Soviet diplomatic support in the United Nation's Security Council was helpful. The Soviet vetoes enabled India to liberate these areas from Portuguese rule and remove all vestiges of colonialism from Indian soil.

One of the beneficial impacts of this growing symmetry between India and the Soviet Union was that a new dimension was added to Indo-Soviet relations. This was the beginning of defence cooperation between the two countries. The Soviet Union reacted favourably to India's request for arms. However, according to the former Indian diplomat S. Dutt, the question of securing Soviet arms was considered by Nehru since the end of 1955. Worried by the incidents along the Sino-Indian border in the late 1950s India made a request in 1960 for Soviet helicopters and supply-dropping planes. The Soviets reacted positively.[4] In 1960 India had already purchased twelve MiG-21s and twenty-four IL-21s. Subsequently the licence to manufacture these aircrafts in India was procured. The agreement was invoked in late 1964, when the Sino-Soviet rift had almost become irrevocable. This was the beginning of defence cooperation between India and the Soviet Union. In the three and half decades arms transfer and defence cooperation gained momentum and became a vital component of Indo-Soviet relations.

At the economic level Indo-Soviet interaction has been mutually beneficial. In the task of building a modern, industrial nation, Soviet experiences in transforming a tradition-bound agrarian society into a modern industrial society within a short span of time was useful. The Congress at its session at Avadi in 1955 accepted the goal of building a socialist society. A Planning Commission was set up and the State undertook charge of the commanding heights of industry. From the mid-1950s economic interaction between India and the Soviet Union was accelerated. Importantly, the Soviet Union helped India by accepting the rouble-rupee transactions in trade. This enabled India to conserve its foreign exchange. Over the years mutually beneficial trade became one of the important components of economic cooperation. In fact the Soviet Union was one of the largest trading partners of India.

Another area of economic interaction was the Soviet assistance, both technical and credits, on easy terms to help India build its basic industries. Hence the public sector in India received a powerful stimulus from the Soviet Union. It should be borne in mind that in the mid-fifties the West had refused aid to India to build a steel plant on the ground that a developing country did not need it. The Soviet Union proved to be an alternate source for India for procuring assistance in its quest to build the basic industries. The Bhilai Steel Plant came to symbolize the growing economic interaction between the two countries. Subsequently, several joint ventures came up with the collaborative effort of the Soviet Union.

Thus, as the Khrushchev era was drawing to a close, Indo-Soviet relations were not only friendly and close, but were importantly stable and had acquired a long-term perspective.

Friendship with Pragmatism

Khrushchev was succeeded by Leonid Brezhnev as the General Secretary of the CPSU and Alexei Kosygin as the Prime Minister of the country. By mid-1960s the perception of geopolitical realities in the region by India and the Soviet Union was undergoing a change. This did not, however, affect the cordiality of Indo-Soviet relations. In Soviet Union's South Asia's policy India continued to occupy prime importance. In fact, the Indo-Soviet Treaty of 1971 reflected the time tested nature of Indo-Soviet relations.

For India, Pakistan continued to be a major preoccupation. When the Indo-Pakistani war of 1965 broke out the Soviet Union played a mediatory role between India and Pakistan. Unlike its earlier position when it extended full support to India on the Kashmir issue, the Soviet Union had adopted a neutral position. For the Soviet Union Sino-Pakistani rapprochement of the early 1960s was a matter of concern. The Soviet view was that it was necessary to establish at least a working relationship with Pakistan. In order to do so it was essential that the Soviet Union should appear to be neutral on the Kashmir issue. Soviet mediation in the Indo-Pakistani war of 1965 resulted in the Tashkent Agreement of 1966. The Tashkent Declaration demonstrated Soviet impartiality on this issue. Subsequently no reference was made to Kashmir in the various joint statements issued at the end of important visits exchanged between the two countries. Soviet attempts to befriend Pakistan succeeded when in 1968 Pakistan gave notice to the United States to close down its communication base at Bedebar near Peshawar.

The Bangladesh crisis of 1971 once again revealed the differing perceptions on Pakistan. The initial response of the Soviet Union was to urge Pakistan to resolve the problem peacefully. The American rapprochement with China in the early seventies, which began with the dramatic visit of Henry Kissinger, then Secretary of State, to Beijing heightened Indian and Soviet concerns. From the Soviet point of view what was important was that Pakistan had played a critical role in arranging this visit. In Soviet perception a Washington-Islamabad-Beijing Axis had come into existence. Since the Karakoram highway had been opened China had got an outlet to the Indian Ocean via Pakistan. This had given the Axis a vital link. This apprehension that an American-Islamabad-Beijing Axis had come into existence was not entirely shared by India. Consequently befriending Pakistan acquired an added urgency for the Soviet Union. Even after the Indo-Soviet Treaty was signed, the Soviet Union continued to advocate a peaceful solution of the crisis within the framework of a united Pakistan. In the Soviet view, complete support to India would have alienated Pakistan, the Indian view was that the millions of refugees on its soil were an economic burden. Besides India was sympathetic to the cause of liberation and Indian public opinion favoured a more active role. However, once the hostilities broke out in December 1971 the Soviet Union rendered unstinted support to India. Soviet vetoes in the Security Council helped the liberation of Bangladesh.

As the Bangladesh crisis was unfolding and the dramatic Sino-US rapprochement occurred, an equally significant development took place. This was the signing of the Indo-Soviet Treaty of Peace, Friendship and Cooperation on 9 August 1971. It seems the Treaty had been under discussion for the last two years. The Treaty also had a dramatic effect on the Indian subcontinent. The Treaty has been viewed variously by analysts. According to Peter Duncan, a well-known scholar, the Treaty from the Soviet viewpoint was probably understood as part of the planned network of bilateral treaties which would underpin Brezhnev's Asian Collective Security project and which was designed to isolate China.[5]

Henry Kissinger believed that the Treaty encouraged India to attack Pakistan.[6] On the other hand, Robert Donaldson and Robert Horn, both scholars of Soviet affairs, felt that Soviet diplomacy played a restraining role in India, right up to the end of October.[7] It was only after that the Soviet Union expressed full support to India.

The Soviet military intervention of Afghanistan once again brought to the fore the differing perspectives on Pakistan. Indian fears were that this would lead to the rearming of Pakistan. India was proved right when Pakistan was declared a frontline state and military aid began pouring into Pakistan. In Indian assessment its neighbourhood was no longer peaceful. The Soviet intervention had paved the way for US entry into the region. In the process the region had become a battleground for the newly launched Cold War. The Soviet Union was characterized as an 'evil empire' by President Reagan and a new arms race had begun. Pakistan had gained to the disadvantage of India. Another worrying factor for India was, that if under the pretext of hot pursuit Soviet troops should ever enter Pakistan, it was bound to affect India. There could be an influx of refugees into India. Such a possibility was real because the resistance to Soviet rule in Afghanistan was mounting and taking the shape of insurgency. In Soviet perception, however, Indian apprehensions were unjustified. The Washington-Islamabad-Beijing Axis posed as much of a threat to it as it did to the Soviet Union.

The circumstances that lent strength to the China factor in Indo-Soviet relations changed somewhat in the seventies. Indian and Soviet perspectives on China were no longer as congruent as they had been in the sixties. After the liberation of Bangladesh India was keen to improve its security environment so that it could play a more dynamic role in the region. This required improvement of relations with the neighbours including China. In the mid-1970s India took the step of normalizing relations with China by restoring diplomatic relations which had remained frozen for nearly fifteen years. This was followed by exchange of visits at the Foreign Ministers level. Atal Behari Vajpayee, then Foreign Minister in the Morarji Desai's government, visited China in February 1979, followed by the return visit of Chinese Foreign Minister, Huang Hua in June 1981. India did not support a Soviet initiative for Collective Security in Asia. At that time the prevailing view was that the proposal was an attempt to contain China in a discreet manner. An ailing Brezhnev visited India in November 1973 and made a strong plea for the proposal. In his address to the joint session of the Indian Parliament he said, 'it seems opportune to hold a thorough and comprehensive discussion on the idea of Collective Security in Asia which would help trace a common approach, acceptable to all states concerned. . . '.[8]

On the other hand Soviet relations with China deteriorated further after Brezhnev had assumed power in the mid-1960s. A territorial dispute was added and the relations touched an all time low when in 1969 the two socialist countries fought a short border war. The Soviet view was that China had to be contained by any means, including military ones. In his address to the Twenty-fifth Congress of the CPSU in 1976, he said:

> The Peking/Beijing policy is deeply contrary to the interests of all peoples. We shall continue to repulse this incendiary policy, and to protect the interests of the Soviet state, the Socialist community, and the World Communist movement. Now it is too little to say that the Maoist ideology and policy are incompatible with the Marxist-Leninist teaching. They are directly hostile to it. . . . We shall continue the struggle against Maoism: a principled and irreconcilable struggle.[9]

The Soviet Union must have found the Indian aspiration for improving relations with China inconvenient, if not annoying. The Soviet Union continued to caution India to be wary of China. Soviet commentaries on South Asia have been highlighting the subversive role of China in South Asia. In its desire to keep India on its side the Soviet Union, according to Robert Horn, a well-known scholar acknowledged for the first time in 1974 that 'India's position on the territorial question with China was correct'.[10] From the foregoing it was clear that the Soviet Union had reservations about India's policy towards China.

New Realism: Gorbachev Era

After the assumption of power by Mikhail Gorbachev in March 1985 he launched his *Perestroika* or Reconstruction to improve the lagging economy and rejuvenate society. Similarly his 'New Thinking for our World' visualized a world that was peaceful and secure. In the regional context the thrust was to bring about peace in the Asian continent. In this regard his Vladivostok initiative of 1986 was a milestone. He addressed the three obstacles of China as a precondition for normalization relations. In fact, the Soviet process of normalizing was faster than that of India. In any case, as mentioned earlier, the China factor in Indo-Soviet relations was no longer as significant as it had been earlier. Nevertheless when Prime Minister Rajiv Gandhi paid his first visit to the Soviet Union in May 1985, Gorbachev revived the idea of Collective Security in Asia. It must be mentioned that this proposal was not the same as the one put forward by Brezhnev. Gorbachev's proposal was patterned on the Helsinki Act of 1975 which had brought peace and security to Europe. His proposal had a positive element and wanted all countries of Asia to participate in it. During Rajiv Gandhi's visit Gorbachev said, 'We think that India is a great power enjoying much prestige and respect both in Asian countries and throughout the world, and can play a very important part in this process.'[11] However, Gorbachev was unable to elicit any favourable response from India.

Although Gorbachev had succeeded in withdrawing troops from Afghanistan relations with Pakistan remained frozen. This was because of the presence of *mujahideens* in Pakistan who continued to foment instability in Afghanistan. India also was unable to break the impasse in Indo-Pakistani relations. On Pakistan Indian and Soviet perception coincided.

Meanwhile in his quest for a peaceful and a secure world Gorbachev paid his first visit to an Asian country, that is, India in November 1986. Their common concern for peace found expression in the signing of the 'Delhi Declaration on Principles for a Nuclear Weapon Free and Non-Violent World'. In 1988 Gorbachev paid his second visit to India. The Festival of India was observed in the Soviet Union and Prime Minister Rajiv Gandhi led the Indian delegation. Thus, we find that whatever the skeptics may say, Indo-Soviet relations in the Gorbachev period were warm and friendly. However, the domestic developments in the Soviet Union demanded Gorbachev's attention and energy, and finally culminated in the break up of the country. President Boris Yeltsin of the Russian Federation inherited a rich legacy of Indo-Soviet relations. It took the new government nearly two years to find the bearings of Indo-Russian relations.

Meanwhile in the field of defence, Indo-Soviet defence cooperation has been highly successful. The cooperation began in the early sixties and the Indian armed forces have been dependent on this cooperation. Some of the hallmarks of this cooperation have been licensed production of defence equipments so as to enable India to achieve a certain amount of self-sufficiency, easy installments and the offer of latest weaponry and equipment. India is perhaps the only country to have been offered the latest weaponry and equipment from the Soviet inventory.

This is not to suggest that Indo-Soviet relations did not have their differences. For instance, while abstaining on the Czech crisis situation in the Security Council of the UN (1968) the Indian Parliament nevertheless passed a resolution which 'hailed the brave efforts of the people of that country (Czechoslovakia) to liberalize and democratize their nation's way of life'. Similarly on the issue of declaring the Indian

Ocean as a zone of peace or on the nuclear question or Leonid Brezhnev's proposal for Collective Security in Asia or on the question of Soviet intervention in Afghanistan there were differences between India and the Soviet Union. But these differences were contained and never allowed to impinge on the friendly tenor of the relationship. This speaks for the maturity and the sound foundation on which the Indo-Soviet ties were built. The Treaty of Peace, Friendship and Cooperation of 1971 symbolized the all round character of Indo-Soviet relations.

NOTES

1. Jawaharlal Nehru, *Soviet Russia: Some Random Sketches and Impressions*, Allahabad, 1929, p. 142
2. Jyotsna Bakshi, *Russia and India: From Ideology to Geopolitics*, Delhi, 1999, p. 10.
3. S. Nihal Singh, *The Yogi and the Bear: A Study of Indo-Soviet Relations*, New Delhi, 1986, p. 25.
4. Ibid., p. 29.
5. Peter J.S. Duncan, *The Soviet Union and India*, London, 1989, p. 20.
6. Ibid., p. 21.
7. Ibid.
8. Jyotsna Bakshi, op. cit., p. 130.
9. *Twenty-fifth Congress of the Communist Party of the Soviet Union: Documents and Resolutions*, New Delhi, 1976, p. 9.
10. Robert C. Horn, *Soviet-Indian Relations: Issues and Influence*, New York, 1982, p. 84.
11. Jyotsna Bakshi, op.cit., p. 171.

Indian Muslim Perceptions of the West during the First Half of the Nineteenth Century—Karim Khan Mushtaq Jhajjari (1839-41)

Gulfishan Khan

INTRODUCTION

The closing decades of the eighteenth century saw the establishment of the British rule in the Indian sub-continent. In the wake of British ascendancy gradual penetration of Western ideas and influences on Indian soil began to be felt. During the expansion and consolidation of the British imperial rule several social groups were exposed to various aspects of the European culture in general and the British in particular. This interest in the Western civilization could be seen as the result of two mutually non-exclusive historical experiences—colonial rule, and contact with a totally different culture. To begin with, this influence though strong, was not all pervasive. This was confined to a particular segment of society which came into contact the most with the new and alien culture. The literate class was both the sufferer as well as the beneficiary in this encounter. It saw in the Western culture something different from what it was used to, and hence, it often attempted at comparisons. The Indian intellectuals came to identify Britain with Europe and the West as a whole. This was true to such an extent that one could generalize and claim that the Indian intelligentsia's experience of the contemporary Western civilization became, in fact, its experience of the British society and culture. During the latter half of the eighteenth century several Indians visited Europe and recorded their experiences of the West. Some of them traveled there to gain political concessions from the Directors of the East India Company, while others went to satisfy their natural inquisitiveness about a different world. All of them were members of the aristocracy and the gentry. They recorded their first-hand experiences in the form of travelogues, memoirs, and autobiographies. There were others who did not have an opportunity of visiting Europe, but wrote about the British life and culture based on knowledge they obtained from various sources available in the Indian soil itself. Their perceptions of the Western life were rich and varied ranging from socio-cultural to scientific, technical, religious, economic and political life of contemporary Britain. Their experiences can be located within a narrow spectrum of social and intellectual experience of the West during the eighteenth century.[1]

However, the central concern of his paper is to trace briefly the Indo-Muslim awareness of Western civilization in the Indian sub-continent during the first half of the nineteenth century. Here, we are going to focus on the perceptions and ideas of a single Indian traveller to Britain—Karim Khan Mushtaq Jhajjari. In the history of Europe too, this half-a-century, when Karim Khan visited Europe, is considered the most revolutionary period when the economy of the nineteenth century was shaped under the influence of the British Industrial Revolution while the French Revolution gave rise to new ideologies and policies. Terms like industry, industrialists, factory, middle-class, working-class, railways, liberals, conservatives, scientists, engineers, etc., were largely, products of this period. No wonder that all these terms have been mentioned in the works of the writer under study—sometimes vaguely conceived but most often clearly understood. For Great Britain, it was an age of rapid industrial change, social distress and class conflict. Mid-nineteenth century Britain was plunged into a prolonged Depression, which lasted from 1837 to 1842. Industrial Revolution at this stage was a social experience. The period was fraught with tension and frustration. It witnessed intense class struggle in the form of Chartism: both the Industrial Depression and Chartism, the working class radical movement, had divided the nation. Britain was also fighting wars in China and Afghanistan. The observer endeavoured to comprehend this entire complex phenomenon and expressed these in his own cultural categories.

BIOGRAPHY

Family Background

Karim Khan 'Mushtaq' Jhajjari belonged to Jhajjar, which was a small town (*qasbah*) in the province (*suba*) of Shahjahanabad, i.e. Delhi.[2] We do not have detailed account concerning our author's family background and personal life except what we can gather from indirect clues he provides in his works. He gives his family genealogy in the concluding lines of his *Siyahatnama* (Book of Travels). He writes his full name thus: Karim Khan son of (*wald*) Qaim Khan ibn Talib Khan ibn Taiyyib Khan bin Daud Khan Afghan Saraban, a resident of the *qasbah* Jhajjar in the *suba* of Shahjahanabad. This suggests that Karim was of Afghan extraction and among the Afghans too, he descended from the Saraban clan, 'Jhajjari' devotes the place of his birth. 'Mushtaq' was his *nom de plume*, which indicates his interest in poetry. Thus, Karim Khan came from an aristocratic Afghan family of Jhajjar. As far as his educational background is concerned, like the other traditional literati of the period he must have received education in an Islamic *madrasa* of his town, as these towns were the repositories of Islamic culture. He would also have acquired higher education at home, which was customary among the upper classes. His writings portray him as a man of cultivated taste, refined manners and sober temperament.[3]

Reasons of Visit

Karim Khan visited England as an envoy (*wakil*) of Nawab Hasan Ali Khan of Jhajjar. Hasan Ali Khan was the younger son of Nawab Nijabat Ali Khan (d. 1814), founder of the *riyasat* of Jhajjar.[4] Hasan Ali Khan occupied the high office of a General in the army of his brother Nawab Faiz Muhammad Khan (1814-35) and received a salary of Rupees three thousand per month for his maintenance. Besides, he also enjoyed other privileges during his brother's regime. However, when Nawab Faiz Ali Khan (1835-45), son and successor of Faiz Muhammad Khan occupied the *masnad* of Jhajjar, the latter refused to entertain his uncle except allowing him fixed amount of salary, which could not suffice for the aristocratic lifestyle of the Nawab. First, the Nawab petitioned his case before the British Agent/Resident of Delhi, when no success was achieved, he sent Karim Khan to England as his envoy to plead his case before the Directors of the East India Company to increase the monthly emoluments. True to his aristocratic pretensions, nowhere in his travelogue did Karim Khan explicitly mention the reasons for undertaking the journey to England. It is only after a scrutiny of *Siyahatnama* that one gets the hint of his actual mission, which was to obtain political concessions for Nawab Hasan Ali Khan.[5] Again, it is only in the last pages of his account that he allows glimpses of the fact that he failed to accomplish his mission. Consequently, in a separate section of his account he undertook to discourage his compatriots from visiting England. He warns them that their efforts to visit England to obtain political concessions, and to lodge their complaints and grievances against the oppressions of the Company, would not be successful. It was obvious that after more than a year of frustration he had to return empty-handed. But he did advise those who wished to take pleasure trips to England, to carry more cash rather than servants since over there they can live comfortably without retainers and helpers.[6]

Karim Khan embarked on his journey to England from Delhi by boat on 1 December 1839, and reached Calcutta from where he sailed by steamer on 14 March 1840 and arrived at London on 28 July 1840. The date and details of his return journey are not known. He compiled his travelogue in London and recorded 8 November 1841 as the last day of his stay in the British capital. During the course of his journey, he also visited Ireland, France and Greece apart from the country of his destination. Karim recorded his impressions of the daily happenings and named it *Siyahatnama* (Book of Travels). What distinguishes *Siyahatnama* from the other pre-1857 travelogues is that it is an accent by an Indian traveller on the British soil, which renders it as a unique document, composed it. The second feature of this literary piece is that it was composed in simple and easy Hindustani/Urdu at a time when Persian was the most prevalent form of communication among the elite and it was still the language of administration, historiography, and *belles-lettres*.[7] Upon his return to India, Karim Khan wrote yet another book, *Mirat-i gitinuma* or (The World Reflecting Mirror) which is essentially a geographical encyclopedia.[8] Some of the information of *Siyahatnama* has been duplicated in the *Mirat*. The incentive to compile the latter work came from Sir Henry Hardinge (1785-1856), the then Governor-General to whom the work is also dedicated.[9] As Karim narrates in the preface of the *Mirat* on 13 *Zulqadah* 1261/14 November 1845, in his ninth year of reign, Abul Muzaffar Siraj al-Din Muhammad Bahadur Shah Zafar (the last Mughal emperor who reigned from 1837 to 1857) visited the tomb of the Sufi saint Khwaja Qutb al-Din Bakhtiyar Kaki.[10] He used this opportunity to meet the Governor-General, probably in expectation of employment, in which it is not clear whether he could succeed. According to the author, first Hardinge discussed Karim's experiences of the West and subsequently the two discussed ancient buildings and monuments located in the imperial city. Karim claimed that during the course of the above discussion the latter was commissioned by Hardinge to write about the ancient buildings and monuments of Delhi especially about the Qutb Minar and the historical monuments lying in its precincts. Finally, he resolved to write based on his knowledge that he had derived from authentic books and from his trustworthy friends. He also decided to communicate his message in a easy and clear medium so that even a common person will be able to comprehend it. While Karim complied with the desire of the Governor-General but he could not appreciate any rationale in merely describing the ancient monuments of the city of Delhi, and to present to his superior. He says:

> I thought to write an account of the buildings only, situated near Qutb Sahab, for presentation to the higher authorities, will not be an act of wisdom. Having this in mind, I decided to compile a work wherein I will discuss the views of the Greek, European and Indian philosophers about the universe and the earth. These views are mutually contradictory. In addition, I will include a description of the Old (*qadeem*) and New World (*jadid*) to enlighten my compatriots. In all probability, such work will be beneficial for all (*fawaid i a'm*).[11]

Sources of Information

Before examining our author's perceptions and ideas of the British life, the question may arise as to what his sources of information were. As he frankly confesses, he did not possess the knowledge of English language, which hindered even day-to-day communication during his visit to England.[12] Therefore, throughout the period of his stay, he utilized the services of an interpreter, probably employed on a fixed salary. True to his aristocratic habits, he played chess with his interpreter in his leisure hours while conversing on various matters relating to the British society and polity. His interpreter was also his main informant on various topics of his interest.[13] Karim Khan also had some experience of working with the British officials before he visited England. For about two years, he was with the Governor-General[14] in Simla, and he accompanied the latter during his tour of the Punjab. There he had the opportunity of a close interaction with the British Agent/Resident in the region of Delhi, such as William Fraser, who enjoyed close relations with the Muslim aristocracy of the region.[15]

While in England, Karim Khan mainly had social contact with those Britishers who were associated with the Company as its Directors or subordinate officials. Obviously, a large number of these Britishers had some experience of Indian life and culture as they had served the Company. Among those, whose names he mentions frequently were Captain Grantlay, Charles Forbes,[16] Charles Grant,[17] Duncan Forbes,[18] and John Shakespeare.[19] Majority of these Britons were acquainted with the Indian languages namely Urdu/Hindustani which was fast replacing Persian as the lingua franca of India. Two of the above mentioned, namely Forbes and Shakespeare had scholarly interest in the Oriental languages. Karim already seems to have read indigenous Persian sources, which he quotes in his narrative. Foremost among those works are *Tarikh-i Firishta*, *Hadiqat al-aqalim*, and *Shigarfnama-i wilayat*. His impressions of Europe represent an advance over the existing literature. The historical context within which Karim Khan visited Europe was also different; mid-nineteenth century Victorian Britain presented a picture of a highly industrialized society with a highly technical level of social life. It was different from the Britain seen by earlier visitors who had arrived during the last quarter of the eighteenth century. He sought to unravel the secrets of British progress and he found the key in its political institutions based on law. Perhaps it lay even more in the modern science and technology. Consequently, the main emphasis of our author was on twin aspects of the British life—its political institutions and modern science and technology. In the representation of the social realities of the west, Karim often proclaims impossibility or his own inability to describe what he saw. Nowhere in his discourse did Karim asserts the superiority of Indian culture, neither did he regard the other culture in any respect inferior. Nowhere does he attempt comparison of the two cultural systems. It was more an attempt of translation of a cultural phenomenon into another. Following is the picture of the various facets of the British/European life as presented in the works of the author under consideration.

A New World-View/Rise of the West

Karim Khan wrote two works namely *Siyahatnama* and *Mirat-i gitinuma*. The first is a travelogue while his second work *Mirat-i gitinuma,* as the name itself suggests, is a geographical encyclopedia. The title of the work reflects the author's desire to embrace new geographical discoveries about which he came to know during his visit to Europe. Karim Khan realized that the new geographical discoveries had changed the concept of the universe, now, instead of division of the world into seven climes (*Haft Iqlim*) the European scientists had devised a new system of classification namely division into four parts known as continents, namely Asia, Africa, Europe and America. The author expressed his sincere desire that in this respect he, too, would like to follow the European system of classification of the inhabited globe. Accordingly, he sought to delineate the human and physical geography of all the four specified continents and of their countries. Further, he sought to delineate the circumference, capital, nature of government, armed strength, and main agricultural and industrial products of every country of all the four continents. In case of the European countries, the author specifically mentioned their possessions in America as well as in the Afro-Asian countries.[20] Some of the information, it seems, he culled from a Persian treatise written by Jonathan Scott for Nawab Asaf al-Daula of Awadh. This treatise was available to our author while he was in London.[21] But not all the information was copied from the above mentioned treatise. Karim had his own observations and comments to offer, as we shall see.

Such was his description of France, the prime European rival of Britain. In the French capital Paris, he encountered the newly introduced Passport system. For Karim, a document to certify the identity and citizenship of a person was totally alien and strange custom; being the *ashraf* of his own society his identity was not obscure, and thus did not require official sanction. Moreover, could the mere possession of such a document check the entry of a thief or criminal into any country, the visitor argued with the French diplomats in Paris. Karim also claimed to have met the French monarch Louis-Philip (1830-48), but the visitor found nothing attractive in the French constitutional monarch. It was the person of Napoleon Bonaparte (1769-1821) which seemed to have fascinated him. He attempted to provide a brief biographical sketch of Napoleon, his phenomenal rise to power from a General to the Emperor, and his achievements especially his brilliant campaigns of conquest in Italy, Austria, and Russia and finally a description of the battle of Waterloo (1815) with utmost accuracy. Karim Khan concluded that such a ruler Europe had never seen before.[22]

About the two other countries, Ireland, and Greece, visited by the author, he had very little to say. He spent several months in Dublin the Irish capital, and noted only briefly that a representative of the British King ruled there.[23] In Greece, he took note of the lately concluded War of Independence (1821-32) which he interpreted as a successful rebellion of the natives, majority of whom were Christians, against the centuries old Ottoman rule. Upon victory, the rebels placed a king on the throne of their country from their own community, i.e. a Christian, whose name was Otho. He specifically informed his readers that when the latter visited Greece, the same king Otho (1833-62) ruled this newly established kingdom with his capital at Athens.

Karim was also aware of the discovery of Australia in the Southern Hemisphere, and knew that it was also known as the New Holland (obviously, he did not mention it as a separate continent). To him, it was an island of a large size almost equal to the size of Hindustan. He came to know that the British convicts were transported to that colony therefore, it was popularly known as the 'black waters'. Similarly, he was well aware about Canada and New Zealand both and noted that the latter was an island while the former, he remarked, was a British ruled province.[25]

America

Among all the four continents it was America, the newly discovered land which was of major interest to our commentator. He provided his readers with an account of the New World including the reasons of its discovery, as to why the Europeans discovered it, course of the discovery and a small biographical sketch of Christopher Columbus, and finally its colonization and consequent ruthless exploitation by the European powers. Karim elaborated upon the reasons of discovery which the latter commented were purely commercial, to find an unhampered trade route to India. Karim opined that before its discovery by the Europeans, the New World was beyond the geographical horizons of the people of the Old World, although some philosophers through their reasoning already conjectured about its existence and that the Western and Southern Hemisphere of the world could be inhabited like the Eastern and Northern part of the terrestrial globe. Moreover, wrote Karim, the Holy Koran also has an allusion to the existence of the New World in the verse, 'The God of the two Easts and the Gods of the two Wests.'[26] Karim seems to have realized that the discovery of the new and vast land required additions to the map of the Old World. Therefore, he attached a world map in the *Mirat* based on the then modern European cartography and entitled it 'Map of the Old World and New World' (*Naqsha-i-qadeem wa jadid*).[27]

First, the commentator carefully noted that North America was largely occupied by the British, while the South came under the possession of the Spanish, French, Dutch and the Portuguese. Herein, like the other three continents, Karim sought to delineate the physical and human geography of Americas and a description of various states of the North and South America, viz., their size, circumference, physical geography, main characteristics, natural resources and the major agricultural and industrial products. In natural resources such as the silver, gold, iron, and other precious metals, the New World was far richer than the Old World. The Europeans exploited these resources for their own advantage. Its natural resources, particularly the Peruvian silver and tobacco—the cash crop have immensely enriched the European settlers. Similarly, European merchants derived enormous profits from the sugar production in the island of Jamaica, which was called West Indies (*Hind maghribi*).[28] Of this new discovery, Karim regretted, there were some adverse impact also such as the fashion of tobacco smoking, a social evil which came from America. Tobacco was an American product, the very word tobacco (*tambaku*) itself was of American origin and four hundred years ago it was unknown in the known world. In the beginning, its use was restricted to medicinal purposes. Gradually, its use spread among various sections of society. Its production immensely expanded during Jahangir's reign since it was a lucrative product, the Indian farmers eagerly cultivated it. The fashion of tobacco smoking went unchecked for a long time and it is still widely prevalent.[29]

Karim evinced similar interest in North America and especially the War of Independence (1775-83), the insurrection by which thirteen of Great Britain's North American colonies won political independence and went on to form the United States of America. The author provided a similar description of the North American states, their size and circumference, major industrial and agricultural products and the British settlements therein.[30] Gradually, this part of the New World become the foremost country in the Western hemisphere in population and economic development, and its prosperity was increasing day by day. It naturally spurred a desire for independence on the American's part, majority of whom were of British descent, and these immigrant settlers began to aspire for equality with the British living in Britain. Even at the present time, waves of the British immigration to the North America continued unabated, almost fifty thousand wealthy British citizens every year leave their country to settle down permanently in the New World. For these British settlers cheap and fertile agricultural land was the major attraction. (Karim added that the cultivable land was only two rupees per *bigha*.) In spite of this growing wealth and riches Americans refused to pay taxes (*taxha*, *mahsul*) to the British Crown; instead when demanded they argued that they were not represented in the British Parliament like Ireland, England and Scotland, and they raised their heads in insurrection.[31] The representative of the British monarch declined to accept their demands. Eventually the imposition of taxes over and above what was customary became the immediate reason of war. Open fighting broke out between the British and the Americans, which was to continue for several years. The British monarch set naval forces to crush the rebels, but the Americans put up strong resistance to the British naval and land battles and both sides suffered heavy casualties. Finally, the Americans succeeded in eliminating the British domination from their own country. Nonetheless a fourth part continued to be under the British control.[32] Ultimately, peace was concluded because after all both were of the same racial stock, i.e. British. Above all, the reason for the peace was that trade and commerce had suffered heavily on both the sides.

One of the results of the American success was the organization of the system of government, that is the formation of the American Republic. Karim appreciated that this system of government was such that no one was subordinate or tributary (*kharaj guzar*), not was any one superior (*hakim*) to others. This form of government was known as *Ijma*, which means government by collective consent.[33] Karim elaborates that according to the system, one socially eminent person was appointed for a term of four years with the consent (*razamandi*) of the populace (*riaya*). For the previously mentioned period a ruler (*hakim*) who was known as President looked after all political and economic affairs. After the expiry of the previously mentioned period, the Vice-President (*naib*) assumed this office, but, in case, two or more persons deserved this exalted office, one with a greater support of the people was appointed as the President. The former retired (*ma'zul*) President was counted among the common people.[34] Karim Khan tells us further that America in his time was divided into twenty-one provinces (*suba*) each under one separate governor. These governors were under the control of the President who had the authority to appoint diplomatic envoys, etc. to other countries.[35]

SOCIAL LIFE

Historical Background, Ancient/Medieval Britain

Karim's description of the British social life begins with a detailed narrative of the British history from pre-historic to present times, followed by a discussion of the physical and human geography of the United Kingdom. Karim Khan posited that he was seeking to explore Britain's historical past in order to understand its modern development.

Also people in India were desirous to know the racial origins (*asl wa nasl*) of their new masters. The author provided a detailed narrative of the British history: the pre-Roman Britain, Roman conquest of the island and four hundred years of Roman rule, Anglo-Saxon settlements, and finally Britain under the Tudors and the Stuarts. First, he sought to describe the pre-Roman Britain. He came to know that in pre-Roman time tribes with primitive organization and institutions inhabited Britain. They were barbarous, uncivilized and savage—mostly dependent on animals for food and their skins for clothing. They worshipped idols, and they did not have any knowledge of the world around them. Each tribe had a leader whose duties and responsibilities were to protect the life and property of his people. They were constantly at war against each other on one pretext or the other, fighting with their crude weapons and methods. The Anglo-Saxons, now called English, was a brave race, but more than that according to the British historians, they settled in Britain by deceiving her ignorant population, the aboriginals. Above all, the land was also very fertile, that was another reason of their settlement in England. Later, feudal structures developed and then, through successive changes the modern state system came into existence. This perception of evolutionary process on the part of our writer is remarkable. From his knowledge of the British historical past Karim concluded that until fairly recently Britain lay at the periphery of civilized world. That was the reason that the author of the *Hadiqat al-aqalim*—an encyclopedia written in 1781 placed it in the seventh clime as a small an insignificant island, argued Karim.[36] Britain in his opinion became significant only in recent times. At this point Karim Khan conjectured that the reason why the Chinese dubbed the English as chimpanzee was due to the primitive and tribal structure of the British society.[37] Another people called Scots attained dominance in Scotland. The Scottish people were known for their bravery and courage and they were considered a martial race. Scotland was a separate country before its unification with England. It has a distinct legal system (based on Roman law). Some of the ancient customs and traditions of Scotland still survived; for instance, the law of primogeniture was not applied to the Scottish society.[38]

Religion

However, Karim Khan did not pay any special attention to one aspect of the British social life, religion. In fact, he consciously avoided any details of this subject. Nonetheless, he seems to have been aware of the major developments, which occurred in Christianity in Europe in general, and Britain in particular. Karim employed the usual Persian/ Hindustani terms to denote the faith: *Din-i Isawi*, *Isa-i Mazhab*. He did not discuss such issues as whether the Christianity was a 'revealed' religion and consequently its followers enjoyed the status of people of the book (*Ahl-i Kitab*). He only briefly noted that one of oldest texts of the New Testament was in Greek language. It is in his narrative of the British history that he wrote that the people of Britain remained rooted in pagan traditions until late. They used to offer human sacrifices and worshipped idols and their religious leaders (*murshid*) believed in the transmigration of soul in the sense that if anyone had committed sin in this world, he was to be reborn in the form of animal (*Khalqat-i haiwanat*) in the next life. It was in the seventh century AD under the Saxon king Aethelberht that St. Gregory I the Apostle of the English, a Christian leader (*Mujtahid Din-i Ilawi*) introduced Christianity in Britain, the King himself being the first to embrace the new faith. (In 597 Pope Gregory I the great, sent St. Augustine to England from Rome.) Karim was also aware of the break with the Roman papacy and the establishment of an independent Church of England as the latter wrote that during the reign of Henry VIII (1509-47) a new religion (*mazhab-i jadid*) came into existence, i.e. an allusion to the Anglicanism. Our author did not use the actual terms Catholic or the Protestant or Anglican to denote the Christian faith.[39] However, he was also aware of certain Christian rituals like the White Sunday and appreciated the social role of clergy. He visited the St. Paul's Cathedral (*girja*) and proudly informed his readers that he sat next to the Archbishop. The Cathedral's classical baroque style of architecture impressed the visitor. It seems he viewed St. Paul's Cathedral more in terms of its splendid architecture and more as a historical monument than purely a place of religious worship.[40]

Modern Britain

Karim sought to described the physical and human geography of Britain. There are found copious observations on the flora and fauna of Britain particularly in his *Siyahatnama*. He sought to described the various facets of Great England: its circumference, climate, land, soil, rivers, main agricultural and industrial products, livestock, trade and manufacturing, finance, banking, insurance, sources of, transportation, and the provincial and local administration.[41] The observer found it a highly urbanized and industrialized nation. Above all, it was a country of easy communication and transportation. Its cities and towns were well developed and magnificent buildings dotted the landscape of the country. The observer emphasized that it was a well-populated and flourishing country, and its people were well-fed and rich. In this period, the prosperity of England is such that if he were to describe it in detail, Indians would not believe it, remarked the commentator. Karim Khan wrote that Britain was a small, compact and beautiful island. There were numerous such islands in the continent of Europe but what distinguished this island from others was its economic growth and prosperity. Its longitude was one hundred and seventy *kuroh* and latitude one hundred and fifty *kuroh*, including Scotland the entire island comprised of three hundred and seven *kuroh*. The oldest name of the country was Great Britain, i.e. large Britain (Karim himself employed the term *Inglistan*).[42] The whole country was divided into *mahals* known as the counties, which were fifty-two in numbers. Its principle crops were wheat, barley, oats, sugar beets and potatoes. They employed horses for farming inspite of the availability of the bullocks. The rivers were rich sources of revenue, apart from their being a source of irrigation, especially the river Thames.[43]

London: A Portrait

In Britain, it was London the British capital city which was the centre of his attraction. It was obvious since our observer spent more than a year in London therefore; his observations are also that of the British capital. It was the period when the British metropolis had become hub of the empire politically, commercially and financially. It was also the industrial, commercial and political centre of the vast empire. It was the pivotal point for world trade in commodities. Some of the British products were famous throughout the world especially in textiles, broad cloth and silk, war equipments such as the cannons, muskets and swords and consumer products and paintings, pottery telescopes and watches.[44] In return, the British enjoyed the desired products from other countries like India, America, Turkey, Syria, China, Iran, and other countries. He informed his readers that London the national capital was situated on the River Thames. In his portrait of London the visitor sought to describe its bridges, colleges, churches, historical monuments, roads, means of transportation and communication, market-places and water-supply, lighting arrangement, its paving, cleansing and sanitation with interest and curiosity. Its beautiful cityscape, rich greenery, and open spaces were pleasant and he liked its weather. He appreciated its spacious roads, which were paved and lighted. Cleaning and sanitation was the responsibility of the joint stock companies, they in turn collected regular revenues in the form of taxes. He also came to know of the insurance system of life and property especially that of houses. This was perhaps due to recurring fire incidents.[45]

In his travelogue, England's prestigious financial and intellectual institution such as the Bank of England, and the British Museum also found a place. About the central bank of England, he remarked that it was a magnificent building and an organization like any other company, i.e. a joint stock bank. The bank had a governor and a deputy governor. It notes were widely circulated. Karim succeeded in obtaining the precise figures about the assets of the bank. He mentions that the then Bank of England had two hundred and eighteen million and one lac, forty one thousand pounds equivalent to twenty-eight crores, fourteen lacs and ten thousand rupees.[46]

Karim went to the British Museum where he saw that whatsoever was on display was dead not alive. He was surprised to see the wealth of archaeological and ethnographic specimens from various countries. The latter was especially fascinated with its collection of the antiquities of Iran and Egypt, especially the Egyptian mummies, and carefully noted the method of burial coffin in ancient Egypt. Karim estimated that about one crores rupees would have been spent in the construction of this magnificent royal building.[47]

During his sojourn in England Karim mainly socialized with the Scots. Karim Khan's main informant about the British society was Duncan Forbes, a Scot. Karim Khan most of the time employed *Angrez* for the British irrespective of their English, Scottish and Irish origins. Karim himself had very little consciousness of the geographical and racial differences among the British as English, Irish and Scot in spite of his awareness of the evolution of the British social structure. It seems this description of the Scots as a distinct race could be attributed to his informant Duncan Forbes. A large number of Karim's acquaintances were those who were related to the Company as its directors, proprietors and administrators. Majority of these British with whom the traveller felt at ease were those with whom he was already acquainted in India, while they served the Company. Most of these officials had also acquired conversational skills in Persian and Hindustani languages. That was another reason for closer intercourse with them.

Socially, our writer saw Britain as a class-based society divided into several social orders, viz., the upper class (*Sharif wa najib*) and the lower classes (*ghurba, awamunnas*). Our traveller mainly socialized with the upper and upper middle classes and, therefore, his observations, too, were focused on the higher strata of the society. And clearly he was more interested in the British upper classes than the underprivileged ones.[48] Karim was impressed by the life-style of the Britain's nobility, aristocracy and its landed gentry. At the same time, he found this group proud and haughty. Their income from their estates as enormous and their rent from the urban property and houses as well as shops was also very high. A medium size shop could yield a rent of rupees five thousand per year. The law of primogeniture was applicable in the personal property as well. He sought to elaborate the titled nobility of Britain thus. He came to know that there were seven titles: that of the Sir, which was also known as the Knight. This title was conferred on the individual and was not hereditary. The second was that of the Baronet, his wife was called Lady, and it was a hereditary little. The third title was of Lord and the fourth was of Earl, and his wife was called Countess, the fifth was of Marquess, this was also hereditary and his wife was called Marchioness, and the sixth was that of the Viscount and his wife was known as Viscountess and seventh was that of the Duke and his wife was called as Duchess. The last was the highest royal title and it was hereditary. These hereditary titles were pure badges of honour, he fully appreciated, and the royal services were not dependent on these, i.e. were not hereditary and the careers were open to talent. This was in the interest of the state as well. For instance, for the smooth running of the administration, it is desirable that an individual capable of handling the affairs of the state should hold the office of Prime Minister. The latter should possess skill, tact and wisdom as the monarch had to depend on the advice of his minister. He cited the example of the two British Prime Ministers William Pitt and Robert Peel and argued that both of them did not claim aristocratic backgrounds, arguably Peel held the title of the second baronet and yet, the Lords and the Dukes were bound to obey his orders.[49] In fact, Karim was appreciating the rise of the intelligent middle class. The affluent classes were not only beneficiaries in every respect; they had to bear the burden of heavy taxation, which was archaic and regressive. The rich had to pay tax even for keeping servants, hunting dogs, horses and carriages, etc. Tax was paid even for the window glasses. But a house with less than six windows was not supposed to pay any tax since the owner was regarded a pauper.

Similarly, an income tax was imposed by the parliament during the massive Napoleonic Wars. Every adult with an annual income of more than two thousand rupees was made to pay a tenth part of his income to the state. This tax was discontinued after the battle of Waterloo. Karim Khan looked upon this tax as strange and unnecessary. Karim came to know that Britain has a long history of oppressive system of taxation going back to early medieval period. In the past during the reign of King Richard in 1377, a similar tax had been imposed: every person above the age of fifteen years had to pay six *annas*. This led to the revolt of Tyler, an ironsmith. Evidently, Karim was referring to the popular rebellion—the Peasant Revolt of 1381—when a poll tax of four pence a head was introduced. There seems to have been two reasons of Karim's interest in British taxation system, first his friendship with Charles Grant, who at the time was appointed Commissioner of Taxes and the second reason was that he had to pay some taxes as a rich Indian aristocrat, while he was in England.[50]

Karim Khan admired the humanitarian works of the British upper classes especially their efforts to abolish the slave trade and slavery and this, the author tried to sketch briefly:

> A few years ago the people of Britain accumulated crores of rupees on their own initiative and deposited the sum in the state treasury. They spent this money for settling the slaves by paying for their freedom to their masters (*malik*). Probably no other country in the whole of the world is so prosperous and rich as is this country. This material prosperity is increasing day by day, which is justifiable, since it is one of the signs of the Day of the Judgement.[51]

However, Karim was not an uncritical admirer of the British society. According to the observer, the British society suffered from two social evils. First social evil was that the dead bodies of the poor (*ghurba*) and especially that of a foreigner were stolen from their graves and were sold to the British scientist (*hukma-i angrez*) and the latter used it to carry out different experiments and observations. Karim concluded with lamentations that the poor had no status in the British society. Second social evil, according to Karim Khan, was the bizarre British custom of duels. Karim Khan sought to find out the reason as to why the duels were fought and its social implications for the persons involved. This was looked upon as a strange social custom. It was disapproved for being a violent practice causing grave physical injuries and sometimes even deaths to the individuals involved.[52]

Position of Women

Karim appreciated the widespread female literacy in Britain. He wrote that women were usually regarded inferior beings in comparison to men. They were thought deficient in intellect (*naqis al-aql*) in comparison to men and quoted Firdausi's verses to substantiate it further. However, women in this part of the world, writes Karim, are not only educated, in fact they have far surpassed men in various fields. They were found superior to men intellectually. He had the opportunity of meeting a few educated British ladies and was highly impressed with their intellectual capabilities. Some of them had distinguished themselves in the art of music and painting, at the same time they had acquired knowledge of abstruse subjects such as the arithmetic (*handasa*). They were capable of arguing on works such as *Tahrir-i uqlidis*.[53] Inspite of Karim's appreciation of high literacy among the British women, he strongly defended the purdah system as a true sign of a noble family's women. Once conversing with an educated British lady in London, he defended the *purdah* system and as a conservative elite, emphasized that *purdah* was the privilege of the upper class aristocratic Muslim ladies. *Purdah* was a status symbol of the upper class women.[54] He also noted that a British woman could divorce her husband like a man.[55] Karim noted that there was some interest about the Indian social customs and practices among the educated British. In this respect he found that Mrs. Mir Hasan's book was quite popular among the British reading public, and her opinion that in India , birth of boy was considered more desirable than a girl, were widely discussed. Karim counter-argued that the British upper classes also had similar attitude in this regard.[56]

To conclude, Karim's analysis of the British socio-cultural life is far from comprehensive and his remarks are mostly peripheral. Yet our writer could analyse the British social structure in the same fashion as he examined his own society. The traditional categorization of *ashraf* and *awam un nass* (elite-masses dichotomy) pertaining to the Indian milieu, finds its echo in his reflections on the British society. This indicates his ability to use the same parameters for studying alien societal structure (hitherto unknown to him) with which he perceived his own. Perhaps Karim was involved in the similar process as Lienhardt has described: 'we try to represent (the other society's) conceptions systematically in the logical constructs we have been brought up to use'.[57]

SCIENCE AND TECHNOLOGY

Modern Astronomy

More than the socio-cultural life of Britain, Karim Khan evinced deep interest in the scientific and technological developments of Europe. Among the sciences too, it was the modern European astronomy, which was an abiding passion for our author during his sojourn in England. As the preliminary remarks to his discourses on the European sciences, Karim Khan explained to his readers, and not without an expression of surprise, that the Copernican system had acquired the status of a philosophy under the epithet of 'Copernicanism', firmly established in scientific thought of European scholars.[58] Thereafter, he began by mentioning the Greek contribution to the scientific thought. He explained to his readers that the Greek philosopher called Pythagoras proposed the notion of a spherical earth but his views could not receive acceptance. It was another celebrated ancient Greek astronomer called Claudius Ptolemy, who put forth a conception of earth-centred geo-centric universe that has influenced astronomical thought until now. According to Copernican perspective contrary to the Aristotelian-Ptolemaic concept, the planet earth orbits the Sun rather than the Earth. Karim Khan clarified that in this revolutionary system the Earth attended by the Moon becomes one of the planets revolving around the Sun. Copernicus also proposed the daily axial rotation of the earth from the west to the east. Karim sought to elaborate the solar system and the relative position of the planets and the distance of various planets for the understanding of his readers. He provided a accurate description of the modern astronomy. He sought to provide his readers with the basic elements of modern astronomy such as the planetary motion, sizes and relative distance from the Sun, annual periods and their axial rotation, the motion of the planets around the Sun, axial rotation of the Sun, four satellites and the fixed stars. He summed up that the Polish astronomer, Copernicus' revolutionary helio-centric theory ushered in the age of modern astronomy. The European scientists had also speculated about possibility of life on these planets like the planet Earth.[59]

The author also emphasized the importance of telescope and wrote that it had revolutionized the entire study of astronomy. It was an invention of the European scientists and it was being constantly improved. Our writer was fully convinced that modern astronomy was based on observations carried out with the aid of this accurate optical instrument—telescope. He mentioned the reflecting telescope and its use at the Royal Observatory. Perhaps the author was referring to the reflecting telescope used by William Herschel to discover the planet Uranus in 1781.[60]

He also refers to Newton's classical theory of gravitational force without explicit mention of the scientist. He alluded to the scientific fact that both human beings and the living creatures on the earth as well as the movement of celestial bodies such as the planet Sun, the Moon, the Stars, and the comets all remain in their own respective place due to this universal force of attraction acting between all matters. Similarly, the same universal force of attraction determines the free fall of objects on earth. This phenomenon of nature in English language is known as attraction and gravitation which means the power of attraction (*quwat-i jazba*) and power of expulsion (*quwat-i dafi'a*). Karim opined that the scholars have written volumes on this subject, but at the same moment, our commentator admits his inability to elaborate this scientific and natural phenomenon.[61]

Interestingly enough, Karim explicitly accepted the Copernican theory and indeed argued in its favour. He discusses the difference of opinion among those who favoured the geo-centric cosmology and those who stood for the helio-centric view and against the Copernican system. In fact, he accepted the latter and considered it to be more reliable. Furthermore, Karim Khan addressed himself to the question as to why the Greek cosmological ideas were still entertained by the Muslims. What were the reasons of Muslims' attachment to Greek philosophy? He refers to the crucial period of transmission of Greek philosophy to Arab world under the Abbasids through translation of Greek scientific literature into Arabic under Caliph Mamun (753-75). He further wrote that it was precisely the period when Prophetic traditions (*hadith*) were also compiled. Does Karim Khan's above statement imply that Muslim philosophers endeavoured to assimilate these ideas into religious discourses? We do not know, as Karim Khan does not elaborate this aspect any further.[62]

To satisfy his intellectual curiosity, Karim Khan frequently visited the Royal Observatory at Greenwich in the company of several British friends and scholars (*hukma-i farang*). Clearly, these academies, observatories, and museums were the reflection of intellectual advancement of Europe for the visitor. Karim Khan frankly admitted his extreme bewilderment at the way astronomical observations were carried out in the Greenwich Observatory with the aid of telescope. The writer amused himself by viewing the planets and ascertained that there were mountains on the Moon. There, the author availed himself of the opportunity of holding scientific discourses with Sir John Herschel, the Royal Astronomer on his favourite subject.[63] He specifically mentions that John Herschel is the son of the famous astronomer William Herschel who discovered a new planet known after his name and now called Uranus, which is a Greek word.[64]

Furthermore, Karim utilized this opportunity to discuss the causes of earthquake with the Royal Astronomer. In this respect, he first sought to explore the nature and composition of the Earth. He came to know that the shape of the planet earth was like an onion having layer upon layer and like the human body, it had liquids consisting of water and fire. Its surface is made up of a number of large, rigid plates and move relative to one another and interact at their boundaries. If one place descends beneath the other it results in a severe earthquake.[65] However, the occurrence of the earthquake cannot be predicted in advance unlike the solar and lunar eclipses, as no method has yet been devised to predict the time, place or magnitude of earthquakes. Karim also informed his readers about a major earthquake which struck Lisbon and heavily damaged the Portuguese capital. Perhaps he was referring to a major earthquake, which occurred in Lisbon on 1 Nov. 1755. Karim felt relieved to know that the major zones of seismicity were Russia, China and Japan. India, his own native land, was comparatively safe from this natural calamity. Yet, the reverberations of the occurrence of any major earthquake were felt in India too. At this point, to seek an opinion of Sir John Herschel, he related an occurrence of a kind of volcanic eruption, which took place in Jhajjar, his own town in 1782. Karim says that after serious reflections the British scientist informed him that it was an earthquake of lower magnitude; consequently, the town remained safe from this natural calamity.[66]

Technical Developments

Britain was seen as a country where both agriculture and industry were developing and expanding. Trade was the major source of income and hence it was perceived a rich country primarily because of its trade and commerce. With the advent of the Industrial Revolution, it had moved from agricultural to a predominantly industrial economy. It witnessed the growth of heavy industries, iron and steel, textile and shipbuilding. The new technology reached its peak in the age of railway and steamship. The railway age may be said to have begun by 1830 and by 1840s when the contemporaries talked of 'railway mania'. This British technical progress was evident to the visitor.

During this sojourn in London, Karim Khan visited the Royal Arsenal and the Dockyard of Royal Navy at Woolwich in the company of an interpreter, where the visitor observed the introduction of labour-saving and labour-facilitating devices in the shipbuilding industry and manufacturing of the cannons. At the Arsenal (*topkhana*), he was impressed with the technological advancement in the manufacturing of cannons and other weapons. He noted that in the Arsenal there were about forty thousand cannons, besides a large collection of the cannons manufactured in other countries. Karim carefully examined various types of cannons manufactured in various European countries such as France, Germany, Spain, Prussia, Austria, Portugal and Russia. There were also cannons manufactured in Arab countries as well as in India, which are Asian and African countries, specified Karim. Amongst this collection, the observer appreciated Tipu Sultan's cannon, which was brought to Britain after the fall of Seringapatam. Karim opined that in no way was it inferior to those of Europe, especially in exterior decoration (*naqqashi*). During his visit to the Dockyard, he admired the British warships (*jahazat-i jangi*). At the Dockyard, he noted that five-hundred and seventy-eight naval ships were ready, while fifty-three were under construction. He noted the process of mechanization in these industries, specially the novel methods of iron smelting and cutting of the wood, which simply bewildered the visitor.[67] Karim noted that the steam played a vital role in the industrialization process of Britain; in fact, almost all the machines were operated with the power of steam.[68]

Karim frequently visited a polytechnic in London to satisfy his intellectual curiosity and frankly admitted that the various scientific and technical innovations were nothing less than breathtaking. At the polytechnic, he saw 'a certain device through which two persons could communicate with each other from a distance of hundred miles'.[69]

Karim saw the introduction of the gas illumination in London for the purposes of street lighting. A large and influential body of those persons who were in charge of public street lighting in London opposed this innovation as they had already invested enormous sums for the above purpose.[70]

Karim Khan's observations about the British Industrial Revolution relate to its second phase, as the latter visited Britain in the fourth decade of the nineteenth century when Britain was throbbing with railway construction. Karim records his visit to the Great Western Railway. References to railways occur at numerous places in his travelogue, mainly in connection with his journeys within the city of London and outside. He reports that railway construction was an enormous project, usually undertaken by private companies. It carries both passengers and freight. Karim noted with immense curiosity the use of electric telegraph to transmit signals along the wire for railroad signaling.[71] This, he wrote, had immensely increased the communication efficiency of the railway system.[72]

Karim carefully describes various bridges of London and the enormous sums which went into their construction.[73] He held lengthy discussions with the French-emigre engineer and inventor, Sir Mark Isambard Brunel (1769-1849), (who solved the problem of underwater tunneling), about the construction of Thames tunnel and the cost involved in its undertaking. He came to know that Brunel had been knighted in 1841 for his engineering feat.[74] At the same time, he noted that the contractors and the private companies on behalf of the government undertook these vast projects.

To sum up, Karim Khan had an articulated interest in the technical progress of Britain. But it seems, in spite of all such amazing details, there were some constraints on the vision of our observer. For instance, he did not have any insight into the basic transformation undergoing along with the industrial progress. Impact of industrialization was clearly apparent at the mid-nineteenth century. Yet Karim Khan could not discern the socio-economic results of industrialization on the various strata of society. Obviously, he was unable to understand the nature of the emerging economy, i.e. capitalism that was transforming the British society. He appreciated that the pursuit of profit led to technological innovations. But he could not correlate the reasons for technical changes with the increase in demand. In spite of his appreciation of the introduction of labour-saving devices, he failed to point out the basic underlying fact that the process of mechanization occurred in the absence of cheap labour. Most of the time he discussed the British technical progress as isolated events without noticing their inter-relationship. He often frankly admitted his lack of comprehension of the various aspects of this transformation; the observer did not conceal his extreme bewilderment at the industrial and technological advancement in Britain. His narrative constantly displays his extreme consciousness that Indians (*ahl-i Hind*) may not be able to follow or appreciate his account of the workers of the British society.[75]

BRITISH POLITICAL INSTITUTIONS

Parliamentary System

The King

Perhaps even more than the science and technical advances of Europe, it was the political ideas and institutions of Britain which aroused Karim's interest the most. British political institutions, the constitutional monarchy and the parliamentary democracy were regarded superior to industrial inventions and technical innovation like the Railways, the steamship, the weaving machine and other inventions. The above were not the object of curiosity and wonder, but the political parties, i.e. Wings and the Tories were. We shall now concentrate on this aspect.

At the outset, Karim explained to his readers that the British government consists of three elements: the King, the hereditary and appointed House of the Lords (*majlis-i amiran*), and the elected House of Commons (*majlis-i umdat ur riaya*). The country's head of the state is the reigning king or queen. A well laid down law of primogeniture regulated the succession of throne. It was a great source of stability. It eliminated the possibility of rebellion of the younger princes and thus peace was not disturbed. Karim specifically pointed out that female succession to the throne was also a recognized principle through which Victoria became Queen of Great Britain. Victoria came to the throne after the death of William IV (d. 1837), as the latter left no heir to succeed him. Although the former king had three brothers, but according to the above law his niece, the only child of the Duke of Kent, became the queen.[76]

The actual sovereignty resides in Parliament and its two houses. The British monarch was a nominal head of the state. He cannot impose or raise the taxes without the consent of the Parliament. The British parliament has the right to impose the taxes. Whenever a necessity arises, a meeting of the members of the parliament is convened where its members discuss that particular issue. Each member of the House of Commons represents one parliamentary constituency. The members must be twenty-one years of age or older. He should be a property owner. The House of Commons is elected for a maximum term of seven years. The decisions are taken based on the majority opinion prevailing over the minority.

Growth of the Parliamentary System in Britain

Karim Khan traces the origins of Parliament and the genesis of the two houses from the reigns of the King Henry and Edward onwards respectively. Under the former, the nobility (*amir*) revolted and created an assembly at Oxford, which later came to be known as the House of Lords. Encouraged by the success of aristocracy, the officials of the state, the military elite demanded their share in the formulation of the state policy, which ultimately led to the formation of the House of the Commons.

Karim Khan explains the origins of the British parliament and its two houses during the thirteenth century as follows:

> After the death of King John in 1216, his son Henry the minor, was seated on the throne by the Padres (*padriyan*) at Gloucestor, with full pomp and ceremony. At that time, the king was barely nine years old. When the king grew of age, he acted upon the advice of clergy, and conferred important offices upon the corrupt and incompetent persons. Due to this, the nobility rose in rebellion. The king was left with no option but to concede to the demands of the nobility. The nobles (*amirs*), with mutual consultation, created an assembly at Oxford, known as Parliament. This assembly consisted of twenty four nobles and one head of the assembly (*mir majlis*). This assembly came to be known as Parliament (*diwani jamat*). The members of this assembly made desirable changes in the existing rules and regulations of the state. This assembly consisted of 464 Lords.[77]

Karim provided a similar account of the emergence of the House of Commons:

> Later on, other officials (*mansabdars*) of the state, consequent upon mutual consultation (*mushawarat*), decided, that so far we have been wielding power and authority in all affairs of the government (which now has been passed into the hands of the Lords), therefore, they forwarded their petition to King Edward, who at that time was twenty-two years old. He agreed to the demands of his officials and, with the exception of his privy councilors (*Khas umara*) and a few padres, who were not included in the category of his subjects, established another Parliament and ordered that from all over the country two officials (*mansabdar*) and two lawyers (*wakil*), worthy of handling the affairs of the state, should present themselves. This was the foundation of the House of Commons

of the English (*qaum-i Inglish*), which is the representative body of the common people, and at present it consists of six hundred and sixty representatives (*wakil*) from England, Scotland and Ireland'.[78]

The Cabinet

The British monarch has formal powers but the actual responsibility lay with the ministers. Cabinet was free to decide on any matter of the state irrespective of the British monarch's wishes. All political power was concentrated in the Prime Minister and the Cabinet, and the monarch must act on their advice. The Prime Minister chooses members of the Cabinet from his party in the Parliament. The house elects from its members one speaker who presides over and regulates the debates. Similarly, a speaker presides over the deliberations of the Lords as well.[79] The Cabinet places before the Parliament all-important bills. While Cabinet thus controls the law-making machinery Cabinet is also subject to Parliament, it must expound and defend its policy in debate, and its continuation in office depends on its retaining the confidence of the House of Commons.[80] The ministers have collective responsibility: they expound and defend the legislative measures and to which they are directly responsible. In fact, they are the government. If they cannot defend the government policy on the floor of the legislative body, the ministry may be turned out.

The ministers (*wuzara*) are not obliged to execute such command of the king which they consider contradictory to the established constitution (*dastur*) of the country. The ministers hold the right to resign from their responsibility, if the king insists to execute any such measure. However, if they consider his orders appropriate, they had to obey his commands. But, in both the situations, they have to explain their position in the Parliament House, where they are questioned by the other members. If they are found irresponsible, not any explanation will be accepted from them. First, they will be asked to explain whether a particular order of the king, which they had executed, was reasonable or not. Again in both the conditions whether they regarded any order of the king reasonable or unreasonable, they will be questioned. If they come forward with a simple explanation such as they undertook to execute the task because the king, in that situation, too, ordered it they will be asked as to why they did not resign from their responsibility in accordance with the constitution of the country. By every means, and in every condition, the ministers are responsible for every good and evil.'[81]

During his sojourn in London Karim paid several visits to the House of Lords as well as to the House of Commons. He was immensely impressed with the pageantry, pomp and glitter of the Lords. He described such things as the royal carriage, sitting arrangement of the House, and the dresses of its members with curiosity and interest. His account is graphic and accurate, it seems in his endeavours he was assisted by the interpreter who accompanied him on all such occasions.[82]

About the Lords, Karim came to know that it consists of three hundred and fifty members, from amongst the highest ranks of the nobility. It was also the final court of appeal. No one, including the King has the right to dismiss them; therefore, cases were decided without favouritism. As an example of the power of the judiciary he cited the case of King George IV that the latter initiated an annulment action against his wife in 1830. Both the parties had their own lawyers, but Queen Caroline's case was successfully defended by Lord Brougham and Thomas Denmen in the House of Lords. Later on, when William IV, brother of George IV, came to the throne, as a reward for impartial decision, he raised Thomas Denmen to the position of Lord Chief Justice. Here Karim Khan had some reflections on the position of judiciary in India. He wrote that in India as well as the situation is somewhat the same: the judges of the Supreme Courts of Calcutta, Madras and Bombay could not be dismissed except for three reasons, in case of natural death, in case the judge has committed an unpardonable offence, or else he resigns from his position.[83]

On his second visit as recorded in his travelogue, Karim listened to Queen Victoria's speech to the joint meeting of the two houses, in which the Queen expounded her views on the British foreign policy. Our observer carefully noted that the Queen assured the members of the House of Lords that Britain's relations with the Kings of China, Russia and Prussia were cordial.[84] At the same time, she assured the members that attempts were made to improve relations between the kings of Portugal and Spain as well. Karim carefully noted Queen's address read to the joint meetings of the two houses in August 1841 concerning Persia. The Queen expressed satisfaction that earlier the British envoy was recalled from Persia, but again they had sent their ambassador for the same purpose, as now the Shah has agreed to conditions proposed by Britain.[85] The Queen is reported to have expressed her concern about the economy of her country: she said that the present financial year was in deficit, and she proposed to avert the deficit by raising revenues from the country. Karim admired the great poise and grace of the Queen in carrying out her official duties, the Queen's fair complexion and beautiful speaking voice fascinated the visitor. However, he was surprised to know that Lord Brougham could openly criticize the queen for her views on the British foreign policy.[86]

However, he seems to have recorded his visit to the House of Commons only once along with a certain Charles Norris, where he was an eyewitness to the debates on the Corn Laws on 14 June 1841. Karim Khan correctly noted the stand of the two parties. The ministers were seeking to reduce the prices of grain by allowing its import and thus relieving the populace from the prevailing oppressive high prices of the essential commodities, while the members of Parliament led by Robert Peel opposed the ministers. The observer specifically noted the arguments and counter-arguments between Robert Peel and Lord John Russell (d. 1878) the former was defending his party's landed interest while the latter advocated free trade.'[87]

On 25 August 1841, Karim briefly noted that the ministers, i.e. the ruling party, who were not in favour of maintaining high prices of corn were defeated/outvoted, as the majority were of those members who were not in favour of importing the grain.[88] Karim noted that in the House of Lords the majority were of those who were not in favour of importing grain and thus maintaining the prices of grain high. He noted that only ninety-five members were in favour of importing grain while one hundred and sixty-seven members rejected it. Duke Wellington also opposed the motion as the latter argued that it was against the established customs and tradition of his country.[89] He again noted that Queen's proposal as was sent to the House of Lords was defeated in the House of Commons as well, where two hundred and sixty-nine members favoured it, while three hundred and sixty members including Sir Robert Peel rejected the motion.[90] Following this defeat Melbourne's ministry resigned and Karim noted this in his *Siyahatnama* on 30 August 1841.[91] Sir Robert Peel became Prime Minister and a new ministry was formed.[92] Lord Ellenborough was appointed President of the Board of Control, which was earlier held by Sir John Hobehouse.[93] In similar way, the entire ministry was changed. Peel formed a new ministry but he retained the Speaker of the House of Commons.

Later on, upon his return to India, Karim recalled his visits to the two houses of British Parliament and he recounted the debates on passing of the Anti-Corn Laws and especially how he was received with marked attention and kindness by the Queen, and was offered a chair specifically kept for the visitor. Karim very evocatively recounted Queen Victoria's delightful silvery voice in which she argued against the prevailing protectionist legislation that kept the prices of the British grain artificially high. He informed his readers that the Queen said that the high prices of the grain were extremely oppressive for the poor subjects of the country. Therefore, if the members of Parliament would agree the grain would be imported and the prices of corn could be reduced. Karim whole-heartedly supported British monarch's stand since, for Karim welfare of the people lay in the cheap prices of such essential items of consumption as grain. For him the high prices could not be the cause of prosperity of a country. Indeed, for Karim the high prices of the grain were oppressive for the poor. He could not understand the reasons for maintaining the prices high. Karim frankly admitted that the explanation for the above was beyond his comprehension. It was a dilemma which the observer could not resolve. Furthermore, the commentator was bewildered to recall that not only was the Queen's proposal rejected, her views were openly criticized by Lord Brougham, a member of the House of Lords. Had it happened in some other country the sovereign would have got his opponent murdered.[94]

Now the question may arise that Karim knew it well that the British sovereign was a nominal head of the state and bound by law. British monarch did not interfere in the policy of the government, and that she could exercise her political function in accordance with the rules passed by the Parliament with the consent of the nation. Yet, his narrative displays an excessive preoccupation with the institution of monarchy; issues such as the law of primogeniture, rights and duties of the constitutional monarch, relation with the Parliament and the Cabinet are discussed with immense interest. Moreover, kingship is also not an Islamic institution. It would be worth an enquiry, as to what the reasons of this obsession with the British monarchy were, and its titled nobility, i.e. Queen and the Lords.

First, this recurring theme of restraints and balances on the power of the sovereign are probably the indirect reflection of the behaviour of the early and mid-Victorian British who saw themselves as the leaders of progress and civilization and prided themselves on the nature of their government. These middle-class bourgeoisie British were the major informants or the primary source of the author under study. Inspite of his appreciation of the limited powers of the monarch and of the Parliamentary system, there seems to have been some basic misconceptions as to how the system functioned. This is evident from Karim's description and analysis of the Anti-Corn Law debates to which he was an eyewitness. To his surprise and great astonishment, he found that the Lord Brougham could openly criticize the Queen in the House of Lords.

Besides, Queen Victoria's period (1837-1901) witnessed transformation of sovereign's political role into a ceremonial one. After 1830 in Britain, the party system became entrenched and all members of parliament began using a party label. Effective power was passing from the monarch.[95]

Moreover, India, his own country, was under full colonial rule. The Mughal empire had already faded to a secondary role, although the emperor was still based in Delhi and the nominal sovereign Akbar Shah (ruled 1806-1837) was succeeded by another *de jure* ruler, Bahadur Shah Zafar who also enjoyed 'nominal sovereignty' until finally deposed after the Revolt of 1857. The territorial suzerainty of the East India Company had almost been established by this time, and the Company had emerged as a paramount power. It now exercised its sway almost over the whole of the sub-continent, directly or indirectly.

Therefore, the East India Company became another major object of enquiry. First, he deemed it imperative to know the structure and constitution of the Company. It was perceived a purely commercial organization. Then, the question arose: If it was a purely trading concern, was India governed by a Mercantile organization or by a sovereign authority?

Social Equality

Karim knew that in Britain the legislature, executive, as well as the judiciary were free from the control of the monarch. The king did not have the right to appoint the judges (*ashab-i adalat*) nor to dismiss them. Therefore, the judges (*qazis*) were free from any compulsion of superior authority and were independent in deciding the cases. The common people had the right to seek justice from the judiciary. Thus, the oppression of the weak by the strong was eliminated. This form of freedom was derived from law. No one could transgress the bounds of law. Therefore, common people in the British society enjoyed a great amount of freedom and liberty.

The roots of social equality and freedom lay in the historical past of Britain, going back to the thirteenth century, when Britain rose against the injustice, oppression (*zulm*) and tyrannical regime of a despot to safeguard their rights and laid the foundation of the parliamentary system, which was defined and redefined with the passage of time. Historical roots of the constitutional freedom and equality before law lay in the great charter (*ahadnama*) of 15 June 1215 signed between the British monarch and the nobility and barons. This was the basis of English liberty and the earliest foundation of English freedom. The entire episode concerning the Magna Carta is traced accurately. The factors and circumstances leading to the declaration of the Magna Carta, historical places and character involved, all are recorded in detail and in chronological sequence with utmost accuracy. It was interpreted as a revolt of nobility (*amirs*) led by the royal contender, Arthur, the Duke the Brittany, against the absolutism and oppression of the reigning monarch. The very concept of freedom (*ilm-i azadi*) had its genesis in the declaration of the Magna Carta.

Karim Khan thus traced the origins of freedom in Britain to the celebrated Magna Carta of the thirteenth century:

In England, the powerful can not oppress the weak. The king, the rich and the poor—all are bound by the rules and regulations (*qawaid-i saltanat*) of the state. Apart from that, the poor are not considered low and contemptible in the eyes of the rich. The underlying root of this freedom, as given by some historians is this: After the death of Richard, King John ascended the throne of England. But he became a tyrant and oppressive and confiscated all the property (*taalluqat*) of the country. These policies made him very unpopular among his subjects. At last, Arthur, Duke of Brittany, his nephew and legal successor to the throne, rebelled against him. King John got him killed. This action of John further aggravated the situation. The king being short-sighted, imprisoned himself in a fort. The nobles further raised storm and they went towards Stamford with a body of rebel soldiers and thence to Brackley and occupied Northampton and Bradford, and finally reached London. Now, as the King had left (London) with no option, therefore the latter sent some of his advisors (*mushair*) to negotiate with the rebel nobles. At last in AD 1215, after long discussion between the rebel nobles and king's councilor (*mushir*) the king agreed to sing the Charter (*ahadnama*), which is at present in full force and it is regarded the foundation of the freedom of the English nation. This document is known as the Magna Carta. The place where this incident took place lies between Stains and Windsor, and now this particular place is known as Runnymede. Until now some people have sentimental regard for the place where this incident took place as this was the foundation of the concept of freedom (*ilm-i azadi*). Later on, John showed disinclination to execute some of the articles of this document (*ahadnama*) and following him Edward, who succeeded John in AD 1272, also refused to follow some of the clauses of this charter. But his ministers signed the Magna Carta owing to that, after some further thought and deliberations, which were not without practical considerations, the king also signed this Charter. After his signature there was no legal obstacle in the execution of Magna Carta. From that day the country is free and the cause of freedom is further progressing.[96]

At the same time, the commentator noted that the British constitution guarantees equality before the law but it did not extend to economic matters. There existed unequal distribution of income. He writes: 'This is also a misconceived notion that all people in England are equal in the real sense of the term, nonetheless, the majority were from the rich and higher classes (*ashraf*) and very few belong to the lowly groups (*kamina*). These people's main occupation is trade and commerce, which has made most of them rich and prosperous. Even those who may be categorized as poor (or lowly) are better off than the rich of other countries.'[97]

Karim sought to argue that the party system in Britain and the political groups, Radicals and the Chartists, reflected this social stratification. At he same time, these political organizations also balanced the fabric of society to a considerable extent. Karim noted that the society was based on internal dissension and rivalries (*nifaq*). Had there been such mutual jealousies and rivalries among the citizens of any other country a single day was enough for the ruin of whole of the country. But the philosophers of the country had formulated the law in such a manner that the increased rivalries and dissensions further bring happiness and prosperity. In order to elaborate his point the analyst sought to delineate the essential characteristics and policies of the two political parties, the Whigs and the Tories.

> In this country, people raise their voice against the government in such a manner that if it happened in any other country it may cause ruin and disaster, but the ancient philosophers (*danayan-i salaf*) of this country have formulated the rules and regulations in such a fashion that intense competition within the society brings prosperity of the country and stability to the government. The root cause of this strength is that whole of the country's population—rich as well as poor—has four groups (*firqa*). They are the Tories, Whigs, Radicals and Chartists. These four groups are different from each other in their character. The Tories are of the opinion that nothing should be done against the customs and usages of the country, while the Whigs believe that any new measure which will bring happiness and prosperity to the country must be promulgated. The radicals are those who think that what they knew is the best. The fourth group was that of the Chartist, the word Chartist is derived from the Latin language. They are rebellious against anything which, in their opinion, is unjust. They do not differentiate between the poor and the rich. The Chartists were demanding universal franchise and abolition of the property qualification for the election of the members of parliament. In all important offices of the country these four groups had their representatives, one may imagine the kind of arguments which would have followed. But in accordance with the tradition the decisions were taken on the basis of majority.[98]

In other words Karim realized the fact that in the British society competition, and not co-operation was the law of social life. The social cohesion and equilibrium was achieved and maintained by law. To illustrate further Karim cited his own experience of the famous Corn Law debates.

On Friday, 4 June 1841, the ministers and the members of the Parliament were debating the question of importation of the grain to bring down the prices of corn. They carried on discussion throughout the day until at last the law was passed in favour of maintaining the prices of corn high. I was myself present that day in the Parliament to listen to the debates of the Tory and Whig parties. At that time the Prime Minister, Robert Peel (1788-1850), who belonged to the Tory party, and was also a member of the Parliament asked me what I considered the most wonderful and strange (*ajaib*) about this country. I replied whatever I saw in this country were wonders for me. He said this was right but nonetheless what was the most wonderful and striking feature I had noticed. Robert Peel thought I would probably mention the railway (*arab- i dukhani*) and steam ships (*murakkab-i dukhani*), the weaving-machines and other electrical inventions, but contrary to his expectations I replied that for me the debates between the Tories and the Whigs were the most exciting of all experiences.(Apparently) I felt that if there existed such rivalry and jealousy among the people it could become the cause of ruin and disaster, and if this kind of discord and dissension occurred in government affairs it would cause its decline. But I was unable to understand the logic that more of this diversity of opinion and opposition meant greater prosperity for the state and the country.[99]

Karim Khan's comments on the socio-economic and political condition of Britain in the 1840 have come close to the prevailing circumstances. As the Britain of 1840's was simmering with discontent, this was the period when the common people in England were showing their dissatisfaction under the Chartist movement, while the middle class was agitating under the banner of the Anti-Corn League and the labouring masses broadened out the giant movement for the People's Charter. He could not define the reason and nature of this discontent; he was able to perceive that this dissatisfaction was class-based and the class divisions were reflected in the party system, although he has included Radicals and Chartists as political parties along with the Whigs and Tories. Probably this misunderstanding was because the Chartists and Anti-Corn Law League were the two most important organizations and the Chartist agitation was at its peak when Karim Khan was in England. While he could visualize that the class divisions were reflected in the political parties, he was also able to appreciate that these parties that these parties represented different groups, therefore, in spite of economic stratification within the society people were free to express their grievances through parties and hence it helped the maintenance of balance among different groups. His assessment of the causes of the material prosperity of the contemporary Britain came very close to the remarks of French philosopher Voltaire who wrote that, in Britain the whole system is based on a government concerned for the needs of the middle class and commerce which has enriched the citizens which in turn, help to make them free and that liberty in turn has expanded commerce. This is the foundation of the greatness of the state.

EAST INDIA COMPANY

The above was the picture of the dynamic West. The Company was defined as a purely commercial organization. It was a group of merchants, a joint stock company whose purpose was to earn profits through trade and commerce. It was a commercial body of merchants and like this, there existed numerous such companies in the United Kingdom such as the Victoria Company for Life Insurance. For a long time, the Company enjoyed monopoly of trade with India in return for a fixed amount of tribute.[100]

Emperor Jahangir's permission to the Company led to the establishment of a factory at Surat as their first settlement. For this Karim Khan accuses Jahangir for sowing seeds of discord and dissension on Indian soil.[101] Gradually, they built factories in Bengal, Madras and Bombay as well. They fought with the Nawab of Arcot and with the *Subedar* of Bengal, Siraj al-Daulah. At present, almost entire Hindustan has come under their political domination. In essence, Karim's discourses about the Company implied that their organization of merchants, which started as a monopolistic trading body, got involved in politics and acted as an agent of British imperialism in India from the early eighteenth century to the mid-nineteenth century.[102]

The Company in semi-popular legends was thought to be an artificial person—a female—having a legal entity, which could sue or be sued in the courts of law. It consisted of a large body of shareholders who were its actual owners. The shareholders were called proprietors, i.e. the actual owners. The association appointed twenty-four Directors to carry out the workings of the Company.[103] The term of the Directors was for six years, and one fourth of the total members retired every second year. The Chairman and the Deputy Chairman were paid a sum of five thousand pounds per annum whereas the ordinary directors were paid three thousand pounds per annum.[104]

Karim quoted figures from Mountstuart Elphinstone's[105] two-volume *History of India* (1841) that the total income of the Company from the territories under its possessions was around rupees twenty crores. But the expenditures far exceeded the income. Due to this the company was indebted to the merchants and it had to pay about rupees two and half crores as interest to the merchants.[106]

The East India Company's services, civil as well as military, were considered highly lucrative. Nevertheless, in most of the cases, the Directors managed to secure these positions for their sons or relatives. Such an incumbent should have passed the required examinations at one of the Company's colleges and should be less than twenty-two years of age. All the military appointments required royal sanctions.[107]

Karim argued that the Company though a commercial organization yet was an integral part of the British Crown. Our author forwarded a number of arguments in this respect; first, he contested with an explicit reference to the author of *Shigarfnama* that the latter was not correct in his assertion that even a General—a senior army officer—of the Company was considered low by a Captain of the royal army. This was wrong, argued Karim, since all the employees of the Company especially those employed in its armed forces received a certificate from the British king, like their counterpart employed in the British army, apart from the one they received from the Directors.[108] The writer asserted that the Company was not a separate commercial entity because various acts passed by the Parliament and the Ministry for Indian affairs were the extension of British king's power over the Company. Hence the Company's servants, too, were the servants of the King of England and thus they did not hold any inferior status but were of equal rank and status to the royal administrators. In brief, the Company was an integral part of the English Crown, not merely a body of merchants.

Besides, none of the Company's servant who has achieved the rank of the Colonel, could be set aside by the British parliament. Furthermore, he received regular income whether he resided in India or in England.[109] Besides, the Directors could not pass any order without seeking prior permission from the Board of Control, which had a close relation with the Minister for Indian affairs.[110] In case of dispute between the Directors and the Board of Control, the British monarch had the right to give his own decision. But such a situation rarely arose. In fact, apparently, the Company, a purely commercial organization, ruled India but in reality, it was a concern of the British Prime Minister, i.e. had the support of the ruling party. In addition, as such he exercised full control over the administrative as well as the financial matters. It was not always the case that the Governor-General was a Lord, sometimes, Company's ordinary servants were also promoted to this high office such as George Barlow who was an ordinary servant of the Company, a mere Baronet.[111]

Nonetheless, the fact remains that whomsoever occupied this exalted office, was regarded representative of the British Crown. He exercised full control over the administrative and financial matters. In India, the Governor-General enjoyed the status of a King, concluded Karim.[112] Beside, the judicial courts of Calcutta, Bombay and Madras, which were also known as the Supreme Courts, were in fact the Royal Courts of appeal. It is to be noted that the officials of the Company were not allowed to confiscate the *Jagirs* of the local potentates of India. If at all, such a situation occurred, the Company administrators argued that such an act was performed in self-protection. He quoted the case of the confiscation of the *Jagirs* of the Bangash chiefs of Farrukhabad by Warren Hastings and wrote that it led to the latter's impeachment in the House of Lords.[113] Similarly, Lord Auckland was also not permitted by the Directors, although he had the support of Board of Control.[114] Furthermore, the aim of the administrators of the Company was happiness and prosperity of the people of India.[115]

EPILOGUE

In *Siyahatnama* Karim closed his account somewhat abruptly by advising Indians not to visit England to lodge their complaints against the oppressions of the Company. He repeated similar views in his geographical encyclopedia, i.e. *Mirat-i gitinuma* as well. Nevertheless, his epilogue of *Mirat* is more reflective. Here Karim raised the question—was the British rule accepted as a fait accompli? Here he voiced fear of continuation of British rule though somewhat obliquely. He posited that it was a well-known fact that the entire Hindustan had passed under the British occupation. The British administrators (*hakman-i wilayat*) have also formulated laws to govern this country. Had India been conquered by any other power and not by a European nation, and the same laws would have been promulgated as were laid down by the British rulers, in that situation the country would have been recovered from the foreign possession, without any war or bloodshed within a period of two years. Had Indians been people of courage and experience, it was not unlikely that the British rulers would have felt pleased with them. According to Karim the remedy to subvert the foreign domination was with experience (*tajriba*) and courage. But the Indians lacked both—the experience and courage—the twin perquisites for success. According to Karim intellect was the key for human progress. Further, it required experience, the source of all knowledge. He regretted that such a failing was characteristic of the Indians. It was embedded in the Indian soil. Before the arrival of Muslims in India, similar was the mentality of Indian potentates. For the Indians, Europe's scientific and technological advancement was nothing more than interesting stories and fiction.

I hesitate to describe what wonders and inventions I saw in Europe. Once I went to visit John Lawrences, magistrate of Delhi, where an Indian (Hindustani) was also present.[116] I mentioned the railways that within hours it could travel hundreds of miles. At one time it could carry about two thousands passengers. Similarly, the electric telegraph (*dakkhana barqi*) through which message could be transmitted thousand *Kuroh* within seconds and the spinning jenny was mentioned. The Indian did not believe it.[117]

Since the beginning of the eighteenth century European discourse on the 'other', 'exotic' as well as 'Oriental', has been based on a distinction between 'self' and 'other' in terms of having or not having the ability to represent and to replace the 'other'. The 'others' cannot represent themselves. So, they must be represented: this has been the underlying assumption of European discourse of the non-European societies. The 'others' were doing the same what the Europeans viewed as the special and exclusive duty and privilege of their discourse alone: to described and to understand other cultures.

NOTES

1. Indian Muslim perceptions of the West have been studied by the present author of *Indian Muslim Perceptions of the West During the Eighteenth Century*, Oxford University Press, Karachi, 1998.
2. Jhajjar is situated 35 miles south-west of Delhi in the Rohtak district. Cf. *Punjab District Gazetteer, Rohtak District*, Lahore, 1911, for the history of the district see pp. 24-7, 44-5 ff. Also, see Ghulam Nabi, *Tarikh-i Jhajjar* (Faiz Ahmadi Press, 1866). This is an interesting local history of the town compiled by Munshi Ghulam Nabi, a *tehsildar* (revenue collector) of the region.
3. For his family genealogy Cf. *Siyahatnama*, folio 223a. However, we do not know our author's date or birth and death, and his exact occupation. There is a likelihood to assume that like the numerous service-gentry of this period, Karim also had no regular employment; therefore, he was seeking to cultivate patron-client relations with the British officials.
4. Nawab Nijabat Ali Khan's grandfather Mustafa Khan (d. 1745) came to India as a military adventurer during the reign of Muhammad Shah and joined the services of Alivardi Khan, the Nawab of Bengal. Nijabat's father, Murtaza

Khan was in the employment of the Nawab-Wazirs of Awadh but later on he moved to Delhi and joined the imperial services. After the death of his father, Nijabat Ali Khan remained at the Mughal court and was given the title of 'Asad al-Daulah Mumtaz al-Mulk Nawab Nijabat Ali Khan Bahadur' by the Mughal Emperor Shah Alam, in lieu of his distinguished military services. When in 1803, British forces occupied Delhi the imperial capital, and defeated the Marathas, Nijabat Ali Khan joined the army of Lord Lake. Nawab Nijabat Ali Khan was awarded this area of Jhajjar, Dadri and Bahadurgarh including some of the adjoining territories (which already formed part of his *jagir* before the British occupation of Delhi) by Lord Lake in lieu of his military services. However after the death of Nijabat Ali Khan there was continuous dispute among his sons and successors over the issue of succession to the family inheritance. The various claimants appealed to the British authorities, who in turn had to intervene in the internal matter of the family. Succeeding generations of the Jhajjar Nawabs were known for their anti-British attitude. Nawab Abd al-Rahman Khan, a great-grandson of Nijabat Ali Khan and the last ruler of Jhajjar, was hanged for his role in the great revolt of 1857 and the *jagir* of Jhajjar was confiscated. For the details cf. a local history preserved in the British Library entitled *Kaifiyat Ahwal-i Jhajjar*. Also see the above quoted local history *Tarikh-i Jhajjar*, for the family history pp, 152-62ff. The above-cited Gazetteer also contains some information about the house of Jhajjar, pp. 31-2, 38-40ff.

5. *Siyahatnama*, folios, 103b, 104a, and 106a. Also see the two above cited local histories, *Kaifyat Ahwal-i Jhajjar* and *Tarikh-i Jhajjar,* pp. 222-3, for the reasons of Karim's visit to England.
6. *Siyahatnama* folios 221b-223a. Karim Khan was himself accompanied by several servants and cooks, and at times also mentions them by name like Pir Bakhsh and Mahabat Khan.
7. Karim Khan has largely remained unknown to the scholarly world of today. It seems there is only one copy of his travelogue *Siyahatnama*, available in the British Library. Originally it belonged to the French Orientalist, Garcin de Tassy who was probably the first to have utilized it in any manner. Karim Khan Jhajjari, *Siyahatnama*, BM.OR.2163. For details of the manuscript cf. J.F. Blumhardt, *A Catalogue of the Hindi Panjabi, and Hindustani Manuscripts in the Library of the British Museum* (London, 1899). This manuscript consists of 223 folios. The first entry in his Journal is dated 1 December 1839. Every entry consists of dates in both Christian as well as Hijri era. This is an autographed copy, as at the last page it is specially mentioned by the author. This seems to be the only surviving copy of the manuscript. The present manuscript was originally in the possession of Garcin de Tassy who wrote on the flyleaf *Siyahatnama*, 'Journal kept by Kureem Khan of Jhujjur during his travels from Dihli to London and during his residence in England, in 1839-40 and 41 (written in Hindoustanee)'. Garcin de Tassy published an abridged French translation of this text in *Revue d'el Orient De l'algeria et des*

Colonies Bulletin de la Societe Orientale de France, *Quotrieme serie-tome Premier Anne*, 1865, pp. 105-41. This translation relates to his journey from Delhi to Calcutta with the title *Livre de Voyage Siyahatnama ou Itineraire de Dehli a Londres par Karim Khan, de Jhajhar*, with an introduction. This introduction describes the reasons of Karim's visit to England and later his close interaction with Duncan Forbes, pp. 105-7. Garcin de Tassy also compiled a small biographical sketch of Karim Khan in his book. For details, see Garcin de Tassy, *Histoire de la literature hindouie et hindoustanie*, 2nd edn, Vol. II (Paris, 1870), p. 165. Recently Ibadat Brelwi of Karachi (Pakistan) has edited the text. But my study is based on the Urdu manuscript lodged in the British Library now part of the Oriental and India Office Collections (London).

8. There seems to have been three extant copies of this work, all lodged in the British Library. *Mirat-i gitinuma*, Oriental Collections and Records, Delhi, Persian 724, is dated 1847, and it bears the author's seal, which has been utilized for the present work. The other two manuscripts are OR 1891 and 2038. All manuscripts are similar in contents and details. For the contents of the last two manuscripts cf. Charles Rieu, *Catalogue of Persian Manuscripts in the British Museum* (Oxford, 1883), Vol. 3, p. 994. For further details see, C.A. Storey, *Persian Literature: A Bio-Bibliographical Survey*, Vol. II, Pt. I (London, 1958), pp. 159-60.
9. British soldier and statesman and Governor-General of India for three years from 1844 to 12 Janaury 1848, recognized the commercial significance of the railways for India, the First Sikh War took place under him, evinced interest in preservation of native monuments of antique art (cf. *Dictionary of National Biography* (eds.) Leslie Stephen, Sydney Lee (London, 1908), Vol. VIII, pp. 1226-9 (hereafter, *DNB*).
10. Khwaja Qutb al-Din Bakhtiyar Kaki (d.1235) a thirteenth century Chishti sufi saint who settled in Delhi during the reign of Iltutmish (1211-36). His tomb is located near the Qutb Minar at Mehrauli. The Qutb Minar, completed by Iltutmish in 1229, is believed to derive its name from Qutb al-Din Bakhtiyar Kaki (not from Qutb al-Din Aibak). The Chishti affiliation venerates Qutb al-Din as one of the outstanding members of its founder-generation in India and records him in his *silsilah* as the link between Khwaja Muin al-Din and Khwaja Farid al-Din.
11. *Mirat-i gitinuma*, folios 1-3b
12. He says that he is completely ignorant of English language therefore could not order the waiter for anything. Again, in his entry of 27 July 1840 he feels handicapped for not knowing English to communicate with anybody. *Siyahatnama*, folio 83b.
13. The name 'Henry Ukarman' is frequently referred by Karim as his interpreter (*sahab-i mutarajjim*). It seems that it was no other person than Forbes who acted as Karim's interpreter throughout the latter's stay in England. The name Henry Ukarman is a later interpolation in the text of the manuscript,

perhaps by Forbes himself. Karim's bias for Scots and his interest in the game of chess indicates this. Secondly, this was also confirmed by Garcin de Tassy, that Karim had close association with the well-known Orientalist, Duncan Forbes, and also that the latter was his principal informant and tutor concerning his knowledge of Europe.

14. Perhaps the Governor-General in question was Auckland. George Eden, Earl of Auckland (1784-1849), British statesman, a Whig and friend of the Tory Prime Minister Melbourne, was Governor-General of India (1836-42), recalled after his disastrous campaign of Afghanistan in 1841, when he tried to replace Dost Muhammed with Shah Shuja, cf. *DNB*, Vol. VI, pp. 357-8.
15. William Fraser's career was spent entirely as a British Agent in the Delhi territories and cut short by his murder in 1835. Cf. M. Archer and Toby Folk, *India Revealed: The Art and Adventure of James and William Fraser 1801-35* (London, 1989). For the career of William Fraser and his involvement with the Indian aristocracy, cf. Percival Spear, *Twilight of the Mughuls* (rpt, Delhi, 1969), pp. 182-93ff.
16. Sir Charles Forbes (1774-1849) a British politician, lived in Bombay, head of Forbes and Company of Bombay, before 1812, member of the House of Common, an advocate for the justice for Indian people, cf. *DNB*, Vol. VII, pp. 380-1.
17. Charles Grant (1778-1866) born in Bengal, a staunch supporter of the Company, President of the Board of Control 1830-4, became Colonial Secretary in 1835 and finally served as Commissioner of land tax, cf. *DNB*, Vol. VIII, pp. 380-1.
18. Duncan Forbes (1798-1868) Orientalist, had brief experience of India, arrived in Calcutta in 1823, but due to ill health returned to England in 1826, and became assistant to Dr. J.B. Gilchrist. In 1837, he was appointed Professor of Oriental Languages in King's College, London, a post that he occupied until 1861. A successful teacher and writer of useful publications, played chess and wrote, *Observations on the Origin and Progress of Chess*, London, 1855, followed by a work of great research entitled, *The History of Chess From the Time of Early Invention of the Game in India till the Period of its Establishment in Western and Central Europe*, London, 1860. He also wrote a number of elementary manuals on Indian languages, Persian and Hindustani. For the Oriental translation fund he translated the Persian romance entitled *The Adventure of Hatim Tai*, London, 1830, edited *Bagh-o-Bahar*, in 1846, 1849, 1859, 1862; edited *Tota Kahani* in Hindustani in 1852 and 1857, cf. *DNB*, Vol. VII, pp. 386-8.
19. John Shakespeare (1774-1858) Orientalist, appointed Professor of Hindustani at the East India Company's college at Addiscombe (1809-29), compiled various grammars and dictionaries and text books of Hindustani language. He was author of several works: *Hindustani Grammar* published in 1813; *Dictionary of Hindustani and English*, 1817, 1849, *Muntakhabat-i*

Hindi, Selections in Hindustani, 1817, *Introduction to the Hindustani language*, 1845, cf. *DNB*, Vol. XVII, pp. 1283-4.
20. Cf. For an account of the Asian continent *Mirat*, folios 11-66; for an account, of the African countries, ibid., folios 66-74; for a description of European countries, ibid., folios 75-88; and for the New World, ibid., folios 88-103. His account of the Asian countries is almost occupied with India.
21. *Siyahatnama*, folio 195a. The same Persian treatise of Jonathan Scott was incorporated by Murtaza Husain in his *Hadiqat al-aqalim*, Newal Kishore Press (Lucknow, 1879, 1881), pp. 504-33.
22. For his visit to France and an account of the Napoleonic wars, see *Mirat*, folios 75a-77.
23. Ibid, folio 87b.
24. For the above comments cf. ibid., folios 86b-87a.
25. For Australia see *Mirat,* folio 103 and for Canada see ibid., folio 100.
26. Ibid., folio 88a.
27. *Mirat*, folio 9.
28. For a detailed description of Southern and Central America and the urban civilization of Mexico and Peru, ibid., folios 91a-98a, and 101-3.
29. Karim severely criticizes its use because of its injurious effects. For the spread of tobacco smoking in India and its injurious effects for health, *Mirat,* folios 95b-97a. Karim traces the spread of tobacco in India from the period of Akbar with reference to *Khulasat al-Tawarikh*, a seventeenth century work compiled by Sujan Rai Bhandari (Aligarh Muslim University, Maulana Azad Library), University Collection, Farsiya Akhbar 12.
30. *Mirat,* folios 98b-100, for an account of the North America with description of its states, their major industrial and agricultural products.
31. *Siyahatnama*, f. 156 for no taxation without representation.
32. Karim was referring to Canada, which, he noted, was a British-governed province, *Mirat,* folio 100.
33. *Siyahatnama,* folios 156a-157. This was for the first time that the word *ijma* (literally, consensus) was used to describe the democratic form of government. Later on, the term *Jumhuria* came to be used by the Arabic, Persian, and Urdu writers to denote the same thing. In fact, *ijma* seemed to be more a connotation for popular and representative rather than presidential form of government.
34. *Siyahatnama,* f. 156, also see *Mirat-i gitinuma*, f. 99b for presidential system of America.
35. *Mirat,* folio 99b. Also, see *Siyahatnama,* folios 156a-157, for an account of the New World and its discovery and colonization by the Europeans, and the War of Independence, and the presidential form of government. It is interesting to see that Karim was interested in current affairs of the United States; while in London on 2 May 1841, he briefly noted in his travelogue that upon the death President William Henry Harrison (1773-d. 4 April

1841), John Tyler the Vice-President became the tenth President of the United States of America (1841-5), ibid.

36. Murtaza Husain Bilgrami, *Hadiqat al-aqalim*, op. cit.
37. For a detailed narrative of the British history from pre-Roman times to the present. *Siyahaṭnama*, 200b-204a. *Mirat,* folios 103b-107b.
38. *Siyahatnama,* 208a; *Mirat,* folios 113b-114a.
39. *Siyahatnama*, folios 201, 203; for similar information, see *Mirat*, folio 106b, for the spread of Christianity by St. Gregory I in Britain.
40. Mirat, folios 111b; for the author's visit to the St. Paul's Cathedral and the social role of clergy, cf. *Siyahatnama,* folio 163b. Karim carefully narrated that the Cathedral was constructed between 1675 and 1710, replacing the Old St. Paul's, which had been destroyed in the Great Fire of 1616. He also provided details of its measurement and the cost of its construction accurately.
41. For a description of England, *Mirat,* folios 103-109b.
42. *Siyahatnama,* folio 149b.
43. Ibid., folios 206b-207a; *Mirat,* folio 108b. Our author had precise figures that within one year, that is from 5 July 1840 to 5 July 1841, the government collected a net revenue of fourteen crores from river Thames alone.
44. *Mirat,* folio 109.
45. For a portrait of London, ibid., folios 110a-115b.
46. *Siyahatnama*, folio 98.
47. Ibid., folios 197a-198a.
48. For Karim's social contacts with the upper strata of the British society. Ibid., folios 149b-150a, 157b, 162b, 163a, 193, and 197. Karim specifically mentioned his meeting with the Duke of Cambridge, brother of King William IV, with whom he exchanged his views about the British society and culture through an interpreter.
49. Ibid., folio 208a. British Prime Minister 1834-5, 1841-6 and founder of the Conservative Party, who was responsible for the repeal (1846) of the Corn Laws that had restricted imports. On this controversial issue of the Corn Laws the landed interest of his party was very sensitive. He also re-introduced the income tax (originally instituted during the Napoleonic Wars) established the internal revenue on a sound footing. *DNB*, Vol. XV, pp. 655-68.
50. For a detailed exposure of the British taxation cf. ibid., folios 212a-214; *Mirat-i gitinuma*, folios 113b-115b.
51. *Siyahatnama*, folio 206a, Slave trade in Britain was abolished in 1807 and slavery was abolished throughout the British dominions in 1833.
52. Ibid., folios 207-8. Karim described an eye-witness account of a duel between a military official and a member of House of Lords.
53. *Mirat,* folio 124.
54. *Siyahatnama*, op. cit., folios. 207b-208a.

55. *Siyahatnama*, op. cit., folio. 173a.
56. Mir Hasan, an envoy of the Nawab of Lucknow, visited England and married an English lady (*Wilayati bibi*). She lived at Lucknow for a few years, and wrote a book of her Indian experiences. Karim Khan mentions her presence in London when he visited England. Mrs. Mir Hasan Ali, *Observations on the Musulmans of India*, 2 vols. (London, 1832), 2nd edn. with notes and introduction by W. Crooke (rpt. in Oxford in Asia Historical reprint, Karchi, 1974).
57. Quoted in Talal Asad and John Dixon, *Translating Europe's Others*, in Francis Barker (ed.), *Europe and Its Others*, Essex Sociology of Literature Conference, Vol.1, (Colchester, 1985), p. 176.
58. Karim Khan transliterated this word into Persian. Obviously he had no Persian equivalent for it. His account of Copernican system seems to have been based on *Hadiqat al-aqalim* and his personal discussions with John Herschel.
59. For author's discourses on astronomy, *Mirat,* folios 4b-6b; Karim wrote very little on the above subject in his *Siyahatnama,* folios 165b-166a, where the author mentioned his visit to the Greenwich Observatory and meeting with John Herschel and a brief note on the main elements of the modern astronomy.
60. *Mirat,* folio 6b; *Siyahatnama,* folio 165b-166, for the description of the telescope used at the Royal Observatory.
61. *Mirat,* folio 9b.
62. Ibid., folio 5a. This line of argument was later taken up by Sir Sayyid Ahmad Khan who attempted to reconcile modern science with the revealed truths pointed out to similar parallels in the early days of Islam when *Ulama* reconciled the Greek learning with the scriptures of Islam. Sayyid Ahmad first rejected heliocentric theory in 1847 but later he amended his views by providing reasons for discarding Greco-Arab sciences in favour of modern European sciences, which were based on observations, while the former was merely analogical and hypothetical cf. C.W. Troll, *Sayyid Ahmad Khan: A Reinterpretation of Muslim Theology* (Delhi, 1978).
63. *Mirat,* folio 6b. Sir John Herschel (1792-1871), English astronomer and successor to his father Sir William Herschel in the field of stellar and nebular observation and discovery. At this time Herschel was occupied with his book Outlines of Astronomy (1849), a book for educated laymen.
64. *Mirat,* folio 11b. William Herschel (1738-1822) German-born British astronomer, the founder of sidereal astronomy for the systematic observation of the heavens. He discovered the planet Uranus in 1781 earlier known by his name, hypothesized the nebulae are composed of stars, and developed a theory of stellar evolution.
65. Ibid., folio 10b. Perhaps what Karim was seeking to elaborate upon was the phenomenon of the intra-plate earthquakes. Karim's description of the composition of earth was accompanied with a diagram of the planet earth.

66. Ibid., folio 10b.
67. *Siyahatnama*, folios 193b-194b, for Karim's visit to the Arsenal.
68. Ibid., folio 212a.
69. Ibid., folio 93a. Perhaps our observer saw some early experiments in the transmission of voice before Alexander Graham's invention of telephone in 1876.
70. Ibid., folio 211b. Our writer did not mention the scientist by name, but he did specifically mention that the scientist demonstrated his invention in Pall Mall in London. This indicated that he was referring to the German scientist, Fredrick Albert Windsor. Yet, our author's information seems out-dated since, the first street lighting with gas took place in Pall Mall in London in 28 January, 1807, and the first gas company known as the Westminster Gas Light and Coke Company was established in 1812, when the above mentioned scientist obtained a charter from the British Parliament.
71. Karim provides Persian equivalents for all inventions such as the railways (*araba-i dukhani*) and steamship (*murakkab-i dukkani*), but for most of the time, he preferred to use the English terms. Similarly he transliterated the terms Great Western Railways, and electric telegraph (*dakkaana barqi*), etc.
72. *Siyahatnama*, folios 199b-200. The two Englishmen, William F. Cook and Charles Wheatstone introduced the electric telegraphy as an adjunct to visual signals on railways: this, a six-wire, five-needle apparatus that could be read visually was in use on the railway between Paddington (London) and West Drayton in July 1839, and was extended to Slough (18 miles) in 1843.
73. Ibid., folio 205b, *Mirat*, folio 109b.
74. *Siyahatnama*, folio 205b; *Mirat*, folios 110a-111a. In 1825 operations began for building the Brunel-designed tunnel under the Thames river between Rotherhithe and Wapping, the first subaqueous tunnel in history. This scheme, which had no precedent, was completed in 1842, after great physical and financial difficulties and a seven years hiatus in construction brought about by lack of funds. Karim was present at this occasion. Apart from the above details, he also came to know that the tunnel measured one thousand, two hundred and fifty feet and a sum of one crore and three lacs was spent in its construction.
75. *Mirat-i gitinuma*, folios 109b and 131a-132a.
76. For a detailed exposure of the law of primogeniture cf. *Siyahatnama* folios 214a-214b; *Mirat*, folios 117b-118a.
77. *Mirat,* folios 118b-119.
78. For a full account of the origins of the two houses of Parliament cf. *Siyahatnama*, folio 91b; *Mirat*, folios 118b-119b.
79. For the role of speaker *Siyahatnama*, folios 181b-182a.
80. Ibid., folios 185b, 213b; and *Mirat*, folio 118b, for the role of the Cabinet and relation with the monarch.

81. For the above cf. *Mirat*, folio 118b; and for a similar account *Siyahatnama*, folio 213b.
82. Our author faithfully recorded the dates: on one occasion that is on 11 August 1840, he visited the Lords with Captain Grantlay. *Siyahatnama*, folio 91a and second time he visited the House of Lords on 26 January 1841 again with Captain Grantlay.
83. *Siyahatnama*, folios 181a-181b.
84. Ibid., folios 132a-133b; Perhaps Karim was referring to the situation following the First Opium War (1839-42) between Britain and China prior to the signing of the Treaty of Nanking, which was signed on 29 August 1842. Anyhow, these details were not known to our author. Karim continued to follow Britain's foreign relations especially with the Chinese emperor and also with the Shah of Persia.
85. Ibid., folio 184b, for these comments on Britain's foreign policy. In 1837, Persia laid siege of Herat and Muhammad Shah was supported by Russia. The British were alarmed that the Iranian control of Afghanistan would bring Russia to the gates of India; they sought to prevent the Shah through British envoy Sir John McNeil. Karim was referring to the above situation. It seems these details were not known to our author. Cf. M.E. Yapp, Strategies of British India: Britain, Iran and Afghanistan (Calcutta, 1984), pp. 146-9.
86. Henry Peter Brougham (1778-1868), British Whig party politician, lawyer reformer and Lord Chancellor of England (1830-4). He was in favour of free trade, though at the same time he disliked the Anti-Corn Law League. Karim Knew that Lord Brougham was an important noble and member of the Privy Council, cf. *Mirat*, folio 123. For his biography cf. *DNB*, Vol. II, pp. 1356-66.
87. Karim visited the Commons on 14 June 1841. *Siyahatnama*, folio 164.
88. Ibid., folio 183b.
89. Ibid., folio 184b.
90. Ibid., folios 184b-185a.
91. William Lamb Melbourne 2nd Viscount (d. 1848), the British Prime Minister from 16 July to 14 November, and from 18 April 1835, to 30 August 1841. He left office after the Conservatives had won the general election of 1841. Karim noted the change of ministry.
92. *Siyahatnama*, folio 185a. Karim noted that the Prime Minister receives a salary of Rs. 50,000 a year, *Mirat*, 118b.
93. Lord Ellenborough (1790-1871) British Governor-General of India (1842-4) and President of the Board of Control for India from 1828-30, and for brief periods in 1834-5 and 1841.
94. *Mirat*, folios 122b-123.
95. Eric Hobsbawm and Terence Ranger (ed.), *The Invention of Tradition*, Cambridge University Press, Cambridge, 1983.

96. *Siyahatnama*, folios 208b-210a; *Mirat*, folios 115-116a. It is an erroneous conception about Magna Carta being a bill of rights or charter of liberties of common man. It was a feudal document in which the king pledged to respect the traditional rights of nobles. But it had the idea of limited government and rule of law.
97. *Siyahatnama*, folio 210b; *Mirat*, folio 116b.
98. *Siyahatnama*, folio 210b.
99. *Siyahatnama*, folios 210b-211b; *Mirat*, folios 116b-117b.
100. Karim Khan sought to trace the origin and formation of the Company from sixteen hundred onwards, albeit briefly.
101. *Siyahatnama*, folio 204a. Interestingly, this particular comment has been omitted by the author in *Mirat*.
102. *Mirat*, folio 125b. For economic and territorial expansion of the Company.
103. The Directors were popularly known as the twenty-four *mushir*, i.e. advisors. *Siyahatnama*, folio 217a.
104. The condition to become a shareholder of the Company and the value of each share is discussed in detail cf. *Siyahatnama*, folios 219a-220a, and *Mirat*, folios 127a-128b.
105. Mountstuart Elphinstone (1779-1859), entered company's service in 1796, served as assistant to the British agent at Peshwa's court at Poona; Resident at Nagpur; in 1808 appointed Ambassador to the Afghan court of Shah Shuja in Kabul; in 1810 appointed Resident at Poona and finally became Governor of Bombay from 1819-27, when upon his retirement a college was founded in his name by the people of Bombay, cf. *DNB*, Vol.VI, pp. 744-6.
106. Karim sought to provide his readers with exact figures. The annual income of the company from 1840-1 was Rs. 21,67,51,748, while the expenditure amounted to Rs. 19,41,67,074.
107. *Mirat*, folio 128b
108. *Siyahatnama*, folio 220b, *Mirat*, folio 128b.
109. *Siyahatnama*, folio 220b, *Mirat*, folio 129.
110. *Siyahatnama* folio 221a, *Mirat* 129a.
111. Sir George Hilaro Barlow (1762-1846), entered Bengal's civil services in 1778, created a Baronet in 1803, and served on various administrative positions including Governor of Madras from 1807 to 1812 and was for two years Governor-General of India (1805-7), cf. *DNB*, Vol. I, pp. 1140-1.
112. *Siyahatnama*, folio 221b, *Mirat*, folio 130a.
113. *Siyahatnama*, folio 220b.
114. *Mirat*, folio 129b. Auckland was recalled after his participation in British setback in Afghanistan.
115. Karim was an eye-witness to the official ceremony of Lord Ellenborough as the President of the Board of Control. He noted that the latter took oath

that he would not seek his own benefit, rather he would strive for the happiness and prosperity of the people of India. Cf. *Mirat*, folio 130a.

116. John Lawrence was magistrate-collector of the city of Delhi from 1842 to 1846. He was known for his overt Christian stance. For his life see, R. Bosworth Smith, *Life of Lord Lawrence*, 6th edn., 2 vols. (London, 1885).

117. *Mirat*, folio 131a.

Hindustan in the Speeches and Writings of Sir Sayyid

S.M. Waseem

A great visionary, reformer, and educational activist in the true sense of the words, Sir Sayyid Ahmad Khan intensely longed and actively worked for the overall development of his country, Hindustan. He extolled his people, both Muslims and Hindus, and for that matter, all inhabitants of India, to work sincerely for bringing the country on the road to progress. True, his mission was to lift the Muslims of India from the precipice and the deep fall in which destiny had placed them, aided by the flow of things and also due to their own irrational ways in fighting against the times by groping in the darkness. Sir Sayyid was a great Indian whom the editor of the *Times*, London, in April 1898, paid tribute by saying:

> For nearly 50 years, and especially since the Mutiny, Saiyid has stood as an interpreter between the Mohammedens of India and their rulers, as well as between them and the British people. He is ever ready to defend his co-religionists from literary attacks upon them, and our own columns, as well as the pages of some of the leading English Magazines, have borne witness to his learning and his dialectical skill when defending his own people.

Such was Sir Sayyid, deeply infused with love for Hindustan. While referring to his writings and speeches, one would find that he repeatedly mentioned 'Hindustan', urging both Hindus and Muslims to unite and work whole-heartedly for (Hindustan's) progress. A truly dedicated social reformer and great Indian, Sir Sayyid must be read in the right perspective, keeping in view the tides of that time in the nineteenth century, when the people of India were restless to shape their own destiny but were being moulded within the given situation. He expressed himself in one of his articles published in *Tahzibul Akhlaq* wherein he advised the then (British) Government in India (and for that matter all the rulers) thus:

It is the responsibility of the Government to safeguard the rights whether they fall under Right of Property and Belongings or Right to Profession and Livelihood, (or) Right to Freedom of Thought, and Right to Life (so that none is harmed due to inequality of power, to protect the deserving weak against the non-deserving (strong) enabling each one to draw maximum benefit out of his property and also due to his skills.[1]

Urging Hindus and Muslims alike to live in peace for developing a true understanding, he said:

. . . God ordained that Hindus and Muslims will breathe in this country's air and eat from her output: live on her land and die here. These indicate God's sanction that both these communities will live in this very country. *Hindustan*, in (all) friendliness like the two brothers. They (Hindus and Muslims) are the two eyes of *Hindustan's* beautiful countenance. . . . [2]

Further, in another of his article, Sir Sayyid declared:

It is my understanding that the two communities inhabiting *Hindustan* are Hindus and Muslims. If one of these progresses but the other does not then the condition of *Hindustan* is not going to improve. . . .[3]

Adding force to these mentioned views. Sir Sayyid said:

'On this very land of *Hindustan*, be it of Punjab, South or in Himalaya, we both live. The life of both of us is sustained here by this very country's air her water (and) output of this country. . . .[4]

As against the 'two nation theory', Sir Sayyid longed for a united, prosperous strong, and secular Hindustan. His views, expressed as far back as in 1884, deserve our attention. He declared:

By the word *qaum* I take both Hindus and Muslims. It is in this meaning that I interpret the word 'nation'. To me it needs no consideration as to what is the faith (of a person), because I cannot (minutely) see any of their (religious) actions: but what we do observe, is that we all, whether Hindu or Muslim live in one land: are subjects of one ruler. The sources of benefit for all of us is one. We all suffer equally during famines. It is due to all these different reasons that both these people who inhabit *Hindustan*, I describe in one word, i.e. Hindu, meaning thereby the *qaum* living in *Hindustan*. . . .[5]

Likewise, Sir Sayyid stressed at harmony in living, and unity of the two major communities, saying that:

'O' my friends! In your country *Hindustan*, two famous communities inhabit, who are known as Hindus and Muslims. As there are certain vital organs in human body, (likewise) these (two) communities are the vital organs of *Hindustan*. . . .[6]

Digging into the history of migration, Sir Sayyid referred to the influx of migrants to Hindustan, thus:

'O' dear! As the Hindus . . . came to this country, we (Muslims) too came to this country. . . . They considered *Hindustan* as their country. We too took to consider *Hindustan* our country. And, like our forerunners we too opted to live here in this country. Thereby *Hindustan* is the homeland of both of us. We both sustain our lives with its air, drink the pious water of Ganges and Yamuna. We both eat what is grown in *Hindustan*. In death and life we share our existence. Living in *Hindustan* our blood has changed; in appearance both (of us) resemble alike. . . . In fact, in *Hindustan* both of us due to our belonging to this our homeland. We are one nation (*qaum*). . . .[7]

Further, it will be appropriate to quote from his lecture delivered at Gurdaspur, Punjab, wherein he said:

There is no estranged relationship between Muslims and Hindus. As the Arayans [*sic*] (here) are called Hindu, the Muslims, in the same way, may also be called Hindu i.e. the inhabitants of *Hindustan*. I have repeatedly said that *Hindustan* is a beautiful bride and Hindus and Muslims are her two eyes. Her beauty lies in the safety and existence of her two eyes. If any one of them is reduced (in size) then the beautiful bride will become . . . eyes is lost, she will be (called) one-eyed. . . . (You) must have seen and heard (referring) to ancient histories and old books and (we) see now also that the application of *qaum* (nation) is made on those living in a country. Different Afghans are described as one *qaum*. Different people living in Iran are called Irani. Europeans have different views and (they) belong to different religions, but are enumerated as one *qaum* (nation); though (a number of) people belonging to other countries, come to stay here. But counted and living together, they are called on *qaum*.

'O' Hindu(s) and Muslims! Are you inhabitants of any other country than *Hindustan* ? Do both of you not live in . . . of this land (You) die on this land, and live on this (land). Remember that Hindu (and) Muslim is a religious word; otherwise Hindus, Muslims and Christians too, who live in this country, are accordingly one *quam* (nation).[8]

Stressing the need to live in harmony and peace, Sir Sayyid, addressing both Hindus and Muslims, said:

'. . . and, it is due to harmonious relations between us, mutual sympathy and love that the development and welfare of the country and also of both of us, is possible and that in case of disharmony, obstinacy and enmity and thinking bad against each other both (of us) will meet our doom.[9]

Sir Sayyid's concern for Hindustan's development is vividly explained in a letter which he wrote to Mohsinul Mulk from London, England, saying that

I am immersed in my thought for the good of my country. . . . the Minister (In Charge) of *Hind* went out after two or three days of my arrival (there). Let me first have a special interview with him then some progress for the welfare of *Hindustan* will be initiated.

Thus, Sir Sayyid wanted all Hindustanis to take to the cause of her development. This essentially requires proper presentation of Hindustan's case to dispel any doubts by truthfully giving a correct picture of the situation in the light of facts and figures. In another letter written to Mohsinul Mulk from London, Sir Sayyid said:

Most of the people here and (also) the members of the Parliament, are well wishers of *Hindustan*. As they are not fully informed of the situation (in *Hindustan*), some know (the facts) while some others hold adverse opinion. . .

Assessing the situation and the state of intellectual pursuits at the time and concerned with the overall development of Hindustan, Sir Sayyid prescribed that

Any nation which is determined to progress in training and good manners, must transfer all (the available) knowledge into her language. Thus, a clear and stable strategy for *Hindustan*'s development, in training and good manners which after thousand of years and after the experience of a number of countries, has reached us, is this that all knowledge and skills held by the alien nations, be got possessed in our own language. (A number of) clubs and societies and institutes by imitating Europe are being established in *Hindustan*, (these) being useful, are not without some benefit. But the roof of every (beneficial action) is primarily in holding treasures of knowledge.[10]

The spread of education, rather higher education, being Sir Sayyid's foremost goal, he started his magazine, the *Mohammedan Reformer*, *Tahzibul Akhlaq*, whose columns he used for spreading his creative and constructive ideas and also the ideas of others with a concern for Hindustan's people. Explaining the objective of starting *Tahzibul Akhlaq*, he said:

The Magazine, Tahzibul Akhlaq, was initially started to invoke action on the part of the dead hearts of the *Hindustanis*. *Hindustan's* present state is like that of the still water which is wrought with varied losses and dangers. It needed an our to stir it. It accomplished some of its work. Now, there has emerged some movement (activity). On the tongues and from the pen of *Hindustanis* words giving (the need for and concern about) national development and (mutual) sympathy, are being expressed. In the newspapers words rather articles on national welfare and national development are being published (now). This makes (us) understand that this Magazine (*Tahzibul Akhlaq*) has accomplished its task.[11]

Our readers would appreciate what was pointed out by Sir Sayyid, i.e. it is not possible for the government to give jobs to so many people (as large numbers are being educated). Having said this, he encouraged the educated youth to take to trade to earn and prosper with all the benefits flowing for Hindustan and her development:

What is the principle of a country's trade and prosperity? He asked, adding further that that country cannot grow rich where trade is done in foreign goods: rather that country can accumulate wealth whose output is traded in other countries. That country adds to her wealth whose products are traded in other countries. Though *Hindustan's* products are exported to other countries but these, after adding to their prices, are re-exported back to *Hindustan*. Considering the quantum of our home products our entrepot trade, and our inter-city trade is limited (in quantum).[12]

But to achieve success in any aspect of our everyday life, it is essential to develop our human resource, for 'things in this world are shadow of man'. Sir Sayyid, touching this issue, opined, thus:

When we take to attract a *qaum* to civilize itself, it becomes important to tell that *qaum* about the different aspects (of life) in which it has to civilize (cultivate) itself. Considering the conditions of Muslims in *Hindustan*, it emerges in my thought that the following are the aspects in which they have to consider to civilize themselves.[13]

1. Freedom of Thought
2. Reconstruction of Religious Thought
3. (Religious) Thought and Religious Actions
4. Education of the Child
5. Paraphernalia for Education
6. Women's Education
7. Skills, Arts and Crafts
8. Selfishness
9. Honour and Self-respect
10. Time Scheduling
11. Morals
12. Truthful Communication
13. Fair Dealing with Friends

14. Art of Expression
15. Tone in Talking
16. Way of Living
17. Cleanliness
18. Rituals in Marriages
19. Rituals in Mournings
20. Agricultural Development, and
21. Trade

But the development of human personality becomes easy and effective if 'they are caught young'. Sir Sayyid, therefore, established his 'Madarsatul Uloom' for 'national development', 'acquiring of knowledge' of 'European Sciences and Literature', and 'training'. Explaining the purpose of the establishment of his Institution, Sir Sayyid said:

> Madarsatul Uloom is indeed a means for national development. Here by nation I do not mean only Muslims, rather (I mean) both, Hindus and Muslims. Madarsatul Uloom has been established to improve upon the miserly lot of Muslims and also (to remove) the difficulty they have been facing in acquiring the (knowledge of) European Sciences and Literature. Both Hindus and Muslims are enrolled here and the training which is required in *Hindustan*, is imparted to both. We refer here (in *Hindustan*) each other calling someone Hindu and the other Muslim, but outside *Hindustan* we are all referred as natives, i.e. *Hindustani*. Foreigners describe Khuda Bux and Durga Ram both as *Hindustani* (Indian).[14]

The Kothari Commission Report rightly said in 1966 that the 'destiny of India is being shaped in her class rooms'. Sir Sayyid as far back as 1894 said that the 'Boarding House' (here at Aligarh) is a machine to develop a *Qaum* as one Nation:

> The foremost and root of all the blessings is your living with good mutual behaviour and love. All the students of *Hindustan* from Panjab, from East, or South, when they reach the lap of your intelligent mother (Madarsatul Uloom) they all become your brother. If you did not behave with them as brothers, showering brotherly love upon each other, then you have violated the first principle that all of you are the offsprings of one intelligent mother.[15]

Such was Sir Sayyid, a great visionary, championing the cause of Hindustan, preaching and practising large-hearted tolerance, mutual love, urging both, the Hindus and Muslims, to bury their differences and work unitedly for the overall development of Hindustan, truly so, for

Sare Jahan Se Achcha Hindustan Hamara

NOTES

1. *Tahzibul Akhlaq*, Vol. 6, Ramzan, AH 1292.
2. Jalandhar, 4 February 1884.
3. *Tahzibul Akhlaq*, 1 Ziquadah AH 1289.
4. Lecture, Ludhiana, 23 January 1883.
5. Reply to the Address presented by the Indian Muhammedan Association, Lahore, 30 January 1884.
6. Lecture, Patna, 27 January 1883.
7. Ibid.
8. Lecture, Madarsah Gurdaspur, Panjab, 27 January 1884.
9. Lecture, Patna, 27 January 1883.
10. Lecture, Benaras Institute, 20 September 1867.
11. Lecture, Jalandhar, 1884.
12. Maqalaat-e-Sir Sayyid.
13. *Tahzibul Akhlaq*, Vol. I, No. 6, 1 Zilhijjah, AH 1287.
14. Lecture in response to the Address presented by Anjuman-e-Islamia, Amritsar, 26 January 1884.
15. Address to the Students of Madarsatul Uloom, 7 December 1894.

    (Translation of the excerpts from the writings and speeches of Sir Sayyid by the author.)

PART 5
REMINISCENCES

Remembering Nuru Bhai

S.Z. Qasim

First Meeting

I first met Professor S. Nurul Hassan in the year 1949, when, after his return from Oxford University, he had joined the Department of History, Aligarh Muslim University, as a Reader. The occasion was a dinner hosted by Col. Haider Khan, the then Chairman University Games Committee to the Athletics Team, which was going to participate in the All India Inter-Varsity Athletics Meet, scheduled to be held in Colombo (Sri Lanka). I was the General Sports Captain of the University at that time and a student of M.Sc. Zoology. During the dinner, several persons made short speeches and then Col. Haider Khan spontaneously asked Dr Nurul Hassan, a special invitee, to make an after-dinner speech. He got up and spoke brilliantly, full of wit, humour and anecdotes, giving some of his experiences of the Oxford Majlis, of which he probably was an elected Secretary or President. The entire team was highly impressed by his speech. After the dinner, he and his charming wife Dawn shook hands with all the team members and asked a few searching questions about our preparedness for the competition. While departing he said somewhat loudly, 'good luck and success'. On our return from Colombo, we went to meet him at his residence and showed him the prizes we had won. He and his wife were very pleased and besides a lavish tea, they gave us their compliments and good wishes.

As Staff Member in Staff Club

In 1951, when I joined the staff of the University as a Lecturer, Department of Zoology, I also became a member of the University Staff Club and started playing tennis, badminton, bridge, etc. At the bridge table, I used to meet Prof. Nurul Hassan and his wife (as both were keen bridge players). At that time, the bridge room used to have a galaxy of star players of the University staff such as Col. Haider Khan, Prof.

Sheikh Rashid, Prof. Aleem, Prof. Moonis Raza, Dr Anas, Dr. Raza Husain Zaidi and many others.

Decency and refinement were the hallmarks of the character of both Nurul Hassan and his wife and this was also reflected in the way they played bridge at the table. It was a real delight to play with them. Their moods never changed whether they won or lost.

As Member of the Same Family

In July 1953, a pleasantly important event occurred in my life which totally changed my relationship with him. This was my wedding with the younger sister of Mrs Nurul Hassan and thus began our addressing him as 'Nurubhai' and his wife 'Baji Jan'. After marriage, I stayed in Aligarh only for a few weeks in Mrs Haidar's house on Marris Road and then proceeded to the United Kingdom to pursue my higher studies in Marine Science. Before departure, we received a lot of instructions and advice from Nurubhai about the style of living in the UK, how to conduct ourselves with professors and other intellectuals of the university, what types of food to accept or avoid and what types of clothes to wear on different occasions. After completing my Ph.D. degree in 1976, I returned to my former post in the AMU, Aligarh. Since a good accommodation on rent in the University area was not easy to come by, we stayed in the house of Nurubhai in the Shamshad Market area for several months before moving into a rented accommodation in 'Amir Nishan'. While staying with them, I got to know both Nurubhai and Baji Jan rather intimately. Both were persons of outstanding qualities and merit. The sharpness and the intelligence which Nurubhai possessed, are hard to find in any other person.

You pose a problem to him with all its complexities and the way he used to respond to the problem—cigarette between his fingers (he was a chain-smoker at that time) and walking with short steps up and down in his office or living room explaining things with utmost clarity and providing a solution to the problem with all its intricacies. He had excellent foresight and could develop ideas and projects, which seldom failed. It was his idea that I should submit a scheme for starting a Fisheries Section in the Department of Zoology to the University Grants Commission (UGC). He helped me in its preparation, which ultimately got sanctioned, and I got a Reader's position with several additional staff members, research scholars, with grants for equipment, contingencies, etc. Thus the Fisheries Section which began in 1957 is still flourishing in the AMU. If I remember correctly, Nurubhai became a professor at a young age, probably before 1956, and shortly afterwards, the Centre of Advanced Studies in Medieval Indian History was established in the Department of History. He also had a natural ability, an innate talent for designing the layout of gardens, parks and preparing blueprints of houses. The house I built on Marris Road in 1958, next to Mrs Haider's residence, was largely based on his design. It was completed within eight months and at that time it was considered as one of the best-designed houses in Aligarh.

My remembrance of him would not be complete unless I add a few lines about the attributes which Mrs Nurul Hassan (Baji Jan) possessed. She was also a person of outstanding qualities and abilities, highly affectionate, and was an excellent housewife and a loving mother. One can judge about her abilities from the fact that at the time she got married to Nurubhai, she had passed only her matriculation examination, but after marriage, over the years, she completed her intermediate (Class XII), BA and MA degrees in History and had almost finished her Ph.D. thesis. In addition to all the housework and giving excellent support to her husband in his academic pursuits, she was also teaching History to BA and MA classes in a local college affiliated to Agra University. In addition, she was deeply involved in the welfare of handicapped children in the University's School for the Blind.

I left Aligarh in September 1962 for Bombay to take up my appointment as Professor, Fisheries Biology in the Central Institute of Fisheries Education, but my family continued to stay on in Aligarh till 1964. They were looked after by Nurubhai and Baji Jan. However, I kept coming to Aligarh frequently till 1964 to see my family members (wife and three children).

Greatest Tragedy in the Life of Nuru Bhai

In 1968, Nurubhai and Baji Jan had gone for a holiday to Kashmir. This was because they have been too busy for the last several years to take a break from work. Soon after reaching Srinagar, Baji Jan became somewhat uncomfortable (probably high altitude effect) and the first symptom noticed (as told later by Nurubhai) was her giddiness and disorientation, which developed into an irretrievable coma. Despite all efforts to make her conscious by the local doctors, she passed away peacefully shortly afterwards. This was the greatest calamity, which Nurubhai had to face. She was 35 years old when she died. For me it was hard to imagine how he would cope with the rest of his life alone because he was so dependent on his wife for everything. However, he recovered quickly, as a few months later, when I visited Aligarh, I went to her grave with Nurubhai. He remained reasonably calm and composed throughout while I nearly broke down.

Entry into Rajya Sabha

In 1968, he first became a nominated member and subsequently an elected member of the Rajya Sabha. He was a very successful and popular member. During his tenure he participated and excelled in many debates and introduced several bills which were passed, the most notable among them was the 'Antique and Art Treasure Bill' which forbids the sale or taking out of the country of any statue, idol or old manuscript which fell within the category of art treasure.

Union Minister of State for Education

Soon afterwards he was sworn in as Union Minister for Education in the cabinet of Smt. Indira Gandhi. One of his important contributions as Minister was to enhance the status of teachers of the country. Through his continued efforts, he got their salaries increased significantly, and made the jobs of all types of teachers dignified and rewarding.

Multi-faceted Personality

Although he joined the Parliament and became a Minister, he was not really a politician. I shall grade him as an intellectual, an elite, a great orator and a statesman. He had a multi-faceted personality. He was one of those who became equally comfortable in the company of politicians, all types of professionals, intellectuals, academicians, scientists, administrators, in fact with practically every type of person. He could understand and talk to them in their own language with considerable ease. This is not always true of politicians some of whom who become uncomfortable, while meeting a scientist.

Vice-President of CSIR

After the fall of the Janata Party government led by Shri Moraji Desai, when Smt. Indira Gandhi's party was re-elected and she took over as Prime Minister of India, she made Nurubhai Vice-President of CSIR. In that position, he officially visited several CSIR laboratories including the National Institute of Oceanography (NIO), Goa, of which I was Director at that time. Besides visiting important laboratories of the Institute, he also went on board the oceanographic research vessel, *Gaveshani*. He took a lot of interest in various shipboard instruments used for probing the ocean.

During his visit to the Institute I purposely made him stay in the Institute guest house, rather than accommodating him in my own residence, so that all types of my colleagues could freely visit and talk to him on different matters. One evening, the Head of Ocean Engineering Division of the institute went and invited him to inaugurate a seminar on 'Coastal Erosion' which was being held in the Institute the next day, and as is customary, he left behind him a ten page typed note on the subject to be read out as his formal speech. He agreed to inaugurate, put the note aside, and called me the next morning to explain to him the phenomenon of coastal erosion. I talked to him about the definition, importance and significance of coastal erosion, what are the regions where it occurs intensively in the country and the forces and factors responsible for it, etc. He listened to me very carefully, without writing a word, asked several very pertinent questions and that was the end. About an hour or so later, he walked to the podium in front of a gathering of about 300 very knowledgeable oceanographers and engineers and made a beautiful inaugural speech on such a technical subject, which was enjoyed and applauded by the entire audience. Many asked, 'How could he talk on such a complex subject, so beautifully, confidently and comfortably and that too without any script! He is indeed a remarkable person.' This was not the first time I had heard him. There were several other occasions earlier, and particularly after my return from Antarctica, when he spoke very elegantly after getting the required information from me and others in bits and pieces. He was at his best when he spoke extempore.

Thus, I can say without any hesitation that although I have heard the speeches of many famous scientists including several Nobel Laureates, I have yet to find a person better than Nurubhai, who could transform bits of information collected from here and there and put the pieces together in such a beautifully articulate fashion. His gifted eloquence and quality of perception and integration of ideas were *par excellence*, and the quality of brain he possessed is not easy to find and this remark I make without any hesitation or exaggeration. At his office table and also at home, I could find important scientific journals such as *Nature, Science, Current Science* and several others.

Ambassador to former USSR

After finishing his term as Vice-President of CSIR, he was appointed as Ambassador to the Soviet Union. During his tenure, I visited Moscow on two occasions as a member of Indian delegations to sign a Memorandum of Understanding (MOU) on cooperation in Ocean and Antarctic Research between the two countries. On both occasions, he organized large dinner parties which included eminent persons, ocean and antarctic scientists including the Deputy Prime Minister of the Soviet Union, Prof. Marchuk who was a famous Atmospheric Physicist and extremely well-known for his publications on 'modelling' using oceanographic data. On his subsequent visit to India, Prof. Marchuk specially called me to meet him. From these accounts, one can easily guess the level of his popularity in the then Soviet Union.

Governor of West Bengal

On his return form Moscow, Shri Rajiv Gandhi, the then Prime Minister of India, appointed him as the Governor of West Bengal. He was given two terms with a short break in between as the Governor of Orissa. I visited Calcutta many times during his tenure and always stayed with him in Raj Bhawan. I normally used to reach Calcutta by the evening flight which usually landed after 10 p.m., was received at the airport by his Public Relations Officer (PRO) and reached Raj Bhawan close to midnight. He was always awake and I was asked to go straight to his bedroom. The first thing he asked me was about the dinner, and I could see the disappointment on his face when I told him that what I had in the aircraft was enough. We talked for quite a while and after retiring to my room where I was surprisingly amused to find a thermos flask full of soup, a plate arranged with different kinds of sandwiches and a basket full of fruits on the bedside table. The next morning when I woke up and was having tea and going through the newspaper, an orderly came to my room and said that I should get ready quickly because 'Saheb' wanted me to have breakfast with him. When I went to him, I found him walking in front of his private dining room and waiting. I entered the dining room and was astonished to see the variety of food items on the breakfast table. After breakfast, I took leave of him and said that my lunch would be at the seminar which I had come to attend. At about 1:00 p.m., while the seminar session was on, I saw a person with uniform and regalia waiting outside. He said that 'Saheb' wanted me for lunch. I had an excellent lunch with him and a few other guests. At dinner there were at least 10-15 guests including the organizers of the seminar, the Chief Minister of West Bengal and other distinguished persons.

The reason for mentioning those few facts is to provide a glimpse of his phenomenal hospitality, the care and attention he gave to his guests. He became undoubtedly a very lonely man after the death of his wife. The only company he could get at home was from his sister Shaddan Baji and whenever he came to Delhi on official visits, the West Bengal House, where he stayed, was full of visitors who enjoyed his phenomenal hospitality.

Last Meeting

It was July 1993, when I heard that Nurubhai was seriously ill. I phoned Raj Bhawan and was told that he had been hospitalized. I rushed to Calcutta and to my surprise I was received by his staff at the airport and found a transport waiting for me. I went straight to the hospital because it was day time and was allowed to go straight inside his room wearing a mask. He was in a semi-conscious state and sitting beside him were, Dr M. Khalilullah, the well-known heart specialist and Dr Rizvi, a nephrologist, his daughter Talat and his daughter-in-law Sultana. His son Siraj was abroad and could only reach a day later. I kept standing, looking at his pale face when suddenly he opened his eyes, looked at me, his face brightened and said 'Zahoor Mian', as he used to affectionately call me, 'You have come, sit down near me', and then went into a coma again. I sat down on a chair, held his hand, felt his pulse, which was feeble and irregular. A little later we were asked to leave, as the doctors were to carry out their examination and dialysis on him. I stayed in Calcutta for a few days spending most of my time in the hospital. I phoned my wife and told her that if she wanted to see him, she should better hurry up. I returned to Delhi; my wife's ticket to Calcutta was booked and she was getting ready to leave when the news came that he was no more.

Thus ended an era—a glorious and eventful life of a person who gave dignity to whatever positions he held and left behind friends and lots and lots of admirers. He became extraordinarily meritorious and had well-wishers everywhere. I am sure he left with no regrets because he is one of those persons who has probably achieved at the age of 72, practically most of what he had really wished to accomplish. He really became a legend in his own lifetime and a person hard to forget.

A Personal Tribute to Nuru Bhai

S.K. Singh

Professor Nurul Hasan, educationist, researcher, historian, political thinker, parliamentarian, member of our Council of Ministers, Governor of two of the constituent states of our Republic, India's Ambassador to the erstwhile Soviet Union, and above all a man of grace and culture, was a friend capable of giving and receiving loyalty. An aristocrat by birth he became a Marxist-Socialist in his younger days, and through Nehruvian osmosis and politics evolved in his mature years into a Gandhian in his basic thinking. He led a life of scholarly integrity and contribution. His insights percolated through a network of friends who were decision-makers worldwide, and who recognized him as much for his modesty, integrity and personal style as for his wisdom and scholarship.

He would not wish me to talk about his accomplishments, the positions he held, government and academic honours he received, but only about the person he was. Above all he would wish to be remembered as a father. He was proud of both his children, son and daughter in a somewhat coy, shy manner. He allowed them to pursue their own preferred disciplines and to do what they wished to, grow up in the way they desired, and thus he ensured that they became their own persons. Both of them are scientists and in their own respective fields, quite eminent. Nurubhai would also wish to be remembered as a thoughtful person. He believed with Francis Bacon that if one begins with absolute certainties, he or she ends up being full of doubts. However, if right at the beginning doubts are allowed a full play, he or she is most likely to end up with certainties. He set for himself an extremely high standard of personal integrity. The standards he set for himself were higher than what any outside authority could impose. To him honour was more important than reputation. Honour, after all, he used to say is what one thinks of oneself, while reputation is what others think about each one of us.

For a person who attained such eminence as a scholar, and as a teacher, someone who attained high offices of State, Nurubhai remained a modest human being with a twinkle in his eyes. He refused to take himself too seriously even when he discussed weighty and serious matters. With his wry sense of humour he would perhaps wish to be remembered as a person who was wise rather than clever, who pursued excellence rather than success, and who believed that trying to tell others what to do is always a losing proposition.

I had the great good luck of getting to know him at an early stage of my life. As a researcher in the National Archives of India, I was attracted to the work of the Indian History Congress where Nurubhai was already the President of the Medieval India Section. Our first meeting in Bhopal in this context attracted me to him and he was gracious enough to invite me to Aligarh. I was then a young lecturer in History at St. John's College, Agra, also working, off and on, in the National Archives as a researcher. Begum Nurul Hasan was a gracious hostess and a very meticulous one, also in her own right, a scholar. Professor Nurul Hasan was unostentatious even spartan about his personal life. But his home, whether in Aligarh or in New Delhi or the Raj Bhavan in Calcutta or the Embassy Residence in Moscow, was always bursting with books, journals and correspondence. He remained interested in art, archaeology, philosophy, poetry, science, technology, languages, music and miniatures. All his homes which I was privileged to visit as a guest, reflected his scholarly interest in things beautiful and old. Books and papers surrounded him even in his travels. Family photographs and flowers were around him always, wherever he may be.

On two occasions in 1967 and 1971 he and I were both members of the Indian delegation to the UN General Assembly. In 1967 he played a stellar role in getting our candidate for the International Court of Justice elected by a thumping majority in the UN General Assembly. That was the occasion when I first witnessed his extraordinary ability to network, functioning as a lobbyist, pursuing a specific national objective in a multilateral international setting. He had an unerring sense of putting together the right mix of Ambassadors, Foreign Ministers and academic personalities at his luncheon table in the UN so that he could pursue a topic or an issue which at that time was the focus of his attention. As a younger diplomat I learnt a great deal watching this intellectual-aristocrat on the international stage, even though he had functioned until then within the confines of national politics. When I complimented him in this respect, he said, *Mian Sahebzade hum ne to pradesh politics bhi isi tarah chalayee thi, jaise ab yehan international level par chala rahe hain. Bahut sa bhaichara, aur thori bahut favours ka lena-*

dena. Imandari ka deal making itna mushkil kaam nahi hota. Iman or sachaee ko sabhi pehchan lete hain.

However, one poignant remembrance I cherish, is that of Nurubhai visiting us in Vienna when I was Ambassador there. He was then our Ambassador in Moscow. A few weeks after my father had passed away, I received a message that he was on his way to London from Moscow via Frankfurt; and that on his way back to Moscow three days later he wished to make a detour so as to visit us in Vienna. Our residence was under extensive renovation at that time, and my wife and I were living for the duration, in an ancient, cramped building, part of an old Palais with no space for a guest suite. I tried, therefore, to persuade him to defer his visit until the time when we could re-occupy our Embassy Residence. Or we could arrange for his stay in a suitable hotel. He, however, was insistent and said, 'Whether you like it or not, I am visiting you now for a couple of nights and I refuse to stay in a hotel. Whatever the character of accommodation available in your place I am going to be your Guest.' Naturally, we received him at the airport, brought him home and showed him how poorly we could host him at that juncture. He disarmed me totally by saying 'Right from the word go I was determined to visit you because I needed to offer my condolences to you both personally at the earliest after the passing away of your father. This was not a protocol visit and this visit I could not postpone.'

His capacity to be graciously attentive about persons and issues never ceased to surprise. Early in our association, once when I was his guest in Aligarh he discovered that my *kurta-pyjamas* were invariably made of *khadi*. The very next time he visited me, he left a largish envelope containing two types of *khadi*, one suitable for *kurtas*, and the other for *pyjamas*. Thereafter almost every year or every other year when he remembered my birthday I would get from him a gift of *khadi*. I think I am still wearing some of the *kurtas*, etc, made of the material he gave me!

When we were both members of our delegation to the UN General Assembly, sometimes over weekends, we would go scouting for new restaurants near or around New York. I liked driving my large, new car and he liked exploring the North American countryside. On these drives, he and I discussed Indo-Soviet and Indo-US relations on several occasions. He recognized that the might, arrogance and self-assurance of superpowers and their establishments had grown to resemble one another. However, insofar as India was concerned, the two were used to handling India in two different styles. The Soviet Union saw India as one large non-socialist, but sympathetic, friendly land; while the USA then used to consider India a special friend of the Soviet Union, the competitor superpower, and, therefore, worthy of being viewed with suspicion, especially of our motives and perceptions and world-view. USA, however, was realistic in conceding that India was a democracy, and one that in a practical way preferred the free market system, despite its oft-repeated preference for socialism. Nurubhai acknowledged that if and when the national interests of either superpower supervened then all bets on third-country relationships would be off.

I suspected that second only to the company of scholars and teachers, he preferred the company of diplomats, whether ours or those from other countries. To our diplomats, with whom he had constant dealing and interaction, he used to give just one piece of advice: 'Be optimistic about India's future. Have faith in our potential, and never be uneasy about the country's future; even if you have some anxiety don't permit it to show, don't ever hint that you are disheartened or unhappy on this or the other score. All discontent is divine, as discontent is the first step towards self-improvement, but your discontent while representing India, must not become public knowledge or the basis of propaganda against your nation and its functioning.'

He was invariably relaxed about himself, the department of the university he headed, the Ministry he ran, each state he governed, the Embassy which he presided over. He may occasionally have felt somewhat dissatisfied with the performance of a collaborator, but that was never permitted to show. Essentially he was a shy, private person, and at the same time capable of prompt and firm decision-making.

Nurubhai above all was a man of integrity, consideration and largeness of heart. His capacity to be generous was enormous.

His style was never to appear an eager beaver, or to insist on imposing his will on friends. Until the end his style in everything he did, remained scholarly, deliberate, somewhat languid. I found through our many exchanges and interactions in Delhi, when he was the Education Minister of India and I an Additional Secretary in the Foreign Office, that his political and administrative responses were invariably prompt and decisive, but he always managed to appear deliberate, leisurely and courtly.

My wife and I were staying with him just a few weeks before he was to move for the summer weeks, to the hills, from the Raj Bhavan in Calcutta, that beautiful old edifice originally built by Warren Hastings. He asked us to accompany him to Darjeeling. We had to deny ourselves the pleasure, as I was committed to addressing certain Conferences in Delhi and Bombay. Soon after we returned to Delhi we learnt that he had been taken ill at the airport while on his way to Darjeeling and had to be brought back to Calcutta for treatment in what proved to be his last illness and last hospitalization. Even today I bitterly regret that I was not more spontaneous. I wish my wife and I had accompanied him to Darjeeling and given ourselves the chance of looking after him.

A Scholar, A Humanist: A Master Strategist

Vina Mazumdar

I met Prof. Nurul Hassan in 1947 when I was a young undergraduate at Oxford. He was a very senior scholar, and was also completing his term as President of the Oxford Majlis—the association of Indian students at the University. The Majlis had just suffered a major blow: a group of members had separated to form the Pakistani Students Association. At the very first meeting of the Majlis that I attended, Prof. Hassan welcomed and informed me that I had been elected Treasurer of the Majlis. My surprised protest that I was a newcomer, and had not sought any position were brushed aside with a charming smile, and some remark about members' finding it more difficult to delay/evade paying subscriptions on time to women treasurers. I was left dumb holding a responsibility I had never sought.

The next occasion when I saw his particular brand of leadership in action was on 30 January 1948. The news about the assassination of Mahatma Gandhi reached us by late afternoon. Prof. Hassan led a team of Indian students of All Souls College to seek advice from Prof. Sarvepalli Radhakrishnan as to what we should do. The College Porter told us that S.R. had locked himself in his room, with instructions that he was not to be disturbed. 'Oh, he will see us, please inform him that we are on the way'. The door was open by the time we reached along with Prof. Summer, Warden of All Souls.

There was little talk. All of us were too stunned but somehow a decision was taken to hold a meeting two days later, to be addressed by Prof. Gilbert Murry and S.R. The Warden offered the All Soul's Library as a venue. The 500 plus persons who came to pay homage sat on the floor in silence, listening to moving tributes. The Majlis' handwritten notices, announcing the meeting had been spread to a far wider circle of people by many student volunteers who were neither Indian nor members of the Majlis. The Majlis executive committee held no formal meeting to plan this event, though a few of them accompanied Prof.

Hassan in that initial instinctive rush to Prof. S.R. None of the Majlis members present in full strength at the meeting, thought of playing any formal role to introduce the speakers or thanking all those who came so spontaneously.

These few memories from my student days, only strengthened my later assessment of Nurul Hassan as a person who was at his best playing a leadership role behind the scenes—rather than by putting himself forward before the public as the key figure. He was also a past master at manipulating friends on whom he thrust major responsibilities without any prior consultation. The challenge would be weighted with a burden of guilt if the friend attempted to wriggle out of the unexpected, often unwanted responsibility.

The early acquaintance as a student was renewed two decades later, when as a newly recruited officer of the UGC I was asked to work with a Review Committee on History which basically meant functioning as its record keeper, calling timely meetings, and assisting the Committee to produce, eventually, a report. A series of events, some anticipated, some unexpected, expanded and transformed the functions of his Committee far beyond a review of the History Curriculum in India's fast expanding University system. The Committee wanted to stimulate more dynamism in teaching/research, to attract more serious and questioning students. It also wanted to respond to the challenges thrown out to the University system by the Report of the Indian Education Commission (1964-6) and hoped for a positive response to its new ideas from Prof. D.S. Kothari.[1] At the international level, the widespread youth revolts led very often by university students had found echoes in India's campuses, stirring considerable sympathy and hope among members of the History Committee.

Against this backdrop the UGC received a proposal from the British Council to collaborate in organizing a series of study seminars on historical methodology, for which the Council would invite a few British historians, who had specialized in Indian History. The UGC had an on-going collaboration with the US' National Science Foundation for organizing a Summer Institute for young science teachers in India, with a view to giving them an opportunity to acquaint themselves with the most recent developments in scientific research and teaching in the West. The British Council's offer drew on this analogy.

Prof. Kothari asked me to comment on the proposal. After a discussion, I was asked to prepare the note to be placed before the full meeting of the UGC. The Commission decided that the offer should be welcomed, but as in the case of Science Summer Institute, the details of each would be decided by the UGC's own Committee on History, which may, if it thought it necessary, consult the Director of the British Council.

Fortunately, the Director of the Council was himself a history scholar, and knew that the proposal that he had sent was not exactly diplomatic. He appreciated the History Committee's decision to give the Study Seminars a comparative framework in which British and Indian historians could present their research on common themes (e.g. the concept of time) undertaken in the West and in India. The first seminar, very successful and stimulating, was held at Delhi University.

The manoeuvre called for a degree of diplomatic and persuasive skills. Prof. Kothari was a past master, but he also banked on the stature of the members of the history Committee. Prof. Hassan played the leader through the entire episode, and followed it up with a seminar in Aligarh. But within the circle of some members of the History Committee who were friends and observed no formalities, he liked to refer to himself as 'Vina's Stooge'. In reality, I was ordered by him to receive Prof. Eric Hobsbawm who came for the Aligarh seminar and then escort him to Aligarh as Hassan himself would be in Aligarh organizing the entire function.

The twenty years, lapse since our first acquaintances had certainly reduced the maturity/inequality gap between us. I had put in more than ten years teaching, completed a D. Phil thesis, and acquired some reputation among students and teachers in Patna before coming to the UGC. I had also managed these while becoming a mother of a sizable family which inspired some awe among the Committee's members, all male. I was certainly not their equal in scholarship, but it was easy to accept me as a friend and fellow conspirator. When Prof. Hassan needed a personal discussion with DSK to register a protest against some efforts to the Education Ministry to restrict/control international travel by scholars from Central Universities he would call me to fix an appointment. I came to know Mrs. Hassan and enjoyed their hospitality.

I had returned to teaching (at Berhampur University, Orissa) in 1971, when Prof. Hassan joined the Government as Minister of State for Education and Social Welfare. In January 1972 when I was taking part in a Selection Committee for Commonwealth Fellows on the invitation of the Ministry, I received a quiet message from an officer that the Minister would like to see me, after the selection was completed. While complaining at my decision to go to 'the back of beyond', he said persons like me needed to be more mobile. He also called his special Assistant to say that my name (with full designation as Professor and Head of the Department of Political Science) and address should be placed on some list. When I asked for details, he murmured 'confidential' and looked rather mischievous. A few days afterwards I received a letter from the Secretary, Social Welfare informing me that I had been appointed a member of the Committee on the Status of Women in India.

It was only four months later, when I had returned to the UGC, that I learnt from Naik Sahib[2] that my appointment as member to the Committee was 'to ensure that a decent report was delivered'. The Committee had apparently run into some difficulties. Prof. Hassan had had nothing to do with the original composition of the Committee, constituted several months earlier.[3] It was only after the departure of Sri Siddhartha Sankar Ray, Minister for Education and Social Welfare (to take up the Chief Ministership of West Bengal) that the responsibility for the CSWI descended on Prof. Hassan. Some additional members had to be found, hence the list was being compiled in January.

I had major responsibilities in the UGC, and could do little to assist the Committee. I was not even able to join other members on occasional tours, till the summer of 1973, when I participated in the tour of Himachal Pradesh which was an eye opener. The Committee's two year term was about to end in September. In August, we (the Delhi-based members) were informed that the Member Secretary had gone abroad. The Chairperson, Dr. Phulrenu Guha came from Calcutta to take charge of the office. We (Prof. Lotika Sarkar, Mrs. Urmila Haskar, Prof. Leela Dube, Prof. Sakina Hassan and myself) decided to talk to Phulrenudi that we had decided to resign from the Committee, as we could not justify seeking extension of the Committee's term in the existing circumstances. She decided to join us.

When on 29 August 1973 we met Prof. Hassan to submit our joint resignation, it appeared that he was not in the least surprised. All that he would say was that he needed sometime, requested that we should not publicize our decision, and that Phulrenudi should remain in charge of the office, which was being shifted to new premises[4] at her suggestion. On the evening of 10 September I was informed by an officer in the Ministry that the Committee had been reconstituted, and the Minister had written to the Chairman, UGC to release my services for one year to take up the position as Member Secretary of the CSWI. The officer had taken it for granted that I knew about it, and was surprised at my request for an appointment with the Minister the following morning.

To my question as to why was I not consulted, he had a simple answer. He had to get a Report, because it had to be sent to the UN, and depended on 'a friend' to save his and the nation's face! I still asked how he knew that the change would be acceptable to other members of the Committee I was told that most of them had met him independently to say so, including all the rest who had resigned.

When I met the Chairman, UGC, Prof. George Jacob[5] he realized that the news had come to me as a shock, and told me to take a few hours to think things through. 'If you still feel reluctant. I will say a 'no' to the Minister. But he does say it is a work of national importance, and that all the other members feel you can do the job. That is an opinion which I confirm as I have known you for a far longer period'. The conversation ended with my acceptance, but I should be allowed to finish a few important tasks in the UGC, before joining the new position.

The manoeuvre, or politico-administrative strategizing did not end there. By October 1974, i.e. a year after I joined the Committee as its Member Secretary we were in the throes of finalizing our Report. We had been given time till 31 December, and were determined to complete it, so the drafting team of four (the Chairperson Phulrenu Guha, Lotika Sarkar, Urmila Haksar, and myself) worked for 12 hours a day, including holidays. Apart from these four and two or three members of the staff closely associated with the drafting, a few others, especially Naik Sahib and the Minister had become aware that the report was going to be uncomfortable as well as unexpected and the Prime Minister's reaction was unpredictable. Two master strategists set to work.

Two decisions of November 1974 of which we (CSWI members) remained unaware of were (a) The Indian Cabinet's acceptance of Nurul Hassan's proposal to table the CSWI's Report before Parliament, well in advance of the UN's World Conference on Women: Equality, Development and Peace[6] (scheduled for June for which the Prime Minister was a Special Invitee); and (b) ICSSR's resolution to publish a Summary of the CSWI's Report for wider public awareness and appoint me as Chief Editor to publish a series from the research supported by the ICSSR for the CSWI.[7]

The Report, *Towards Equality* was tabled before Parliament on 18 February 1975 and there was a full scale debate, spread over the next three months. The same day, Phulrenudi and I were asked to address a Press Conference in the Ministry at 3 p.m. National and International press were well represented. By the next week CSWI's most glaring/unexpected findings had achieved unprecedented publicity. The national press continued to write for the next few months-until the declaration of Emergency (26 June 1975) silenced them. Earlier, in May, the full Report (*Towards Equality*) and the ICSSR's Summary came out in print. By the end of the year the ICSSR's publisher reported that the initial issue of 7000 copies were finished. Translations of the Summary subsidised by the ICCSR informed me later that the draft statement prepared by the Secretary, Social Welfare had to be discarded. Since Parliament had already debated and adopted a Resolution on the CSWI's Report their presentation could not be a rosy one. Eventually, the modest Indian presentation emphasising more what still had to be done received great applause and earned many allies for us within the international women's movement and the UN system. After the Delegation's presentation participants and organizers of the parallel non-official conference—the *Tribune*—grabbed the 25 copies of the Report carried by the joint Secretary (Social Welfare) and for months afterwards the *Tribune*'s Newsletter carried data/quotes from *Towards Equality*. It took me all that time to appreciate the historic role of the Conspiracy of Silence of the master strategist.

Recently I asked Anil Bordia, who had represented the Education Ministry (of which he was a Joint Secretary then) on the ICSSR, if he remembered why the Council decided to bring out a Summary of *Towards Equality*, weeks before it was submitted to the Government of India. He remembered Naik Sahib expressing a fear that the Report might not be published like the Report of the Committee on Unemployment.

Prof. Hassan's role in ensuring the publication went far beyond the decision to place it straight before Parliament in a cyclostyled form, and the Press Conference on the same day. The cyclostyling was done in the ICSSR, under my supervision. Only three typed copies were given by us to the Minister on 1 January 1975. One stayed with him, one with a Joint Secretary, and the third was given to a brand new Under Secretary, to prepare a Press note. The officer's special qualification for the task, according to the Minister, was that he had been my student. B.B. Sahay, the Under Secretary, informed me that the Minister had 'trusted' him 'not to tamper with the nuances of the Report'-since the primary author had been Sahay's teacher.

A few weeks earlier, delivering the Convocation Address at the SNDT Women's University, Prof. Hassan raised a question about the 'special role of a women's university in relation to the status of women in the country as a whole'. The University responded by establishing a Research Centre on Status of Women under the direction of Prof. Neera Desai, who had played a leading role in the CSWI's Task force on Social Aspects. The Research Centre acquired an Advisory Committee which included some members connected either with the CSWI or the ICSSR' Programme.

Krishna Patel, working in the ILO through the 1970s and beyond reported a conversation with Prof. Hassan years later, when he admitted that but for the Cabinet Resolution to place the CSWI's report before Parliament, the document 'would never have seen the light of day'.

I have tried to inform various participants in the twin movements of Women's Studies/movement of the contribution this great scholar and humanist made to their struggle. To me personally he remained a good friend, who always took the trouble to enquire about the state of my concerns on the rare occasions that I met him in later years.

The Editors of this volume perhaps expected a scholarly paper from me. But trends in my life towards which Nurul Hassan made a certain contribution have turned me into an activist. I chose to pay my tribute by drawing on my memories of the individual.

NOTES

1. D.S. Kothari served as the Chairman of the Education Commissions as well as the UGC.
2. J.P. Naik, Member-Secretary, ICSSR and Hony. Adviser to the Minister of Education. He had earlier (1964-6) been Member Secretary of the Education Commission.
3. The original list of members, decided in the PMO, had not included either Leela Dube, or myself. Our addition was entirely due to Prof. Hassan's suggestion.
4. The ICSSR, which occupied the major part of the building, was making part of one floor available to the CSWI.
5. He succeeded D.S. Kothari in 1972. He had been Vice-Chancellor, Patna University in my last few years there, and had always been very kind to me.
6. Mexico, June 1975. The Conference also signalled the adoption of the International Women's Decade (1975-85).
7. I was informed by JPN on 2 January 1975 that instead of returning to the UGC, I would take up this office on 7 January, after winding up the CSWI Secretariat, and that the UGC (my original employer) had agreed to this move.